STUDIES IN THE
SOCIAL HISTORY OF
CHINA AND SOUTH-EAST ASIA

STUDIES IN THE SOCIAL HISTORY OF CHINA AND SOUTH-EAST ASIA

ESSAYS IN MEMORY OF VICTOR PURCELL

(26 JANUARY 1896 – 2 JANUARY 1965)

EDITED BY

JEROME CH'EN

Senior Lecturer in Asian History
University of Leeds

AND

NICHOLAS TARLING

Professor of History
University of Auckland

CAMBRIDGE
AT THE UNIVERSITY PRESS
1970

Published by the Syndics of the Cambridge University Press
Bentley House, 200 Euston Road, London N.W.1
American Branch: 32 East 57th Street, New York, N.Y.10022

© Cambridge University Press 1970

Library of Congress Catalogue Card Number: 69–13791

Standard Book Number: 521 07452 5

Printed in Great Britain
at the University Printing House, Cambridge
(Brooke Crutchley, University Printer)

CONTENTS

Foreword   *page* vii

Portrait of Victor Purcell   *facing page* 1

V. W. W. S. Purcell: a Memoir   *page* 1
by SYBILLE VAN DER SPRENKEL, *Lecturer in Chinese
Sociology, University of Leeds*

PART I CHINA

Anti-imperialism in the Kuomintang 1923–8   23
by P. CAVENDISH, *Lecturer in History (Chinese Studies),
University of Glasgow*

The origin of the Boxers   57
by JEROME CH'EN, *Senior Lecturer in East Asian History,
University of Leeds*

The high tide of socialism in the Chinese countryside   85
by JACK GRAY, *Senior Lecturer in History, University of
Glasgow*

The Sino-Indian and Sino-Russian borders: some comparisons
and contrasts   135
by ALASTAIR LAMB, *Professor of History, University of
Ghana*

Unpublished Report from Yenan, 1937   153
by OWEN LATTIMORE, *Professor of Chinese Studies, University
of Leeds*

The Use of Slogans and 'Uninterrupted revolution' in China
in the early part of 1964   165
by JAMES MACDONALD, *Lecturer in Political Science, University of Leeds*

The Optick Artists of Chiangsu   197
by JOSEPH NEEDHAM, F.R.S., *Master of Gonville and Caius
College, Cambridge, and* LU GWEI-DJEN, *Fellow of Lucy
Cavendish College, Cambridge*

CONTENTS

PART 2 SOUTH-EAST ASIA

Canton and Manila in the Eighteenth Century *page* 227
by W. E. CHEONG, *Senior Lecturer in History, University of Hong Kong*

Sino-British Mercantile Relations in Singapore's Entrepôt Trade 1870–1915 247
by CHIANG HAI DING, *Lecturer in History, University of Singapore*

The Dutch and the Tin Trade of Malaya in the Seventeenth Century 267
by GRAHAM W. IRWIN, *Professor of History, Columbia University*

Early Chinese Migration into North Sumatra 289
by ANTHONY REID, *Lecturer in History, University of Malaya*

Revolution in Education 321
by KENNETH ROBINSON, *Deputy Director of Education, Sarawak*

Sikh Immigration into Malaya during the Period of British Rule 335
by KERNIAL SINGH SANDHU, *Lecturer in Historical Geography, University of British Columbia*

The Entrepôt at Labuan and the Chinese 355
by NICHOLAS TARLING, *Professor of History, University of Auckland*

China and South-East Asia 1402–1424 375
by WANG GUNGWU, *Professor of Chinese Studies, Australian National University*

Bibliography of the Writings of Victor Purcell 403
by THE EDITORS

Index 407

vi

Victor Purcell

(*photograph by Edward Leigh*)

FOREWORD

Victor Purcell died early in 1965 soon after he had retired from his lectureship at Cambridge University. Typically he was full of plans for his retirement. This volume can hardly compensate for the fact that they were not realized. But it can perhaps serve as some sort of tribute to his achievements on the part of friends, colleagues, and erstwhile pupils.

Volumes that are the work of several pens are open to many criticisms. In this memorial volume the editors, with the co-operation of the contributors, have sought to concentrate on a number of topics in East and South-east Asian history, and in particular on the role of the Chinese people and civilization that Victor Purcell so much admired.

We are, however, less concerned that the volume may lack a unifying theme than that it fails to reflect the many-sidedness of Victor Purcell's personality and the multiplicity of his interests. In it we pay tribute to him as a scholar. But we think of him also as a controversialist, a colonial civil servant, a raconteur, a traveller, a delightful autobiographer, and a poet. He was a man who loved his friends and enjoyed his enemies, and is much missed.

JEROME CH'EN
NICHOLAS TARLING

Leeds and Auckland, 1968

V. W. W. S. PURCELL

C.M.G., Ph.D., D.Litt. (Cantab.)

A MEMOIR BY
SYBILLE VAN DER SPRENKEL

I should like to thank all those who have helped by answering my enquiries, particularly Dr Hugh Purcell for allowing me to have access to his father's papers. S. v. d. S.

The man whom we honour in these pages attained distinction in several different fields—as colonial and later international civil servant, poet, historian, publicist and teacher.

Most of those who have contributed to this volume came to know Dr Victor Purcell when he was already a distinguished and a rather imposing figure, both in bulk and reputation, and anyone could have been forgiven for supposing that the position he occupied in our society was the natural culmination of a career begun in favoured circumstances. This was not so. Though it would be wrong to describe his origin as humble, he had in fact had to make his own way, for, in terms of the distinctions of class in English society, the family had suffered a decline in the previous generation. Victor Purcell's grandfather, as an agent on the estates of the Earl of Warwick, may be counted as having enjoyed minor professional status—he lived in a rather large, solid house and was on friendly (if inferior) terms with the Warwick family. However, this grandfather died relatively young leaving a large family, so Purcell's own father did not have the benefit of much formal education. He made the Royal Navy his career, but having once entered as a petty officer, it was impossible in those days for him to attain commissioned rank. (He was nevertheless a man of literary and scholarly leanings: he published a story for children[1] and translated a number of books into Basic English.) Victor Purcell felt his father's lack of worldly success keenly, and this is thought by some to have been a factor in his own motivation, as well as a reason for his sympathy with others who were still struggling.

Purcell himself was educated at Bancrofts—a public school, but not among those most esteemed—which he left shortly before the first world war. He made one or two false starts, but he had found no real sense of direction before he was drawn into the war. At the time, these years seemed to be an interruption of his activities and a marking time in his education, but they were in fact a forcing-house of experience, as, later, he realised himself. They gave him a lot of time for thinking as well as a lot to think about, and he learned a good deal about the smallness and the greatness of which human beings were capable. Through the interest of the Warwick family, he obtained a commission (slightly sooner than he would have done merely by reason of having been in

[1] *Into the Heart of Make-believeland.*

3

the O.T.C. at school) and in 1914 he became, in his own words, 'a temporary gentleman'. The significance this had for him is a reminder of the rigid social distinctions of those days (and perhaps, some have suggested, he never to the end of his days quite lost the awareness of his promotion). He saw service in some of the grimmest battles in France, and was twice severely wounded. In the 1918 'push' he was taken prisoner and spent the rest of the war in a German P.O.W. camp. There the prisoners were resourceful in organizing their own entertainment and education in ways that became familiar in the second world war. (These experiences furnished material for an autobiographical novel.[1]) It is typical of Purcell's fairmindedness that he never became embittered by his experiences, and he was among those who deplored the British blockade of Germany after the armistice and the suffering it caused to the civilian population.

After the war the veteran admission scheme enabled Purcell to spend the next two years at Cambridge University, reading history at Trinity College. The horrors of the preceding years made the intellectual and other activities possible there doubly enjoyable. He made his mark by becoming secretary of the Union and editor of *Granta*, but it seems that in those days he was not specially interested in politics (nor in political science!). Nor does he appear at that stage to have contemplated an academic career, though he said himself that he always wanted to become a writer and, from this time on, writing was always an important part of his life.

With his way to make, in 1921 he left Cambridge and entered the Malayan Civil Service. Given a choice of training, he elected to specialize in Chinese affairs (though he was warned at the outset that by thus becoming a 'specialist' he might jeopardize his career prospects). Some interruptions apart, he spent 25 years serving in various posts in the Chinese secretariat of the M.C.S. He was sent to China to study the language and, given this opportunity, applied himself with characteristic energy to understanding Chinese civilization and Chinese problems, and he found in these studies the reward of an abiding interest. Purcell has given his own account of the years in Malaya,[2] so perhaps they may be briefly passed over here. The country then

---

[1] *The Further Side of No-Man's Land*, London 1929. This he thought himself would be chiefly valued for the evidence it gave of the way prisoners were treated by the Germans which he summed up as 'little ill-treatment but much neglect'.

[2] *Memoirs of a Malayan Official*, London (Cassell) 1965.

consisted of the Federated and Unfederated Malay States, over which Britain had advisory powers, and of the Straits Settlements (Singapore, Penang and Malacca), which were under the direct control of the Colonial Office (and which contained the majority, though by no means all, of the Chinese residents). In the absence of representative constitutions, as Purcell has himself written, the M.C.S. played a more important part in government than the civil service does in democratic countries. Its servants were moreover expected to be able to undertake administrative work of any kind, no matter what expertise it might require. Over the years, therefore, he enjoyed a great variety of responsibility and experience—at different times conducting a census, supervising immigration, and inspecting schools, as well as acting as magistrate, and supervisor of prisons.

Among the problems which particularly engaged the attention of the Chinese Protectorate in those years were the activities (in Malaya) of Chinese secret societies, the suppression of the traffic in women and girls, the regulation of conditions of Chinese labourers and—by no means the least—the question of Chinese schools. The processes of education assumed new significance in the 1920s when nationalism and anti-imperialist sentiment were growing in China and political parties there took an increasing interest in Chinese communities overseas. One major problem was the content of school text books, which had to be imported from China. The matter was complicated by the inclusive Chinese idea of nationality. The Chinese thought of this as based on descent and cultural identity without regard to place of birth or residence. In Malaya, as elsewhere in South-east Asia it raised the question of the ultimate loyalty of the generation being educated (a matter still on the agenda for clarification at Bandung in 1954).

Purcell has described the duties of the local Protector of Chinese as being more like those of a village headman than of a mandarin, and he seems to have entered into the role with gusto. Each morning the Protector held an unofficial court for domestic and other cases, which the parties attended voluntarily: the decisions did not have binding force (with the exception of certain labour cases), but they were usually accepted. This particular Protector made it his business to 'visit every nook and cranny of the places of labour', whatever the difficulties of travel or distance. All this must have afforded a wonderful insight into the ways of life and thought of the Chinese community. An

English friend visiting Malaya watched him at work, and impressed no doubt with Victor's official title, describes the court sessions as follows:

It seemed to be entirely a matter of protecting the Chinese against one another, and he was prepared to listen in three or four dialects. There would be a tremendous noise, and then he would beat the table for silence and say, 'Split the difference. Next case.' It seemed a very popular form of justice.

Having in the course of his official duties become particularly interested in problems of Chinese education, he returned to his old university in 1939 and presented a dissertation on the subject for the Ph.D. degree (at the same time qualifying in law, the better to equip himself for duties as a magistrate in Malaya). This work led to an invitation to serve on a committee on the teaching of English in secondary schools set up by the Chinese Ministry of Education, an activity which involved travel in both China and the U.S.A.

He returned to Malaya, and was there in the early years of the second world war—by this time as Director General of Information and Publicity—until ordered to leave, shortly before the capitulation to the Japanese (1942). For the rest of the war he held various official appointments in the Pacific area, travelling also in Australia and the United States, and ending up with the rank of colonel, attached to Admiral Mountbatten's staff in Ceylon.

In 1945, he returned—now as Principal Adviser on Chinese Affairs to the British Military Administration in Malaya—to face some of the most difficult problems of his career, and for his work at this time he was awarded the C.M.G. When the civil administration took over from the military in 1946, he was appointed Acting Secretary for Chinese Affairs. He had then to take a decision affecting his future career. He was fifty, the minimum age for retirement, and had a choice: to stay and grapple with new problems in the country he knew well—and, presumably, to reach the honours that usually mark the peak of a conventional career—or, with this experience behind him, to make a break and embark on something new. After weighing the question carefully, he decided to resign because, he said, he wished to lead the rest of his life according to the dictates of his own nature. He had no exact idea where this would lead him and he looked around for a suitable opening.

His first assignment after leaving the M.C.S. was as a U.N. consultant, first as secretary to a Working Group on 'Devastation and Reconstruction in Asia and the Far East', and then as a consultant to

A Memoir

E.C.A.F.E., in which capacity he visited and reported on conditions in Hong Kong, Malaya, Sarawak, Siam (Thailand) and Burma, attending an economic conference in Calcutta in December 1947 as U.N. representative.

Meanwhile he conceived the idea of making a comprehensive study of Chinese communities in the various countries of South-east Asia and, under the joint auspices of the Institute of Pacific Relations and the Royal Institute of International Affairs, he spent 1948 in the United States on research for the study which has become a standard reference work on the subject.[1]

Back in England, he found himself a specialist in an almost unexplored field—in the universities, at least. The involvement in Chinese affairs which he had found a handicap in his career as a colonial official, combined with his knowledge of a wide area of Asia, made him a notable authority on a region now recognized as one of interest and importance, and entitled him to a place in the ranks of scholars trying to make up for the almost total neglect of these subjects in British universities hitherto. In 1949 he was invited to a lectureship in Far Eastern history at Cambridge, and there as scholar, writer, teacher, and publicist he spent the rest of his life. (It was during this period that most of the contributors to this volume came to know him: that they were mostly younger men follows from the facts of academic demography.) He continued to make occasional journeys to the scenes of his earlier life, and by these personal visits and through his regular and vast correspondence, he remained at the centre of a network of relationships accumulated in the course of his former experiences. He worked untiringly to spread interest in this region to a wider public. He was in demand as a public speaker and regularly addressed audiences of widely differing character. He received the Litt.D. from Cambridge in 1951, and in 1952 he was elected to membership of the Athenæum, a privilege he claimed that he enjoyed because it offered distinguished company recruited on the basis of merit and achievement without consideration of birth or wealth. (Many of us owe our acquaintance with this particular microcosm to Victor Purcell's generosity.)

As a member of the history faculty at Cambridge he gave courses on the history of the Far East and offered two special subjects for Part II of the History Tripos—the first on the Opium Wars and the second on

[1] *The Chinese in South-East Asia.*

7

the Boxer Movement (which led up to his published study on this subject). The pioneering nature of his work is attested to by the diffidence of the Seeley librarian concerning the library's ability in the first days to provide for 'subjects such as yours'.[1] Whether for this or other reasons, he did not succeed, it must be recorded, in communicating his enthusiasm for his subject to undergraduates, and he was disappointed that over the years his courses did not attract more interest. Rather surprisingly, this particular medium does not seem to have suited him. While he gave a polished paper occasionally to a learned society and discoursed fluently with popular audiences, his routine lectures were delivered in a rather jerky style and on these occasions he tended to discourage students' questions. He was, however, much in demand, and a popular speaker, with undergraduate societies and he was very successful both with adult education audiences and as a supervisor of postgraduate researchers: to these he gave generous encouragement, and none for whom he was responsible ever gave up without finishing his work.

For one who had known the pomp of imperialism in its heyday, the style of Purcell's life at Cambridge was modest (though he was always ready to enjoy—and to offer—the pleasures of good food and wine). Having lost most of his possessions in Malaya during the war, he made a simple home in which, apart from a much-loved Chinese vase and a scroll or two, books were the only treasures. Here he entertained students and friends to tea or coffee brewed with no little ceremony, while he also entertained a wide circle of friends in restaurants or at his club in London, both casually and at parties which were planned with much attention to detail and were greatly enjoyed by his guests.

After his retirement from the university in 1963, he continued to live in Cambridge (using the University Combination Room as he would his club), with an even simpler retreat in the country—a caravan tethered in a paddock belonging to friends in Hampshire, where he could work undisturbed, or, in relaxed moments, enjoy talk about the days in Malaya. From these bases he pursued his many activities with what appeared as only slightly diminished vigour until he completed the last sentence of his last chapter the night before his death.

From his undergraduate years at Cambridge, writing was for him

[1] Letter from the Seeley Librarian. (The Seeley Library is the special library for History at Cambridge University.)

always an important and regular activity. He wrote a great deal, and published work of many different genres—a novel, poetry, essays, periodical-articles, historical studies, works of reference, a book of travel[1] and countless reviews. (Though he enjoyed the theatre, he never seems to have attempted a play.) He was a master of the effective use of words, a good classical scholar, and wrote verse with facility. These talents enabled him to write surveys that were hailed as masterpieces of compression, and on occasion, when roused by the seriousness of a matter in which he was concerned, to write a telling letter to the press—often acting as spokesman for informed but less articulate opinion. Under a pseudonym which did little to conceal his identity (indeed it has been suggested to me that the name 'Myra Buttle' suited him perfectly), he published a series of skilful and witty parodies which he used in the best eighteenth century manner to attack a host of *bêtes noires*, ranging from Gertrude Stein, through various established 'worthies', to modern architecture. These he took trouble to bring to the notice of his friends, whose reactions varied according to their own complexion; they brought him some new admirers (but must have annoyed as many others) and have sometimes been quoted in anthologies. The last of the 'Myra Buttle' series, *Aere Perennius*, privately circulated two months before his death, was a passionate plea for action to preserve the best in our cultural heritage from erosion by the mass media, pop culture, and the threat of mass destruction.

It was his firm belief that in the twentieth century as in the eighteenth, clear English prose should be immediately intelligible to anyone who could read at all. And he took pains to achieve this in his own writing. (It was his habit to read aloud whatever he had just written to a selected listener, chosen often for the sake of getting the reaction of an ordinary member of the non-scholarly world—so that he could be sure that he had conveyed his meaning unmistakably.) This insistence, valuable as it may have been in his own work, was responsible for one gap in his scholarly armoury. Reluctance to allow that technical advance in a subject might require a vocabulary and style that was not immediately comprehensible to the lay public (in this he differed from Bertrand Russell, with whom he was in agreement on most other subjects) prevented him from appreciating the work of scholars

[1] See List, p. 403.

9

working in disciplines he had not made his own—notably of those in the social sciences.

His interest in China and the Chinese endured to the end of his life. Few Westerners have had the opportunities Purcell enjoyed for observing China itself at first hand over five decades, from the twenties to the sixties of this century, which gave him knowledge of it in depth. In the twenties he spent three years as a language student in Canton (1921–4), during which time it was the seat of Sun Yat-sen's government, and for a time he had Sun's Russian adviser, Michael Borodin, as his next-door neighbour. He first visited Peking and the Great Wall in the autumn of 1923. 'If I were asked to say which of my experiences in the Far East had made the greatest impact on my imagination,' he later wrote, 'I would without hesitation give Peking the position of honour.'[1] In 1937 he went to China again, this time as a member of a Chinese government committee and, cut off by the Japanese advance, he made the journey across south China which is recorded in his very readable travel book, *Chinese Evergreen*.[2] Wartime missions took him to Chungking in the forties, and later, as a U.N. consultant, he spent some weeks in Shanghai in June 1947, a witness of the inflation and the utter demoralization of the Kuomintang. Twice after 1949—in 1956 and 1962—he visited the People's Republic of China as a self-financed private observer of the transformation going on there.

He came early to an appreciation of Chinese poetry and art, and he did much to introduce these enjoyments to the English-speaking world. The list of his writings characteristically reflects his growing pre-occupation with Chinese language, poetry and education. He invented an original system for identifying Chinese characters using a numerical code[3] which though it was never widely adopted was found useful by no less a scholar than Lionel Giles. A Chinese vase of ox-blood porcelain, his most treasured possession, inspired what he himself considered one of his best poems. The practical sense and rational temper of much of Chinese thinking was congenial to him: his own life as meritocratic scholar-official ran parallel to the Confucian ideal—

---

[1] *Memoirs*, p. 150.
[2] This would deserve attention if, for no other reason, for the thinly veiled—and very lifelike—portraits of William Empson and I. A. Richards in whose company he travelled.
[3] Published as *An Index to the Chinese written language on a new non-radical system with reference to the dictionaries of Kanghsi and Giles*, Singapore Government Printing Office, 1929.

his temperament led him to pay less attention to the contemplative aspects of Chinese civilization.

His attitude to the new China was one of sympathetic interest, tinged with considerable but not uncritical admiration for the achievements of the Communist regime. 'I am not sold on it,' he said to one of the contributors to this volume in 1963. He observed realistically how slow a process reconstruction must be. The exclusion of China from normal diplomatic intercourse he considered a tragedy for the world. 'There are many [who] believe (as I do),' he wrote, 'that the policy of the "containment" of China, involving the denial to her of part of her sovereign territory, is the greatest single factor in making co-existence between the two world blocs impossible . . .'[1] Perhaps it should also be remarked that he was among the first to observe that there was nothing natural or inevitable about the Sino-Soviet alliance in the fifties.[2]

Nor was Malaya forgotten. In the years before the war Purcell had been, in the tradition of the M.C.S., a conscientious civil servant, responsible for the execution of policy, not for its formulation. This, as he later wrote, did not include preparing the country for self-government. It was as true in 1941 (when the Japanese invaded) as it had been in 1880 that all the colonial government was doing was 'teaching [the people of the country] to co-operate with us and govern under our guidance'. Nothing was done either to fuse the separate communities or foster a sense of belonging to an integrated society. The separate entities remained too much divided for any significant nationalist or independence movements to arise among the people themselves. All this was changed, however, by the experience of the Japanese occupation and anti-Japanese resistance, and a very different situation faced the British Military Administration in 1945. The hope in those first days was that the still separate communities, Communists and others, might be won over to work *with* the British towards a Malayan Union based on common citizenship. The critical issue, if this was to be accomplished (as Purcell saw and continued to urge), was to win the loyalty of the numerically and economically important Chinese element by granting them rights of citizenship on reasonable conditions. The task for statesmanship this entailed was to find a way

[1] 'What Russell has meant to me' (unpublished).
[2] *Asia Redux* (1956), ch. x (unpublished).

11

of granting the Chinese these rights without injuring the interests of the other communities in Malaya. In the event the problem was not to be dealt with simply. The situation underwent rapid changes and various expedients were adopted in the attempt to reach a solution. It is well known that, in the context of the Cold War, inter-communal dissensions and frustrations resulted in insurgency which the British had great difficulty in quelling until finally pacification was achieved by a combination of military measures, social reform and officially sponsored political development.

Inevitably Purcell continued after his retirement to take an interest in all that affected Malaya. He returned on visits in 1950 and again in 1952, on the latter occasion in the capacity of Adviser to the Malayan Chinese Association, whose guest he was while in Malaya. He was distressed at the atmosphere of distrust and suspicion he sensed on all sides. During the course of his 1952 visit an incident occurred which he allowed to assume great significance, in this perhaps showing more of his readiness to fight for causes he espoused than of his usual good sense. Some account of this must be attempted.

The situation as Purcell saw it was that by appointing a soldier (and the man recently responsible for repressing the disorder in Palestine at that), General Sir Gerald Templer, to the post of Governor, the British Government appeared to have abandoned the search for a political solution in Malaya, thus throwing away what he and others had patiently worked for. Though with the benefit of hindsight, and especially after what has since happened in Indo-China and Vietnam, we may question his judgment, it seemed to him that the 'Communist Emergency' was being made the occasion for repressive military measures. To these, and consequently to General Templer, he was strongly opposed. 'The only alternative to a communist Malaya is a strong, democratic, independent Malaya,' he wrote in a letter to the press, which continued, 'and of this there is no sign whatever.'[1] For his part, the General could not view with much favour anyone who appeared in the guise of protagonist of one racial interest when progress depended on creating inter-communal harmony in a multi-racial political community. (It is reported that he was equally hostile to champions of Indian group interests.) Moreover, he had other Chinese experts on his staff, and he may have doubted the relevance, in a

[1] *The Daily Telegraph*, 15.xii.1952.

rapidly developing (or deteriorating) situation, of the expertise of one who had been away from the country for some years and who no longer had access to official sources of information.

Following the publication of an article in *The Straits Times* which the Governor had regarded as subversive, Purcell was summoned to an interview (28.viii.1952) at which the Governor upbraided him in strong language, showing in Purcell's words 'gross and gratuitous offensiveness'. Though he undoubtedly also felt this as an affront to his personal dignity, Purcell declared that he resented the Governor's attitude as being offensive to the Chinese community whose chosen representative he was. The result was a lasting antagonism which many of Purcell's friends regarded as a waste of his energies and influence. He became an outspoken and intransigent critic of what he regarded as the General's terroristic methods.

This was probably the first time that Purcell had found himself directly ranged against authority—hitherto in his career, the tide had mostly flowed his way—and it was for him a chastening experience, not lightly to be forgotten. The shock was probably responsible for his eyes being opened to aspects of affairs that had previously escaped his notice. He wrote in a letter about this time, for example, of the effect of 'too much paternal rule for too long'.[1] It is to be noted though that neither this nor anything else shook his belief in the feasibility of ordered change, i.e. of bringing about reform by constitutional means. He urged the Malayan Chinese Association (M.C.A.) to break with the government and, in alliance with UMNO, to pursue a policy of far-reaching social reform which could win broad popular support. (In this he evidently under-rated what the government were trying to do to this end. He believed that the reforms it offered were intended only to delay self-government.) 'Malayan nationalism can arise only in opposition to the present government,'[2] he wrote, drawing a parallel with India, and continuing 'MCA policy must be anti-Government, but this does not of course mean "revolutionary" or "seditious".' The M.C.A. in a difficult position were understandably cautious but were not to be persuaded by the government to disown their Adviser.[3]

Whether it be that feelings of resentment temporarily clouded his

[1] Letter 12.ii.1953. [2] Letter of Nov. 1953.
[3] The file of correspondence between Purcell (in London) and the M.C.A. reveals his awareness of situations, patience in trying to move the M.C.A. along in the direction he felt they should be proceeding, and other qualities.

judgment or for more complex reasons it must be admitted that Purcell was wrong—though not alone in this mistake—in his assessment of British policy in Malaya at this time, both in castigating it as solely terroristic[1] and in denouncing its political bankruptcy. There is also something a little unrealistic about expecting the conventions of Westminster to be applied, by any person or group, in the conditions then existing in Malaya. It was a situation for which it would be difficult to find precedents.

When later the policy against which he had protested so vehemently did nevertheless ultimately have positive results, viz. the establishment of Malaysia, Purcell welcomed this development and was one who argued that Britain should continue to feel a special responsibility for this 'succession state'.[2]

This stand Purcell took in opposing the official British policy in Malaya brought him some new and rather unpleasant experiences. In contrast to the authority and respect he had enjoyed formerly, he was made to feel in various ways 'in the wilderness'. It involved him, for example, in a breach—never afterwards healed—with many of his old colleagues and associates, who regarded him as little better than a traitor to his country. His income from broadcasting and public lectures dropped suddenly. One incident may be quoted to illustrate the sort of thing that happened. Purcell was at the time a member of the Council of the Royal Central Asian Society. A move was made by the officers of the Society to force him to resign; Purcell refused to do so and had the heartening experience of being re-elected by the membership. For the persons concerned, in the heated atmosphere of the time, such incidents assumed what may in retrospect appear as disproportionate significance. One lesson he learned from this whole unpleasant affair was thereafter to avoid controversy for the sake of preserving whatever influence he had.

In his years of service before the war, Purcell had accepted colonialism as part of the natural order of things; then, having as part of his wartime duties and indeed throughout his life defended the British record in Malaya, he found himself afterwards taken to task by critics (some of

---

[1] An example he is said to have quoted often to justify the use of this term was the destruction of 16 houses at Permatong Tinggi. I leave the reader to decide what epithet would have been appropriate. Others who were on the spot at the time have admitted to having had similar views which they have revised in the light of subsequent events.

[2] Letter to *The Times*.

them close friends), as an apologist of imperialism. This impelled him to look at colonialism again with as much detachment as he could.[1] While he sympathized with the peoples of these areas not only in their aspiration for independence but also in their striving for forms of modern development that would not do violence to their own traditions,[2] he could not in honesty agree with the sweeping condemnation of his critics. As he contrasted the British, the Dutch, and the French records, he observed that the metropolitan powers had differed in their strengths and weaknesses but all, in his view, performed an indispensable service in bringing their dependencies into the age of science and technology; if they erred, it was not in maintaining authority, but to the extent that they refused to recognize changing circumstances and adapt their policies to suit them. This was his final judgment.

Central throughout his life was his outspoken and uncompromising rationalism. The Enlightenment, as he saw it, 'was not, as presented by the orthodox historians, merely a period in the eighteenth century when it was fashionable to rely on the unassisted reason, but a serene, philosophic and civilized state of mind which has persisted in varying degrees and in limited circles since the time of the Greeks', and his intellectual heroes, Socrates, Lucretius, Gibbon and, in his own day, Shaw, Wells and Bertrand Russell, were all men who could be identified as belonging to it. Religious faith and opinions sincerely held he was prepared to respect, and he was careful to avoid giving offence to those —of his friends, at least—whose views differed from his own. He was strongly opposed, however, to any kind of hypocrisy or obscurantism; more particularly, to the respectability and prestige accorded to established views and organized churches. In his opinion Lyell's geology and Darwin's theory of natural selection had destroyed the foundation on which Christianity rested, and the church had consolidated its social and political hold on English society in an age when its doctrines had become untenable and when no fresh inspiration was forthcoming to support its outmoded ethic. (New thinking on these subjects seems to have passed him by.) Having been sheltered during his years in Asia from external religious pressure, it came as something of a shock on his return to find that England, far from having become secularized, as is

---

[1] 'The Colonial Balance Sheet' in *The Revolution in S.E. Asia*, pp. 167–77, London, 1962.
[2] His travel diaries tell of the effort he made to come to terms with the rapid developments taking place, and how well he realized the crucial importance of education in this process.

commonly claimed, seemed to have undergone what he regarded as an irrational revival of religious orthodoxy. He compared the claims to exclusive adherence to Christianity, Judaism and Islam with the mutual tolerance of the religions of East Asia, and the western mind/body dichotomy with oriental philosophies of organism—in each case to the advantage of the latter—and despaired. Poetry, 'a sure index to the spiritual health of society', had [in the person of Eliot] taken 'a headlong plunge into mysticism and credulity', to which science, 'indifferently dedicated to man's welfare and destruction', had failed to provide a corrective. Historians and novelists (even bearers of the honoured name of Huxley) had added to the confusion and Purcell lost no opportunity for hitting out at them all, making use of his satirical verse as a vehicle for his attacks. While these views isolated him from some circles, they also brought him into contact with others. Towards the end of his life he was a member (for a time President) of the Cambridge Humanists, and it was a matter of pride and satisfaction when, in his last years, he came to enjoy the friendship of Bertrand Russell.

Of all men, it was Russell who came nearest to his ideal—'the last of the Europeans whom Socrates and Spinoza would have acknowledged as their countryman'.[1] Attracted early in his career by Russell's interest in Chinese problems (though his analysis was quite different from Purcell's own assessment at the time) and by Russell's educational experiments, he went on to examine his political opinions and was please to find that the socialism Russell advocated was in fact a kind of aristocracy—free from 'specious egalitarianism'. But it was in the matter of religion that the views of the two most nearly coincided. As the friendship ripened, they discovered much common ground, and they worked together on a number of vexed problems in the field of international relations and nuclear disarmament. The qualities in Bertrand Russell which particularly aroused Purcell's admiration were his freedom from vanity, the consistency of his career, his continued activity and influence in public affairs right into his nineties, the scrupulous fairness of his judgments ('being constitutionally compelled to admit what was good even in St Francis and Spinoza') and, above all, his compassion, which Purcell thought was Russell's outstanding characteristic.

[1] He thus paraphrased Gibbon on Boethius in a contribution to a broadcast in honour of Bertrand Russell's 90th birthday.

Purcell had a powerful mind and was prodigiously industrious. All his life he read voraciously and his memory was phenomenal—it has been suggested that he must have trained it deliberately: certain it is that he could recite his favourite poets for hours on end. He possessed great intellectual curiosity: encyclopaedias were a favourite form of bedside reading. He had a taste for literature, and especially for poetry. Besides being a good classical scholar, he had mastered a good many living languages. He was a man of strong views, which he expressed readily and forcefully; he relished an argument as a form of intellectual exercise. Apart from the subjects mentioned already, on which his views were fixed, he was otherwise and normally a fair-minded man. His entry into any circle immediately enlivened the atmosphere. Whether pro or con, he was not a man who could be ignored; and he aroused correspondingly strong reactions in others.

There are few parts of the world where he had not journeyed. He took off for a holiday in Europe, a tour in the Far East, a conference in Moscow, or a visit to his son in Persia, with as little fuss as he would for a weekend with friends in the country, and he would stay at modest rest-houses, the local barber's shop or as a pampered guest of a colonial governor with equal zest. He wrote—of a four-month journey through China and South-east Asia undertaken with the aim of bringing his knowledge of the political and economic situations existing (in 1956) in those countries up to date for the sake of his work at Cambridge:

I have never been an 'explorer' in the sense that Richthofen or Sven Hedin were explorers; my journeys have all been along well-beaten tracks. But this has been due less to a lack of enterprise than to design, for my interest was primarily in *people* and it is along the 'beaten track', rather than in deserts or on barren mountains, that human beings are to be found.

It was from people that he got a sense of what was happening. 'Human contacts are all-important in sizing up a situation,' he wrote. And among the people he met, it was among those of middle rank, he said, that he found his best 'informants'. (Whereas, by contrast, all that could be obtained from their seniors were either platitudes or indiscretions.)

He was a man to whom people mattered—not just for their services as informants. But he was also a man of principle; so issues mattered too. Occasionally differences led to rupture, though a good many old friendships endured, and he continued to make new friends among all kinds and conditions of men and women right up to the end of his life. The year before he died he gave a party for an admirer of 90 who had wanted to meet him because of their common interest in China. College servants at Cambridge are said to have reckoned it a privilege to have the opportunity of serving and talking with Purcell. He aroused their interest in reading and was never a man to 'talk down' to anyone.

Some of his relationships with women he has himself described—inimitably. He was twice married, but in neither case was the relationship successful in a conventional sense—nor did these partners play a decisive part in shaping his career. With the Atlantic between them, he remained on terms of cordiality and, to the end, exchanged witticisms with his second wife. Probably more important to him were the friendships he enjoyed with a number of women, gifted either intellectually or artistically—though he expressed himself as antagonistic to feminists as such. He liked to feel that with friends who were married he enjoyed friendship equally with each one of the pair.

He was proud of his son Hugh, taking pleasure in the fact that he should follow him in the Green Howards, and also in his oriental (though in Hugh's case Middle Eastern) and literary interests. In his last years he enjoyed spending time occasionally—usually in rather short periods—with Hugh and his wife and their two sons. It was for the grandsons that he wrote a fairy-story one weekend shortly before his death.[1]

More than is true of most people, there was internal consistency and coherence about the pattern of Victor Purcell's different activities. He lectured and wrote to create a public informed regarding the region where he had lived and worked. Poetry, to him the most significant form of literature, he used both to express his own philosophical outlook and to prick the pretensions of his opponents. Country walks could be combined with conversation with congenial companions or with visits to historical sites and to places with literary associations. Friendships formed a pervasive and sustaining network, threading through all his activity.

Purcell once claimed (writing of Cambridge as he had known it as an undergraduate) that nothing that was the creation of human beings, fallible like himself, could have legitimate claims to his uncritical appreciation. Until late in his life, however, two qualities in him—the

[1] See List, p. 405.

tolerance he felt to be due to human beings as such and his capacity for becoming engrossed in the detail of the scene or activity currently engaging his attention (which militated against detachment)—combined, perhaps, with the success of his own career, predisposed him nevertheless to a philosophy of acceptance: acceptance of the patriotic attitudes of 1914, of the colonial system as he found it or the authorities he consulted in his research. (Even his rejection of religion may perhaps be seen as acceptance of his father's outlook.) Comparison may perhaps be made with another ex-colonial civil servant turned writer and publicist, Leonard Woolf (though one must ask the reader to make some allowance for differences between Ceylon and the multi-cultured community in Malaya, where political advance presented a more complicated problem). Woolf enjoyed the life and learned to like and respect the people in his charge, and he clearly had gifts —and prospects —as an administrator, but a very short experience sufficed to convince him that imperialism as a system was evil. Purcell's judgment, even in retrospect was different, and his honesty compelled him to admit this. It appears that experiences in England and Malaya (after he ceased to exercise authority himself), brought him up with a jolt and persuaded him that he had been too trusting, and the shock of this realization made him ready thereafter to do battle energetically for any cause which aroused his sympathy (or against others) with what one of the contributors to this volume has called 'an endearing combustibility'.

It seems to be generally agreed that in his scholarly work he was probably better at amassing and presenting data than in the critical assessment and analysis of his documentary authorities. He was not much at home with abstract conceptualization: his intellectual world (even in his poetry) was essentially that of concrete reality; but of actual situations he had a sure grasp, learned through years of experience. In the broad surveys he attempted it was inevitable that in dealing with the whole sweep of a complex region there should be unevenness of treatment and—especially in the revision of his book on the Chinese in South-east Asia in the light of the rapidly accumulating research—that there should be some errors and omissions. It is unlikely that any other individual could have attempted such a gigantic task: such a work would nowadays be undertaken as a team project. Others have taken much further the study of the Boxers Purcell pioneered: what may be said, to judge from later work, is that the features that engaged his attention were important and the questions that he raised were worth answering. Mention must be made finally of what he contributed by active participation in conferences of both scholars and men of affairs, for it was not only to his juniors and the lay public that he spoke. In December 1964 (a month before he died) he wrote to Bertrand Russell:

Since I last saw you I have been much involved in discussions on peace in the Far East. For example, I spent nearly four days last weekend at a very high-level conference between British and Americans on China. Needless to say, I was very often in a minority of one, but I feel that it is worth while participating in conferences of this sort if only to try to introduce a note of reality into the discussions.

He was above all a very likable human being. More than one contributor to this volume has written that on all reasonable grounds he would have expected to detest Purcell, but the fact is that he nevertheless actually liked him, and the same has been said by others who are not admirers of his work. He was a warm person, with a sense of the dignity of all human beings, ready to enter into the concerns of any—save those with pretensions of their own. I have been given many examples of his generosity: he was generous with his money to anyone in need who crossed his path (and particularly to struggling poets who were brought to his notice); he was generous with his time and any special help he could give to younger scholars; he was generous too in praising the work of other men.

Though the choices of his life made it inevitable that he should be an isolated figure, if he remained alone it was from choice. In a good many homes he was an always welcome guest who was counted on to enliven the scene from the moment of his arrival. But he himself chose the way of life which permitted him to achieve a prodigious output of writing. His passing robbed public life in England of a significant figure. It was also felt as a personal bereavement by his many friends.

PART 1
CHINA

ANTI-IMPERIALISM IN THE
KUOMINTANG 1923-8

BY P. CAVENDISH

Anti-imperialism made a considerable impact upon the Chinese revolutionary movement in the 1920s, and it has influenced Chinese politics ever since. It was a leading theme not only of the Communist Party but also of its senior partner and later antagonist, the Kuomintang. The present paper examines the nature of anti-imperialism in theory and in practice in the Kuomintang between the approximate dates 1923 and 1928. This was the period of the rise and decline of the National Revolution and anti-imperialism and the problems of foreign relations played key roles in all phases of the revolution. It will not be possible to analyse Nationalist foreign policy here in any detail nor to discuss the accuracy of anti-imperialist views. The nature of Kuomintang anti-imperialism, the relationship between anti-imperialism and foreign policy, and the connection between external issues and the internal development of the regime are the main themes of this paper.

THE ADOPTION OF ANTI-IMPERIALISM
BY THE KUOMINTANG

For some time before the 1920s foreign pressures had been the most important single spur to constructive political action in China. Approaches to national problems, sometimes directly opposed to each other, were largely responses to the same basic problem of China's survival and regeneration in a threatening environment. Anti-imperialism, as a particular and systematic explanation of the contemporary world and of China's ills, began to influence these approaches in the May Fourth period (c. 1919–23). The subject of imperialism and of foreign economic and political pressures had been raised before 1911 in the debate between reformers and revolutionaries, but it was essentially marginal and attitudes on external problems remained confused. Certain political movements, such as the anti-American boycott of 1905 and the anti-Japanese boycott of 1915, could also be held to foreshadow the anti-imperialist movements of the 1920s, but these

23

movements were limited in aims and outlook and different in inspiration.[1]

The May Fourth Movement of 1919 itself marks a transition in that it clearly anticipated certain features of anti-imperialism, such as the United Front and the close coupling of domestic and internal issues, yet at the same time it, too, proceeded from different assumptions. It was aimed against Japan alone and the bitter disappointment at Versailles did not immediately lead to a general revulsion against the Treaty Powers and the existing structure of international relations. Though the Chinese attempted unsuccessfully to raise the whole question of China's international status at the Peace Conference, both Chinese diplomats and public continued to accept the basic Wilsonian goodwill of the Powers other than Japan. Only a handful of intellectuals, important though they later proved to be, were beginning to adopt more radical views. The May Fourth Movement demonstrated the existence of a vigorous public opinion on external issues and the importance of the students as its most vocal element. It also led certain sectors of society in the larger cities, especially the commercial and student groups, to join together in political activities. But the significance of the Movement for the development of Chinese opinion on external issues was still obscured by the absence of any enduring political organization, by a confusion of attitudes, and by the lack of a compelling general concept of China's position.[2]

The most notable event in China's foreign relations in the early 1920s was the Washington Conference, for the policy of the Conference formed one of the chief points of reference for Chinese policy over the following decade. The Chinese attempt to secure China's general release from treaty restrictions, and especially from the web of formal and informal burdens associated with extraterritoriality and the conventional tariff, was met by the Powers' view that China should be released as and when her judicial and administrative institutions were brought into line with those of other countries. This approach has

---

[1] Among the controversialists of the late Ch'ing period Liang Ch'i-ch'ao was particularly aware of the dangers of foreign pressure. He argued against revolution on the grounds that it would open China to spoliation by the foreign powers. These arguments were refuted by Sun Yat-sen's supporters.

[2] For the May Fourth Movement see Chow Tse-tsung, *The May Fourth Movement: Intellectual Revolution in Modern China*. Cambridge, Mass. 1964, esp. chapters 5 and 6. For a later Communist judgement on the movement, which resembles that made here, see *Hsiang-tao Chou-pao* (Guide Weekly) no. 113 (3 May 1925), p. 1044.

been referred to as the 'Washington formula'.[1] The Conference was intended to end the period of the Japanese domination of China and to usher in an era of enlightened and constructive international relations in the Far East. China's efforts at regeneration were to be regarded with sympathy and the Powers were to act together in support of these efforts.

By 1925, however, when the Washington Powers had at last acquired a sense of urgency about the China problem, Chinese politics had been transformed by the growth of the Nationalist movement and of anti-imperialism. The roles of Soviet diplomacy and of the Comintern in this development have been described elsewhere.[2] The two most important events in Chinese politics in this connection were the creation of the Communist Party of China in 1921 and the adoption of an anti-imperialist outlook by the Kuomintang. This was an important aspect of the revival and reorientation of that Party under Soviet influence in 1923 and 1924.

Sun Yat-sen, the party's leader, had previously been generally well-disposed towards the foreign powers. His career had owed much to foreign sympathy and aid at certain points and his admiration for many aspects of Western and Japanese life tended to give him a characteristic outlook which was the opposite of anti-imperialist. He had generally believed that a more extensive foreign involvement in China's economic and political life would bring benefit to his country, and this idea was still alive in 1923. In October of that year, moreover, he told a student audience that the true solution to China's problems was internal rather than external. Internal and external problems, he said, were only connected in so far as domestic progress and self-strengthening would lead to an improvement in China's international status. He thus explicitly rejected the anti-imperialist view which was now taking root in advanced circles. Indeed, he mistakenly equated the views of those who feared the 'joint control' of China by the Powers with those of the reformers of the late Ch'ing period who had argued that revolution might facilitate China's dismemberment. He had not

---

[1] The discrepancy between Chinese and foreign institutions, it is needless to say, had determined the form taken by the treaties. The 'formula' had first made its appearance in the treaties contracted between China and the U.S.A., Great Britain, and Japan in 1902 and 1903; see D. Borg, *American Policy and the Chinese Revolution, 1925–1928* New York, 1947, pp. 11–12.

[2] See A. S. Whiting, *Soviet Policies in China, 1917–1924*, New York, 1954.

yet understood that such fears were now to be a particularly compelling motive for pushing ahead with domestic revolution, rather than an argument against doing so.[1]

Nevertheless, his outlook had not remained unchanged, as his reference in the same speech to the enslavement of China demonstrated. The content of his 'nationalism' (*min-tsu chu-i*), one of the original planks in the Kuomintang platform, had been significantly enlarged by January 1923 when he issued a manifesto which included a call for the revision of China's treaties. This passage, however, was based on an appeal to the principle of self-determination and was cloaked in liberal democratic terms. The general trend of the modern world, to which the manifesto referred, was that of 1776 and 1789 rather than that of 1917.[2]

By January 1924, three months after the arrival of Borodin in Canton, the First National Congress of the Kuomintang had adopted a much more radical document calling for the abolition of the 'unequal treaties' and of all similar aspects of foreign privilege in China. The termination of tariff restriction became an important part of Kuomintang policy. The specific influence of anti-imperialist ideas was evident in many of the documents of the Congress. All classes of Chinese society were said to be suffering under imperialist oppression and exploitation. Chinese industry was being held back by the conventional tariff, and imperialism was said to be ruining the Chinese countryside. Above all, the imperialists were alleged to be hand in glove with the warlords, covertly supporting them in order to keep China backward and disunited.[3] Such views constituted a total rejection of the pretensions of the Washington Powers.

[1] Text in *Kuo-fu Ch'üan-shu* (Complete Works of Sun Yat-sen), III, 252–258. In 1923 he was considering the possibility of American intervention in Chinese politics to secure a negotiated conclusion to the endless civil wars; see Li Yun-han, *Ts'ung Jung-Kung tao Ch'ing-tang* (From the Admission of the Communists to the Purge), Taipei, 1966, p. 209.

[2] Text of the Manifesto in *Chung kuo Kuomintang Li-nien Hsuan-yen Hui-k'an* (Collected Declarations of the Kuomintang), December 1928. The attitudes of Sun and his colleagues towards external issues in the decade before 1923 are still somewhat obscure, but it appears that by the summer of 1922 Sun was losing sympathy with the Washington Powers; see, for example, *Sun Chung-shan Hsuan-chi* (Selected Works of Sun Yat-sen), Peking, 1962, I, 440 and *Kuo-fu Ch'üan-shu*, p. 1030. (His antipathy for Britain had a longer background, dating back to about 1913.)

[3] *Ko-ming Wen-hsien* (Documents on the Revolution) VIII, 1122–36 gives, the text of the Manifesto and of the resolutions from which these points are taken. The warlord-imperialist link, in so far as it concerns groups other than the Anhwei and Mukden Cliques, has often been uncritically accepted. It should be subjected to a much closer examination than any it has so far received.

There is some evidence that Sun was reluctant to commit himself openly to these novel views, as he was afraid of the effect on some of his long-standing supporters, but his mood was changing and there is little doubt that his quarrel with the Diplomatic Body over the Canton portion of the Maritime Customs surplus greatly contributed to the change. The customs dispute came to a head in December 1923, shortly before the Congress, and resulted in a humiliating defeat for Sun. It also coincided with the earliest period of the Soviet mission, a period in which the prospect of effective Soviet assistance only accentuated his disillusion with the West.[1]

In the last months of Sun's life events further sharpened his sense of disillusion and stimulated more strident calls for a new era in China's foreign relations. The local conflict between Sun and the British naval authorities in August 1924 and certain incidents in the course of his journey from Canton to Peking in the last few weeks of the year strengthened his belief that the Western Powers were actively opposed to him. He spent his last active weeks, in November and December, planning a People's Convention which would bring all the democratic forces in the country to bear against imperialism and militarism. Propaganda movements were launched by the Kuomintang for the promotion of the Convention policy and, slightly later, in connection with Sun's death. Anti-imperialism was an important issue in both movements.[2]

[1] Sun's hesitation is described in a contemporary note made by Borodin and reprinted in A. I. Cherepanov, *Zapiski Voyennogo Sovietnika v Kitaye* (Notes of a Soviet Adviser in China), Moscow, 1964, pp. 67–72. Sun apparently particularly feared the effect of his new stand on his Overseas supporters who might worry about their position in the colonial territories of South-east Asia. For the customs dispute see S. F. Wright, *The Collection and Disposal of the Maritime and Native Customs Revenue since the Revolution of 1911* (2nd ed.) Shanghai, 1927, pp. 185–7. For Sun's attitude see Lo Chia-lun, *Kuo-fu Nien-p'u Ch'u-kao* (A Draft Chronological Biography of Sun Yat-sen), Taipei, 1958, vol. II under dates 7 and 30 December 1923, and the Kuomintang 'Manifesto on the Customs Problem' in *Chung-kuo Kuomintang Li-nien Hsuan-yen Hui-k'an*, 1928, p. 50 ff.

[2] In August 1924 the British consul in Canton warned Sun not to bombard the merchant quarter of the city in furtherance of Sun's dispute with the merchant community. The Kuomintang manifesto of 1 September was strictly anti-imperialist in tone and content; see text in Lo Chia-lun, *Kuo-fu Nien-p'u Ch'u-Kao*, II, pp. 686–7. The Convention Policy was outlined in a manifesto of 10 November 1924, text in *Sun Chung-shan Hsuan-chi*, II, 880–883. It is impossible to discuss here other relevant events, such as the anti-imperialist movement in Peking in the summer and autumn of 1924, which was connected with Soviet diplomacy, or the Shamien strike of July and August, or the movement in the Hunan mission schools later in that year.

Sun's lectures on 'Nationalism', given early in 1924, provide further evidence of the Soviet influence upon his outlook. He spoke warmly of the Russian Revolution and denounced the betrayal of self-determination since the first world war. Tai Chi-t'ao's contemporaneous rejection of the Washington Conference for the speciousness of its good intentions can also be regarded as an indication of Sun's attitude.[1] Sun was, moreover, aware now of an alleged drain of 'not less than 1,200,000,000 dollars' per annum from China to the imperialists, and he spoke of China as an exploited 'sub-colony'. It is important to note, on the other hand, that he and his followers continued to believe that the introduction of foreign capital on satisfactory terms was a necessity for China's development.[2]

It is well known that Sun did not accept Marxism, and his lectures show no important concessions to Marxist viewpoints. He did not, therefore, give any further analysis of imperialism and the concept did not figure in his discussions of democracy and popular livelihood. The rest of his observations on Nationalism demonstrate his pride in China's past and his belief in China's moral superiority over the 'advanced nations'. The lectures taken as a whole, with their superficial application of a simplified anti-imperialism and their nationalistic tone, were typical of the outlook of the majority of his non-Communist followers. The speech on 'Greater Asianism', which he gave in November 1924 during his short visit to Japan, also dealt with a theme which had a lasting appeal for Chinese Nationalists and which shows once again the thinness of the anti-imperialist veneer over the nationalism beneath.[3]

The link between evil foreign influences and domestic warlords or other political opponents and the idea of economic exploitation were the two leading notions derived from anti-imperialism which really fastened hold on Chinese political opinion. Both became commonplaces

[1] Text of the lectures in *Sun Chung-shan Hsuan-chi*, II. For Tai, see his 'Kuomintang ti chi-wang k'ai-lai', dated 27 January 1924, in *Ko-ming Wen-hsein*, VIII, 1174.

[2] On the need for foreign capital see Sun's lectures on 'Popular Livelihood', in *Sun Chung-shan Hsuan-chi*, II, 804, and see also Article 2 of his 'Fundamentals of National Reconstruction' (*Chien-kuo Ta-kang*), April 1924.

[3] The lectures on 'Popular Livelihood' were not given until August 1924. The speech on 'Greater Asianism' was given on 28 November 1924, text in *Kuo-fu Ch'üan-shu*, pp. 1022-1026. M. B. Jansen discusses the last period of Sun's life and his pro-Japanese sentiment as a facet of his hostility towards Western imperialism in *The Japanese and Sun Yat-sen*, Cambridge, Mass. 1954, chapter 9 and Conclusion.

of nationalist thinking from one end of the political spectrum to the other. At the Communist end of the spectrum these views were wedded to a comprehensive theory of modern history and society. At the other end they were widely accepted without such a basis and were combined with the kind of ideas and sentiments which have been preserved in Sun Yat-sen's lectures. The broad acceptance of the theory of economic imperialism is suggested by the prefaces to Ch'i Shu-fen's study of the subject, published in 1925. These were contributed by T'ang Shao-yi, Wu Chih-hui and Kuo Mo-jo, three men of very different character.[1] And allegations of underhand links between political opponents and some foreign power became a standard feature of Chinese politics.

Anti-imperialism had important implications for Kuomintang ideology and policy. It served as the leading argument for the identity of the political interests of the different sectors of Chinese society, thereby reinforcing the Kuomintang's hostility to concepts of class division. All but a tiny minority of political outcasts such as warlords, bureaucrats, compradores, local bullies and other parasites of imperialism were suffering under the same yoke. The Kuomintang claimed to be the champion of the minimum demands of the individual sectors of society, but at the same time deplored the promotion of individual sectional interests at the expense of the people as a whole. The clearest application of this United Front argument was to the labour movement. The workers were adjured to strike against foreign management only and to co-operate with the Chinese bourgeoisie in the national movement, for they were told that their real exploiters were the imperialists.[2]

The tendency to attribute all of China's afflictions to imperialism grew from 1924 and gave rise to the view that external problems were more fundamental and more urgent than the internal issues which were merely their final products. Equivocation in the actual strategy of the anti-imperialist movement was introduced, however, by the fact that the primary means of struggle was not to be a direct struggle with the imperialists but a civil struggle against their catspaws, the warlords. A

---

[1] *Ching-chi Ch'in-lueh hsia chih Chung-kuo* (China under Economic Aggression), Shanghai, October 1925.

[2] See, especially, Sun's speech of May Day 1924, in *Sun Chung-shan Hsuan-chi*, II, 839–846. Communists reconciled the United Front principle with the promotion of the labour movement by regarding the proletariat as the vanguard of the entire revolutionary movement and of the anti-imperialist movement in particular.

convincing case could be made to support this approach, but it did tend to obscure the clarity of the aims of the revolution and it opened the door to the indefinite postponement of the realization of anti-imperialist aspirations.

It was also realized that the evils of imperialism, being largely invisible to the uninitiated, were more difficult to explain to the masses than the patent evils of militarism. This was all the more true since a distinction was generally drawn between anti-imperialism and mere anti-foreignism. Sometimes, however, the older and cruder type of appeal was used.[1]

ANTI-IMPERIALISM AND NATIONALIST
FOREIGN POLICY 1925-7

The difficulties of promoting anti-imperialism were very greatly reduced by the 'incidents' or 'tragedies' of the May Thirtieth period, that is, from the summer of 1925. A foreign observer complained that 'even the soberest Chinese' were feeling the effect of the incidents.[2] The May Thirtieth and subsequent incidents directly accelerated the growth of the Kuomintang and of the Communist Party and caused a general strengthening of the urban revolutionary movement. The Hupeh branch of the Kuomintang, for example, described the period after the Incident as the one in which the provincial organization had for the first time acquired a certain standing with the public, and the establishment of formal provincial branches in a number of areas was closely related to the movement of protest. Kuomintang membership figures are difficult to use, but it cannot be doubted that the May Thirtieth Movement accounted for a very large part of the approximately fourfold increase in registered membership between 1924 and

---

[1] The distinction was made, for example, by Wang Ching-wei in his *Kuo-min Hui-i Wen-t'i Ts'ao-an* (Draft Resolution on International problems for the National Convention), Peking, 1925, p. 116. For the use of the older appeal see Wu Chih-hui's speech of 9 May 1927, in *Wu Chih-hui Wen-chi* (Writings of Wu Chih-hui), p. 20. See also the Kuomintang propaganda manual on the abolition of extraterritoriality issued in July 1929, entitled *Shou-hui Ling-shih Ts'ai-p'an-ch'üan Yun-tung Hsuan-ch'uan Ta-kang* (Outline of Propaganda on the Recovery of Consular Jurisdiction). Extraterritoriality, it was alleged, had led to the establishment not only of race-tracks and brothels, but also of foreign hospitals, in which medical experiments were performed on Chinese. The Kuomintang was drawing here on the popular fears which had caused so much trouble in the nineteenth century.

[2] The American Minister, MacMurray, quoted in D. Borg, *American Policy and the Chinese Revolution, 1925–1928*, p. 63.

1926.[1] The effect on the Communist Party can be traced more accurately for the 994 members enrolled in the Party and the 2,365 members of the Communist Youth Corps at the beginning of 1925 increased to 4,000 and 9,000 respectively after the Incident.[2]

In Nationalist and Communist terms the anti-imperialist movement was a mass or public (i.e. extra-party) movement and a valuable vehicle for their influence, and it functioned in this way in many different parts of the country. The united front of 1919 was revived on a wider basis and, being linked now to a substantial political movement, the agitation of 1925 did not turn into an influential political episode, but became the basis of a continuing political process.[3] This was especially so in Canton and Kwangtung where the response to May Thirtieth and to the much bloodier Shakee Incident of June 23 contributed a great deal to the strengthening of the Nationalist regime.

The anti-imperialist movement which now got under way was largely confined to the ports and cities but now for the first time also began to affect certain parts of the countryside, especially those under the Kuomintang's control. [4] The most important groups concerned in the movement from 1925 were the students and the unionized workers, though the commercial sector was also active more intermittently. This was perceived by the American Minister, who spoke of

[1] Hupeh Branch report in *Chung-kuo Kuomintang Ti-erh tz'u Ch'üan-kuo Tai-piao Ta-hui ko Sheng-ch'ü Tang-wu Pao-kao* (Provincial Party Reports to the Second National Congress of the Kuomintang), May 1926, pp. 37–9. For the establishment of provincial branches see *Chung-kuo Kuomintang Ti-erh Chieh Chung-yang Chih-hsing Wei-yuan-hui Tsu-chih Pu Pao-kao* (Report of the Organization Department of the Kuomintang Central Executive Committee), March 1929, pp. 2–4. For the general political effect in various areas see reports in *Hsiang-tao Chou-pao*, pp. 1387–8, 1424, 1809–10, and 'Nan-ch'ang Ta Shih Chi' (Record of Important Events in Nanchang) in *Jindaishi Ziliao* (Materials of Modern History), 1957, no. 4, pp. 113–4. The official figures for Kuomintang membership were these: in 1924, no contemporary figure, but an official estimate of 1929 gave it as 'less than 50,000' within China; in January 1926 T'an P'ing-shan reported to the Second Congress a total of 175,875, but this was certainly a minimum figure, and the branches claimed a total of 284,987 either registered or in process of registration.

[2] Figures from E. H. Carr, *Socialism in One Country*, III, 693 n. and 728.

[3] There were indeed still fluctuations in the revolutionary movement outside Kuomintang territory. The movement in Shanghai ebbed from July onwards. In Peking the arrival of the Manchurian forces in the spring of 1926 dampened the movement there. It was not long, however, before the Northern Expedition reopened the situation.

[4] See the Manifesto of the Second Provincial Congress of the Kwangtung Peasants' Association, May 1926, in Chang Yu-i, *Chung-kuo Chin-tai Nung-yeh Shih Tzu-liao*, Peking 1957, II, 708. And see A. L. Strong, *China's Millions*, New York, 1935, p. 165, for Hupeh.

'the importunities of artificially formed unions of coolies and school-boys'. As in 1919 the students were in the forefront of the agitation but they now had behind them a political movement and an anti-imperialist ideology. Students and their teachers, including those in middle schools, henceforth became one of the chief pillars of the Kuomintang and its vanguard in the areas outside its control.[1] The workers played an important part in the movement partly because of the concentration of industry in the areas under foreign influence and partly because of the anti-imperialist zeal of the Communists, who made the labour movement their special concern. Indeed, apart from the students in missionary schools and colleges, the industrial workers in foreign establishments were the group at closest quarters to 'imperialism'.[2]

Among the organizational forms of the anti-imperialist movement the boycott committees, the student unions, the Chambers of Commerce, and the Leagues of All Sectors of the People had already appeared by 1919. But the rejuvenated Kuomintang, the Communist Party and the new trades' unions had now entered the scene. The boycotts are particularly interesting as they illustrate most clearly the characteristic features of Chinese mass movements. A number of boycotts had been staged since 1905, generally against Japan, and boycott movements were to recur until the early 1930s.[3] With the sanction of patriotism boycott organizers attempted to apply restraints to trade in the goods of the country concerned and to withhold daily necessities and services from the foreigners involved. Fines, bonfires, imprisonment and various forms of public shaming were used on occasion to persuade or punish recalcitrant Chinese merchants. Chambers of commerce and commercial organizations inevitably played a major role in all boycotts but between 1925 and 1927 they were somewhat overshadowed by the labour and student organizations. The great Canton and Hong Kong strike and boycott, which was supported by the Nationalist regime in Canton, built up a powerful coercive organization which its Communist leaders deliberately compared to a small state. The example of the Canton Strike Committee

[1] The words are those of MacMurray, quoted in D. Borg, *American Policy and the Chinese Revolution, 1925–1928*. p. 62. The importance of intellectuals as a vanguard in warlord areas is attested by the reports in the first work cited in note 1, p. 31, above.
[2] For the workers in the May Thirtieth Movement see J. Chesneaux, *Le Mouvement Ouvrier Chinois de 1919 a 1927*, Paris and The Hague, 1962, chapter 11.
[3] C. F. Remer, *A Study of Chinese Boycotts*, Baltimore, 1933, provides an outline of these movements.

was followed on a smaller scale at Wuhan in 1927 where the pickets of the Hupeh General Trades' Union took on the specialized functions of a revolutionary and anti-imperialist police force.[1] Outside Kuomintang territory the authorities were likely to curb such activities.

It may be true in many cases, as anti-imperialists always alleged, that local military authorities suppressed patriotic agitation in order to oblige foreign interests but, on the other hand, most forms of public activity were liable to arouse suspicion under a military autocracy, especially in a society where sectional groups or organizations tended to assume political powers in the matters which concerned them. Sun Yat-sen, for example, showed his appreciation of the political value of all types of public body in his scheme for a People's Convention, for he had included within the scheme educational bodies, associations of Overseas Chinese and of journalists, and trades' unions. The connection between anti-imperialist or nationalist agitation and domestic revolution had in any case become obvious by this time. It was clear that the 'awakening' of the people on which the Nationalist movement depended would, if successful, bring an end to militarism as well as imperialism.

Response to external pressures, therefore, was beginning to have a decisive effect on domestic politics now that the Nationalist regime was gathering strength for the territorial expansion on which it embarked in 1926. Since the nationalist impulse was the chief *raison d'être* of the revolutionary movement and was the bond between its otherwise diverse components, it is not surprising that the tide of indignation which arose in 1925 stimulated its growth. The anti-imperialist movement continued to sustain the Kuomintang over the following two years, but, with the rising power of the regime, the relationship between anti-imperialist ideology and Nationalist foreign policy becomes the most interesting facet of the revolution in its external aspect.

The chief implication of anti-imperialism for Nationalist foreign policy was the Kuomintang's adherence to the World Revolution

---

[1] Methods of shaming included the use of cages and of 'kneeling and weeping teams' which applied moral pressure against the merchant or his employees.

The comparison with a small state was made by Teng Chung-hsia in a speech printed in *Jindaishi Ziliao*, 1958, no. 5, p. 104. For the Hupeh General Trades' Union see e.g. Chiang Yung-ching *Pao-lo-t'ing yü Wu-han Cheng-ch'üan* (Borodin and the Wuhan regime), Taipei, 1963, pp. 101, 141.

centred on Moscow. This relationship, which had begun to form from 1923, was greatly strengthened from the time of Sun's final illness early in 1925. For two years thereafter Nationalists of all but the further reaches of the right wing spoke of their movement as a part of a larger whole. The documents of the Kuomintang's Second National Congress (January 1926) show how anti-imperialism came to overshadow all other aspects of the Kuomintang programme in Party statements.[1] It was held to imply three grand strategies: alliance with countries treating China as an equal, that is, the U.S.S.R.; alliance with the oppressed peoples of the world, that is, with the colonial movements stretching from the Riff to Korea, and thirdly, alliance with the oppressed classes within the imperialist countries. Only the alliance with the U.S.S.R., however, had any real significance for the revolution, though Canton served as a useful base for other Asian revolutionaries until 1927.[2]

Far from involving the Kuomintang in a concerted assault on imperialist interests and outposts wherever they were to be found, anti-imperialism was sophisticated in its application, for the Nationalist offensive was almost exclusively directed against the British. Though the French were involved in the Shakee Incident and the Japanese in the events leading up to May Thirtieth, the anti-imperialist movement acquired this bias from the beginning and it retained it until the summer of 1927.[3] One of the Soviet military advisers has recalled his difficulties on two occasions when he was taken for an Englishman, and an American journalist in Canton was warned by a Kuomintang press official not to wear short trousers in the city. Again, early in 1927 the Chinese Minister in Washington, answering complaints of acts against Americans, suggested they wear some kind of mark to distinguish

---

[1] The Manifesto is printed in *Chung-kuo Kuomintang Ti-erh tz'u Ch'üan-kuo Tai-piao Ta-hui Hsuan-yen chi Chueh-i-an* (Manifesto and Resolutions of the Second National Congress of the Kuomintang), February 1926. The identification of the proletariat as the vanguard of the world anti-imperialist revolution in this manifesto shows the extent of Communist influence upon the Kuomintang at this time.

[2] The interest of some moderate Kuomintang leaders in the British Labour movement was the only important example of the third strategy.

[3] The boycott of June 1925 was directed against the Japanese for a while. It is interesting that the Communist labour leader, Teng Chung-hsia, in his early (1930) history of the labour movement, regarded the exclusively anti-British line as an aberration of warlord-capitalist origin; see his *Chung-kuo Chih-kung Yun-tung Chien-shih* (Brief History of the Chinese Labour Movement), n.p., 1949, p. 159. A. Iriye has also attributed a similar policy to the non-Nationalist authorities during 1925; see his *After Imperialism*, Cambridge Mass. 1965, p. 62 where he draws on Japanese archives.

themselves from the British.[1] The policy of concentration against a single power was a generally successful one, for it undoubtedly accentuated the differences between the leading Powers and probably hastened the moderation of British policy in the second half of 1926.

The identification of the British with the treaty system as a whole was still reasonable despite the increased importance of Japan and the United States in China since 1914. The British community also tended to dominate the foreign concessions, especially the International Settlement in Shanghai, and ran an influential English-language press which was extravagantly hostile to Chinese nationalism. The proximity of Canton to Hong Kong was another more pressing motive for the Kuomintang, and a state of extreme tension between the two cities prevailed for many months after the Shakee Incident. At a deeper level of policy the Soviet Union's belief that Britain was the centre of a world anti-Soviet front and that China was the weakest link in the imperialist perimeter must also have influenced Kuomintang policy.

During this most expansive and revolutionary phase of the Nationalist movement the foreign policy of the National Government was remarkably moderate. Though there were local incidents in mission schools and hospitals and in connection with boycotts, there were almost no attempts to denounce the 'unequal treaties' unilaterally, to confiscate foreign property or invade foreign concessions. The tension between Canton and Hong Kong was a local problem and was in any case reduced when the Kuomintang began to expand to the north. Foreign policy was centred on two elements. The first and most superficial was the maintenance of protest on the many 'incidents' of the period. Secondly, at a deeper level, the Government rejected the tardy implementation of the policies of the Washington Conference and reserved its position on all the major questions of foreign relations. The Commission on Extraterritoriality and the Tariff Conference were denounced by the Nationalists, who were opposed in principle to a conditional release from international restrictions and who could not recognize the competence of the Peking Government. In fact, the

---

[1] Memoir of Ye. V. Teslenko in A. S. Perevertailo, *Sovietskiye Dobrovol'tsy v Kitaye v 1923–1927 gg.* (Sovet Volunteers in China between 1923 and 1927), Moscow, 1961, pp. 98 and 121. Teslenko had the double misfortune to arrive in Canton on 23 June 1925 and in Kiu-kiang on 7 January 1927. He was also obliged to explain himself in English. The American was Hallett Abend, see his *My Years in China*, p. 17. The Minister's suggestion is in *Foreign Relations of the United States: 1927*, p. 53.

political situation in China had deteriorated to such an extent by 1926 that the whole approach of the Washington Conference appeared to be unworkable. The prolonged civil war induced the Powers to shelve once more the larger issues.[1]

The first phase of the Northern Expedition, from May to November 1926, brought a great increase in Kuomintang morale. When the regime moved its headquarters from Canton to Wuhan and Nanchang at the end of the year the mass movements were at their height and foreign interests seemed to be bending before the storm. The British statement of December 26 was felt to indicate that Britain was in retreat, British and Japanese envoys began to show a more respectful interest in the regime, and there was even some thought of gaining British recognition. Finally, on 3 and 7 January 1927, Chinese crowds overran the British Concessions at Hankow and Kiukiang. These events were the outcome of a month of protest against the extradition of Nationalist organizers from the British Concession in Tientsin to the Northern authorities. They were subsequently converted by Nationalist diplomacy into the formal retrocession of the concessions, the climax of the anti-imperialist policy.[2]

In the prevailing atmosphere of confidence there was much talk of the invincibility of the 'economic weapon', that is, of strikes and boycotts, as a means of routing the now unnerved imperialists. All eyes were turned to Shanghai, the repository of about one third of all the foreign investments in China and the chief refuge for the many foreigners who had fled the interior. The sturdy growth of the democratic and anti-imperialist united front in the city encouraged great hopes.[3]

[1] The Tariff Conference had to be discontinued when the Peking Government foundered after April 1926. With reference to Kuomintang policy it is true that the Nationalists began to levy the so-called 'Washington surtaxes' unilaterally from October 1926, but they knew that Britain would not oppose this step.

[2] The best description of the events of January 1927 is to be found in Chiang Yung-ching, *Pao-lo-t'ing yü Wuhan cheng-ch'üan*, pp. 91 ff. For the question of recognition see the same work, pp. 93–4, and see Eugene Ch'en's 'Report on Foreign Relations', dated 13 March 1927, in *Ko-ming Wen-hsien*, XIV, 2369–70. A Kuomintang commentary on this question, dated December 1926, was translated by 'Asiaticus' in *Von Kanton bis Schanghai*, Vienna–Berlin 1928, pp. 108–9. Foreign diplomats visiting the Nationalist regime at this point included the Japanese Sadao Saburi and the British Miles Lampson.

[3] For the confidence which prevailed up to the Nanking Incident see the end of E. Ch'en's report just cited, p. 2378. On the power of economic boycott see Sun Fo's speech of 24 January 1927, in *Sun Che-sheng Hsien-sheng Yen-lun Chi* (Collected Speeches of Sun Fo), ed. Keng Wen-t'ien, 1933, pp. 83–6, in which he suggested that the technique of physical withdrawal, so successful against Hong Kong, should be used against Shanghai.

On the other hand, by February 1927 the growing tension between Left and Right in the Nationalist movement was causing great anxiety within the Kuomintang. It was feared that Chiang Kai-shek and other more conservative forces in the Party were prepared to come to an arrangement with the Imperialists and also with the warlords to the detriment of the more radical forces. There was enough evidence of contact between Chiang, the Japanese and the North, whatever its exact nature, to justify such fears. The dominant Party group, which had assembled in Wuhan by the beginning of March, was anxious to preserve its authority, especially in the field of foreign relations.[1] Meanwhile, the landing of the Shanghai Defence Force by the British and increasing trouble between Chinese and foreigners in Nationalist territory were other sources of apprehension. For though violence against foreigners was officially discouraged, the beginning of 1927 saw a number of anti-foreign incidents in widely separated areas, and these were no longer directed solely against the British. Eugene Ch'en, the Foreign Minister in Wuhan, did what he could to deal with such incidents. By now, indeed, he was describing the mass movements as a 'diplomatic hazard', even though he owed the greatest success of his career to the disorders of 3 January.[2]

A new period in the internal development and in the external relations of the Nationalist movement opened at the end of March. While the anti-Communist forces in the Kuomintang started to organize a coup against Wuhan, the Nanking Incident of 24 March began to exercise a decisive influence on Nationalist foreign relations. Several foreigners were killed during the Nationalist occupation of the city and British and American naval vessels laid down a light barrage to ensure the safety of a party of foreign fugitives. The Incident was a blow to Ch'en, who was at first dismayed by the killings, and the Hankow *People's Tribune*, a semi-official Kuomintang organ, at first took an indulgent view of the foreign barrage. It was not clear for a while

---

[1] The best description of these events is in C. M. Wilbur and J. L. How, *Documents on Communism, Nationalism and Soviet Advisers in China, 1918–1927*, New York, 1956, pp. 388 ff.

[2] For incidents involving Americans and other foreigners see *Foreign Relations of the United States: 1927*, pp. 51, 52, 85, 86, and D. Borg, *American Policy and the Chinese Revolution, 1925–1928*, pp. 268–9. For Ch'en's attitude to the mass movements see Chiang Yung-ching, *Pao-lo-t'ing yü Wuhan cheng-ch'üan*, p. 112, quoting remarks made on 2 February and 2 March. But note the appreciation of popular support which he expressed at the end of his report cited in note 2, p. 36 above.

whether the offenders had been retreating Northerners or advancing Southerners. Only on further reflection did Ch'en make the barrage a major Chinese grievance and only later did the sensational figure of 2,000 Chinese casualties begin to circulate.[1]

The public attitude of Chiang Kai-shek was at first no 'softer' than Ch'en's. He, too, emphasized the need for further information and the seriousness of the foreign bombardment. His willingness to take appropriate action after an enquiry and his assurances that no violence against foreigners would be permitted could have been matched by any Nationalist leader. Nevertheless, the Japanese Government, which had been carefully following the Kuomintang's dissensions since the beginning of the year, very quickly adopted the policy of using the Incident to promote the prospects of Chiang and the 'moderates' at the expense of the more radical Wuhan leadership. It wished to delay foreign sanctions in order to give Chiang time to give satisfaction and to establish himself. The American Government, which was taking a generally sanguine view of the whole course of the revolution, grasped this point though it was opposed to sanctions in any case.[2] While Eugene Ch'en remained truculent over the Incident, Chiang Kai-shek took steps to find and punish culprits, Nanking being within the area of his immediate command. The Powers eventually allowed the Incident to pass without insisting on proper amends, but this course was easier to take in view of the foundation of a new anti-Communist regime in the south-east in April.

Wuhan and Moscow regarded the new Nanking Government which came into existence on 18 April as the product and client of the imperialists. It is clear, indeed, that the Powers did regard Nanking as a better, if still unsatisfactory, alternative to Wuhan, and their diplomacy reflected this view. Yet there is no evidence of any substantial foreign role in the evolution of the Nanking Government. The success

---

[1] Kuomintang documents on the Incident, including the first reports by local commanders, are in *Ko-ming Wen-hsien*, XIV, 2378 ff. The most useful collection of foreign documents is to be found in *Foreign Relations of the United States: 1927*, pp. 146 ff. Ch'en's changing reactions can be studied in *Foreign Relations of the United States: 1927*, p. 164, and Chiang Yung-ching, *Pao-lo-t'ing yü Wuhan cheng-ch'üan*, pp. 117–18. For the rumours see *People's Tribune* (Hankow) 30 March. On 21 April this paper reported 12 dead and 19 wounded as a result of the barrage.

[2] See Chiang Kai-shek's statements of 26 March and 1 April, in *China Weekly Review*, 2 April 1927, pp. 121–2, and *People's Tribune*, 5 April, p. 2. The Japanese role was first described by D. Borg, *American Policy and the Chinese Revolution, 1925–1928*, but has been dealt with much more fully by A. Iriye in *After Imperialism*, pp. 128 ff.

of the anti-Communists in the Kuomintang was determined by Nationalist politics, not by foreign manipulation.[1]

Meanwhile, the radicals in Wuhan were unable to pursue a more uncompromising anti-imperialist policy than their rivals in Nanking and Shanghai. Immediately after the Nanking Incident the Wuhan Government adopted a policy of rapprochement with Japan, ostensibly because Japan had not taken part in the Anglo-American barrage. Behind this policy lay the beliefs that deep conflicts had developed between the Powers and that Japan had not decided how to deal with the Chinese revolution. It is probable that this policy was also connected with Comintern strategy. Even after the Hankow Incident of 3 April in which Japanese marines killed several Chinese, Wuhan was not prepared to abandon the attempt at a rapprochement, and on 3 and 5 April the *People's Tribune* carried *in extenso* Sun's famous speech on 'Greater Asianism'. Eugene Ch'en, encouraged by Borodin, was preparing to deliver a message of goodwill towards Japan when, on 10 April, he learnt that identic notes on the Nanking Incident were to be presented to him the next day by the five interested Powers, including Japan. The notes jeopardized the pro-Japanese policy and the projected message was not sent, but expressions of the same outlook continued to be made by those in authority for a few weeks thereafter. It is clear, however, that this attitude was not reciprocated by the Japanese who, of all the Powers, hoped for and obtained a good relationship with the Nanking regime.[2]

This approach to Japan took place against the background of a general retreat in policy by Wuhan. Anxiety among foreigners about the rising tide of Chinese hostility and of militant trades' unionism had been greatly increased by the Nanking Incident. The Wuhan

---

[1] It must be observed, however, that the local co-operation of the foreign authorities in Shanghai was an important asset for the anti-Communists. It might otherwise have been more difficult for them to retain the advantage of surprise on 12 April. Nevertheless, similar events took place in many cities where there were no foreign enclaves.

[2] This account is based upon Chiang Yung-ching, *Pao-lo-t'ing yü Wuhan Cheng-ch'üan*, chapter III. For later expression of the pro-Japanese view see Sun Fo's speech of 25 April in *People's Tribune* 26 April, p. 2 and the article entitled 'Whither Japan' ('Wohin treibt Japan?'), published in the *Chinese Correspondence* (organ of the Kuomintang Central Executive Committee) on 1 May, translated by 'Asiaticus' in *Von Kanton bis Schanghai*, pp. 229–33. The presumption of a Soviet role in this policy is reinforced by G. Z. Bessedovsky, *Revelations of a Soviet Diplomat*, London, 1931, pp. 155–60. (The author was then the Soviet Ambassador in Tokyo.) The Japanese attitude towards the Nanking regime of 1927 is one of the more important points in Iriye's study, *After Imperialism*, pp. 144 ff.

Government was compelled to take steps to reassure foreign interests in order to stabilize its position. The war had aggravated unemployment in Wuhan and had led to a reduction in the volume of trade in Central China, a development which affected the prospects of the regime. Labour troubles and militant anti-imperialism had also played their part in demoralizing foreign and Chinese enterprise. After the Incident of 3 April foreign business in Hankow came to a virtual standstill, and after talking to the Standard Oil manager, the Japanese consul and foreign shippers, Eugene Ch'en began to insist that foreign confidence be restored. The Kuomintang Political Council rejected the suggestion of the Hupeh General Trades' Union that the Japanese factories should be confiscated and run by the state, and the alternative policy of 're-volutionary discipline' was evolved. This involved the curbing and stricter supervision of the anti-imperialist and labour movements. This policy was even more firmly promoted after the schism between Nanking and Wuhan led to isolation and greater insecurity.[1]

At the beginning of the year a Nationalist spokesman had confidently declared that, if attacked with the 'economic weapon', the British would find they had acquired a 'field of stones'. The experiences of April showed that, given the nature of the National Revolution, it was the revolutionary regime which would suffer this fate if the economic relations between Chinese and foreigners were cut off.

After the schism of April neither the Wuhan nor the Nanking Government was in a position to take any positive steps in the diplomatic field and the civil war continued to delay any substantial dealings with the Powers. The Wuhan Government was ignored by the Powers from the middle of May and was by then entirely absorbed in its internal problems. Late in July, however, the Nanking Government launched

[1] This paragraph is based on Chiang Yung-ching *Pao-lo-t'ing yü Wuhan cheng-ch'üan*, as just cited, and upon *People's Tribune*. The employment situation in Wuhan was the subject of a special article in *Hsiang-tao Chou-pao*, 8 May 1927, pp. 2129, 2130. Some information on rising prices was printed in *People's Tribune* 24 April, pp. 1 and 5. The decline in trade, as reflected in the Shanghai customs revenues for March 1927, was reported in *United States Daily* on 26 May (in Chatham House press cuttings). A meeting between E. Ch'en and American interests is recorded in *Foreign Relations of the United States: 1927*, pp. 115, 116. Ch'en spoke of the 'immediate restoration of trade conditions within Nationalist territory'. The policy of 'revolutionary discipline', as applied to labour, is spelled out in the resolution of the Central Committee of the Communist Party and of the Hupeh General Trades' Union, dated 25 April 1927, Document no. 9, in R. C. North and X. J. Eudin, *M. N. Roy's Mission to China*, pp. 186–7.

an ambitious taxation programme aimed at breaking down the fiscal immunity of foreigners, and declared its intention of unilaterally introducing a new tariff. This programme involved an acrimonious local conflict between the impoverished Nanking authorities and the indignant foreign interests of Shanghai. But the Government was too weak to carry out its intentions and the crisis passed. A similar contrast between the policy of the rival regimes occured in connection with the anti-Japanese boycott which broke out after the despatch of a Japanese force to Shantung in July. While the Kuomintang in the Nanking areas fostered the movement, it was discouraged in Central China.[1]

The Nanking Government was not the pliant tool of foreign interests, nor was its rival in Wuhan a more effective champion of anti-imperialism. Both shared the same insecurity and both, one sooner than the other, turned against the mass movements. The populist politics of the preceding period came to be seen as a source of weakness rather than of strength in the existing circumstances, and the boycott movements, which had long antedated the rise of the revolutionary movement, were the only survivors of the change. The experience of both regimes demonstrated the close links between external and domestic policy, and it is interesting to find financial pressures inducing one to increase and one to decrease the pressures on foreign interests. All factions, though not all individuals, remained anti-imperialist in the general Nationalist understanding of the term, but at the same time concrete policies were needed to deal with difficult situations and these anti-imperialism could not provide. After the purge of the Communists anti-imperialist sentiment continued to prevail in the Kuomintang, but the organization and activation of such sentiment became increasingly unacceptable to the authorities for both domestic and diplomatic reasons. There was also a growing feeling that the Nationalist movement was losing its momentum, and not least in the sphere of foreign policy. The preoccupation with military and factional struggles, the decline of the mass movements, and the complete isolation of the regime after the estrangement from the U.S.S.R. all contributed to this feeling.[2]

[1] For Nanking's taxation campaign see *Foreign Relations of the United States: 1927*, pp. 393, 396, 494 ff., and *China Weekly Review*, 2 and 6 July 1927. Contrasting policy towards the boycott in Nanking and Wuhan was noted by the Japanese Foreign Ministry in *Saikin Shina Kankei sho-mondai Tekiyo* (Summary of Problems of Current Relations with China), II, December 1927 pp. 32, 37, 38.

[2] For examples of anti-imperialist sentiment among the anti-Communists in 1927 see Wu Chih-hui's speech of 9 May as cited in note 1, p. 30 above, and the anti-British

ANTI-IMPERIALISM REINTERPRETED 1928

Early in 1928, after nine months of confusion, the Kuomintang began to revive under the renewed leadership of Chiang Kai-shek. The Fourth Plenum of the Central Executive Committee which met in February was the first major session of the leadership after the turmoil of 1927 and was an important stage in the formation of Kuomintang policy. It met at a time when several developments affecting foreign policy and anti-imperialism were taking place. The Communist rising in Canton on 11 December 1927 had further intensified certain already established trends in Nationalist policy.

The involvement of the Soviet consulate in the rising had led, three days later, to the closing of all Soviet consular and commercial establishments in Kuomintang territory and the deportation of Soviet citizens. Nationalist comment on this final rupture of relations with the U.S.S.R. varied from speaker to speaker. Some regarded the breach as regrettable and Chiang Kai-shek himself, observing that it did not mean that China would join an anti-Comintern front, professed to believe that normal relations could be restored after the civil war was over. Kuo T'ai-ch'i, on the other hand, in a speech to the American University Club in Shanghai, emphasized the global and moral significance of the step.[1] The Canton rising also provoked a renewed repression of popular organizations. The regional military authorities stepped up the 'restoration of public order', Canton, Hankow and the Kiangnan region being the areas of the most severe repression. Suspension of the mass movements was nevertheless regarded in most Party circles as a temporary expedient.[2]

The abolition of the 'unequal treaties' and the attainment of inter-

'Manifesto of the Shanghai Branch of the Kuomintang Propangada Department' in Tai Wei-ch'ing ed., *Kuo-min Cheng-fu Hsin Kung-wen, Hsin Fa-ling Hui-pien* (Official Documents, Laws, and Orders of the National Government), I, part 2, 1928, pp. 12, 13.

[1] The Government publication *Kuo-min Cheng-fu San Nien Lai Wai-chiao Ching-kuo Chi-yao* (Brief Account of the Diplomacy of the National Government over the last three years), 1929, chapter 6 gives details of the breach with the U.S.S.R., which was a virtual, not a formal rupture of relations. See also *North China Herald*, 7 January 1928, p. 3. The reference is to Chiang's statement of 13 December 1927, in *Ko-ming Wen-hsien*, XVI, 2884, 2885. Kuo's opinion was reported in *China Weekly Review*, 24 December 1927, p. 91.

[2] The Kwangsi generals in Hupeh, Hunan, Kwangsi, and parts of Kwangtung, were especially severe. Southern Kiangsu was also greatly disturbed by several local riots and risings, of which the one in Ihsing in November 1927 was the most notable.

national equality still dominated the Fourth Plenum's views on foreign policy, but the methods of achieving these aims were entirely redefined. It was now declared that it was economic and political reconstruction, rather than slogans and processions, which were required. The emphasis was shifted away from popular political activities, which were now considered useless as well as dangerous, towards a long-term programme of reconstruction and rearmament organized from above. 'Communist methods', the methods of the United Front period, could only turn China into the battleground of Red and White imperialisms. Henceforth the Nanking leaders constantly emphasized the contrast between 'mere words' and 'real work'. No passage in the Plenum's manifesto was more significant in this connection than that dealing with the student movement. The criticism of youth for joining in political and social struggles which did not concern it marked the beginning of an increasingly unsatisfactory relationship between Nanking and the nationalist youth which had played such an important part in the growth of the movement. This was important for the future of anti-imperialism.[1]

The priority given to reconstruction rather than to revolutionary agitation might perhaps be considered reasonable in itself, though it concealed important problems, but it ran counter to the generally accepted concept of anti-imperialism. Reconstruction had been regarded as impracticable while imperialist exploitation persisted, and the imperialist pressure had been singled out as the root cause of China's backwardness. The emphasis now placed upon reconstruction seemed to deny the primacy of the external problem and to contain, by implication at least, a concession to the 'Washington formula'. When accompanied by arguments against political activities it conflicted with the Kuomintang's mission to 'awaken' the people.[2]

These altered perspectives naturally affected the leaders' presentation of the international context of the revolution. The phenomenon of

---

[1] Text of Manifesto in *Chung-kuo Kuomintang Ti-erh Chieh Chung-yang Chih-hsing Wei-yuan-hui Ti-wu tz'u Ch'üan-t'i Hui-i Chi-lu* (Proceedings of the Fifth Plenum of the Central Executive Committee of the Kuomintang), 1928, pp. 7–15. On youth see also J. Israel, *Student Nationalism in China, 1927–1937*, Stanford, 1966, pp. 17–28.

[2] It is interesting that Ch'en Kung-po, who was shortly to become the spokesman of the radical wing of the Kuomintang, also held a negative view of the old anti-imperialist movement and believed that more 'preparatory work' should have preceded any attempt to tackle foreign interests. See his *Kuo-min Ko-ming ti Wei-chi ho Wo-men ti Ts'o-wu* (The Crisis of the National Revolution and Our Mistakes), 1928, esp. pp. 75 ff.

'world imperialism' was no longer described in Leninist or supposedly scientific terms. Instead, an extended metaphor was employed. Imperialism was described as a world-wide 'feudal system' in which Western Imperialism, which had fomented the world war, was compared to the Warring States, while the Comintern, a product of that war, was compared to the rapacious state of Ch'in. Both were 'tyrants' though the Red was far more dangerous than the White. In these circumstances, it was declared, China's friends might well be found in any quarter.

While the Plenum laid out new ground-lines, the civil war continued to obscure the diplomatic prospect. The North China Campaign, the last phase of the Northern Expedition, did not begin until April 1928 and lasted until June. Two important facts, however, can be extracted from the somewhat confused events of these early months of 1928. The first is that the Nanking regime was clearly anxious to reach a better relationship with the Western Powers, particularly the U.S.A. and was determined to avoid antagonising the Japanese. Secondly, there was increasing criticism of the government within Kuomintang circles, especially among the young.[1]

Huang Fu, a moderate who was regarded in some Kuomintang circles as a 'bureaucrat' (career politician) of little Party standing, took up office as Foreign Minister on 21 February. His first task was to close the Nanking Incident of March 1927 with the Powers concerned, but only the United States would enter into an agreement on this question at this time. The text annoyed and disappointed Nationalist party opinion for it included an apology by the Nanking Government but, on the American side, only contained an expression of regret for the barrage, which was described as unavoidable.[2] An important current of Kuomintang opinion regarded the agreement as evidence of the general impotence of Nationalist foreign policy. It is not clear whether there was a similar response to the Government's indulgent attitude towards Japanese anxieties about North China or towards the obvious exclusion of Manchuria from Nationalist war plans.[3]

[1] For criticism among the young see Chou Keng-sheng, 'Chin-hou ti Wai-chiao', dated 2 May 1928, in Chou Keng-sheng, *Ko-ming ti Wai-chiao* (Revolutionary Diplomacy), Shanghai, 1929, p. 74.
[2] See Chou Keng-sheng's article on the agreement in *Ko-ming ti Wai-chiao*, pp. 64–74.
[3] Indulgence towards Japan was revealed in Huang Fu's statement of 22 February; see text in *Foreign Relations of the United States: 1928*, p. 407. For the exclusion of Manchuria see Chiang Kai-shek's press conference of 6 March, in *Ko-ming Wen-hsien*,

Perhaps the most important feature of this period was the fact that the civil war was expected to end by the early summer. For the victory of the Expedition was deliberately associated in Party propaganda with a general advance on the diplomatic front. This prospect drew closer at a time when evidence of a division between Nationalist leadership and Nationalist opinion had emerged.

ANTI-IMPERIALISM AND SELF-STRENGTHENING 1928-9

In the event, the problems of foreign policy and Nationalist sentiment could not be deferred until the moment of victory. On April 19 the Japanese Government announced its decision to send an expeditionary force to protect Japanese nationals in Shantung and by the end of the month a substantial force was stationed in Tsingtao and Tsinan. Finally, on 3 May, Japanese and Chinese Nationalist troops in Tsinan became involved in a serious conflict with each other. Though it is quite probable that the initial spark was provided by undisciplined Chinese soldiers it is clear that the Nationalist authorities were surprised and alarmed by the outbreak and that they did all they reasonably could to resolve it. The Japanese, however, adopted an intransigent and aggressive attitude and by 11 May they had cleared the last Nationalist troops out of a wide zone around Tsinan and the railway to Tsingtao. They remained in control of this area for a year.[1]

Nationalist policy was formulated after the initial despatch of troops by Japan. It consisted in avoiding at all cost any deliberate conflict with the Japanese and in pressing ahead with the Northern Expedition. From the political point of view it consisted in stimulating foreign sympathy and restraining opinion at home. These policies were re-affirmed and made more urgent by the Incident, which had a profound effect on Chinese opinion in both North and South. The policy of restraining domestic opinion was particularly difficult to implement and from 4 May Nationalist leaders spared no efforts to call for public calm. Envoys were sent from Nanking to Shanghai to supervise public activities and to explain government policy to the press, a part of which favoured war with Japan. Ch'en Pu-lei, Chiang Kai-shek's aide, who was then the editor of a non-Party newspaper in Shanghai, recalls how

---

XVIII, 3191 ff. A. Iriye, in *After Imperialism*, p. 207, has pointed towards a measure of collusion between Nanking and Tokyo early in 1928.

[1] Iriye discusses the Incident in *After Imperialism*, pp. 196–205. Chinese documents are collected in *Ko-ming Wen-hsien*, XIX.

his first reaction to the Incident was to call for retaliation and how, on further reflection, he decided to promote the official policy of 'unification first'.[1]

Official propaganda was based on the idea of the non-recognition of Japanese pretensions, on the international isolation of the enemy and on the long-term self-strengthening which had been a leading theme at the Fourth Plenum. General Ho Ying-ch'in expressed the official attitude thus: 'Let all the youths of China remember the example of many Occidental powers before us. Let them prepare and train themselves. We must as a nation, persevere and check this temporary outburst of indignation ... In a decade or two we shall be able to meet any enemy in the field and wipe out once and for all the humiliations and insults which have been heaped upon us.'[2]

The government was afraid that popular violence might provoke further trouble and might alienate foreign opinion. The people were discouraged from any activities other than the boycott but they were at the same time expected to support the government. A government directive requiring the people to obey central orders and to combine 'patience and ardour' epitomized the dilemma which patriotic agitation posed for the insecure Nationalist regime. The government was very much aware of the strength of its antagonist and of the political dangers which might follow at home if its circumspect tactics were to fail.[3]

Public opinion was mainly expressed in the boycott movement. Important sections of the Kuomintang including its Shanghai leaders and the Central Propaganda Department gave it strong support and the Party clearly considered it a legitimate movement.[4] Another manifestation of opinion was the 'Student Army' established in Shanghai. By 10 June this body could muster 5,000 students in uniform but

[1] For Kuomintang policy see the 'Instruction to Party Members' of 24 April in *Ko-ming Wen-hsien*, XIX, 3544, and P'eng Hsueh-p'ei's article in the official *Chung-yang Jih-pao* (Central Daily) of 24 May, reprinted in *Ko-ming Wen-hsien*, XIX, 3640, 3641. See also *North China Herald*, 12 May, p. 215 and contemporary Chinese press reports in Hatano Kenichi, *Gendai Shina no Kiroku* (Records of Contemporary China), Peking, 1932, May 1928, pp. 104 and 108. For Ch'en Pu-lei see his *Hui-i Lu* (Memoirs) Taipei 1962, pp. 59–60.

[2] Speech of 5 May translated in *North China Herald*, 12 May p. 216.

[3] The reference is to the message to army and provincial authorities issued by Li Lieh-chün on 14 May; text in *Ko-ming Wen-hsien*, XIX, 3554.

[4] For the boycott movement see Hatano, *Gendai Shina no Kiroku*, May 1928, pp. 107 and 122–3. For the Kuomintang's attitude see *Chung-yang Chou-pao* (Central Weekly, internal organ of the Central Propaganda Department), VIII (slogans) and XII, pp. 1, 2.

unarmed. Strong reactions were not confined to the south, and the Peking Educational Association, for example, called for preparations for war with Japan.[1]

It soon appeared that the solution of the Tsinan Incident would have to await the outcome of a general readjustment of Sino-Japanese relations.[2] No solution was in sight, therefore, on 15 June, when C. T. Wang, the new Foreign Minister, opened the campaign for new and equal treaties with his first statement on foreign affairs. In this general statement he looked forward to a 'new era' in China's international relations and to material and non-material assistance from abroad after new treaties had been signed. His assurance that only legitimate means would be used to secure such treaties was not novel, but the friendly and positive tone was much more marked than that of any previous Kuomintang statement.[3] There is little doubt that many Nationalists, particularly in professional circles, placed great hopes in the U.S.A. and it was for this reason that many were very pleased by the Sino-American Tariff Treaty of 25 July.[4]

Though Wang's general policy was to attack tariff restriction and extraterritoriality simultaneously, the tariff issue was given priority. The government was determined to secure tariff autonomy by the new year, the date originally envisaged by the Tariff Conference of 1926. The chief tactics on the treaty question were to annul unilaterally at their term all the treaties which could be held to be expiring, to subject the foreigners concerned to Chinese jurisdiction and taxation on a provisional basis, and to persuade the powers with extant treaties to negotiate. The government accordingly informed five minor powers that the extraterritorial and commercial provisions of their Treaties of Amity and Commerce were no longer valid. Finally, on 19 July, this policy was applied to the much more important Sino-Japanese Treaty of 1896. The line of attack was not new, for it had been pioneered by the Peking Government from the end of 1926, but by the summer of 1928

---

[1] *The Times*, 11 June 1928, and see Hatano, *Gendai Shina no Kiroku*, May 1928, p. 107. See also J. Israel, *Student Nationalism in China, 1927–1937*, p. 22. The *North China Herald*, 12 May, p. 220, reported deep anti-Japanese feeling in the capital.

[2] Unresolved problems included the Sino-Japanese Commercial Treaty, the Nanking and Hankow Incidents and the question of Manchuria.

[3] See *Kuo-min Cheng-fu San Nien Lai Wai-chiao Ching-kuo Chi-yao*, chapter 10, and compare Nanking statements on the treaty question during 1927, in chapter 5.

[4] See, e.g. *Chung-yang Chou-pao*, IX, p. 2, and Chou Keng-sheng's article of 9 September, 'A new era in foreign relations', in his *Ko-ming ti Wai-chiao*, pp. 155–66.

it could be applied more widely. Wang's boldest move was to apply it to the Japanese treaty which had been renewed for successive short terms since its expiry in 1926 by the more cautious Peking administration.[1]

Government policy was not making a favourable impression on Nationalist opinion, however. Wang's statement of 15 June was far removed from the anti-imperialist sentiment which prevailed among much of the rank and file of the Kuomintang, and the unilateralist spirit fostered over the preceding three years was not to be assuaged by diplomatic manoeuvres. In fact, the whole conduct of foreign relations had been subjected to much more criticism after Tsinan, such criticism being ultimately based on the concept of 'revolutionary diplomacy'. In Nationalist usage this term indicated a bold and aggressive approach ignoring precedent and convention, dedicated to overturning the status quo and constantly keeping the initiative. Based on a definite strategy, it was not to be confined merely to dealing with crises as they occurred. Its two leading characteristics were 'revolutionary spirit' and popular support. The former was interpreted as the rejection of all timidity and compromise while the latter was to be the substitute for the arms which China did not possess. The revival of the organized mass anti-imperialist movement and the opening of foreign relations to full publicity and discussion were two important corollaries of these views. Chinese leadership of a specifically Asian revolution and direct contact between the Kuomintang and foreign peoples, thus avoiding the corrupt apparatus of international diplomacy, were other features of discussions of this subject. Finally, the substitution of bilateral dealings with individual powers for relations with the Treaty Powers as a single and powerful bloc was regarded as a hallmark of revolutionary diplomacy.[2]

Ch'en Kung-po, now the spokesman of the more radical wing of the Kuomintang, had reacted to Tsinan by calling for the revival of the mass movements as the basis of a more forceful foreign policy and had drawn attention to the government's failure to present China's views either at home or abroad. He complained of 'Peking-style diplomacy' in which it was not considered necessary to inform, let alone to convince, Chinese opinion on questions of foreign policy. These points,

[1] A. J. Toynbee, *Survey of International Affairs 1928*, pp. 422, 423, contains a useful summary of treaty problems between 1926 and 1928.
[2] For the idea of 'revolutionary diplomacy' see Chou Keng-sheng *Ko-ming ti Wai-chiao* pp. 1–10, 74–84 and *passim*.

and especially the desire for a revival of the mass movements, were echoed by a large number of Party branches. Many branches appealed to the Fifth Plenum (August 1928) for 'thorough' or 'revolutionary' measures and some demanded the formal denunciation of the treaties and the rejection of all talk of 'revision'.[1]

There was also a distrust of the professional diplomats and a desire to replace them with good Party men. C. T. Wang himself, a Christian as well as a 'bureaucrat', was considered in many Kuomintang circles a doubly unsuitable person to hold his particular office. The Kwangtung Party Branch, the largest in the country, called for greater care in diplomatic appointments and observed: 'The so-called "diplomatic" personnel of the present, the men with experience, are merely skilled in striving to please and in manoeuvring for advantage. As for national interest or diplomatic strategy, they just have no conception of what they are.' Behind this view lay the idea that China's diplomatic champions since 1919 had mistakenly tried to play the game in the style and according to the rules laid down by China's oppressors, an enterprise that was bound to lead nowhere. One commentator, indeed, commended the U.S.S.R. for its uncouth attitude towards established rules.[2]

Frustration and conflict on the subject of foreign relations came to light most clearly during July when the Centre canvassed Party branches for their views on current problems. Dissatisfaction with the Government's approach increased during the remainder of the year, for the Foreign Ministry made no bold moves. Nationalist suspicions that the Government lacked the firmness of will which was required were redoubled by the authorities' reluctance to inform the public about their activities. The general political background also had a strong influence upon opinion and tended to aggravate this situation. In August the conflict between the radical and moderate factions within the Party passed the point of reconciliation and in September the

[1] 'Proposals' of Party branches in *Chung-kuo Kuomintang Ti-erh Chieh Chung-yang Chih-hsing Wei-yuan-hui Ti-wu tz'u Ch'üan-t'i Hui-i Chi-lu*, pp. 348–353. Ch'en's views were expounded in *Ko-ming P'ing-lun* (Revolutionary Critic), no. 2, p. 3.

[2] The Shanghai and Anhwei branches proposed that no Christians should be given diplomatic appointments, while the Kwangtung branch wished to see Christians excluded from the Kuomintang altogether; see the work cited in the previous note, pp. 348–53. The Kwangtung opinion cited here is from *Chung-yang Chou-pao*, VIII, p. 1. Chou Keng-sheng praised Soviet diplomacy in an article of 8 August 1927, in *Ko-ming ti Wai-chiao*, pp. 8–10.

moderates, who retained control of the Centre, began a counter-attack upon their critics. The Party crisis which developed over the next six months was occasioned mainly by the organizational policies of the Centre, but questions of foreign policy also played their part. Those who criticized the leadership for its authoritarianism and its tendency to compromise with feudalism and bureaucracy tended to be the same as those who complained of failure and weakness in the field of foreign policy. The Foreign Minister, for his part, claimed to welcome 'urban organizations for the treaty abolition movement' but he appealed for a careful study of external problems and warned against the unbalanced pursuit of 'ideological thoroughness'.[1]

Protest reached its furthest point early in December. Rumours that China was about to recognize the Nishihara loans (contracted in 1917 and 1918) were compounded by the publication of new treaties with Belgium and Italy on 29 and 30 November. Nationalist opinion was disappointed to find most favoured nation provisions attached to the extraterritoriality clauses of the treaties. More offensive still was the annexe to the Belgian treaty, which would entitle Belgians to trade, live, and own property anywhere in China on the expiry of extra-territoriality. Though this was an inescapable consequence of getting rid of extraterritoriality it awakened fears of being swamped by acquisitive and troublesome foreigners, particularly if the Japanese should acquire similar rights. Finally, China's promise to introduce suitable civil and commercial codes by January 1930 was felt to be an affront.

Dissatisfaction with the treaties, rumours about the loans and, finally, the unexplained arrival of an eminent Japanese politician in Nanking provoked an angry demonstration there on 13 December. The Anti-Japanese League, the universities, the middle schools and the Kiangsu section of the Kuomintang organized a rally to protest against C. T. Wang and his policies. Chiang Kai-shek himself argued with the demonstrators on the theme that discipline and legality were essential aspects of the struggle with imperialism. A more peaceful rally with the same purpose was held two days later in Peiping, as Peking had recently been renamed.[2]

---

[1] Wang made this claim in a press interview of 10 September; see *Chung-yang Chou-pao*, xv, p. 6. It should be noted that strong feeling on external issues was not confined to opponents of the regime on domestic grounds.

[2] For the treaties see *Kuo-min Cheng-fu san nien lai Wai-chiao Ching-kuo Chi-yao*, chapter 10 and appendices. For public criticism and for the demonstrations see 'Nan

Chiang Kai-shek had already tried to stem the tide of criticism on 10 December in a speech at the Central Party Headquarters. He had attacked those who disliked the annexe to the Belgian treaty on the grounds that their ideas were out of date and betrayed a fear of the foreigners. China could no longer close her doors, but the foreigners would not be so intimidating if China could only become united and acquire a strong army. The main significance of Chiang's speech and of central policy in general was that the timetable of anti-imperialism was being completely recast. Abolition of the treaties, Chiang declared, would take 'at least three years, or a bit more slowly, five or ten years'. Such a long period would be necessary for 'self-strengthening' because the Chinese now needed to become men of the twentieth century and this meant 'adopting present-day culture, law, economy and politics'. While this effort was going forward the spirit of antagonism would have to be kept alive, but the agitation and the inflammatory tactics of the previous period would be eschewed. Chiang explained that the masses were indisciplined and inconstant in their patriotic resolve and went on to say that the Party members were not capable of giving them the guidance they needed.[1]

He was clearly shifting the main tasks from the people to the state, a shift of emphasis which had been most clearly expressed by two of the moderate leaders at the Fifth Plenum: '. . . the imperialists are afraid not of processions, lectures, societies and assemblies of our people, but are afraid of our country having a strong and united government and of us having a strong central force to reform political life.' This passage shows how the leadership's preoccupation with the apparatus of central government, a feature of Nationalist politics in 1928, had an important bearing on the future of anti-imperialism.[2]

'Self-strengthening' was the key term in Nanking's pronouncements

hsing Tsa lu' pp. 1, 2 in *Kuo-wen Chou-pao* (National News Weekly), VI, no. 1, and press reports in Hatano *Gendai Shina no Kiroku*, December 1928, pp. 97, 118, 119, 213 ff. 222–5, and see account of a meeting between a deputation of protest and C. T. Wang on 16 November in the above title, pp. 231, 232.

[1] Chiang's speech is printed in *Chiang Tsung-t'ung Yen-lun Hui-pien*, IX (Speeches of President Chiang), IX, pp. 105–13. See p. 105.

[2] The quotation is from the motion put before the Plenum by Miao Pin and Ho Ying-ch'in, in *Chung-kuo Kuomintang Ti-erh Chieh Chung-yang Chih-hsing Wei-yuan-hui Ti-wu tẓ'u Ch'üan-t'i Hui-i Chi-lu*, pp. 126 ff. One of the chief reasons given by Nanking leaders for the establishment of the Five Yuan Government was the need to impress foreign nations, see T'an Yen-k'ai's of 8 October in Hatano *Gendai Shina no Kiroku*, October 1928, p. 141.

on external problems. Historically, it was associated with the ultimately unsuccessful movement to strengthen China without substantial internal change in the latter part of the nineteenth century.[1] Tai Chi-t'ao complained that the term had become unfashionable in recent times, especially among the young. Concerned to place the idealistic and nationalistic strands of Kuomintang ideology in perspective, Tai pointed out that though Sun Yat-sen had taught 'universal love' and 'global harmony' he had spoken even more frequently about wealth and strength as national aims. Nations, Tai maintained, were established by arms, and military life and military needs, however regrettably, were of great cultural significance for the development of society and the individual. It was in this context that Tai and Chiang both emphasized the importance for the new China of the Japanese example.[2] Professor Mary Wright's brilliant essay on the increasing influence of the T'ung Chih Restoration upon Chiang Kai-shek's outlook may be referred to for the background and the wider significance of the concept of 'self-strengthening' in this period.[3]

Tai's remarks show the leadership's concern with the problem of rearmament and, more generally, with the problems of the state. In his lectures on Nationalism Sun Yat-sen had argued that the nation or people was the product of nature while the state was the product of force. He had drawn a contrast between the natural growth of China and the violent extension of the British Empire, and Nationalist writers commonly castigated the West for its cult of 'organized homicide'.[4] Nevertheless, Tai's nationalism was probably as close as that of any Nationalist leader to the nationalism of Sun Yat-sen, for the difference in their approach on these two occasions reflected the Kuomintang's rise to power rather than any incompatibility in their views.

[1] S. Y. Teng and J. K. Fairbank *China's Response to the West: A documentary Survey*, Cambridge Mass., chapters 5 and 17.

[2] Tai's argument is contained in his article, probably a broadcast given in December 1928, entitled 'Cheng-li Chün-shih shih Fu-kuo Ch'iang-ping ti Chi-tien' (Military Reform is the foundation for the achievement of 'A wealthy nation and a strong army') in the Kuomintang publication *Ts'ai-ping Chien-kuo chih yi-yi* (The meaning of disbandment for the building of the state), 1929, pp. 164–9. For acknowledgements of the Japanese model see Tai's words of 22 September in the 'I chou chien ta shih shu-p'ing', pp. 1–2 in *Kuo-wen Chou-pao*, V, no. 38, and, among a number of statements, Chiang's speech of 1 January 1929, in *Ko-ming Wen-hsien*, XXIV, 4842.

[3] M. C. Wright, *The Last Stand of Chinese Conservatism: The T'ung-chih Restoration: 1862–1874*, Stanford, 1957, chapter 12.

[4] The phrase quoted is from T'ang Leang-li *China in Revolt*, London, 1927, p. 128.

Rearmament was now becoming a major concern of the Kuomintang leadership despite China's adherence to the Kellogg Pact in September 1928. Military reform, naval construction, aviation and the security of the frontier regions were all subjects of current interest. The arrival of Colonal Bauer's German military mission in the autumn of the year inaugurated a period in which professional armed forces backed by modern communications and provided with modern equipment became an important preoccupation of the regime.[1] This concern with military revival was not out of line with Nationalist opinion on the level of principle. The conflict derived from the fact that patient rearmament was the Centre's alternative to the anti-imperialist movement.

If the implications of rearmament brought back echoes of the late Ch'ing period, the old dichotomy of 'fundamental principles' and 'practical application' could not be revived, though many Nationalists including Sun Yat-sen harboured something of the old idea. Not only had circumstances changed, but the very programme of the government involved the Westernization of China's institutions on a large scale.

Hu Han-min once summed up the policy of the new state under the two headings 'laws' and 'arms', and laws form the second aspect of state policy which is closely connected with the reinterpretation of anti-imperialism. The position that diplomatic progress depended on internal improvements was well established at the Centre and this view lay behind the extensive legislative programme which was launched in November 1928. In his review of the first year of the Legislative Yuan's work Hu Han-min recalled that an average of one hundred clauses had been produced each day—'laws as numerous as hairs', as the Ancients had said.[2]

Halfway through this year of codification Hu spoke of motives. 'We must quickly complete these codes, on the one hand for the protection of the property and lives of the whole people, and on the other hand to remove the foreigners' excuse for preventing the abolition of extraterritoriality. Actually these words are addressed entirely to

[1] For the German mission see F. F. Liu *Military History of Modern China*, Princeton, 1956, pp. 61–63 and 74–76.

[2] Hu's speech of 15 July 1929 in *Ko-ming Li-lun yü Ko-ming Kung-tso* (Revolutionary Theory and Revolutionary Work I and II, 1932, p. 122 and Chiang Yung-ching 'Hu Han-min Hsien-sheng Nien-p'u Kao' (Draft Chronological biography of Hu Han-min) in *Chung-kuo Hsien-tai Shih Ts'ung-k'an*, III, 275. For the established position on diplomatic progress see Hu's speech of 21 December 1928 in *Ts'ai-ping Chien-kuo chih yi-yi*, p. 153.

ourselves. We never speak in this way to foreigners. When I speak on this subject to foreigners I do not admit that we are only hurrying to compile these codes in order to recover extraterritoriality.'[1]

Hu's approach amounted to a full but covert acceptance of the 'Washington Formula' against which nationalist feeling had rebelled over the previous four years. As in many other respects, the Nanking Government merely took up the policies pursued by the Peking governments of the preceding era. But to satisfy the Powers the Nanking Government, like its predecessors, would have to do far more than draft new laws: it would have to make its authority really effective at every level of government. The success of Nanking's policy would therefore depend very largely on the effectiveness of its domestic policies. Here the outlook became increasingly discouraging with the aggravation of the Kuomintang's grave internal weaknesses and the renewal of civil war within the Nationalist camp from March 1929. In the period up to the Mukden Incident local conditions closely resembled those prevailing during the era of the Peiyang warlords (1916–28).

CONCLUSION

The approach of the Nanking leadership to the problems of foreign relations ran counter to the main stream of Nationalist opinion in three major respects. It involved an acceptance of domestic reform as the condition for China's elevation to full sovereignty, it stressed the importance of armaments, and it expressed a distrust of popular involvement. All three positions had previously been regarded by Nationalists as characteristic of the 'old-style bureaucratic diplomats', while the last was frankly opposed to the populism of the earlier period of the revolution.[2]

Despite the contrast between anti-imperialist hopes and the rather disappointing diplomatic achievements of the Nanking Government in its first years in office, the authorities did not have to deal with any serious disturbances occasioned by external issues after December 1928. The new treaties, the solution of outstanding Sino-Japanese problems and the attainment of qualified tariff autonomy were the main events of the years 1928 and 1929. In 1929 a renewed and more determined diplomatic assault on extraterritoriality was launched by the Govern-

[1] Speech of 15 July 1929 as cited in previous footnote.
[2] Chou Keng-sheng discussed the second position in *Ko-ming ti Wai-chiao*, pp. 27, 28.

ment, an assault behind which the Powers correctly discerned the uncomfortable pressure of Chinese opinion.[1] None of these events can have given much satisfaction to anti-imperialist sentiment, but such opinion was now subsumed in the general movement of Party and military opposition which came into the open in March 1929. Democratic development and a more vigorous foreign policy were the chief slogans of this movement in 1929 and 1930.

Fainter echoes of the great upheaval of the mid-twenties continued to reverberate in Nationalist politics until the Mukden Incident of 18 September 1931 opened a new period. By that date the main political features of the Nanking regime were well established. After the Incident the Japanese problem completely dominated Chinese foreign policy and the diplomatic campaign against extraterritoriality, already weakened by the dissensions of 1929–31, was suspended. The old anti-imperialism of the revolution was revived on a narrow front in the form of an unofficial anti-Japanese movement. This movement came to resemble in many respects the anti-imperialist agitation of the Peiyang and National Revolutionary periods as it had developed outside the areas of Nationalist control.

Popular support for Nationalist diplomacy was always regarded as desirable, and often as essential, by the Nationalist leaders, yet few steps were taken to obtain such support. The explanation lies in the general political development of the Nanking regime after the end of the Northern Expedition. An acute awareness of the regime's insecurity, in which the Communist threat was only one of a number of factors, led to the discouragement of most forms of public opinion or activity. National security was itself urged as a reason for dampening domestic 'dissensions'.[2] External problems, however, were by far the most pressing issues to those urban groups which alone were effectively involved in Chinese national politics at this time. The gap between promise and achievement was therefore particularly unfortunate in the field of foreign relations.[3] More important still, the wider circles

[1] For the extraterritoriality question between 1929 and 1931 see W. R. Fishel, *The End of Extraterritoriality in China*, Berkeley, 1952, pp. 153–87.

[2] For examples of the latter argument see *Chung-yang Chou-pao*, xxv (26 November 1928), p. 2, and Hu Han-min's speech of 3 December 1928 in *Chung-yang Chou-pao*, xxviii.

[3] The urban character of the Kuomintang in 1928–9 is supported by membership figures and analysis in *Min-kuo Shih-pa Nien Chung-kuo Kuomintang Nien-chien* (Kuomintang Yearbook 1929), p. 752.

outside the urban middle class, which had begun to play a really important part in Nationalist politics between 1925 and 1927, were now no longer effectively involved in political life. Much of the wind had gone out of the Kuomintang's sails. It remained to be seen whether a modern state could be created on the narrow base which had been selected.

The connection between internal political development and the realization of China's external aspirations had come to light more clearly after the May Fourth Incident, when patriotic protest became increasingly associated with agitation for domestic political change. The militant anti-imperialist movement of the National Revolution was also only one aspect of the development of revolutionary democracy in Nationalist China up to 1927. Later, in the 1930s, the anti-Japanese movement was clearly associated with left-wing currents of opposition to the authoritarian Nanking regime. In other circles, the Mukden Incident persuaded some Kuomintang leaders that the national crisis required a widening of the political base of the regime. The pressure of Japan was undoubtedly a most important stimulus to the constitutional developments of that decade.

The Nationalist attempt to build a new state in the decade following 1928 through 'self-strengthening' has not yet been assessed as a whole. It was launched initially upon a very narrow basis and amid widespread disappointment and conflict. The internal weakness of the regime in its early years limited the effectiveness of its foreign policy, and diplomatic failure, in its turn, reduced its domestic strength. In view of the Nanking leaders' acute awareness of the strength of their foreign antagonists, the question should also be raised whether the reunification and regeneration of China could be achieved in the twentieth century without the help or protection of a foreign power.

THE ORIGIN OF THE BOXERS

JEROME CH'EN

INTRODUCTION

What may be called the militia theory of the origin of the Boxers is nothing new; it made its first appearance in 1901 even before the signing of the Protocol.[1] But it had been generally ignored until the publication of G. N. Steiger's thesis in 1927.[2] For lack of evidence, Steiger had to rely on commonsense and conjecture to a dangerous extent to arrive at his conclusion, thus failing to convince either Chinese historians or his Western colleagues like G. G. H. Dunstheimer[3] and the late Dr Victor Purcell.[4] Having surveyed the entire ground of the Boxers' connection with various religious sects and secret societies, Dunstheimer and Purcell, working independently, came to the same conclusion: the Boxers were definitely from a sectarian root. Aware of the political implication of all this, Purcell goes further to devote two chapters of his book to answering the question: Were the Boxers pro-dynastic or anti-dynastic? The significance of it, I regret to say, has escaped many scholars.[5]

Chester Tan's position is slightly different from Dunstheimer's and Purcell's. 'The Boxer Bands', he says, 'were not militia recruited in response to Imperial decree. They were officially reported to have appeared in Shantung as early as May 1898, while the first decree ordering the organization of the militia was not issued until November of that year. Our record shows that they began as volunteer associations under the influence of the heretical sects.'[6] 'Under the influence

[1] Sir Robert Hart, *These from the land of Sinim*, London, 1901, p. 4; Ku Hung-ming, *Papers from a Viceroy's Yamen*, Shanghai, 1901, p. 17.

[2] *China and the Occident*, Yale, 1927.

[3] 'Religion et magie dans le mouvement des Boxeurs d'après les textes Chinois', *T'oung Pao*, vol. XLVII, Livr. 3–5 and 'Le mouvement des Boxeurs,' *Revue Historique*, Avril-Juin, 1964. Particularly section 1 a of the former.

[4] *The Boxer Uprising, a background study*, Cambridge, 1963.

[5] If the Boxers were originally pro-dynastic militia, they could in no sense be a revolutionary, nationalistic movement, hence reactionary and even absurd; if they were anti-dynastic heretical sects, their political complexion would be entirely different, perhaps progressive and patriotic.

[6] *The Boxer Catastrophe*, Columbia, 1955, p. 237.

of' does not mean 'led by' the heretical sects; indeed Tan finds it difficult to ascertain on slender evidence 'to what extent the Boxer movement was initiated by the heretical sects. For if they played an important role in organizing the movement, their illegal status made it impossible for them to reveal themselves. There are no records as to exactly how and when the I Ho Ch'üan were first organized. Our evidence indicates that they began as volunteer associations. It is quite possible that the secret society operated in the background.'[1] This may be described as the 'front organization' theory.

In 1963 Tai Hsüan-chih of Taiwan in a remarkable manner revived Steiger's theory in his notable monograph, *I-ho-t'uan yen-chiu*.[2] Remarkable, in two senses: nowhere in his book does Tai refer to Steiger; almost everywhere Tai brings, in sharp contrast to Steiger, a great deal of documentary weight to bear on his argument. Both Steiger and Tai begin by doubting the judgement of Lao Nai-hsüan.[3] Steiger argues:

... it is impossible to believe that a secret society, holding heretical doctrines and known to have revolutionary aims, would deliberately go out of its way to institute a campaign of bitter hostility against Christian missions, and thus stir up against itself the activities of the officials and the complaints of the foreign diplomats. Such procedure would have been contrary to all that is known of the history of secret societies in China, and is without precedence in the history of the country.[4]

Tai, on the other hand, attacks Lao's reliance on one solitary document, Na-yen-ch'eng's memorial to the throne of 3 December 1915, by pointing out that Lao confused the I-ho-ch'üan of the 1810s with the I-ho-t'uan of the 1890s. He uses the Boxers' (I-ho-ch'üan's) aid to the magistrate of Chinhsiang, Wu K'ai, in defending the town against the Eight Diagrams sect to prove their hostility to the sect in 1813. He goes on to say that the magical powers—acting as mediums for divine manifestations, reciting spells, and claiming invulnerability—practised by the Boxers of the 1890s were unknown to the I-ho-ch'üan of the earlier period.[5]

---

[1] *The Boxer Catastrophe*, p. 45.

[2] Taipei, 1963. An English synopsis of this was published in 1964, but it does not do justice to his book.
Lao's often quoted pamphlet, *I-ho-ch'üan chiao-men yüan-liu k'ao*, was published in 1899 and republished in Chung-kuo shih-hsüeh-hui, *I-ho-t'uan* (hereafter *IHT*), Peking, 1951, IV, 431 ff.

[4] *China and the Occident*, p. 129.   [5] Tai, *I-ho-t'uan, yen-chiu*, Tapei, 1963, p. 3.

Since, according to him, Lao Nai-hsüan is not to be trusted, Tai feels the need to reopen the issue of the origin of the Boxers. As he points out, 'the Yi Ho Boxers of the Kuang-hsü period made their first appearance in a religious incident at Pear Garden Village Liyüant'un, Kuan County, Shantung Province, in the 13th year of Kuang-hsü (1887)'.[1] The incident had its beginning in 1870 over the trivial matter of half an acre of land, the site of the Taoist temple, Yü-huang Miao, owned by the county, which was to be given to a missionary for building his church. The church was extended in 1887, which event provoked a dispute between the Christian converts and the rest of the community. In 1891 and 1892 the dispute deteriorated into a fight between the two groups in which the Plum Flower Boxers (Mei-hua-ch'üan) played a prominent role by inviting a Taoist priest to the scene and by taking 'the guns used in earlier years to equip militia' to the temple for its defence. At this point, the government intervened by force, bringing the matter to an end after much bitter fighting. Thereafter, in 1898, the persecuted Plum Flower Boxers changed their name to the I-ho-t'uan.[2]

Quoting from the governor of Shantung, Chang Ju-mei's memorial to the throne on 17 June 1898,[3] Tai proves that the I-ho-t'uan were the descendants of the I-ho-ch'üan of the Hsien-feng and T'ung-chih reigns, who, in the intervening period, were called the Plum Flower Boxers. Their aims were for defence against thieves and robbers[4] and for mutual assistance between villages in Shantung. Theirs was an open, legitimate village militia (*hsiang-t'uan*) which had no connection whatever with such secret and heretical organizations as the White Lotus and Eight Diagrams.[5]

If this brief summary has not done too much injury to Tai's theory, it appears to me that Tai raised more questions than he answered. First, to prove that the Boxers were unconnected with either the White Lotus or the Eight Diagrams is not the same as to prove that they were unconnected with any secret society at all. Second, the Boxers' reliance

---

[1] *Ibid.* pp. 5, 6 or the *Synopsis*, p. 33.

[2] *Ibid.* p. 7 or the *Synopsis*, pp. 33, 34.

[3] According to Tai, this is included in a collection entitled *Kuan-hsien Liyüantun chiao-an* (the religious incidents of Liyüant'un of Kuanhsien, to which I have no access) but not in Kuo-chia Tang-an chü, *I-ho-t'uan tang-an shih-liao* (hereafter Tang-an), Peking, 1959, perhaps because of its similarity in content with another memorial by Chang dated Kuang-hsü 24.v.12 (30 June 1898), to which Tao also refers.

[4] The Nien rebels.　　　　　　　　[5] Tai, *I-ho-t'uan yen-chiu*, pp. 4, 23.

on magic spells in the 1890s in contrast to their reliance on sheer physical prowess earlier on may have been caused by their confrontation with a totally new and far more powerful foe—the foreigner equipped with fire-arms—as well as by a change in the popular belief in magical powers. Third, the most important and hitherto unexplored area of study is the actual difference between the village militia and secret bands in Shantung. From these initial doubts, we may proceed to ask: How were the village militia of Shantung organized before 1898? Who organized and who joined them? What did they do? What affiliations, if any, did they have with the secret societies and heretical sects? Did they have surreptitious dealings with rebels and bandits? Were the political principles and aims of the village militia and those of the sects and societies irreconcilably opposed to each other? To answer these, one will have to study the relationship between the Boxers and all the unofficial organizations, not just the Boxers and the secret societies. In a limited and tentative way, this is the principal task of the present paper, an endeavour to find a compromise between two apparently opposing views. The procedure I propose to use is to begin with the militia of Shantung and then go on to secret societies and bandits of the 1850s and 60s before coming to the Boxers themselves.

SHANTUNG MILITIA

Chang Ju-mei made it clear in his two important memorials of 17 and 30 June 1898 that the I-ho-ch'üan began in the Hsien-feng and T'ung-chih periods, in other words, at the time of the Nien rebellion. The simultaneity suggests a connection which S. Y. Teng elaborates in a plausible, but speculative way:[1]

Many Nien remnants who escaped the wholesale slaughter of 1868 resumed their original underworld life under various new names; and the Boxers and the Nien were indeed sister organizations, which came into existence in 1808, derived from the same source and active in the same area. The membership of these two societies was probably interchangeable. During the period of Nien activity the Boxers were seldom mentioned. When the Boxers later became active, the Nien remnants doubtless were included in their ranks.

During the Nien rebellion, the inhabitants of Shantung took two measures for their own protection against pillage. One was to build *yü*

---

[1] *The Nien Army and Their Guerrilla Warfare*, Paris, 1961, p. 230. Teng's authority is Chiang Ti, *Ch'u-ch'i Nien-chün-shih* lun-ts'ung (Essays on the History of the Early Stages of the Nien Army), Peking, 1959.

(forts) which on the whole were not as successful as expected. In addition, they created very many administrative problems by being obstructive to both the government and the rebels alike, as is described in an exaggerated manner by such popular novels as the *P'eng-kung An* (Prefect P'eng's cases).[1] In Shantung, Honan, and Anhwei there were 'forests of *yü*' manned by armed local inhabitants against rebel attacks (described vividly on pp. 53 *a* and *b* in *chüan* 117 of the *Shantung t'ung-chih*). The other measure pursued with much energy but little planning was the organization of village militia starting in the second month of Hsien-feng third year (March 1853).[2]

In the second year of this attempt, the task of organization was entrusted to officials in retirement or on leave or the scholar-gentry of whom some were said to be 'upright supported by other upright people and others unworthy aided by other unworthy people'.[3] It is safe to say that right from the beginning the gentry-led militia in Shantung were divided into the law-abiding and the intransigent types, side by side with which there emerged another group of village militia units led not by the gentry but by people of modest origins[4] often described by the government as *chia-t'uan* (bogus militia) or *fei-t'uan* (insurrectionary militia). Disputes and fights occurred between government troops and the intransigent and bogus types and among the militia themselves. The situation grew uglier and uglier in the middle of the Hsien-feng reign, when it was necessary for the Grand Secretary, Wen-ch'ing, to propose to the throne a change of policy. His memorial in the fifth month of Hsien-feng fifth year (June 1855) said this:

Since the rebellion of the Kwangtung bandits [the T'aip'ing], militia units have been organized. At some places, they have been helpful [in local defence]

---

1 The attack on the Yenchiaying of Hsinhsien, as reported in the *Shantung t'ung-chih*, *chuan* 117, 42*b*, bears a strong resemblance to the attacks on various *chai-tzu* (fortresses) in the *P'eng-kung An*. For details about the *yü*, see Nieh Ch'ung-ch'i (ed.), *Nien-chün tzu-liao pieh-chi* (Further collection of source materials on the Nien Army), Shanghai, 1958, pp. 41, 67, 87, 104–5 and Hsüeh Fu-ch'eng, *Jung-an wen-chi hsü-pien* (sequel to the Jung-an essays), II, 22, and *Jung-an hai-wai wen-pien* (Jung-an essays written abroad), IV, 11*b*–12*a*.
2 *Shantung chün-hsing chi-lüeh* (A Brief Account of the Military Campaigns in Shantung) in Chung-kuo Shih-hsüeh-hui, *Nien-chün*, Shanghai, 1955, IV, 416. This is by far the best source for Shantung militia activities of that period.
3 *Ibid.* IV, 417, 321. The quotation is from pp. 418, 419.
4 Yang Wu (Yang the dark), Wang Ch'i ho-shang (Wang the seventh, a monk) and so on, but without any reference to their 'official position' or 'degrees' as in other cases.

and at others the matter has been treated perfunctorily for years. The reason is that those who are taking the matter seriously often feel a lack of authority [in their own hands] and those who are keen but light-hearted trifle with it. Moreover, unscrupulous people of the gentry, in the name of organizing militia, impose heavy taxes on the people, thus driving them to the verge of rebellion. When the [Nien] rebels come the good militia show their loyalty while the bad ones take to their heels. There are even leading members of the gentry in charge of organization who have been hiding themselves at safe places, never to appear on the scene of fighting. From this one can see that it is better to entrust the matter to the officials rather than to the gentry. But when the task of organization was given to the ordinary people of Honan, village unions (Lien-chuang-hui) emerged to cause a great deal of trouble. The ideal way is to order the officials to lead the gentry and the gentry to lead the ordinary people.[1]

The emperor considered this proposal but did nothing. Two years later the triangular conflict among the local governments, the gentry, and the militia in Shantung deteriorated even further.[2] However, it was in the tenth year of Hsien-feng (1860) that Tu Ch'iao was appointed the commissioner of Shantung militia who in nearly a year's time managed to do nothing to relieve the tense situation in the province. He and his successors, nonetheless, introduced a new category of militia through their effort—the *kuan-t'uan* (government-sponsored militia units) were thus born.[3] In the 1860s there existed four kinds of militia units—the government-sponsored, the law-abiding and the intransigent led by the gentry, and the 'bogus' led by people of the lower classes.

The military situation of Shantung in the 1860s was as grave as that of Hunan in the previous decade, and yet the province lacked a man of Tseng Kuo-fan's calibre to make good use of these local forces. Whether under the leadership of the gentry or that of people of modest origins, the Shantung peasants, once organized, became defiant and quarrelsome. Between 1860 and 1863 they exploited the weakness of the local

[1] *Ibid.* p. 425, the memorial being referred to in Liu Ching-tsao (ed.), *Ch'ing-ch'ao hsü wen-hsien t'ung-k'ao*, *ping*, IV, 9622 a, b.

[2] *Nien-chün*, IV, 426.

[3] *Shang-tung tung-chih*, IV, 440, and Nien Ch'ung-ch'i, *Nien-chün tzu-liao pieh-chi*, p. 108. Tu has been variously reported as the Vice President of the Board of Revenue, of War, or of Rites (see *Tengchow fu-chih* in *Nien-chün*, III, 434, also IV, 427, *Yehsien chih*, in *ibid.* III, 481, and A. Hummel, *Eminent Chinese of the Ch'ing Period*, p. 779. His ineptitude was noticed by Seng-ke-lin-ch'in (*Nien chün*, IV, 430) and Hsüeh Fu-ch'eng, *Jung-an hai-wan wen-pien*, IV, 11 a.

governments and made full use of their newly acquired strength to fight for reduction or suspension of taxes, particularly of the *ts'ao-liang* (Grain Tribute), as Shantung was one of the tributary provinces, and to redress what they considered as miscarriages of justice. They also demanded money and supplies for running their organization and on occasion they fought among themselves over jealousies, grudges, and other personal reasons.[1] Some of them were even hand in glove with the Nien and other rebels, playing a similar 'amphibious', but less prominent, role to Miao P'ei-lin in Anhwei.[2] The chaos caused Yen Ching-ming (appointed acting governor in 1862) and Ting Pao-chen (appointed commissioner of law in 1863) to take urgent steps for their suppression and transformation. In a memorial to the throne in 1863, Yen commented:

The men recruited everywhere in the north now are simply a lawless and undisciplined motley who known neither respect for their emperor and their superiors nor the way to fight and win. Those who are selected to lead them are avaricious for fame and money and are utterly unreliable. As commanders they can cause only mutinies; as leaders of militia they can provoke only riots.[3]

A year later he spoke even more forthrightly:

[The militia] squeeze money out of villagers for their own pay and collect the peasants together to form fighting units. They have done no good at all. Even Fu Chen-pang, the provincial commander in charge of militia affairs of Teng [chow], Lai [chow], Ch'in [chow], and I [chow], has said that people of Shantung origin should not be put in a position to control militia units. On my part, I can do no more than supervise local officials to strengthen the defence and to empty the countryside against the rebels, and refrain from insincere tribute to the militia's part in resisting the bandits.[4]

The area in which the government troops and militia often clashed lay in a semi-circle round the central plateau of the province, starting in the north from Chanhua, moving along the north bank of the Yellow River up stream to the west, then turning southward to end at Feihsien. The principal geographic features of this region are its bordering on Chihli and Honan and its complicated waterway system

[1] *Nien-chün*, IV, 427–42.
[2] *Ibid.* III, 362–5; IV, 439, 440, 444.
[3] *Ch'ing-shih lieh-chuan* (Biographies of the Ch'ing History), *chüan* 57, 13 *a* and *chüan* 57, 15 *b*.
[4] *Ibid. chüan*, 57, 16*b*.

consisting of the Yellow River, the Grand Canal, and three lakes—the Tungp'ing, Shushan, and Weishan. The former gave Shantung outlaws, and in this case the militia, an easy access to a refuge in Chihli or Honan when they were persecuted by Shantung authorities; the latter provided a barrier against troops sent northward and westward to conduct campaigns of suppression and against effective co-operation

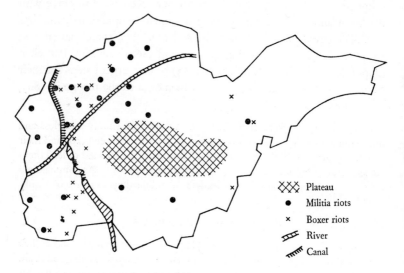

between the popular organizations in uprising. It was consequently the home of the defiant militia in the 1860s as thirty years later that of the troublesome Boxers.

The clashes, riots, and protests tend to make nonsense of any clear distinction among militia, secret societies (including religious sects), and bandits in Shantung in the 1860s. In many areas these organizations overlapped and on many occasions they were the same people. It also seems futile to insist that the militia units, in contrast to other local organizations, were named after their places of origin such as Chinhsiang, T'angyi, and so on. In fact here were the Shang-yi (Exalt Rectitude), Hsiao-chung (Be Loyal), and I-hsin (One Mind) militia in Ts'aochow, the Hsiao-chung and T'ung-hsin (United Hearts) militia in Feich'eng, the T'ai-ho (Great Harmony) militia in Shouchang, and the Hung-ch'üan-hui (Red Fists) in Kuant'ao.[1] In 1961 M. Dunstheimer

---

[1] Respectively, *Shantung t'ung-chih, chüan* 117, 42*b*, *Nienchün*, IV, 422, 424; *ibid.* 433, 442; *ibid.* III, 522.

in his well-known study, 'Religion et magie dans le mouvement des Boxeurs d'après les textes Chinois', observed:[1]

Dans ce passage, le mot *t'ouan* est employé dans deux sens différents: milices officiellement reconnues et bandes illégales. Malheureusement le fait est cité sans aucune référence. Nous [Dunstheimer himself] espérons trouver plus tard des indications plus précises.[2]

and he is right.

So much for the militia; now a few words about the secret societies.

SECRET SOCIETIES

In dealing with the secret societies, one pertinent question to ask is: Since the militia of the 1850s and 60s were organized for defence against the prowling Nien and since the secret societies are understood to be anti-dynastic organizations, then how could members of the latter join the former, transform their organizations into militia units, and even in some instances use the militia organization as a front for their clandestine political activities? The obvious answer is that not all secret societies were actively anti-dynastic. Such a society was the Ch'ing-men (later known as the Ch'ing-pang, the Green Gang).[2] The history of this politically moderate society, like those of other secret societies of China, is a blend of facts and fiction, often more fiction than facts; everyone knows that it must be used with the greatest possible care and yet no one knows how to reduce it to reliability. In any case, my account below is likely to have facts and fiction confused.

It is reported that the Ch'ing-men was inaugurated in Ch'ingchiang, north Kiangsu, in 1676,[3] for the purpose of protecting the interests of transport workers along the waterway of the Grain Tribute.[4] This date may be taken as accurate, for three years earlier the Hung-men (Hung League) had staged an uprising against the Ch'ing government which ended in disaster.[5] The abortive rising might have caused

---

[1] *Loc. cit. T'oung Pao*, XLVII, 338.

[2] See *Shih-liao hsün-k'an*, XI, 373*a* and Wei-ta fa-shih (Wei Chü-hsien), *Chung-kuo ti pang-hui* (The Secret Societies of China), Chungking, 1949, pp. 3, 4.

[3] Ch'en I-fan, *Ch'ing-men k'ao-yüan* (The Origins of the Ch'ing-men), Peiping, 1933, p. 1.

[4] Chu Lin, *Hung-men pang-hui-chih* (The Society, Hung-men), 1940, Taipei, 1964 ed. 1, 2, 3 and Hsiao I-shan, 'T'ien-ti-hui ch'i-yüan k'ao (The Beginnings of the T'ien-ti-hui),' in the *Fan-kung* (Counterattack) fortnightly, no. 173, quoted from *Chung-hua min-kuo k'ai-kuo wu-shih-nien wen-hsien*, Taipei, 1963, I, part 2, 301.

[5] Liu Lien-k'o, *Pang-hui san-pai-nien shih* (300 Years of the Secret Societies), Macao, 1940, pp. 68, 69.

disagreement over policy among the members of the League, which led the dissidents to prepare for the establishment of their own group without risking an open breach with the mother body. At this stage, indeed even much later, the Hung-men remained united ostensibly under the slogan of 'Restore the Ming and Overthrow the Ch'ing'. As late as 1725 the three grand leaders of the Ch'ing-men—Weng Yai, Ch'ien Chien, and P'an Ch'ing—were still concurrently members of the T'ien-ti-hui, which name the Hung-men adopted in 1723.[1] Before long, however, the three leaders of the Ch'ing-men parted ways as two of them, Weng and Ch'ien, left for Inner Mongolia, traditionally a place for Han-Chinese exiles.[2]

It is not clear whether these two leaders were compelled by P'an to take such a long journey from Chekiang to the north as a result of a disagreement or banishment by the government. The truth is obscured by euphemism. Their departure left P'an the unrivalled leader of the society which under his guidance was said to have received imperial approval.[3] Whether the approval was actually given or not is irrelevant; what is relevant was a distinct change in the political outlook of the society. Thereafter, as all evidence shows, the society became tolerable from the official point of view. In 1786, three years after the death of P'an,[4] the governor of Chekiang reported on his investigation into the affairs of the Lo-chaio, saying that the society showed no sign of insurrectionary tendencies. When the followers of the T'ien-li-chiao under the leadership of Lin Ch'ing and Li Wen-ch'eng rebelled in Ts'aochow and Tingt'ao in 1813, a member of the Ch'ing-men, Wang Cheng-chi, broke away from the society, established his Ch'ing-ch'a-men-chiao (Clear Tea Sect), and joined forces with the rebels.[5] The main body of the Ch'ing-men, however, remained indifferent to the insurgency, and it must be remembered that the I-ho-ch'üan were fighting in this rebellion on the government side in the county of Chinhsiang.[6]

---

[1] *Ibid.* 69, 70, 73, 74, and 78–80, and Ch'en, *op. cit.* 52, 53.

[2] Ch'en, *Ch'ing-men k'ao-yüan*, p. 59.

[3] Ch'en, *ibid.* p. 56; *Ta-ch'ing li-ch'ao shih-lu*, Ch'ien-lung, 1462, p. 13 and *Ch'ing-shih-kao*, Tao-kuang, *chüan*, 204, 31 and *chüan*, 211, 19.

[4] Ch'en, *ibid.* p. 59 and Wei, *Chung-kuo ti pang-hui*, pp. 66–8. *Shih-liao hsün-k'an*, no. 12, pp. 404a–407a, and memorial dated 20.x.1768.

[5] Ch'en, *ibid.* pp. 3, 61, 62; Lao Nai-hsüan, *I-ho-ch'üan chiao-men yüan-liu k'ao*, in *IHT*, iv, 435; *Shantung t'ung-chih*, *chüan* 117, 3a.

[6] *Shantung t'ung-chih*, *chüan* 117, 3a, and Tai, *I-ho-t'uan yen-chiu*, p. 3.

In the reign of Tao-kuang, it seems, official tolerance had generated moral corruption and political unawareness among the members of the secret societies in general. The *Chiu-shih chen-pien* (methods to save society) commented:

As I see our brethren today, they are reckless and quarrelsome. They are fond of visiting prostitutes, gambling, and smoking opium. They are treacherous and greedy. They instigate law suits, scheme against others, and kill ... They are said to be courageous because they have no regard for their own lives. Debauchery and opium addiction are considered by them as the qualifications for being members of the societies. They do damage to others by their treachery. If you disapprove of their ways, they will tell you that you are inexperienced and lack understanding. . . . All our bretheren say that our family background and ourselves must be respectable. The fact remains that many who are not are either our leaders or members of our societies.[1]

This depraved picture is confirmed by Liu K'un-i and Chang Chih-tung in their joint memorial of July 1900:

Along the [Yangtze] River, secret society bandits, salt smugglers, and the An-ch'ing Taoists (An-ch'ing Tao-yu, i.e. the Ch'ing-men) are numerous and they and the Boxers have their separate societies. In peace time, they rob others. The names of their societies show clearly their insurgent propensities.[2]

And in a letter dated 8 July 1898, Sheng Hsüan-huai related:

Having received a joint telegram from the gentry of Ch'angchow [Wuchin], I and others, in view of the food shortage, asked the local officials to arrange money for the transport of rice, and on the 16th day (4 July) soup kitchens began operation. However, the two secret societies—the An-ch'ing and Ko-lao—gathered a large number of their members and robbed more than 3,000 piculs of rice at three places between morning and evening on that day. The authorities of Wuchin arrested some ten people before the robbers dispersed. The chief culprits, however, are still at large.[3]

The above description yields these points: (1) in the nineteenth century there was a general decline in the moral standards and political consciousness of the secret societies; (2) the Ch'ing-men was a moderate society in regard to the Manchu government; (3) the defence of Chinhsiang by the I-ho-ch'üan in the Lin Ch'ing–Li Wen-ch'eng uprising of 1813 strongly suggests that the Boxers were in association

---

[1] Wei Chü-hsien, *Chung-kuo ti Pang-hui*, p. 88.
[2] Sheng Hsüan-huai, *Yü-chai ts'un-kao ch'u-k'an* (Official Papers of Yü-chai), *chüan* 36, 14*b*.
[3] *Ibid. chüan* 32, 19*b*.

with, if not actually members of, the Ch'ing-men; and (4) most of the members of this society were transport workers along the Grain Tribute route.

When Shantung was seriously threatened by the Nien and militia units were organized through the length and breadth of the province, several heretical and other illegal bands made an opportunistic bid for local power. They were therefore regarded by the government as bandits. The first to deserve some attention here is the Fu-fei (turbaned bandits), most of whom, like the members of the Ch'ing-men, were transport workers along the Grain Tribute route. It would be surprising if some of the Fu-fei were not actually members of the Ch'ing-men, playing a role similar to that of Wang Cheng-chi and his followers in the 1813 uprising. As the Tribute was commuted to monetary payment in 1863, 'several hundred thousands' of transport workers became unemployed and destitute and took up armed banditry in south Shantung.[1] Not only did they co-operate with the Nien, they also allied with the religious bandits of Tsouhsien. In a report in 1861 T'an T'ing-hsiang, the governor, stated:

> ... the turbaned bandits have been a real menace for years. Wherever they go they intimidate defenceless people. As soon as a handful of them break into a *yü* [normally defended by local militia], the bad elements [in the *yü*] give them support, thus leaving the upright people with no choice but to be obeisant.[2]

In this way, they also coerced the militia to help them. Their allies, the religious insurgents of Tsouhsien, belonged to the Wen-hsien sect,[3] which Yüan Chia-san[4] regarded not as bandits but merely objectors to heavy taxation.[5] This observation might have been true before 1860, for up to then the sect had been organizing militia in co-operation with the local gentry. Their surreptitious activities of kidnapping, plundering, appointing officials, and even using

---

[1] *Nien-chün*, IV, 322–76. See also S. Y. Teng, *The Nien Army*, 126–8.

[2] *Nien-chün*, IV, 374.

[3] Very little else is known of this sect except that its followers recited classics of the sect, wrote incantations, and practised spiritual healing. Because it began at a place called the White Lotus Pond (Pailiench'ih), S. Y. Teng calls it a branch of the White Lotus sect (*The Nien Army*, p. 123). However, the names of the Pond and of the sect suggest no more than its being a Buddhist sect. See *Shan-tung t'ung-chih, chüan* 117, 62*a*.

[4] A. Hummel, *Eminent Chinese*, p. 949.

[5] S. Y. Teng, *The Nien Army*, p. 123.

'T'ien-tsung' as their reign title were not known until then. After 1860 persecution began in Tsouhsien itself and four or five adjacent counties. Their alliance with the turbaned bandits was chiefly due to the fact that their area was immediately to the north of the bandits'. To the west, across the lakes and the Grand Canal to Ts'aochow and Hotse,[1] there were the Long Spears (Ch'ang-ch'iang-hui), originally consisting of members of the local militia selected to fight against the Nien in 1853–4. Gradually, however, the *hui* replaced the militia in these counties, assumed a new name, the I-hsin militia, and joined forces with the Nien.[2] Across the Yellow River from the Long Spear area to Kuant'ao and Kuanhsien, there were situated the centres of the bandits under the control of the Eight Diagrams; these fought the government under yellow, blue, green, white, and black banners. The black banners were those of Sung Ching-shih, whom I shall discuss presently. Although these bandits lived in the same town as the Hung-ch'üan-hui (Red Fists), they were hostile to each other.[3] It is therefore wrong to say that the Red Fists were affiliated to the Eight Diagrams.

Near the provincial capital, Tsinan, there had flourished for years the Huang-yai-chiao (Yellow Rock), a sect mild in its political outlook but rigorous in its puritanic discipline. Its influence grew steadily in Feich'eng and areas nearby, and, despite its non-involvement in insurgent activities, the sect was considered a threat by the government of Shantung. Official investigations were therefore conducted, followed by rigorous persecution in 1865. In the end the sect was forced to transform itself into the Tsai-li-chiao (Observe Rites) or the Li-men.[4]

This brief account shows two significant points. In the first place nearly all the illegal organizations in Shantung in the 1860s had the support, voluntary or otherwise, of village militia. Some of them even organized militia themselves, presumably to collect money openly in the name of local defence. In a situation such as this, it is impossible to draw a clear line of demarcation between the militia and the secret

---

[1] Other counties under their control were Yünch'eng, Chüyeh, Tingt'ao, Ch'engwu, and Tanhsien.

[2] Nien-chün, IV, 229, 424.

[3] *Ibid.* IV, 250–80; III, 373, 522.

[4] *Ibid.* IV, 409–15 and S. Y. Teng, *The Nien Army*, p. 123. See also T'ao Ch'eng-chang, *Chiao-hui yüan-liu k'ao* (Origins of Secret Societies) in Hsiao I-shan, *Chin-tai mi-mi she-hui shih-liao* (Documents of Modern Secret Societies), II, appendix i, p. 4a.

organizations. The only exceptions, as far as can be ascertained, were the Eight Diagrams, a branch of the White Lotus, and the Yellow Rock. Indeed, the Eight Diagrams were reliably reported to have fought the Red Fists. The reason, I think, was the former's un-compromising hostility to the government as evinced by the guerrilla activities of the religious bandits under their leadership, in Kuanhsien, Hsinchi, and T'angyi. Perhaps because of this, they failed to enlist the co-operation of their fellow townsmen, the Red Fists, who, as available evidence shows, were not formally organized into a militia unit.

Paradoxically, the apolitical outlook of the Yellow Rock, its grow-ing influence, and its adjacency to the provincial capital, aroused the suspicion and a sense of insecurity of the governor, Yen Ching-ming. Its transformation after the suppression proved that it had been a sect of the Li-men. This leads to the second point: when a secret society or a sect openly or semi-openly disseminated its doctrines near a seat of power, it had to dissimulate its political interests so as to avoid per-secution.

MILITIA AND REBELS

To illustrate these points even more concretely, let me use the well-documented and complicated relations between the rebels and militia of Hsinchi, T'angyi, Kuanhsien, and Kuant'ao in northwest Shantung as an example.[1] The notable militia groups there are shown opposite. The top leaders of local militia groups listed here might not actually take charge of training them, nor command them in battle. The instructors they employed were naturally people who had acquired some martial skill and such people were mostly Sung Ching-shih's teachers, friends, sworn-brothers, or fellow students under a boxing master. Take the Liulin *t'uan*, for instance. Among its instructors, Wang Hsi-lu was a bandit leader and a friend of Sung; he left the Black Ban-ners because of a quarrel with Sung. Ai Lao-mei was Sung's teacher; he hated the Black Banners because they had murdered a disciple of his. Yang Ch'un-shan was a fellow student of Sung's under Ai Lao-mei; he broke away from the Black Banners. Mu Ching-hua was also a fellow student of Sung's; having quarrelled with Sung, he joined the militia group to become the commander of the much feared Black Tiger

---

[1] Unless otherwise indicated, all the information on Sung Ching-shih and the village militia of these counties comes from Chen Po-ch'en, *Sung Ching-shih li-shih tiao-ch'a chi* (a report on the investigation of the history of Sung Ching-shih), Peking, 1957.

Name of militia group	Leaders	Attitudes towards the Eight Diagrams and the Black Banners
Liulin *t'uan*	Yang Ming-ch'ien (big landlord, government student)	Dared not fight the Eight Diagrams at first; changed to hostility to them with the support of T'an T'ing-hsiang (the governor)
Fanchai *t'uan* (*Chungyi t'uan*)	Fan Ching-t'ang (military *hsui-ts'ai*, landlord)	Hostile to the Black Banners
Hsinchi *t'uan* (*Such'ing tuan*)	Ting Ping-t'ang (military *chü-jen*, landlord) Wang Chiu-ling (military *chin-shih*, poor)	Maintained a peaceable relationship with the Black Banners
Houku *t'uan* (*Yunghsing t'uan*)	Liang Chao-hsiang (landlord, government student)	Friendly with the Black Banners
Hsiaot'un *t'uan*	Ma Kuang-jen Ma Ching-san (big landlords)	On good terms with the Black Banners
Tangyi *t'uan*	Wang Pai-ling (*hsiu-ts'ai*, small landlord)	Employed Sung Ching-shih as militia instructor; maintained peaceable relationship with Sung and then turned against Sung
Yenchiaying (*Chungyi t'uan*)	Yen Lung-hsiu	Centre of the Eight Diagrams

Group. In the Fanchai *t'uan*, the situation was similar: its instructor, Wang Chan-ao, was related to Sung, and Wang Chan-chi was Sung's teacher and a convict on a murder charge. It was through people like these, who shared the same social background as the leaders of the rebels, that contacts with the rebels were made and attitudes were formed.

Their social background can be illustrated by the life story of Sung Ching-shih. Before becoming a bandit leader, Sung had been a student for a couple of years, a farmhand, a salt smuggler, a horse dealer in Inner Mongolia, a riot leader against heavy taxation, and a convict. He was a man of good physique and outstanding boxing skill. These qualities and his ability to read, together with his experience in travelling, made him an adequate leader at a time of crisis. For a living he exhibited his boxing skill, taught boxing, and acted as an escort for convoys of goods. Indeed, before his career as an outlaw, he had even led Wang Pai-ling's militia in T'angyi. Through boxing exhibitions and lessons as well as through leading militia units, he became widely known and had extensive local contacts so that it was possible for him to organize anti-tax risings in his native town. Not all his teachers and friends turned against him when he raised his Black Banners; many joined him or joined the T'aip'ing rebellion, such as Liu Hou-i and Sun Ju-ching.

This then was the subterranean picture of Shantung society in the 1860s. On the extreme left, as it were, there stood the White Lotus, hostile and uncompromising, co-operating with the Nien and fighting the government. Their sister organization, the Eight Diagrams, was perhaps less belligerent at the beginning of the Nien rebellion. (For instance, the Yenchiaying, the centre of the Eight Diagrams in west Shantung, even attempted to form its own militia group, but was eventually pulled into the arms of the rebels.) At the other extreme, there was the Ch'ing-men, corrupt and politically vague, some of whose members perhaps broke away to take up arms against the government by joining the turbaned bandits in the same way as Wang Cheng-chi had done in 1813. With or without a religious hue, these underworld organizations cut right across the province's militia units. This makes any attempt to differentiate them from the militia impossible.

ORIGINS OF THE BOXERS

The situation of the 1860s can throw a good deal of light on that of the 1890s. There is no sound reason to suppose that in the 1890s the subterranean scene of Shantung could be radically different from that of a generation earlier.

However, with regard to the origin of the Boxers in the 1890s, scholars remain poles apart. The exponents of the militia theory maintained that the Boxers were members of law-abiding militia who had never entertained any insurrectionary thoughts whereas the secret society theory under the influence of Lao Nai-hsüan insists on the origin of the Boxers being the White Lotus.

Tai Hsüan-chih argues that the Boxers were in no way associated with the White Lotus on the grounds: (1) the magical powers claimed by the Boxers as referred to already were unknown to the White

Lotus;[1] (2) the Boxers had never been an anti-dynastic organization whereas the White Lotus had always been so.[2] Contrary to Tai's position, historians in China are anxious to establish the fact that the Boxers were originally members of the White Lotus, but unfortunately none of them have so far succeeded in doing so. Fan Wen-lan, for example, regards the White Boxers as descendants of the White Lotus, therefore anti-dynastic.[3] Another example is the hasty Lü Chen-yü, who makes out a case that the slogan 'Supporting the Ch'ing' was put forward not by the true Boxers (the peasants) but by the bogus Boxers (the gentry). In the final analysis, according to him, the Boxers, the true ones, were anti-dynastic.[4] Whereas Fan ascribes the decision to support the Ch'ing to Chu Hung-teng and the monk, Pen-ming, Shih Ch'un, without citing a shred of evidence, says that these two were 'pursuing a clandestine revolutionary activity under the slogan of "Overthrowing the Ch'ing and Restoring the Ming".'[5] These historians' effort goes to show only a poverty of historiography.

Tai's first reason, a different type of magical power, I think, is not really important, not even relevant. Concepts of magical powers, like other things, undergo changes from time to time, even among the members of the White Lotus. Early risings organized by the sect left behind no records of any claim to magical powers at all.[6] The uprising led by Wang Lun in 1774 boasted no more than boxing skill and spiritual healing.[7] It was as late as the Chia-ch'ing reing (1796–1820), or more precisely in the nineteenth century, as Tai points out, that the White Lotus and the Eight Diagrams began to assume magical capabilities such as the *chin-chung-chao* (the Golden Bell 'Armour', invulnerability), high-speed (flying) walking, transmigration etc.[8]

---

[1] Tai, *I-ho-t'uan-yen-chiu*, p. 3.

[2] *Ibid.* pp. 16, 17.

[3] *Chung-kuo chin-tai shih* (A Modern History of China), 1, 348, 349.

[4] 'Wei-ta jen-min ti wei-ta li-shih ch'uang-tso—tu *I-ho-t'uan ti ku-shih pi-chi*,' (A Great Historical Work by a Great People—A Review of *Stories of the I-ho-t'uan*) in the *Min-chien wen-hsüeh* (Popular Literature), no. 3, 1959.

[5] *I-ho-t'uan yün-tung liu-shih chou-nien chi-nien lun-wen chi* (Commemorative Essays on the 60th Anniversary of the Boxer Movement, hereafter *Lun-wen chi*), Peking, 1961, p. 35.

[6] *Chiu Yüan-shih* (The Old History of the Yüan Dynasty), *chüan* 42, and *Ming-shih* (The History of the Ming Dynasty), *chüan* 117, 120, 154, 185, 206 and 256.

[7] *Shantung t'ung-chih*, *chüan* 117, 3 *a*, *b*, and J. J. M. de Groot, *Sectarianism and Religious Persecution in China*, 1904, II, 299, 400.

[8] Tai, *I-ho-t'uan yen-chiu*, 3; *Tang-an*, I, 4; *IHT*, I, 346; and Ch'ai O, *Fan-t'ien lu ts'ung-lu* (Jottings of the Fan-t'ien Studio), Shanghai, 1936, XIII, 18 *a*, *b*.

Towards the end of the nineteenth century, as novels on supernatural performances enjoyed unprecedented popularity due to the modern printing press, there was a considerable change in the concepts of magical powers. These grew more and more fantastic in order perhaps to sustain the readers' interest. A feature of these supernatural performances is that they not infrequently occur in passages where a Chinese hero meets a foreign (seldom European) or a religious foe (such as a Buddhist or a Taoist). By his superior magical ability he succeeds in preserving the superiority of the Han-Chinese. Such magical tricks as the *fei-chien* (flying swords remotely controlled by their users), it must be remembered, were figments of Chinese imagination after the deadly qualities of the foreign gun had become common knowledge and they were the Chinese answer to them. I have, by relying on Sun Kai-ti's study of popular novels, tentatively put forward this view in my previous paper on the Boxers.[1] Here I would like to draw the reader's attention to the fact that the Boxer movement was the only one in the entire history of China to have had such an elaborate and boastful system of magical powers.

Tai's second point is of much greater significance. Hitherto scholars of the opinion that the Boxers were originally associated with the heretical sects and were anti-dynastic have hinged their theory on the Boxer leaders, Chu Hung-teng and Pen-ming, and the P'ingyüan incident of October 1899.[2] Chu, according to a recently revealed source,[3] was born in Ssushui of Shantung, a travelling medicine man with no living relations when he was arrested; Pen-ming was a native of Kaot'ang whose secular name was either Yang Hsi-shun or Yang Shun-t'ien and who became a Buddhist novice at the Ting-chia-ssu of Yüch'eng in his boyhood. Of the local officials who had reported on Chu, Pen-ming, and the P'ingyüan affair,[4] Lao Nai-hsüan was the

---

[1] 'The nature and characteristics of the Boxer movement', *the Bulletin of the School of Oriental and African Studies*, XIII, 2, 1960.

[2] Quoted extensively from *IHT* in V. Purcell, *The Boxer Uprising*, chapter IX.

[3] Quoted in the *Lun-wen chi*, pp. 72, 100. The sources are a report from the prefect of Tsinan dated Kuang-hsü 25.xi.1 (3.xii.1899) and another from the magistrate of Lich'eng dated Kuang-hsü 25.xi.17 (19.xii.1899). Both documents are in the Academy of Sciences, Peking.

[4] By Yü-hsien, *Tang-an*, I, 34–6, 39, 41, 42 and also an earlier one quoted by Yüan Ch'ang, *IHT*, IV, 159; by Chiang K'ai, *IHT*, I, 354, 360; by Lao Nai-hnsüa, *IHT*, IV, 438; by Chih Pi-hu (who inherited Lao's theory), *IHT*, IV, 443; and by Yüan Shih-k'ai, *Yang-shou-yüan tsou-i chi-yao* (Collected Memorials of the Yang-shou-yüan), 1938, II, 3a (after reading Lao Nai-hsüan, he too was influenced by him), *ibid.* IV, 14a.

only one who stated definitely that the Boxers came from the White Lotus sect, although nearly of all them said that Chu claimed to be a descendant of the imperial house of the Ming. Later developments, however, were baffling. To begin with, it is established beyond any doubt that the Boxers used the Eight Diagrams to designate their branches and according to a recent on-the-spot investigation conducted by Chinese scholars,[1] there were in fact, contrary to earlier suspicion of only three, eight groups of the Boxers in Chihli, each having its own leaders and one of the eight diagrams as its designation. This tends to indicate their connection with the Eight Diagrams sect. In my view, this indication cannot be read as conclusive evidence of such a connection. There was no reason for the syncretic Boxers to refrain from using the Diagrams as group designations, but it would be rash to conclude from this that they were a branch of the Eight Diagrams or the White Lotus. Had they been, there would have been no explanation of the second development, their persecution of the members of the White Lotus in Peking in 1900.[2] Perhaps greater importance should be attached to this latter fact to repudiate the hypothesis that the Boxers and the White Lotus were one. In this Tai Hsüan-chih's analysis in section 2 of chapter 2 is, to my mind, acceptable in principle.

It is not only impossible to establish definitely the relationship between the Boxers and the White Lotus, but it is also difficult to find any definite associations between the Boxers on the one hand and the Big Swords (Ta-tao-hui) and the Red Fists (Hung-ch'üan-hui) on the other. The only two pieces of evidence on the relationship between the Big Swords and the Boxers, as far as I know, are furnished by Chiang K'ai and Liu T'ang; both are, however, sketchy, shifty, and unconvincing. Although Chiang inclined to think that the Big Swords and the Boxers were closely linked, neither he nor Liu stated unambiguously that there existed an alliance between them. With regard to the Red Fists, there are at least four edicts referring to them of which the first one issued in the seventh month of Kuang-hsü 25 (August 1899), quoted by Chiang K'ai, evoked Chiang's incredulity.[3] To say the least, the connection between the Boxers and the other groups, in a formal and organizational sense, is far from clear.

---

[1] *IHT*, II, 7 and *Lun-wen chi*, p. 265.
[2] Purcell, *The Boxer Uprising*, pp. 220–21. See also *IHT*, I, 20 and Huang Jui, *Hua-sui-jen-sheng-an chih-i* (Reminiscenses of the Hua-sui-jen-sheng-an), 1943, p. 21.
[3] *IHT*, IV, 8; *Ta-ch'ing li-ch'ao shih-lu*, Kuang-hsü, 435, 14*b*; and *IHT*, I, 355.

To refute the Boxers being a branch of the White Lotus is not the same as to say that they were loyal and law-abiding. It is impossible to deny that Chu Hung-teng did claim to be a descendant of the Ming ruling house. In addition, Chiang K'ai has given us a piece of information—Chu left behind many private letters in which he talked about his plan for an attack on Peking.[1] From these two items of information, one forms the impression that Chu was politically a hot-headed fellow with rebellious intentions. It would be very hard for such a man, however fickle he may have been, to have raised the slogan of 'Supporting the Ch'ing and Wiping Out the Foreigners' as ascertained by Chinese communist historians.[2]

After the suppression of Chu and Pen-ming, the Boxers of Ch'ihp'ing came under Wang Li-yen,[3] of Kuanhsien under Chao San-tuo,[4] and of Tungch'ang under Wang Ch'ing-i.[5] It was at this juncture the slogan of 'Supporting the Ch'ing' appeared to signify a change in policy. At the same time, the Manchu Court, influenced by Yü-hsien's memorials, sacked Chiang K'ai, and issued the following edict through the Grand Council to the viceroys and governors, dated 21.xi.1899:

Recently, the viceroys and governors were obsessed by the idea of keeping peace upon entering into negotiations with foreigners on important matters. Therefore they appeared ill prepared for such negotiations. This bad habit represents the worst type of ingratitude to us ... Henceforth ... the word 'peace' must be removed not only from their lips but also from their minds.[6]

What this edict did not spell out was the Court's *volte face*—time and again before the P'ingyüan incident the government ordered its local officials to deal with the Christians and others, including the Boxers, as people of the same stock, a policy in effect favouring the Christians as they were hated by the rest of the community in which they lived; after that event the policy of repression gave way to one of differentiating between good and bad Boxers. This policy was first defined in an edict of 11.i.1900:

... not all the societies are the same. Although it is inadmissible to forgive the unruly people who form cliques and create incidents, there are also law-abiding subjects, following the principle of mutual aid, practising skills

[1] *IHT*, I, 361. [2] *Lun-wen chi*, p. 94.
[3] *IHT*, I, 361.
[4] *Kuanhsien chih*, ed. by Ch'en Hsi-hua, 1933, *chüan* 10, 17, 18.
[5] *IHT*, IV, 443. [6] *Tang-an*, I, 37, 38 and *IHT*, IV, 7, 8.

[boxing?] for self-defence and forming village organizations for maintaining law and order. If the local officials listen to rumours, regard them as secret society bandits, and persecute them ruthlessly without making a differentiation between the good and bad, this will result in a panic among the people.[1]

This edict was aiming at restricting Yüan Shih-k'ai, who, swimming against the tide in Peking, mercilessly suppressed the Boxers; it also induced Yü-lu to adopt an ambivalent attitude towards the Boxers. Its substance was repeated in the edict of 17.iv.1900[2] which said: 'The question to be asked is not whether they are members of the Boxing society but whether they are outlaws.'[3] It was on the basis of this kind of understanding that the Dowager Empress could donate money to the Boxers on 25.vi and 6.vii.1900.[4]

The P'ingyüan incident therefore marked a drastic change in the attitude of both the government and the Boxers, bringing their views closer to each other. In a letter to the late Dr Purcell, I said:

Generally speaking, the officials in the Court were in favour of a compromise which was eventually achieved. The reason I say that the compromise came after Chu Hung-teng's arrest and the Ming Monk's [Pen-ming's] disappearance is that they were the last of a series of arrests and executions. Chronologically, this coincided with the change of policy of the Ch'ing Court and should also synchronize with a change in the Boxers' political aims if we grant their leaders a normal share of political alertness.[5]

I am not yet in a position to revise what I said then, beyond adding that Chu Hung-teng and Pen-ming were arrested on 22.xi.1899[6] and executed on 26.xii.1899.[7]

Having refuted Lao Nai-hsüan, Tai goes to the other extreme by reviving the militia theory. In his view, the Boxers were apolitical[8] to the extent that they did not even worship the insurrectionary characters of the *Water Margin*.[9] Theirs was an open organization, consisting of solid, upright, and law-abiding peasants.[10] Their only aims were self-defence against robbery and pillage, and mutual aid among villagers.[11]

---

[1] *Ibid.* I, 56.　　　　　　　　　[2] *Ibid.* 80 and *IHT*, IV, 12.
[3] *Tang-an*, I, 82.　　　　　　　[4] *IHT*, IV, 128, 132.
[5] Purcell, *The Boxer Uprising*, p. 220. For slogans, see *IHT*, IV, 443.
[6] *Tang-an*, I, 34–6, 39.
[7] *Lun-wen chi*, p. 101.
[8] Tai, *I-ho-t'uan yen chiu*, p. 31.
[9] *Ibid.* p. 22, Ai Sheng's assertion that the Boxers worshipped Sung Chiang and Wu Sung (*IHT*, I, 444, 456) is regarded as hearsay by Tai.
[10] *Ibid.* pp. 16, 22.
[11] *Ibid.* p. 14. This echoes the imperial edict quoted above.

What they had inherited was the tradition of the *hsiang-t'uan* (village militia), not the *kuan-t'uan* (government-sponsored militia) of the Hsien-feng and T'ung-chih periods.[1]

This, I regret to say, is an untenable position to maintain. To insist that the Boxers in their initial stages in Shantung consisted only of law-abiding peasants is to oversimplify the matter, as will be discussed presently. It is no exaggeration to say that the law-abiding characteristic and the tradition of the *hsiang-t'uan* simply could not exist in the same organization. The innocence of the militia units portrayed by Tai was not a fact in the 1850s and 60s, as has already been discussed above; nor was it so in the 1890s. When the Boxers were beginning to play havoc in Shantung, the same incongruous and chaotic subterranean situation remained in that province as shown by the decrees issued from Peking and reports despatched from Shantung counties. Besides the Boxers, there continued to exist a great variety of secret societies and heterdox sects. The Boxers in a few independent cases might have begun as self-defence organizations as Ai Sheng's conversation with Ku Jui-hsiang, a militia leader of Hsipao village of Tinghsing, shows:

I asked Jui-hsiang what are the advantages of learning boxing. He replied: 'Speaking of my own village, every winter there are scores of arson cases which we can't report to the officials, burglaries which even if we reported nothing would be done about them, and gambling which we can't stop. Once we have learnt boxing, all these things are completely wiped out and we can live in peace. We have no other intentions.[2]

But, generally speaking, once the peasants were organized under whatever leadership, a tension began to grow, as in the 1850s and 60s, between them and their local governments. Their organizations, be they boxing groups or ordinary militia units, needed money to run and when they were run smoothly gave them a position of strength. The very fact that they needed these organizations for their own protection was a comment on the ineptitude of the authorities. Inevitably they would demand the lowering of taxes as generally they felt they were too burdensome and the revision of miscarriages of justice of which there were not few. The murder of the magistrate of the city of Tientsin, Liu Kuo-t'ang, by the Boxers of Yangchuang is a case in point. Before his death there had circulated in Tientsin a ballad which ran as follows:

[1] *Ibid.* p. 14. [2] *IHT*, I, 454.

Origin of the Boxers

'The Boxers in front of us;
The Red Lanterns behind us.
Let's kill Liu Juo-t'ang first
Before dealing with the Catholics.'[1]

In the 1890s the troubles the militia stirred up were similar to those created by their forerunners in the 1860s—they were disobedient to their local authorities,[2] jealous of each other,[3] and, in addition, hostile to the missionaries and Christian converts. The government in Peking was not unaware of these and its solution was that since it was impossible to suppress, it might be possible to appease them. Indeed, the decrees for the organization of the government-sponsored militia units in Shantung issued on November 1898 and later were designed precisely to prevent the Boxers from making further troubles,[4] and to put their anti-foreign sentiments under the guidance and exploitation of the government.[5] The lessons of the 1860s, so it seems, had not quite sunk in and, worse still, the government had no new methods to deal with the exigencies arising from militia organization except by relying on the good sense and leadership of the gentry.[6] These decrees provoked Yüan Shih-k'ai (appointed the governor of Shantung on 6.xii.1899) to voice his strong disagreement:

Leaving aside the impossibilities of reassembling the already dispersed and restoring the already suppressed, the commissioner and leaders of militia appointed by the government must be people of sensibility. But of the officials and gentry, the sensible simply would not undertake such a task. Even if they could be persuaded, how can they understand the feelings and aims of the Boxers, who after all practise a heterodoxy and use magical incantations, and how can they control them? Furthermore, the financial needs of the militia have always been met by the ordinary people. Now if hundreds of thousands are to be organized into militia units, there will be need of money. Whence can the money come if not from the people? Please allow me to speculate on the evil consequences of this. As soon as bandits can use the name of militia and heterodox sects are given legitimate authority, they will operate openly and can never again be disbanded. They will take the opportunity offered to

---

[1] *I-ho-t'uan ku-shih*, pp. 162–3, also p. 157. The Red Lanterns were girl Boxers.
[2] *Ta-ch'ing li-ch'ao shih-lu*, Kuang-hsü, p. 446, 10*a* and p. 461, 10*b*; *Tang-an*, I, 30; and *I-ho-t'uan ku-shih*, pp. 211–2.
[3] *IHT*, I, 492 and *Keng-tzu chih-shih* (1900 Chronicles), Peking, 1959, p. 157.
[4] Dated 19.vi.1899, Yüan, *Yang-shou-yüan tsou-i chi-yao*, V, 2*b*.
[5] *Ta-ch'ing li-ch'ao shih-lu*, Kuang-hsü, p. 448, 15*a*, *b*.
[6] Yüan, *Yang-shou-yüan-tsou-i chi-yao*, IV, 16*b*–17*b*.

them to satisfy their selfish ends while no one can check them. How then can the general situation not become chaotic and the ordinary people not suffer at their hands?

He added: 'It is absolutely inadvisable to place private militia units under governmental supervision.'[1]

Indeed, when the government-sponsored militia came into being, local ruffians and other undesirable characters found room in them[2] as they had done before. The origins of the leaders of the Shantung Boxers that can be traced bear witness to this:

	Secular leaders	
Huimin	Chang He-hsiao	bandit
	Chao Ch'an	boy
	Chao Ch'ang-ming	salt smuggler
	Chao Lin-sheng	boy
	Li T'ung-fang	local ruffian
	Nei Hung-wen	soldier
	Sun Yü-lung	soldier
	Wang Cheng-nan	local ruffian
	Wang Chih-ts'ai	convict
	Wang Wei	salt smuggler
	Wang Yü	salt smuggler
P'ingyüan	Chu Hung-teng	medicine man
	Tung Yüan-pang	peasant
Tungp'ing	Wang Erh	peasant
Yenshan	Liu Erh	bandit
	Buddhists	
Shantung	Ta-kuei	—
P'ingyüan	Hsin-ch'eng	—
	Pen-ming	—

As to their following, they were mostly peasants and sons of educated people in Huimin[3] and mostly army deserters in P'ingyüan.[4] In Chihli, the general impression was that they were unemployed and rootless people one might describe as the 'lumpen proletariat'[5] and country bumpkins.[6] According to a recent investigation conducted at Tientsin,[7] they were mostly landless peasants, part owning farmers,

[1] *Ibid*, IV, 16*b*–17*b*.
[2] *Ibid*, V, 3*a* and *IHT*, I, 497, 499.
[3] *IHT*, I, 403.   [4] *Ibid*. 356.
[5] *Ibid*. 290, 307, 477; II, 141, 146; IV, 13.
[6] *IHT*, I, 290, 307 and *Keng-tzu chi-shih*, p. 12.
[7] *Lun-wen chi*, pp. 260–3.

transport workers, handicraft workers, pedlars, deserters from the Ch'ing army, *yamen* clerks and orderlies, teachers, students, and a few well-to-do persons. Their ages were strikingly young.[1] Although they were known to have used the names of their places of origin as the designations of their units, such as the Hsiangho *t'uan* and Wuch'ing *t'uan*, they were known as a whole as the I-ho-t'uan, which was subdivided into eight branches according to the names of the Eight Diagrams. Each branch was then further divided into the basic units of *t'an* (altar). It is well known that all their members, male and female (the Red, Blue, and Black Lanterns), practised magical tricks and worshipped their deity.

The Boxers' social composition shows no difference from that of either the militia or the secret societies (including religious sects). This ambiguity made their transformation from one into another quite easy and formed the basis of the government's decision to transform them into militia units under government supervision. But organizationally the Boxers showed a predominant religious character which distinguished them from ordinary militia groups.

The social ambiguity and easy transmutability among the militia, secret societies, and bandits imply that any attempt to distinguish the Boxers from the others is an effort of little historical significance and that any insistence on a distinction represents a methodological mistake or misconception. It is on the social and ideological ambiguity rather than organizational connection of these popular groups that one should focus one's attention.

The Boxers had no formal connections with the White Lotus, Eight Diagrams, or the Hung-men (including the Triad, the Three Dots, and the Tien-ti-hui,) They were no ordinary militia either. As a movement, they did, however, have some unique characteristics. The movement was predominantly anti-foreign, strongly religious both organizationally and ideologically, hierarchically pyramidal but without an apex, and socially similar to other popular groups but with very little participation of the gentry in the initial stages. As a political movement among the uneducated and semi-literate, these characteristics indicate an eclecticism aiming at the broadest possible support of the individual members of all popular organizations who did not mind jettisoning some unimportant doctrinal and political differences. To put it in

[1] *IHT*, I, 8, 139, 238–40, 354. Also *Keng-tzu chi-shih*, p. 12.

anachronistic terms, the movement was an anti-foreign united front of all except for the White Lotus, Eight Diagrams, and Hung-men.

The observation can be supported by other reasons. The missionaries were known to have interfered in the litigations between Christians and other people, influencing the local officials to give verdicts in the Christians' favour; so were likely the secret societies on the opposing side in a magistrate court. The defeat of a non-Christian Chinese meant a loss of prestige, most probably, of a secret society. The Kuanhsien incident which developed into a fight between the Christians and the Plum Flower Boxers was a case in point. The same might be applied to other popular organizations, hence their common hatred of the foreigner and the Christian. Another reason which may be used to supplement the point under discussion comes from the deities of the movement. Tai classified them into four categories—immortals (*shen-hsien* such as the Jade Emperor, the Eight Fairies, and etc.), loyal and righteous people (such as Kuan Kung and K'ung-ming), knights errant (*hsia-k'e*, such as Huang San-t'ai and his son, Huang T'ien-pa), and brave soldiers (such as Hsiang Yü).[1] His categorization, I am sorry to say, is unreliable, having left out two important groups of gods and demi-gods, namely the Buddhist deities such as Ta-mo (Darma), Chi-kung and all main characters in the novel, *Monkey*, and the anti-foreign officials of the Ch'ing dynasty such as Ch'i Chün-tsao and Li Ping-heng.[2] The worship of both the Buddhist and Taoist gods on the same altar meant that the movement was syncretic, but the fact that most of their gods were Buddhists ones, particularly those of Zen Buddhism, and that no Taoists appeared in any list of their leaders confirmed their claim to being a Buddhist movement.[3]

The worship of Zen Buddhist gods and of Huang San-t'ai and Huang T'ien-pa, heroes of the novels, *Shih-kung An* and *P'eng-kung An*,[4] together with other supplementary pieces of evidence, indicates a rather peculiar origin of the Boxers hitherto unnoticed. This origin was the Ch'ing-men. According to the tradition of the Ch'ing-men, it was a Zen-Buddhist-dominated secret society[5] consisting, as has been

---

[1] Tai, *I-ho-t'uan yen chiu*, p. 22.   [2] *IHT*, II, 8; III, 373.

[3] *IHT*, IV, 152.

[4] The former was published in 1839 and the latter in 1891–4. The biographies of Shih Shih-lun and P'eng P'eng are in A. Hummel, *Eminent Chinese*, pp. 613, 614, 653, 654.

[5] Ch'en I-fan, *Ch'ing-men k'ao-yuan*, pp. 1–32, 40.

shown above, of transport workers along the Grain Tribute route. The fact that Shih Shih-lun was made into the hero of the novel *Shih-kung An* was not only due to his fairness and incorruptibility, but also due to his incumbency as the director-general of the transport of the Grain Tribute from 1715 to 1720, the period in which the Ch'ing-men was developing under the guidance of the three grand masters, Weng, Ch'ien, and P'an. His success in discharging the duties as the director-general no doubt had the co-operation of the Ch'ing-men. Therefore in the novel, as P'eng P'eng in the *P'eng-kung An*, he was depicted as an official who welcomed the service and co-operation of those members of secret societies who desired to render loyal services to the government. Huang San-t'ai and his son, described as natives of Shaohsing of Chekiang, the province in which the Ch'ing-men flourished, were such men. These two novels and all the operas and stories incorporated into and derived from them went to praise those members of secret societies like the Huang father and son who had served the dynasty. These people, fictitious as they were, could be construed only as the personifications of the principles and aspirations of the members of the Ch'ing-men.

In addition to this, the Ch'ing-men, like the Boxers, attached the greatest importance to the master-disciple relationship and the tie among the disciples under one master. This was quite different from the Hung-men practice which gave priority to sworn brotherhood.[1] Again, like the Boxers but unlike the Hung-men, the Ch'ing-men followers were disciplinarians, law-abiding in principle, and filial to their parents.[2]

If these indications can be taken as meaningful, I would like to put

---

[1] *IHT*, I, 90, 144 and Ch'en I-fan, Ch'ing-men Rao-yuan, p. 210.

[2] The 'commandments' of the Ch'ing-men are: obey the law, be filial to one's parents, be respectful to gods (Heaven, Earth, Confucious, Kuan Kung, and the grand masters of the Society), follow the right path in life, take care of one's health, quickly correct one's misdeeds, be careful in what one says, take up a legitimate job, reform one's character, get rid of vices (opium, drinking, prostitutes, and gambling); those of the Boxers are: do not violate the law, do not go against the wishes of one's parents, kill foreigners, hang one's head low when walking in the street, do not stare left and right greet fellow Boxers on meeting them, do not be greedy for money, kill corrupt officials, and purge one's lust. (See Ch'en I-fan, *op. cit.* pp. 97–98 and *IHT*, II, 142.) After the initial stages of their respective movements, neither the Ch'ing-men nor the Boxers observed their rules of conduct rigorously.

It is however, interesting to note that both the Ch'ing-men and the Boxers worshipped Kuan Kung, the god of war, more than any other deity.

forward the view that the membership of the Boxer movement and that of the Ch'ing-men overlapped, perhaps to a considerable extent. The Ch'ing-men may not have been the dominant nucleus of the movement which treated the movement as a front organization, but its followers probably played an important role in it. In this case, as in the case of other secret societies, the association forged between the Boxers and the societies perhaps existed not on the organizational level, only on the individual level.

The Boxer movement on the whole was doctrinally eclectic and organizationally complicated, comprising individual members of a large number of sects and societies who were united by their anti-foreignism. The White Lotus, Eight Diagrams, and Hung-men were not in it. Therefore neither the secret society theory connecting the movement to the White Lotus nor the militia theory depicting it as a law-abiding organization can be accepted as it stands.

THE HIGH TIDE OF SOCIALISM IN
THE CHINESE COUNTRYSIDE

BY JACK GRAY

THE PEASANTS AND THE STATE

In the modern revolution of China the peasant at first played an insignificant role, in both theory and practice. Their problems were recognized, and usury and landlordism were universally deplored, and there was a general sentiment in favour of a redistribution of the land, but little clear thinking about how land reform should be carried out.

As the economic implications of modernization became clearer, the reform of rural conditions assumed a new theoretical importance. It was seen that low productivity and the low purchasing power of the peasant majority were of decisive importance as a factor in the inhibition of economic growth; and it was universally accepted that the chief obstacle to growth in the countryside was the rural social system, in particular the prevalence of tenant farming at high rents, none of the profits of which were ploughed back for the improvement of the farms.

In the 1920s there was a sharp revival of the peasant disaffection which, in the nineteenth century, had kept China in turmoil.[1] Although these movements of protest were to some extent organized by the new Communist Party, the evidence is overwhelming that most of the hundreds of cases of rural revolt which then took place were spontaneous. This peasant movement turned the attention of many of the new western-educated intellectuals to the study of rural conditions,[2] and what they found confirmed Chinese public opinion in its alarm at the decay of rural society and in its belief that a social revolution in the countryside was one of the first essentials for the strengthening of the nation.

[1] Chung-kuo Hsien-tai Shih Tzu-liao Ts'ung-k'an, ed., *Ti-i-tzu kuo-nei ko-ming chan-cheng shih-chi ti nung-nien yün-tung* (The Peasant Movement in the Period of the First Revolutionary Civil War), Peking, 1953.
[2] The most copious and convenient collection of material on this subject is Feng Ho-fa, ed. *Chung-kuo nung-ts'un ching-chi tzu-liao* (Materials on the Rural Economy of China), Shanghai, April and August 1935. The best brief introduction in English is R. H. Tawney, *Land and Labour in China*.

In this way the basis was laid for bringing the farmers into the political system to an unprecedented extent. Discontent over tenancy and taxation made them active, and their projected place in the national revolution obliged them to become active and not merely passive citizens.

The entry of the peasants into politics took place through a number of stages. First, the first united front between the nationalists and communists brought together communist interest in the peasants as allies of the working class in the revolution, and Sun Yat-sen's personal belief (not widely shared in his party) that the new nationalism must embrace all classes. Second, the idea of the usefulness of the peasants as a revolutionary force was confirmed by their part in the Northern Expedition. Third was the emergence of Mao Tse-tung to predominant influence in the Party after his demonstration that the Party could survive and grow on the basis of peasant revolutionary fervour alone. Fourth, the necessity of a revolution from below was confirmed by the failure of the Nationalist Party to keep their new and theoretically democratic local government and rural organization out of the hands of the rural upper classes, who were the chief obstacle not only to rural improvement but to the creation of a national government whose writ would run everywhere. Finally, the communist-led guerrilla war against Japan mobilized the rural population of North China for a nationalist purpose and one which was simple enough for them to appreciate and directly related to their own lives.[1]

The Japanese invasion thus created the mass nationalism which Sun Yat-sen had desired but of which in his own lifetime he had seen no more than the faintest foreshadowing. It would be a mistake, however, in this context to make a distinction between nationalist and revolutionary sentiment. The poor of North China, suffering from plain and universally acknowledged injustice, were attached to the nation not as it was, but as it could be. Their nationalism, therefore, had revolutionary implications; the achievement of social justice by redistribution of the land was the condition of their participation in national life.

By the beginning of the second world war, however, Chinese public opinion as a whole had accepted that traditional family farming could provide neither a substantial rise in the peasants' standards of living nor an agricultural surplus sufficient to support the strengthening of

[1] See Chalmers S. Johnson, *Peasant Nationalism and Communist Power*, Stanford, 1962.

the nation by rapid industrialization. It was generally agreed among experts and among politicians that some form of co-operative agriculture had to be established. The projected part of the peasants in the national revival was now, therefore, to involve them in a far higher degree of organization and mutual dependence than was natural to them and a far closer and more constant relationship with the State than they had ever conceived.

Only the communist minority among politically conscious Chinese desired that co-operative agriculture should take a form similar to the Soviet collectives; but in the general acquiescence in Communist rule, brought about by the collapse of the Nationalist alternative, there could be little wholehearted opposition to the fact that under Communism co-operative farming would take the Communist form.

The dilemma of the development of co-operative agriculture everywhere is the paternalism essentially involved. The theoretical justification of the co-operatives is based largely upon concepts outside the experience of the dwarf family farmer, just because he *is* a dwarf family farmer. He is unlikely to be persuaded of the advantages of co-operative farming except by experience of it under the direction of those who know what to demand of it. Verbal persuasion is therefore ineffective, whereas coercion was recognized by the Chinese communist party as liable in this matter to defeat its own ends. This was the dilemma of the Chinese Communist Party's rural policy and the supreme test of their ability to induce the Chinese peasants to accept their projected place in the new polity.

THE EARLY CO-OPERATIVE MOVEMENT

The first campaign for the co-operativization of Chinese agriculture was launched in December 1951 by an unpublished resolution of the Central Committee which was revised and published in February 1953, after a year's experiment, as part of the General Line for the Period of Transition.[1] In the years since completion of land reform in the north, the organization of agriculture had gone back rather than forward. The restoration of public order and economic stability and the rapid expansion of urban markets had strengthened independent farming, so

[1] See Chung-kuo k'o-hsüeh-yüan Ching-chi Yen-chiu-so, ed. *Kuo-min ching-chi hui-fu shih-ch'i nung-yeh sheng-ch'an ho-tso tzu-liao hui-pien, 1949–1952* (Source Materials for the Study of Agricultural Co-operatives during the Period of Economic Recovery), Peking, 1957.

that middle peasants tended to withdraw from the Mutual Aid Teams, rich peasants flourished in increasing numbers, and conscientious Party farmers were apprehensive about their own prosperity which threatened to turn them into exploiting rich peasants.[1] Morale was wavering. This is one possible reason for the decision to speed up co-operativization. Another possible reason was the necessity of allowing time for tentative experiment before the beginning of full-scale industrial planning demanded greater control over agriculture.

Between 1951 and 1955 there were several changes of pace and intensity in the successive campaigns for the collectivization of agriculture, reflecting controversies within the Party, and carried on against the background of diminishing confidence in collectivized agriculture elsewhere in the communist world. This article, which is concerned primarily with the model for the political process of collectivization put forward with the authority of Mao Tse-tung himself, will not deal with the history of the process; it is sufficient for our purpose here to describe the assumptions with which the process began in late 1951,[2] and to compare these with the assumptions underlying the justification of rapid collectivization in late 1955.

On a preliminary examination of materials published then on the basis of the Party's Resolution, it is clear that the Party had a consistent view of the prerequisites for success in the co-operativization of agriculture. They are summarized as follows:

(1) *Mutual Benefit.* Agricultural Producers Co-operatives (hereinafter referred to as A.P.C.s), in bringing together the land, labour and capital of poor and middle peasants, must avoid the exploitation of labour by those with more land, on the one hand; and, on the other, must avoid becoming a means of redistribution of income to the disadvantage of the more prosperous. Elaborate recommendations and a large choice of arrangements were suggested and the A.P.C.s left to choose. The result at first was a system heavily biased towards payment to land.

(2) *Voluntarism.* The insistence that adherence to A.P.C.s must be voluntary was re-enforced in local instructions to cadres with sufficient

---

[1] This was especially true in Manchuria, where land reform had been completed earliest.
[2] See especially *Source Materials*, etc. (above, p. 87, n.), *passim*; these volumes treat the early stages of the A.P.C. movement province by province, mainly at the level of such practical instruction.

detail concerning the application of this principle to leave no doubt that it was meant to be applied and to suggest that it probably was in fact generally applied at this experimental stage of the co-operative movement; the Party could not afford at this 'demonstration' stage the failures which coercion might cause and their programme was, at this time, too tentative to offer much temptation to coercion among the local cadres.

(*3*) *Gradualism.* This meant not merely that the farmers would pass through the two stages of the Mutual Aid Teams and the A.P.C.s before reaching full collectivization, but also that within these two stages there would be gradual changes which might serve to soften considerably the transition from one stage to another.

(*4*) *Collectivist Consciousness.* Successful development of the co-operatives pre-supposed the development among A.P.C. members of a rational consciousness of the relation between individual, communal and national economic interests, as well as presupposing the ability of the members to work together in discipline and to accept rational sharing of rewards. Collectivist consciousness was expected to be much improved by the increase of common property within the Mutual Aid Teams and within the co-operatives.

(*5*) *Increased Production.* This was the fundamental point. Increased production would provide the only argument which in the end could be decisive, not only in the establishment but in the consolidation of the A.P.C.s; and only increased incomes could lubricate the anticipated process of transition from one form of organization to another.

It must be stressed that the documents upon which all this is based are not high-level propaganda documents but practical instructions to cadres, nor does their caution represent a retreat after a period of forceful advance; they were in fact produced at a time when the process of co-operativization was to be speeded up. The result of failure to take these prerequisites seriously, illustrated profusely in the documents, is the resignation of members or the break-up of A.P.C.s and Mutual Aid Teams.

By March 1955, about 14% of China's farming households were in the A.P.C.s and predictions for the future made upon this basis were still very cautious. In July, however, came the speech of Mao Tse-tung which insisted that there was a 'high tide of socialism' in the Chinese countryside, that many local Party Organizations had failed to appreciate the possibilities of rapid popular progress in agricultural organization and advocating that the process should be speeded up. By November 1955, over 60% of China's farming households had entered the co-operatives.

Mao Tse-tung claimed to have based his new and more optimistic analysis upon the reports made by local cadres at the enlarged plenum which met in July. In December, a selection of these reports, with the addition of many more similar documents illustrating development in the later part of the year, were published, with a preface by Mao himself, to justify the new policy, under the title *The High Tide of Socialism in the Chinese Countryside*.[1] The rest of this paper is based upon the material in this collection on the provinces of Hopei, Honan, Heilungkiang, Kirin, Kiangsu, Chekiang and Kwangtung. Clearly this is not a balanced source. The aim of the compilers was to prove that rapid co-operativization was possible, and in particular that there was a widespread popular demand for it. The compilers do not try to prove this, however, by selecting examples only of smooth co-operativization or of perfect co-operatives; rather, they were concerned to prove that all the problems of the process of founding and of consolidating co-operatives had been solved somewhere and could therefore be solved elsewhere. It is of the essence of this approach that the problem must be described and analysed. Being a collection of articles and reports of a local nature, the collection does not provide a consistent systematic comparison of co-operatives. It is consistent only in its use of a single criterion of choice, the successful solution of a general problem in a particular instance. It gives a wide range of information about every aspect of the co-operative movement. It makes, one can assume, the best case which could in honesty be made for rapid further progress. If it fails to prove that the speeding up of co-operativization was justified in terms of the conditions which the Party itself predicated, then it forms an *a fortiori* argument for subsequent policy.

[1] Chung-kung Chung-yang Pan-kung T'ing, ed. *Chung-kuo nung-ts'un ti she-hui-chu-i kao ch'ao* (The High Tide of Socialism in the Chinese Countryside), Peking, 1956. [Hereafter referred to as *High Tide*.]

The purpose of this essay is to examine the model for the process of collectivization represented by the *High Tide* material. Clearly this material cannot serve as a basis for generalization about the actual practice of the process of collectivization, nor can the picture of Chinese conditions which emerges from it be taken to be accurate or representative, either with respect to the natural conditions described or with respect to the responses of the Chinese peasants.

The *High Tide*, however, is not merely the ephemeral propaganda of a particular moment in the history of collectivization. It is a body of political and social theory, couched in terms of examples of actual development, with comments interspersed. It is in this respect in the Chinese tradition, in which political theory was usually expressed in the form of commentary on historical texts. It is perhaps difficult to appreciate the purpose and significance of the *High Tide* collection unless one remembers the precedents, such as Wang Fu-chih's examination of the idea of the Mandate of Heaven, expressed as a commentary on the history of Sung, and Ku Yen-wu's examination of decentralization as a means of limiting imperial power, expressed in a vast historical gazetteer of the Empire. It is this tradition to which Mao Tse-tung was consciously or unconsciously appealing. By interpreting the historical events in the Chinese countryside in the preceding two years he sought to prove that a new level of social and political consciousness was appearing, and to show the conditions of its appearance. It is important not only for the history of collectivization, but for the subsequent history of Chinese Communist thought; it contains the germs of ideas later expressed in the communes and the Great Leap Forward, and latterly in the Cultural Revolution. The *High Tide* awaits full analysis in this respect; the present essay is limited merely to describing, with some explanatory comment, the political ideas and assumptions involved, as they applied to the co-operativization of agriculture.

Among the editorial comments attached to individual articles and providing exegesis on Mao's preface is one which sums up with a degree of frankness characteristic of these volumes the current objections to rapid co-operativization.[1] These objections are described as superstitions destroyed by the events in the countryside of the second half of 1955, and they are then listed:

[1] See *High Tide*, p. 56.

The idea that co-operativization within three years was childish; that co-operativization in the north could be speeded up but not in the south; that backward villages could not be co-operativized, nor mountain villages, nor villages in minority areas or racially mixed areas; that co-operativization was not possible in places where natural disaster had occurred; that it was easy to found A.P.C.s but difficult to consolidate them; that the peasants were too poor; that there was no means of centralizing capital; that peasants had too little education to permit them to keep proper accounts; that too many co-operatives had already been founded; that the co-operative movement produced too much 'disturbance'; that development had gone ahead of the consciousness of the masses and of the experience of cadres; that the Party's unified grain purchase and supply policy and its co-operative policy had reduced the incentives of the peasants to produce; that as far as the co-operative movement was concerned, if the Communist Party did not promptly 'get off its high horse' there was danger of the worker-peasant alliance being broken up; and that co-operativisation had produced a mass of surplus labour which had no outlet, etc. etc.'

These are the objections which the compilers of the collection seek to meet.

In the event, the conditions described in the *High Tide* collection were used to justify not simply the absorption of the rest of the Chinese farmers into the co-operatives, but in the immediate wake of this the changing of the co-operatives into full collectives so that collectivization was completed by the end of 1956, although Mao's preface had predicted only that by that time co-operativization would have been complete.

THE HIGH TIDE

The Principle of Voluntarism

The whole tenor of policy prescriptions in the collection suggests that as far as the principle of voluntariness is concerned, the Party had not changed its attitude; in this campaign for speedier progress, as in the first campaign against 'dependence upon spontaneity' in 1952, coercion and pressurization are condemned. The collection provides a large number of individual examples of peasants who refused to join the A.P.C.s, and we need not doubt that whatever pressures were present they were not such as to make it impossible (although they might make it very difficult) for the average middle peasant to stay out.

There is also ample evidence that it was possible (in practice as well as in theory) to withdraw from an A.P.C. Of about 40 A.P.C.s individually described, three were dissolved, and two lost almost half of their membership, and there were half a dozen individual resignations (usually of middle peasants discontented with a particular arrangement which they felt worked to their disadvantage). The implication throughout the collection is that the consolidation of all A.P.C.s founded in a particular area is a matter exceptional enough for special mention and for praise.

Three examples may suffice to illustrate the Party's notion of voluntarism at this time. The first concerns a village in Chekiang where, with 40% of the population in the A.P.C.s, the Mutual Aid Teams were suffering from neglect to such an extent that they had become largely nominal, and had to be rebuilt.[1] Among the severely practical prescriptions for dealing with this situation, is one which concerns the present argument: 'Entry into the Mutual Aid Teams is to be voluntary, resignation is to be permitted and will carry no consequences.' On the other hand: 'All those who join voluntarily must attend Team meetings, accept production plans, and carry out their Mutual Aid undertakings.' In other words, the opportunity was provided for the reluctant and the indifferent to resign, while at the same time, the responsibilities of those who chose to stay were re-affirmed and emphasized. New elections of Team leaders were held; but of ten leaders considered unsatisfactory by the Party, only one was changed by election; three committee members were also changed. About one hundred and forty families appear to have been involved; only three resigned, and one was expelled.

The second example concerns an A.P.C. in the Sian suburbs.[2] Here, though the political methods used were on the whole praised, two points were chosen for criticism. The cadres had used the argument that if the middle peasants did not join the A.P.C.s, they were showing ingratitude to the Party and to the State for the benefits enjoyed since Liberation; this argument was condemned as a form of pressure. Also, subscription to the A.P.C. was done in a full meeting of the village population, so that a section of the middle peasants joined 'under this constraint', and were discontented and wanted to resign.

The third example concerns the condemnation of a cadre for having permitted the voluntary dissolution of an A.P.C., in Shaho *hsien*

[1] See *High Tide*, p. 669.
[2] See *High Tide*, note 10, p. 1211.

Hopei.[1] This was a large society with three hundred and twenty-three member households, among whom there had been constant bickering. Middle and poor peasants could not agree, the Party branch was split on the issues involved, and there is evidence behind all this of a division of the village based upon rivalry between two surnames. The head of a county Party work team sent to examine the problems of the village found that the majority of the members wanted to leave the society, and he accepted this. The county committee roundly condemned his action, but not on the grounds that the A.P.C. had no right to dissolve itself. He was condemned for having apparently made no effort to solve the specific problems which had led to the deplorable state of the society, for having failed to listen to the representations of those members of the Party branch who thought that the problems could be solved (and they were apparently a majority of branch members), and above all for having bowed his head to a village feud. There is no indication that the A.P.C. was reconstituted; the consequences of its mistaken dissolution fell not upon the heads of members but upon the head of the unfortunate cadre who had advised dissolution.

Thus in these local examples, we see the Party (1) emphasizing in the case of a particularly difficult and suspect group (the peasants remaining after about 50% co-operativization) that the gurantee of positive participation in the work of mutual aid teams is that participation must be voluntary, (2) that the use of the majority to constrain the minority into joining the A.P.C.s is wrong, and that even the appeal to gratitude to the Party is an undesirable form of pressure, (3) that the responsibility for the successful consolidation of the A.P.C.s lies squarely upon the Party, and that it is the Party and not the A.P.C. membership which has failed when an A.P.C. fails.

Even if the A.P.C. movement remained voluntary, however, in the sense that having heard the Party's arguments (and having been shielded from the organized expression of counter-arguments), a man could still stay out, or having come in experimentally could still leave, the question of what degree of 'spontaneity' existed in the co-operative movement remains a quite separate one. The Party argument at this time was that cadres in many parts of the country were dragging behind in the midst of a mass movement into the co-operatives. If this were so,

---

[1] See *High Tide*, p. 63.

we should find a substantial number of cases in which A.P.C.s were formed spontaneously or even in defiance of discouragement from local cadres; and we should expect this collection to over-report rather than under-report such cases.

In fact, only a very few spontaneous A.P.C.s are mentioned, and they were obviously not taken very seriously.

There are also a number of cases in which the initiative was taken in forming an A.P.C. by a local man who had seen examples of successful A.P.C.s elsewhere, or had read about them in the newspapers. In every case recorded here, however, these men appear to have been Party members, and in at least one case,[1] the Party member had to persuade his fellow-members of the Branch into forming an A.P.C.; and this A.P.C. when formed was formed of the Party Branch members only and of the whole Party Branch, except for one dissident member who thought he had too much to lose. This having been done, the next step, as the article says, was to 'bring in some non-Party people'. The fact that this was in an Old Liberated Area where production was said to have been tripled through the Mutual Aid Teams which had existed since 1942 does not suggest a high level of non-Party initiative in the country as a whole—even although in this case the call for subscription to the new A.P.C. resulted, to the embarrassment of its sponsors, in an almost unanimous response.

Another article is devoted to a village where several attempts had been made to found co-operatives by the inhabitants of the village, and where their efforts had been discouraged by the county committee who thought that the village was backward.[2] This is the only such case; in a collection constructed as this is, in the form of whole articles on particular points by way of illustration rather than in the form of statistical analysis, the fact that there is only one detailed case of such spontaneity is not in itself disproof of spontaneity in the movement; but by itself it can hardly be called proof, and it is very surprising that the compilers did not put up a stronger case for the idea, which was after all the best possible argument for the speed-up of the movement.

While the widespread spontaneous formation of A.P.C.s would have provided the strongest argument for the existence of a 'High Tide of Socialism in the Countryside', the lack of evidence on this point does not disprove the existence of such a tide. This would be

[1] See *High Tide*, p. 44.   [2] See *High Tide*, p. 56.

sufficiently proved by the existence of widespread support for the Party-directed formation of A.P.C.s. We must estimate the potential support for co-operativization in the average Chinese village; and if this seems to amount to the support of a majority of the population, we must then see how far the Party had succeeded upon realizing this potential by 1955.

Some idea of potential support for the co-operatives can be reached by considering the economic interests of the peasants at various relative levels of income. The poor peasants were mainly those who in spite of land reform still had less land than was enough to give them subsistence without other sources of income; a small section of them, however, consisted of families who had enough land but who, because of illness, widowhood, or other misfortunes, had not sufficient labour power to make full use of their land. A minority of poor peasants had an interest in petty trade or in handicrafts, and by virtue of their double source of income might in fact be tolerably well off by village standards although classified as poor because they were not self-supporting in grain. Those with too little land and inadequate opportunities of additional employment could expect to gain from membership of an A.P.C.; but it is important to remember that the advantages they would reap would be related to the land and capital available to the A.P.C., and this in turn depended upon the adherence to it of a sufficiently strong middle peasant element.

The middle peasants were a group whose interests were by no means the same.[1] Their attitude to the A.P.C.s would depend very much upon the land-labour ratio of their farms. All middle peasants, by definition, had adequate land for the support of the family; but while, in the typical case, this land sufficed and no more to provide profitable employment to the labouring members of the family, some middle peasants had less land than the family could work (having more than average labour available), while others with less labour power might have more land than they could work at the most profitable degree of intensity. To both these groups, co-operative working of the land might offer advantages, in the first case by providing through more intensive cultivation, construction work and organized handi-crafts an outlet for surplus family labour, and in the second, access (in

---

[1] See the author's 'Political Aspects of the Land Reform Campaigns in China, 1947–52', *Soviet Studies*, October 1964.

political conditions which discouraged the employment of labourers by the individual farmer) to labour necessary for more intensive cultivation.

The prosperity which the restoration of peace and the development of urban markets had brought since 1949 had increased the proportion of the peasant population in two categories. Some poor peasants had become middle peasants, and were distinguished as 'new lower middle peasants'; and some middle peasants had risen to new prosperity and become 'new upper middle peasants'. The latter represented a loss to the potential supporters of the A.P.C.s. The former were often in a position of some perplexity. As men who had risen as independent farmers, they could hope to go on rising as such, and therefore tended to resist entry into the co-operatives. On the other hand, they were as a class particularly conscious of the benefits of Communist rule; many of them had risen to prosperity through taking the advice of the Party on the new methods of agricultural production, and there is evidence that because they were to some extent formed of the most vigorous-minded and politically active of the poor peasants, their connection with the Party was very close and they probably made up a larger proportion of the rural Party (especially of the rural Party committees) than their mere numbers would warrant.

The Party had still other sources of strength in the village. One quarter or so of the population on average would be in adolescence and early youth, and everything suggests that in the early nineteen-fifties the Party could depend upon their support. They could depend also upon a number of individuals even among the more prosperous groups who were politically convinced of the place of co-operative farming in the national revival, regardless of their own short-term economic interests. They could depend upon a proportion of women who had been convinced that their emancipation would be materially assisted by the opportunities within the co-operative of gaining an income independent of that of their husbands.

Finally, and this was probably by no means negligible in importance, the closeness and strength of family ties in the Chinese village, crossing the lines of class division, provided a means by which the aversion of the more prosperous peasants to co-operativization might be eroded away to some extent by the adherence to the A.P.C.s of poorer or more politically enthusiastic members of their family. This must have been specially so with the relatives of village, Party, and A.P.C. cadres, who would tend to be supported as a matter of principle (and ancient habit) because they had won authority.

This suggests that potential support for the A.P.C.s was quite high. In a village in which 40% of the farmers were poor peasants, 10% new lower middle peasants, and 30% middle peasants: if the Party had the potential support for co-operative farming of eight in ten of the poor, one in two of the new middle peasants, and, say, one in five of the rest of the middle peasants, this would give a percentage of potential support of 43%. If the adherence of youth, women activists, and other politically convinced elements, along with the operation of family influence, gave as little as another 7% support, then we reach a percentage of fifty; and this seems fairly conservative.

The complexity and variety of the situation in the villages was such that statistical treatment of the relationship between class structure and co-operativization would require a very substantial sample of villages; and descriptions in the Chinese records so seldom give adequate information on this point that a quite enormous amount of material would have to be read before a sufficient sample would emerge. On the basis of the present collection, we can say no more than that the most striking examples of very rapid complete co-operativization come from places where either there was substantial equality among the village population or there was a very high proportion of poor peasants. The two villages where the movement went most slowly had 30% or more of upper middle peasants, the proportion of which in village populations was said to vary usually between 20 and 30%. The middle range of villages, however, reveals no clear correlation.

At one end of the scale was a village in Yent'ai *hsien*, Hopei[1] which as part of an Old Liberated Area had had by 1952 ten years of Communist government and Mutual Aid Teams, and had reached such a stage of prosperity as a consequence of the steady growth of production that by 1952 only one household out of 77 was still classified as poor, while 38 households were classified as new middle peasants. The first tentative attempt to set up an experimental A.P.C. produced virtually unanimous subscription, and in little over one month the whole village was in a single co-operative. Another village in the suburbs of Sian was completely organized in a single co-operative in

[1] See *High Tide*, p. 44.

the course of one year; here the explanation is obvious in that almost 70% of the population were poor peasants.

At the other end of the scale was a village in Ch'engteh *hsien*[1] Hopei, which by mid-1955 had only one co-operative of 30 out of a population of 190 households. Here, the poor peasants were about one-third of the population, and the upper middle peasants were almost as numerous. The County Party so despaired of doing anything with this village that the poor peasants were positively discouraged in their attempts to set up co-operatives.

It is clear enough that the class structure played a part in determining the speed and success of co-operativization; but its part is often obscured by other factors. For example, Yeht'ai *hsien*[2] as a whole had succeeded by the end of 1955 in bringing two-thirds (66·8%) of the rural population into the co-operatives, although between 40 and 50% were classified as upper middle peasants. This *hsien* thus reached the national average in spite of an apparently adverse class structure; but it may be significant that it took four years to do it—twice as long as the average for the A.P.C.s in this collection.

There is another way of examining this question: how many of each class in the village adhered to the A.P.C.s at successive stages in their growth? Little information is available on this point, in a collection largely devoted to showing how the middle peasants could be brought in. The available information, moreover, cannot give a neat answer, for two reasons, one geographical and the other economic. The geographical reason is that the land of an A.P.C. had to be as compact as possible, so that expansion by the creation of new A.P.C.s or even by the growth of the original A.P.C. involved a spread to untouched parts of the village, and in consequence the later stages might involve (with the very probable exception of the most prosperous families) much the same proportions of different classes as the first stage. The economic factor is that cadres were reluctant to create A.P.C.s based upon poor peasants whose pooled resources would be insufficient to sustain a co-operative; generally speaking, development had to wait for the adherence of at least a few families with more land and more capital.

This second point is well illustrated by an A.P.C. whose policy in this respect went too far. This was in Anyang *hsien* in the extreme north of Honan.[3] An A.P.C. was formed in late 1954 out of a large Mutual

[1] See *High Tide*, note 10, p. 1211.   [2] See *High Tide*, p. 66.   [3] See *High Tide*, p. 788.

Aid Team of 30 households, and some other families. A total of 50 households were prepared to join; of these 19 were poor, 11 were new middle peasants, 19 were old middle peasants, and one a re-classified rich peasant. This would have made up an A.P.C. of 30 poorer and 20 more prosperous families. The village Party branch, however, preferred to pick their own more economically healthy team, and chose 8 poor peasants, 10 new middle peasants, and 17 old middle peasants, some of whom had no wish to join, thus giving the poorer members a bare majority. To do this, they had to rush subscription to the A.P.C. through in public meetings on three successive evenings. The more prosperous peasants joined under this public pressure and without a clear knowledge of what was involved. One wife of a middle peasant said, 'Some A.P.C.! You turn away the poor and drag the rich in stiff!' and the motive of the cadres appears very plainly in the remark of another peasant: 'Land reform didn't go far enough, but the A.P.C. will soon fix that!' The result was that the richer members refused to work on the co-operative and six of them decided to leave.

Most co-operatives were started with perhaps 15 poor households and perhaps 5 others, one of which might be a prosperous middle peasant. Progress from this point depended very much upon the circumstances of the village and the success of the original society. In the 'backward' village of Ch'aoliangts'e, the existing A.P.C. consisted of 30 families, of whom 17 were activists and Party members and presumably the usual majority were poor. When subscription was opened for the expansion of this society, 94 further families were willing to join (the adjacent villages had co-operatives and the harvest had been a bumper one); of these 28 were poor, 50 lower middle, and 16 upper middle families. Of these, 61 were accepted; their status is not given, but it is clear that the bias was towards the lower middle peasant group, and those remaining outside the society at this stage were equally composed of poor and upper middle households, the one group economically and the other politically undesirable until the society was well consolidated.

Tables concerning I-t'ao village in Shuyang *hsien* in North Kiangsu[1] show the proportions joining the first four A.P.C.s and those joining at a later stage.

This was a village in an area which the breakdown of water-

[1] See *High Tide*, p. 56.

conservancy had depopulated, a frontier zone where labour was scarce and cultivation crude. The repair of the dams made rapid expansion of production and incomes possible, but only if organization could overcome the shortage of labour. This probably accounts for the high level of participation and the relatively slight difference between classes. The extreme cases in this respect (as we will subsequently see) were those in which the acute shortage of labour and the relatively low value of land made possible rapid advance to full collectivization.

	Old A.P.C.s	New membership	Outside
Poor	136	135	21
New lower	35	50	5
Old lower	17	12	6
New upper	40	21	11
Old upper	28	30	5

The other extreme is represented by an A.P.C. which at first won no support from any but poor peasants, and won the adherence of the more prosperous only at the final stage of the complete co-operativization of the whole village. This co-operative was begun in a village in Anyang *hsien*, Honan, in the spring of 1953.[1] It was formed out of the membership of two Mutual Aid Teams, but the five middle peasant members of the teams would not join the new society. After a successful year, it was joined by 17 more families, of whom 14 were lower middle peasants, and meanwhile as a result of its example two more co-operatives were formed, presumably with a similar class structure. It was only after another year of increasingly successful production that the rest of the village joined the societies, which were then merged into one. In terms of the whole of China, and not just of the highly selective source used here, this was nearer the average case. Several other A.P.C.s formed wholly by poor peasants are described. The difficulties in attracting the upper middle peasants into the co-operatives were usually considerable.

The case of the village in Yeht'ai *hsien*[2] which was brought wholly into a single co-operative in little over a month provides, one must suppose, an example of these difficulties at a minimum. In this Old Liberated Area there had been Communist government for a decade,

---

[1] See *High Tide*, p. 777. [2] See *High Tide*, p. 44.

and the village had been organized in Mutual Aid teams for six years. When it was decided to form a co-operative, the 19 Party members (of whom 18 were new middle peasants) were joined immediately by eight more new and five old middle peasants. The rest hesitated. They believed that grain would be divided out equally. They feared that fertilizers would be requisitioned. The women were worried about vegetable production.

In this place, fears over production and over future Party policy were probably minimal. Elsewhere, however, the main fear was the obvious one; that the societies would not produce as much as the most prosperous individual farmers involved; or would do so only with the use of a wasteful amount of labour which would depress the value of a labour-day and so in effect bring about a redistribution of wealth in favour of the poor by providing them with paid but relatively un-productive employment.

There were two further causes of apprehension. The first was that membership of the co-operatives would make it impossible to sell on the free market at free prices, as their rich peasant neighbours who were excluded from the co-operatives could (illegally) continue to do. The expansion of one A.P.C in the Sian suburbs[1] was prejudiced because the society sold its potato crop to the state trading organs at a price only half that obtained on the free market by the independent farmers. It was also hard to convince the farmers that state prices and quotas would not be arbitrarily changed.

The second was the belief that however liberal the society's arrange-ments might be at the start, there was no guarantee that they would not be changed; indeed it was the Party's avowed policy to secure a gradual redistribution of the profits in favour of labour as opposed to land, though in theory this would only take place as rising production and incomes permitted.

Increased Production

In China as in the case of the rest of under-developed, over-crowded Asia, the main obstacle to improved productivity was the deterioration of the soil through over-cropping, inadequate fertilization, and con-sequent erosion of the top-soil. The main necessity in this respect was the provision of adequate humus through heavy applications of organic manures; the second necessity was deeper tillage, to give the maximum

[1] See *High Tide*, p. 56.

root-run and cut the effects of drought on the impoverished top-soil; the third was improved rotation of crops.

The traditional problem in China, however, was water conservancy. In spite of the immense efforts made throughout her history, the problem of flood remained serious—more serious than ever, since the decay of the previous century had been compounded by the destruction of the second world war. As for irrigation, it was severely limited by the lack of capital in the hands of the peasants, so that very little of the North China Plain was irrigated at all although the possibilities of irrigation by the sinking of small wells were immense. In the Yangtse estuary only about 8% of the land surface was irrigated. The yields on irrigated land could be 40% higher than on the same ground watered merely by rain. Just as important, the uncertainties of the monsoon could be very much reduced by an extended irrigation system. The control of flood might require enormous public works and the control of whole river systems, but an immense amount could be done to improve and stabilize production by small-scale irrigation works requiring little capital, or by labour-intensive operations on a village scale.

Of almost equal importance in increasing productivity—a point as paradoxical as the implicit recommendation in the previous paragraph that the Yangtse Valley should grow more paddy rice—was more intensive cultivation. Substantial increases of crop weight could be got simply by the virtual elimination as opposed to merely the control, of weeds; and this involves usually no more than one or two extra summer hoeings.

The gestation period of these improvements is nil. The restoration of humus, deeper cultivation, the irrigation of a dry field, the elimination of weeds by hoeing, are all measures which will have a substantial immediate effect, although their maximum effect may come later. It is to be noted also that the capital cost is low; the new production is created mainly by extra labour, in collecting and spreading organic manures, digging ditches, and hoeing. The only important capital expenditure would be on the purchase of deeper ploughs and in some cases of stronger beasts to draw them; if the more prosperous villagers could be brought to contribute by investment in the co-operatives, this was well within the capacity of most village communities.

Labour, the first necessity in Chinese conditions for the improvement of agricultural production, China apparently had in plenty. One of the doubts which we have seen expressed over the A.P.C.s was that in so far as co-operative farming succeeded in rationalizing the use of labour, it would intensify the surplus of labour. Conversely, the use of the co-operative organization to provide further work for the under-employed would simply result in the withdrawal of the middle peasants if this new employment did not result in substantially increased production. There was a strong tendency in almost all the new co-operatives to waste labour either through inexperience of the organiza-tion of a body of labourers larger than the family, or through reluctance to record individual contributions of labour in ways which inevi-tably led to odious comparisons among neighbours. Some A.P.C.s were content to remain like this because of the egalitarian preconcep-tions of the poorer members.

Circumstances varied widely, however, and in many areas of recent reclamation or recolonization or of intensively worked cash crops, there was, as already seen, a labour scarcity; and Mao Tse-tung pro-phesied that with the continuous growth of opportunities for profitable production this labour scarcity would become general and acute, and permanent.

It is difficult to generalize about this problem. We find, in the *High Tide*, cotton-growing A.P.C.s in Chekiang where a campaign to get women out to work was an urgent necessity, and a village outside Sian where labour was sufficiently scarce to justify considerable investment in the supply of electric power to irrigation pumps. Round the cities as land was changed over to vegetable production as city markets grew, labour became acutely scarce. In most of Manchuria, human labour is quite inadequate to the scale of cultivation and heavy investment in horses or tractors is the key to the growth of production. Tractor stations grew up there and in the recolonized Huai River area. On the other hand, the besetting problem on the A.P.C.s of Kwangtung was how to provide employment; and a substantial part of the effort of the A.P.C.s was put into the planning of auxiliary, non-farming work.

In general, however, the immediate problem was to make use of an existing but absorbable surplus of labour in intensified cultivation and local construction work, on the lines described.

In addition to these general prescriptions for profitable intensive cultivation, many of the villages described offered considerable opportunities for economic expansion.

In North Kiangsu, these opportunities arose from the fact that the precariousness of agriculture in this area, which had kept its population low and its agriculture crude and extensive (dependent upon silt with no use of fertilizers) had been and was being reduced by the repair of the dams, and with the help of tractors and increased animals, it could be turned into an intensively cultivated area yielding two crops per year. In one case, the consequence was the raising of the working year in agriculture from 65 days to 156 days in three years,[1] with substantial increases in production through land reclamation, double-cropping, and fertilization.

In Hochien *hsien* in south Hopei, an area of light land with gravelly bottoms, but fairly heavily populated, one village[2] invited an extension team to plan its future production and explore its possibilities. Part of the gravel was planted with shelter belts of willows, productive in themselves and underplanted with suitable vegetables, and the rest planted with red thorn and mulberries. Canal banks and roadsides were planted with flax, and steeper river banks with fodder crops. By these means about 100 acres were brought into useful cultivation. Sandy areas which normally grew kaoliang and gave a poor crop were heavily fertilized and planted with wheat, dry rice and flax. Cotton acreage and vegetable acreage were extended, and ponds stocked with fish and planted with reeds. The extension team hoped by these means almost to double income. In contrast to the Huai area, this is an area where only marginally more intensive land use is possible; but even then, the possibilities seem considerable.

In general, few Chinese villages did not offer considerable chances for more intensive land use or for reclamation or for the use of hillsides for the planting of trees or increased grazing of livestock, in addition to the very great possibilities of increasing yields on existing land; and in conditions where the average farmer had worked only between 120 and 160 days, depending on the length of the growing season, sufficient labour existed to exploit a great many of the opportunities. Most of them depended, however, on large-scale co-operative organization to permit the flexible use of land and labour.

The *High Tide* gives, for the provinces under discussion, 15 examples of dramatic increases of production. Such a small sample will not of course bear statistical analysis; but the order of magnitude of these

---

[1] See *High Tide*, p. 611.   [2] See *High Tide*, p. 75.

increases can be summarized as follows. Production increased on these 15 farms by an average of 23% per year, for periods varying from one to four years. In 10 cases, the increase was between 20 and 40%. The lowest figure is 10% and the highest 110%. The figures are for staple crops; at this time substantially higher increases were commonly recorded for auxiliary products. They are for weight of crop and do not take into consideration changes from high value to low value crops (as from grain to tubers) or vice versa (as from kaoliang to peanuts). The basis of comparison varies; it is usually with the production of the same farmers in the preceding year, but may be expressed as a comparison with that of local mutual-aid farmers in the same year.

In most cases plausible reasons are given for the achievement of these increases, usually taking the form of the extension of irrigation, the increase of the intensity of cultivation by more regular cultivation or by deeper ploughing, the increase of inputs of organic manures, or the use of marginal land to diversify crops. No attempt is made to conceal the operation in some cases of exceptionally advantageous local factors. The methods, which in general are well approved for China and comparable countries, epitomize the Maoist idea of agricultural growth in the first stages before industry has developed to the point of providing substantial assistance to farming.

There is no reason to be sceptical about the possibilities suggested by these examples (which are repeated a thousandfold in almost daily articles in the Chinese press, with immense elaboration of detail as to methods), especially as the examples concern achievement under quasi-experimental conditions involving a concentration of technical expertise as well as political zeal. The farms concerned would certainly be used for purposes of demonstration and so would be open to the inspection of local farmers.

In these quasi-experimental conditions, the lessons of such achievements are important as illustrating the basic potentialities of the Chinese soil, rather than as economic lessons. Questions of costs, the alternative use of resources, and of incentives are not raised. The assumptions are important: they are that, given massive under-employment and a level of income both extremely low and extremely precarious, costs are not critical and incentives are overwhelming. Again, these are characteristic Maoist assumptions; and again one can say that while they were clearly applicable to wartime Shensi where they were first fully applied, and perhaps generally applicable in North China and in other relatively poor and under-developed areas, they are much less certainly useful in the rice-bowl areas of the centre and south.

Indeed such examples, with their emphasis upon heroic solutions by hard labour and self-reliance, point to an aspect of Maoist thought which has since increased with the years. The line of descent from the Wang Kuo-fan A.P.C. of 1954 to the Tachai Production Brigade of 1965 is plain.

Gradualism

One of the key concepts of policy in China was the idea that the co-operative farms could gradually be brought nearer to collectivization by a change in the system for the distribution of income made politically possible by the increasing incomes of members. The question is whether the increases in production recorded were sufficient to yield the incomes necessary for a smooth transition of this sort. There are only a few cases in which both production and income figures are given, and not always in ways which make comparison possible; they certainly do not make generalization possible. In one case, with an annual increase of production of 38%, incomes rose by an average of 188% (accounted for, if at all, by a vastly increased income from auxiliary production); in the second, production rose by 227% in two years, but income rose only 150%—a reasonable result assuming (as was the case here) that heavy investment was necessary to ensure the increase of production; in the third case, production rose by 40% and income by 100%, this being a co-operative which had gone over to highly profitable vegetable production.

Income figures are quoted as a table for one A.P.C. in Kirin:[1]

In 1955 as compared with 1954
12 families had reduced incomes
8 families increased incomes by 1–10%
10 families increased incomes by 11–20%
11 families increased incomes by 21–50%
13 families increased incomes by 51–100%
15 families increased incomes by over 100%

In the six cases in which incomes are given in a usable form (with or without information concerning increases of production), the average

[1] See *High Tide*, p. 426.

per annum increase for the years quoted is 90%. This, for what it is worth, is a great deal higher than the figure for per annum increase of production.

Of the twelve families who suffered in income, four suffered because members of the family had gone to work elsewhere. Assuming that these were poor families, this leaves eight families who were clearly prosperous peasants—they suffered in income because they had formerly practised usury or employed labourers. If one assumes that the next two groups, eight and ten families, along with the first eight, are the upper middle peasants of the village, it seems that most of the prosperous peasants gained from joining the A.P.C. but it is questionable if in this case they gained enough to permit any change in the distribution of income to land and labour.

A model of the possible growth of income of an A.P.C.[1] will show what would be needed to make this transition smooth: Take the imaginary case of an A.P.C. with 100 members of which half are poor peasants and half are middle peasants. Assume that total land is 1500 mou, that poor peasant holdings are 10 mou, and middle peasant holdings 20 mou. Assume that net income for the whole group of members as individual farmers in the last year before co-operativization is 250,000 catties of grain; and that both groups work equal labour-days.

The A.P.C. is set up with a 50/50 distribution system, and in its first year it achieves a 20% increase in net income, which then rises to 300,000 catties. The income of the two groups in the first year of the A.P.C. will then be:

		Income in respect of land	Income in respect of labour	Total income
300,000 catties	Middle peasants	100,000	75,000	175,000
	Poor peasants	50,000	75,000	125,000

[1] This model is deliberately schematic. To make it realistic, it would have to include:
    (a) the effects of progressive land-tax on incomes;
    (b) distribution of income from co-operative auxiliary occupations (which might increase at this time much more rapidly than income from agriculture);
    (c) the individual incomes of members from the private sector (which in some cases might be stimulated by the advantages of co-operative grain production);
    (d) the possible loss of ability to sell at higher prices on the free market;
    (e) the income received by the more prosperous as instalment payments for beasts and tools purchased by the A.P.C.;

In the second year, on the basis of last year's success, a further 20% increase is planned, and it is decided to change to a 40/60 land/labour distribution; and the 20% increase is achieved.

		Income in respect of land	Income in respect of labour	Total income
360,000 catties	{ Middle peasants	96,000	108,000	204,000
	Poor peasants	48,000	108,000	156,000

In the third year, a further 20% is planned and achieved, and it is decided to change to 30/70 land/labour distribution.

		Income in respect of land	Income in respect of labour	Total income
432,200 catties	{ Middle peasants	86,400	151,200	237,600
	Poor peasants	43,200	151,200	194,400

In the fourth year, if there is a further 10% rise (to 475,200 catties) and the A.P.C. becomes a collective, the whole net income being distributed to labour, the middle peasants would get *237,600* or the same income as in the previous year, and the transition to the collectives would be made without loss to the middle peasant group as a whole.

Thus only on farms which achieved the levels of increased income claimed could the transition to the collective form have been made between 1953 and 1956 without absolute loss to the middle peasants as a whole (though they would have suffered a relative decline in income). The increase of agricultural production on the national scale, however, was much less, being not more than 4% per annum. The increase within the co-operatives may have been faster, but clearly not a great deal faster or the 1955 harvest figures (which were in fact unprecedented but which can have owed little to the co-operatives), would have been still higher. Experience may have proved that some co-operatives *could* reach the rate of production increase necessary for

(*f*) interest on loans to the A.P.C.;
(*g*) the variation of individual income among the middle peasants.

gradual transition; but this was for the future: in the event it was too far in the future for the Party to wait for it.

One would expect that in this selected group of A.P.C.s, so many of which covered virtual whole villages, and so many of which had increased production and incomes to a dramatic extent, there would be ample evidence of this process of gradual transition. In fact there is none. We have an account of only one A.P.C. where any advance is specifically mentioned as having been made in this respect. This was an A.P.C. in P'iaoyang *hsien*,[1] west of the T'ai Hu in Kiangsu, which had begun with a division of the profits very favourable to labour, but under the protests of the middle peasants (of whom of there were seven including one upper middle peasant, as against 17 poor peasants), this was changed to 50/50; it was then the turn of the poor peasants to protest. The Party branch secretary did a calculation to find out at what ratio of distribution no member of the A.P.C. would suffer in income; the result was a ratio which gave only 38% to land, and this was agreed. While this represents an advance and concerns the distribution of a product much increased over the preceding three years, it is not what the Party said they meant. The point here was that income had been increased in the last year only by a tough fight against drought which had cost a very large number of labour days and depressed the remuneration for a labour day below the local wage-level; by members 'not suffering in income' was meant that the poor peasants received what they regarded as a normal wage for their work; presumably it also meant that out of the increased income, even at a 38% distribution, the middle peasants also did not suffer.

The only other case concerning the remuneration to land was a defeat for the Party's policy. An A.P.C. in Anyang *hsien*, Honan,[2] began with a 40/60 land/labour distribution, but when the middle peasants realized exactly what was meant, they were discontented, and the A.P.C. was on the point of breaking up. The Party branch finally accepted a 60/40 distribution in favour of land, with the landowner paying the land tax (15% plus local levies), bringing his share out of 100 to about 50; and this, calculated presumably on that year's production, became a fixed rent except in case of natural disaster when the A.P.C. would revert to the original 40/60 distribution. The Party branch, moreover, had to promise to maintain this unchanged for five years.

[1] See *High Tide*, p. 635.   [2] See *High Tide*, p. 788.

There is thus no evidence here that this particular facet of gradualist policy had been seriously applied; presumably the assumption still was that the lower-level A.P.C.s had three or four years to run before collectivization, as Mao's preface predicted.

The main and the simplest desideratum of the gradualist policy was that the A.P.C.s would develop from small to large, from few to many, from simple to complex, at a speed which would enable them to be consolidated on the basis of the increasing experience of the cadres and of the members of the societies.

In a group of about 40 usable examples in this material, we find that the average time taken for the successful consolidation of a key-point A.P.C., or for the successful extension of the movement to a majority of the village (two developments which usually went parallel), was just over two years. In the typical case, the experimental small A.P.C. might be set up after the autumn harvest in 1953 or before spring cultivation in 1954. If its operation in the first year was such as to encourage other peasants to accept membership of it, it would expand (often considerably) after the autumn harvest of 1954, while at the same time other A.P.C.s would be set up around it on the basis of its experience. If these were successful the following year, then the whole or a large part of the village might be induced to join in after the autumn harvest of 1955. There are, of course, many variations of this pattern; but on the whole, development in this selected group of co-operatives conformed.

There is one general qualification to be made. As one would expect, the north has a greater number of cases of abrupt co-operativization following upon long preparation, and a higher proportion of village populations were in the co-operatives by late 1955. In the south the level of participation is less (though not much less in this selected group), and the results up to this date more erratic. In the country as a whole, as in the village, the principle of operation was that with the benefit of the experience of those A.P.C.s (or those areas) with the longest history, the rest of the village (or of the country) could catch up and the whole be brought to a uniformly high level of co-operativization at the same time. This was clearly a dangerous analogy. The 'key-point' A.P.C. in the village could directly teach the rest of a village whose conditions and circumstances it shared; but Hopei's successes meant very little in the different conditions of Kwangtung.

There is no evidence whatever of any co-operatives having received or having given advice from or to any other outside the boundaries of its own *hsien*. The south could not be effectively proselytized from the north, but would have to find its own solutions locally, village by village, as the north had done; so the analogy scarcely held.

The differences between north and south, which are bound to have been very great, are to a large extent obscured in the *High Tide* collection. One of the opinions which it was compiled to combat was that the organization of farming would be much more difficult in the south. The chosen examples of southern co-operatives, therefore, conform as closely as possible to the earlier northern pattern. It is noticeable that in the material selected to represent the provinces of Kiangsu, Chekiang, and Kwangtung, there appears only one village of the characteristic southern type—based upon intensive rice cultivation as the most important source of income. That one example comes from K'unshan[1] and it shows quite clearly the difficulty of dealing with the much more productive, sophisticated and highly commercialized agriculture typical of the most populous areas of the south. All the other examples from these provinces are of mountain co-operatives, farms precariously working coastal sands and others more than half dependent upon non-agricultural sources of income, or of cash-crop areas such as the cotton areas of upland Chekiang. The typical rice-growing village is not dealt with thoroughly at all. Nevertheless, some of the difficulties characteristic of the central and southern regions come through.

The village in K'unshan (traditionally one of three most productive *hsien* in China) is introduced as an example of rapid co-operation in a late-liberated area. The editors preface the description with an attack upon those who think that the late-liberated areas cannot be co-operativized in three years along with the old liberated areas, and point out that this village was completely brought into co-operative agriculture in only two years.

The village, *Hsisohsiang*, was in an area where the proportion of tenants among farmers was perhaps the highest in China, although the tenancy figures are misleading in that the tenants included a significant proportion of prosperous commercial farmers enjoying a unique local form of tenancy giving very great security of tenure at exceptionally

[1] See *High Tide*, p. 598.

low rents; the real victims of the tenancy system here were sub-tenants, whose conditions approximated to those of tenants elsewhere. Even most of these, however, were commercial farmers to a degree certainly not typical of China as a whole. The system was much less 'feudal' and much more like capitalist farming, stimulated by the fertility of the soil and the existence of a ring of great cities within easy reach—Shanghai, Soochow, and Nanking. There was, in these circumstances, a high degree of polarization in the rural population: 77% of the population were poor peasants or new lower middle peasants (that is, former poor peasants); the proportion whose status had risen is not given, but whatever it was, it was offset by the decline of others: 34 households had sold land and 57 were in debt by 1953 out of a total population of 607 households, while the number of rich peasants had grown by 11 from their previous number, which was probably about 30. The Party deplored the 'get rich' outlook which prevailed, especially as all nine members of the weak Party branch either engaged in commerce or had bought land. It is significant also that the author can quote a case in which a rich peasant bought back 'for five bushels of rice' three mou of land which had been requisitioned from him during land reform— an indication that, in this commercialized area, the rich peasants enjoyed some sympathy; for it is highly probable that the man who sold the land back for a song would be the former tenant of the rich peasant concerned. In spite of the high proportion of poor peasants and former poor peasants in the population, the Party had an uphill fight. First the branch was lectured on the evils of participation in commercial dealings and of its nine members seven were induced to volunteer for two experimental A.P.C.s. Then nine more activists were absorbed into the Party, and a strenuous campaign for the development of co-operative farming created 10 A.P.C.s in one year. The history of the consolidation of the two formed first involved an unusually tough struggle with the more prosperous members. They joined, but they refused to hand over their boats to the A.P.C. at any price, and they would not pool their fertilizers but insisted upon their being used only on what was still nominally their own land. They refused to invest in the societies. They were bitter because their beasts and tools had been bought at 10% under the market price, while the poor peasant members were equally bitter about the system of grading of land adopted, which gave many of them an income for their land insufficient even to pay their grain tax.

The unusually numerous group of rich peasants provided a focus for discontent (this is one of the few cases where the rich peasants and former landlords appear as a factor of political significance). The Party kept the A.P.C.s in being by strenuous education and continual compromise between the prosperous and the poor, and were efficient and lucky enough to have good harvests for two successive years. At the end of the second year, virtually the whole village, except of course for the rich peasants and former landlords, were absorbed. A factor characteristic of the centre and south clearly in operation here was the fact that the middle peasants tended to own irrigated land, and the poor tended to own dry land on the slopes above the paddy fields, so that the reconciliation of their interests—which inevitably tended to be crystallized in the production brigades—was made much more difficult.

It must be obvious that this village could not have been exceptional. Although it is arguable that K'unshan *hsien* and perhaps its neighbours Ch'angshu and T'aits'ang would show these problems at their maximum, many of them were clearly problems which would be severe throughout all the highly developed southern rice areas. This was perhaps implicitly recognized, in so far as the choice of K'unshan as an example implies an *a fortiori* argument of which Party leaders could hardly have been unconscious. It is of equal importance that in the account of the consolidation of the A.P.C.s here, the author is at pains to stress that success was won by moderation and compromise, by education (the influence of the rich peasants was overcome, it is indicated, not by attacking them but by educating the rest of the farmers), and by the successful organization of production. The price paid for beasts and tools was adjusted, and the lowest grade of land was done away with as a *quid pro quo*. A 'face-saving' formula on investment confined this to the supply of fertilizers; and these were to be supplied 'in proportion to the family's own land'; in other words the Party gave in on this point.

In other parts of the south, especially the far south, extremes of poverty uncommon in the centre and north provided new problems, and the most heroic solutions were sometimes necessary. In the remote coastal districts of Kwangtung, from which the *High Tide* examples are drawn, the situation was made worse by the fact that in the crucial year 1954 there seem to have been local vagaries in the weather. Unusual frost which destroyed winter crops and killed large numbers of cattle (which did not normally require shelter), was succeeded by spring drought, then heavy rain and floods, then drought again, and finally a destructive typhoon on the very eve of the autumn harvest. Even without these adverse, one might almost say perverse, weather conditions, poverty arising from very great underemployment and precarious agriculture provided a new range of problems. It is characteristic that after some hesitation, the Party threw away its ideological prejudices, and where necessary put a quite heretical stress upon *fu-yeh* (side lines), assured village Party branches that commercialism in these circumstances was justified—and even accused them of being pettyminded when the survival of their fellow-villagers was at stake—and encouraged the Party to become entrepreneurs, which they did with their usual verve in the examples given.

The almost stupefying concatenation of disasters was treated in these descriptions as a challenge, to be turned to the good of the cooperatives. The A.P.C. appears as the busy organizing centre of the affected village; the boundary between the society-member and the *tan-kan* (individual) farmer disappeared for the duration; and so disappeared for good.

Thus although as far as the scale and scope of the co-operative movement were concerned, even if gradualism was adhered to in the expansion of individual A.P.C.s and in the spread of co-operative farming in the individual village, the same notion of gradualism applied to the co-operative movement on the national scale involved a false analogy which led policy-makers, as represented by the compilers of the present collection, to obscure the greater difficulties which the movement faced in central and south China, and so in the most productive parts of the country.

Gradualism needs definition, however. There is a distinct difference between gradualism and experimentalism. The one dictates a steady though accelerating growth; the other is compatible with a period of trial in particular places followed by a sudden general application. Perhaps this distinction was never quite explicit in Chinese thought. Mao's preface, and indeed the whole idea of the *High Tide*, is an experimentalist idea, and contradicts the notion of gradualism. It is enough that the manifold particular problems of co-operativization and co-operative working have all been solved *somewhere*. They are therefore capable of solution everywhere. This is acceptable on the level of the leadership and the cadres; but it is not a substitute for gradualism at the level of the farmers, who can only be convinced, in the last resort, by their own practical experience over a series of agricultural seasons; and who must *get used gradually* to a new form of discipline and a new concept of shared profit. This is the nub of the politics of the co-operative movement; it sets an irreducible minimum period for success, and in the event most Chinese farmers were not given this minimum.

Gradualism and the Problems of Increasing Scale

The co-operative of twenty families, working very much like a family unit, with the minimum division of labour and with the remuneration of labour remaining essentially egalitarian, was never regarded as anything more than the first step to effective co-operative farming. It was too small for the most important economies of scale to operate, and labour incentives were undeveloped. The ideal was the unified co-operative working of the whole land of the hamlet, the *hsiang*, and in some cases of several adjacent *hsiang*. Only this would make possible an adequate pool of labour and a concentration of capital sufficient for planned construction (particularly in water conservancy) for the whole village, the specialization of labour, and (even more important) specialization of land use in place of subsistence farming in which the same crop-mix might be grown on quite different soils. It would make possible planned production on that basis, and finally it would permit a degree of impersonality in the remuneration of labour which would facilitate the sharpening of labour incentives.

We have seen how the gradualist approach worked in the absorption of the whole of a village or a large part of it into a single co-operative or a federation of co-operatives. Side by side with the increase in scale went a series of changes in organization which greater size made both possible and necessary.

Twenty families was about the maximum for working with a simple quasi-family organization (the figure was much lower than this in the north-eastern areas of extensive cultivation). When the A.P.C. increased beyond that size, it was subdivided into brigades; very often these were simply the A.P.C.s or mutual-aid teams which had merged with the original A.P.C. in the course of expansion. It was necessary at the same time to define the relation of the brigades to the society, and this was usually done by the introduction of a simple system of short-term contracts, referring to one season or one agricultural task. The brigades having contracts to fulfil, then had an incentive for ensuring that their members worked adequately and well. They were induced to adopt a system of remuneration of labour which reflected the actual labour of an individual more closely. This might be the change from a fixed wage for members, paid per labour day, in accordance with the general opinion of his strength and skill, to the 'ssu-fen huo-p'ing'[1] system where his rated ability became merely a norm, with increases or decreases made according to his actual performance. It might involve a further change, in the direction of a piecework system. In this connection, it is important to realize that in the early years of co-operative farming, the object of increasing the incentives to labour was not to squeeze work out of a population already fully engaged in co-operative labour, but to provide incentives which would increase the small number of days traditionally worked by Chinese farmers, and to provide a disincentive to the distractions of private plots, peddling, and handicrafts; in fact the aim was the simple one of ensuring that a sufficient number of workers turned out on a calculable number of days. This is the basic disciplinary problem involved in turning under-employed individual peasant-farmers into labourers whose habits are regular enough to permit even the simplest planning. As impersonality increased with increasing scale, it was both possible and necessary to systematize rewards for regular attendance and conscientious performance of tasks. The *High Tide* material shows this clearly. The complaints are all concerned with irregular attendance and to a lesser extent with skimped workmanship; not at all with dissatisfaction with the speed at which work is done.

One change was a particularly vital one, involving considerable political difficulty. The brigades, being mainly former independent co-operatives or mutual-aid teams, would have unequal land and unequal means of production. Sometimes these inequalities were very large, and consequently unless the richer brigades in effect subsidized the poorer heavily, through the terms of the contract system, there would be disruptive inequalities of income.[2] The land and the means of

---

[1] 'ssu-fen huo-p'ing', fixed individual norm, with actual payment allowing increase or decrease according to work done.

[2] When in 1958 the A.P.C.s were combined in communes which were the units of a free-supply system, these disruptive inequalities were even more serious, and were a major factor (perhaps the decisive one) in the failure of the communes as originally conceived.

production had therefore to be equalized as far as possible between brigades, and this was a change which although it is played down in the records was as revolutionary—more revolutionary in a sense—as the formation of the co-operative. It meant the first real divorce of many families from the land which had formed their own farms and which was still in their ownership: they would come to own land in Brigade A's area, while they worked on Brigade B's land. The richer brigades, that is, those whose members as a whole were least enthusiastic about co-operative farming, might have to relinquish equipment and beasts to another brigade which would get the use of these things and might neglect them; and a brigade might have to give up irrigated land and receive dry land in its place. It is no wonder that one dismayed middle peasant faced with this is said to have exclaimed, 'This is worse than land reform was for the landlords!', and that cadres and Party members in the brigades bargained as jealously as ordinary members in order to maximize their own brigade's advantage in the new deal. Like any other measure of redistribution on the co-operatives, however, the degree of difficulty involved depended very much upon whether or not incomes were rising; if they were, then the adjustment, which equalized the remuneration of labour as between brigades without affecting income from land, might take place fairly smoothly; but there is so little evidence on this point that it is impossible to say whether or not the adjustment usually waited for an opportune time. Indeed, the *High Tide* pays surprisingly little attention to this vital problem of transition, although several cases of fully developed 'four-fixed' contract systems strongly imply that the change had been made in at least a few cases.

Further increases in scale involved a still greater degree of organization. The society management would become a planning centre, and the brigades would become management units carrying out society plans independently and in accordance with their own particular conditions. Instead of contracting for the completion of seasonal tasks, they contracted for fixed volumes of production. The actual working unit, which allocated labour for day-to-day work was the subordinate group, the production team. The brigade laid down the norms for the completion of routine tasks; it had its allocation of labour days from the society management, and allotted shares of labour days to the teams. In most of the cases recorded here, a full system of individual piece-work had been implemented by the teams.

When the A.P.C. had reached this scale, at which it covered the whole or a large part of the village, the members of the management committee would each have their own special functions, and there would be sub-committees for finance, technology, etc., while ideally even at brigade level, there would be brigade cadres for production, finance, technology, and care of public property. The deputy chairman of the society usually took the responsibility for political work.

For both cadres and members, none of these adjustments was easy to make. Even the actual increase in scale by mergers had to be justified by experience, and in many areas the mergers were preceded by various forms of association; networks for the exchange of information, and then federated societies, were ideally the intermediate stages. The decentralization of production to the brigades was not possible until there were enough cadres with experience of the planning of production and of the recording of labour, and in the early stages even the society cadres themselves very often lacked this experience. The gradual evolution of a piecework system by trial and error was a long process involving perpetual argument and adjustment, and quite plainly many cadres refused to take the trouble. For the members, the whole process involved the increasing tightening of the screws of a kind of discipline wholly unfamiliar; piecework was never accepted without dismay and resentment, and in every case here it was preceded by the partial adjustments represented by the 'ssu-fen huo-p'ing' system and short-term contracts.

Thus gradualism was unavoidable in the solution of the problems of increasing scale.

Collectivist Consciousness

The phrase 'collectivist consciousness' has to liberals a sinister ring. Its meaning in this context, however, was simple enough. It indicated little more than the degree of consciousness of common interests necessary for co-operative effort. The practical problems which a sufficient degree of collectivist consciousness would overcome included irregular attendance at co-operative work, inattention to the quality of work done, the faking of labour records to secure higher wages, carelessness in the use and maintenance of common property, lack of co-operation between production brigades (shown for example in the hogging of equipment), stubbornness on the part of either poor or middle peasants over the compromises necessary to maintain the principle of mutual benefit, and reluctance to accept a system of remuneration more or less closely related to work done. Such a level of 'collectivist consciousness' is no more than one expects from most members of any group of reasonable and experienced workers in a common enterprise, capitalist or socialist. The innumerable examples of the lack of collectivist consciousness show how low the standards of communal responsibility could be and how far the newly formed A.P.C.s were from the standards normal in any advanced society. As in so many other aspects of Chinese life, the slogans which sound so overdone—'love the society like the family'—prove on examination to aim at no more than the achievement of minimum standards of honesty, competence, and responsibility.

Collectivist consciousness applied, however, not only to relations between members of the co-operative, but to the relations between the co-operative and the state, especially as regards the fulfilment of deliveries to the state trading organs, and to a lesser extent at this time, to the planting of such crops as would assist the state in achieving its economic plans. It is this aspect of collectivist consciousness which has strong political implications. But is the situation any different from the previous one? Throughout the twentieth century, the Chinese farmer had been subjected to advance payment of taxes, military requisitions, forced sales and state quotas, and crippling rents. The Communist procurement system differed from its predecessors only in that it was not so arbitrary and that the burden imposed upon agriculture was almost certainly lighter, in conditions of rapidly increasing production; and yet in order to get the laws which laid down this improved system obeyed, the Communist Party had to resort to a vast annual campaign of national propaganda and individual persuasion, which was never at this time fully effective. There had never been a government in China which deferred so far to the interests of the peasants, but many peasants still evaded their responsibilities. It would perhaps be difficult to argue that they showed a lower standard in this respect than is prevalent elsewhere; but in terms of their own past experience, they were not being asked to do anything very unreasonable. It is quite possible to accept the Party's explanation that many peasants were reluctant to meet their legal responsibilities in this matter simply because they had not yet reached the stage of sophistication at which they would appreciate the interdependence of industrial and agricultural development. Again, it can be argued that the Party, in this aspect of collectivist consciousness also, was not asking for the moon, but simply for a rational degree of co-operation.

The point of this argument is not to justify the actual system of labour discipline or the level of procurement. We are only concerned here with how far the Party was able to achieve this particular condition of successful co-operativization, and we must not prejudge the evidence by arbitrary assumptions that the Party could never have succeeded because it was asking for more than human nature could be expected to give. It was asking for no more than what a large part of the human race gives habitually and with very little complaint.

By the end of 1955, it could claim that on the whole, in the co-operatives analysed in this collection, the major difficulties had been overcome. If the level of responsible behaviour sought had not become habitual, systems had been worked out which minimized the possibilities of backsliding. Labour incentives were provided by a piece-work system. Planning in consultation with the whole membership of the society, with individual members pledging themselves to play a specified part in the fulfilment of the plan, put the individual on his honour. Emulation campaigns opened the work of teams, brigades, and societies to mutual and critical inspection. Brigades were charged with the care of tools and beasts, and allowed a certain sum for the purpose; if they were careless, they paid. In the brigades, one individual cadre was made personally responsible for the care of common property. The effects on the behaviour of society members are not readily measurable, but the impression remains that the worst faults had been eliminated by the end of 1955 in the co-operatives described.

The Development of Common Property

No figures are given which permit an estimate of the average value of common property in the A.P.C.s, and very few are given for individual co-operatives. Figures were hardly necessary, as the whole process implied its accumulation. The small sum of 1 to 5 %, depending upon the prosperity of the A.P.C., put aside each year as a common fund was the least of the accumulation of assets. Investment at interest by the more prosperous members of the co-operative was probably more significant than this fund, at least in the society's first two or three years and perhaps beyond; but the purchase of the equipment and plough-beasts of individual members was the greatest initial step in acquiring property in which all members had a stake.

This, however, was only the beginning of the process, and the acquisition of further equipment and animals bought with investment funds or with loans from the state or the credit co-operatives might add considerably in most cases to the stock of common property.

The main increases of common property, however, were those which resulted directly from the investment of labour. Central to this was the reclamation of land, and the creation of new areas of irrigated land by the development of local water conservancy; and besides the widespread possibilities of such expansion, most co-operatives could expand in other ways depending upon local circumstances, by the development of forestry, grazing on hillsides, stocking of fishponds or their creation by damming, the breeding of animals, the planting of orchards and copses of bamboos or willows, the restoration of derelict mulberry plantations, and so on. The *High Tide* collection, in its effort to cover the widest possible range of circumstances, probably exaggerates these possibilities because it gives less weight than is reasonable to the restricted but all-important areas such as the level ground of the loess plains and the crowded estuary lands of the Yangtse and the Pearl River where there was much less room for expansion of this kind. Unfortunately, it was precisely in these areas that the more prosperous peasants saw least advantage in co-operative farming and so had the greater need of being committed to it by solid advantages. It would be a mistake, however, to assume that even here the opportunities were too slight to be useful in this respect. It would be a reasonable conclusion that most co-operatives after two or three years of successful operation might acquire assets which members would value highly.

The Principle of Mutual Benefit

Unless the A.P.C. could increase production, it would be merely an instrument for the redistribution of existing incomes to the disadvantage of the more prosperous members. The mere association of the greater landholdings of the middle peasants with the under-employed poor peasants in itself would only have improved production if the middle peasants had been over-employed; and our existing knowledge of Chinese agricultural conditions would suggest that most of them were not.

It was necessary to ensure that the more prosperous peasants:

(1) Joined the A.P.C. in the first place. Fundamentally this meant convincing them that production would rise.

(2) Were guaranteed against loss if production did not at first rise as expected, by giving them substantial dividends on their land invested. As we have seen, according to the implicitly prescriptive material in the *High Tide*, the Party was prepared in 1955, as in the initial stages of the movement in 1952 and 1953, to compromise to a quite remarkable extent on this.

(3) That the prosperous peasants (i) invested a substantial part of their land, so that they would not have so much 'retained land' that they were tempted to hold back fertilizers, labour, and investment; at this time it appears that, in the formation of a co-operative, the peasant was formally free to invest as much or as little of his land as he chose, but in fact would be under considerable pressure to retain for his own management only a small part, (ii) invested their best land as well as their poorest. This was met by adequate differences in share-value for different grades of land. In particular, irrigated land and land capable of bearing a rational rotation of crops, had to be paid for at a high rate. There are cases of compromises being made in this respect, and of complaints of the owners of poorer land that they were being unjustly treated.

(4) Sold or hired their equipment and beasts to the society. This was of vital importance, as the better utilization of these forms of capital was the chief hope of rapid improvement in productivity.

(5) Were prepared to invest part of their savings in the society. This was the most difficult problem of all.

How far was this principle of mutual benefit still maintained in the *High Tide's* prescriptions? We cannot know in detail, but we can say that:

(*a*) There seems to have been little pressure to secure the predicted changes in the distribution ratio in favour of labour, even in conditions of rapidly rising productivity and incomes. As long as a part of the *increase* of production sufficient to sustain a high level of incentives went to labour, the Party seems to have been willing to leave the proportion of *traditional* production paid to land unchanged.

(*b*) Nothing significant appears in the collection concerning 'retained land'. There seems to have been at this time no overt pressure to reduce it; but it is possible that plans for the expansion of production and the fuller use of local resources drafted by the Party involved inducements to submit retained land to planning, if not actually to invest it in the societies; and it is clear that in co-operatives struggling with natural disasters the distinction between society land and private plots disappeared.

(c) With respect to the quality of land invested, we find cases of adjustment in both directions—the differential for high-quality land increased, or that for the lowest quality decreased. In recorded cases the differential is quite substantial.

(d) In the acquisition of equipment and animals, it is clear that nothing less than payment of the market price by instalments over a reasonable period, with at least a rate of interest on instalments equal to that payable on loans from the credit co-operatives (17%) would induce the peasants to sell. There is even one case recorded here where the society management had to pay more than the market price because the middle peasants argued that prices were rising.

(e) The problem of members' investments was acutely difficult. The savings of a middle peasant were his only hedge against the un-certainties of the successful development of the co-operative. To invest them in the co-operative was to put all his eggs in one basket with a vengeance. It is clear that the problem of investment provided a task of the utmost difficulty, and it is here that one's suspicions that undue pressure was exerted are greatest. We find the financial member of a management committee refusing to canvass members for invest-ment, saying that this invidious job should be done 'by all concerned', that is, in the full meeting of the membership and not by an individual. Other evidence shows that 'small-group discussions and individual conversations' were sometimes necessary. In one case, the Party members and activists held a meeting and decided how much they personally could invest. They decided that each of them, mainly lower middle peasants, could provide 100 yuan. On this basis, they decided that it would be reasonable to ask for 30 yuan per family from the other members of the society, to bear no interest; any additional investment was to bear interest. It was stressed that the interest paid should be at the rate normally paid on deposits with the credit co-operatives. In the event in this case the members were persuaded that they could do no less than the Party members had done, and a sum representing an average of 119 yuan per family was raised. This was in support of specific production plans. The poorest members who had nothing to invest gave their spare time for the winter to collect fertilizers. The average sum per family probably represented between 12 and 15% of the average family earnings for the year. This may not have been an unduly heavy drain on past savings if production and incomes increased at a reasonable rate, and if it was spread among members. On the other hand, a case of a co-operative is described, with approval, where a similar sum was raised and where over 20% of the sum invested came from the only two middle peasant members of the society. Other examples, however, suggest that an effort was made to ensure that the investments of more prosperous members were matched by comparable efforts of the poorer members. Indeed the most often quoted objection by the prosperous was not the risks involved, but the fact that the poor might contribute little or nothing. The puzzle is why the Party laid such stress upon direct investment by members, when they could have got the same effect by encouraging deposits with the local credit co-operative, with the risks thus spread. Whatever the reasons, it is probable that it was the Party's insistence that the A.P.C.s must find their own capital (with the state stepping in only when a co-operative had proved its capacity for self-help and even then only in times of distress or to support a particularly hopeful piece of local enterprise) which put the biggest strain on the 'solidarity of the poor and middle peasants'.

The strongest argument for the belief that the Party wished to maintain to the end its determination to compromise as much as was necessary to secure middle-peasant participation in the co-operatives comes, however, less from the few individual cases we can quote than from the patent fact that the arrangements involved were still being arrived at by a bargaining process the results of which differed widely. A highly pragmatic attitude was taken, and within very wide limits, local societies were free to make the best bargain they could. It is equally plain that the penalty for ideological rigidity was still the withdrawal of those who felt injured and the collapse of the society.

Conclusion: The 'High Tide' Prescriptions and Subsequent Policy
On the Party's own showing, the development of the consciousness of the masses to the point where it could sustain the working of the large

A.P.C.s which were the aim of the movement was a slow business. Participation in an A.P.C. for at least three or four harvests was necessary for its development. In most of the cases quoted here, this scheme was adhered to. Those in which development outran the norm were exceptionally well prepared—in Old Liberated Areas mainly—or ran into trouble.

It is clear, however, that if Mao's prediction of the future pace of co-operativization was fulfilled (and it was over-fulfilled), the norm would disappear. It cannot in fact have applied to more than about 10% of China's farmers at the most. Does this mean that in the most important aspect of preparation, the psychological preparation of the farmers themselves, gradualism was given up by 1955. For most of the increase from 16 to 60% co-operativization between July and November 1955 must have consisted of farmers who certainly had not had the normal experience; and a substantial part of this increase took place presumably in the south, where experience was on the whole shorter.

The suddenness of their absorption, however, as we have seen, was softened to some extent by

(1) the fact that almost all had had some years of experience in rapidly developing mutual-aid teams, or at least in observing their operation;

(2) the fact that many were joining already developed co-operatives —this is the real crux of the problem; we do not know in fact how far the increase in families participating (from 14 to 63%) resulted from the foundation of new A.P.C.s and how far from the enlargement of existing co-operatives;

(3) the fact that almost all *in the north* at least had had plenty of opportunity to observe closely in their own village the way in which a co-operative worked, and what would be expected of them if they joined.

In these circumstances, Mao's affirmation in his Preface to the *High Tide* that there had been a sudden landslide of rural opinion in favour of the co-operatives is not entirely implausible, at least as regards the north of China; but the *High Tide* cannot be held to have given adequate evidence for this.

It is reasonable to assume that rapid and successful co-operativization depended to some extent upon the local strength of the Party. The sample which emerges from the collection is too small, however, to do more than demonstrate that, at the extremes, Party strength is correlated with success in the development of the A.P.C.S. Of 14 examples in which the strength of the Party is given, the average strength at the beginning of the A.P.C. movement was one Party member to 16 households. In the case of those examples where the Party was stronger than the average, 92·3% of the village populations referred to in the examples were in co-operatives. Where the Party was less than average strong, the average in co-operatives was 68%. This seems decisive, but in fact the result reflects the very great strength of the Party in Old Liberated Areas (in one case there was one Party member to every 3·5 households) on the one hand, and the weakness of the Party in the most recently liberated areas. Between these two extremes, there is little correlation. Given the scarcity of cadres almost everywhere, the success of the movement depended as much on how existing leadership resources were used as upon the size of the resources. It depended to a large extent in fact upon the opinions of the local Party members concerning co-operativization, and also on their administrative ability. The backwardness of Ch'aoliangts'e village in Ch'engte *hsien* already referred to was due not merely to the fewness of Party members (one to 24 families) but to the fact that only half of them were active, and that the Youth League was moribund. Its inactivity indeed probably accounts for its limited membership. On the other hand, the rapid success of the movement in Hsisohsiang in K'unshan, where 89% of the population were brought in although the Party strength was only one member to 37 households, was due to the reinforcement of the existing unsatisfactory branch membership by nine new members determined (and no doubt authorized) to overcome the faults of the rest. In fact a weak branch might result in the higher Party level stepping in and producing quick results, to the confusion of statistics based simply upon village branches. This, however, was apparently unusual, and on the whole the movement depended very much upon the village Party branch and especially on its committee; which meant in effect that there is a very strong personal element in the equation. A vigorous secretary could keep the movement going, while if a minority of branch members were opposed to co-operativization or indifferent to it the efforts of the majority could be largely nullified. Party unanimity mattered as much as total Party strength.

Rural Party members were still far too few for the responsibilities which they carried. The development of the A.P.C.s was only one of their tasks, and at least two other major pre-occupations competed for their time and attention—annual procurement and conscription—besides the actual administration of the village. The figures for the growth of the Party show that there was some improvement in the period 1952–5.[1] Total membership of the Party increased by more than one-third. We have seen that the average for the cases quoted was one Party member to 16 rural families, averaging the period as a whole. We have seen also that there were enormous differences from village to village (the ratios ranging from 3·5 to 37). In 1956 with a rural Party membership of about 7,000,000 and about 150,000,000 farming facilities, the national ratio was only one Party member to about 21 rural families, as against about 30 in 1952. In most of the places described, there was a Party sufficiently strong to ensure the presence of Party members in every society and in most production brigades, although the rapid increase of co-operativization in late 1955 must have imposed a strain in this respect. In these conditions, the Youth League, activists, and Party probationers were fully employed, bringing the total of those in the process of gaining political and administrative experience up to perhaps three or four times the number of the Party.

We have seen, however, that numbers were not the whole answer. The effectiveness of the local Party depended upon two other factors: political commitment and administrative ability. At the early stages of the movement, both were problematic.

There is sufficient evidence to suggest that in the early stages of the campaigns, local Party members were far from unanimous about the co-operatives. Even in the village co-operativized in one month, where the Party was very strong, one Party member out of the total membership of twenty refused to join, and came in only when the whole village, except for eleven families, had accepted. The backwardness of Ch'aoliangts'e village was due to the fact that less than half of the Party membership were politically active, and the efforts of the rest to develop co-operatives were not supported. There are several cases of individual Party members who said, 'I will wait a year or two until I am a little better off and then come in.' It is clear that a considerable amount of 'rectification' was necessary before all or nearly all

[1] See John Wilson Lewis, *Leadership in Communist China*, New York, 1963, pp. 108–120.

Party members would commit themselves to the movement in the only effective way—by joining the A.P.C.s. By 1955, as one would expect, after three years of constant propaganda and two or three years of involvement in co-operative work, this problem seems to have been solved, although after the completion of collectivization Party doubts were to appear again on a considerable scale.

We also find of course a great deal of confusion at first over the implications of mutual-benefit policy. There seems to have been equal deviation towards using the A.P.C.s to redistribute income to the poor, and permitting the middle peasants to dominate the societies, and towards excessive pressure and excessive caution. There is no evidence that right deviations were treated with any less mercy than left deviations. The practical nature of the implied prescriptions in the collection are some guarantee that our impressions are not too far out, but in any case the bargaining and constant adjustments which we have seen going on must have been an increasingly effective solvent of dogmatic attitudes, while the increasing complexity of A.P.C. institutions left much less room for the wilder deviations.

More important perhaps than ideological attitudes was the question of administrative ability. The creation of agricultural enterprises on a wholly new scale offered an enormous problem, and one must admire the heroism of their creators. It must be emphasized that they were not workers from the cities familiar with large-scale organization, or minor intelligentsia. They were the villagers themselves. The surnames of village cadres (which are invariably given when their individual part, good or bad, is described) in all the Chinese material are almost always those of the villagers. There is only one recorded case in the collection where a cadre is stated to have come from outside the village to reside there and establish the co-operatives, and he remained only for a matter of weeks. Some of the village Party committee may have had experience as NCOs in the PLA, but there is no evidence that such men were given any preference.

The lack of experience of the co-operative cadres showed itself in two chief ways. First, only a very small minority of them knew enough simple arithmetic to keep accounts. In Lalin *hsien*, Heilungchiang, in 1953, where there were 27 A.P.C.s, of 150 'otherwise capable comrades' at *hsien and ch'u* (not A.P.C.) level, only six could keep accounts.[1]

---

[1] See *High Tide*, p. 391.

A society chairman from Kwangtang, giving his experience in a growing and increasingly complex A.P.C., admitted that he could follow the accounts and calculate labour requirements himself, only 'with occasional help from the accountant';[1] and he was probably lucky to have an accountant who could help. In some co-operatives, the village children who were at middle school kept the records; in one, a sixteen-year-old boy was made accountant. The breakdown of co-operatives because of muddled or unkept accounts was widespread. The higher Party levels sent out work-teams to assist in this, and more experienced A.P.C.s helped the newer ones. Short courses were put on for A.P.C. accountants, and 'accountancy networks' were set up. The importance of accountancy can hardly be exaggerated. It was not just a question of recording labour days, income, and disbursements, but the cost accounting of future plans. It had considerable political importance, in several ways. The society management had to be seen to be impartial among individuals and classes. Many of the choices before societies could only be made intelligently if the financial consequences of the choice could be clearly stated: 'the Party chairman drew up two statements, showing what the effects would be in each case' is a constant description of how problems of loans versus direct investment by members, of alternative systems of distribution of profits, of hiring versus buying of equipment and animals, etc. were put before an A.P.C. Finally, the planning upon which in the last resort the solidarity and the enthusiasm of members depended was impossible without a fairly high level of accounting skill.

Second, many Party members had remarkably little notion of what was expected of them simply as Party members. They had to be reminded constantly that their first duty was to be sufficiently informed about what they were directly concerned in to be able to assist the Party branch or the society management in coming to decisions, and that when the decisions were made they had the responsibility of carrying them out. As leaders of the A.P.C.s, they had to teach their committee members to accept the same responsibilities. They had to learn to delegate authority and to ensure that they got information when it was needed. Once more, we are observing not the organization of a political force of great subtlety, but merely a sustained attempt to

[1] See *High Tide*, p. 951.

familiarize the lowest levels of the Party with the bare fundamentals of administration and committee management.

On the whole, however, it is difficult to believe that the continuous education in these respects over the preceding three years had not solved most of the problems involved, at least in the older co-operatives. In spite of the strictures still made at this time, the collection shows an impressive number of examples of competent management and good organization.

On both these points—the consciousness of the masses and the experience of cadres—very great progress had been made by 1955.

Given the dilemma of co-operative development, that neither argument nor coercion is likely to be effective, the object of the Party's political organs in the countryside was not to strengthen its power to dictate. Its object was to ensure not the maximum of control but the maximum of communication. The first A.P.C.s were founded with Party members and activists forming most of the membership. These first A.P.C.s were supported by all the resources of administrative experience and technical knowledge which could be mobilized, and were given tremendous local publicity. It would not be surprising if most of them succeeded in impressing their villages with the possibilities of co-operative agriculture. The mutual-aid teams were associated with them, and under their influence went beyond the simpler forms of exchange of labour to the planned use of their labour force and to a certain degree of unified planning of production. In most areas a mutual-aid and co-operative network was formed, with a committee composed of leaders and representatives of the teams and societies who kept in constant touch. The result was that many teams began to approach the co-operative level of organization, while the local Party was able to ensure that new co-operatives were begun only on the basis of the mutual-aid teams most likely to succeed. When the village contained several small and simple co-operatives, these were often associated for the furtherance of their common interests, sometimes by a formal federation. By this means the newer teams learned from the older and were gradually brought up to the level of the most advanced, until they had gained sufficient experience to be merged into one or more large co-operatives. The villages where development had been most successful sent teams representative of all the interests involved—poor and prosperous peasants, youth, and women—to advise on such practical problems as accounting, the keeping of labour records, the estimating and distributing of profits, the setting of piecework norms, and the planning of labour.

The key-point A.P.C.s held open days to permit local farmers to inspect their work, and to demonstrate the use of co-operative methods.

When it came to estimating production, it was recommended that members of the mutual-aid teams should be invited to participate as observers. In every way, the operations of the society were laid open to inspection.

In their relations with the individual farmers, many Party branches went beyond the negative instruction that they should not be discriminated against. Numerous cases are given in the *High Tide* (for their effect upon local opinion) of co-operatives which assisted sick or otherwise distressed individual farmers to get in their harvest, or lent equipment or animals, and the local A.P.C. was the source of modern equipment (insecticide sprays for example) for any farmer who wanted to use it. And as we have seen, in times of natural disaster the A.P.C. might come into its own as the only organization which could lead the defence or the restoration of the village.

These local descriptions and recommendations are not merely theory. They are practice, though they may represent practice at its best. In total, they add up to an impressive campaign of practical persuasion. They do not prove that coercion was negligible; but at least they suggest that before the Party's own frequent condemnations of coercion are taken to mean that it was general, it is worth asking how much coercion is likely to have been necessary when the means of persuasion were so well developed and when, as has been suggested, potential support for the co-operatives is likely to have been a majority of the population of the average village.

THE FINAL CAMPAIGN

In March 1955, 14% of farming households were in co-operatives. By the end of the year the proportion had risen to 63%. This was a startling increase, but the *High Tide* collection provides *prima facie* evidence that it was not wholly unlikely. At the beginning of the 1955 agricultural year there were 600,000 A.P.C.s, so that there was a society in almost every village. Of these, almost three quarters had had at least two years' experience of operation by the end of 1955.

If the means by which the more experienced societies spread their influence by their patronage of other A.P.C.s and mutual-aid teams was as successful as the *High Tide* collection suggests, many mutual-aid teams must already have been approaching the transition to co-operative farming by the end of 1955. Much if not all of the expansion might be accounted for by the promotion of the most successful teams.

The expansion described in the collection, however, was not the end. Without further comparable justification, the movement swept on against all current predictions into its final stage of collectivization. By the end of 1956 almost the whole rural population were in not merely co-operatives but collectives. The question which must now be asked is, how far this new policy can be supported by the information given in the *High Tide* collection, in terms of the Party's professed methods and conditions.

It can be said immediately that the descriptions given of the collective farms in existence in 1955 do not in themselves support the policy of rapid collectivization. They suggest that collectivization had up until that date proved possible only in exceptional conditions. Some of the collective farms described were vegetable-growing market gardens in the suburbs of Peking and Tientsin.[1] Others were specialized cotton-growing farms.[2] All the examples given have one thing in common, an acute scarcity of labour in relation to crops whose demand for labour was very high; a situation in which the payment of dividend to land was much more easily abolished than it was on the typical grain-growing farm worked by plentiful, indeed underemployed, labour.

In spite of this, it is still possible to ask if the material gives any support of a less direct kind for rapid collectivization. But first it is necessary to look at what actually occurred.

The figures for the development of collectivization strongly suggest that, first, the decision was taken to collectivize the A.P.C.s with the longest history, that is those represented by the 10% of the population already in the co-operatives by early 1955. Success in this led immediately to the spread of collectivization to the rest of the mutual-aid/co-operative networks which, we suggested, had formed the basis of the rest of the 63% brought into the co-operatives at the end of 1955. This (if we exclude landlords and rich peasants) left about 30% of the population still apparently unorganized, until a figure of 27.8% of the

---

[1] See *High Tide*, pp. 285 and 294.   [2] See *High Tide*, p. 651.

population in A.P.C.s appears side by side with 60% in collectives. Presumably this represents the hitherto unassimilated upper stratum of the middle peasants, organized in new co-operatives. By the end of the year these new A.P.C.s had all become collectives. If this is so, the final collectivization campaign, though drastic, had a certain logic.

The significance of the change from co-operative to collective depended very much upon the level of development of the co-operative concerned. To some extent, the experience of one successful A.P.C. could be transferred ready-made to its neighbours; every A.P.C. did not have to go through an equal gestation period in order to apply new agricultural methods or the principles of co-operative organization and planning. With the most highly organized societies, the change to collectivization meant only that payments to land ceased; but this could hardly have applied to more than the hard core of old societies representing 10% of the farming population. For the rest, the change must to a greater or less extent have involved the simultaneous enforcement of piecework, the equalization of the means of production among brigades, and the reduction and equalization of retained land—steps which as the Party itself had been at the utmost pains to insist, were not mere matters of administration, but social and political changes, important steps in the rural class-struggle, which should be undergone slowly and successively in relation to the development of collectivist consciousness. Even the experienced 10% had by no means all completed these transitional stages, for we have seen that the *High Tide*, whose compilers had clearly an incentive to show the maximum progress in these respects, fails to show this.

Yet it must be stressed that collectivization was completed with relatively little trouble. Communist China was the only post-1945 Communist regime to achieve full collectivization; and unlike the U.S.S.R., she achieved it without major social disruption, and bloodshed, and drastic economic losses. It may be suggested that there were two reasons for this: the possibilities of rapid growth through labour-intensive improvements in farming, perhaps unique to China; and the political prescriptions of Maoism developed in 20 years of experience of the Chinese village and epitomized in the *High Tide* collection.

THE SINO-INDIAN AND SINO-RUSSIAN BORDERS: SOME COMPARISONS AND CONTRASTS

BY ALASTAIR LAMB

Western observers have sometimes become so fascinated with the ideological aspects of modern Chinese foreign policy that they have tended to overlook a number of practical considerations which have but little to do with Marxist theory; and nowhere, perhaps, has this been more the case than in the interpretation of the significance of tensions along the Sino-Indian and Sino-Russian borders. A historical analysis will show clearly enough that there are many parallels between Chinese Communist and Chinese National attitudes towards the landward limits of the Chinese state, attitudes whose origins can in many instances be traced far back into dynastic times. The object of this essay is to explore some of these non-Marxist, traditional, facets of the Chinese frontier system which today divides the Chinese People's Republic from the Soviet Union, Pakistan and the Indian Republic, and which, not so long ago, separated the Manchu Empire from the Empires of Great Britain and Tsarist Russia.

GEOGRAPHY

Except for its extreme western end, the Sino-Indian border region is marked by a single dominant geographical feature, the southern edge of the Tibetan plateau. Here the Himalayan range, stretching for nearly 2000 miles from Ladakh to the remote northern corner of Burma, marks a zone of transition between the Tibetan plateau, dry, cold and much of it over 16,000 feet high, and the monsoon plains of the Indian subcontinent. The transition is accomplished by means of a mountain belt between 50 and 100 miles wide in most places; and it is the location of the political boundary within this belt that provides most of the raw material of the Sino-Indian boundary dispute. The Himalayan range possesses a feature which is lacking in many other frontier ranges elsewhere in the world, like the Andes or the Alps. It does not mark a divide between rivers flowing into widely separated outlets. The major rivers of the Tibetan plateau with their sources north of the Himalayan range, like the Indus, Sutlej and Tsangpo-Brahmaputra, cut southward through the range to join rivers rising on its southern side, like the Ganges, Jumna, Chenab and Jhelum. In other words, the Himalayan range does not provide a major waterparting (geographers apparently prefer this term to watershed) of the kind provided by the Andes with rivers on the west flowing into the Pacific and rivers on the east flowing into the Atlantic. While there is no universal law of nature which declares that international boundaries in mountainous country shall follow lines of waterparting, yet in many cases practical advantages do tend to lead to a degree of correspondence between boundaries and waterparting lines. The geographical nature of the Himalayan range to a significant extent denies to it these advantages. In the Sino-Indian boundary dispute there has been much talk of watersheds; but neither side has in fact been able to point to a major waterparting line so obvious as to help produce any general agreement on the basic principles of boundary definition.

For much of its length the Himalayan range possesses, from the point of view of boundary evolution, a threefold structure. On the one hand lies the Tibetan Plateau, on the other the Indian plains: in between is a mountain tract which has tended to acquire a political history of its own and to interpose a buffer of sovereignties between Plateau and Plain. Looking north from the plains, the foot of the hills has tended to be the natural border rather than some point along the Himalayan crests nearer the river sources.

A major system of waterpartings absent from most of the Himalayan range does begin to emerge at its western extremity; and along the Karakoram range from the Karakoram Pass to the edge of Wakhan in Afghanistan this waterparting becomes a clearly marked geographical feature separating the basins of the Indus to the south and of the Tarim in Chinese Turkestan to the north. This waterparting line had evolved into some kind of political divide long before the British set foot in India, and it continued administratively in this role in the British period even though there were times when the authorities in Whitehall and Simla saw fit to lay out on maps boundary lines lying well to the north of this waterparting. The Indus–Tarim waterparting, with one or two extremely minor deviations, today marks the Sino-Pakistani border in the north of Pakistani-held Kashmir.

Like the Sino-Pakistani border, the western end of the Sino-Russian border which divides the Soviet Republics of Tadzhikstan and Kirgizya from Chinese Sinkiang also follows more or less a water-parting line. The Indus–Tarim divide of the Sino-Pakistani border, indeed, leads directly to a divide between the Tarim and the two great rivers which flow into the Aral Sea, the Oxus (Amu Darya) and the Jaxartes (Syr Darya). This divide is marked by the eastern edge of the Pamirs and by the crests of the T'ien Shan range.

At a point east of Lake Issyk-Kul the Sino-Russian border, now separating Kazakhstan from northern Sinkiang (Dzungaria), leaves the T'ien Shan range. For more than 2000 miles, until it reaches the Argun river, and Manchuria, the Russian border follows a geographical pattern for which no parallel can be found in the Indian subcontinent.[1] This pattern is largely determined by the courses of rivers which rise in Sinkiang and Mongolia and flow into Russian territory, draining either into inland seas like Lake Balkhash or into the upper reaches of the great rivers of northern Asia like the Irtysh (a tributary of the Ob), the Yenisey and the Lena. The border cuts across the rivers, the valleys of which often provide easy channels of communication between Russian and Chinese centres. Between river crossings the border tends to follow the crests of mountain ranges like the Alatau, the Tarbagatay, the Tannu Ola and the Sayan: but these mountains have played a less important role in the determination of border alignment than has the selection of points where the border cuts across rivers.

The final, and easternmost, sector of the Sino-Russian border, from the eastern end of Mongolia to the Pacific, also has a shape not to be found along the Sino-Indian or Sino-Pakistani borders. It follows the *thalweg* of rivers, the Argun, the Amur and the Ussuri, except for the last few miles in the neighbourhood of Vladivostok.

This brief geographical description of the Sino-Russian and Sino-Indian borders reveals, to sum up, four main categories of frontier landscape. First, there is the glacis of the Himalayan range, a fairly

---

[1] For the greater part of the history of Sino-Russian contact Mongolia lay on the Chinese side of the frontier. Much of the line of the present Russo-Mongol border was set out in the Sino-Russian treaty of 1727. In this geographical survey I have treated the Russo-Mongol border as if it were a sector in the Sino-Russian border. The present Sino-Mongol border, except at its extreme eastern and western ends, is marked by its own characteristic feature, the unpopulated wasteland of the Gobi, which provides an effective if not too precise divide between Inner Mongolia in China and the modern independent Mongolian People's Republic.

narrow strip of hill country separating the hot monsoon plains of the Ganges and Brahmaputra systems from the cold dry highlands of Tibet. Second, there is the waterparting line in the Karakoram, Pamirs and T'ien Shan which marks the western and north-western edges of the Tarim basin in Sinkiang. Third, there is the long sector of Sino-Russian and Russo-Mongol border line marked by an alternation of mountain crests and the crossing at right angles of rivers flowing from Mongolian and Chinese sources into Russian territory. Finally, there is the Amur sector, which is by far the longest river border in Asia. These geographical features are obvious enough; and a glance at a good map should reveal them. However, in the discussion of Sino-Russian and Sino-Indian border arguments they are often ignored, by the participants as much as by outside observers. Yet the fact remains that the basic pattern of Sino–Russian and Sino–Indian frontier history has been shaped by these considerations of physical environment.

FRONTIER PEOPLES AND THEIR PRE-IMPERIAL HISTORY

The present Sino-Russian and Sino-Indian borders are in the main the product of the evolution of British and Russian policy during the nineteenth and early twentieth centuries. In many regions, however, the British and Russians encountered existing forces of frontier formation which they either adapted to their own advantage or were obliged to counter. Much of the Sino-Indian and Sino-Russian frontier zone, though lying in regions which in many places are to this day extremely remote, yet possesses populations, even if very small, with political histories of their own. One of the problems of boundary formation which both the British and the Russians had to face was the reconcilia-tion of the consequences of such political histories with their own imperial needs. The kind of political history of the various frontier zones, of course, was to a great extent shaped by geographical factors of the type that has been touched upon above.

The Himalayan range, as a transition between Tibetan Plateau and Indian Plain, tended to evolve politically as a kind of buffer between these two regions. This process was far from uniform throughout the length of the range. In the extreme east, where the Himalayas may perhaps be considered as a westward extension of the hill tracts of south-west China and mainland South-east Asia, the mountains were inhabited by tribal groups with cultural affinities with the hill tribes of the Burma–Assam border and with but the remotest of political ties with either the Tibetan plateau or the Indian plains. Here was a real no-man's-land within the Himalayan range which the British had only started to penetrate when they left the Indian subcontinent in 1947.

Towards the west the isolation of this part of the Himalayas breaks down. At the point where the North East Frontier Agency of India (N.E.F.A.) meets Bhutan there is a strip of territory where direct Tibetan political influence penetrated right down to the edge of the plains. Here the shape of the river valleys was such that quite far down in the foothills they continued to serve to cut off the full impact of the monsoon, thus creating a cool and dry environment of the kind favoured by Tibetans. Similar conditions apply in Bhutan and Sikkim; but here, instead of direct Tibetan influence, there developed states on the Tibetan cultural and political pattern but enjoying a considerable degree of autonomy. The main direction of political relationship here, however, was certainly northward rather than southward.

To the west of Sikkim is Nepal, another state lying along the Himalayan range. Tibetan influence, following climatic conditions comparable with those in Sikkim and Bhutan, flowed southward over the edge of the plateau and down the Himalayan slopes. In Nepal, however, unlike Sikkim, Bhutan and N.E.F.A., geographical factors, the pattern of rivers and the proximity to centres of Hindu–Buddhist civilization in the plains, have resulted in a meeting of northern and southern political influences far deeper in the hills than has been the case to the east. The Gurkhas who in the eighteenth century conquered the whole of what is today Nepal as well as a considerable extent of hill country to its west, claim a southern ancestry. But Nepal under the Gurkhas remained, as the region had been before them, essentially a Himalayan body politic rather than an extension of the polities of the plains. Thus here the traditional *Indian* frontier still tended to follow a foothill line.

West of Nepal up to the Sutlej valley the influence of the plains made its greatest penetration into the Himalayan range, in places approaching the very edges of the Tibetan plateau. Even here, however, the tradi-tional pattern had been the evolution of petty states confined to a Himalayan environment, even though with political ties of some kind to the powers in the plains; and in the northern fringe of this tract, as elsewhere to the east, Tibetan influence had established itself. In the

late eighteenth century the Gurkhas took over most of the hills between their present western frontier and the Sutlej; but for British intervention this area would today be part of the Himalayan state of Nepal.

West of the Sutlej the Himalayan range runs sharply northward into
a tangle of mountains where it meets the Karakoram and the K'unlun,
the last range marking the northern edge of the Tibetan plateau. Here
the physical environment of the Tibetan plateau extends into a kind of
'little Tibet', Ladakh, centred on the upper valley of the Indus.
Ladakh, until the Dogra conquest of the 1830s incorporated it into the
State of Jammu and Kashmir, was really a minor Tibetan state, with
ties with Lhasa which were real enough even though weakened by the
effects of distance. Culturally this is an extremely interesting region.
Ladakh has long been in very close contact not only with Tibet but also
on the one hand, with the Vale of Kashmir which was once a major
centre of Hindu civilization, and on the other hand with the Islamic
world of Turkestan and Afghanistan. In Baltistan the meeting of the
Tibetan and Islamic civilizations is clearly visible in the local population,
the Baltis, who speak a Tibetan dialect and obviously possess a strong
Tibetan ethnic strain, yet are Muslims. In this region the divisions of
the Himalayan slopes further to the east become much blurred; and it
should cause no surprise that here exist no less than two of the most
complex and intractable frontier problems in the world today.

In the Karakoram, as has already been noted, there begins a true
waterparting line which, starting as the Sino-Pakistani border, con-
tinues more or less as the border between China and Russia along the
Pamirs and the T'ien Shan. This waterparting line does not mark one
of the major cultural divides of Asia, for Islam has spread across it. In
minor ways, however, it has had its impact upon the pattern of cultural
and ethnic distribution. For example, the Karakoram separates the
Dardic speakers (and in the main non-Mongoloid) of the Gilgit region
from the mainly Turcic populations of the Tarim basin. Politically,
moreover, the waterparting line along the western and north western
edges of the Tarim basin has long tended to mark a separation between
the two halves of Turkestan, that is, what is now Russian Turkestan, with its centre between the upper reaches of the Oxus and the
Jaxartes in the neighbourhood of Tashkent, and what is now western
Sinkiang with its centre around the oasis towns of Kashgar, Yarkand
and Khotan. In the eighteenth and nineteenth centuries relations

between Kashgar and the Khanate of Kokand were very close; but they were not close enough to lead, in periods of the loosening of Chinese control in Eastern Turkestan, as for example between 1864 and 1877, to an eastward political expansion of Kokand. Thus it was, indeed, that the Russian occupation of Kokand did not lead inevitably to the Russian annexation of Kashgaria.

Along and across the waterpartings of the Karakoram, Pamirs and T'ien Shan there has been, of course, a history of nomadic occupation. Across the Karakoram, where the country is rugged in the extreme, seasonal migration has never been of much significance. In the Pamirs and the T'ien Shan the migrations of Kirgiz pastoralists was a factor noted by Russian and British observers in the nineteenth century; but it took place on a scale too small to provide an effective challenge to the natural advantages as a frontier of the waterparting line. The Chinese in Kashgaria in the nineteenth century certainly possessed some suzerain status over Kirgiz groups within the Pamirs and the T'ien Shan; but they showed no great determination in clinging to these rights in the face of Russian pressure.

From the T'ien Shan all the way to the Amur tributaries in the Far East the Russian frontier passes through a region far less effective as a political divide than the Karakoram–Pamirs–T'ien Shan waterparting line. The border crosses a number of river valleys which have throughout recorded history provided channels of communication eastward and westward across the nomad world of the steppes and deserts of northern Asia. Perhaps the most obvious of these gaps in anything like a natural frontier line is the land between Lakes Balhkash and Issyk-Kul and along the valley of the Ili, a river which rises on the northern slopes of the extreme eastern end of the T'ien Shan, deep in Sinkiang, and flows westward into Lake Balkhash. Fairly easy country links the Ili valley to that of the Chu, which rises in Issyk-Kul and runs westward until it disappears in the deserts to the east of the Aral Sea. The Ili–Chu route connects the Kazakh population of modern Sinkiang with the Soviet Republic of Kazakhstan; and along it in the eighteenth century marched and countermarched Kazakh and Dzungarian hordes in what was to be one of the last great nomad conflicts of Central Asian history. Parallels to the history of the Ili frontier can be found elsewhere to the east, on the upper reaches of tributaries of the Yenisey for example.

At first it looked as if the final stretch of the Sino-Russian border, from Mongolia to the shores of the Pacific, would also involve a frontier zone cutting across the upper tributaries of a major Asian river, in this case the Amur; and that here, as for example on the Ili, a river valley would provide a channel of communication across the frontier zone. In the event, however, the Amur border evolved into something quite different, a line following a clear natural feature, the *thalweg* of the Amur and its tributaries the Argun and the Ussuri. It was perhaps inevitable that here natural features should predominate. The Amur basin has never been a major region of nomad occupation. It is largely forest country which until very recently was inhabited by a few small tribal groups of mainly Tungusic affinities. Some of these groups may well have acquired rather remote political relationships with the Manchu clans further south; but the evidence would suggest that Manchu influence was in effect confined to scattered settlements along the Amur, Argun and Ussuri, and that to the north of the rivers lay what was virtually terra incognita. Manchu diplomats certainly found it very difficult to provide anything like a coherent geographical account of the trans-Amur districts when they were negotiating the Sino-Russian border agreements of 1689 and 1727.

CHINESE FRONTIER EVOLUTION

From the Chinese point of view the Sino-Indian and Sino-Russian borders form part of the same frontier system which, in its present form, owes much to Manchu policy in the eighteenth and nineteenth centuries. The traditional Chinese frontier problem has been, for at least two millennia, to isolate the Chinese heartland from the nomad world of inner Asia. A number of devices have at different times been adopted to achieve this objective, the most dramatic being the construction of vast systems of fixed fortifications. Chinese Walls, however, have not been noted for their impermeability. More successful, perhaps, has been the policy of establishing some measure of Chinese control, albeit exercised by indirect means, over the centres of nomadic power. In pursuit of such a policy the Manchus created what might perhaps be called 'protectorate' systems in Tibet, Eastern Turkestan, Inner and Outer Mongolia and Manchuria. Within these 'protectorates', at least until the very end of the nineteenth century, the Manchus did not attempt to extend the structure of the provincial government of metropolitan China. Instead, they made good use of a diversity of indigenous powers and institutions, ranging from the Lama incarnations of Tibet to the 'feudal' princes of Mongolia.

The Manchu 'protectorate' system, which covered the entire area of the Sino-Indian and Sino-Russian borders, was oriented internally rather than externally. The dangers which it was designed to meet lay within the 'protectorates', not outside them. Hence there was no great theoretical urgency in the precise definition of the external limits of the 'protectorates'. In one way, indeed, it might be said that Chinese influence had no precise limits. Like a pebble dropped into a lake, its ripples grew fainter and fainter the further removed they were from the centre; and eventually they just faded away. This analogy is well in keeping with traditional Chinese concepts of sovereignty which admitted of no power which was not in some manner subordinate to the Emperor of the Middle Kingdom.

By the middle of the eighteenth century in only one region had the ripples of the Chinese state broken against the rocks of another power of a kind which could not be absorbed into the framework of the Manchu tributary system. In the North East, in Manchuria and Mongolia, the Manchu 'protectorate' system, while actually in the process of formation and consolidation, encountered the vanguard of Russian expansion into Siberia. The outcome was the Nerchinsk treaty of 1689 and the two frontier agreements of 1727 which produced a Sino-Russian border line from the Sayan mountains west of Lake Baikal to the shore of the Pacific on the Sea of Okhotsk. Part of this line, that from the Sayan mountains to the upper Argun river, was defined with great precision; and this, virtually unmodified, marks today the boundary between the Soviet Union and the Mongolian People's Republic. The eastern end of the line was by no means so precisely defined. It ran through territory along the northern edge of the Amur basin about which neither Russians nor Chinese knew much. Vague references to the division of river basins did not stand the test of time. The 1689–1727 line, essentially that of the waterparting between the middle and lower Amur on the one hand and the Uda on the other, was replaced formally in 1858–60 by the Argun–Amur–Ussuri *thalweg* line.

Geographical principles, such as those implied in the definition of the eastern end of the border in the 1689 and 1727 treaties, were not characteristic of Chinese boundary evolution in Inner Asia. More typical was a definition of sovereignty on the basis of tribal occupation.

In a sense this was, of course, also a geographical definition, but it was a fluctuating one since so great a proportion of the population of the external frontier zone of the Manchu 'protectorate' system was nomadic. Tribal areas varied from time to time and season to season. A boundary definition of this kind is to be found in the 1727 Sino-Russian treaty. It relates to what would now be the extreme western end of the border between the Soviet Union and the Mongolian People's Republic where the Soviet Tuvinian Autonomous Oblast (Tannu Tuva) meets Mongolia. The Tuvinians are a Turcic speaking group who came into the Chinese sphere rather indirectly through their relationship with the Mongols. The 1727 border cut through Tuvinian (or, as the Chinese have it, Urianghai) territory; and the 1727 treaty made border definition follow the pattern of the payment of tribute in sable skins by the Urianghai.

In what is now known as Sinkiang, which the Manchus brought into the 'protectorate' system in the middle of the eighteenth century as the outcome of a long series of campaigns against the Dzungars, the principle of tribal relationship played a most important part in frontier evolution. Chinese power, exercised through officials who might well be compared to the Residents in British colonial territories where indirect rule was practised, was based on oasis cities like Kuldja (Ining) and Kashgar. Here lived settled cultivators. Outside the oases was nomad country where the physical presence of the suzerain power was demonstrated either by the periodic collection of tribal dues, usually indirectly, or by the maintenance of a few picket posts far removed from the outermost limits of tribal country. In the Ili region, for example, in the 1850s and early 1860s it is probable that the Chinese picket line was located up to 200 miles or more to the east of what the Chinese, on the basis of tribal relationships, would regard as the limits of their 'protectorate'.

In practice, in the extreme west of Sinkiang, the effective Chinese border—if we define border as a line beyond which no official of the Chinese central authorities habitually ventured—followed the waterparting line of the T'ien Shan, the Pamirs and the Karakoram. But the Chinese certainly saw their sovereignty as flowing across this line by virtue of relationships they had established with Kirgiz nomads. In the Pamirs in the middle of the eighteenth century a Chinese force made a foray of more than 50 miles across the waterparting line; but this was an isolated episode, and by the middle of the nineteenth century Chinese influence had its direct impact on the nomads west of the line only when they had crossed it eastwards onto territory which now forms part of Sinkiang. In the Karakoram, Chinese influence also can be shown from the early nineteenth century at least to have crossed the main waterparting. The state of Hunza (now subject to Pakistan) certainly accepted at this time—if not earlier—a rather symbolical subordination to the Chinese authorities in Kashgaria. The main effect of this subordination, however, was to be seen not in Hunza itself but in tracts north of the main waterparting like Raskam and the Taghdumbash Pamir where the ruler of Hunza, the Mir or Thum, exercised certain rights of taxing, grazing or cultivating, by virtue of Chinese permission.

The pattern of indirect rule which was to be found in Chinese Turkestan, at least until the 1860s, was also to be seen in Tibet during the latter part of the eighteenth century and all the nineteenth century. A Chinese Resident at Lhasa and Chinese relationships with the petty chiefs and Lama incarnations of Eastern Tibet kept some half a million square miles of territory within the Chinese fold. The southern edge of Tibet was marked by the Himalayan range, which we have already noted was a region where autonomous states could flourish. These states tended to acquire relationships with Lhasa, based on trade and religion as much as on politics; and, by virtue of the Chinese 'protectorate', relationships with Lhasa became relationships with Peking. Nepal, for example, possessed such relationships, which were broken for a short period by the Gurkha conquest in the 1760s, only to be re-established in the 1790s, in this particular case by direct Chinese intervention.

By these relationships, direct or indirect, the Chinese could claim— except, of course, in the no-man's-land of the extreme eastern end of the Himalayan range—that their influence ran right down to the foot of the hills, and even beyond in a few places. The Chinese authorities in Lhasa, however, are not recorded to have shown interest in the precise definition of boundaries on the southern edge of their sphere. Here they were content to let their influence gently fade away with distance much as it did beyond the picket line on the Ili. Thus the Chinese Resident in Lhasa was not concerned with boundary disputes between states like Sikkim, Bhutan and Nepal and their southern neighbours.

The Chinese, for example, did not intervene in the Anglo-Nepalese war of 1814–16, the Anglo-Sikkimese war of 1861 or the Anglo-Bhutanese war of 1865. The Chinese Resident in Lhasa, the *Amban*, however, was very much concerned with boundary disputes within the Chinese sphere. Thus there is a long history of Chinese involvement in the borders between Tibet and Sikkim, Bhutan and Nepal. Here, in order to avoid disputes and conflicts, the Chinese on occasion intervened to the extent of actually marking out boundary points on the ground. We have evidence, for example, that the Chinese Amban in Lhasa personally arranged for border markers, inscribed plaques, to be erected at points—usually on the summits of passes—along the Sikkim–Tibet border on a number of occasions in the early nineteenth century. The Amban even came down to inspect the markers from time to time.

Another interesting example of such Chinese boundary definition can be seen in Ladakh. In the 1680s, as a result of a complicated Mongol–Tibetan–Ladakhi–Moghul conflict, a number of boundary points on the upper Indus were established by Tibeto-Ladakhi agreement as being on the border. In the 1830s Ladakh was occupied by the Dogras of Gulab Singh, the founder of the State of Jammu and Kashmir. In 1840–1 Gulab Singh invaded Western Tibet from Ladakh; but was repulsed. In 1842, in the treaty of peace between the Dogras and the Tibetans, the old boundary points were confirmed. There are a number of interesting aspects of this 1842 agreement (which has been much quoted in the modern Sino-Indian boundary argument) which deserve comment. First, the Chinese and Tibetans do not appear to have minded the effective Dogra control of Ladakh so long as certain forms were complied with in order to maintain the impression that Ladakh still remained within the Chinese 'protectorate' system. Second, the real problem to the Tibetans and Chinese, namely the security of western Tibet from further attack, gave rise to a reassertion of the main points on the Tibet–Ladakh border where it was most likely to be crossed, as for instance along the valley of the Indus. Here the border was established with considerable precision. Third, the Chinese and Tibetans made absolutely no attempt to determine the external, non-Tibetan, limits of Ladakh. These did not appear to concern them.

This survey of the outer limits of the Chinese 'protectorates' of Inner Asia shows clearly that there were two main circumstances which produced boundary definitions of anything like the geographical precision required by the political conditions of the twentieth century. First, some such definition took place where a European power like Russia had actually come into contact with these outer limits; and it took place only after the Chinese had concluded that the Russians had in fact transgressed those limits. Second, in areas where there were territorial conflicts between subordinate states right on the fringes of the 'protectorate' system, then the Chinese might bring about boundary definition; but here there would remain *some* nominally Chinese territory between the defined boundary points and the outside world.

THE EVOLUTION OF THE BRITISH AND RUSSIAN IMPERIAL FRONTIERS

Traditionally Chinese frontier policy in Inner Asia has been defensive. It has been designed to protect the Chinese heartland from external attack. Until very recently, at any rate, the Chinese have not had a particularly 'colonial' outlook. The frontier systems which the British and the Russians erected in Asia around the periphery of the Chinese empire were the products of policies which differed in a number of important respects from the frontier policy of China. The real problem of Russian and British frontier policy, despite much public argument to the contrary, was not defence against external attack but the limitation of the process of imperial expansion. The point is given classic expression in the famous Gorchakov Memorandum of 1864. Prince Gorchakov, Foreign Minister of Russia, explained why the Russians found it so hard to stop their advance into Central Asia. There were turbulent peoples just across the frontier. To pacify them meant an advance of the frontier; but this produced an encounter with yet more turbulent tribes. So the process went on. The point of the Gorchakov Memorandum was that only one more such advance was needed to achieve a final solution; but few diplomats could have deluded themselves that the Russian advance would stop until it had come up against a barrier more formidable than that provided by the nomads and the oasis Khanates of Central Asia.

The Gorchakov dilemma was a major factor not only in the Russian advance in Asia but also that of the British, as even a superficial study of what happened in the half century after Plassey will show. It was not, of course, the only factor. Expansion certainly tended to follow natural lines of communication. The Russian occupation of Siberia was to a great extent a reflection of the Russian exploitation of the waterways of the rivers of northern Asia. The pace of advance was easily halted or slowed down only when it had brought the Russian outposts close to the limits of navigation on any particular river system. The checking of Russia on the upper Amur, such as the Manchus achieved in the 1680s, was bound to produce an unstable frontier, for on the Chinese side of it lay a great waterway which the Chinese found it increasingly hard to block and which the Russians found it increasingly tempting to exploit. The rivers of Siberia brought Russia to the Pacific in just over half a century after the initial Russian crossing of the Urals. By an analogous process the Indo-Gangetic plains brought the British rapidly to the lower slopes of the Himalayas, Karakoram and Hindu Kush.

There were two main circumstances under which, in the British and Russian empires in Asia, the advance of the frontier was checked and the process of boundary evolution could begin. First, a natural physical barrier could be encountered. The British found such a barrier in the Himalayas, the Karakoram and the Hindu Kush, mountains which conveniently bounded the northern fringe of the Indian subcontinent. The Russians encountered similar barriers in the Pamirs and the T'ien Shan. Second, the frontiers of an indigenous Asian power could be met, a power strong enough to be capable of maintaining the required minimum of law and order in its peripheral territory. China was such a power, and so, though to a far less certain degree, were Persia and Afghanistan. Each of these two categories of limitation to imperial advance tended to produce a rather different kind of political or diplomatic boundary situation.

The natural barrier could easily bring about a boundary which was defined unilaterally by the imperial power if it was defined at all. The Sarikol range in the Pamirs presented the Russians with such a convenient and obvious boundary line that they have never seen the need to define it by treaty with the Chinese. Many Himalayan tracts, likewise, did not seem to the British to call for precise boundary definition. Indeed, it was only when the second category was involved that definition could arise. A stable line of contact between imperial and indigenous powers required some form of treaty definition; and where the imperial powers sought such a line of contact, treaty definition was brought about. The line of contact, of course, might run along a natural barrier; and only here do we find natural-barrier-type frontiers delimited or demarcated as the result of bilateral agreements. This point has a particular significance for modern boundary arguments in the Himalayas.

Along the Himalayan range during the British period only two stretches of boundary were defined by bilateral agreements. The first was the short Sikkim–Tibet border which was delimited in the Anglo-Chinese Convention of 1890. The second was the MacMahon Line in the Assam Himalayas, which was delimited by a secret exchange of notes between the Government of India and representatives of the Dalai Lama of Tibet in March 1914. In both these instances delimitation followed a threat of the southward extension of active Chinese or Tibetan influence into the Himalayan range and towards the edge of the Indian plains. In the case of Sikkim this threat, albeit extremely mild in nature, was posed by the Tibetans who had established themselves on the territory of the British protectorate of Sikkim. Boundary delimitation by Anglo-Chinese agreement in this case was intended by the British side to be a necessary measure to secure Chinese co-operation in restraining the Tibetans from such aggressions in the future. The McMahon Line arrangement of 1914 was the culmination of British policy to prevent the extension of Chinese influence into the Assam Himalayas. It was made with Tibet and without Chinese participation because by 1914 as a consequence of the Chinese Revolution and the fall of the Manchus the Chinese had for the time being lost control of Tibet.

Apart from Sikkim and the McMahon Line the British managed to avoid any treaty settlement of the southern borders of Tibet. In places, as in the hills on either side of the Sutlej, they established unilaterally a *de facto* border. This line cut across traditional patterns of Tibetan administration; but Tibetan protests were so feeble that the Indian Government could afford to ignore them. Elsewhere the British managed to keep in being buffer states, Nepal and Bhutan, whose survival was in part the consequence of a British reluctance to create zones of direct Anglo-Chinese contact. The British in effect applied a similar buffer policy at the extreme western end of the Himalayas where that range joins the Karakoram. Here, in eastern Ladakh and the Aksai Chin plateau, the Tibetan border was in theory in British times the concern of the Government of the State of Jammu and Kashmir. In this region in the late nineteenth and early twentieth centuries there was some direct contact, and certain amount of argument, between the British and the Chinese authorities in Sinkiang, which was sufficient to produce formal British boundary proposals but insufficient to lead to the negotiation of any final agreement. Thus the Aksai Chin border in modern times has lacked definition by bilateral agreement.

Geographical factors, the nature of the Himalayan range, produced a lack of treaty definitions of the boundary between the British Indian Empire and the Turkestan and Tibet 'protectorates' of the Manchu frontier system. Goegraphical factors, however, produced quite the opposite effect along all but the extreme western sector of the border between Russia in Asia and the Manchu sphere. From the T'ien Shan to the Pacific there were points of Sino-Russian contact. Contact produced conflict and argument, which in turn gave rise to treaty definition. Thus the Russo-Mongol and Russo-Manchurian borders were defined in treaties of 1689, 1727 and 1858–60; and the Russo-Sinkiang border from Mongolia to the Pamirs was defined in treaties of 1860, 1864 and 1881. Much of this Russo-Sinkiang border was subsequently demarcated on the ground. There can be no doubt that the treaty basis for the Sino-Russian border is far more impressive than that for the border between China and India.

MODERN CHINESE CLAIMS

To the present Sino-Indian and Sino-Russian borders the Chinese can raise two main categories of objections. First, in some regions they can maintain that the border was never defined in imperialist times and now requires bilateral negotiation in order to determine its alignment. Second, the present Chinese Communist regime, like its Nationalist predecessor, can argue that many of the boundary treaties of the imperialist era are invalid in that they were imposed on China by force, and that these treaties should be replaced by new agreements in which due regard is paid to Chinese rights, interests and traditions. The claim of lack of definition has particular importance for the Sino-Indian border, and it is certainly the key to the Chinese position in the Aksai Chin dispute. The claim that imperialist treaties may be invalid has been raised, and with some force, by China in connection with the McMahon Line sector of the Sino-Indian border. It could be raised easily enough to cover all but the Pamirs stretch of the long Sino-Russian border.

It is interesting to note that, in fact, the claim of invalidity has not been raised formally by China with regard to the Sino-Russian border. There has, of course, been much Chinese talk about 'unequal' Sino–Russian treaties and so on, and Chairman Mao may have told Japanese journalists that 'we have not yet presented our account' to the Soviet Union for the long list of Tsarist aggressions against China. The formal Chinese position, however, is quite clear. As the Central Committee of the Chinese Communist Party informed the Central Committee of the Communist Party of the Soviet Union in February 1964:

Although the old treaties relating to the Sino-Russian boundary are unequal treaties, the Chinese Government is nevertheless willing to respect them and take them as the basis for a reasonable settlement of the Sino-Soviet boundary question.

Indeed, it is difficult to see how the Chinese could in practice adopt any other attitude. The Sino-Russian border, in just those regions where the Chinese could make the largest claims, on the Ili or in the Amur basin, is a divide between two powerful sovereign states which runs through well surveyed and by no means unpopulated territory under active administration. For Russia, for example, to go back to the theoretical pre-1864 position on the Ili (at least as the Chinese see that position) would involve the abandonment of the great Russian city of Alma Ata, which by 1939 had a population of 230,000. This is a population at least five times greater than the entire population of all the disputed tracts of the Sino-Indian border. For Russia to retreat in the Amur region from the 1860 line to the line of the 1689 Nerchinsk treaty would involve the loss of cities like Khabarovsk (200,000 in 1939) and Vladivostok (206,000 in 1939). Only war could possibly produce such surrenders. In a way the implications of a Chinese challenge to the validity of the old Sino-Russian boundary treaties would be analogous to a British revival of claims to the possession of Normandy and Aquitaine.

The real problem of the Sino-Russian border does not lie in the unsatisfactory nature of the treaties. It is a product of the unsatisfactory nature of Sino-Russian relations in general. Its main practical impact has been felt in regions like the Ili Valley where the border cuts across populations. The Sino-Soviet border divides about 500,000 Kazakhs in China from some 3,000,000 Kazakhs in the Soviet Union; and in periods of international tension the presence of such ethnic minorities cannot fail to lead to border incidents from time to time. Another region of practical crisis is the Amur and the Ussuri, where a river separates active Chinese and Russian administrations. Normal border problems, like accidental crossings and changes in river course, are extremely hard to solve in an atmosphere of ill will: but this would be the case even had there been no 'unequal' treaties of Aigun (1858) and Peking (1860).[1]

While on the Sino-Russian border it is probable that border problems have been aggravated by international tension rather than the other way about, there are good grounds for believing that on the Sino-Indian border it was the failure to solve border problems that produced a crisis in international relations. These problems, as has already been indicated, are of two basic types. First, there are, because of the nature of the terrain and the course of British boundary evolution, extensive tracts of Sino-Indian frontier which have never been defined and which do not follow geographical features so obvious as to eliminate the need for formal definition. Thus, regardless of the political outlook of the parties concerned, there would at some point have been a need for boundary definition in Ladakh to remedy British omissions. Second, there is an aspect of the treaty basis of one of the two bilaterally defined sectors of the Sino-Indian border which no Chinese regime could accept. The McMahon Line of 1914 was negotiated between the British and Tibetans without Chinese participation. Its validity implies the right of Tibet to make international agreements on her own behalf. This right no Chinese government since the latter part of the nineteenth century, when the question first arose in the context of Chinese relations with the Powers, has been prepared to accept.

The attitude of the Indian Republic has been to deny that either of these problems exists. New Delhi has endeavoured since the 1950s to prove that the undefined sectors have in fact been well defined; and it has attempted to show not only that Tibet had the right to make treaties but that the Chinese have in the past acknowledged this right. This attitude has guaranteed the failure of any Sino-Indian boundary negotiations which, with a different Indian outlook, might well have resulted in no more than minor changes of boundary alignment in the desolate Aksai Chin plateau to accommodate the Chinese road linking Sinkiang with Western Tibet.

---

[1] Since this essay was written in early 1968, just such a problem has arisen over Damansky (or Chenpao) Island in the Ussuri.

UNPUBLISHED REPORT FROM YENAN 1937

BY OWEN LATTIMORE

INTRODUCTORY NOTE

The material printed below was originally written as two articles for *The Times* of London. Following a journalistic convention, I wrote the articles as if I had made the journey alone. I do not at the moment have any material at hand to date or document the circumstances precisely, but I think they were about as follows:

In late May or early June 1937 there came to Peking, where I was then living, two Americans who wanted to go up to Yenan to talk to the Chinese Communists and get material from them for publication. One was Mr Philip Jaffe, editor of *Amerasia*, who was accompanied by his wife, and the other was Mr T. A. Bisson, who was, I think, already (at least he became one later) a research worker for the American branch of the Institute of Pacific Relations, an international organization. They asked if I would go with them as their travel guide and interpreter, and I agreed. We then went to see Mr Edgar Snow, who had recently created a sensation by breaking through the blockade against foreign journalists reaching the Chinese Communists, and was living in Peking and writing *Red Star Over China*, which instantly became and was to remain one of the great classics of the history of the Chinese Revolution. Taking Mr Snow's advice, a letter was sent to Yenan and an invitation received, as described in the report below.

On reaching Yenan we found that the communists had excellent translators of their own, so I had the great advantage of being present when others were interviewing both important and ordinary people, asking hardly any questions myself but 'listening in' on the interpretation both from English into Chinese and Chinese into English. I found this much better than being myself the interpreter, for it has always been my experience that the interpreter has to concentrate so intently on each detail, trying to give a fast and accurate translation, that at the end he has quite lost the thread of the discussion as a whole.

I still remember how impressed I was with the patience of the Chinese leaders and the great pains they took to give simple and clear answers to the questions put to them by Americans whom they must have regarded as extremely amateur students of revolution and notably ignorant of the peculiar conditions of revolution in China.

On our return to Peking I decided to try my own hand at journalism, and wrote two articles which I sent to *The Times*. They accepted the articles, but never published them. I think the reason must have been the Marco Polo Bridge incident, which occurred in July and marked the opening of the full-scale Japanese assault on China. The tone of my articles was governed by my conviction that this time the Japanese would find themselves in a long hard war which they could not win; but 'well informed' opinion at the time was that when the Japanese moved in force they would break through the Chinese armies and cut them up as they had done in Manchuria in 1931. It is likely, therefore, that the editors of *The Times* were afraid that if they published my articles just as the Japanese were beginning a series of sensational victories and advances, it would make both the newspaper and its contributor look foolish.

In this connection I may mention that I wrote at the same time an article for *The Saturday Evening Post* in the United States. In this article I described the juggernaut of Japanese imperialism but said that this time it would not succeed in crushing the Chinese. I based my analysis and arguments not on information from the communists, but on the prevailing mood in Peking and Tiensin, the part of China I knew best. Not only were the intelligentsia and the University students afire with militant patriotism, but the troops of both the National Government and the warlord armies were eager to fight. This time, I was convinced, even if some of the generals were to try to negotiate and withdraw (and some of them did), the majority of the troops would stand and fight, without orders or even against orders. This article was actually in the press when the news of the Marco Polo Bridge incident was flashed round the world, and later I had a letter from the foreign editor of *The Saturday Evening Post* telling me how lucky he had been to be able to save my reputation as a prophet by stopping the presses, taking the article out, and inserting other material. I do not know what has become of that article. I have not been able to find a copy of it among my papers. But the unpublished report from Yenan, the two articles written for *The Times*, follows below, without any change whatever in the original wording.

22 January 1968

THE ARMY LEADERS

Many people at Nanking will tell you that Chinese Communism is finished. The appeal to class war has been dropped. The landlords are no longer being expropriated. The territory held by the Communists is poor in agriculture and almost barren of other resources. The Communists are already accepting subsidy from Nanking, and are offering to accept incorporation into Nanking's armies. This must mean, in the end, the 'fading away' of the Communists as a separate political and military force, unless perhaps they faintly survive as a left-wing group within the orthodox Chinese nationalism.

Yet, if this be collapse, the Communists are not in the least anxious to cover it up. On the contrary, they claim that the present situation is chiefly of their own making. It was they who relaxed the lockjaw silence of the Sian crisis last winter with the magic of their united front slogans. They did not intervene until after Marshal Chiang Kai-shek had been made prisoner by the mutinous remnants of the old Manchurian armies. When they did intervene, it was to save the life of the Generalissimo, their mortal enemy of 10 years of civil war. This they did to show that they were more eager to rally the nation against Japan than to triumph over Nanking. The implication of what they say is that they do not intend to wither away in the ravines and loess plateaux of North Shensi. There is more than a hint, in the assured manoeuvring of the youthful veterans who lead the Red Armies, that they believe already that they have a negative control strong enough to prevent Nanking from doing what they do not like which may yet be converted into positive control and command of the situation.

A Nightmare journey

All of this makes North Shensi not only a mystery but a region in which perhaps can be discovered important clues to the unfolding history of Eastern Asia; the struggle for unity in China; the forces welding illiterate millions into increasingly solid and formidable resistance against Japan; the convergence on China, from different directions, of Japan and the Soviet Union.

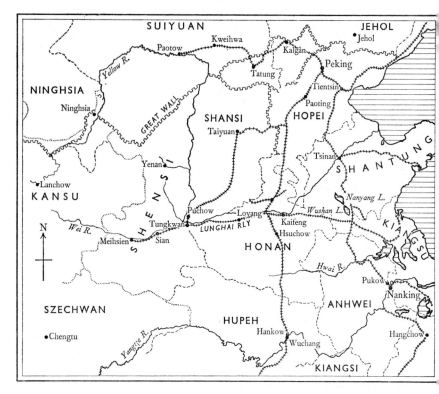

Not knowing of any underground tunnels that would lead me to North Shensi, I set about planning the journey in trustful innocence. I sent a letter to the Red capital, by ordinary mail, with my address candidly printed on the back of the envelope—and got, in answer, a cordial invitation. Accordingly, I went by train to Sian, the capital of Shensi, and then by car to Yenan, the Red capital, about 170 miles to the north, but 250 miles by road.

It took four days to get there from Sian and six to get back, because the rains were on and we were driving through the heart of the loess country. The yellow, wind-dropped soil lies hundreds of feet thick over what used to be the face of the earth. The hills are smothered, but a network of streams has cut down to the ancient valley-beds, so that the formation is now one of innumerable plateaux, some of them higher and some lower, but all flat-topped and all divided from each other by straight-sided ravines. When it rains the whole landscape becomes a nightmare of rather inferior, pale-coloured chocolate. The streams boil up in flood and the cubes of table-land sag and slump. It is not a country made for wheels at all. The local inhabitant prefers pack-mules, when it is dry, and when it is wet he gives up altogether, because even a mule skids on wet loess. Only the foreigner. wincing and flinching from the memory of the fleas indoors, and the revolutionary, who has been trained to follow a line even when skidding, stay out in the wet and strive to make progress. It is not easy, because the newly and crudely made motor road traverses the pale chocolate nightmare in appalling ascents and descents. From each ravine it attacks the next cube of tableland at a corner, climbing at angles that are difficult even for trucks with five gears; it then rushes across the top of the cube and falls over the far edge in a series of even more terrifying swoops.

Place of Pilgrimage

In spite of this, it has become a pilgrim's highway. Chinese educators and students are going up by the hundred, and many of them stay to take courses in the Red Academy. Foreign visitors are welcomed, and missionaries are being urged to come up and see for themselves that their premises are undamaged and the Chinese Christians left undisturbed to preach in public or pray in private, as they like. The only foreign visitors thus far have been Americans, but the Communists profess impatience to see representatives of other nations, and judging from the way they talk, the first Englishman to arrive will be a good deal of a hero.

There is in this a slightly wry contrast with the history of the last ten years, when missionaries fled at a whisper of a Red raid, and when Great Britain, rather than Japan, was the bull's eye in the target of Communist propaganda. What does this reversal mean? Is this the true end of the Long March? When the ghost-army of the Reds was flitting from Kiangsi round by the fringes of Tibet to the uneasy lands of the partly Moslem, partly Chinese, partly Mongol North-West, a curious thing became noticeable. Whenever it was officially reported that a detachment of the Red Army had been surrounded and annihilated, that particular column invariably turned up, a little later, 50 or 100 miles farther ahead on its appointed line of march. Bearing this in mind, I was particularly eager, when the Sung pagoda overlooking Yenan came in view, to find out whether the famed—almost fabulous— leaders of the Red Army showed any signs of that fading out so knowingly predicted of them in the best semi-official quarters. One of the first things I heard was that in a blockhouse on another hill, opposite the pagoda, built before the Reds came, to defend the town from them, there still stand the proclamations offering large rewards for Mao Tse-tung and Chu Te, dead or alive. The Reds had never assaulted the town. It was the defence that faded out, leaving only the notices behind it. Another omen?

Mao Tse-tung, the first of the leaders that I met, did not look faded. In fact, they say he has put on a little weight during the recent months of relative inactivity. It is absurd, looking at him, to think of the rumours current for years that he was about to die of tuberculosis. It would be equally absurd to think of him as a ravening bandit or as a cold doctrinaire. In the course of a few days I saw him in many moods: at interviews that lasted for hours; at meals; at the theatre (in the church of the English Baptist Mission), where sketches and short plays were being put on that substituted united front propaganda for Communist indoctrination. One of my most vivid impressions was on the evening of my departure. The room was full; Chu Te and Chou En-lai had their heads together over a statement to the Press; others were arguing, laughing, giving verbal and written messages to be taken 'out' —for communication between the Red world and the outside world is not yet entirely free. I happened to glance at Mao Tse-tung, who was sitting in the middle of it all. His head had sunk forward a little, his arms hung limp, his face was expressionless, and his eyes without lustre. He had completely withdrawn himself from his surroundings. Then someone spoke to him, and he joined in at once, as though he had subconsciously kept up with all the conversations going on around him.

Range of Knowledge

This is a trivial example of a flexibility that is really amazing. Mao Tse-tung can range from the widest philosophical concepts on which the Communist policy is based to the narrowest detail of practical application, without haste, without delay, and without the slightest blurring of focus. He has fire and passion, but so matured and tempered that there seems to be no personal warping of his thought; and yet, in a long extemporaneous discussion of a complicated subject there will not be a single cliché (and Chinese is more full of clichés than English even); every phrase has a personal stamp.

It would be misleading, however, to give too many personal details about Mao, Chu Te, and other leaders. So little is known of the inside workings of the Communist movement in China that it is almost always spoken of in terms of its leading personalities. At Yenan a contrast is immediately noticeable; the Communists themselves never speak of Nanking in terms of Chiang Kai-shek or any other leader. They stick to estimates of groups and movements and economic, social, and political forces. From this alone it is obvious that they are not either bandits preying on society or *condottieri* aiming at power for the sake of power. This is as true now that they have compromised on a united front as it was when they were at open war with Nanking.

Resistance to Japan

The area in which the Chinese Communist armies are at present concentrated extends from North Shensi into East Kansu and South Ninghsia. It has a total population of about 1,400,000, within which the Chinese Moslems form an important minority. To this Chu Te added the information that the Red Army now numbers from 80,000 to 90,000 men, counting only the regular forces under central command and in touch with each other. There is an indefinite number of partisan irregulars, mostly in mountainous strongholds on the borders between provinces where the Communist armies have passed. Chu Te is the wiliest old campaigner of them all—soldier under the Empire, official under the Republic, general under the Soviets. Now that he is not campaigning, he lectures on Leninism in the Red Academy and reads widely. He commented to me acutely on the divergences between American and British policy revealed in a Chinese translation of Mr Stimson's *The Far Eastern Crisis*.

Political Strategy

No other Communist party, in bargaining for a United Front, has ever started with a great area like this—however poor and remote—under its own rule; with a large civilian population—however ignorant and economically backward—in addition to a seasoned army which has been fighting, marching, and organizing peasant support for ten years. If Nanking has never been able to crush them, why should the Communists themselves ask for a cessation of civil war? To this and other questions it is of interest, I think, to give the Communist answer; partly in order to give a personal impression of the little-interviewed Communist leaders, and partly, I confess, because I was not in the Red region long enough to make a close check between the facts as represented and the facts as they are.

The Communist answer reveals a mixture of political manoeuvring, in the narrow sense, of historical reasoning and of regard for the balance of national politics and world politics. Nanking was never able to crush them; but neither were they able to make head against Nanking by frontal attack. The Communists lost more men in counter-offensives when they were in Kiangsi, according to Chu Te, than they did in the whole of the long, circuitous 'retreat', which they proudly call the Long March, from Kiangsi to Shensi. In the meantime, Japan was able to take advantage of the deadlock to increase its gains in North China.

The Communists had appealed for a United Front long before the capture of Chiang Kai-shek at Sian last December. That was only the incident which gave them a chance to intervene, to demonstrate that they really wanted a United Front more than they wanted the Generalissimo's head and that they were prepared to make concessions even when, temporarily, they held the kind of advantage that terrorists would have used ruthlessly.

Does this mean the abandonment of the Revolution? It seems to me as foolish to think so as to suppose that the Soviet Union is on its way back to capitalism. Primarily, the Communists must have felt that the United Front as a rallying cry against Japan would have a wider popular appeal than the demand for revolution; while, secondarily, a democratic phase in China would mean a filtering down of political education among the common people, making it possible to renew Communist demands in the future. Mao Tse-tung, when asked whether the United Front would not result in smothering the Communists under the increased prestige of Nanking, replied that leadership within a United Front does not depend entirely on which party commands the larger military force. What reveals the quality of leadership is the programme advocated and the efforts made to carry it out. If things go as the Red Army has long demanded that they go; if the Japanese are driven out and China democratized (with the free popular election of Communist and other representatives, instead of the arbitrary appointment of all executive officials by the Kuomintang), this will mean that Communist leadership had been followed, by Nanking.

Complicated Issues

Chu Te confirmed this, arguing that it is not the numbers of an army which count. No matter how large, well-armed, and liberally financed the armies of Nanking, they must remain 'semi-colonial' armies, in the Communist view, and therefore inferior, as armies, to the invading forces of Japan. Semi-colonialism can only resist imperialism by bringing the aid of a mass movement to the support of whatever army it may have; and the Communists believe that they alone can unite the people—the politically ignorant as well as the politically conscious—behind the armies of Chiang Kai-shek.

Is this arid phraseology, or does it mean something? It means, so far as I could see, that the stiff and simplified Communist vocabulary covers a flexible understanding of complicated issues. When it was pointed out to him that the Chinese Communists demand war against Japan at a time when all the other Communist parties demand peace, Chu Te replied that the paradox of the Communist demand for world peace and the Chinese demand for war against Japan is tied up with the many-sided struggle in China, where the Communists are simultaneously moving towards the world peace front, struggling against Japanese aggression, and working for a revolution. The implication would appear to be that the Chinese Communists agree that peace, all over the world, is favourable to the general development of Communism; but that once aggression has been started, as Japan has started it in China, it must be boldly resisted.

The importance of the Communist theories is that they have already begun to put them into practice. Chinese Communism has more than once been described as violent peasant rebellion, of a kind not at all new in Chinese history. The ease and thoroughness with which the Communists have already changed their land policy in the area controlled by them indicate that on the contrary their ideas are of a new order, but that they have been able to win the confidence and support of the peasants. Formerly, landlord property was seized and distributed to the peasants, who were allowed to hold it as private property. Under the new policy, the landlords may keep their land, but they may not demand from a tenant more than 30 per cent. of his produce in rental. Landlords whose property had already been taken will not have it returned to them, but if they return to the district they will be granted a share of land equal to that of other farmers.

The size of land holdings is not, I was told, the most important question. There is a great deal more arable land than can be farmed by the present population. Landlords controlled the wealth of the country-side by virtue of the fact that they alone had enough capital to invest in plough cattle and the implements of farming, and the peasants had to compete with each other in the rates which they offered for the use of these necessities. Because of this initial scarcity, and because in addition the Kuomintang troops destroyed everything they could lay hands on before abandoning North Shensi to the Red Army, there was at first a real danger of famine. In order to save both the population and the Communists it was necessary to form peasant cooperatives to make the maximum use of all the farming implements and resources available. Success in doing this was the basis of the present good feeling between the peasants and the Communists. Although this kind of reform sounds very well, it seems to me that it will have strong competition from the cooperatives sponsored by Nanking and backed by the Shanghai Chinese banks.

Improved Relationship

Friendly relations with the non-Chinese minorities were also absolutely imperative if the Communists were to hold their ground. With the Moslems they are already on excellent terms, and contact with the Mongols of the Ordos deserts is being improved. Two regiments of non-Communist Moslems are already serving with the Red Army, I was told, and are considered thoroughly reliable troops.

The Communists have worked on the theory that relations between the Chinese and their minority subject peoples are bad because the regular method has always been to select a Moslem or Mongol chief and give him arms and power which place him above other leaders, thus creating division and rivalry. The Communist method is to give the arms first and bargain afterwards, so as not to seem to be using unfair pressure. The arms are given to the constituted authorities, whatever they may be: but at the same time the common people are told that if their rulers use these arms merely for civil war or tribal war or to collect extra taxes, the people will be supported against the rulers. In this way Mongol princes (for instance) are not forced into negotiation with the Japanese for fear of the Communists, but at the same time the

Mongol tribesmen are made to feel that the Communists are not (like so many Chinese provincial officials) in alliance with the princes to exploit them.

Nor is any attempt made to convert these peoples into Chinese. They are not forced to use Chinese schools, but are given help in teaching their own languages. In the case of the Moslems this includes Arabic, the religious language. Every effort of this kind is coupled with the appeal to realize that the danger from Japan, to the Chinese and the minority peoples alike, is much greater than the danger from Chinese to Moslems or Mongols. This principle, it is pointed out, can be applied equally to all the nations which stand in fear of the danger to world peace from unprovoked aggression; and therefore the Communists believe that their participation in a Chinese United Front will not cause alarm in either Great Britain or America.

Thinking it over myself on the journey back, it seemed to me that if Japan does not fight the Communists will emerge as a legal party with influence all over China and a sort of provincial status in the region they already control. If Japan fights, and the Communist theory of the relation between army and population in a 'semi-colonial' country is correct, a large part of both army and people will go over to the Communists.

6-2

THE USE OF SLOGANS AND 'UNINTERRUPTED REVOLUTION' IN CHINA IN THE EARLY PART OF 1964

BY JAMES MACDONALD

This paper describes briefly the Chinese Communists' technique of the use of slogans, and examines the actual use of slogans in the columns of *The People's Daily* in a recent period.

The basis of the technique is that common to Communist parties—first the identification of the general policy, or line, appropriate to each major phase of development and the identification of particular policies to give effect to the general policy, then the encapsulation of these policies in short, readily intelligible, readily propagated forms, slogans, and finally the 'advancing' of the slogans as signals for bringing into play the maximum organizational effort for the realization of the content of the slogans.

The two classes of slogan are distinguished by Mao Tse-tung in his report to the national party conference of 1937, 'The Tasks of the Chinese Communist Party in the Period of Resistance to Japan', in which he said:

How does the proletariat give political leadership through its party to all the revolutionary classes in the country? First, by putting forward basic political slogans that accord with the course of historical development and by putting forward slogans of action for each stage of development and each major turn of events in order to translate these political slogans into reality.[1]

The use of slogans is thus a key technique in making policies known and taking action to achieve them.

The need for flexibility in political leadership subsequently led to a refinement of the technique. The decisions on methods of leadership taken by the Central Committee of the party on 1 June 1943 emphasize first the need for combining a general and widespread call to action with particular and specific guidance derived from personal experience.[2] Such general calls are to be arrived at by relying on the

---

[1] Mao Tse-tung, *Selected Works*, Foreign Languages Press, Peking, 1961–5, vol. I, p. 274, para. 17. [2] Mao, *ibid.*, vol. III, p. 117.

'mass line' and are to be formulated out of particular guidance given in a number of cases and widely tested. The decisions specify further that steps must be taken to avoid confusion of tasks: 'At any one time there can be only one central task, supplemented by other tasks of a second or third order of importance.' The person with overall local responsibility is told to undertake his own planning, so as not to act automatically on each instruction from higher up thereby creating 'a multitude of "central tasks" and a state of confusion and disorder'. Equally, when assigning tasks to the lower levels, higher organizations must indicate which task is central, and what is the order of priority and urgency.

After the establishment of the People's Republic of China, the technique was described again in the first issue of 1952 of the magazine *Study*:

We know that revolution is a mass movement. In one period the activity of the broad masses must concentrate on one or at most a few clear objects. Therefore the strategic leadership of the party must be able to put forward the most appropriate tasks and the most appropriate slogans. These tasks and slogans must clearly be the central tasks. That is to say, the tasks must clearly be the most pressing and important ones of that period and after completing them it may be said that there has been an all-round improvement...After completing one central task putting forward another central task, for one central slogan exchanging another central slogan, this is the law of the forward development of revolutionary movement, and also the law of steadily raising the level of consciousness and organizational strength of the broad masses.[1]

It will be seen that the keys to the successful use of slogans lie in three activities. The first is the correct formulation of basic political slogans that 'accord with the course of historical development'. The second is the correct ordering and limiting of immediate tasks and their adaptation to local circumstances. The third is reliance on the 'mass line' both in arriving at correct slogans and also in propagating them.

All three activities seem to have been put in question by the Great Leap Forward. In his keynote speech for the Great Leap, Liu Shao-ch'i spoke of the Chinese party and Mao Tse-tung's having always guided the Chinese revolution by the 'Marxist–Leninist theory of uninterrupted revolution', putting forward new tasks in good time so as

[1] *Study* (Hsüeh-hsi), no. 1, 1952, p. 44.

to maintain the 'revolutionary fervour of the masses'.[1] This way of speaking implied a high degree of certitude in the ordering of revolutionary tasks, and Liu did claim that the party's general line for socialist construction had proved its correctness at every step in the course of practical work. While allowing for its future testing, developing and perfection, he asserted that its basic correctness was established. However, after a year of the Great Leap Forward the Chinese economy was experiencing considerable dislocation, especially in its organization at lower levels. During the period 1959–61 the dislocation grew increasingly severe, compounded by natural disasters, and in 1961 the order of economic priorities was reversed. At the same time a rectification campaign was set in motion against the party cadres, who were exhorted to adhere faithfully to the mass line,[2] which was described and recommended anew by the highest level of leadership.[3]

This whole experience cast doubt on the idea of uninterrupted revolutionary development kept moving by a successive exchange of central tasks and slogans as demanded by the growth of 'social productive forces' (a phrase also used by Liu). By 1961 the Chinese party seemed to be on the horns of a dilemma: for either the growth of the social productive forces did not pose tasks to which Marxism–Leninism gave special insight, or the persons exercising the insight had been mistaken. In the meantime, economic problems demanded emergency measures.

The present paper looks into how the exchange of the tasks of revolution was being put into effect in general and particular slogans during a more recent period in the history of the People's Republic of China when stability had been restored, to see what slogans were in existence and to see how the slogans were handled when a major new policy was introduced. The place of search was limited to *The People's Daily*, the central propaganda organ of the Communist Party of China, and the period to 1 January–31 May 1964. It would be useful to compare the results of this search with the results of a similar search of local

---

[1] Liu Shao-ch'i, 'Report on the Work of the Central Committee of the Communist Party of China to the Second Session of the Eighth National Congress', in *Second Session of the Eighth National Congress of the Communist Party of China*, Foreign Languages Press, Peking, 1958, Section II.

[2] Communiqué of 18 January 1961, of the ninth Plenum of the Eighth Central Committee.

[3] Liu Shao-ch'i, *Address at the meeting in celebration of the 40th anniversary of the founding of the Communist Party of China*, pp. 9 and 13, Foreign Languages Press, Peking, 1961.

Chinese newspapers during the same period, if they were available, particularly as local authorities have the duty in certain activities of adapting slogans to local conditions. Some light is thrown on local activities by the columns of *The People's Daily*, however, since that newspaper regularly publishes reports of local activities in the course of development of a campaign, and local slogans are frequently quoted in these reports. Indeed, as will be seen, they are so common that among the slogans to be found in *The People's Daily*, they form a category of their own.

The slogans which actually were found were, as was to be expected in the fifteenth year of the revolution, very numerous. This was partly a product of the fact that the tasks of the revolution in the period of the construction of socialism included many which were long-term, so that although particular slogans might be moved from the centre of the picture they could not fall into total disuse unless the activity they promoted could be considered wound up. It was also partly a product of the complications of the society which was being constructed, together with the manifold complications of the society in which the building was taking place, bearing in mind that *The People's Daily* is an organ of the central authorities, but speaks to the nation as a whole.

For the purposes of description, the slogans are arranged in seven groups. In practice there is close linkage between members of various groups.

The first group here are called 'background slogans'. These are a very large number of slogans, having general rather than particular application.

The second group are the slogans of current campaigns of a generalized nature, capable of being applied to all sections of the community and to all of its activities.

The slogans of the third group are also directed to the whole community but aim to achieve one objective.

Fourth are a group of slogans directed to a section of the community only, but still on a high level of generality and capable of being applied to all activities of that section.

The slogans of the fifth group are of a different order, in that although coming from a higher level they aim at more specific achievements in a section of the community, sometimes deriving from general campaigns, sometimes from the activities of particular functional groups.

The sixth group of slogans are on a lower level, being those produced locally, perhaps in adaptation of a national campaign, or perhaps to achieve a purely local purpose.

The seventh group are of a different category altogether—the slogans deriving from the persons or units selected to act as models. Such slogans might occur in any of the other groups but are isolated because of their method of coinage, and because of their special place in Chinese techniques of mass mobilization.

These classifications will now be discussed in more detail.

First, background slogans. Most of the editorials and reports published during this period used a standard selection of phrases of this sort, and they were especially common in reports of speeches. Many of them consisted of four characters, and, as with the four-character phrases of the pre-Communist era, they often appeared in strings in sentences. They were also commonly used as small headings over the main headlines of a news story or an editorial. Among the four-character slogans so used, the following thirty were found:

> endure and struggle ever on
> be diligent and frugal in building the nation
> use our own strength to rise up again
> strive with gusto for the nation's strength
> fight on to better things
> spur up every effort
> more, faster, better, cheaper
> increase production and economize
> be red and expert
> find the right way from the facts
> study with an open mind
> upraise the proletarian, extinguish the bourgeois
> unite together
> advance shoulder to shoulder
> advance forward with the current
> actively study, actively use
> make good still better
> get down to things and be practical
> investigate and research
> change customs and conventions
> work without thought of self

build the country economically
be public-spirited, forget yourself
don't spare yourself for others
see what is just and do it with enthusiasm
help others as a pleasure
facing hardship, live plainly
relate with the masses
remould the natural environment
give help to each other.

This is probably not a complete list. Most of these slogans can be used in any situation; all can be used in more than one.

Not all background slogans are four-character phrases. On 9 February 1964, the Chinese armed forces were told in detail about (among many other things) the 'san lao' (san lao)[1] and the 'si yan' (ssu yen)—'the three honesties' and 'the four stricts' (be an honest man, speak honest words, do honest deeds: have strict requirements, have strict organization, have a strict attitude, and have strict regulations). These were propagated as being part of the working style of the general population, and one found general references to upholding 'the three honesties' or 'the four stricts' in all matters. The full version of the three honesties does in fact consist of three four-character phrases, and these were found sometimes at the top of a general news story.

All these slogans were an important part of the moral environment in which the nation was to be made strong and socialism was to be built, although some of them were likely to have staled with repetition.

Turning to the second group, the slogans of current campaigns of a generalized nature, we find a situation of considerable complexity, for as we come in, on 1 January 1964, three major campaigns are going strong all over the nation. Pre-eminent is the great new emulation campaign, which had begun early in the previous year, with the slogan 'Compare, learn, catch up with those in front, and help those behind' ('bi, xue, gan, bang—pi hsüeh kan pang'). Second there was the campaign 'Learn from Lei Feng' (the deceased model soldier) with youth as its prime, but not its only, target. Third there was the campaign for 'The three great revolutionary movements', i.e. the class struggle, the struggle for production, and the encouragement of

---

[1] The pinyin form of transcription is used, followed by the Wade–Giles equivalent.

scientific experiment. Another very widespread campaign also capable of generalized application was also in existence, the continuing campaign to study the works of Chairman Mao, always ready to rise up again.

In this category the dominant slogan at this time was the emulation slogan 'bi xue gan bang'. The campaign had been running for nine months and was intended to reach into all activity. Its main application was in the field of production. But it was not allowed to stop there. The editorial on New Year's Day specifically called for emulative competition in political study, thus providing a link with the developments of the next month.

The main emphasis being on industrial production, there were numerous stories of different enterprises comparing themselves with others and benefiting thereby; stories of iron-making factories, which compared methods and increased their output; of two hundred factories in Peking which by comparing and studying 'with open mind' had improved their products; a story from Hupei province of a light industry which at first did not take the trouble to join in the movement, but afterwards 'with open mind' did; a Shanghai weaving-mill which had been studied for years by others now suddenly awoke to the fact that it had fallen behind a Nanking mill and decided to catch up. This last became the subject of an editorial on self-satisfaction. And so the reports continue throughout this period. Stories come from Shanghai, Tientsin, Chungking and Canton, indeed from all over China. They deal with weaving, cement-making, coal-mining, the manufacture of bicycles, pencils, vacuum flasks, sewing machines, with oilfields, steel-making, acid-making, hub-cap making, a rubber factory, food-canning, and so on.

Editorially, the slogan continued unchanged at this time, although it was extended later on. It was accompanied by various exhortations, and by explanations of the significance of its different parts, and discussion of how best to carry each out. One editorial, for example, dealt with why 'comparing' was the first thing that had to be done. Another explained the importance of 'helping those who were behind'. Another explained why fundamental priority should be given to 'thinking' in all these processes.

The development of the campaign involved many activities from which emerged slogans belonging to other categories, but which it will be convenient to mention here.

Among the different types of industrial enterprise a common method was for the appropriate national organization to hold a national meeting, and for their respective constituent bodies at the levels of province, big city, county, commune, production brigade, and factory to hold their own meetings, at all of which 'advanced experience' was exchanged, comparisons were made, and model units and workers were chosen. These then usually became a source of slogans and all engaged in the particular form of activity were urged to study them and catch up with them.

In agriculture, the emulation campaign was linked with seasonal activities and to lesser, specifically agricultural campaigns.

Additional impetus was given by linking the campaign to existing older general slogans. For example, take the slogan 'More, quicker, better, cheaper', which has already been listed in the background slogans. This was in fact part of the existing 'general line' for the construction of socialism. It was now prayed in aid in numerous ways: for example, in proposals for the reform of agricultural technology as being demonstrated in certain villages in Shantung province, and as demonstrated in a Shanghai hub-cap factory. All national industries were told how to guarantee it and the ninth national conference on the sickness bilharzia expressed determination to tackle their problems in that way.

The same thing happened with the slogan 'Use our own strength to rise up again' ('zi li geng sheng—tzyh lih geng sheng'). A wide variety of enterprises and units were praised for showing this spirit, and for a time the slogan was used regularly as a headline.

In this period one of the current great 'models' was extolled, as a triumphant example of self-reliance; it became widely imitated and revivified the slogan to some extent. This was the village of Da jai (Ta Chai) which will be mentioned again.

A similar quite wide use was made of the background slogans 'Build the country economically' and 'Increase production, and economize'. But the talismanic quality of some of the older slogans seemed to have waned with the transfer of energy from the campaigns in which they had been central, and the use made of them seemed routine.

Although the emulation campaign was still in full spate in January 1964, however, and full of life, it was about to be joined by a new major campaign, with a whole crop of its own slogans. This was the 'Learn from the Liberation Army' campaign. The subject of learning from the army's political work was mentioned on New Year's Day, and was also mentioned towards the end of January. But it is on 1 February that it appears as a full-scale national campaign. The army's own campaigns really belong to the next category for description but what the new campaign meant for the populace at large in terms of slogans and activities can only be understood by introducing at this point an account of how the army organized itself.

The army had begun intensive campaigns to raise the level of political consciousness in all ranks some three and a half years before and the effort had been continually refreshed. Military training tends to be systematized and reduced to simple code form, and these political campaigns were no exception. They also employed the common Chinese fondness for numerical mnemonics. What this meant by this time can be seen from the report on 18 January 1964, of a meeting of the General Political Department of the People's Liberation Army, at which the following activities were mentioned in references to army training, and were being used in various slogans:

> the 'four good' companies
> the 'four firsts'
> the 'three-eight working style'
> the 'five good' soldiers
> the 'five "more's"'
> the 'twelve lessons for building a company'
> the 'ten lessons for grasping the living thought'
> the 'seven measures for company leadership' and
> 'learn from the good 8th Company of the Nanking Road'.

On 22 January more army slogans were given in a report made by a Deputy-Chairman of the General Political Department:

> 'learn from the model exploits of the heroes of the Sino–Indian border counter-attack' and
> 'thoroughly master the thought of Mao Tse-tung'.

He also recommended the cadres to use 'the three memories and three comparisons' method and cited Lei Feng's formula for political study:

> 'question, study, practise, sum up'

and also that of 'the good 8th' Company:

> 'one, read, two, discuss, three, compare, four, put into practice'.

Next day, in a list of explanations of some of these terms another new one was included:

> 'the five principles for managing education.'

The army was thus a centre of slogans and campaigns of some variety. Generally speaking, however, the army's activities centred on two poles: the cultivation of political thought, and the cultivation of military skill.

When on 1 February, the call came to the whole country to learn from the army, the editorial in *The People's Daily* made its impact by concentrating on the army's political work, the two main slogans which it took being the 'four firsts' and the 'three-eight working style'. These were commended and recommended as having general significance. The four firsts are:

> put the human element first
> put political work first
> put ideological work first
> put living thinking first.

The three-eight working style consists of three phrases and eight characters; the three phrases advocate:

> a fixed and correct political direction
> a plain, enduring working-style
> flexible strategy and tactics;

the eight characters advocate:

> solidarity,
> alertness,
> seriousness,
> liveliness.

The main slogan of the movement, however, was (and continued to be) 'Learn from the Liberation Army'. As the first paragraph of the editorial put it, 'An upsurge of learning from the Liberation Army is just arising over the whole country. In the communist competition to compare with the advanced, learn from the advanced, catch up with the advanced and help those behind, "Learn from the Liberation Army" has already become a fighting slogan.'

In support of the editorial were a number of news stories. In every factory, school and organization in Shanghai, common subjects of conversation were reported as 'Learn from the Chinese People's Liberation Army' and 'Take the good 8th Company of the Nanking Road for your own model'. On the same page it was reported that a mining village in Hopei province had studied the People's Liberation Army's 'ten lessons for grasping the living thought'; this had taught them how to put political ideology first, and the result had been an increase in production. This emphasis was brought out in the slogan which headed a report next day of a conference of industrial communications workers, which ran 'Learn from the Liberation Army—strengthen ideological work'. The new slogan began to take precedence over the emulation slogan which in a number of stories was relegated to being one of a number of activities carried on. The emulation slogan *was* still being used as a slogan, and there were still regular reports of emulation activities. The movement was not suddenly eclipsed. But instead of being one activity to which the emulation movement might apply, the study of politics now became a central activity which might be undertaken by emulation movement methods but to which the key was the practice of the army, a force represented as, at once, active, disciplined and correct.

Great efforts were made so that the two slogans did not appear to conflict. But as editorial and news stories made clear, the new intention was that political work was to be conducted as the key to production. 'Politics in Command', in fact, to recall the 1958 slogan. For example, the experience of the Yumen oilfield was cited under a series of slogans: they 'actively studied, actively used' the experience of the Liberation Army. Taking 'the three-eight working style as a model', they established a 'three honests, four stricts, four sames' style of work.

As the movement to learn from the army developed, it began to appear that the core of the army's political work was the study of the works of Mao Tse-tung.

This campaign bestrides the second and the third groups, since it was directed to the single object of actually studying Mao's works, but the uses to which they could be put were represented as very general indeed. In March and April slogans relating to this began to receive new prominence, while other slogans continued to stress the primacy of political work in general. As one headline put it, 'In learning from advanced experience there are thousands of lessons, and political thought work is the first.' For five days running *The People's Daily* had an enormous banner line 'Hold high the red banner of Mao Tse-tung'. Both slogans were used on numerous occasions, and the movement was supported with very many stories illustrating the variety of uses of the works of Mao, ranging from their application by factory reform groups to that by a research team in the Metallurgy Department, and that by the Shensi Meteorological Department, all of whom were reported as having used their study in solving practical problems.

In addition to the well-known basic slogans of 'Study the works of Chairman Mao' and 'Raise high the great red banner of Mao Tse-tung's thought', the movement was promoted with many other slogans, dealing with methods of study, and attitudes to study. 'Actively study, actively use', was the commonest, but there were also 'Study and use together', 'After studying, use; after using, study again', 'Be a revolutionary for a life-time, study the works of Chairman Mao for a life-time', 'Live to old age, study to old age, reform to old age', 'Before studying get the circumstances clear, while studying relate to the facts, after studying be severely practical', 'Keep on studying, keep on using, more self-awareness, more results', 'Bring questions to your study, actively study actively use, join study and use together, impatient to use study first, study the implications of what you learn', plus the formulae of Lei Feng and the Good 8th Company.

These movements for political study were linked with the socialist education movement and the class struggle part of 'the three great revolutionary movements' and these, too, had related slogans, used to organize activities, or to bring out the wider significance of particular incidents. Among these one finds the slogan 'xing wu mie zi' ('hsing wu mieh tzy')—'Raise up the proletarian, extinguish the bourgeois', and a large number of associated slogans explaining how the process should be carried out. One method was to use the history of local people, and there were movements for 'telling the five histories' (and also 'the four histories' and 'the three histories'). Other slogans aimed at the same end were 'recall the past, compare it with now' ('hui yi dui bi—hui yi tui pi'), 'recall the old bitterness, think of the new pleasantness' ('yi ku si tien—yi k'u ssu t'ien'), 'Dig out the old misery' ('Wa ku gen—Wa k'u ken'), 'three memories and three comparisons' ('San yi san bi—San yi san pi'), and 'One explain, two show, three visit, four discuss, five recall, six pass it on' ('Yi jiang, er jan, san fang, si yi, wu ji, liu chuan—Yi chiang, erh chan, san fang, ssu yi, wu chi, liu ch'uan'). This last should be further explained: when expanded it means

> Explain the wickedness of the exploiting classes,
> Show real things which compare the new and old,
> Visit the homes of the worker and peasant masses,
> Discuss the reason for the class struggle,
> Recall the exploits of the former revolutionary generation,
> Pass on the experience of class education.

A basic test which could be applied to all activity was whether it tended to raise up the proletarian or do the opposite. Whether it was in a factory, a production brigade, an infantry platoon, or a youth club, 'remember the bitter and think of the sweet' were a recommended means for advancing socialist education.

It is difficult to categorize the 'four good' 'five good' and 'six good' campaigns, which were run vigorously for organizations and individuals during this period. They were both general and particular, and served a combination of ends. The 'five goods' were not the same in each case, being adapted for the type of organization under consideration. They were also adapted for application to individuals, and the two sorts of campaign were run together. In essence they were important subordinate parts of the other campaigns, but as they reached into every aspect of activity, this naturally encompassed ideological work and so raised them to a higher level.

Part of the stimulus came from the 'Learn from the Liberation Army' campaign, since a main army movement was the establishment of 'four-good units' and 'five-good soldiers'. Almost every day there would be a report of a meeting in some army command which established 'four-good units', or else of some particular 'four-good unit', whose merits were described. The four goods of the good army units, by the way, are:

> ideology good
> three-eight working style good
> military training good
> way of living good.

The five goods of the 'five-good' soldier are:

> ideology good
> military skill good
> three-eight working style good
> fulfilment of duty good
> physical training good.

One of the merits of the 'four-good' and 'five-good' campaigns was that everyone could succeed in them. In one army unit it was reported that one half the companies were 'four-good' companies, and over half of the soldiers were 'five-good' soldiers. In civilian life, the 'five-good' method was also known and it received a special fillip as part of the emulation campaign: organizations were advised to use it, and choose 'five-good enterprises' and 'five-good workers' or 'five-good production teams' and 'five-good team members'. The number of goods was not uniform, and some areas were choosing 'six-good team members' and 'six-good workers'. The 'five-goods' did not vary all that much. For an industrial enterprise, they were:

> ideology good
> fulfilment of plan good
> management of the enterprise good
> way of living good
> cadres' working style good.

The six-goods of commercial enterprises were:

> political thought good
> operating the policy for fulfilling the plan good
> solidarity and mutual help good
> care for public property good
> regular study good
> service attitude good.

Not only were the main parts of factories and their workers included: so were their auxiliary services, e.g. a canteen might qualify as a 'five-good canteen'.

The 'five-good' activities did not stop at industry, agriculture and the army. The Young Communist League also ran 'four-good' and 'five-good' competitions. The League's 'four goods' were:

political thought good
'three-good' activities (body, study and work) good
all-round daily life organization good
    way of uniting with the masses good.

There were 'four-good' P.T. teams, and 'five-good' P.T. exponents. In a Wuhan glass factory, not only were 'five-good' workers selected, the hostels associated with the factory also ran 'five-good family' competitions. A further development of the 'five-good' movement came in a story of 1400 students and teachers from Peking Teachers' Training College going for two months to work in six communes in Tahsing County. One hundred teachers and students were given a 'five-good' title: they were good at studying the works and policies of Chairman Mao, their practical work was good, their hardening through labour was good, their investigation and research was good, and their thought reform was good. In Wuhan, where there was a ten years' history of 'five-good' family activities, nearly 10,000 'five-good' families had been nominated over that period. Their 'five-goods' were:

> ideology,
> domestic economy,
> educating children,
> solidarity and mutual aid,
> safety and hygiene.

This was an example of an excellent campaign for mass mobilization: it focused on essentials—politics, production and social conscience; at one and the same time the 'five-good' slogan promoted unity but was also capable of adaptation to any circumstances. It is a question whether it is simple.

Another kind of major national campaign directed at a single objective was the campaign to show support for a declaration of foreign policy. Here the effort was usually short and the slogans readily coined. An important example occurred on 13 January when Mao Tse-tung gave an interview in which he proclaimed solidarity with the Panamanians in their dispute with the U.S.A. The slogan at once raised was 'The Chinese people resolutely support the Panamanian people's just patriotic struggle'. Over several days this was repeated and as mass demonstrations took place all over China was joined with slogans like 'The Yankees must lose, Panama must win', 'Panama—yes, Yankees

—no' and 'Resolutely support Panama's just struggle for sovereignty'. In the month of April a similar campaign was raised with the slogan 'U.S. imperialism get out of Japan'.

While these campaigns of general application were going on, there were also sectional campaigns, the slogans of which make up the fourth group. In the army, for example, in addition to the slogans of which examples have already been given, another slogan was added during the period when the nation was being exhorted to learn from the army. The new slogan exhorted and called on the army to 'study the local people'. This meant that at the same time as the people were studying the army's 'four firsts' and 'four goods' and 'five goods' and 'three-eights', to help their emulation and education campaigns, so the army were studying the methods of the civilians—the 'four importants', the 'three honesties', the 'four stricts' and the 'four sames'—to help it in its construction work.

On various other occasions we find the army urged to develop 'the Yenan', and 'the Nanniwan' spirit. We also find the army and the public security forces organizing 'Support the government and love the people' activities on a broad front and the public security forces holding a 'Love the People Month'.

Perhaps the most common target of sectional appeals was the agricultural sector. Some of these were very general and some more directly related to the seasons. As an example of the former we find throughout the period a constant campaign 'In drought and flood guarantee stable production and high production'. In exhortations addressed to the countryside, at conferences on production, in stories from the country, this was a prime policy. Various angles were given to it. Research work in agricultural science was exhorted to promote it. Technical knowledge was reported as being spread to help it. An important means advocated for the achievement of it was to 'summarize experience' (itself a common slogan). Some areas ran appropriate emulation campaigns. At a general conference it was concluded that there were tens of thousands of lessons for high production and stable production, and that the first of these was 'Do well ideological work'. Stories emphasized the need to 'Rely on the masses' and 'Use the spirit of self-reliance'. One commune which struggled for five years to achieve high and stable production reported its experience to a meeting in Canton of representatives of over one thousand units. State farms were told that they must struggle for it. All were exhorted to bear it in mind as the spring ploughing approached. 'Putting thought first and combining management, technique and science' was the method practised by one commune.

An example of a general agricultural slogan with more limited application, is 'A bit more preparation, a bit more harvest', which began to be used before the spring ploughing, and again as the early harvest time approached.

A different aspect of agricultural production was promoted with the slogan 'Study science, use science, and develop agriculture'.

The first editorial on this campaign came in, as seems usual, as this kind of activity was already being promoted in different parts of the country. As in the case of the 'Learn from the Liberation Army' editorial it was accompanied by appropriate news stories from various places. National organizations joined in. The Agricultural Department's Broadcasting Bureau and the Scientific Technical Alliance jointly called on all provinces and special districts to increase their propagation of scientific technique. The importance of cadres' taking part in this work began to be regularly emphasized, and methods of doing so described. Experience began to be 'summed up' and 'generalized', and a particular organizational form was adopted—the scientific experiment small group. That name was not, however, at this time, used as a slogan itself.

Another prime target of sectional slogans was the Young Communist League. A conference of the Central Committee of the League was reported as raising the following slogans for its work in 1964:

Raise the red flag of Mao Tse-tung's thinking still higher
Study the Liberation Army
Actively move young people to take part in the socialist education
    movement and the produce and economize movement
Fiercely grasp class education
Forcefully create 'four-good' branches
Establish, unite and educate youth front activities
Promote the revolutionary competition of comparing, studying,
    catching up and helping
Strive still further to revolutionize youth.

(This is not a complete list of the tasks decided on by the conference.)

In an entirely different field one finds an example of the width of the coverage of the government. In a report on a conference of the small arts practitioners—the story-tellers, singers and cross-talk performers —is adopted the slogan 'Create the new, edit the new, tell the new, sing the new'.

The fifth group of slogans illustrate the production of slogans for particular activities in various fields. A good example was provided in May by the Forestry Department. They adopted a policy of 'Three parts make, seven parts tend' for the creation of forests. Later in the month this slogan was taken up by five provinces as a system for looking after the early rice plants.

In hygiene work there was the standing slogan 'Eliminate the four evils' (flies, mosquitoes, rats and snails).

In the industrial field, economy was emphasized by the raising of the slogan 'The word "Save" in the lead'.

Inevitably, various demands were made of cadres. The principal object was to get cadres to leave their offices and get down to the place where production work was actually being carried out. 'Get down to the bottom level' ran the call. They were also asked to hold fewer meetings and to stop asking for so many reports from the lower levels. On other occasions they were enjoined to practise the 'four togethers', a slogan of long standing, prescribing methods of establishing close and firm links with the masses.

In April came a call to cadres to 'keep a cool head', however warm their hearts might be. The term occurred in a report from Canton, where one cadre was said to have been dissatisfied with a very successful harvest, and by study to have discovered contradictions the resolution of which would lead to even higher production.

A different slant on cadre activities was provided by the Youth League which had to deal with the problem of retiring those who were getting too long in the tooth and bringing on the new blood. For this branches were recommended to use three principles: choose courageously, combine the old with the new, and keep hold of essential workers.

The sixth group of slogans derive from local activities. Participation in campaigns at the lower levels produces a rich crop of activity which finds expression in slogan, motto or code-form. Some are not heard of again. Others are taken up and given extended use. The richest source is again agriculture. One of the most interesting stories came from the

Nanp'ing Special Area in Fukien. (This is a large area comprising one city and thirteen counties.) At the previous new year they had held a meeting, and concluded that their political work was falling behind. Some cadres had gone as far as to call political work 'soft' and economic work 'hard'. In May they had begun a political campaign, with 'the four firsts' as its principal content. The cadres had had to study the works of Mao Tse-tung, and thereafter the general sanction for the cadres and members of the communes became 'Obey the words of Chairman Mao; take the socialist, collectivized road pointed out by Chairman Mao; be the good cadre (or member) that Chairman Mao desires'. In their general political work they 'used living people and living deeds to promote a living education'. For their work among the communes they invented the following methods:

'Tell three bitternesses; remember three histories; settle three accounts; make three comparisons; and invite three old ones to tell revolutionary stories.'

The three bitternesses were those of feudal exploitation, capitalist exploitation, and poor peasant economics. The three histories were the changes in the villages, the development of the communes, and the reform of the family. The three accounts to be settled were the political, the economic and the cultural. The three comparisons were of past and present, the good and the bad models of today, and the present and the future. The three old ones were old army men, old poor peasants, and old cadres.

These cadres also ran emulation campaigns to produce 'four-good brigades' and 'six-good commune members', and propagated examples of 'good people and good deeds'.

At the end of the year, in this special area, one hundred thousand people had become 'six-good' and five thousand units had become 'four-good'. To maintain the momentum of this movement they invented a further device by appointing 'the three officials' (a reporting official, a branch education official and a propaganda official) so that responsibility for future development was clearly allocated. Some brigades established a 'three-day' system. The tenth of each month had originally been Party day; the twentieth of the month was League day; now they added a third day, a 'Love the country, love the commune, love the brigade day', when they discussed their work, both past and future.

In March a story from Kweichow Province mentioned a method of instruction which was afterwards taken up on a large scale by the army. This was the 'one taking two' or 'one taking three' method whereby one member of an advanced team transmitted his experience to two or three persons attached to him for the purpose. The system was evidently also in use elsewhere, particularly in Shansi both in commune and factory. The army adopted it, specifically referring to it as 'the Shansi movement' and saying it was worthy of imitation. For army purposes it was modified to one soldier helping one other and called 'one helps one' or 'one pair red'. It was directed to linking those who were 'four-good' and 'five-good' and those who were not.

The experience of an individual commune in Shansi should not be overlooked. After the cotton harvest some teams were reported to have started looking to their own selfish interest and following a policy of selling to the state only the bare necessary minimum of cotton. In consequence the Party committee undertook local education work in patriotism and internationalism. Coincident with these events, there appeared the news of the help that China was giving to Cuba. Seizing their opportunity, the committee explained their idea of the significance of this news and put forward the slogan 'Support Cuba, sell more cotton'. The result was said to be a quick change of heart by all members of the commune. (This is a noteworthy case indeed: how few years before, during the Japanese war, peasants in remote parts of Shansi had not even known what the word 'Japanese' meant.)

In Szechuan, a subsidiary activity involving cadres was described. This was the 'two-five' system of working. (Many similar systems had been devised in other parts of the country in previous years.) The 'two-five' system was part of the general 'Lead on the job' movement, which had been started to encourage cadres to take part in physical work. The 'two-five' refers to a division of the seven days of the week into five days spent in physical production—in this case the running of ex-perimental plots—and two days on office work and study. Among other objects, this division permitted them to implement another policy, known as 'the three combinations'—combining physical work with scientific experiment, combining labouring, being on the spot and investigating and researching, and combining work in a definite place with work over a larger area.

At the same time the Provincial Party Secretary was starting a similar campaign in Kiangsi. He called on all areas to make their emulation movement work more practically by implementing the 'five down to earths'. In Kiangsu there were six pieces of work to be done 'down to earth'. On another day cadres in a Kiangsi brigade, an advanced model for guaranteeing high and stable production, were putting into effect another method of leadership. Theirs was the 'early morning study, forenoon work, afternoon investigate, and evening help' method.

Leadership methods were also prescribed in Fukien. There every level of cadre was required to operate a 'three dont's and three downs' policy. These were:

> don't wildly call meetings
> don't wildly give out jobs
> don't wildly demand material from the lower levels
> do all work down to the production team
> do ideological work down to the individual
> make production measures go down to the ground level.

In Liaoning they were just propagating the 'three ditch' experience, named after three villages, all with 'ditch' in their names and encouraging the correct adjustment of 'the three relationships and the use of a 'four not-plant' system. The relationships were

> one, agriculture, forestry and pasturage;
> two, present and future production;
> three, high production and stable production.

Two of their troubles in the past had been the use of bad seed and failure to prepare the ground adequately. They summarized the needs of their experience in four conditions—preparation of the ground, selection of good seed, testing of seed, and treatment of the seed by chemicals—and developed the 'four not plant' system to prevent planting in the absence of the four conditions.

In Hopei a well-known production brigade, the leading brigade of its county, was reported to have become self-satisfied, which was leading to deficiencies in their work. The local party branch helped to put this right by organizing a general 'five comparisons, five examinations and five look-to's' movement.

In the world of industry, local slogans were also being created. In the emulation movement, a Wuhan cotton factory adopted their own slogan 'Don't let one man drop out of the team'. In a Nanking wireless factory the current slogan was 'to make a resolution, make it on using your skill'. In a Szechuan food factory, it was discovered that the amount of pig bristle being wasted each year was equal to $2\frac{1}{2}$ chin ($3\frac{1}{4}$ lb) of fertilizer for 680,000 mou (110,000 acres) of land per year. This was carefully explained to the workers and a movement began with the slogan 'Don't waste a single pig bristle'. On the walls of a Shanghai spinning factory were found the three injunctions 'Before you do your work, first study the Party policy', 'Before making a decision first look into the real circumstances', and 'Before doing things first listen to the opinion of the masses'.

In Shansi, at a conference of 'five-good' enterprises and 'five-good' brigades and teams and workers' representatives, a coal-digging team were selected as the province's leading unit. The whole province was called on to study them and their 'put the word "strict" in the lead' and 'absolutely never careless' working style. This team was notable for adopting a 'five-ones' system for maintaining safety, referring thereby to the five last activities which they carried out below ground, each team leader being in each case the last one to do each thing and so take responsibility for that activity.

In a Chengtu (Szechuan) embroidery factory, they selected 'the whole factory mosts'—signifying in each 'most' the area of superiority of the particular model.

The Chinese army creates its own slogans, usually at a high level, to judge by their propagation in the *Liberation Army Daily*. A particular case of army sloganizing which *The People's Daily* reported is worth describing in some detail. The slogans derived from a course of study of the works of Marx, Engels, Lenin and Stalin by high-ranking army cadres. The main part of studying, it was said, was reading, discussing and thinking. Some comrades, according to the report, made this still more concrete in the form of 'three readings, three relations, one discussion and one writing'. The readings were:

> One, read the whole work, understand the main meaning and find the important questions
> Two, read the important parts and understand their spiritual quality
> Three, read the important paragraphs, ask questions, join the thought together and get a deep impression.

The relations were:

> One, relate to Chairman Mao's works and directives
> Two, relate to the facts of the present struggle
> Three, relate to the thinking of the individual.

The 'one discussion' was 'to take the state of one's own mind, questions and realizations and discuss them with comrades, or discuss them with or explain them to the lower ranks'.

The 'one writing' was 'to annotate the text, note selected paragraphs, make notes of one's impressions, and write essays'.

These examples of 'local' slogans do not exhaust the subject as it appears in *The People's Daily* for the period under review, although they do give a fair impression of their variety, and the generality of coinage.

The final category of slogan has already frequently been mentioned but that vast source of slogan material which is constituted by 'models' has still barely been touched. The conscious search for models of all forms of approved activity was going on in Yenan days and has been going on even more vigorously since the present government set itself up. It was going on at all levels throughout this period. The activity of establishing models is itself the subject of slogans:

> One person has merit, everybody congratulates; one person
>   makes progress, everybody learns from him
> Praise good people and good deeds
> Put praise first, make criticism an addition
> Forcefully praise advanced persons
> Widely set up models.

and so on they run. And models are set up on the national, provincial, county, town, factory, shop, commune, brigade, and team levels, and, it would appear, in every form of approved activity. A model may appear nationally, for a national campaign, or locally for a purely local campaign. It may be an organization or an individual. The slogan then becomes 'Learn from . . .' whatever or whoever it is. This conscious fabrication of slogans is multifarious and unending. It may concern 'model' work. It may concern 'model' study of the works of Mao Tse-tung. It may concern outstanding examples of selfless conduct.

Two of the models celebrated during this period must be mentioned. They are the village of Tachai, and the oilfield of Tach'ing. Both were advanced as national symbols—the former for relying entirely on their own efforts to cope with and recover from the effects of natural disasters, the latter for being a native-produced, modern and efficient industry. 'Learn from Tachai' and 'Learn from Tach'ing' have been national slogans ever since, and slogans of the greatest generality. (They have been adapted during the 'Cultural Revolution' and now symbolize the application of the principles of Mao Tse-tung.)

This, then, roughly describes a selection of the slogans actually used during this period. The questions must now be discussed whether the slogans are efficient in terms of themselves and the ways of using them and what effect they were likely to have as propounding the central task of the 'forward-going' movement of the revolution.

As a slogan for work-appraisal expresses it, 'Put praise first, make criticism an addition.' One problem for an industrializing government, or even a simple nationalizing government, is to express its policies in such a way that at the lowest levels actual physical tasks are presented to those who have to do the work. The national plans of many countries seem to have foundered on insufficient grasp of this fact. This is not simply a matter of arriving at a policy and then deriving from it the jobs which will achieve it. A prior requirement is that the policy-makers shall understand the practical possibilities at the lowest levels, so that policy is conceived in terms of attainable goals.

Despite the somewhat chequered history of the policies of the central authorities of the People's Republic of China, the impression remains that this problem has been understood, even although on some occasions it has been forgotten. In the first place, understanding of it was forced on the Chinese Communists during the period of the Kiangsi Soviet.[1] Thereafter, it was formally expressed in terms of the cadre policy adopted in 1938,[2] and when a cadre-force building programme was subsequently drawn up the duties of the cadres were seen not only in terms of what the Central Committee might want, but also of what the people amongst whom they worked could be expected to achieve.[3] This attitude was preserved in the Common Programme of 1949 and also in the 1954 Constitution. If one refers to this attitude as 'realism'

[1] Mao, *Selected Works*, vol. I, 'Pay attention to economic work', esp. pp. 134–5.
[2] Mao, *ibid*. vol. II, 'The Role of the Chinese Communist Party in the National War', p. 201 'Cadres Policy'.
[3] Mao, *ibid.*, vol. III, 'Some Questions Concerning Methods of Leadership' esp. p. 120, para. 6.

it may plausibly be asserted that the first five-year plan, despite its successes, saw a loss of realism, since the plan was insufficiently adapted from the Soviet model, e.g. in the production of technically qualified personnel. One result of this falling-off was the strikes which took place in 1956. These and other related experiences cast doubt on the whole planning process as conceived in China at that time. After the experiences of 1959–61 equivalent doubts should reasonably have been entertained. In all these cases, however, the explanation of the discrepancies between expectation and performance included substantial criticism, either directly or by implication, of the methods of task-articulation at the lowest levels. This was sometimes unfair on the low-level cadres. For example, the criticism of cadres which followed the Great Leap Forward did not seem to take account of the obvious effects of the optimism of the central authorities. Nevertheless, this criticism was itself a re-affirmation of realism in Chinese Communist policies.

One of the striking aspects of the present survey is the continuing realization shown in the organization of campaign activity that it is at the bottom levels that success has to be sought, once a campaign has been decided on. The accent is always put on some real activity, so that no person is left in doubt as to what he should do in order to further the current task. The central organizers seem aware of the possibility of substituting the raising of slogans for acting upon them, and support their propaganda with copious news stories of local activities so that local inspiration is passed on and no small area can fail to have the opportunity of identifying itself with similar areas as part of the greater whole.

From this point of view, the emulation campaign was a good one. It fitted in well with the background slogans, and derived happily from the necessary concentration on economic work which had preceded it. It allowed for local initiative and contained within its main slogan opportunity for varying the particular point of main attraction, thus freshening up efforts, without detracting from overall objectives. Equally, it dovetailed with non-economic work and could be applied to all forms of activity. The spreading of 'advanced' experience was one of the main methods then open to the government of improving general standards and the emulation campaign had the further advantage of encouraging this through local activism.

In practice, it was not as simple to operate as it may sound.

For example, some news items about the campaign reveal the kind of difficulty that was met in some localities. In some cases representatives who were sent to other enterprises in order to study advanced experience spent their time sitting in offices writing up notes, instead of getting onto the factory floor and finding out just what the processes they were supposed to study involved. Others who went elsewhere to study 'advanced' experience would not, on their return, pass it on to others. Some peasants, when they were required to make comparisons with the crops of others, merely expressed words of praise, when the crops inspected were in fact inferior to their own, and they might have given advice. In some places, then, a fair amount of local work was needed to bring the campaign home, and to get some positive results from it. In other places, it appears that the process of comparing and studying was taken up so energetically that the effects of coming and going began to be felt on the enterprises concerned: at one point a new slogan had to be raised: 'Study on your own doorstep.'

Nevertheless, here was a campaign which was translatable into action with verifiable results.

At the same time, it would have been improved if it could have been articulated within a more specific general framework. If we admit that national construction will take several decades, that admission seems to make all the more necessary the setting of targets on local and national scales and their co-ordination. For their own reasons, the government was not at this time publishing national production figures, so that this national co-ordination could not be achieved openly. The various reports of factories and communes fulfilling and overfulfilling their plans show that the individual efforts were not short of any yardstick at all, but the general impression is one of sporadic efforts. In view of the high social contribution which the worker at the bottom level made in the form of surplus labour, any satisfaction would have been increased by the linking of the general with the particular.

This is particularly important because of the possibility of 'slogan-fatigue'. The marginal benefit of exhortation falls off quickly. The collection of slogans from what is itself a central organ of publicity naturally leads to a much greater density of 'sloganeering' than one would meet at the lower levels. The further from the centre, the less the concentration, one would expect, and the effect of the examples given should not be allowed to obscure this. But this was the fourteenth year of the revolution, and it had been attempting mass mobilization in pursuit of very numerous goals throughout that period. The danger of slogan-fatigue existed throughout the nation, but the worst part of the danger lay in how far that fatigue might be felt by the lower-level cadres, and the extent that it might be counter-productive.

Here arises the main question in connection with the overlaying of the 'Learn from the Liberation Army' campaign. Despite the overt integration of the two it cannot be denied that these campaigns are different in quality. The most obvious expression of the 'emulation' campaign was in economic work. The 'Learn from the Liberation Army' campaign and its derivative upsurge, the campaign to study the works of Mao, were so to speak 'whole man', 'whole society', 'whole revolution' campaigns. By pursuing the goal of revolutionization, they placed productivity in an ideological context.

In view of the events of 1966 and afterwards, it may be asked whether these successive campaigns were in competition, the more particularly as their two ideas are now plainly differentiated and identified with individuals. Clearly some competition was there. But there would still be no grounds for expecting irresolvable conflict to result from it: what could be expected was a certain amount of conflict, but while few disturbances with an ideological basis had not in the past involved the casting out of Party members, this had been done without the loss of Party unity. In 1964 it might as justifiably be said that a comprehensive ideological campaign was due, so that the 'New Economic Policy' of the previous three years might be put back into the perspective of the construction of socialism. It is true that the form of the new campaign—learning from the army, which had since 1960 been undergoing intensive in-doctrination in the writings of Mao—might give us pause for thought, and equally true that occasional items of news, such as that dealing with the methods of study adopted by 'senior army officers' for the study not only of Mao but of Marx, Engels, Lenin and Stalin, might have covert implications bearing on the question. But the mere fact of the new campaign cannot support this case. On the contrary, 'revolution-ization' might well have been generally agreed as the central task of the revolution at that stage, in preparation for a renewed attempt to increase the amount of savings, say in the context of a new five-year plan. The very variety of campaigns in existence might be adduced as grounds for believing that there was a need to establish greater overall coherence. If such was the hope, however, it must be said that while the new campaign did introduce for a period a certain simplicity into the 'tasks of the revolution' as advanced through the columns of *The People's Daily*, at the lower levels there was a clear danger of confusion. The general slogan 'Learn from the Liberation Army' not only is not itself an energizing slogan, it is not a clear slogan. It does not say what has to be learned. For these tasks, other slogans have to be coined. These slogans are in fact civilian adaptations of military slogans. Consider then the position of the lower level cadre and the worker or peasant. Before the new campaign began he was immediately involved in 'emulation' activities of some variety: the four elements, comparing, studying, catching up and helping, all required separate attention; any of them was liable to be the subject of 'model' selection and imitation; this was linked with the selection of five-good units and workers. These movements might also enter his life outside the sphere of work. In the background were the socialist education movement, and the three great revolutionary movements, and associated with all the campaign to study the works of Mao.

Just how many of these campaigns any worker was involved in would naturally vary, and how they were put to him locally would be all-important. But he could not avoid hearing about them, being involved in some, and knowing people connected with others.

As soon as the 'Learn from the Liberation Army' campaign began, he would at least come into contact with the 'four firsts' and the 'three-eight working-style'. Anything more than minimal promotion of this campaign might lead to contact with a large body of new slogans. The number of 'active' slogans that were then about may be judged by the slogans already cited which the Army and the civilians were to learn from each other.

As opposed to the worker, the cadre was in theory not so free to choose his activities. Local circumstances allowed a certain leeway in the methods to be adopted, but some methods had to be adopted, or the cadre was to be found wanting.

It is in this context that the 'Learn from the Liberation Army' campaign takes on new meaning. The 'emulation' slogans were not simple (in some places they were misunderstood) although their prime activity was simple. The new slogans were more complicated and, if given effect, far-reaching. (In these circumstances the adventitious foreign policy campaigns, requiring large-scale mobilization, probably provided a measure of relief.) At the same time, a possible 'contradiction' between economic and ideological work was emerging which might lead to further confusion. The core of the new campaign was political and the core of its politics the study of Mao's works. In so far as the new tasks required organized study and new practices in productive work they were immediately competitive with that work, as it was being carried on. In the long run, to be sure, heightened political consciousness might generate a climate in which productivity would leap ahead. But the immediate effect of the new activities was likely to be hiatal. Moreover, in re-orientating the structure which had been built up since the emergency, they had to overcome the memory of the recent past, in which emphasis on ideology had been associated with a general hiatus in production.

The new object-lessons were the political heroes of the armed forces, and the two civilian models, the agricultural one, Ta-chai, and the industrial one, the Yumen oilfield. In both the latter the revolutionary spirit was immanent. Their essential quality was self-activation: having the right basic attitudes they were able to exert themselves wholeheartedly in their economic tasks. They were thus living examples of the proposition that giving first place to politics proved itself in the better performance of economic tasks. The army provided a more general example of the same position. They showed in detail how to develop a revolutionary will and apply it in any circumstances.

Evidence was then not wanting that cadre performance was giving rise to complaint. As we have seen, campaigns existed to try to get cadres to be more active and less bureaucratic. Many cadres found it hard to get out of their offices, for good or bad reasons; but whatever the reasons, office-bound cadres were not good cadres. Some cadres were officious, some had bureaucratic manners. Later on evidence was to show that in 1964 a major movement, called 'the four clean-ups', was introduced to reprove and often purge cadres throughout the country.[1] But, while remedial measures were obviously called for, it should not be overlooked that complaints about cadre malfeasance of

---

[1] See 'Letter from the Central Committee of the Chinese Communist Party' of 20 February 1967, in Peking Review, no. 9, 1967, which says that cadres removed from office in the 'four clean-up' movement 'are not allowed to counter-attack in revenge'.

various sorts had been common ever since the establishment of the People's Republic, and, for that matter, before it.

For the moment this was, perhaps, malfeasance of the lesser sort. There were also the cadres who called political work 'soft' and economic work 'hard'. Some of them might know that the army itself had not satisfactorily adjusted its relations between political work and technical work.[1] And it was these cadres who might pause at the introduction of the new object lessons.

The last previous campaign to put ideology in command of production had preceded extreme economic difficulties. Since then the tasks of government had seemed less amenable to attack by storm than by siege, the work of construction increasingly complex, the tradition of success no longer there as a support. Once the 'forward development of revolutionary movement' had been put in question that movement was made to seem more subjective than the earlier formulae for it had implied. The impulse to minimize any conflict with economic work would accordingly be strong, and would be encouraged by the failure of the 'Learn from the Liberation Army' campaign completely to supplant the emulation campaign. The effect was not what the 1943 instruction of the Central Committee on methods of leadership had advised—the masses were not being rallied around one major slogan and a small number of subsidiary slogans with a clear notion of priority.

Since *The People's Daily* was calling for the restoration of priority to ideological considerations its call would be met. The nature of the response, however, could easily be confined to advancing slogans, in the absence of any new sanction; the models selected need not be those fulfilling the criteria of the centre.

And here an additional significance of the slogan 'Learn from the Liberation Army' emerged. The army was the foundation of 'the dictatorship of the proletariat', and the ultimate guarantor that its policies would be implemented. It was in this period that soldiers were seconded to the civilian ministries to help them organize the new political departments that were to ensure the supremacy of the spirit of revolutionization.[2] Conditions were being created for the restoration

---

[1] See the editorial in *The Liberation Army Daily* of 1 August 1966, for reference to three major struggles over the place of technique in military training.

[2] They were set up in 1964 (see *The People's Daily* of 1 March 1964). *The People's Daily* of 18.v.1965 reported that 200,000 servicemen were at work in the new political network.

of clarity in the pursuit of revolutionary goals, but in circumstances suggesting that the revolution had, in fact, been interrupted.

THE OPTICK ARTISTS OF
CHIANGSU

JOSEPH NEEDHAM, F.R.S., AND LU GWEI-DJEN

Every province and city, indeed every famous district in China, has its own local history and topography carefully recorded by local scholars in the form of books which in some cases go back to the Middle Ages, and have often been amplified, edited and re-edited through recent centuries. These local histories contain a wealth of information about science and technology as well as many other things, but so far they have been very little used in the work that has been done on the history of these subjects in Chinese culture. For example, we knew of one mediaeval bridge which had employed cast-iron columns and beams, but a search by Lo Ying through the local 'gazetteers', as they are called, revealed a dozen more, all of Sung, Yuan and Ming date, i.e. from the tenth century onwards. The use of this source material is unfortunately difficult in this country, because in general these local gazetteers were not collected by British sinologists in the past and our libraries are rather poor in them.

During a visit to the provincial museum at Suchow in Chiangsu in the autumn of 1964, we became acquainted with the life-stories of two men of the seventeenth century who achieved great renown in southeast China by their mastery of spectacle-making and the construction of optical apparatus. Their lives were recorded in the local history but their names did not get into the national literature. Although their dates are not very certainly known, the decades of their activity are fairly clear. So, for example, the older one, Po Yü, was born not later than 1610 and was active more or less in the period between 1628 and 1640. The younger man, Sun Yün-ch'iu, was born some time between 1628 and 1644, and died between 1662 and 1735.[1] Sun's most probable life-span was between 1630 and 1663, for it is known that he died young, and it is fairly certain that he was active in the decade 1650 to 1660.

[1] This late date enters in only because it was the end of the K'ang-hsi and Yung-cheng reign-periods, and (as we shall see) there is no reason to think that Sun Yün-ch'iu lived into the eighteenth century at all.

Let us first read the brief biographies of these two men from the *Wu-hsien chih* (History and Topography of Wu-hsien, i.e. Suchow).[1] They both come in chapter 75 B, which includes the *lieh chuan*, or biographies, of men of art (*i shu*):

Po Yü's *tzu* name was Tzu-chio and he came from Ch'angchow. He lived in Chia-hsing. His knowledge was excellent and profound. He understood all sorts of things, such as the variations of *Yin* and *Yang*,[2] astrology and astronomy, strategy and tactics, agriculture and animal husbandry (*t'un-mou*), the manufacture of things, engraving and carving. He was a man whose hands could perform what his mouth could not explain, and whose mouth could explain what he could not express in writing. People were sorry for him and respected him, but no one could understand how he came to have so much knowledge. In the Ch'ung-chen reign-period (1628 to 1643) when the rebels invaded Anch'ing (i.e. Anhui) the Hsün-fu (Provincial Governor) Chang Kuo-wei commissioned Po Yü to make bronze cannon. These had a range of 30 *li* and whenever they were shot off they did great execution because (the gunners) had telescopes (*ch'ien li ching*) which showed just where the enemy had concentrated. Po Yü also made water-raising machinery (*shui ch'e*) and pumps (*shui ch'ung*) for extinguishing fires, as well as explosive mines (*ti lei*) and spring-trap guns (*ti nu*, literally earth cross-bows[3]) etc., which destroyed countless numbers of the enemy forces. (Chang) Kuo-wei recommended him to the Imperial Court but the authorities gave him no reward. Instead Po Yü retired to Wu-men (Suchow), his homeland, and lived in a humble house where he continued to make all kinds of instruments. Once he constructed an armillary sphere (*hun t'ien i*) planetarium, not more than a foot in circumference, yet the sun was shown and the moon waxing and waning, together with the lunar mansion constellations and the planets moving forward and retrograding, all without the slightest inexactitude. In building this, he used a straight line (or thread) to divide the circumference and get the angles right, regulating in such a manner the varying distances north, south, east and west, so that although they might really be as much as a thousand million *li*, it was in the model as if they were less than a foot; in short, he used the methods of geometry.[4]

[1] The first edition of this book appeared in 1642, too early therefore to contain the biographies, but a revision was made by Sun P'ei in 1691 and this time was doubtless that of their compilation, not at all too late to profit from the local records then existing.

[2] On Chinese natural philosophy in general reference may be made to our *Science and Civilisation in China*, vol. 2, pp. 253 ff., 273 ff. Hereinafter abbreviated as *SCC*.

[3] The old term was carried over into the firearm era.

[4] It may be significant that the expression used here is *kou ku fa*, implying geometry as it was known in traditional China (cf. *SSC*, vol. 3, passim), not the Euclidean geometry introduced by the Jesuits (see p. 209 below), which was known as *chi ho hsüeh*. The expression *kou ku* was retained however as a literary term for all geometry, as may be seen in book titles of the late nineteenth century, of which we have half a dozen in our own working library.

Before proceeding to comment upon this interesting passage, it will be best to examine the parallel biography of Sun Yün-ch'iu. The *Wu-hsien chih* says in the same chapter:

Sun Yün-ch'iu had two *tzu* names, Wen-yü and Ssu-pin. He lived at Hu-ch'iu (Shan) . . . He used to use rock crystal to make spectacles (*yen ching*) for people to aid their vision, whether old or young, with confused sight (*hua*), or of the far- or near-sighted types, etc., corresponding to their need, and never by a hair's breadth wrong. Those who heard of it paid no attention to the high cost, but bought. To Wen K'ang-i of T'ien-t'ai, who was afflicted with myopia, (Sun) Yün-ch'iu presented a telescope (*ch'ien li ching*) and took him to the top of Hu-ch'iu (Shan) to test it—thence they could see from far away all the towers and the terraces, the pagodas and the temples of the city (of Suchow), just as if they were quite close; moreover they could see the mountain tops of T'ien-p'ing (Shan),[1] Lingyen (Shan)[2] and Ch'iunglung (Shan)[3] each more beautiful than the last in the jade-like caerulean distance. When he had done looking at all these lovely things, he was delighted and exclaimed 'This is like magic! That art could reach this pitch!' But (Sun) Yün-ch'iu smiled and answered 'This is not the last of my wonders.' Then, taking out several dozen other pices of apparatus, he showed him (*a*) 'a keeping-in-the-eye glass' (*ts'un mu ching*) which increased (size and) brightness a hundredfold, so that with earnest gaze there was nothing too small to be seen, and (*b*) a 'myriad transformations (literally flowers) glass' (*wan hua ching*), an optick glass which could make one shape turn into a dozen other shapes. There were also (*c*) 'mandarin duck' or 'one-of-a-pair glasses' (*yuan ching*); (*d*) (a pair of?) 'half-glasses' (*pan ching*); (*e*) some 'glasses that turned the daylight into evening' (*hsi yang ching*); (*f*) some 'many-faces glasses' (*to mien ching*); (*g*) some 'illusory-appearance glasses' (*huan jung ching*); (*h*) a glass for the investigation of exceedingly tiny things (*ch'a wei ching*); (*i*) a light-projecting apparatus (*fang kuang ching*); (*j*) a 'brightening-the-night glass' (*yeh ming ching*), etc., etc., all so magically ingenious that one could never have thought of it. He (Sun Yün-ch'iu) also wrote a portfolio of manuscript entitled *Ching Shih* (History of Optick Glasses). He asked the craftsmen of the city to make optical instruments according to his methods, and thus they began to circulate widely in the world.

Beyond this, we know very little indeed about the lives of either of these two men. Our colleague, Wang Chin-kuang,[4] who lives in Hangchow, has searched other local records[5] but without much

---

[1] About 6·5 miles away.   [2] About 9·5 miles away.   [3] About 12·5 miles away.

[4] Author of an interesting paper on the two men in question which we saw only after having copied the passages from the book in the museum. We then had the pleasure of meeting Dr Wang while at Hangchow.

[5] Such as the *Wu-men piao yin* (very rare), *Wu-men pu ch'eng*, *Su-chou fu chih*, etc.

success. We know nothing else about Po Yü, but it appears that Sun Yün-ch'iu came from a poor family and when young earned his living by selling drug plants in the street. His mother nevertheless was an educated woman and wrote the preface for his book; it is most unfortunate that this has not survived. In later times Suchow was a city especially famous for its spectacle-makers, and there is one shop still in Shanghai which began as a branch office of a Suchow firm established in 1719.

The question arises whether Sun Yün-ch'iu could have been a direct pupil of Po Yü. It is known that Sun died at the early age of thirty-three, so if the most probable dates of his life are 1630 to 1663 he would have been entering the principal decade of his activity in 1650, by which time Po Yü would have been a man of about forty or forty-five, with the main period of his activity behind him (1630 to 1640). It is noteworthy that the Manchu conquest of 1644 lies like a shadow across the careers of both these men, Po Yü having been more active just before it and Sun Yün-ch'iu after it. If Po Yü was born as early as 1600 he may have had two decades of activity, between 1620 and 1640. It is quite likely that Po Yü out-lived Sun Yün-ch'iu, dying perhaps in his sixties between 1670 and 1680. Thus the date of the *Ching shih* would have been about 1660; we do not know whether it was ever printed.

One of the most interesting and important questions which present themselves is whether Po Yü could have been a Chinese Lippershey. We need not here go into the general history of the knowledge of lenses and mirrors in Chinese civilization, for it has been given in another place.[1] Suffice it to say that much quite sophisticated knowledge of reflection and refraction phenomena grew up from the Warring States period (fourth century B.C.) onwards, and that by the tenth century all the four chief geometrical forms of lenses were known.[2] Besides this, it may be taken as established that the invention of spectacles for correcting eye defects was a Western one stemming from Italy at the end of the thirteenth century and finding its way with rapidity during the Ming period to South-east Asia and to China.[3] Putting all these facts together, it is evident that any Chinese artisan or scholar interested in natural phenomena during the early decades of the seventeenth century could have assembled biconvex lenses in such a way as to give the effect

[1] *SCC*, vol. 4, pt 1, pp. 81 ff.   [2] *SCC*, vol. 4, pt 1, p. 117.
[3] *SCC*, vol. 4, pt 1, p. 120.

of 'the proximity of the top of the church steeple' that the Dutch apprentice is said to have obtained.

Exactly who was the true inventor of the telescope in the West is of course a matter of great dubiety, and now perhaps impossible to be determined.[1] Thomas Digges, in his preface to the *Pantometria* of 1571, seems to have claimed the honour for his father, its author, Leonard Digges (born *c.* 1510), saying (in celebrated words):[2]

> my Father by his continuall painfull practises, assisted with Demonstrations Mathematicall, was able, and sundrie times hath, by proportionall Glasses duely situate in convenient Angles, not only discovered things farre off, read letters, numbred peeces of money with the verye coyne and superscription thereof, cast by some of his freends of purpose upon Downes in open Fields, but also seven Myles off declared what hath beene doone at that instant in private places . . .

This would refer to the fifties and sixties of the century, for the father seems to have died in the year the book was printed. What may be his own statement appears in the body of it:

> Maruelyouse are the conclusions that may be perfourmed by glasses concaue and conuex of circulare and parabolicall fourmes, using for multiplication of beames sometime the ayde of glasses transparent, which by fraction should unite or dissipate the images or figures presented by the reflection of other. By these kinds of glasses or rather frames of them, placed in due angles, ye may not only set out the proportion of an whole region, you represent before your eye the lively image of euery towne, village, etc., and that in as little or great space or place as ye will prescribe, but also augment and dilate any parcell thereof, so that whereas at the firste appearance an whole towne shall present it selfe so small and compacte together that ye shall not discerne any difference of streets, ye may by applycation of glasses in due proportion cause any peculiare house or roume thereof dilate, and shew it selfe in as ample fourme as the whole towne first appeared, so that ye shall discerne any trifle or reade any letter lying there open, especially if the sonne beames may come unto it, as playnly as if you wer corporally present, although it be distante from you as farre as eye can discrye . . .

Singer's comment was that Digges was the first to whom could definitely be attributed the construction of a bilenticular system; other historians have been less impressed. But Digges' contemporaries, such

---

[1] Cf. the standard histories of the telescope (Favaro; King; Ronchi; Rosen; Singer), and of the microscope (Clay & Court; Rooseboom). See also Gerland, pp. 340 ff.

[2] '*A Geometrical Practise, named* Pantometria . . .' London: Bynneman, 1571, p. 5 of the unpaged preface; 1591 ed., p. 2 of the unpaged preface.

as William Bourne, accepted the claim, and John Dee (T. Digges' tutor at Cambridge) foresaw important military uses for 'perspective Glasses' as early as 1573. To us Leonard Digges seems a strong contender.[1] If he really made a telescope it must have been of the Galilean type with a biconcave eyepiece, not the doubly biconvex Keplerian type, as otherwise the image would have been inverted.

Then there were stirrings in Italy. The famous 'natural magician', G. B. della Porta (1535 to 1615), if we may so call him, spoke oracular words (as usual) in the later twenty-book edition of his *Magia Naturalis* (1589).[2]

With a Concave (glass) you shall see small things afar off, very clearly; with a Convex, things neerer to be greater, but more obscurely: if you know how to fit them both together, you shall see both things afar off, and things neer hand, both greater and clearly.[3]

And again,

I spake of *Ptolomies* Glass, or rather spectacle, whereby for six hundred miles he saw the enemies ships coming; and I shall attempt to show how that might be done, that we may know our friends some miles off, and read the smallest letters at a great distance, which can hardly be seen. A thing needful for mans use, and grounded upon the Opticks. And this may be done very easily; but the matter is not so to be published too easily; yet perspective will make it clear.[4]

After which he goes on to speak of a biconcave lens, presumably the eye-piece of his bilenticular combination.

And if you know how to multiply Lenticulars, I fear not but for a hundred paces you may see the smallest letters . . .[5]

Opinions have been rather divided about della Porta's claim, but his contemporaries Kepler and Stelluti accepted it in some measure,[6] while

---

[1] His son Thomas (died c. 1595) was the civil engineer in charge of the construction of Dover Harbour, but he also ventured at sea. 'In 1590 the Queen issued a commission to [Sir] Richard Greynevile of Stow, Cornwall, to Piers Edgecombe, Thomas [Digges] and others, authorising them to fit out and equip a fleet for the discovery of the lands in the antarctic seas, and especially to [sail to] the dominions of the Great "Cam of Cathaia",' (D.N.B.) This was none other than the Wan-Li emperor. So far as we know, the expedition never came to anything, but twenty years later English ships were beginning to touch at Chinese and Japanese ports, notably John Saris in 1613 and John Weddell in 1637. See further in Cordier, vol. 3, pp. 191, 198 ff., 211, 212 ff.

[2] Cf. Thorndike, vol. 6, pp. 418 ff.

[3] Bk. 17, ch. 10, para. 7.

[4] *Ibid*, ch. 11, para. 1.

[5] *Ibid*, ch. 10, para. 6.

[6] See Rosen, pp. 19, 21.

Caspar Schott supported it in his *Magia Universalis* of 1657–9.[1] In modern times Price is dubious, Rosen ironical and King condemnatory; Singer allows him a microscope but not a telescope, and Spencer-Jones upholds him, largely on the basis of a letter he wrote to the Cardinal d'Este in 1586 saying that he could make *occhiali* with which a man could be recognized several miles away.

Next it was the turn of the Dutch. In 1618 Isaac Beeckman wrote in his diary that he had seen a picture of Galileo's telescope with diaphragms, adding that earlier someone (Zacharias Jansen, 1588 to *c.* 1631)[2] had made a telescope without diaphragms at Middelburg in Holland.[3] This certainly enlarged distant objects but left them fuzzy. Later on, in 1634, he made another entry to the effect that

Johannes Zacharias[4] says that his father (Zacharias Jansen), made the first telescope here (in Holland) in the year 1604, copying one which had been brought from Italy and bore the date 1590.[5]

If this statement was true it disposes of any claim for independence on the part of this Dutch spectacle-maker.[6] But the possible originality of others is not weakened by similar evidence. Sirturi recorded that a telescope had been presented to Prince Maurice of Orange by Johannes Lippershey,[7] also of Middelburg, in 1608.[8] Lippershey's invention, according to a persistent story, was made accidentally, by children or an apprentice; and documentary evidence still extant proves that in the same year he petitioned for a patent or monopoly.[9] He was not the only one to do so. Later in the very same month a similar petition was put in by Jacobus Adrianszoon[10] of Alkmaar, one of the two sons of a professional mathematician Adrian Anthoniszoon (1527 to 1607), well

---

[1] Thorndike, vol. 7, p. 230; Clay & Court, p. 19.

[2] Really Janszoon, i.e. not a surname. The family name was Martens. Zacharias' father Jan or Hans had settled in Middelburg.

[3] de Waard ed. vol. 1, p. 208 ff. See also de Waard's book on the history of the telescope.

[4] Really Jan Zachariaszoon.

[5] de Waard, ed. vol. 3, p. 376; cf. Ronchi, pp. 84 ff.

[6] That there had been telescopes in Italy before 1600 appears from a letter which Raphael Gualterotti wrote to Galileo after the appearance of *Nuntius Sidereus* in 1610, saying that he had been using one since 1598. See Gerland, p. 353, who alludes to evidence that Italian glassmakers migrated to Middelburg.

[7] Or Jan Lipperhey, d. 1619.

[8] P. 24, cf. Beeckman, de Waard ed. vol. 1, p. 209. The thought was military. See also de Waard's book on the history of the telescope.

[9] See the classical paper of G. Moll based on the researches of J. H. van Swinden; also King, p. 30, Rooseboom, p. 13, etc.

[10] Or James Metius, so called because his father came from Metz.

known for his computation of the value of π to seven decimal places.[1] Lippershey's priority was upheld by Schyrlaeus de Rheita writing in 1645,[2] and that of Adrianszoon by Descartes in 1637.[3] It is remarkable that the question of priority was already a raging one by 1645, for Pierre Borel (1591 to 1689) then made a special investigation which he published in his *De Vero Telescopii Inventore, cum Brevi Omnium Conspiciliorum Historia* of 1655. Some witnesses favoured Zacharias Jansen, others Jan Lippershey. If people of that generation could not solve the problem it is hardly likely that we shall.[4]

As for Galileo, his statements are extremely well known. He always attributed his knowledge of the idea of the telescope in the spring of 1609 to the Dutch, but asserted that he then constructed his own instruments entirely on the basis of optical reasoning, 'making use of the doctrine of refractions'.[5] He admitted that it was a comfort to be 'certain of not being in search of the impossible' and that the knowledge of what the Dutch had done 'did indeed stimulate me to apply myself to the notion' but he had no model to copy, and gained his thousandfold magnification by deductions from known principles. Before the year was out Galileo hurried to Venice and had the high officials of the Signoria observing sails and shipping from the top of the highest church towers. The naval significance was not lost upon them, and they confirmed him in his professorial chair for life.[6]

It may have seemed unnecessary to rehearse so many well-known pieces of information, but we have done it with design and purpose. The invention of the telescope begins to look more and more like that phenomenon so rare before modern times, almost simultaneous achievement by a number of individuals when an idea is once 'in the air'. Although it would no doubt be possible to establish a chronological

---

[1] See *SCC*, vol. 3, p. 101. The same result had been anticipated by Tsu Ch'ung-chih about A.D. 490.

[2] *Oculus Enoch et Eliae, sive Radius Sidereo-Mysticus*, p. 337.

[3] *Dioptrique;* in *Oeuvres*, ed. Adam & Tannery, vol. 6, pp. 82, 227.

[4] While still with the Dutch in mind we should remember the clear claim of Cornelius Drebbel (cf. p. 215 below), made in a letter to King James I in 1613, that he could construct a telescope magnifying objects up to 10 miles away (see Beeckman, ed. de Waard, vol. 3, p. 440; Harris, p. 146, cf. pp. 130, 182). Harris says (p. 129) that before he came to settle in England Drebbel had been friendly with the two sons of Adrian Anthoniszoon.

[5] *Sidereus Nuntius*, Venice, 1610, and *Il Saggiatore*, Rome, 1623; both passages given in Singer, pp. 412 ff.

[6] This incident was not lost upon Bertold Brecht, who brought it in with much effect in his play on Galileo.

chain such that Digges begat della Porta, and della Porta begat Lippershey or Adrianszoon (through Zacharias Jansen), and that the Dutch begat Galileo (though this last is a pretty clear case of stimulus diffusion);[1] surely it is much more likely that between 1550 and 1610 half a dozen people at least played about with bilenticular combinations, using biconcave as well as biconvex lenses, and got the effect of a startling enlargement of far-away objects.[2] If this may be admitted then the possibility that Po Yü himself was one of them becomes quite reasonable, and in view of the difficulties of transmission and communication may even be the easiest supposition. These are what we must now examine.

The first mention of the telescope in Chinese was in the book of the Jesuit missionary Emmanuel Diaz (Yang Ma-no) entitled *T'ien Wen Lüeh* (Explanation of the Celestial Sphere) of 1615, but here there was no explanation of how it was constructed or how it worked.[3] Galileo's name was not transliterated, and there was mention only of 'a famous scholar of the West, particularly learned in (astronomy and) calendrical science'. Nor was the telescope given any special term.[4] Some of the most important results obtained by its aid were however related.[5] An account of the construction of the telescope did not come until the *Yuan ching shuo* (Account of the Far-Seeing Optick Glass) written by another Jesuit, Adam Schall von Bell (T'ang Jo-wang), in 1626.[6] This was not, as has sometimes been said, a translation of the book of Girolamo Sirturi, *Telescopium, sive ars perficiendi novum illud Galilaei Visorium Instrumentum ad Sidera* (Frankfurt, 1618), though it was probably based on it. The book contains diagrams explaining the Galilean telescope with biconcave eyepiece lens, though not the Keplerian one.[7] Attention is drawn to its possible uses in war,[8] and

---

[1] *SCC*, vol. 1, pp. 244 ff.

[2] This is in fact the view that was held both by Favaro, p. 2, and by Gerland, p. 354.

[3] We have reproduced and translated a couple of pages of this in *SCC*, vol. 3, figure 185, opposite p. 444. On the whole subject of the knowledge of Galileo's work in China, see the monograph of d'Elia.

[4] It was just called *i ch'iao ch'i*, an ingenious instrument.

[5] E.g. the moons of Jupiter, the phases of Venus (so vital for the Copernican theory), the rings of Saturn (unresolved), and the multitude of small stars in the Milky Way.

[6] Here the Chinese text was due to Schall's collaborator Li Tsu-pai, an astronomer forty years later one of the martyrs of modern science during the controversies of the beginning of the K'ang-hsi reign-period.

[7] Pp. 24, 25 of the text. The doubly biconvex compound instrument occurs in Kepler's *Dioptrice* of 1611.

[8] P. 13 of the text.

there are diagrams of the resolution of many stars in the nebulae of the Crab and Orion.[1] Further relevant Jesuit books followed in 1628 and 1637.[2] The famous minister Hsü Kuang-ch'i, the friend of Matteo Ricci (Li Ma-tou), called upon the emperor in 1629 to decree the construction of three telescopes, and two years later he used one to study an eclipse.[3]

It is thus indubitable that during the twenties of the seventeenth century, when Po Yü was young, there was a considerable transmission of Galilean astronomy to Chinese culture, and a rather lesser dissemination of Western optical knowledge. Unfortunately there is no evidence whatever that Po Yü, or for that matter Sun Yün-ch'iu, was in touch with the Jesuits at any time; their scientific work had been concentrated at Peking since about 1610, while our men were working at Suchow, a long way away in the south.[4] Of course there is no reason for doubting the reality of Jesuit influence in other directions. For example, that very remarkable scholar Huang Lü-chuang (1656 to c. 1684) was at the capital (Peking) in the decade 1675 to 1685, where he made microscopes and probably also telescopes as well as much other apparatus,[5] but that was a long time after the Jesuits had stimulated their construction in the official government Bureau of Astronomy. The whole question thus remains open, and further research will be required to throw light upon the possibility of Jesuit scientific influence at Suchow in the early decades of the seventeenth century; so far at any rate Wang Chin-kuang has not been able to find evidence of it.

[1] It will be remembered that the Crab nebula is considered the remains of the first supernova recorded by man; it appeared in 1054 and the only astronomers who recorded it were the Chinese and Japanese (see *SCC*, vol. 3, p. 427).

[2] Notably the *Ts'e t'ien yo shuo* (Brief Description of the Measurement of the Heavens) by Johannes Schreck (Terrentius), (Teng Yü-han) in the former year, which emphasized the significance of the phases of Venus, and described the studies newly being made on sun-spots by the aid of the telescope. The only thing Schreck omitted to mention was that they had been known and systematically recorded in China for a dozen centuries before Europeans discovered them. The first transliteration of Galileo's name, as Chia-li-le-a, came in 1635, when Schall gave an account of him in his *Li fa hsi chuan* (History of Western Astronomers), first printed as part of the *Ch'ung-chen li shu* collection.

[3] In 1631 the Korean ambassador Chong Tuwon, eager for science, as the Koreans always were, took back home with him several of the Jesuit tractates on astronomy and an actual telescope. In 1634 another of the modern Chinese astronomers, Li T'ien-ching, presented a telescope to the emperor with a full description.

[4] In the same way della Porta has no known connection with Digges, nor Lippershey with della Porta.

[5] Cf. *SCC*, vol. 2, p. 516, and for all detail Chang Yin-lin.

We must shortly turn to the interpretation of the different kinds of optical apparatus constructed by Sun Yün-ch'iu. First, however, we must recognize that there can be no doubt that both men did construct telescopes (*ch'ien li ching*). The technical term permits no other interpretation.[1] In 1964 we had an opportunity of checking the credibility of Sun Yün-ch'iu's telescope mounted on Hu-ch'iu Shan, for we spent an afternoon there during the time that we were in Suchow. This beautiful hill, crowned with temples and a fine pagoda of 961, lies about three or four miles to the north-west of the city of Suchow, and from what one can see with the naked eye at the top of the hill, it is obvious that it would have been an excellent place to try out the paces of an effective telescope.

One would give a good deal to have specimens in our museums of Chinese telescopes of the time of Po Yü and Sun Yün-ch'iu—Chinese, Korean and Japanese telescopes of course there are, but always of rather later date. In 1963 the Old Ashmolean Museum at Oxford acquired a three-draw telescope of pasteboard, lacquered in red and black with gold tooling which includes a phoenix motif. The eye-piece has a perforated disc of horn defining the aperture, and there are caps for both ends. Chinese or Japanese writing can be made out on the paper from which the pasteboard was made. The general style is characteristic of the latter half of the seventeenth century, so that it could date back as far as the time of Huang Lü-chuang, though of course it might have been made much later.[2] Another telescope, brought back from China by the navigator-sinologist and historian of astronomy Léopold de Saussure, may be seen in the Musée d'Histoire des Sciences at the Perle du Lac park in Geneva, but it is clearly of late seventeenth-century London manufacture and must have been exported east.[3]

As yet we know almost nothing of the use of the telescope in late seventeenth- and eighteenth-century China or Japan.[4] Astronomy as part of modern world science did not 'get off the ground' there

---

[1] Cf. Suter, but he adds nothing. The other term later generally accepted, following the Jesuit phrase, was *wang yuan ching*.

[2] Personal communication from Mr Francis Maddison.

[3] Personal communication from Mr Gerard Turner.

[4] There are only occasional glimpses. Between 1716 and 1745 the enlightened shogun Tokugawa Yoshimune ordered the erection of a telescope at the Kanda observatory, and later in the century one such instrument appears in a book of pictures entitled *Ehon yotsu no toki* (The Four Seasons), by Kitao Shigemasa.

(because of adverse scoial conditions, the lack of modern university education, etc.) till the second half of the nineteenth century. But the local records and clan or personal documents, as may be seen from the present communication, are only beginning to be tapped, so that surprises may be in store. The government Bureau of Astronomy, which lasted down to the end of the Ch'ing dynasty, also had its archives, and so far as we know no study of these has ever been made.

Whether or not Po Yü was an independent inventor of the telescope, it would seem that he deserves much credit for applying the instrument to gunnery. It is clear from his biography that besides all his other accomplishments he was a successful cannon-founder. On the history of bronze-founding in China and of gunpowder weapons, including metal-barrel cannon, there is of course a considerable literature which will give the background to Po Yü's work.[1] His equipment of the artillery of the provincial forces with 'telescopic sights', or rather spotting telescopes, an invention which seems to have been put into practice as early as 1635, would appear to precede by some time any application of the same kind in battle anywhere else. As has been apparent from several references and quotations given above, a recognition of the potential naval and military value of the telescope came early in Europe, but when was it actually first used in a campaign? We have not been able to find the date of the first use of spotting telescopes for artillery in the West but we believe that it may be distinctly later in the seventeenth century.[2] The 'rebels' referred to in the passage translated must have been the peasant armies under Li-Tzu-ch'eng, who succeeded in overthrowing the effete government of the last Ming emperor and capturing the capital, Peking; only to be overthrown in his turn by the traitor general Wu San-kuei, who opened the gates to the Manchus from the north with the intention that they should help him to recover the country for the Ming. As events turned out, they took it for themselves.

[1] Pending our relevant chapters in *SCC*, vol. 5, there is no study in a Western language which incorporates all the discoveries of contemporary Chinese historians, but the paper of Wang Ling is still, broadly speaking, a correct outline account of the development of gunpowder weapons. For the wider comparative background there is the monograph of Partington. On bronze-founding the book of Barnard covers the earlier historical stages though some of his conclusions are still under discussion.

[2] We expected surely to find something in vol. 4 of the *Works* of Simon Stevin, edited by W. H. Schukking, but no reference occurs in the index, and within the time at our disposal we could find none in the mass of detailed documents which the book contains.

There is not much else to say about the translation concerning Po Yü. It should however be mentioned that the pumps referred to were no doubt force-pumps of Alexandrian type. These were also a relatively new thing in Chinese culture, introduced either by the Jesuits or by the Portuguese merchants who had preceded them, and their principal use was as 'fire-engines' for putting out fires. The reader may be referred to the full discussion of pumps and water-raising machinery in China which has been given elsewhere.[1]

There remains the planetarium of Po Yü. It would be good to have much further information about it, but again its background can be appreciated by a study of what has already been written on the subject of orreries and planetaria operated by clockwork of various kinds in China.[2] The idea of such instruments goes back far in Chinese history, indeed to the Han period (second century), and relatively accurate instruments had been constructed since the beginning of the eighth century (in the T'ang dynasty) when there occurred the first invention of an escapement. For the history of the hydro-mechanical clock in China during six centuries before the introduction of Western weight-driven mechanical clocks, the reader is also referred to a separate publication.[3] Some comment ought to be made perhaps upon the concluding words of the passage on Po Yü, where it is said that he used the methods of geometry. This might sound at first sight very like evidence of Jesuit influence, because as is well known, the first six books of Euclid were translated by Matteo Ricci and Hsü Kuang-ch'i in 1607 and entitled *Chi ho yuan pen*, but it is doubtful whether this would have reached our master-artisan at Suchow.[4] Moreover, the existence of a considerable fund of non-deductive empirical geometry in Chinese culture should not be overlooked, and indeed we have drawn attention above (p. 198) to the fact that the phraseology used distinctly indicates this rather than the geometry of Euclid. The planning of the magnificent monumental clock-tower at K'aifeng in 1086 by Han Kung-lien, described in the book of Su Sung, *Hsin i hsiang fa yao* (Design for a New Armillary Clock), was clearly stated to have been done by

[1] *SCC*, vol. 4, pt 2, pp. 138, 222, *passim*, and esp. pp. 141 ff., 149.
[2] See *SCC* vol. 4, pt 2, pp. 466 ff., 481 ff., 492 ff.
[3] Needham, Wang & Price.
[4] *SCC*, vol. 3, pp. 52, 106. What is not so generally appreciated is that an Arabic version of Euclid seems to have existed in the library of the Imperial Observatory about 1270 (*SCC*, vol. 3, p. 105). Of course this source would have been even less likely to influence Po Yü.

geometrical methods, and these were certainly not Euclidean.[1] For the earlier history of geometry in China the reader is referred to work already published.[2]

The moment has now come to take up the biography of Sun Yün-ch'iu and see what can be got out of it. We found a little difficulty in translating to the best purpose the terms used early in this text about the defects of vision of Sun's clients.[3] It has been suggested that the 'confused sight' (*hua*) was probably diplopia (possibly resulting from a squint) rather than astigmatism, but we think the latter is more likely. The essential feature of *hua*, according to the Chinese medical dictionaries, is blurred vision of all objects, whatever the distance.[4] Since it was not possible to correct for this optically until the nineteenth century, one wonders what success Sun could have had. The 'far-sightedness' would be as likely to have been presbyopia as hypermetropia, but no doubt he made slightly convex lenses to correct for them. The earliest spectacles had been of this kind. We can assume at any rate that myopia was certainly one of the things he had to deal with; concave lenses were surely familiar to him.[5]

We shall now discuss in order the series of pieces of equipment marked by the letters inserted by us in the translation. The first one of these, (*a*) the 'keeping-in-the-eye glass'[6] (*ts'un mu ching*) we take to have been a magnifying glass or a simple microscope.[7] The former may be thought more probable than the latter since, as we know, the instrument with an almost spherical single lens was a development which in Europe came later than the compound microscope; permitting

[1] The memorandum concerned bore the words *kou ku* in its title (*SCC*, vol. 4, pt 2, p. 464).

[2] *SCC*, vol. 3, pp. 91 ff.

[3] Cf. Singer, pp. 317 ff.; Singer & Underwood, pp. 640 ff.

[4] It corresponds to the more classical literary terms *hsüan* and *hsüan*. See *Chung i ming tz'u tz'u tien*, p. 126 and *Chung kuo i hsüeh ta tz'u tien*, p. 2662. The modern term for astigmatism is *san kuang* or *san shih*.

[5] On spectacles in China and the spectacle-makers there see *SCC*, vol. 4, pt 1, pp. 118 ff. where much literature (e.g. H. T. Pi; Ch'iu K'ai-ming; Rakusen and Rasmussen) is summarized and evaluated. A more recent paper is that of Nieh Ch'ung-hou; it confirms the general view. Actual examples are not uncommon in our museums, e.g. the Old Ashmolean at Oxford, and in a new exhibition of Chinese medicine (cf. Poynter) at the Wellcome Historical Medical Museum in London a number are on show.

[6] Or conceivably, the 'preserving-the-eye glass'—by preventing it from straining when examining very small objects.

[7] This is also Wang Chin-kuang's view.

the wonderful work that van Leeuwenhoek did with it from 1673 onwards.[1] The remark about the increasing of brightness by a hundred-fold might perhaps indicate rather a magnifying glass, since the concentration of light rays which occurs when such an instrument is used as a burning-glass might have been in the author's mind. But the nuance of the Chinese text (if we are to take it literally) is that size as well as brightness was increased a hundredfold, which must imply a lens more powerful than any ordinary magnifying glass.[2] Besides, the evidence is that simple biconvex lenses were used habitually in the Sung period (eleventh to thirteenth century) by judges, for example, when studying difficult manuscripts,[3] and it is therefore not obvious why any particular fuss should have been made about such a thing as much as five hundred years later. Moreover there had been in the Ming a special name for the magnifying glass, *tan chao* or 'single shiner', so why should another term have been invented if not to designate another thing? Interpretation as the simple microscope may well therefore be right after all.

There is however an entirely different possibility which ought to be mentioned. For the understanding of Chinese technical terms a certain philological awareness is desirable, and there may thus be 'more than meets the eye' (if such a metaphor may be excused in the present context) in the phrase *ts'un mu ching*. For *ts'un* also means to examine or investigate, and is therefore interchangeable with a word[4] used in one of the most venerable and widely known texts of the Chinese classics, precisely in relation to the study of the stars—the Shun Tien chapter of the *Shu ching* (Book of History), where there is mention of the circumpolar constellation template,[5] oldest of Chinese astronomical instruments. Moreover *mu* need not mean the eye at all; it has the subsidiary meaning of a list, index, contents table,[6] muster or roster, so that here it might allude to the company of the stars. The increase in brightness so clearly mentioned in the text might therefore go better with the making more distinct of very distant light-sources, and the phrase would thus be 'glass for examining the array (or tally) of the stars'. So possibly this instrument was a more powerful version of the

---

[1] Rooseboom, p. 31; Clay & Court, pp. 32 ff., etc.
[2] Van Leeuwenhoek's simple microscopes magnified by a few hundred times and had a resolving power of about 1μ.
[3] *SCC*, vol. 4, pt 1, p. 121.
[4] I.e. *tsai*, equivalent to *ch'a*.
[5] *SCC*, vol. 3, pp. 336 ff.
[6] As in familiar *mu lu*.

ch'ien li ching. The essential difficulty in the Chinese wording is exactly the same as in some of the early European descriptions; one does not know whether 'smallness' was that of some very small object near at hand or whether it referred to some object small because it was very far away. On the whole the simple microscope may be the best solution.

Next (*b*) the *wan hua ching*, the 'myriad transformations glass', which could make one shape turn into a dozen other shapes, may have been, one would suppose, either a kaleidoscope[1] or some form or forms of distorting mirror.[2] The invention of the kaleidoscope is usually attributed to David Brewster in 1817, but in fact it had been current in a less perfect form during the last half of the eighteenth century.[3] Its appearance in the early seventeenth, especially as far away as China, would therefore be a rather remarkable circumstance, though the basic effect of multiplication of images by mirrors at angles of 120°, 90° and 72° was noted by Athanasius Kircher as early as 1646. As we shall shortly see in the case of item (*f*) below, experiments with multiplied images were much older than that in Chinese culture. Moreover regarding the second possibility, the silvering of mirrors had been known in China for many centuries before Sun Yün-ch'iu's time,[4] so that it would only require the casting of a glass surface into various curves to give a variety of distorting appearances. Such experiments were already presaged by what scholars were writing about mirrors of different curvatures at the end of the eleventh century.[5] But this may be better for item (*g*) below. Of course the early Jesuit missionaries brought optical apparatus among their paraphernalia. Wang Chin-kuang has noted one reference to a *wan hsiang ching* or 'ten thousand images glass', but we do not know what the proper interpretation of this should be.[6]

We do not know what the 'mandarin duck' (*c*) or 'one-of-a-pair

---

[1] A name later adopted for this in China was *wan hua t'ung*, the 'myriad transformations (lit. flowers) tube'.

[2] One might also think of a many-faceted piece of glass or rock crystal, but this is probably less likely here than in the case of item (*f*) below.

[3] Feldhaus, col. 547.

[4] *SCC*, vol. 4, pt 1, p. 91.   [5] *SCC*, vol. 4, pt 1, p. 93.

[6] It was one of the Jesuit possessions sent to the capital in 1643 when the Ch'ing forces occupied Szechuan and took prisoner Louis Buglio (Li Lei-ssu) and Gabriel de Magalhaens (An Wen-ssu). The former was later much concerned with the introduction of the rules of European or optical perspective to China, and the latter was a capable instrument-maker and horologist. In 1655 they petitioned to have their property returned to them. See Li Nien, vol. 3, p. 48.

glasses' (*yuan ching*) were either, unless perhaps they were separate eye-glasses or monocles, that is to say single lenses without ear-pieces rather than spectacles with them. As for the 'half-glasses', (*d*), (*pan ching*), they certainly could not have been bifocal spectacles in the modern sense, but they might perhaps have been semi-discoidal spectacles of the type which is sometimes still seen today, namely the lower halves of lenses only, permitting the use of the unaided vision for long distances as the wearer looks out above them. These are known as 'half-eye spectacles' and go back to an invention of Benjamin Franklin. This seems rather a striking development to find in early seventeenth-century China.[1]

As for (*e*), the 'glasses that turned daylight into evening' (*hsi yang ching*), we can only suggest that these were dark glasses or 'sun-glasses', made perhaps of smoky quartz or tinted rock-crystal, possibly wearable over ordinary spectacles.[2] There is evidence for the use of these, again by judges, as early as the Sung,[3] and specimens are not uncommon in our museums. The value of tinted glasses in all forms of eye inflammation,[4] iritis and photophobia, must not be forgotten; and a search of the Chinese ophthalmological literature would undoubtedly bring to light interesting textual evidence concerning them.[5] Now philologically the expression *hsi yang* is an ancient phrase for that side of a mountain facing west which receives the rays of the afternoon and evening sun. While this would not disagree with the interpretation already given, it could also be compatible with a 'mountain-shaped'

---

[1] It might indeed imply the recognition of hypermetropia, which did not come in Europe until about 1750.

[2] For observations of sun-spots and the phenomena of eclipses, the Chinese had used something of the same sort since ancient times (cf. *SCC*, vol. 3, pp. 420, 436). We have suggested thin slices of jade or dark mica.

[3] *SCC*, vol. 4, pt 1, p. 121.

[4] Trachoma was rife in traditional China.

[5] This may be the point to make a protest against the too easy dismissal of the large planar 'mandarin' spectacles (also common in museums) as worn purely for affectation or prestige. In fact they were more the ancestors of goggles, giving some protection against wind drying and dust, and especially useful after cataract operations.

As is well known, operating for cataract goes far back in Hellenistic, Arabic and Western mediaeval medicine, though it was generally 'couching' (the displacement of the opaque lens to the floor of the posterior cavity) rather than radical extraction (see Singer, p. 320; Singer & Underwood, pp. 643 ff.; Mettler, pp. 1006 ff.). In China cataract was called *nei chang* (inner obstruction), and was operated for many centuries before Sun Yun-ch'iu's time. Whether 'couching' goes back in China to the Hou Han period, corresponding to the age of Galen and Celsus, we do not yet know, but it was certainly practised in the T'ang (seventh to tenth centuries); cf. the paper of Li T'ao.

piece of glass, i.e. a prism. But whether or not Sun Yün-ch'iu was seeing strange phenomena with prisms, a John the Baptist of what came later, must be left for further research to elucidate.

With the 'many-faces glass' (*f*) (*to mien ching*) we have another puzzle. It could conceivably be interpreted as a kaleidoscope, but perhaps more probably it was a many-faceted piece of glass or rock crystal giving multiple images with spectral colours.[1] There are in museums, e.g. the Old Ashmolean at Oxford, some nineteenth-century examples of such glasses, mounted like pocket magnifying glasses. Their exact purpose is not known but it is assumed that they were used for amusement only. Such an explanation could of course apply also to item (*b*) above. However there is a curious background to the *to mien ching* not generally known, namely that in the early Middle Ages in China (e.g. eighth century) some Buddhist monks experimented with plane mirrors placed in such a manner as to give an infinite regress of images. Details of this have been given elsewhere,[2] and we have been interested to notice a number of recent advertisements in technical journals which have made use of the principle.[3] The Buddhist philosophers were interested in this because of their theories of the unity of the universe, all beings, actions and things reflecting themselves in all other beings, actions and things. We are therefore inclined to propose that the *to mien ching* was some kind of arrangement of plane (or curved) mirrors giving any number of images.

Item (*g*), the *huan jung ching*, or 'glasses giving illusory appearances', would seem to be *par excellence* the term by which we should understand distorting mirrors of some kind or another (cf. item (*b*) above). Perhaps their curvatures were more extreme than those of the *wan hua ching*. But there are at least two other interpretations. They might have been 'magic mirrors', a speciality of Chinese life, of which a full account has been given elsewhere.[4] Throughout the Middle Ages the Chinese made mirrors with designs of characters or pictures cast at their back and then the whole polished in a special way under pressure

---

[1] To go further into this would involve the practices of jewellers and the history of their tools.
[2] *SCC*, vol. 4, pt 1, p. 92.
[3] Notably those by Messrs. Pilkington and Sons in *Far East Trade and Development*, December 1964 and December 1965. It seems that multiple reflections of an object are used to provide a test for the flawlessness of plane mirrors. Everyone has seen the effect in the many mirrors beloved of French *restaurateurs*.
[4] *SCC*, vol. 4, pt 1, pp. 94 ff.

so that the design on the back of the mirror made itself seen in vague outline when light was reflected from the mirror on to a plane wall, though no pattern could be seen on the face of the mirror itself.[1] Sometimes an additional item of puzzle was introduced by giving the mirror a false back with an entirely different picture or inscription upon it. One example of this kind is in the Old Ashmolean Museum at Oxford.[2] These mirrors, however, were known for centuries before Sun Yünch'iu's time as 'light-penetration mirrors' (*t'ou kuang chien*) and it does not seem obvious why any new name should have been invented if this had been what the *huan jung ching* was. The third alternative is an image or images projected by some kind of magic lantern. But this would seem to be a more probable explanation of the penultimate item in the list, (*i*).

For the next one, (*h*), the instrument for investigating very tiny things (*ch'a wei ching*), we favour the possibility of a compound microscope.[3] The inventor of the compound microscope in Europe is of course not identifiable, and as in the case of the telescope there are several possibilities; we only know that Willem Boreel saw one in London in 1619 when he visited Cornelius Drebbel.[4] The instrument did not receive the name *microscopium* until 1625, when John Faber, one of the Lyncean Academy, so christened it.[5] The first sketch of it was drawn in 1631 by Isaac Beeckman in his diary, where he called it 'instrumenta Drebbeliana'.[6] Seeing that Sun Yün-ch'iu could make a telescope, there seems no reason at all why he could not have combined lenses in a slightly different way to make a compound microscope, either of the Galilean or the Keplerian type.[7] It is sad that he died so

[1] Such was the prehistory of multiple-beam interferometry.
[2] See the account by Turner.
[3] Wang Chin-kuang in principle concurs.
[4] His opinion, afterwards recounted in P. Borel's *De Vero Telescopii Inventore* (The Hague, 1655) was that the first compound microscope had been made by the same Zacharias Jansen already mentioned and his father Jan (or Hans) some time during the last decade of the sixteenth century, and that one of their make had come into the possession of Drebbel. Huygens and his father, on the other hand (1621), believed that Drebbel himself was the inventor (Gerland, p. 363; Harris, p. 183). See the standard histories of the microscope such as Clay & Court; Rooseboom, etc. and the papers and monographs of Singer.   [5] Rosen, pp. 24, 66.
[6] de Waard ed. vol. 3, p. 442. It accompanied a copy of Drebbel's famous letter to King James I (1613).
[7] Presumably by having the two lenses much farther apart. It is proved beyond doubt that Galileo himself made use of his telescope as a microscope in this way, for we have two good eye-witness accounts of his experiments, one by a Scottish student, John

young, for otherwise we might have had some interesting observations at this early date of very small objects such as snowflakes (afterwards prominently studied by the Japanese), plant parts and insects.[1]

As in the case of the telescope (p. 207 above) we know little or nothing of the use of the microscope in seventeenth- and eighteenth-century China, but it would be most unwise to conclude that we never shall know anything. One instrument, at any rate, which dates from the mid-eighteenth century, was brought back from China by Léopold de Saussure and is now in the Musée d' Histoire des Sciences at Geneva; close examination would no doubt show whether it was Chinese-made or an export from Europe. It is of the Culpeper type but with the possibility of inclining the barrel.[2] For Japan so far there is more information than from China.[3] The first picture of a microscope and the first illustrations of microscopical objects occur in a book called *Komo ʒatsuwa* (Miscellaneous Information about the Red-Haired People, i.e. Europeans, especially Dutch), written by the physician Morishima Churyō[4] (1754 to 1808) and published in 1787.[5] The microscope depicted is of early Culpeper or pre-Culpeper type (i.e. *c.* 1730) in a tripod mounting,[6] and it seems that two examples of the same kind are still preserved in Japan.[7] The name of the apparatus is given as *kembikyo* (*hsien wei ching*), 'glass for making manifest very tiny objects', but from other sources we know that the characteristic European term 'flea-glass'[8] passed directly into Japanese as *mushi-*

Wodderborn, in 1610 (*Quatuor Problematum* . . ., p. 7), and another in a MS letter by Jean Dupont, Canon of Sarlat, for 1614 (Paris MS, *Bib. Nat.* (Fonds Perigord), VI, cart. 20 ff.). See Clay & Court, p. 11; Singer, in *J. Roy. Mic. Soc.* p. 328.

[1] To the identification of the earliest investigation carried out with the microscope in Europe Charles Singer devoted a great deal of work; and for the claims of George Hüfnagel (1592), Fabio Colonna the botanist (1606), and Francesco Fontana (1646), Singer's papers and monographs must be consulted. His final conclusion was, we believe, that one must regard the drawings of the minute anatomy of bees, contained in the *Apiarium* of Federigo Cesi and Francesco Stelluti (Rome, 1625), and in the *Persio Tradotto* of Stelluti alone (Rome, 1630), as the earliest figures of microscopic objects. Galileo certainly published nothing of this kind.

[2] Private communication from M. Cramer and Mr Turner.

[3] It has been set forth recently in an interesting paper by van der Pas.

[4] A quasi-pen-name; his real name was Katsuragawa Hosan. His grandfather had changed the family name from Morishima.

[5] The oldest mention of a microscope so far found is in a book of the same kind, *Komo dan*, written by Gotō Rishun in 1765. He used the term *kembikyo*.

[6] Only two supports are actually shown in the drawing.

[7] One of them may have been made there.

[8] This generally applied to the simple microscope in Europe; we do not know whether in Japan also.

megane (*ch'ung yen ching*). Morishima also gave a number of figures of crystals, seeds, and insects (aphid, louse, gnat, fly with egg and pupa, mosquito with its larva, ant with egg and larva). It has been suspected that most of these drawings were copies from J. Swammerdam's *Historia Generalis ofte Algemeene Verhandeling der Bloedeloose Dierkens* (Utrecht, 1669), but although the parallelism is close it is not so complete as to suggest that Morishima and his friends did no observing themselves.

The microscope was later used in Japan for quite another purpose, namely the delineation of snowflake patterns. When Kepler published his celebrated New Year's Letter on snowflakes in 1611 he did not know that the hexagonal symmetry of snowflake crystals had been appreciated and constantly commented upon in China since about 135 B.C.[1] The great naturalist Ono Ranzan began to examine them microscopically about 1799 but his work was never published. Then just a dozen years after William Scoresby had laid the foundations of the systematic classification of snowflake forms, a daimyō of Shimōsa, Doi Toshitsuru (1789 to 1848), published an outstanding collection of drawings, the *Sekka zusetsu* (Illustrated Discussion of Snow Blossoms). This was in 1832 and a supplement followed in 1839. Together with those of James Glaisher in 1855, these drawings were the best before the coming of microphotography. The Japanese work was entirely independent, and not known to microscopists in the West till long afterwards.

It is for item (*i*), the *fang kuang ching* or 'light-projecting apparatus', that we have in mind the magic lantern. The invention of the so-called magic lantern[2] takes one back again to Cornelius Drebbel, whose specification, not too obscurely worded, was printed in a book by Daniel Schwenter in 1636,[3] just in Po Yü's prime. 'Coloured pictures shown upon a wall by perspective glasses' were then expounded by Athanasius Kircher ten years later,[4] using sunlight with a transparent slide or a picture painted on the lens, or lamp-light with a transparent slide. When he brought out his second edition in 1671 he made use of an improvement which the Dane Thomas Walgenstein had introduced

[1] The story has been traced in a paper by Needham & Lu Gwei-djen.
[2] We can leave out of account mediaeval transparencies and shadow-plays without lens systems. See Feldhaus, col. 823; Gerland, p. 310; Thorndike, vol. 7, p. 496.
[3] *Deliciae Physico-Mathematicae*, p. 263.
[4] In his famous *Ars Magna Lucis et Umbrae*, pp. 912, 915.

by 1665, namely the mounting of the transparent pictures on a sliding or rotating plate so that they could be changed more rapidly. Another pioneer hardly later than Drebbel was J. F. Nicéron, whose 'Perspective Curieuse . . .' of 1638 clearly described a magic lantern.[1] By the last quarter of the century it had become a familiar thing.[2]

What is very little known is that Martin Martini (Wei K'uang-kuo), one of the Jesuit missionaries from China, lectured with lantern slides on a tour in Europe in 1654.[3] We therefore thought at one time that further research might indicate that this particular piece of optical apparatus using two plano-convex lenses was transmitted from the Far East to the Far West, but the dates of Drebbel and Nicéron make this impossible, and if Sun Yün-ch'iu really threw designs on a screen with his 'light-projecting apparatus' he was once again an independent rather than an initiating discoverer.

The last item on the list (j), is the 'brightening-the-night glass' or *yeh ming ching*.[4] For this we suggest some kind of searchlight, torch or dark lantern,[5] giving a less concentrated beam than that of the *fang kuang ching*. A sketch by Leonardo da Vinci in the *Codex Atlanticus* is the oldest in Europe, apparently, to depict a single large plano-convex lens with a light behind it, and presumably a concave mirror behind the light source; he did not forget to draw in the diverging rays.[6] Lights in front of concave mirrors had been well known in China at the same time, and were called *han kuang wa* (light-containing dishes), so undoubtedly Sun's new lamp had a lens. It looks as if Huang Lü-chuang's *jui kuang ching*, (auspicious beam glass) made about 1680, was an enlarged version of Sun's lamp, for it had a diameter of 5 to 6 ft. and shot a beam for several *li*; those who sat near it in winter felt the warmth coming from it.[7] Searchlights in modern times, however, got other names, *t'an chao teng* or *t'an hai teng* (revealing light or sea-revealing light).

1 See Thorndike, vol. 7, pp. 594 ff.
2 Thorndike, vol. 8, p. 223.
3 He was a pupil of Athanasius Kircher. See Liesegang; Bernard-Maître; Duyvendak; and the comments in *SCC*, vol. 4, pt 1, p. 123.
4 The name may perhaps have been derived from a pit which was dug in ancient times at the mid-autumn festival to contain a pool of water in which the moon was reflected. This was called *yeh ming*.
5 The term is redolent of Bow Street Runners and Dr Watson, but it was just a lantern with a shutter which could readily be closed or opened.
6 See Feldhaus, col. 611.
7 See Chang Yin-lin, p. 83.

This brings us to the end of Sun Yün-ch'iu's recorded optical devices. It may be convenient to summarize the interpretations we regard as certain or most probable:

ch'ien li ching	telescope
ts'un mu ching	simple microscope
wan hua ching	kaleidoscope
yuan ching	monocle
pan ching	spectacles with lower halves only
hsi yang ching	dark glasses
to mien ching	plane mirrors for infinite regress of images, or faceted glasses
huan jung ching	distorting mirrors, or 'magic' mirrors
ch'a wei ching	compound microscope
fang kuang ching	magic lantern
yeh ming ching	searchlight, or dark lantern.

In conclusion, Po Yü gives the general impression of having been a very clever artisan, indeed a personality quite like those of the 'mathematical practitioners' or 'higher artisanate' who formed so extremely important a part of the personnel during the rise of modern science in the West. He was evidently an extremely practical man, and in his inarticulateness reminiscent of a classical figure in the history of Chinese engineering, Ma Chün, whose amusing biography is well worth reading in this connection.[1] Sun Yün-ch'iu, on the other hand, gives the impression of coming from a more educated, though poor, family, and being rather more scholarly, since we know that he composed a book on optical apparatus. In contrast to Po Yü's longer life, Sun Yün-ch'iu seems to have been something of a youthful genius and did not live long enough into the Ch'ing dynasty to make his name on any national scale.

It is truly remarkable to find Chinese scientific and technical men following so closely upon the heels of the pioneers of optical apparatus in Western Europe, in spite of the great difficulties of communication between the alphabetic and the ideographic culture-areas. These difficulties indeed rather emphasize the extent to which the 'optick artists' of Chiangsu in the early years of the seventeenth century were probably building upon their own immemorial traditions, stimulated,

[1] *SCC*, vol. 4, pt 2, p. 39.

as they surely must have been, by rumours of what was on foot in the great days of modern natural science in the Western world. The chief moral of the whole story, perhaps, is that it illustrates the speed with which Chinese mathematics, astronomy and physics could fuse with these sciences in their Western forms to give modern universal world science. The process took only a few decades, and later on, in the nineteenth century, the fusion of chemical knowledge took hardly any longer. But with a science such as botany a century at least was needed, and with medicine the process is even now not completed. Contrasts such as these we hope to discuss in another place.

ACKNOWLEDGEMENTS

The thanks of the authors are due to Dr Hu Tao-ching in Shanghai and Professor Wang Chin-kuang in Hangchow, as also to Mr Francis Maddison, Mr G. l'E. Turner and Dr J. Levene of Oxford, for many consultations and help in the elucidation of the work of the two 'optick artists' of seventeenth-century Suchow.

REFERENCES

BARNARD, N. *Bronze Casting and Bronze Alloys in Ancient China*, Australian Nat. Univ., Canberra, and Monumenta Serica (*Monumenta Serica Monographs*, no. 14). Tokyo, 1961.

BEECKMAN, ISAAC. See de Waard.

BERNARD-MAÎTRE, H. Les Sources Mongoles et Chinoises de l'Atlas Martini (1655), *Monumenta Serica*, 12, 127. 1947.

BOREL, P. *De Vero Telescopii Inventore, cum Brevi Omnium Conspiciliorum Historia*. The Hague, 1655.

CESI, F. & STELLUTI, F. *Apiarium*. Rome, 1625.

CHANG YIN-LIN, Chung-Kuo Li-Shih shang chih Ch'i Ch'i, chi ch'i Tso-che, (Scientific Inventions and Inventors in Chinese History). *Yenching Hsüeh-Pao*, 1 (no. 3), 359. 1928.
Reprinted in *Chang Yin-lin Wen Chi*, (Collected Works of Chang Yin-lin), p. 64. Hongkong: Chung-Hua, 1956.

CH'IU K'AI-MING, The Introduction of Spectacles into China, *Harvard Journ. Asiatic Studs.* 1, 168. 1936.

CLAY, R. S. & COURT, T. H. *The History of the Microscope, compiled from Original Instruments and Documents, down to the Introduction of the Achromatic Microscope*. London: Griffin, 1932.

CORDIER, H. *Histoire Générale de la Chine*, 4 vols. Paris: Geuthner, 1920.

DIGGES, LEONARD. *A Geometrical Practice [Practical Treatize,] named* Pantometria, *divided into three Bookes*, Longimetra, Planimetra *and* Stereometra, *containing Rules manifolde for mensuration of all Lines, Superficies and Solides; with sundrie strange conclusions both by Instrument and without, and also by Perspective Glasses* [*Glasses*] *to set forth the true description or exact plat*[*te*] *of an whole Region; framed by Leonard Digges, Gentleman, lately finished by Thomas Digges his sonne.*

[*First published by Thomas Digges Esquire, and dedicated to the Grave, Wise and Honourable Sir Nicholas Bacon, Knight, Lord Keeper of the Great Seale of England, With a*]

Who hathe also thereunto adjoined a Mathematicall treatise [*Discourse*] *of the five regulare Platonicall bodies* [*Solides*] *and their Metamorphosis or transformation* [*Metamorphosis*] *into five other* [*other five*] *equilater uniforme solides* [*compound rare*] *Geometricall* [*Bodyes, conteyning an hundred newe Theoremes at least*] *of his owne invention, hitheto not* [*never*] *mentioned* [*before*] *of by any* [*other*] *Geometrician*[*s*]

London: Bynneman, 1571. London: Jesses, 1591 (alterations of the title in the second edition shown in square brackets).

The *Longimera* reprinted as: *The Theodelitus and Topographical Instrument of Leonard Digges of University College, Oxford, described by his son Thomas Digges in 1571.* Oxford: ed. R. T. Gunther, 1927. (*Old Ashmolean Reprints*, no. 4.) This also contains the preface in which Thomas Digges claimed the invention of the telescope for his father.

DUYVENDAK, J. J. L. Early Chinese Studies in Holland, *T'oung Pao*, **32**, 293. 1936.

D'ELIA, PASQUALE. Echi delle Scoperte Galileiane in Cina vivente ancora Galileo (1612–1640), *Atti d.r. Accademia dei Lincei* (*Rendiconti, Ser. Mor.*), (8e ser.), **I**, 125. 1946.

Republished in enlarged form as *Galileo in Cina. Relazioni attraverso il Collegio Romano tra Galileo e i gesuiti scienzati missionari in Cina* (1610–1640). *Analecta Gregoriana*, 37 (Series Facultatis Missiologicae A, no. 1). Rome, 1947.

Eng. tr. *Galileo in China*, with emendations and additions by R. Suter & M. Sciascia. Cambridge, Mass: Harvard University Press, 1960.

FAVARO, A. La Invenzione del Telescopio secondo gli ultimi Studi, *Atti del Istituto Veneto di Scienze, Lettere ed Arti*, 66. 1907.

FELDHAUS, F. M. *Die Technik der Vorzeit, der Geschichtlichen Zeit, und der Naturvölker* (encyclopaedia). Leipzig and Berlin: Engelmann, 1914.

GERLAND, E. *Geschichte d. Physik* (erste Abt.), *Von den ältesten Zeiten bis zum Ausgang des 18ten Jahrhunderts.* Oldenbourg, München and Berlin, 1913. (Geschichte d. Wissenschaften in Deutschland, vol. 24.)

GUTHRIE, D. The Pursuit of the Infinitely Small; the Evolution of Microscopy, *London Hospital Gazette*, 5. 1949.

HARRIS, L. E. The Two Netherlanders, Humphrey Bradley and Cornelis Drebbel. Cambridge: Heffer, and Leiden: Brill, 1961.

HUGHES, A. F. W. Studies in the History of Microscopy; I, The Influence of Achromatism, *J. Roy. Mic. Soc.* **75**, 1. 1955.

KING, H. C. *The History of the Telescope*. London: Griffin, 1955.

KIRCHER, ATHANASIUS. *Ars Magna Lucis et Umbrae*. Rome, 1646. 2nd ed. 1671.

LI NIEN. *Chung Suan Shih Lun Ts'ung* (Collected Essays on the History of Chinese Mathematics), 5 vols. K'o-Hsüeh, Peking, 1955.

LI T'AO. A Short History of Old Chinese Ophthalmology, *Chinese Medical Journ.* **50**, 1513. 1936.

LIESEGANG, F. P. Der Missionar und China-geograph Martin Martini als erster Lichtbildredner, *Proteus*, **2**, 112. 1937.

LO YING. *Chung-kuo Ch'iao Shih* (A History of Bridge-building in China). Peking, 1961.

METTLER, CECILIA C. *A History of Medicine*. Toronto: Blakiston, 1947.

MOLL, G. On the First Invention of Telescopes, collected from the Notes and Papers of the late Professor [J.H.] van Swinden, *J. Roy. Institution*, **1**, 319 and 483. 1831.

NEEDHAM, JOSEPH (with the collaboration of Wang Ling, Ts'ao T'ien-ch'in, K. Robinson, Ho Ping-yü, Lu Gwei-djen et al.). *Science and Civilisation in China*, 7 vols. in 11 parts. Cambridge, 1954–.

NEEDHAM, JOSEPH and LU GWEI-DJEN. The Earliest Snow Crystal Observations, *Weather*, **16**, 319, 1961.

NEEDHAM, JOSEPH, WANG LING & PRICE, DEREK J. DE S. *Heavenly Clockwork; the Great Astronomical Clocks of Medieval China*. Cambridge, 1960. (Antiquarian Horological Society Monographs, No. 1.) Prelim. pub. *Antiquarian Horology*, **1**, 153. 1956.

NICERON, J. F. *Perspective Curieuse, ou Magie Artificielle des Effets Merveilleux de l'Optique*. Paris, 1638.

NIEH CH'UNG-HOU, Chung-Kuo Yen-Ching Shih (A History of Spectacles in China), *I Hsüeh Tsa Chih (Chinese Journ. Hist. of Med.)*, **4** (no. 1), 9. 1952.

PARTINGTON, J. R. *A History of Greek Fire and Gunpowder*. Cambridge: Heffer, 1960.

VAN DER PAS, P. W. The Earliest Microscopical Observations in Japan, *Arch. Internat. d'Histoire des Sci.* **17**, 223. 1964.

PI, H. T. The History of Spectacles in China, *Chinese Medical Journ.*, **42**, 742. 1928.

DELLA PORTA, J. B. (Giambattista). *Magia Naturalis*. Naples, 1558, 1589. Anvers, 1561. English trans. R. Gaywood. London: Young & Speed, 1658; London: Wright, 1669. Facsimile of the 1658 edition, edited by Derek J. de S. Price. New York: Basic Books, 1957.

POYNTER, F. N. L. (with the collaboration of J. Barber-Lomax and J. K. Crellin). *Chinese Medicine; an Exhibition illustrating the Traditional System of Medicine of the Chinese People* (catalogue with introduction). London: Wellcome Historical Medical Museum and Library, 1966.

RAKUSEN, C. P. History of Chinese Spectacles, *Chinese Medical Journ.*, **53**, 379. 1938.

RASMUSSEN, O. D. *Old Chinese Spectacles*. Tientsin: North China Press, 1915. 2nd ed. enlarged, *Chinese Eyesight and Spectacles*. Privately printed, Tonbridge, 1949.

DE RHEITA, SCHYRLAEUS. *Oculus Enoch et Eliae, sive Radius Sidereo-Mysticus.* Antwerp, 1645.

RICHARDS, D. W. The History of the Microscope; Selected References and Notes, *Trans. Am. Mic. Soc.* **68**, 55, 206, 275. 1949.

RONCHI, V. *Galileo e il suo Cannocchiale*. Turin: Bornighieri, 1964.

ROOSEBOOM, M. *Microscopium*. Leiden: Rijksmuseum voor de Geschiedenis der Natuurwetenschappen, 1956.

ROSEN, E. *The Naming of the Telescope*. New York: Schuman, 1947.

ROSEN, E. The Invention of Eyeglasses [Spectacles], *Journ. Hist. Med. and Allied Sci.* **11**, 13, 183. 1956.

SCHOTT, CASPAR. *De Magiae Universalis Naturae et Artis*. Herbipoli, 1658.

SCHUKKING, W. H. (ed.). *The Principal Works of Simon Stevin*. Vol. 4, The Art of War. Amsterdam: Swets & Zeitlinger, 1964.

SCHWENTER, DANIEL. *Deliciae Physico-Mathematicae*. Nürnberg, 1636.

SINGER, C. Steps leading to the Invention of the First Optical Apparatus. Art. in Singer (1921), vol. 2, p. 385. An earlier and shorter version of the same paper appeared as: The Earliest Steps in the Invention of the Microscope, *Trans. Faraday Soc.* **16**, 1. 1920.

SINGER, C. (ed.). *Studies in the History and Method of Science*. Oxford, vol. 1, 1917; vol. 2, 1921. Photolitho reproduction, London: Dawson, 1955.

SINGER, C. The Dawn of Microscopical Discovery, *J. Roy. Mic. Soc.* 317. 1915.

SINGER, C. Notes on the Early History of Microscopy, *Proc. Roy. Soc. Med.* **7**, 247. 1914.

SINGER, C. The Earliest Figures of Microscopic Objects (observations of F. Cesi & F. Stelluti on bees, 1625), *Endeavour*, **12**, 197. 1953.

SINGER, C. The First English Microscopist, Robert Hooke (1625 to 1703), *Endeavour*, **14**, 12. 1955.

SINGER, C. *A Short History of Medicine*. Oxford, 1928.

SINGER, C. & UNDERWOOD, E. A. *A Short History of Medicine*. Oxford, 1962. This is the rewritten form of Singer (1928) but it does not supersede it, as in order to include much new material, more than doubling the size of the book, some valuable and interesting text, and some figures, had to be omitted.

SIRTURI, GIROLAMO. *Telescopium, sive Ars perficiendi novum illud Galilaei Visorium Instrumentum ad Sidera*. Frankfurt, 1618.

STELLUTI, F. *Persio Tradotto*. Rome, 1630.

STEVIN, SIMON. See Schukking.

SUTER, R. The Chinese Word for 'Telescope', *Isis*, **50**, 152. 1959.

SWAMMERDAM, J. *Historia Generalis ofte Algemeene Verhandeling der Bloedeloose Dierkens.* Utrecht, 1669.

THORNDIKE, L. *A History of Magic and Experimental Science.* 6 vols. New York: Columbia University Press, vols. 1 and 2, The First Thirteen Centuries, reprinted 1947; vols. 3 and 4, Fourteenth and Fifteenth Centuries, 1934; vols. 5 and 6, Sixteenth Century, 1941; vols. 7 and 8, Seventeenth Century, 1958.

TURNER, G. L'E. Amida's Mirror, *Roundabout*, I (no. 3), 14. 1965.

DE WAARD, C. (ed.). *Journal tenu par Isaac Beeckman de 1604 à 1634,* 4 vols. The Hague: Nijhoff, 1942–53.

DE WAARD, C. *Die Uitvindung der Verrekykers* (The Invention of the Telescope). Rotterdam, 1906.

WANG CHIN-KUANG, Ch'ing Ch'u Kuang-Hsüeh I-Ch'i Chih-Tsao Chia, Sun Yün ch'iu (On the Early Ch'ing Maker of Optical Instruments, Sun Yün-ch'iu), *K'o-Hsüeh Shih Chi-K'an* (*Chinese Journ. Hist. of Sci.*) (no. 5), 58. 1963.

WANG LING. On the Invention and Use of Gunpowder and Firearms in China, *Isis*, **37**, 160. 1947.

WODDERBORN, JOHN. *Quatuor Problematum quae Martinus Horky contra 'Nuntium Sidereum' de Quatuor Planetis Novis disputanda proposuit Confutatio.* Padua, 1610.

PART 2
SOUTH-EAST ASIA

CANTON AND MANILA IN THE EIGHTEENTH CENTURY[1]

W. E. CHEONG

In the seventeenth and eighteenth centuries elaborate control systems were developed by Western powers in order to exclude rival European commerce from their respective spheres of trade in maritime Asia. To a lesser extent even traditional indigenous carriers were brought under these regulations. This was the essence of Western mercantilist trade in Asia. Simultaneously with the rise of Western mercantilism in maritime Asia, new indigenous rulers in the states of mainland Asia were imposing disabling laws upon the external trade of their respective domains regardless of whether such trade was conducted by Europeans or Asians. In nineteenth-century diplomatic jargon this type of control system became known as the closed-door or the exclusionist policy. Although differently motivated, Western mercantilism and Oriental exclusionism had ultimately the same effects on trade. Both systems sought to employ political boundaries as commercial perimeters, thereby obstructing free trade.

But the laws of supply and demand are not entirely governable by state legislation and few political units are so self-sufficient as to be able to afford complete commercial exclusion. Thus in most parts of Asia, whether under the one or the other system, concessions were granted for the sale of surplus products and in order to obtain necessary but otherwise unobtainable commodities. To ensure continued political control of the commercial sector, such concessions were made to facilitate specific commercial functions and usually served only prescribed lines of trade. Hence concessionaires in the eighteenth century tended to develop a high degree of specialization in their particular spheres of activity or handling of commodities. Nevertheless, within the limits defined by law, these concessions were the *instruments* for external commerce. The instruments therefore relaxed the *controls* but

[1] This paper was originally read by invitation at the Third International Congress of Economic History in Munich, 23–8 August 1965, in the section on 'The Instrumentalities of International Trade', under the chairmanship of Professor K. Glamann of the University of Copenhagen. Acknowledgment is made to Asia Foundation for a grant which enabled research to be carried out for this paper in Manila.

only within the limits demarcated, forming in sum the enabling factor.

The various types of instruments and control used in the two systems are best illustrated in the trade and regulations of Canton and Manila in their eighteenth-century contexts. These two ports were models of their respective systems. Canton was the classic example of a port within the exclusionist system. Its permissive trade served an extensive hinterland as well as a considerable overseas market for teas and silks. Manila was the centre of another large and important complex of trade, supplying Spanish American markets with Asian textiles and returning silver to Asian markets where dollars were the principal medium of exchange. Trade to and from Manila was conducted under one of the oldest European monopolist systems in Asia. Because foreign trade at Canton depended to a large extent on the silver brought to Manila, and the Manila trade to Acapulco relied predominantly upon Chinese textiles, the trade partnership of Canton and Manila in the eighteenth century became a necessary one despite the controls at both ports.

Trade under closed-door conditions was not special to eighteenth-century China. The Japanese *sakoku rei* lasted from 1640 to 1853; in India, Mughal governors often acquired special monopolies at ports under their control; the export of precious stones was a royal prerogative in Burma; in Siam certain food or strategic commodities such as teak or rice were often placed under restriction either as a price control or as a punitive measure against a dependent neighbour. But the formal growth of the Hong system in China finds no parallel in contemporary Asia. The prototype of this arm of Chinese administration—the Superintendency of Foreign Trading Junks—was first established during the T'ang period for the maintenance of an orderly relationship with foreign traders, the collection of imperial and local taxes, and the organization and reception of tribute missions. The number of Superintendencies varied in the following dynasties and the ports over which they had competence changed accordingly.[1] In the early part of the

---

[1] The Imperial Customs Collectorate established in the tenth century brought Canton, Chu'anchow and the Kiangsu and Chekiang ports under control. The Mongols started with Chu'anchow, Wenchow, Hangchow, Ningpo, Shanghai and Kan-fu, dropped Chu'anchow in 1293 and ended in 1329 with Ningpo alone. In 1368–70, the Mings centralized control at Huang-tu and Tai Ts'ang in Kiangsu, but reverted to Canton, Ningpo and Chu'anchow. In Yung-lo's rule the Tongking and Yunnan Superintendencies were added. T. T. Chang, *Sino-Portuguese Trade, 1514–1644*, Leiden, 1934.

fifteenth century, this largely functional bureau acquired a new ceremonial prominence in the aggressive Ming tribute system which was
dominated by the court eunuchs.[1] The subsequent decline of eunuch
power and the abandonment of the overseas policy enabled the Board
of Rites formally to confirm the specialized division of the administration of commerce from tribute. The official prohibition of trade notwithstanding, the collection of imperial and local taxes from foreign
commerce was officially desirable and privately lucrative for both
officials and Chinese merchants alike. But the use of force in the early
sixteenth century by the Wakos and the Portuguese fidalgos forced
Chinese policy on to a more restrictive plane. Even after the cession of
Macao to the Portuguese in 1557, events between that date and 1637—
when they expelled the Portuguese from Canton—showed that concessions by the Chinese varied in direct proportion to the military
power of the Portuguese and their commercial importance as carriers
of the suspended Sino-Japanese trade.[2] By the end of the Ming period,
therefore, some of the instruments and conditions of trade of which
European traders later complained had already made their appearance.
The general southward drift of China's maritime trade had been underlined by the coming of Western shipping from the south, and the
Japanese *sakoku rei* had shorn the trade of the northern ports of its
golden fleece.[3] The closing of Ningpo and Chu'anchow in 1522 during
the Wako raids had presaged the one-port system centred at Canton, in
which the merchants at Canton were to play an increasingly important
and monopolistic rôle under the following dynasty.[4]

After the fall of the Mings in 1644, many of the southern ports
continued to be administered by officials of the old régime, thus
ensuring a measure of continuity of method and institutions of trade

---

[1] Professor Wang Gungwu (University of Malaya), read to the Eighth Collogue of
Maritime History, Beirut, 5–10 September 1965, a paper underlining Ming innovations
in the tribute system.

[2] Sino-Japanese trade was suspended in 1549. Apart from the Macao–Nagasaki line the
Portuguese had a controlling interest in the Macao–Manila runs after 1580. In seven
years after 1635 the Portuguese lost Malacca, were driven from Nagasaki, signed their
monopoly of the Macao trade over to the English Company, surrendered Ceylon, and
lost the lucrative Macao–Manila monopoly.

[3] Chinese trade, though much reduced, could still reach Japan through Deshima after
1640. The clandestine trade of the Shimazu family of Satsuma by way of the Ryukyu
Islands kingdom continued uninterrupted.

[4] Many of the Canton merchants were from Amoy and Chu'anchow and one later famous
merchant house—that of Chunqua—came from as far north as Nanking.

regulation.[1] The prohibition of foreign trade during the campaigns against Koxinga (1661–83) had not prevented the continuance of English trade along the coast, but with the pacification of Formosa the ports of the empire were thrown open in 1685. The increasing efforts of Western traders to establish regular trade at Canton called for a more elaborate and effective control of maritime revenue income, for, despite the distinction between 'state trade' (tribute) and 'private trade' (commerce) and the traditional disdain of officials towards the merchants, the need to replenish imperial and provincial treasuries was an argument for allowing the trade. The official gratuity arising from the revenues,[2] and the unofficial gifts from the merchants, strengthened the devotion of officials to the task. Hence the appointment of two revenue commissioners—the Hoppos—was for this reason among many others a significant and a much resented event at Canton.[3] Although all senior officials then were Manchus, the provincial officials were freemen and administrators by training and profession, whereas the Hoppo belonged to the 'boyi' class, one hereditarily committed to the service of the imperial family, but often untrained and inexperienced.[4] Yet he ranked equal with and independent of the other three senior local officials—the Viceroy of the provinces of Kwangtung and Kwangsi, the Governor of Kwangtung, and the Tartar-General of the permanent Manchu garrison stationed at Canton.[5] His coming tended to divide the allegiance of the lower bureaucrats who were obliged to execute his orders, but were in fact

1 By 1650 the Ming prince Kwei Yang had been driven from Canton, but three Chinese vassal princes were then nominated to rule the south during the period of the consolidation of Ch'ing power.

2 A Viceroy earned taels 180 and 90 piculs of rice per year. A second income of taels 13,000–20,000 was paid in gratuities to him from the revenues of his provinces to ensure his loyalty. Gifts and private gratuities were his third income. The proportion between them is estimated at 1 : 6 : 93, if an average is taken of the income of the officials filling the two thousand key posts. Lower officials, according to their power and accessibility to gifts, probably earned proportionately less. R. M. Marsh, *The Mandarins, The Circulation of Élites in China 1600–1900*, Illinois, 1961, p. 64.

3 References are made in English Company records to the second Hoppo: 1699, 1703, 1735/6, 1796, 1800. In Kiangsu and Chekiang the provincial Governors were in charge of maritime revenues, although in the early period Hoppos are mentioned by English records. In Fukien the Tartar-General assumed the rôle. H. B. Morse, *The Chronicles of the East India Company Trading to China 1635–1834*, Oxford, 1926, II, p.329.

5 Below them were the provincial Treasurer, the Judge, the Prefect and the sub-Prefect in that order. Then came the Hien—the local police superintendent, tax-collector and magistrate all in one. He had daily contact with the foreigners.

answerable to the Governors. And in the first quarter of the century, to obtain the co-operation of the Chinese merchants, he had to seek the support of the highest Chinese authority—the lowly ranked Titu—provincial commander of the Green Banners.[1] Hence the constant appeals of traders over the head of the Hoppo to the Viceroy or the Governor often led in the first half of the century to the Hoppo's being overruled. The Co-Hong set up in 1720 by the Hoppo and Titu was dissolved in 1721 on the Viceroy's intervention. Between 1724 and 1729 the post of Hoppo was suspended and, when restored, it underwent the indignity of having its first tenant dismissed in 1732. In 1741 the Viveroy refused to issue the Grand Chop for the departure of foreign ships until all the Hoppo's records for the five previous years were scrutinized. Between 1730 and 1747 the maritime revenues were controlled at various times by the Viceroy, the Governor, the Tartar-General, the provincial Treasurer and the second Hoppo.[2]

The tightening of regulations over Western trade in the fifties closed official ranks generally and strengthened the Hoppo's hand, but he had to make joint reports to the Court with the Governor and the Viceroy, and this new strength failed to save the career of the Hoppo in 1759. Official bickering retreated behind the screen of the Hong merchants after 1760, and little was reported of officials until the failure of several Hong merchants in the late seventies brought renewed official intervention. From 1782, the firmer enforcement of the prohibition of direct intercourse with the Viceroy and the Governor, and the grant of supervisory powers to the Hoppo over the Hongs, brought this official's power to its full measure, his rapacity augmenting with his power.[3] Throughout the century the post of Hoppo had been in safe Manchu hands,[4] yet from the last decade of the century his annual reports were being compared with the secret monthly reports of the

---

[1] Many decrees were issued regularly under the chop of both the Titu and the Hoppo in Amoy and Canton in the early part of this century, and in 1722 the Titu was even able to obstruct the issue of the Grand Chop for the departure of a ship at Canton.

[2] Morse, I, *passim*; v, pp. 1–8.

[3] The repeated complaints of European traders and the many failures of Hong merchants bear testimony to this. One Hoppo was reputed to have netted $240,000 in six months as Hoppo of Canton in 1794.

[4] In 1777 the Manchu Viceroy, acting as Hoppo, was ordered to Yunnan and replaced by the Chinese Governor of Shantung who was precluded from control of the maritime customs. The Manchu Governor of Kwangtung became acting Hoppo. Another Chinese Viceroy in 1800 was so maligned at Court by the Manchu Governor that he committed suicide in the latter's residence.

Governor and the Viceroy, severally.[1] The rise of the Hoppo had facili-
tated the control of the Chinese merchants, the trade and the revenues,
but the growth of the Chinese merchants into a defined and organized
group to handle the foreign trade administration simplified this process.

The emergence of the Canton merchant in the eighteenth century
may be studied in three main contexts: in his rôle as an individual and
head of a family business, as a member of a trade guild purveying for
Western trade, and as part of an instrument of administration and
control of Western trade and traders. To protect his individual interests,
he had to be a member of the guild—the Hong—and as a member of
the Hong he exercised progressively more administrative powers. First
drawn together in 1702 with the Hoppo's support to resist the greed of
an imperial favourite, in 1720 the Hong had turned into an instrument
of monopoly against Westerners. Like the 'nakama' of the contemporary Tokugawa era, the Hong stabilized the commercial dominance
of its members by serving as a guarantee in commercial transactions and
providing joint bargaining powers in their relations with local officials,
foreign trade partners and suppliers from the interior. Its being made
up of the principal merchants of the market added respectability and
exclusiveness to the organization and their influence and intervention
often moderated the demands of their foreign partners. Within ten
years the administrative potential of this commercial group had been
harnessed by the authorities. By 1728 the Viceroy, then also acting
Hoppo, was advising foreigners to trade only with the Hongs so as to
avoid debts and disputes.[2] The French, the Ostenders, the Dutch
(1729), the Danes (1731), and the Swedes (1732),[3] had multiplied the
tasks and the anxieties of the officials, and each dispute was accompanied by a threat to move up the coast.[4] The case for the confinement
of Western trade to Canton, and for regulating it even within the port,
was strengthened. In 1736 Chinese merchants were made to stand

---

1 J. K. Fairbank, *Trade and Diplomacy on the China Coast 1842–1854*, Cambridge, Mass.,
1953, p. 49.
2 Morse, I, p. 188.
3 For the French activities, see L. Dermigny, *La Chine et l'Occident. Le Commerce à
Canton au XVIIIe Siècle, 1719–1833*, Paris, 1964. The Danes: K. Glamann, 'The
Danish Asiatic Company 1732–1772', *Scandinavian Economic History Review*, VIII,
no. 2, pp. 109–49. The Dutch: K. Glamann, *Dutch-Asiatic Trade 1620–1740*, Copenhagen and The Hague, 1958. A summary of Swedish activities: S. Roth, *Chinese
Porcelain Imported by the Swedish East India Company*, Gothenburg, 1965.
4 Between 1710 and 1760, six English ships actually traded or tried to trade at Chusan
(1), Amoy (2), and Ningpo (3).

security for Western ships, and this beginning of the 'security merchant' system was formalised in 1745 and strengthened in 1755 by the
addition of a monopoly to the powers of the Chinese merchants. The
closure of the empire in 1757 made the monopoly even more effective,
and the imperial decree of 1760, which confirmed the existing system,
gave a legal stamp to the Hong system.[1] In everything but in name the
Hongs had become a branch of the Chinese port administration, the
principal partners of each Hong actually buying the title 'shaw' or
'qua' in the ninth rank of the mandarinate.

While giving a legal guise to the Hongs' actions, the chartering of
the Hongs added little to the merchants' commercial capacity, nor
could they be held answerable for their actions. On the other hand it
committed them to official policy, and made all the powers that they
previously exercised independently of official recognition dependent
upon membership of the Hong. The appointment of Hong merchants
being at the disposal of officials, the whole career of the merchant
became orientated to the cultivation of official goodwill: seasonal gifts,
given previously as an act of appreciation and politeness, began to be
exacted as a right and a fee for official recognition. Once purchased,
membership of the select group had to be financially 'maintained'.[2] As
their official status advanced, the merchants' vulnerability to extortion
increased, and their responsibilities and financial obligations accrued.
Yet their basic commercial commitment ensured their continued and
efficient performance as agents of the officials. Hence from 1760 official
disfavour became almost a worse fate than commercial failure. Failure
was invariably followed by a period of incarceration, beatings, and
finally confiscation of all properties and the exile of the merchant or
his partner to Ili.[3] Official disfavour led to exorbitant extortion and
enforced tenure of the impoverished Hong, until death in harness
transferred the burden to one of the sons.[4]

By the fifties many of the Hongs were already indebted and ten

---

[1] Morse, v, p. 94, Regulations for the control of Trade at Canton, 1760.
[2] Membership of the Hong was most sought after by pursers or cashiers of the old
Hongs wishing to strike out on their own. Sons of established Hong merchants, however, sought every possible means to evade the duty of succeeding to their father's
title.
[3] For example Yngshaw and Kewshaw (1779), Wyequa and Shykinqua (1794), Gnewqua
(1813), and Exchin (1828).
[4] For example, Munqua (suicide, 1796); Mawqua (died 1812); Phuankhequa (forced
from retirement and died in harness, 1820); Chunqua (forced from retirement and died
a bankrupt, 1829); Inqua (Chunqua's partner, suicide, 1829).

years later their indebtedness had become chronic. Only by the exercise of their original powers as a commercial group in controlling prices, and by credit trade despite official prohibition, were the Hongs able to continue commercially viable and meet their official burdens as well. The abolition of the Co-Hong in 1771 removed even this last safeguard of Hong finance and within seven years five of the nine Hongs were embarrassed.[1] From then on, although each attempt to form a Co-Hong was fiercely contested by the English, the Committee of the English Company at Canton was repeatedly forced to take the finances of some of the Hongs in hand in order to keep them solvent, to protect them from the Hoppo (whose extortion was usually passed on to the Company in raised prices or demands for advances), and generally to keep the trade going.[2] A special Consoo Fund, set up in 1782 by obligatory contributions from the Hongs for the liquidation of debts of the Hong merchants, was conveniently misappropriated by the Hoppo to pay imperial duties whenever more direct means failed.

The practice of resorting to the wealthiest Hong merchant as the intermediary between the Europeans and the officials became formalized after 1782. The Hoppo now had virtual control of the Hongs through a mandarin specially appointed to supervise Hong affairs, and the senior viable merchant was answerable to him for the misdeeds of the Europeans and the Hongs. An order of seniority emerged below the chief merchant which became a veritable order of succession to the dreaded post and served as the order according to which contracts and the securing of foreign ships were allocated. This enabled the Hoppo to attain his mercenary ends even more easily than before. On the other hand the senior merchant became such a butt of the Hoppo's rage and extortion that, in the last forty years of Hong history, the wealthy senior Hongs exhausted guile and excuse to avoid the honour. By refusing the Hongs of deceased fathers, by retirement, by transferring the Hong to a poor relative, by deliberately ceding contracts and the right to secure ships, the great Hongs tried to avoid ostentation and exposure. But only the famous Howqua was rich enough to bribe his way back into the ranks each time a death or retirement threatened to make him the senior merchant. The three generations of Phuankhequas who were singled out for this honour probably had more than their

[1] Four of them, Coqua, Seuqua, Kewshaw and Yngshaw, failed in 1779.
[2] Co-Hongs were established or attempts were made to establish them after 1771, in 1775, 1776, 1777, 1779, 1780, 1782 and 1795.

share of imprisonments, fines and bullying from the officials, but their incredible record of stability suggests that they either had another source of income or that with diplomacy in dealing with officials, business acumen in handling the trade and ruthlessness in extortion from other Hongs, it was possible to hold the post and survive.[1] But the rank and file never recovered complete viability in the sixty years after 1782.

The path to the security of official recognition was, for many, also that to chronic indebtedness; for some, to bankruptcy. Whereas in 1843 there was one Hong of ninety years' standing, two reaching their fiftieth year and one its fortieth year,[2] fifteen failures had been recorded in the last quarter of the eighteenth century, and eight others followed in the first thirty years of the nineteenth century.[3] A few even disappeared unnoticed. Although up to as many as thirteen Hongs have been mentioned as operating in any one year during the period 1760–1843, in fact at no time was the number of merchants considered viable enough to be allowed to secure ships more than eleven. Even this last figure was attained only during a period when the English Company was helping more than half the Hongs along.[4]

[1] *Senior Hong Merchants 1760–1833:*
1760–1788   Phuankhequa I (deceased 10 January 1788).
1788–1796   Munqua (suicide 10 April 1796).
1796–1807   Phuankhequa II (retired).
1807–1814   Puiqua (reputedly brother of Howqua, probably died). During this period Mawqua I held the post briefly in 1808 and 1810–12, having retired in 1807 and 1809, but being brought back both times, and dying in yoke.
1815–1820   Phuankhequa II (died in harness). He was brought back from retirement. His son Shinqua refused the Hong on the grounds that he was in too high a rank—2nd rank of the mandarinate. A poor relative Tinqua was put up.
1820–1821   Mawqua II (interim measure). He was otherwise Kowqua, the eldest of Mawqua I's three sons who were made to take the Hong in 1813.
1821–1833   Phuankhequa III—otherwise Heemqua, younger son of Phuankhequa II. He was forced to take the partnership with the useless Tinqua. From about 1830 onwards, Howqua became a joint leader with Phuankhequa.

[2] These were Phuankhequa, Howqua, Mawqua and Goqua.
[3] The number of failures after 1800 would have been greater had not the English Committee spent ten years in the second decade of the century in liquidating the debts of most of the Hongs. Failures: 1777, Wayqua; 1779, Yngshaw; 1779, Kewshaw; 1779, Coqua; 1779, Seunqua; 1788, Howqua; 1790, Eequa; 1793, Chowqua; 1793, Pinqua; 1794, Shykinqua; 1794, Wyequa; 1796, Munqua; 1797, Munqua Jr.; 1797, Seequa; 1798, Geowqua; 1810, Gnewqua; 1821, Conseequa; 1827, Exchin; 1827, Poonequa; 1828, Manhop; 1830, Chunqua; 1830, Inqua.
[4] *Hong merchants who secured English ships 1760–1833:*
1760, 3; 1761, 3; 1764, 4; 1768, 4; 1772, 8; 1773, 6; 1774, 3; 1775, 5; 1776, 6; 1777, 6; 1778, 5; 1779, 5; 1780, 5; 1781, 4; 1782, 4; 1783, 7; 1784, 7; 1785, 8; 1786, 8; 1787, 8; 1788, 8; 1789, 7; 1790, 6; 1791, 5; 1792, 6; 1793, 8; 1794, 7; 1795, 9; 1796, 9; 1797, 9; 1798, 8; 1799, 8; 1800, 8; 1801, 8; 1802, 8; 1803, 8; 1804, 9; 1805, 9; 1806, 9;

The Co-Hong had developed originally as an instrument of commerce, but from the fourth decade of the eighteenth century it had become also an instrument of control. After 1760 it exercised powers with the force of law, and yet it was without the responsibility of a department of state administration. Nor were the Hongs functional in the formulating and making of the laws on trade, but only in the administration of them. But these developments had not occurred in a vacuum: they had been shaped and influenced by organized Western reaction. It is perhaps no accident that the establishment of the first Co-Hong (1720) should have coincided with the organization of the English Company's rotative seasonal council of supercargoes at Canton, nor that the first English resident council came in 1758, just before the charter of the Hongs in 1760. The firm establishment of the Co-Hong in 1782 was to be expected after the spate of failures in the late seventies had nearly led to a show of force from the English. On the other hand, effective though the Committees of the East India Companies may have been, and vocal in their grievances, they did not really constitute a legal body, and were powerless to prevent 'human' incidents arising from the frequent contacts of European traders and sailors with the Chinese. It was perhaps presumption on their part to have expected anything more than their due—that is, direct negotiations of any kind only through the complementary Chinese instrument, the Co-Hong. It is, however, true that official-to-official rapport on parity would have been unacceptable to the Chinese government, for although the Canton system developed to handle an essentially eighteenth-century situation, the system was in conformity with Chinese traditions of foreign relations, and of the place of private trade (commerce) as distinct from state trade (tribute). The type of administration offered for commerce aimed at the collection of taxes, the maintenance of a respectable distance between traders from states considered tributary to China and the imperial officials, and the regulation of an orderly intercourse in which the fixing of the terms of trade and the conditions of residence were merely a normal corollary.[1]

1807, 10; 1808, 10; 1809, 9; 1810, 7; 1811, 7; 1812, 9; 1813, 10; 1814, 10; 1815, 11; 1816, 11; 1817, 11; 1818, 11; 1819, 11; 1820, 11; 1821, 9; 1822, 9; 1823, 10; 1824, 10; 1825, 9; 1826, 9; 1827, 8; 1828, 7; 1829, 6; 1830, 10; 1831, 10; 1832, 9; 1833, 11.

[1] The material used in this part of the paper was from the China and Japan Section of the records of the English East India Company, to be found in the India Office Library. The three principal series were the Consultations of the Canton Committee, the Diary and the Court Letters.

Canton and Manila in eighteenth century

Most of the instruments of trade and control used in Manila in the eighteenth century developed from the earliest Spanish days in the islands, and did not undergo any striking changes in the eighteenth century despite the dynastic change at home. The Manila trade consisted mainly of an import trade in textiles from India and China, and an export trade of the same commodities to the Mexican port of Acapulco, which yielded silver dollars—the principal circulating medium in international trade in maritime Asia at this time.[1] The two lines were therefore organically interdependent, and the colony's economy became so dependent upon the incomes from the trade that agricultural and other enterprise was stultified.[2] The government benefited from direct taxation at Manila, from the licences issued to Chinese traders in the colony, and indirectly from a Mexican subsidy which was in fact remitted from the duties on goods entering Acapulco from Manila;[3] the *obras pias* made fortunes from investments in the trade and from loans to other investors;[4] and the Manileños profited from the trade itself. Officials had an interest in the trade in their own right as citizens of the colony and as officials administering the port's commerce and also because of the levies which they exacted from the trade for themselves. It was therefore a matter of administrative adeptness and economic expedience that the Asian supply trade should be regulated and taxed, and the re-exportation to Mexico organized and restrained.[5]

<hr />

[1] W. E. Cheong, 'Trade and Finance in China 1784–1834: A Reappraisal', *Business History*, VII, pt. 1, January 1965, pp. 34–56.

[2] The effect of the galleons on the Filipino economy is explained in British Museum MSS. [BM hereafter] Egerton 518 ff. 91–115, 'Direccion de la Campania de las Filipinas ... en contestacion a la representation hecha a S.M. por el Consulado de Manila', 11 January 1788.

[3] The 'situado' or 'socorro', as the subsidy was called, varied greatly: 1700—$140,000 (fixed by law); 1725—$72,801; 1742—$211,000; 1786—$346,912; 1787—$74,383; 1788—$298,138; 1797—$500,000. It was abolished in 1804 when the colony became self-supporting. W. L. Schurz, *The Manila Galleon*, N.Y., 1959, p. 180. Seville Archives, Filipinas Section [Filipinas hereafter] 976, Cargo of San José (1788); Filipinas 977, Cargo of San Andrés (1797).

[4] For example, between 1734 and 1766 the Misericordia loaned $3,319,787, and eight other *obras pias* together, another $5,000,000. In the fifties Governor Arandia borrowed from the Misericordia ($100,000) and the Franciscans ($30,000) to finance the ill-fated mestizo retail firm. In 1803 the Royal Philippine Company borrowed $180,000 from the Franciscans to tide over a bad season in Canton. E. H. Blair and R. Robertson, *The Philippine Islands*, Cleveland, 1906–9 [hereafter B & R], XLVIII, p. 183; Schurz, p. 168; Filipinas 990, Madrid Directors of Philippine Company to C. Soler, 9 September 1803, with enclosures.

[5] Overloading of the galleons was often the cause of wrecks and of gluts in the Mexican markets. To escape official detection some galleons dragged flotillas behind them

The trade to Mexico was regulated by a series of juntas each with a specialised function. The allocation of shipping space on the annual galleons was undertaken by the *junta del repartimiento* which was set up in 1604. It was headed by the Governor and included the Oidor (normally a listener, but here the Dean of the Audiencia), the Archbishop, the Fiscal of the Audiencia and two *regidores* or city councillors. After this junta had completed its work, in dividing the holds among those of the Manileño Spaniards with ten years' residential qualification, the *junta de evaluo* began producing a manifest of the cargo and evaluated the shipment. This junta was made up of the Fiscal and two other officials of the treasury, and the evaluation was based on an established scale of values for specific goods, fixed every five years for imported products, and at ten-year intervals for insular products.[1]

The ship's clearance could be given only by the Governor, and from 1619 was personally supervised by the Fiscal. As these two officials had the key posts in the port administration, a pattern of rivalry developed. The Governor was technically supreme in military and civil affairs, but the Fiscal, as Attorney-General and member of the Audiencia, was independent of and equal to the Governor in his field, and moreover he was considered as an overseer of the metropolitan government.[2] Until the establishment of the juntas the Governor had previously been supreme in the matters of the trade, but by 1619 the Fiscal's approval on all financial affairs of the colony became mandatory.[3] With the *junta de evaluo* already in his charge, in the seventeenth century the Fiscal gained control of the *junta del repartimiento*, often deputizing for the Governor, and when not doing so, opposing him. By 1703 the 'city and commerce' were demanding a special *junta del repartimiento* of three under the Fiscal.[4] The Governor successfully resisted this proposal, and in 1721 Governor Tore del Campo attempted to interfere in the Fiscal's competence by appointing two special observers to

crammed with goods and, on returning, unloaded their silver cargoes in a provincial port before entering Cavite. The arrival between 1800 and 1804 of eight galleons—*Magellanes, Fama, Lucia, Montanez, Rey Carlos, San Rafael* (of the Philippine Company), *N.S. de Guia, N.S. de la Concepcion*—ruined the Mexican markets for years.
[1] As duties in Acapulco were 33⅓%, goods were grossly undervalued at Manila. Mexican authorities, however, always raised the invoiced valuation before imposing the taxes.
[2] The Oidor, Dean of the Audiencia, had equal ranking in the judicial branch but played only a secondary rôle in this matter; the Archbishop also had immense influence when he chose to use it.
[3] B & R, xxv, p. 24, Law no. 46, Felipe IV, Merida, 4 May 1619.
[4] B & R, xliv, p. 232.

supervise the lading of the galleons. Valdés, his successor, continued this practice, but repeated and fierce remonstrances by the 'city and commerce' finally procured the dismissal of the Governor's two spies. But in 1753, Obando, the first of three authoritarian Governors with extreme 'mercantilist' views and anti-Chinese inclinations, dropped the Fiscal from the *junta del repartimiento*, which was then reconstituted under the Oidor. Arandia, his successor, kept the system, but before the British invasion it had been abandoned, and the Fiscal resumed his powers when Manila was restored to Spain. Despite the establishment of the powerful Consulado in 1769, the Fiscal's powers remained unimpaired, and they were strengthened immensely in 1784 when a second title—that of Intendant-General—was conferred on the Fiscal. The new post gave the Fiscal sweeping powers over all the Filipino ports,[1] enabling him to outrank the Governor in this branch of the administration, but increasing his already renowned rapacity.[2] It was with this official that European traders came into contact when Manila was thrown open in 1790.[3] The rise of the Fiscal was underlined by his increasing alignment with the emergent 'city and commerce' of Manila.

The term 'city and commerce' in the sixteenth and the seventeenth centuries referred generally to all the Manileño Spaniards with the ten-year residential qualification who thereby qualified for an allocation of shipping space on the galleons to Acapulco. In the main they were made up of the trading community which formed the 'commerce' side,

---

[1] B & R, L, p. 56, Royal Order no. 17, 26 July 1784.

[2] The connivance of most high officials in the contravention of the port regulations was well known. Such acquiescence was fully rewarded. Several cases in the 1760s involved Governor de la Torre and the Archbishop, and had to be dropped. Ciriaco G. Carvajal, the first Intendant-General, was the centre of another scandal in 1788, when, after his promotion to the Mexican Audiencia, the new Governor, Marquina, accused him of having accepted, apart from thousands of dollars of gifts, 'un coche de quatro asientos a la moda Ynglesa', while Fiscal of Manila. B & R, L, p. 28; B & R, XLVIII, p. 310; Filipinas 986, F. B. de Marquina to A.Valdés, Manila-Madrid, 15 December 1788, no. 5.

[3] Manila was opened to Asian shipping from 1785. A decree in 1789 opened it for three years to European shipping from 1790, but it was closed during the Nootka Sound crisis. Thereafter it remained opened most of the time, with periodic sanctions against the English, as in 1797 during the proposed invasion of Manila, and in 1803 upon the resumption of war in Europe. Canton Consultations, India Office Library [IOCC henceforth] 145 (1803–04) p. 26, 31 October 1803; BM Egerton 518, ff. 47–77 (printed) Cedula for founding of the Royal Philippine Company, and opening of Manila to native craft; Home Miscellaneous Series, India Office Library, 606, Manila Invasion Plans 1797; Copy of Cedula opening Manila, 15 August 1789, enclosed in A. Merry to Leeds, 24 August 1789, No. 27, *F.O. 72/15*, Public Record Office.

and of the local authorities, of which the principal was the *cabildo* (city council) headed by the *alcalde* (mayor), who formed the 'city' part of the group.[1] In many cases the two groups overlapped—thus a merchant could also be a regidor (justice of the peace or alderman). By the eighteenth century, however, the trading power had concentrated in the hands of the religious orders[2] and a few established families, and repeated abuse of power in the juntas had caused a drift of the 'city and commerce' from official policies. There ensued a fight to remove official power over the trade and to recover the shipping space misappropriated by officials. In 1703 the 'city and commerce' had demanded an independent administration of the galleon trade, and sustained pressure for representation led in 1734 to the appointment of eight representatives to a board called the *compromisario* who were to act as a whole as a moderator in the juntas handling the galleon trade. One of its members would alternate with one of the two regidores on the *junta del repartimiento*.[3] Three years later they had procured the dismissal of the governor's two observers of the galleon-lading, but the *junta del repartimiento* continued to lend itself to considerable maladministration, from which the Governors were not reluctant to profit.[4]

By 1751 officials were invoking their various qualifications in order to acquire additional space on the galleons. They were prohibited the trade as officials, but the Oidor took ten additional units of space, the Fiscal and other Audiencia judges took five more each, and the regidores claimed eight additional lots. Obando also granted extra units to naval and military personnel, and all the ports of the Philippines were granted lots according to the number of Spanish inhabitants. But many who qualified did not have the funds to fill their quota with cargo and were

[1] There were two *cabildos* in Manila, one civil and the other religious. The Audiencia Section of the Seville Filipiniana lists their work separately, for example in the following *legajos* (in bundles): Ecclesiastical Cabildo: 77, 78 (letters 1586–1700), 294, 295 (letters 1645–1764), 1015, 1016, 1017 (duplicates of papers 1688–1835); Secular Cabildo: 27, 28 (letters and minutes 1570–1699), 187 (letters 1700–59).

[2] The religious orders had official permission to trade from 1638. In 1751 their lot was fixed at 132 units, and this was confirmed in 1769. Individual members of orders were prohibited the trade, but in practice this prohibition was not observed. The main houses were Jesuits, Dominicans, Franciscans, Augustinians, la Mitia, Misericordia and Archicofradias. J. Montero y Vidal, *El Archipelago Filipino*, Madrid, 1886, p. 225.

[3] Schurz, p. 154.

[4] 'También los governadores abusaban de su poder, reservandose un gran parte de la cabida del buque para su uso y el de sus amigos.' F. G. Calderon, *Enciclopédia Filipino*, Manila, 1908, p. 38. ('Also, the Governors used to abuse their powers, reserving a large portion of the holds of the ship for their own use and that of their friends.')

not restrained from selling them; some mortgaged their trade to Chinese or Portuguese traders from whom they bought goods on credit. Others borrowed from religious houses at exorbitant rates.[1] Wealthy Mexicans commissioned agents to obtain residential qualifications and trade on their behalf, passing themselves off as the Mexican consignees of the Filipino principal when in fact the Filipino consigner was merely an agent for the Mexican investor.[2]

The situation became so bad that in the last thirty years of the century after the establishment of the Consulado in 1769, only some twenty-five Manila traders of a Consulado membership of 150 were possessed of sufficient funds for private investment in the galleons; fifty-six others traded through these twenty-five.[3] It was sensibly acknowledged in the founding of the Consulado that the participants were no longer Manileño Spaniards of ten years' standing. Many who did not qualify were obvious assets to the trade; others who qualified were in no position to participate. To admit the latter and exclude the former was to aggravate the tendency to speculate on the resale of shipping lots.[4] The basis of qualification thus widened to include members of the Consulado, residents of more than ten years in Manila, any person who had more than $7000 or was a 'regidor, militar, haciendero, banquero o viuda de aquella ciudad'.[5]

As the galleon trade declined, the 'city and commerce' threw itself behind efforts to save it, but the Governors steadily transferred their force to the development of other sectors of the colony's economy.[6] When the Royal Philippine Company was established to trade directly between Spain and the Far East in 1785, the Consulado obtained special

[1] G. Anson, *The Manila Galleon* (undated, in Lopez Memorial Museum, Manila), p. 7; J. White, *A Voyage to China*, Boston, 1823, p. 126. Montero y Vidal, p. 225. Interest charged ranged from 50% for Acapulco, 35% for India and 25% for China.

[2] B & R, XLIV, p. 248, Report of Antonio de Abreu, Madrid, 1736.

[3] Schurz, p. 163.

[4] Tickets for a unit of space on the galleon were normally priced at $80–$100 each, and were assessed for taxation purposes at Manila at $125. In 1766 each space-unit was being sold for over $200. B & R, I, p. 64.

[5] BM Egerton 518, ff. 188–201, 'Reflexiones imparciales que D. Vicente Vasadre propone al Ministerio', Madrid, 14 January 1791. ('alderman, military personnel, landed proprietor, banker, or widow of that city')

[9] Governor Vasco y Vargas (1778–87) took the most important steps in this direction, trying through the Sociedad de los Amigos del Pais to diversify the colony's economy. The sugar-cane and tobacco industries remain as evidence of his efforts. Maria Aguilar (1793–1806) also played an important part in freeing the colony from dependence on Mexico and the galleons.

veto powers in the Company's Manila junta in order to safeguard the galleon interests. For the next twenty years the Consulado fought a losing rearguard action against the higher peninsular interests which the Royal Company represented.[1] The cessation of the galleon runs in 1813,[2] and the eventual abandonment of sailings to Mexico after 1820 finally brought this chapter of the 'city and commerce's' history to an end.[3] The rise of the select mercantile middle-class to representative status in the principal commercial activity of Manila, thereby acquiring an administrative function in the port administration, is the nub of the developments which the Spanish mercantilist system underwent in the export trade of eighteenth-century Manila.

The Spanish regulation of the supply trade from Asian countries forms part of the greater problem of Chinese immigration to Manila, and was further conditioned by certain special factors. Spanish prohibition of the visits of Spanish shipping and nationals to Asian ports confined the Manileños to a sedentary rôle in this line, while exclusion laws prevented the participation of other European traders apart from the Portuguese.[4] But the Portuguese, after a brief but intense struggle in the early seventeenth century, ceded the main carrying trade from China to Chinese junks issuing from the Fukien and later Kwangtung coasts.[5] The supplies from India were dominated by Armenian carriers

[1] The Consulado feared the inflationary effect of the Company's trade on the prices of Asian goods at Manila. The Company's direct trade from Manila to Callao destroyed an important sub-outlet for the Acapulco ships. Clashes also occurred over the Company's cartel with private British Indian and Canton Agencies, direct trade from Spain to Canton, the opening of Manila to the West and overloading of the galleons. IOCC 84 (1786–87), 17 March 1787, Fitzhugh to Canton Committee, Manila–Canton, 12 February 1787; Filipinas 976, Junta de Estado to Directors of Philippine Co., Madrid, 12 July 1788; Filipinas 989, Madrid Directors to D. Gardoqui, 15 August 1794; M. Aguilar to Gardoqui, Manila–Madrid, 30 October 1793; Filipinas 986, Junta del Gobierno de la Compania de Filipinas, 27 December 1787; BM Egerton 519, ff. 97–103, Directors of Philippine Co. to A. V. de Faranco, Madrid, 7 November 1794.

[2] Filipinas 932, Decree of Regents, 27 September 1813.

[3] Contrary to W. L. Schurz's assertion which most historians have taken for granted, the Philippine Company's Canton Factory was in full operation into the second decade of the century and did not cease operations in 1805. In the twenties the Factory still existed but the supercargoes were engaged in opium speculation. W. E. Cheong, 'Opium Trade and Agencies at Canton 1821–1834', unpublished Imperial History Prize monograph, 1964 (Institute of Commonwealth Studies, London).

[4] Following the union of the Iberian crowns in 1580, Portuguese trade interests were specifically excluded from the field of Spanish endeavour in 1593. B & R, xxv, p. 29, Law no. 38, Felipe IV, Madrid, 31 December 1622. Calderon, p. 36.

[5] The Portuguese dominated the Macao–Manila trade between 1618 and 1632, but priced themselves out of the trade. B & R, xxv, p. 141.

of British investments from the Coromandel and later Malabari and Bengal coasts.[1] Chinese traders were thus monopolists of the principal supply line for the lifeline of the colony—the galleon trade. This monopoly left the Manileños virtually at the mercy of the Chinese, while some Manila merchants wanted a share of the trade themselves. Yet the *junta de pancada*, set up in 1589 for the purchase of Chinese goods by the junk-load, satisfied neither the sellers, who felt imposed upon, nor the buyers, who were forced to accept government-purchased goods and were deprived of the possibility of making better bargains. By 1703 a 'feria' system had become current. For a charge of eight thousand dollars the Chinese were allowed every 4 June to conduct a grand sale, but again this method had fallen into disuse by 1777. Nor did the government-backed mestizo-Spanish firm for retail established in the fifties by Governor Arandia rally those who wished to appropriate the trade for themselves.[2] The government on its part recognized that the Chinese trade could not be suppressed as it was crucial to the galleon trade; nor was it in a position to take a measure which would deprive the coffers of a substantial income in taxes in various forms from the Chinese.[3] Officials were even more reluctant to surrender an easy second income in the form of bribes. But the presence of Chinese settlers in large numbers engendered official disquiet.[4] Policies therefore alternated between periods of fierce application of expulsion orders and phases of accommodation.[5] In between these two types of policies, house and head taxes, levies for licences to trade and physical

[1] S. D. Quiason, *The English Country Trade*, Quezon City, 1966; W. E. Cheong, 'An Anglo-Spanish-Portuguese Clandestine Trade between the ports of British India and Manila', read at the International Conference of Historians of Asia, Hong Kong, September 1964.

[2] B & R, XLVII, p. 180. Schurz, p. 75.

[3] Figures on the income vary substantially by the year. Over a thirty-year period between 1606 and 1635, incomes went as high as $162,941 (1634–5) and as low as $5,770 (1618). A report of the eighteenth century gives $23,000 as derived from licences to trade and $37,000 from taxes. These are probably understated, as the same report cites the Mexican subsidy to Manila as between $50,000 and $60,000, which is much lower than any of the figures cited in footnote 3, p. 237 above. B & R, XXV, pp. 74–86. Receipts from Chinese licences, *ibid.* p. 141. Revenues on China Trade, B & R, XLIV, p. 276.

[4] These figures suggest the potential Chinese menace: 1586—10,000; 1636—30,000. A period of administration generally unfavourable to Chinese settlement followed. 1749—40,000. In contrast the figures for Spanish nationals were: 1636—230; 1702—400; 1722—882. B & R, XLIV, p. 271, Report of Antonio de Abreu; Schurz, p. 81.

[5] Anti-Chinese Governors of the eighteenth century were Conde de Lizaraga (1709–15), Gaspar de la Torre (1739–45), Obando (1750–3), Manuel de Arandia (1754–9), José Raon (1765–70), Simon Anda (1770–6), Berenguer de Marquina (1787–93).

ostracization helped to keep the numbers down.[1] In the application of tax laws and policies of expulsion, due distinction was made between the non-Christian and the Christian Chinese, for the powerful church found in the affinity between the pursuit of their substantial commercial interests and their missionary zeal irresistible arguments for a policy of moderation.[2] But the opening of Manila in 1790 broke the Chinese monopoly, and enabling laws soon encouraged the establishment of Spanish houses in Bengal, Madras and Canton. Thus the first step towards the abandonment of port controls according to mercantilist tenets was taken from within, but another fifty years separated this initial step from the complete opening of the Philippine Islands.

Chinese relations with the West at Canton in the eighteenth century hinged upon the development of a system which would keep the trade going without conceding any of the traditional practices of diplomacy and trade. The traders on both sides were committed to the maintenance of this trade by their vested interests, and as the trade expanded, even more were they committed. For the officials the replenishment of the imperial and provincial treasuries was the ostensible reason for the trade, but the making of their own fortunes played a significant part. Beyond this point of general agreement that the trade should continue, the three parties were most concerned with their particular interests, and these did not exactly coincide. The Western traders, small in numbers but organized, were always fighting for better terms of trade; officials were bound to keep the barbarians at a distance, but were not loth to levy taxes on their shipping and trade, and to make a little on the side; and the Chinese merchant had to buy the goodwill of the officials and keep his foreign partner within terms which would not render trade unlucrative. The institutionalization of the Hongs as an instrument of commerce as well as of control in fact

[1] The Chinese could trade in the districts of Tondo, Laguna Bay, Pampanga and Bulacan. Arandia actually confined Chinese trade in Manila to the San Fernando Trade Pavilion. The Chinese Parians were at Tondo, Binondo, Santa Cruz and later Pampanga at Lake Candaba. A Chinese Headman was usually appointed. Non-Christian Chinese paid $8 residential registration fees, 5 reales tribute, and 12 reales house tax. The capitation tax was at $6 in 1790. B & R, XLIV, p. 136; XLVIII, p. 180; L, p. 200. See also E. Wickberg, *The Chinese in Philippine Life, 1850–1898*, New Haven, 1965, chapters 1 and 2.

[2] The Dominican Governor *ad interim* Arrechedera was one remarkable instance. In Anda's governorship, he complained bitterly that the protection of the Chinese given by the religious orders went to the extent that it adversely affected Spanish interests.

accommodated most of these diverse interests. It was not a perfect system: Western traders still felt imposed upon, and were made to accept the terms of the Hongs; the officials did not always escape the pressure of foreigners or get away with their extortion; and many Hongs were ruined. But at least Westerners thought it worthwhile to stay on and trade, the conditions notwithstanding; officials had their taxes and gratuities; and some of the Chinese merchants managed a fair trade.

The eighteenth century was a period of decline for the Manila system, and by the opening years of the nineteenth century the stock of the colony's 250-year-old commercial system had reached its nadir. The same basic elements were at play in Manila as at Canton: the struggle between local and metropolitan interests as typified by individual officials in positions of ill-defined power; a growing middle-class mercantile group which worked with officialdom till it ceased to be of service; and a foreign trade partner who was much resented, often demanding and problematical, but always largely indispensable. The use of juntas in Manila was, however, distinctly Spanish in inspiration and was an administrative device to divide work, eliminate over-dependence upon individual officials, and provide a built-in control of malpractices. The Spaniards had the additional problem of handling an amorphous group of Chinese settlers whose very lack of organiza-tion made control imperative and at the same time more difficult. The growth of the Consulado which took final form in 1769 was not a development in the constructive sense that the Hong was. Both had developed to cope with eighteenth-century situations, but in Canton it was the establishment of the Hongs which launched the Canton system, whereas in Manila the Consulado was the last stand of the already un-representative galleon interest. This conservative instinct, given form and made vocal in the twilight of the galleon's career, was struggling not for a new era but to preserve an anachronism. Officialdom, graft, maladministration of the juntas, and the Philippine Company were not the real enemies of the galleon interests. The revolution of Western ideas of trade and political events had created a new economic infra-structure for the colony which militated against the galleon trade. The diversification of the colony's economy with plantation activities and other commercial interests, the opening of Manila to Western shipping and the establishment of direct trade from metropolitan Spain to Asia, had created a self-supporting and viable economy for the islands by 1804. The suspension of the Mexican subsidy in 1804, and the outbreak of the Spanish American independence revolts from 1809, disrupted the markets of New Spain and took the silver mines and mints from the hands of the metropolitan rulers, thereby largely destroying the basis for the eastward-oriented economic life of the Philippine islands, of which the galleon trade was the principal instrument. The official abandonment of the line in 1813 and the final cessation of crossings in 1820 were therefore little more than footnotes to the more important changes which the Filipino economy had already been undergoing for some fifty years. There was to be no spring to this winter of the galleons' days, but only, as so often happens in nature, raw and cruel extinction. But already the half-light of free trade, however wintry then, played upon the walls of the mercantilist ruins at the further end of the 'empire where the sun never sets', at twilight time in the metropole.

Neither the Chinese nor the Spanish system aimed at preventing all trade, but rather at facilitating a considerable volume of trade conducted in an orderly manner within the terms acceptable to the respective governments. In the main these terms may be summed up as the control of the foreign sector, the monopoly of the home sector, and the restriction of foreign activities. The main gain from the system was from taxes, profits from transactions, the maintenance of peace and order, and, for the officials directly involved in supervising the trades, large secondary incomes accruing therefrom. Price control, a fair amount of intervention with the mechanics of the laws of supply and demand, and a large number of threats to close the trade, carefully built into the system, may be seen both as means of acquiring further invisible advantages and as means of keeping the foreigners in line. Officially instituted bodies were the instruments of trade as well as of the administration of the legislation for the foreign traders. The choice of the foreign partner was therefore either to overcome these conditions, to abandon the trade altogether, or to accommodate them. The desire for trade being mutual, the foreigner was not prepared to abandon the trade, and the host partner was not unprepared to make concessions to ensure its continuance.

SINO-BRITISH MERCANTILE RELATIONS IN SINGAPORE'S ENTREPÔT TRADE 1870–1915

BY CHIANG HAI DING

Singapore's immediate success in attracting Chinese and other traders in South-east Asia and its demonstrable usefulness for the protection and expansion of British trade in Asia guaranteed its retention by the British Government in spite of Dutch opposition. Singapore was extremely well situated for trade with South-east Asia, South and East Asia, and Britain and Europe. It was very close to and easily accessible to small boats from Siam, Indochina, Indonesia and Borneo, and it was a convenient port of call for ships (sailing and subsequently steam) setting out from Britain or India and bound for Siam, Indochina, China and the Philippines. It was further endowed with other natural advantages, such as a magnificent harbour, excellent sheltered anchorage, and a plentiful supply of fresh water.

Chinese traders were immediately attracted to Singapore because it was precisely the kind of port for which they were looking. Chinese trade in South-east Asia (the Nanyang or 'South Ocean') could be divided into two sections by drawing an imaginary north-to-south line through the middle of Borneo: that of the Eastern Nanyang which was based at Luzon in the Philippines, and that of the Western Nanyang for which there was no satisfactory base. The second section was the richer, and after the decline of Palembang in the fifteenth century and the fall of Malacca to the Portuguese early in the sixteenth century, Chinese traders had sought in the region of Siam, Johore and Java for an alternative base. In the last years of the eighteenth century and at the beginning of the nineteenth, they had established settlements in Sambas in west Borneo, in Bangka and Billiton, and on both sides of the Straits of Malacca. Penang and Jakarta (Batavia) were not sufficiently well located for the needs of Chinese trade in this area, but Singapore was.[1]

British private traders also quickly realized the value of Singapore

[1] Wang Gungwu, *A Short History of the Nanyang Chinese*, Singapore, 1959, p. 19.

as a base for their trade with China. They had obtained in 1813 the opening of the trade to India, which hitherto had been the monopoly of the East India Company.[1] Since Singapore constituted part of the Company's Indian possessions, private traders could participate in the trade with China by using Singapore as a trans-shipment base: they took Chinese silks from Singapore and left English cottons there to be forwarded to China in Chinese junks.

In 1833, however, the trade to China was thrown open, and Singapore's rôle as a mere trans-shipment port came to an end. But its importance as a trading emporium grew. Singapore's trade with South-east Asia increased from about a quarter of total imports and exports in 1833 to almost one half in 1860; in this period its trade with China declined from almost a quarter of total trade to less than a fifth.[2]

Singapore's importance as an entrepôt port continued to increase. Singapore was a market-place where goods were brought and exchanged: its economic rôle was that of middleman. Its foreign trade grew steadily during the years 1870–86, and more rapidly but with irregular ups and downs between 1887 and 1896; thereafter imports and exports expanded very rapidly until 1903. Then a period of decline set in until 1909, when they rose again until the opening years of World War I (see Table 1). Singapore's trade with South-east Asia continued to increase in this period: imports from South-east Asia increased from two-fifths of total imports in 1870 to almost three-fifths in 1905 and more than two-thirds in 1915, but exports to South-east Asia remained quite steady at about half of all exports. The port's trade with South and East Asia declined in importance: imports accounted for a steady 20–30,% but exports fell from almost 20% in 1870 to about 10% in the twentieth century. The importance of imports from the Western countries declined very markedly, from a quarter of total imports in 1870 to 10% at the end of the century; the importance of exports to the West, however, showed a steady increase from 30% in 1870 to over 40% by 1900 (see Table 2).

The flow of trade from Asia (especially South-east Asia) to the West was therefore more important than the reverse flow from the West to Asia.

---

[1] See Arthur Redford, *Manchester Merchants and Foreign Trade 1794–1858*, Manchester, 1934, pp. 111–18.
[2] C. D. Cowan, *Nineteenth-century Malaya, The Origins of British Political Control*, London, 1961, p. 21.

TABLE I *Foreign trade of Singapore 1870–1915 ($000)*
(including treasure and trade with Penang and Malacca)

	Imports	Exports		Imports	Exports
1870	39,059	31,731	1895	157,969	135,126
1871	36,767	32,034	1896	156,947	133,485
1872	43,415	39,020	1897	179,297	153,167
1873	47,880	41,752	1898	197,632	164,157
1874	46,887	41,509	1899	222,186	185,393
1875	43,766	41,620	1900	251,790	205,535
1876	45,466	40,615	1901	254,128	213,109
1877	49,327	41,428	1902	280,517	234,225
1878	47,259	40,022	1903	299,266	257,708
1879	56,278	49,250	1904	274,675	243,556
1880	60,676	54,579	1905	248,982	211,692
1881	70,700	58,001	1906	252,835	228,873
1882	74,344	61,192	1907	262,368	218,659
1883	79,176	68,174	1908	230,509	191,562
1884	79,572	65,164	1909	228,976	197,333
1885	74,289	61,428	1910	273,194	234,931
1886	77,278	60,579	1911	285,192	240,281
1887	92,120	75,066	1912	320,755	260,237
1888	108,112	87,143	1913	349,667	272,355
1889	110,747	88,683	1914	289,713	236,499
1890	112,634	94,132	1915	345,335	308,534
1891	103,012	91,225			
1892	106,970	97,850			
1893	123,975	108,456			
1894	164,001	137,040			

(SOURCE: *Straits Settlements Blue Books*, 1870–1915)

The foreign trade of Singapore can be divided into two sections: the European or Western and the Asian or largely Chinese and partly Indian. The European merchants handled the imports from and exports to Western countries: their trade was conducted mainly at the wharves in New Harbour and their shops were concentrated in Raffles Place. The Chinese merchants handled the distribution of Western manufactures from Singapore to South-east Asia and the collection of its produce at Singapore. Their business was conducted on the Singapore River and most of their shops lined Boat Quay along the river. The Indian merchants handled the trade between Singapore and West Asia and South Asia. Thus Raffles Place was the centre of the trade in Western manufactures brought thither by ocean-going vessels, whilst

TABLE 2 *Regional distribution of Singapore's foreign trade 1870–1915 (by percentage)*

	1870	1875	1880	1885	1890	1895	1900	1905	1910	1915
IMPORTS										
Malaya	14·29	18·20	14·94	14·25	18·79	21·05	20·45	23·35	19·03	30·34
British Borneo	2·43	1·75	1·71	1·54	1·84	1·76	1·93	2·60	2·19	1·90
Indonesia	13·99	15·66	15·61	20·24	17·24	16·03	18·60	18·07	18·15	17·40
Siam	4·26	6·82	7·90	6·30	6·43	7·26	6·38	9·60	9·48	11·63
Burma	1·53	3·83	3·61	3·48	5·36	3·99	3·26	3·06	2·55	0·94
Indochina	4·05	0·84	0·55	3·69	2·61	3·46	2·78	1·73	2·78	5·36
(i) South-east Asia	40·55	47·10	44·32	49·50	52·27	53·55	53·40	58·41	54·18	67·57
South Asia	8·49	15·53	12·49	8·40	7·80	10·19	13·25	10·32	11·95	4·80
East Asia	13·50	10·61	13·50	14·13	16·50	19·73	15·01	13·02	14·02	12·38
(ii) South and East Asia	21·99	26·14	25·99	22·53	24·30	29·92	28·26	23·34	25·97	17·18
(iii) Asia (i) and (ii)	62·54	73·24	70·31	72·03	76·57	83·47	81·66	81·75	80·15	84·75
United Kingdom	26·97	19·81	25·13	20·94	16·58	10·91	10·80	10·59	11·26	8·15
Europe	4·00	4·07	2·70	4·08	4·14	4·06	5·41	5·26	4·53	2·59
United States	0·05	0·20	0·73	1·52	1·14	0·24	0·62	1·11	1·35	1·72
(iv) West	31·02	24·08	28·56	26·54	21·86	15·21	16·83	16·96	17·14	12·82
Others	6·34	2·68	1·13	1·43	1·57	1·32	1·51	1·29	2·71	2·43
TOTAL	100	100	100	100	100	100	100	100	100	100
EXPORTS										
Malaya	11·82	18·54	10·43	11·46	10·85	13·91	14·33	18·85	17·98	18·36
British Borneo	3·39	1·68	1·19	1·35	2·22	1·73	1·96	3·05	2·87	1·41
Indonesia	14·60	23·11	25·74	24·48	15·34	21·12	19·62	18·90	15·70	16·43
Siam	8·08	8·49	7·73	6·94	10·08	8·36	5·93	6·87	4·47	3·68
Burma	1·88	1·83	2·53	1·78	2·16	1·81	2·12	1·76	1·66	0·84
Indochina	6·85	0·67	0·75	5·19	3·40	2·19	1·51	0·95	0·82	0·95
(i) South-east Asia	47·52	54·32	48·37	51·20	44·05	49·12	45·47	50·38	43·50	41·67
South Asia	6·90	7·08	8·29	1·66	6·13	2·45	2·50	2·71	3·83	5·92
East Asia	11·79	8·83	11·22	11·36	8·55	9·94	8·93	8·05	6·17	4·77
(ii) South and East Asia	18·69	15·91	19·51	13·02	14·68	12·39	11·43	10·76	10·00	10·69
(iii) Asia (i) and (ii)	66·21	70·23	67·88	64·22	58·73	61·51	56·90	61·14	53·50	52·36
United Kingdom	17·42	16·00	16·40	21·42	19·40	14·75	19·00	14·94	19·55	12·15
Europe	1·29	5·11	4·67	7·14	11·73	14·10	10·84	11·63	15·21	8·78
United States	9·30	7·00	9·40	4·55	7·98	8·05	9·89	10·36	9·33	24·84
(iv) West	28·01	28·11	30·47	33·11	39·11	36·90	39·73	36·93	44·09	45·77
Others	5·78	1·66	1·65	2·67	2·16	1·59	3·37	1·93	2·41	1·87
TOTAL	100	100	100	100	100	100	100	100	100	100

(SOURCE: calculated from *Straits Settlements Blue Books*, 1870–1915. Singapore's imports from and exports to Penang and Malacca are included in 'Malaya'.)

Boat Quay was the centre of the trade in South-east Asian produce, brought there in small coastal steamers and native *prahus*. The two sections of trade were even distinguished by the language used: English in the 'foreign' market and Malay in the bazaar.[1]

TABLE 3 *Import-export firms in Singapore's foreign trade 1870–1915*

	Western	Chinese	Indian	Japanese	Total
1870	42	9	6	–	57
1875		not available			
1880	38	8	3	–	49
1885	36	9	13	–	58
1890	48	16	21	–	85
1895	47	14	15	1	77
1901	66	24	22	3	113
1906	62	20	23	3	108
1911	56	26	22	3	107

(SOURCE: see Appendix, p. 266)

The actual number of import-export merchants involved in the trade of Singapore is difficult to determine, though there is little doubt that they increased steadily in number and in variety, so that by 1895 there was a Japanese firm, the Mitsui Bussan Kaisha, and in 1901 there was a Russian one, Stcherbatchoff, Tchokoff and Co. A close examination of the *Trade Directories*[2] will give an insight into the structure and operations of these firms.

Six European firms will be examined closely for this purpose: Boustead & Co., Guthrie & Co., Paterson, Simons & Co., Gilfillan, Wood & Co. (later Adamson, Gilfillan & Co., now Harper, Gilfillan & Co.), the Borneo Co., and Behn, Meyer and Co.[3] (All six firms are still operating today.) The first five were British and had their head offices in London, while the last was German and had its offices in Hamburg. The firms were so organized that some partners remained in Europe

[1] Ralph M. Odell, *Cotton Goods in the Straits Settlements*, Department of Commerce, Bureau of Foreign and Domestic Commerce, Special Agents Series No. 115, Washington Printing Office, 1916.

[2] The trade directories used were of the series: *Straits Calendar and Directory* (1870–74), *Singapore Directory for the Straits Settlements* (1877–9), *Singapore and Straits Directory* (1880–1921).

[3] Some details about European firms operating in Malaya can be found in G. C. Allen and Audrey G. Donnithorne, *Western Enterprise in Indonesia and Malaya*, London, 1957, pp. 53–60.

while the others went out to the East. In some cases, partners alternated between Europe and Asia, as in that of Thomas Shelford and William Gulland of Paterson, Simons. Both were partners in 1870, with Gulland in London and Shelford in Singapore, where he became a member of the Straits Settlements Legislative Council in 1880. The 1885 *Directory*, however, reveals that Shelford had returned to England, while Gulland replaced him in Singapore as resident partner and, incidentally, also as member of the Legislative Council. But in 1890 they exchanged positions, and thereafter Gulland remained in London. There were also cases in which a partner did not move back and forth but remained in Singapore: such as that of John Anderson of Guthrie's who was a partner in 1880.

As a general rule the more senior partners were to be found in Europe and the junior ones in Singapore. Thus in Bousteads, Thomas Cuthbertson was a partner in Singapore in 1880, 1885 and 1890, but was in London in 1895, 1901, 1906 and 1911. In Gilfillan, Wood & Co., James Miller was a partner in Singapore in 1885, 1890, 1895 and 1901, but was in London in 1906 and 1911. A progression was also discernible from the low status of assistant in Singapore to partner in Singapore and on to partner in Europe. In the firm of Bousteads, for example ,W. P. Waddell and W. A. Grieg were assistants in 1885, 1890 and 1895. They had become partners in Singapore in 1901 and 1906. Waddell was a member of the Legislative Council in 1906 and a partner in London in 1911. In the Borneo Co., Andrew Currie was manager in Singapore in 1880 and 1885, with Charles Sugden as his assistant in 1885. By 1895 Currie was a partner in London and Sugden the manager in Singapore. In Behn, Meyer & Co., Ad. Laspe was an assistant in Singapore in 1890, a partner in Singapore in 1895, and a partner in Hamburg in 1901.

Familial connections no doubt assisted the aspirant to partnership status, although men of ability made the grade anyway. Certain surnames predominated in some firms: in Behn, Meyer that of Meyer (Arnold Otto Meyer, partner from 1870, Edward Lorenz Meyer, partner from 1885), in Bousteads that of Young (Jasper Young, partner from 1870, T. S. Young, assistant in Singapore in 1885, Arthur Young, partner in London in 1901, and J. B. Young, assistant in Singapore in 1901 and partner in 1906, and partner in London in 1911). In the firm of Gilfillan, Wood & Co. (later Adamson, Gilfillan & Co.), the surname of Adamson was particularly prominent (William Adamson, partner in 1870, G. F. Adamson, assistant in the Penang branch in 1885, 1890, and 1895, H. Adamson, assistant in 1901, and D. L. Adamson, assistant in 1911). In the firm of Paterson, Simons, the name Paterson occurred frequently (William Paterson, partner in London in 1870, Cosmo G. Paterson, assistant in Singapore in 1885 and partner in Singapore from 1890, Graham Paterson, assistant in 1895, partner from 1901). The name of Shelford was also associated with this firm (Thomas Shelford, partner in 1870, and William H. Shelford, assistant in 1890 and partner from 1901).

Sometimes, however, assistants or even partners branched out on their own. James Sword of Gilfillan, Wood & Co., an assistant in 1880 and a partner in 1885, struck out and joined F. C. Muhlinghaus to form The Straits Trading Company which survives to this day.[1] The best example of fission among business houses was provided by Katz Brothers. In 1880 it numbered as partners Herman Katz in Frankfort-am-Main, August Huttenbach in Penang, and Max Behr in Singapore, with Meyer Behr, Joseph Heim and Heinrich Huttenbach as assistants. In 1885 there were two new partners, Ludwig Huttenbach in Penang and Meyer Behr in Singapore, and two new assistants, Louis Katz and Sigmund Katz. In 1890, however, the firm of Katz had only Herman, Louis and Sigmund Katz. But two new firms had appeared. The first was Huttenbach Brothers, which had Ludwig Huttenbach as the partner in London and August Huttenbach as the one in Penang and Joseph Heim as assistant. The other firm was Behr & Co. which had Max Behr as partner and Meyer Behr as assistant.

The European business houses extended the area of their operations. While they continued to be primarily concerned with trade between Singapore and Europe, they set up new branches and agencies in other regions as well: in South-east Asia, East Asia, and in one case (Guthries in 1901), even Australia. For example, the Borneo Co. in 1870 had branches in Manchester, Calcutta, Batavia, Bangkok, Sarawak, Hong Kong and Shanghai, besides London and Singapore. By 1880 it had closed its branch in Calcutta but it set up branches in Surabaya in 1895, in Rahang and Chiengmai in Siam in 1901, and in Labuan in 1906.

The nature of business also underwent changes. Though these

---

[1] Allen and Donnithorne, p. 159.

houses were primarily concerned with import–export trade, they handled other types of business also. Some of them were even agents for governments: the Borneo Co. for Labuan from 1870 to 1885; Paterson, Simons & Co. for Johore from 1885 and for Sarawak from 1895; and Guthrie & Co. for the Federated Malay States and the British North Borneo Co. from 1906.[1] The six firms collectively accounted for

TABLE 4 *Agencies of six European firms in Singapore 1870–1911*

	Insurance	Shipping	Banking	Goods and others	Managing	Govern- ments	Total
1870	24	1	6	0	2	1	34
1875				not available			
1880*	(20)	(5)	(7)	(0)	(0)	(1)	(33)
1885	48	18	7	1	5	2	81
1890	49	28	7	4	9	3	100
1895	63	30	12	11	10	3	129
1901	65	34	9	38	9	3	158
1906	70	47	10	89	13	4	233
1911	74	57	11	144	75	4	335

(SOURCE: *Singapore and Straits Directories*)

Notes: (i) In 1880* no details were given for Behn, Meyer (which held 13 agencies in 1870 and 18 in 1885).

(ii) The column 'Goods and others' includes agencies for companies outside South-east Asia.

(iii) Agencies of companies operating in South-east Asia are listed under 'Managing'.

34 agencies in 1870, of which insurance companies totalled 24 (see Table 4). Though this type of agency remained important and increased in absolute terms, the trend towards the end of the nineteenth century was towards agencies of foods and drinks, industrial and engineering products, such as alcoholic beverages, tobacco, flour, dynamite, machines: the six firms had no such agencies in 1870, 11 in 1895, 38 in 1801, 89 in 1906 and 144 in 1911.

More significant was the management of companies floated overseas, mainly in the United Kingdom and Europe, which were involved in production in South-east Asia. In 1870 there were only two such agencies, both of which were held by Paterson, Simons: the Singapore

[1] The agencies for Sarawak and the British North Borneo Co. were formerly held by A. L. Johnston & Co., another merchant house.

Patent Slip and Dock Co. and the Johore Steam Saw Mills. There were only nine such companies in 1890 and in 1901. The number of agencies rose to 13 in 1906, of which two dealt with tin-mines and none with rubber estates. Up to the end of the nineteenth century the European merchant firms by and large did not actively participate in the tin-mining industry in the Malay states, and it was Chinese capital and labour from Singapore and Penang which were responsible for its rapid development.[1] Nor did the European merchant houses actively participate in the planting industry, though it was one in which other European investors took a great interest. Only after the failure of coffee planting and the introduction of para rubber did the merchant firms become involved, and then largely in a managerial capacity, for companies floated in Britain and Europe.[2] Thus in 1911, the six firms held between them the agencies of 75 companies, of which 58 were rubber companies operating mainly in Malaya, Borneo and Sumatra. The largest number, 31, was held by Guthries.

In their primary business activity between 1870 and 1911, that of importing and exporting, the European firms depended on their Chinese employees and agents. Writing in 1900, a traveller through Singapore observed that 'the business of the European firms—and this is true of the whole Far East—could not be carried on for a week without their Chinese shroffs, compradors and clerks'.[3] These Chinese employees negotiated with the Chinese firms on behalf of their European employers. They themselves never rose to partnerships, although in many firms they were more numerous than the Europeans.

The Chinese merchants were the middlemen in Singapore's middleman economy. They stood between and effected the exchange between the European importers and the South-east Asian producers. They obtained manufactured goods from the European importers and distributed them all over South-east Asia, and collected in exchange the produce of the area which they passed on to the European merchants.

[1] See Wong Lin Ken, 'Western Enterprise and the Development of the Malayan Tin Industry to 1914', in C. D. Cowan, ed., *The Economic Development of South-east Asia*, London, 1964, pp. 131–8.

[2] Loh Weng Fong, *Singapore Agency Houses 1819–1900*, unpublished academic exercise, University of Malaya, Singapore, 1958, pp. 45–9.

[3] Henry Norman, *The Peoples and Politics of the Far East, Travels and Studies in the British, French, Spanish and Portuguese Colonies, Siberia, China, Japan, Korea, Siam and Malaya* London, 1900, p. 42.

This exchange could be effected in one of three ways. First, the Chinese merchant could barter manufactured goods for produce brought by native traders to the Singapore River.[1] The second way was for the merchant himself to seek out the consumers-cum-producers. For this a greater degree of enterprise was required, and he invariably took along not only manufactures such as cotton piece-goods, but also such necessities as salted fish, rice, salt and matches, to barter for gutta-percha, rattans, areca-nuts and similar produce, which he then brought back to Singapore. A contemporary Chinese described the risks taken by his compatriots thus:

As commercial travellers they penetrate into many islands where a white man is never seen. In the past they have watered with their blood many a savage territory and paved the way for the introduction of civilization and better government into many lands.[2]

There were also merchants (presumably the wealthier ones) who chose the easier and less risky way of appointing agents at various points in South-east Asia. Such agencies were possible because the Chinese

have established connexions in almost all the islands to which our foreign [that is, Western] commodities are carried. Their agents reside on the Indochinese mainland, collecting produce by barter with the natives, to whom they are not infrequently related by social as well as by commercial ties.[3]

The third way in which Chinese merchants engaged in trade in South-east Asia was by financing the production or collection of commodities they required and thus assuring themselves of a supply. Singapore was a financial centre from which capital flowed to surrounding areas to finance mineral and agricultural exploitation. In tin-mining it was not uncommon for wealthy merchants in Singapore (and Penang as well) to grant credit to merchants and advancers in the Malay States who in turn granted credit to tin-miners, the arrangement being that all the tin obtained should move back along the line down to

[1] Wong Lin Ken, 'The Trade of Singapore, 1819–69', *Journal of the Royal Asiatic Society, Malayan Branch*, XXXIII, Pt. 4, December 1960, pp. 76–77.
[2] Tan Teck Soon, 'Chinese Local Trade' (10 August 1901), in *Noctes Orientales, Being A Selection of Essays Read Before the Straits Philosophical Society between the Years 1893 and 1901*, Singapore, 1913, pp. 195–204.
[3] J. Thomson, *The Straits of Malacca, Indochina, China, or Ten Years Travels, Adventures and Residence Abroad*, London, 1875, p. 12.

Singapore.[1] Another good example was pepper and gambier production in Johore, the large state immediately north of Singapore. Some Chinese merchants in Singapore financed the cultivators in Johore 'on the understanding that they were to have the monopoly of all produce from the plantations of their debtors'.[2] These merchants even formed their own Association, the Pepper and Gambier Society or *Kongkek*, to regulate the trade in these commodities: in 1887, for example, its representatives met with those of European firms dealing in pepper and gambier to discuss ways and means of improving quality.[3] The *Directories* recorded that 'most of these [Johore] cultivators go from Singapore; the capitalists for whom they cultivate are Singapore traders and some of Johore's, and all of their produce and most of their earnings find their way back to Singapore again'.

It is difficult to select representative Chinese firms for closer examination, since many of them did not advertise in the *Directories*, and, furthermore, most of them do not appear to have survived the demise of their founders. For example, the firm of the famous Whampoa (Hoo Ah Kay, first Asian member of the Straits Settlements Legislative Council, 1870) was founded in 1849 but made its appearance in the *Directories* only in about 1880; it had ceased to be an import-export firm by 1906, but was listed as provision merchant, baker and contractor. It was managed by his widow and several relatives, probably sons: Hoo Ah Yip Whampoa, Hoo Hoong Kee, and one Tchun Chun Fook. The firm of another famous Chinese, Seah Eu Chin, also fell into disarray soon after its founder's death. His sons, Seah Liang Seah (sometime member of the Legislative Council), Seah Song Seah, and Seah Peck Seah, merely managed the estates left to them, although Liang Seah engaged in financing pepper and gambier production in Johore and became President of the Pepper and Gambier Society in the 1880s.

Three Chinese firms can be examined which lasted throughout the period under survey: Kim Seng & Co., established in 1842, Lee Cheng Yan & Co., 1858, and Kim Cheng & Co., 1865. Two of them were located in Boat Quay, where most of the Chinese firms were, while Lee Cheng Yan & Co., which made its appearance in the *Directories* only in 1885, was in Telok Ayer Street.

---

[1] Wong Lin Ken, *The Malayan Tin Industry to 1914*, Tucson, 1965, p. 63.
[2] Song Ong Siang, *One Hundred Years of the Chinese in Singapore*, London, 1923, p. 37.
[3] *Singapore Chamber of Commerce Annual Report* [hereafter referred to as *SCCAR*], 1887, Appendix E.

All three were family concerns. Kim Seng & Co. was founded by Tan Kim Seng, a third-generation Malacca-born Chinese, who retired to Malacca and died in 1864, leaving his sons Tan Beng Swee and Tan Beng Guan to succeed him.[1] They were followed by Tan Jiak Kim (member of the Legislative Council 1890–3), Tan Jiak Chuan, Tan Jiak Lim, and Tan Jiak Ong. Lee Cheng Yan & Co. bore the Lee imprint; in addition to Lee Cheng Yan there were Lee Cheng Guan and Lee Keng Tit and Lee Choon Guan. The firm of Kim Cheng & Co. was founded by Tan Kim Cheng (son of the famous Tan Tock Seng, also a Malacca-born Chinese who was attracted to Singapore). He was sometime Siamese Consul-General and Special Commissioner in the Straits Settlements in Singapore, and he was succeeded by his widow and relatives Tan Boo Liat and Tan Swee Hong, for all his sons died before him.[2]

The nature of the business of these firms is not very clear, as few details are available about them in the *Directories*. However, they extended beyond Singapore: Kim Seng & Co. had branches in Shanghai and Malacca in 1870, and at the time of the death of the founder Tan Kim Seng in 1864, the firm was engaged in planting and mining as well.[3] Kim Cheng & Co., as might be expected, had a branch in Bangkok. They engaged in other types of business; Kim Seng in 1880 was an agent for tramp steamers and Kim Cheng by 1880 owned a rice mill in Siam,[4] and by 1911 was primarily interested in the rice-trade.

A look at other Chinese firms reveals that they held agencies for insurance companies, banks, and shipping companies, most of which had headquarters in China. In this regard they appeared to be catching up with and rivalling the European firms, and some of them even obtained the agencies for Western commodities.[5]

---

[1] C. S. Wong, *A Gallery of Chinese Capitans*, Ministry of Culture, Singapore, 1963, pp. 32–33.

[2] C. S. Wong, pp. 36–7.

[3] C. S. Wong, p. 32.

[4] According to C. S. Wong, p. 35, Tan Kim Cheng also owned steamers and a rice-mill in Saigon.

[5] In 1906 the firm of Yap Whatt & Co. held agencies for eight British companies (e.g. Jones Sewing Machine Co. Ltd, Manchester, and Whalley's Sanitary Fluid Co., London) and for two French ones. In 1911 the firm of Kim Hin & Co., which specialized in wines and spirits, held the agencies for eighteen British and European companies: five wines, four each whiskies and brandies, two each stout and champagne and one beer.

A number of Indian firms were engaged in trading activities in Singapore. By and large they appear to have been primarily concerned with the trade between Singapore and South and West Asia, though in common with European and Chinese firms they were also reaching out into South-east Asia, and in some cases, even to East Asia and Europe. A few examples can be given. In 1885 the firms of Burjojee Khodadad & Co., Hakimjee Rajbhoy & Co., and Hormusjee Pestonjee & Co., all had branches in Bombay, and the last-named firm had an agency in Calcutta as well. In 1890 the firms of Abdultyeb Esmailjee, J. M. Oosman, and Abdulkader Husenally, which had headquarters in India, listed branches or agencies in South and West Asia: Surat, Mauritius, Aden and Jedda; in South-east Asia: Bangkok, Pnom-Penh, Saigon, Moulmein, Macassar, Batambang; and East Asia: Hong Kong and Hodeida.

Indian firms, like Chinese ones, were not long-lived. Of the six firms named, which made their appearance in the *Directories* in 1880, the first and third did not survive into 1890 nor the second after 1895. The fourth firm failed to appear in 1901 and the last two in 1911. Virtually no Indian firms were listed continuously from 1870 to 1911. However, four firms which were listed from 1885 to 1911 can be examined more closely.

The first, the firm of Syed Mohammad bin Ahmet Alsagoff, was founded in 1864 but appeared in the *Directories* only from 1885. It was a Singapore firm and its owner had large interests in landed estate and other enterprises besides trading. The firm established a branch at Jedda in 1890 and by 1911 had branches in Mecca and Taib (in Arabia), Cairo and Alexandria (in Egypt), and in the Moluccas. The firm of S. Manasseh & Co. had a head office in India, a branch in Singapore. The other two firms were more India-oriented companies and their interests were more widespread. The firm of Saiboo Mohammad Meerah & Co., established in 1866 but advertising in the *Directories* only from 1885, had branches in Karikal (in 1885) and in Negapatam (1890), and branches and agencies throughout South-east Asia: branches in Macassar, Cambodia and Tongking (in 1890), in Menado and Amboina (in 1895), in Padang and P. Brandan (Sumatra), Telok Anson and Pontianak (in 1901), and agencies in Medan, Labuan, Deli, Sandakan, Bangkok, Bali, Banjermassin, Penang and Oleh-Oleh. The firm of Mohamadally Abdul Gaffoor, which originally had its head

9-2

office at Bangkok, though by 1906 it was at Bombay, also had connections in Jedda.

The nature of the business done by these companies is not clear from the *Directories*. Only in respect of Alsagoff is it stated that in 1895 the firm was agent for a steamship and in 1906 for a saw-mill.

At least three of the four firms appear to have been family organizations. In the firm of Alsagoff the partners in 1890 were Syed Mohammad bin A-Alsagoff, Syed Sallay bin O. Boftaim, and Syed Omar bin M. Alsagoff. Between 1890 and 1906 Syed Sallay had disappeared, but in 1901 one Syed Abdulkader bin Adbulraman Alsagoff replaced him. In the firm of S. Manasseh the partners in 1885 were Salleh Manasseh and Saul Jacob Nathan. When the first passed on, he was replaced by his widow, Mrs S. Manasseh, and relatives: Maurice Saleh Manasseh, Ezckiel Manasseh and Reuben Manasseh. The firm of M. A. Gaffoor had him as sole partner until 1901, when he was replaced by three men whose names suggested that they were relatives: Ahmedbhai Abdool Gaffoor, Abdoolkayoom Abdool Gaffoor, and Abdeally Abdool Gaffoor. The firm of Saiboo Mohammad Meerah, however, had four partners, of which one was Ana Hajee Saiboo and another Haji Mohammad Meerah. But the partners who succeeded them did not appear to be related to the original partners, except for one M. Osan Saiboo.

European and Chinese merchants were the intermediaries between the industrialized nations of the West and the undeveloped regions of South-east Asia, which produced raw materials and foodstuffs in exchange for manufactured goods. The activities of these merchants were therefore complementary, and they were interdependent: only in the twentieth century were they in some degree competitive. The European merchants imported manufactures in bulk from the home markets, which they broke down into manageable lots to be entrusted to their Chinese counterparts to dispose of in South-east Asia. They received in return the produce of the region, which the Chinese merchants collected, and which had to be assembled, graded and packaged for re-export back to the home markets. The Chinese merchants obtained manufactures on credit from the European merchants, which they traded for produce and foodstuffs. In turn they sold these to their creditors.

Sino-British mercantile relations

Upon this credit nexus rested the relationship between Chinese and European merchants.

As early as 1835 a meeting of European merchants tried to draw up rules to regulate the granting of credit to Chinese merchants. It was agreed that credit was to be reduced from the six months then customary to three months, payment to be strictly enforced after three days' grace. But in practice credit continued to stretch over six months, repayment coming in instalments proportionate to the degree of pressure applied. In 1852 the Singapore Chamber of Commerce resolved that none of its members should grant credit for longer than three months. That this resolution was probably not strictly carried out is suggested by its reaffirmation in 1858. In 1864 there was a commercial crisis and two European firms failed, due, it was said, to insufficient care in granting credit to Chinese merchants who were encouraged to over-trade. The laxity was occasioned by keen competition between European firms to dispose of their goods to Chinese middlemen, the newly arrived German firms granting extended credit in order to attract business.[1]

Prior to 1870 insolvency was punishable by imprisonment. A cause of grave concern to the Europeans was the dishonest Chinese merchant who set out to cheat his creditors by declaring himself bankrupt. While his European creditors were trying to make something of his business books, he was secretly sending his assets to China. After a term of imprisonment he retired to China to enjoy what he had saved from his creditors. In 1870 imprisonment for debt was abolished by the Bankruptcy Ordinance (XXI of 1870). The result, claimed the Chairman of the Singapore Chamber of Commerce, was that 'the majority of our trading bankruptcies are tainted with fraud'.[2]

In 1885 a Commission of Enquiry[3] found that 'special circumstances' in the Straits Settlements assisted fraudulent debtors. Firstly, a great deal of the trade of the colony was with remote places: this made it practically impossible to follow assets, with the result that creditors were forced to accept small compositions, while debtors later sold off their hidden goods to realize a neat profit. Secondly, the accounts of

[1] Wong, 'Trade of Singapore', p. 165.
[2] *Straits Settlements Legislative Council Proceedings* [hereafter referred to as *SSLCP*] *1885*, 17 August, p. B105.
[3] *SSLCP 1885*, Appendix 46, 'Bankruptcy Commission Report', 29 December 1885. There was one Chinese member, Tan Keong Saik, a merchant. There was no doubt that the Commission was particularly concerned with the problems of fraudulent *Chinese* bankruptcies.

Asian traders were kept in languages other than English, and false accounts could be prepared against failure. Thirdly, the clannish nature of Asian traders, particularly the Chinese, enabled the dishonest ones to hand over their property to friends and relatives for safe-keeping until the storm resulting from their dishonesty had blown over. Fourthly, Asian traders could easily retire to their own countries to avoid legal proceedings against them. Fifthly, some moneyed persons traded in the name of young relatives and friends of no means, 'taking the profit if successful, without incurring losses in the case of failure'. The 1870 Bankruptcy Law was subsequently amended to make insolvency 'something approaching a crime'. Disabilities were heaped on the bankrupt, who could not, for example, institute court action nor leave the colony without the consent of the Official Assignee or the Court.[1] But the situation did not improve. One disgusted merchant declared that spending money on lawyer's fees to take a debtor to court was 'in fact throwing good money after bad'.[2] Finally, in 1895, imprisonment for debt was re-imposed,[3] despite a massive Chinese protest that it was 'contrary to the usage of civilized nations'.[4]

The fifth reason for fraudulent bankruptcy in particular troubled European merchants. The Chinese were unwilling to reveal who the partners in a firm were; there were only rumours that certain well-known wealthy men were partners. Quite often they were *de facto* partners, participating in the profits from a business venture which they financed or in which they had a share. But they disclaimed partnership and legal responsibility if the business failed, and the European merchant was then left to deal with a Chinese merchant of no wealth and no standing who had traded on the strength of a claimed, but not proven, relationship with rich Chinese 'partners', and on the European credit which he was thus able to obtain. The legal position was well stated by the Chief Justice of the Straits Settlements in 1885:

[1] *SSLCP 1887*, 15 August, p. B 104, first reading of 'A Bill to Amend the Law of Bankruptcy'.
[2] *SSLCP 1893*, Appendix 1, 23 February 1893, 'Report of the Committee appointed to enquire into the working of the Bankruptcy Department and Ordinance', 24 December 1892, Evidence of C. H. Valtriny, a merchant, p. C 25.
[3] *SSLCP 1895 and 1896*, Bankruptcy Ordinance Amendment Bill, 25 November, 6 December, etc., passed 18 June 1896.
[4] *SSLCP 1896*, Appendix 16, 2 April 1896, pp. C 169–73. Petitions to the Governor came from the Chinese in Singapore (333 signatures), Penang (238), and Malacca (81).

There is no difficulty as to a person who represents himself to be a partner because he *is* a partner to those to whom he makes these representations. He cannot say afterwards he is not a partner to third parties; he is a partner. A difficulty does arise when a person wishes to obtain goods on the credit of another person who is not a partner but whom he represents as one. Such a person is not bound by the other's representations, and as there is probably no time to follow up representations made in that way, difficulties arise.[1]

To overcome these difficulties the registration of firms was proposed.[2] Details of a firm's name, head office, branches and agencies, *chop*[3] and the names, addresses and description of all partners or persons holding the power of attorney, were to be kept in a register for reference. The sole purpose was to enable European merchants to be able to ascertain the partners in a firm before granting credit.

It was then pointed out by the Chinese member of the Legislative Council that there was little to prevent Chinese from registering anybody or even any name as a partner.[4] In 1895, when the bill was again discussed, it was proposed that partners be required to hand in statutory declarations of their identity or Certificates of Identity signed by a Solicitor of the Supreme Court, a Magistrate, a Justice of the Peace, a Commissioner of Affidavits, a bank manager, accountant or cashier, a member of the Singapore or Penang Chamber of Commerce, or a Police Officer not below the rank of Inspector.[5] In 1900 a further amendment was proposed, that photographs of partners should accompany statutory declarations and Certificates of Identity. If a woman partner was registered, the 'name of her father and the name of her husband or reputed husband if any' were also required.[6]

Chinese opposition to the registration of partnership was well based. Such an ordinance would have introduced many serious inconveniences without any compensatory advantages. Yet for a long time there was

[1] *SSLCP 1885*, 17 August, p. B109.
[2] *SCCAR 1887*, Appendix C, pp. 18–24, 'A Bill Intituled An Ordinance for the Registration of Parnership Firms, 1887'.
[3] A kind of stamp or identifying mark of a Chinese firm. A firm had both a name and a *chop*, in much the same way as a European firm might have a name and a trade mark for its products.
[4] *SSLCP 1895*, 3 August, p. B177.
[5] *SCCAR 1895*, Appendix E, Col. Sec. to SCC, 5 September 1895, with proposed amendments to the bill.
[6] *History of the Movement for the Registration of Partnerships in the Straits Settlements*, Penang Chamber of Commerce, 1916, pp. 224–8, 'A Bill Intituled An Ordinance for the Registration of Partnerships and Firms', November 1905.

considerable Chinese support for the principle of registration. The Chinese spokesman in 1892 suggested that firms trading on their own capital be given the option to register, but that firms trading on borrowed capital be compelled to do so.[1] In 1905, when further discriminatory measures were proposed, he declared:

The Chinese do not want registration and the supporters of it are limited to a few European firms doing business with a small section of the Chinese. If therefore, registration is to be enforced, I am of opinion that it should be limited to the European firms and to those Chinese trading with them.[2]

This sensible compromise went unheeded and Chinese opposition rose to a high pitch in 1906. The Chinese Advisory Boards and the Chinese Chamber of Commerce of Penang and Singapore (newly founded in 1906) protested vigorously.

Yet it was not Chinese but European opposition that led to the rejection of the bill. The Chinese as a community were not at first opposed in principle to registration, and indeed tried to suggest ways and means of achieving precisely what the Europeans had in mind. It was principally European opposition to the bill that caused its withdrawal—Chinese protests were merely in support of a resolution of the Singapore Chamber of Commerce to reject the bill.[3] Opposition came from the older and better-established European firms in Singapore. In 1905, when the bill was discussed by the Singapore Chamber of Commerce, nineteen firms voted that the bill was 'not desirable in the trading interests of the Port'.[4] Of these ten were import-export firms and of the ten seven were responsible for 60% of the export trade to Europe.[5] In favour of registration were seven firms, five of which were relatively small or new import-export firms. The conflict of interests between the older and better-established firms and the new small and weak firms was described in ironical terms by a supporter of registration:

[1] *SSLCP 1893*, Appendix J, pp. 17–18.
[2] *SSLCP 1906*, Appendix 61, 30 November 1906, 'Report of Select Committee on the Registration Bill 1905', Rider by Tan Jiak Kim, the Chinese member.
[3] *SSLCP 1907*, Appendix 4, 8 February 1907, SCC to Col. Sec., 12 December 1906, p. 9.
[4] *SCCAR, 1905*, p. XXXI, 'Report of the Special general meeting of the Chamber held on 19 December 1905'.
[5] They were Gilfillan, Wood & Co., Behn Meyer & Co., Boustead & Co., Paterson, Simons & Co., Huttenbach Brothers, Brinkman & Co., and the Borneo Co. See *SSLCP 1908*, Appendix 27, p. C99, and *Royal Commission on Shipping Rings, Evidence*, Cd. 4668, 1909, IV, p. 180, Evidence of R. D. Holt of the Ocean Steam Ship Co.

Let the man with the largest purse, the man with the best sources of information, the man longest here, win. We can afford to give credit on our own accounts, you cannot afford to do; if you follow our example, you must take the consequences. If a smash comes, we can afford to write off the loss; you are a small man, and it will break you. Do not introduce legislation which will facilitate the introduction of new firms into the Colony, which gives small capitalists as much chance as large capitalists.[1]

This was in fact the crux of the problem. New firms were anxious to obtain a share of the market, but their experience and knowledge of Chinese merchants were limited. They were often compelled to grant more generous terms while, because they were new or small, their trading positions were relatively weak. Such firms therefore favoured registration because they would thereby be assured of at least some safeguards—the men they traded with would have been legal partners, answerable in a court of law. The older and stronger firms opposed registration. Possessing better financial resources and better knowledge of the market than their competitors, they argued that the granting of credit was a matter of individual judgment, and that if some merchants had better information than others, it was not the rôle of government to interfere.[2]

In the final analysis, relations between Chinese and European merchants were surprisingly harmonious. It would appear that their dependence on each other in the entrepôt trade of Singapore and their mutually profitable co-operation more than compensated for the temptations before Chinese merchants to defraud their European counterparts. Thus the deliberations of the Commission of Enquiry in 1892 attracted little interest,[3] and in 1904, when the total Straits Settlements import and export trade was valued at $710 million, the total value of business failures recorded by the Official Assignee came to only $1·5 million.[4]

[1] *SSLCP 1906*, 12 January, p. B15. The punctuation is mine: except for full stops this speech was originally not punctuated at all.
[2] *SCCAR 1905*, 'Memorandum on the Registration of Parnerships Bill at present before Council' (by the Committee of the Chamber), p. xv.
[3] *SSLCP 1893*, etc.
[4] *SSLCP 1906*, etc.

APPENDIX

R. D. Holt of the Ocean Steam Ship Company (the Blue Funnel Line) is reported to have said that in 1897 there were only twenty European import-export firms engaged in the trade westwards from Singapore to the United Kingdom and Europe and that in 1908 there were sixty such firms. However, he neither named all the firms nor indicated how he identified an import-export firm (*Royal Commission on Shipping Rings*, *Evidence*, Cd. 4668, 1909, p. 18). Figures similar to ones given by him were used by a member of the Straits Settlements Legislative Council in 1910 and were not challenged, which suggests that Holt's figures were probably not incorrect (*Straits Settlements Legislative Council Proceedings 1910*, 11 April, p. B55).

However, the Straits *Calendar and Directory 1870* and the *Singapore and Straits Directories 1880, 1885, 1890, 1895, 1901, 1906, 1911*, showed a large number of firms listed in a variety of ways: as merchants, general merchants, merchants and commission agents, etc. It is difficult to determine which were engaged in import-export business and to distinguish these from those engaged merely in local trading.

The figures in Table 3 represent those firms listed as merchants, or as merchants and commission agents.

It will be noticed that the figure for European firms in 1895 is very much greater than that given by Holt for 1897, but Holt was concerned only with the export of goods from Singapore *to the United Kingdom and Europe*. The figures for the Chinese and Indian firms are probably too low, as some firms engaged in import and export trade did not bother to list themselves in the *Directories*, or did so only towards the end of the nineteenth century. The figures for Chinese firms given in Table 3 are certainly lower than in 'List of the Principal Chinese Firms in Singapore', also published in the *Directories*, which included merchants of all descriptions such as 'sago manufacturers', 'tin dealers', 'ship-chandlers', 'shop-keepers' and others, who were unlikely to be involved in import-export business. Furthermore, for the sake of consistency, it was decided to obtain figures for the European, Chinese and Indian firms from the same 'Commercial Directory' for Singapore.

Though the resulting Table 3 cannot be considered very reliable, it probably is a useful indication of the growth in the number of firms engaged in Singapore's foreign trade.

THE DUTCH AND THE
TIN TRADE OF MALAYA IN THE
SEVENTEENTH CENTURY

BY GRAHAM W. IRWIN

In the days of the Malacca Sultanate merchants came from all over Asia to purchase Malayan tin. They came from Gujerat and Malabar, from Coromandel and Bengal, from the islands of the Indonesian Archipelago, and from Tongking and China.[1] Some of the requirements of these merchants could be met by the great entrepôt of Malacca itself, for tin was one of the items of tribute the Malacca Sultans received from the northern rivers under their jurisdiction. The *Suma Oriental* of Tomé Pires mentions Sungei Ujong, Klang, Selangor, Perak, Bernam, Dinding and Bruas as areas from which an annual tin contribution was expected.[2] But the amount of the metal available for purchase at the Sultans' capital was small. The staples on which Malacca's fame and prosperity rested were high-value, luxury commodities like Banda and Moluccas spices, Timor sandalwood, Borneo camphor, and Sumatra pepper and gold. Goods such as these could be, and were, carried over long distances and bought and sold many times before reaching their final destinations, without transportation and handling costs rising to unacceptable levels. But a heavy, bulky, low-value commodity like tin could not be economically handled in the same way. To make steady profits in the tin trade, the overseas merchants had, so far as possible, to tap the sources of supply and keep their trans-shipment costs to a minimum. The pattern of the Malayan tin trade thus became established: ore was mined in the uplands, smelted into rough blocks of about fifty pounds weight, and floated down the rivers to loading-points on the Bay of Bengal; there it was purchased by merchants from India, Java and China who shipped it direct to their own lands.

The coming of the Portuguese produced no basic changes in this

---

[1] Armando Cortesão, ed., *The Suma Oriental of Tomé Pires*, II, London, 1944, pp. 268–71.
[2] *Suma Oriental*, II, p. 248. Paul Wheatley, *The Golden Khersonese*, Kuala Lumpur, 1961, p. 317. M. A. P. Meilink-Roelofsz, *Asian Trade and European Influence in the Indonesian Archipelago between 1500 and about 1630*, The Hague, 1962, p. 29.

pattern. As heir to the Malay Sultans the Portuguese Crown reserved to itself the whole of the tin of Perak, and part of the production of other tin districts. The right to trade in tin was conferred on the Captains of Malacca for six months in the year and on the town of Malacca for the other six. In time the Malacca Captains succeeded in engrossing almost all the trade at the expense of the townsmen, and one commentator claimed that a Captain could amass from his tin monopoly a profit of ten thousand cruzados over a period of three years.[1] This may have been true of the mid-sixteenth century, when Portuguese power was at its height. But the rise of Acheh on the one hand and the advent of the Dutch on the other combined to reduce drastically the ability of the Portuguese to dominate Malaya's external trade. After the Achinese had conquered Perak in 1575 and again in 1620, the profits on the tin trade of that region went increasingly to the Achinese themselves and to the Asian merchants who traded both at Perak and at Acheh, while Dutch naval superiority, particularly after the imposition of the blockade of Malacca in 1634, gradually strangled that town's communications with the western Malayan coast. The decline in Portuguese profits from tin may be illustrated by two Portuguese estimates of tin production in Perak. Eredia (1618) states that Perak supplied 'more than three hundred *bares* [*bahar*]' (about 115,000 lb) for 'the Captain of Malacca and the trade of the merchants from India',[2] while Barretto de Resende, writing just before the Dutch conquest, put Perak's annual output at 'five or six quintals' (500–600 lb).[3] These figures are very low—Resende's absurdly so—and if they have any meaning at all they must refer to tin brought to Malacca, not to the total production of Perak. It is clear that, as Portuguese control over the regions north of Malacca dwindled, Asian traders resumed their practice of collecting the smelted ore directly from the tin rivers, a practice they had never, indeed, been forced entirely to abandon. Even merchants from places in India under Portuguese rule, like São Tomé and Negapatam, traded with the Malayan coast without calling at Malacca (where they would have had to pay customs dues), and exchanged their cloth for Malayan tin undisturbed.[4]

[1] Joost Schouten, cited in Meilink-Roelofsz, pp. 168–9.
[2] Cited in R. O. Winstedt and R. J. Wilkinson, 'A History of Perak,' *Journal of the Royal Asiatic Society Malayan Branch* [*JMBRAS*], XII, pt. 1, June 1934, p. 14.
[3] Barretto de Resende, 'Account of Malacca', *Journal of the Royal Asiatic Society Straits Branch*, LX, 1911, p. 11.   [4] Meilink-Roelofsz, p. 169.

From the figures of annual tribute levied on the dependencies of the Malacca Sultanate[1] and from the small number of production estimates in the available Portuguese sources, it is not possible to determine the total tin production of the Malay Peninsula before the seventeenth century and, even then, not with any precision. The English East India Company's factors at Surat early became aware of the flow of Malayan tin into that city, but in their reports home spoke only of the 'very great quantity' of the metal, and stated in 1609 that 'somewhiles there comes such store from Cadar [Kedah] with other places near unto Malacca that it is of a very base price'.[2] The Dutch at Batavia, closer to the scene and from the beginning of the century anxious to deny Malacca to the Portuguese, were better informed. 'Pera, it is said,' states a Dutch account of 1638, 'produced between 6,000 and 7,000 *bahar* of tin annually; Kedah somewhat less, though at a higher price.' In the same year the Dutch sent a commercial reconnaissance to the Malayan tin districts. Its commander was able to buy 26,906 lb of tin at what his masters regarded as a reasonable price, even though he arrived late in the season and found that most of the available stock had already been sold to traders from Bengal, Pegu and Coromandel.[3]

The value of the *bahar* of three *pikul* varied from place to place in South-east Asia and from commodity to commodity. As a measure of weight of Malayan tin, however, it seems to have remained fairly constant throughout the Peninsula at between 360 and 375 lb. If the Dutch estimate of 1638 is accepted as correct, Perak and Kedah between them must have been producing at that time over three million pounds of tin annually. The output of the northern districts, moreover, of which the chief were Ujong Salang (Phuket) and Bangeri, was not inconsiderable, and the Dutch found it necessary later on to negotiate commercial treaties with both. It may well be that, when the Dutch entered the competition for the Malayan tin trade in strength after their capture of Malacca from the Portuguese in 1641, the total annual production of the Peninsula tin-fields was in excess of four million pounds, or nearly two thousand tons.

[1] Wheatley, p. 319.

[2] Surat Letter, 30 August 1609. F. C. Danvers, ed., *Letters Received by the East India Company* (O.C. Series), I, London, 1896, p. 33.

[3] Generale Missive, 22 December 1638. P. A. Tiele, *Bouwstoffen voor de geschiedenis der Nederlanders in den Maleischen archipel*, II, 's-Gravenhage, 1890, p. 360. [Hereafter cited as *Bouwstoffen*.]

This estimate can be partly supported by statistics from a later date. In 1790 A. E. van Braam Houckgeest stated that Perak 'at one time, according to the old books, delivered 4,500 *pikul* annually, though now, because of the emigration of its miners, not more than 2,800'.[1] John Anderson, writing at the beginning of the nineteenth century, put the yearly output of Perak at 9,000 *pikul*.[2] There is a marked discrepancy here, but the figures at least seem to show that the total output of Malayan tin (on the justifiable assumption that Perak was still the largest supplier) was less at the end of the eighteenth century than it had been in the seventeenth.

That such a decline did in fact take place is likely. Throughout the seventeenth century western Malaya was an important source of tin for India and Western Asia in general, while Ligor and other places subject to Siam supplied the China market. During the eighteenth century both areas lost their earlier privileged position. In 1710 tin was discovered in Bangka, and the Dutch began to exploit that island in 1755.[3] Thereafter the Bangka mines, with those of Biliton, became the chief Dutch, and a major Asian, source of supply. Not only was the ore available there considered to be of higher quality than Malayan ore,[4] but the mines, from the Dutch point of view, were easier to control. In Malaya by mid-century the tin quarters had been thrown into confusion by the commercially dislocating incursions of the Bugis,[5] and although the Dutch reacted to the extent of bringing Perak under a measure of control again, the Malay Peninsula had by then ceased to be a major focus of their interest.

It was from the 1640s until roughly the end of the seventeenth century that serious competition existed for the product of the western Malayan tin mines. Because of their naval superiority and aggressive tactics the primary initiative lay with the Dutch who, as elsewhere, tried to create and maintain a monopoly of trade. Their rivals were, on

---

[1] J. de Hullu, 'A. E. van Braam Houckgeest's memorie over Malakka en den tinhandel aldaar (1790)', *Bijdragen tot de Taal-, Land- en Volkenkunde van Nederlandsch-Indië*, LXXVI, 1920, p. 299. [Hereafter cited as *BKI*.]

[2] John Anderson, *Political and Commercial Considerations Relative to the Malayan Peninsula*, Prince of Wales Island, 1824, p. 187.

[3] J. S. Furnivall, *Netherlands India*, Cambridge, 1944, p. 202. Wong Lin Ken, 'The Malayan Tin Industry: a Study of the Impact of Western Industrialization in Malaya', in K. G. Tregonning, ed., *Papers on Malayan History*, Singapore, 1962, p. 11.

[4] J. H. Croockewit, *Banka, Malakka en Billiton*, 's-Gravenhage, 1852, p. 5.

[5] Richard O. Winstedt, *A History of Malaya*, Singapore, 1962, pp. 144–51.

The Dutch and tin trade in Malaya

the one hand, the Asian merchants, chiefly from India and long established on the Malayan coast, and, on the other, the Europeans—Portuguese, English and Danish—some representing their nations' great trading companies, some acting for business interests in India, some trading on their own account, but all endeavouring to poach on what the Dutch chose to regard as their commercial preserve.

For the merchants of India, in particular, it was natural to resent Dutch pretensions, since Indian pre-eminence in the Malayan trade had been clearly recognized by the Malacca Sultans, and had been maintained under the Portuguese. Of the four *shahbandars* appointed to control trade at Malacca in Sultanate times, one was for Gujeratis and one for 'Indians, Burmese and traders from Pasai'. The port regulations at Malacca were based on the Indian pattern. When the city came under attack from the Portuguese, it was the 'Moors' who tried to stiffen Malay resistance with assurances that Albuquerque's threatened assault was only a bluff, and it was the Gujeratis who worked 'day and night at the fortifications' to repel the invader.[1]

Even after the Portuguese gained footholds at Malacca, on the Coromandel Coast and in Ceylon, trade in the Bay of Bengal remained substantially in Indian hands. 'Under Portuguese domination,' states W. H. Moreland, 'Indian merchants could carry on almost any trade they wanted to, provided they understood how to set to work and were prepared to pay the sums demanded for the privilege.'[2] When the Portuguese began to operate a licence system, Indian merchants paid for the licences when they had to and sailed without them when they thought they could get away with it. They were entirely familiar with *farmans*, passes and permits. Trade, in their experience, could rarely be conducted without bribes and payments of one kind or another, and, lacking the strength to challenge the Europeans, they were obliged to come to an accommodation with them.[3] In September 1642 a Surat ship arrived at Kedah with passes issued by the English, Dutch *and* Portuguese,[4] and in 1680 Indian traders arriving on the Malayan coast

[1] Winstedt, *History of Malaya*, pp. 64, 67.
[2] W. H. Moreland, *India at the Death of Akbar. An Economic Study*, London, 1920, p. 201.
[3] Tapan Raychaudhuri, 'Jan Company in Coromandel 1605–1690', *Verhandelingen van het Koninklijk Instituut voor Taal-, Land- en Volkenkunde*, XXXVIII, 's-Gravenhage, 1962, p. 126.
[4] H. T. Colenbrander, ed., *Dagh-Register gehouden int Casteel Batavia . . . 1641–1642*, 's-Gravenhage, 1900, p. 171. [Hereafter cited as *D-R.*]

were reported as having accepted 'passes and flags' from the French.[1] The extra expense involved in satisfying European demands could be tolerated, but only so long as trade routes were not unduly obstructed and profits could still be made. Even claims by European companies to the possession of the monopoly of a particular commodity were acceptable provided, as under the Portuguese, such claims were not strictly enforced. The crisis in the seventeenth century Malayan tin trade came, as will be shown, when the Dutch not only proclaimed a monopoly but took the unprecedented step of trying to make it a reality.

For their part the rulers of Malaya sought to extract the maximum advantage from foreign trade, both by participating in it themselves and by taxing overseas merchants entering their ports. Van Leur's summary of the means by which at this period the commercial acumen of the princes of Indonesia found expression may be taken as applying to their Malayan contemporaries as well: 'levies and tolls, enforced stapling, monopolization, exploitation of some kinds of production for sale in trade, occasional trade, shipowning, and *commenda* investments, and the practising of salvage rights and piracy.'[2] The only monopolies the Malayan rulers favoured were their own. When they lacked the power to control a particular export trade, they followed a policy of 'free trade with all nations . . . desiring no enemy'.[3] They never voluntarily granted exclusive purchasing or selling rights to any foreigners, whether Asian or European, but were quick to adjust to a changing balance of power. 'Let this suffice for the present,' wrote the *pengeran* of Jambi with some sarcasm to the Portuguese at Malacca in 1630. 'I will protect them [the Dutch], and when your force shall be stronger than theirs you shall have the trade which you desire.'[4]

If rulers like the Sultans of Perak and Kedah had had their way, they would have kept the export of all commodities in their own or their agents' hands, including that of tin. That they were unable to do so was

---

[1] Generale Missive, 30 November 1680. Rijksarchief, 'Brieven en Papieren Overgekomen', 1681, Boek 1. [Hereafter cited as *BPO*.]

[2] J. C. van Leur, *Indonesian Trade and Society. Essays in Asian Social and Economic History*, The Hague and Bandung, 1955, p. 92.

[3] Pieter van Dam, *Beschryvinge van de Oostindische Compagnie*, Tweede Boek, Deel 1, ed. F. W. Stapel, 's-Gravenhage, 1931, p. 18.

[4] Cited in William Hoare to Court of Directors, 6 December 1630. W. Noel Sainsbury, ed., *Calendar of State Papers, Colonial Series, East India and Persia, 1630–1634*, London, 1892, Doc. 104.

partly due to military and naval weakness, but even more to their chronic shortage of capital. An Indian merchant bringing cloth to Malaya was prepared to surrender it in return for the promise of tin to be delivered at some future date. He had no choice in the matter, since the tin would not be produced except against an advance of cloth; the Malays involved in the tin trade were unable to secure up-country tin unless they had cloth with which to pay for it. Often many months went by before the appropriate quantity of the metal could be assembled. Only then was the visiting Indian merchant able to load it aboard his vessel, transport it to India or Persia for sale, and return with more cloth the following year to begin the cycle all over again.

Inevitably such commercial procedures had two results, neither beneficial in the long run to the rulers of the Malay states. In the first place, the Indian traders took to residing on the Malayan coast for longer and longer periods, and in the end semi-permanently, the better to supervise their investments. Secondly, the rulers got more and more into debt to the Indian merchant community established on their soil. Direct evidence of the extent of this indebtedness, and of the consequent hold that resident Indians gained over the Malayan export trade, is lacking, but many passing references in the contemporary accounts show that it existed and, further, that it increased as the seventeenth century progressed.

In 1641, for example, the Sultan of Kedah told the Dutch factor, Jan Hermansen, that the trade of the 'Moors and Bengalis' in his lands did him no good, since their activities deprived him of his profits. He expressed himself willing to order all Indians out of his country under a guarantee of Dutch protection,[1] but subsequently thought better of this decision. The following year, when a Dutch soldier was murdered at Ujong Salang, the trouble was settled only after the intervention of the Indian resident community.[2] In 1645, when the Danish skipper Simon Thorstenson, brought his ship, the *St Michael*, into Kedah harbour, he had instructions to deliver all trade goods aboard to 'Sayed Nina, and if he is dead to Juan Fernandez'; Thorstenson was explicitly forbidden to participate himself in commercial transactions, which were to be left in the hands of the Danish Company's Indian agent at Kedah.[3] In 1666 the Dutch at Malacca learnt of 'a certain

---

[1] *D-R, 1641–1642*, pp. 83–4.   [2] *D-R, 1641–1642*, p. 161.
[3] Johannes Brønsted, ed., *Vore gamle tropekolonier*, Copenhagen, 1952, I, p. 88.

Moor named Mira', who had bought a vessel from the Sultan of Johore for '2,000 gold *mas* at 48 rixdollars each', and bewailed their inability to stop him using this vessel in the Perak tin trade, despite the fact that he was a resident of Malacca.[1] At Ujong Salang it was the economic stranglehold gained by Indian *chulias* that provoked the massacre of 1677, an event applauded by the contemporary English observer, Thomas Bowrey, with the words: 'I am not at all Sorry for this Massacre, but doe rather wish they [the *chulias*] were Served soe in Bantam, Achin, Queda, Johore, Syam, and many other Places they are crept into.'[2] Finally, and most revealing of all, a Dutch report of 1686 complains of 'the Moor Sedelebé', who was drawing 'the whole production of tin of Pera' to himself and had persuaded the Sultan of that state to order the up-country tin miners to deliver their product to himself alone.[3]

It was not only the willingness of the Indian merchants to grant credit that won them a privileged place in the Malayan export trade. In several other ways they had an edge on their competitors. Cloth, for example, which was the staple exchange commodity in Malaya as elsewhere in the area of the Bay of Bengal, came mainly from the Coromandel coast. The demand for it was highly specialized: a particular market would accept only certain varieties of cloth, and these were often manufactured in equally specialized centres of production.[4] Indian merchants resident in, or trading with, Coromandel thus possessed a powerful competitive advantage when it came to procuring the limited quantities of cloth available. An Indian trader, too, whether operating on his own account or for a rich and powerful magnate like Muhammad Sayyid, *mir jumla* of the Carnatic, had fewer overhead costs to pay than the representative of a European company. He had no large establishment to keep up, no fleet to provision or service, no fort or army to maintain. He could afford to be content with a smaller profit margin than the European factor, and was in consequence able to offer higher prices.[5]

[1] Generale Missive, 25 January 1667. *BPO*, 1667, Boek 1.
[2] Thomas Bowrey, *A Geographical Account of Countries Round the Bay of Bengal, 1669 to 1679*, ed. R. C. Temple, Cambridge, 1905, p. 258. D. K. Bassett, 'The Historical Background, 1500–1815', in Wang Gungwu, ed., *Malaysia. A Survey*, New York, 1964, p. 120.
[3] Generale Missive, 13 December 1686. *BPO*, 1687, Boek 1.
[4] P. Geyl, 'The Dutch in India', *Cambridge History of the British Empire*, IV, Cambridge, 1929, p. 35.   [5] Raychaudhuri, pp. 12, 123.

The Dutch and tin trade in Malaya

In the most favourable circumstances the Indian traders were strong enough to shut out European competitors entirely. A good example of this is provided by the Malayan elephant trade. Elephants were in strong demand in seventeenth-century India and, after the capture of Malacca in 1641, the Dutch laid plans to supply this demand from the resources of the Malaccan hinterland. They learnt that the countryside around their new possession was full of elephants,[1] and eight of the animals were rounded up and shipped to Bengal. The speculation was a total failure. No one in Bengal would buy Dutch elephants, and the authorities at Batavia inveighed against the 'collusion among the Moors' they believed was responsible for their agents' lack of success.[2] Another cargo of eight beasts was picked up at Kedah in 1648,[3] but thereafter the efforts of the Dutch to cut in on the Bay of Bengal elephant trade went unrewarded. The Dutch Company's animals became ill, fell into the sea and drowned during transshipment from one vessel to another, and refused to eat and 'died of sorrow' (*sturff van spyt*) when in captivity.[4] By the 1650s the Dutch were resigned to being worsted by their Indian rivals in the elephant trade. 'It is always the case that we cannot compete with them,' they reported in 1654. 'They are better bargainers than we, and know better where and how to dispose of their goods.'[5] The Dutch continued to exploit the elephants of Ceylon—in the 1660s profits from this trade were the largest single item in the revenue returns of the Dutch Company's factories there[6]—but they had to withdraw from the elephant trade in Malaya. Other Europeans such as the Englishman, Edward Lock, did better,[7] but as country traders working for, or in collaboration with, Indians, and not as representatives of the European national companies.

When at the end of 1638 the Dutch decided to take Malacca from the Portuguese, their motives were military rather than economic. They

---

[1] *Bouwstoffen*, II, p. 59. *D-R, 1641–1642*, p. 156.

[2] *Bouwstoffen*, III, p. 233. *D-R, 1644–1645*, p. 75.

[3] Johann Merklein, *Reise nach Java, Vorder- und Hinter–Indien, China und Japan, 1644–1653*, Den Haag, 1930, p. 44.

[4] *D-R, 1641–1642*, p. 81. *D-R, 1643–1644*, p. 128. Generale Missive, 23 December 1644, in W.Ph. Coolhaas, ed., *Generale Missiven van Gouverneurs-Generaal en Raden aan Heeren XVII der Verenigde Oostindische Compagnie*, II: *1639–1655*, 's-Gravenhage, 1964, p. 241.

[5] Generale Missive, 7 November 1654. *BPO, 1655*, Boek 4.

[6] Sinnappah Arasaratnam, *Dutch Power in Ceylon 1658–1687*, Amsterdam, 1958, p. 152.

[7] Winstedt, *History of Malaya*, pp. 107–8.

saw the capture of the most powerful naval base the Portuguese possessed east of India as a move in an overall strategic design; they did not expect that Malacca would in itself be of much commercial value to them. 'When victory has been achieved', they wrote in December 1638, 'we incline more to the idea of demolishing everything than of maintaining a considerable establishment. Otherwise costs will increase unduly. It will be sufficient for us if we inherit the enemy's commerce, which must necessarily happen, and if we enjoy the fruits of the valuable trade in pepper, tin, etc., which is to be driven in that area.'[1] Malacca, in short, was to pay for itself after the capture, but could not be regarded as a major commercial acquisition.

If the trading interests of the Dutch in Asia are considered as a whole, it is easy to see why Malacca had to be relegated to a minor rôle in their planning. In the first place, the fortress and settlement they won in 1641 was not as necessary to them as it had been to the Portuguese, whether as a fulcrum of political power or as an entrepôt for trade. The Dutch had Batavia, and Malacca always took second place when its interests conflicted with those of the Company's headquarters in Java. The policy of deflecting all Chinese trade to Batavia, for example, which was beginning to be effective by the second half of the seventeenth century,[2] meant that Malacca was deprived of the benefit of the junk traffic from Canton and Tongking. In the Portuguese time and earlier this trade had been one of Malacca's mainstays. The gradual strangling of the overseas commerce of Java, moreover, reduced the prahu trade which had once flourished between that island and Malaya to a trickle. Secondly, to the Dutch western Sumatran pepper was always of greater importance than Malayan tin. Until the negotiation of the Painan treaties in the 1660s[3] this trade was controlled by the rulers of Acheh, who also exercised the powers of a suzerain in relation to their vassal state of Perak in the Malay Peninsula. Before the 1660s, therefore, the Dutch had to treat Acheh with caution. They could not pressure its government too forcefully into granting them free entrée to the Perak tin trade lest that government retaliate by hindering, even more than it was doing already, their access to the Sumatran pepper trade. Thirdly, Dutch intra-Asian commerce could not be carried on

[1] Generale Missive, 22 December 1638. *BPO*, 1639, Boek 1.
[2] Generale Missive, 7 November 1654. Coolhaas, II, p. 753.
[3] J. E. Heeres, ed., 'Corpus Diplomaticum Neerlando-Indicum, Tweede Deel (1650–1675)', *BKI*, LXXXVII, 1931, pp. 165, 251.

without a regular supply of Indian exchange goods, particularly of cloth. In consequence the Dutch, never strong enough in the Indian sub-continent to dictate commercial conditions there, frequently had to yield to the wishes of Indian merchant princes seeking to participate in the trade with Malaya, even when this involved blatant infringements of Dutch monopoly policy and contractual arrangements in the Peninsula. Finally, the vaunted 'naval supremacy' which the Dutch are often presumed to have possessed in Asian waters during their golden century proved quite inadequate for their purposes in Malaya. It is true that their fleets and vessels were individually the strongest afloat, but the total naval forces available to the Netherlands East India Company never enabled it to dominate the seas everywhere at once or even police effectively particular areas against competitors. In December 1643, for example, the Company's ships in the East were disposed as follows: at Batavia, 18 vessels of which 10 were about to leave for Europe, plus 5 smaller craft: in the Moluccas, 4 vessels; in Amboina, 5; in Banda, 1; on the West Coast of Sumatra, 2; in Palembang, 3; in Jambi, 2; in Patani, 1; in Siam, 4; in Cambodia, 3; in Tongking, 1; in Formosa, 5; in Malacca, 3; in Arakan, 3; in Coromandel, 5; in Ceylon 13; on the Malabar Coast, 7; in Surat and Persia, 3; and in Mauritius, 1; in all, 89 ships.[1] The total is impressive, but it is obvious that there could be no question of overall naval supremacy when these ships had to be spread over two oceans from Madagascar to China. By concentrating their strength the Dutch were able to achieve local predominance more or less anywhere they chose. What they could not do was maintain effectively and for decades a series of blockades in widely dispersed areas of the East. Yet, as in the case of the Malayan tin trade, it was precisely this kind of sterile and unproductive police duty that their monopoly policies compelled them time and again to attempt.

When, therefore, the Dutch took over Malacca in 1641, they saw no immediate prospect of bringing the Malay states under their commercial control by force. They were unable, or at any rate unwilling, to spend the resources to achieve this. The alternative was persuasion. 'I conclude', wrote the first Dutch governor, Johan van Twist, in November 1641, 'that we should bring back to Malacca not only the

[1] N. MacLeod, *De Oost-Indische Compagnie als zeemogendheid in Azië*, Rijswijk, 1927, II, p. 345.

locally born people, who are dispersed far and wide, by welcoming them and permitting them the free exercise of their religion ... but also all Portuguese and others, without distinction of person, origin or faith, and permit them free trade (provided they pay toll and other dues as in the Portuguese time).' As for the Indian traders, in whose hands, as the Dutch well knew, the bulk of the Malayan export trade lay, they should be compelled to call at Malacca both before and after any visit to the tin quarters to the north.[1]

In the early 1640s an arrangement of this kind may well have seemed to the Dutch to have a reasonable prospect of success. During the siege the rulers of both Perak and Kedah had written to Batavia in complimentary fashion, praying God for the success of Dutch arms,[2] and the first factors sent to these states after the capture were warmly received. In 1642, indeed, Senior Factor Jan Dirksz. Puijt was granted by the Sultan of Perak an honorific title, raised 'above the *shahbandar*' and given charge of the port, and presented with an Achinese keris and sword.[3] Even the merchants of India, who can scarcely have welcomed the transfer of Malacca to the Dutch since they had been doing so well under the Portuguese, seem to have been willing to give the new authorities at Malacca at least a trial. In July 1642 a vessel arrived there bearing an Achinese dignitary accompanied by various 'Moguls from the Bengal ships' lying in Acheh harbour, and six months later came 'a great Moorish ship belonging to the second son of the Great Mogul', both visits being designed, in the opinion of the Governor of Malacca, 'to test the possibilities of this place'.[4] Ships of all nations, moreover, continued to call at Malacca, as in the Portuguese time, despite the obligation laid on them to pay Portuguese-style tolls. 'In one day', reported a Danish visitor to the settlement in 1644–5, 'arrived here in the roads two Portuguese ships, to wit, the *Kaiman* and *S. Franciskus*, which came from Goa and were bound for Makao in China; also an English ship, named *Snayle*, which came from Masulipatam and was bound for Kambaje; and yet another ship from Mozambique, also bound for Makao.'[5]

---

[1] *Bouwstoffen*, III, pp. 35–36.
[2] *D-R, 1640–1641*, pp. 70–71.
[3] *D-R, 1641–1642*, p. 167. Winstedt and Wilkinson, 'History of Perak', p. 25.
[4] *Bouwstoffen*, III, pp. 99–100.
[5] Adam Olearius, trans., *De beschryving der reizen van Georg Andriesz* ..., Amsterdam, 1670, p. 92.

Equally successful were most of the initial Dutch attempts to win control of the Malayan export trade in tin by means of formal contracts. In July 1642 the Sultan of Kedah concurred in an arrangement whereby half the tin produced in, or imported into, his kingdom would be sold to the Dutch Company at the fixed price of 31¼ reals per *bahar*. In October of the following year the Dutch obtained freedom to trade at Ujong Salang, and in January 1645 the right to the entire tin production of Bangeri. All these contracts contained the stipulation that non-Dutch ships must be refused trade unless they had valid passes issued by Dutch officials in the countries from which they came or from the Dutch government at Malacca.[1]

Before long, however, the Dutch were forced to realize that neither of their two main economic objectives in Malaya—control of the tin trade and prosperity for Malacca—was being achieved. For one thing, Malacca quickly gained a reputation as a place of pestilence, and Indian and Portuguese traders began avoiding it.[2] For another, the Dutch soon learned that, although Malay rulers readily signed treaties and agreements, they were less willing to adhere to them or oblige others to do so. Despite the contracts with Kedah and Bangeri, Indian and other merchants continued to visit these areas without Dutch permission and to trade in tin. The Sultan of Perak, moreover, could not be induced to sign an agreement at all. In 1639 the Dutch had been granted access to Perak tin by that state's suzerain, Acheh, but this arrangement had been disregarded so far as possible in Perak. In an attempt to divert the Indian merchants who traded there the Dutch began patrolling, and in 1644, after an argument about an interloping Cambodian vessel, withdrew their factor from Perak and proclaimed a blockade of its rivers.[3] But neither this blockade nor the commercial links established with the other tin quarters increased the quantity of tin available for the Dutch to buy.

By 1647 the situation, as seen from Batavia, was becoming intolerable. Expenditure at Malacca had exceeded revenue every year since the conquest, and the average annual deficit was running at more than forty

[1] J. E. Heeres, ed., 'Corpus Diplomaticum Neerlando-Indicum, Eerste Deel (1596–1650)', *BKI*, VII, 3, 1907, pp. 364–6, 400–03, 414–17, 437–9.
[2] Generale Missive, 23 December 1644. *BPO*, 1645, Boek 1. The sickness of which the visiting merchants complained was presumably malaria, although the local Dutch believed that 'evil vapours' resulting from the long siege were causing the trouble.
[3] Winstedt and Wilkinson, 'History of Perak', pp. 26–7.

thousand guilders. 'The past year', wrote Governor de Vlamingh van Oudshoorn of Malacca in December 1646, 'we have had some good trade, but only in pepper, brought here from Palembang and Indragiri ... From Kedah not one *kati* of tin have we received, and from Ujong Salang no more than 292 *bahar* 202 lb ... In Perak the Company has had in place of tin fine words and a friendly countenance, and from there has won no more than 10 *bahar*.' By contrast Indian traders carried 488,000 lbs of tin to Surat in three ships in 1646, and during the following year took 1500 *bahar* from Perak alone. Repeatedly the Dutch factors at Malacca and the tin quarters warned their superiors that 'Moorish competition' was so heavy that they could neither buy nor sell with profit; the Indians flooded the Malayan coast with cloth and offered higher prices for Malayan tin.[1]

The only solution, the authorities at Batavia decided, was to use force. In June 1647 they resolved 'to interdict the Moors of Surat, Coromandel, Bengal, Pegu, etc.... from the trade of Acheh and the tin quarters on pain, should they continue to appear there in the future, of being declared prizes of war'.[2] To make this blanket prohibition effective, a blockade was imposed on the rivers of western Malaya. Dutch cruising ships received orders to warn interlopers and, if the offence was repeated, to arrest them.

Initially these harsh measures achieved their objectives. Indian trade with Malaya fell off sharply, and the Dutch found that at last they could buy tin from the Malay states freely and at their own price. During 1650 an unprecedented quantity, 770,000 lb, was purchased. This was sufficient not only to fulfil the demands of India and Persia, but to supply a new market the Company was then engaged in opening up in Taiwan.[3] In August 1650 the Dutch succeeded in pressuring the Queen of Acheh into an agreement whereby her subjects and the Dutch Company were to share the tin of Perak equally, and in this arrangement the Sultan of Perak was obliged to concur.[4] The Sultan also agreed to the re-establishment of the Dutch lodge which had been withdrawn from his state in 1644. Finally, the finances of Malacca, reflecting the increasing volume of Dutch trade in the Peninsula,

---

[1] *Bouwstoffen*, III, pp. 199–200, 331–2, 343. Generale Missive, 31 December 1645. *BPO*, 1646, Boek 2.
[2] Generale Resolutie, 3 June 1646. Rijksarchief, *Kol.* 572. *Bouwstoffen*, III, pp. 354–6.
[3] Generale Missive, 20 January 1651. *BPO*, 1651, Boek 1.
[4] Heeres, 'Corpus Diplomaticum ... Eerste Deel (1596–1650)', pp. 538–40.

sharply improved after 1647. In 1649–50 there was a surplus of f. 1,632 and in 1650–51 this figure increased to f. 28,596.[1]

In July 1651, however, any expectations the Dutch may have been entertaining of a permanent domination of the Malayan tin trade were abruptly shattered when news arrived at Malacca of the 'Massacre of Perak'. This event marked a clear turning point in the history of Dutch–Malay relations in the seventeenth century. The circumstances surrounding it were as follows.

Early in 1651 Factor Michiel Curre, who had already spent some time in Perak and was well regarded there, received orders from the Governor of Malacca to reopen the Perak factory. His instructions were precise: with timber obtained from Cape Rachado he was to erect a building twenty feet wide and seventy-five feet long, divided into three parts, the middle section to be used as a warehouse and the outer sections as living quarters for the factory staff. Accompanied by his wife, Curre left Malacca for Perak on 8 April.

For some time the news filtering down from Perak had been disquieting, and after Curre's arrival there it got rapidly worse. A Dutch soldier, it was learnt, had been assaulted by an Achinese in the open street, thrown to the ground and pinned there by his assailant's foot 'to the disparagement of the Netherlanders'. Junior Factor Nicolaes Mombers was accused by 'a certain foreigner from Coromandel' of having seduced the latter's concubine, and had been 'very murderously removed from this life' with a keris. In neither case had the offender been punished. Even more serious was the persistent refusal of the Sultan and nobles of Perak to dismiss the 'long-resident Moors' from their territory, even though the treaty of 1650 had clearly stipulated that all merchants other than Dutch and Achinese should be denied access to trade.

Finally, in July came word of the massacre of the Dutch in Perak. In accordance with his instructions Curre had gone to the Sultan's palace in order to present a formal letter from the Governor of Malacca. On arrival he was immediately attacked by Malays, and the resistance offered by the eight soldiers he had with him provoked a general outbreak. The Malay assault fell not only on the commercial staff of the factory but on the crews of the ships in the harbour as well.

---

[1] Generale Missiven, 20 January 1651 and 24 January 1652. *BPO*, 1651, Boek 1 and 1652, Boek 1.

In all twenty-seven Dutchmen were killed, the only survivors being Curre and his wife, an assistant, a carpenter, two sailors and the family of a second carpenter. The few who escaped death were rounded up and imprisoned in the houses of various officers of state. Curre owed his life to a direct intervention on his behalf by the Sultan.

The Dutch at once decided that the massacre at Perak had been both unprovoked and premeditated. They based their conclusion on the fact that the Company's Resident at Acheh had heard that an attack on the Dutch was being planned before Curre and his party had even left Malacca. They regarded as absurd the Sultan of Perak's subsequent claim that his people had taken action against the Perak factory because it was being turned into a 'fortress' rather than a mere lodge; and when the Sultan further protested that Curre's men had secretly been bringing heavy guns into the factory from the ships in the harbour, they dismissed this assertion as equally false. How could a wooden building seventy-five feet long be transformed into a fortress?

To preserve their reputation the Dutch felt that they must exact the maximum possible penalty from 'the faithless murderers of Perak'. Four yachts, a sloop, a flute-ship and three war-prahus were quickly assembled, loaded with ammunition and a detachment of three hundred soldiers and, under command of Commissioner Joan Truijtman, rushed from Batavia to Malacca. At Malacca a further 120 men were added and by the beginning of October Truijtman, with this sizeable force to back him up, was demanding from the Sultan of Perak full satisfaction and the surrender of all prisoners. The Sultan temporized, explaining that he could not hand over Curre or Curre's wife until he had received an answer to the report of the whole matter he had written to his suzerain, the Queen of Acheh.

Truijtman promptly set out for Acheh, where the Queen readily agreed to all his demands, professing total ignorance of recent happenings in Perak. She despatched two messengers to her vassal, the Sultan, with a written order instructing him to surrender the prisoners and, in the presence of the Dutch Commissioner, publicly punish the *temenggong* and *shahbandar* as the chief instigators of the uprising, together with their supporters and other guilty persons. Returning to Perak Truijtman obtained the release of the prisoners without difficulty (though in the meantime the two sailors had been put to work in the 'tin-mountains' and had to be sent for) together with a promise that the perpetrators of the massacre would be brought to justice. The Sultan also agreed that compensation would be due in respect of Dutch Company property destroyed. With these results the authorities in Batavia were for the time being content. They must have realized, however, that Truijtman's achievements represented a small return indeed on the expenditure of so much effort, and they were certainly aware that a final and satisfactory settlement of the matter was likely to be far in the future. Meanwhile the naval blockade of Perak was to continue.[1]

Yet scarcely had this decision been reached when Netherlands-Perak relations deteriorated still further. At the end of December 1651 Truijtman, hoping to stimulate the Sultan into taking quicker action against the murderers, returned to Perak. He was making his way up river in a small boat, and had reached the first of no less than five defences erected by the Malays to bar access to the capital, when he was fired on without warning. In the first broadside he lost three men killed and six wounded. This could hardly be interpreted other than as an act of open war, and Truijtman decided to dig in on the river bank and send to Malacca for reinforcements. He and his men survived a dawn attack by the Malays early in 1652, but the coming of the rainy season defeated him. The site he had selected for his defensive position became sodden, and he and his men came down with malaria. He had no choice but to withdraw, leaving the victory with Perak.

Making his way to Acheh Truijtman complained in understandably vigorous terms about the hostile reception accorded him by the Queen of Acheh's insubordinate vassal. But he found little sympathy at the Achinese court. The Queen had plenty of complaints of her own: the Dutch, she said, had been planning to build at Perak 'a stone house' larger than the residence of the Sultan himself and His Highness had naturally resented this; all the common people had now become thoroughly embittered against the Dutch Company; and, in any case, it was not the *temenggong* or the *shahbandar* who had caused the outbreak at Perak but the Indian who had murdered the Dutch soldier. Truijtman had to withdraw from Acheh having achieved nothing whatever.

His misfortunes were not yet over. From Acheh he went to Kedah, where he had instructions to seek payment of some outstanding debts due to the Company from the Sultan. To begin with, the welcome he

---

[1] Generale Missive, 19 December 1651. *BPO*, 1652, Boek 4. Generale Missive, 24 January 1652. *BPO*, 1653, Boek 1. Coolhaas, II, pp. 511–20, 568–72.

received was very friendly. Mounted on a state elephant he was conducted to the Sultan's capital at Bukit Tinggi, and entertained and
flattered for two days. But when he attempted to discuss business the
Sultan's attitude suddenly changed. Pointing to the side-arms carried
by the soldiers of Truijtman's escort, His Highness announced that
there were too many Dutchmen present and that their weapons must be
surrendered. One of the soldiers resisted and there was a scuffle, in
which one Dutchman was killed and another wounded. The whole
party, sixty strong, were then clapped in gaol. The justification for
this extraordinary action, as explained to the prisoners, was that the
Sultan was seeking compensation for a vessel of his which the Company had seized on the high seas four years before. From May to
October 1652 Truijtman and his men were held captive in Kedah.
They were released only after the Dutch had agreed to pay to the
Sultan compensation for his impounded yacht at his own valuation and
had cancelled some of his debts. The net loss to the Company as a
result of these proceedings was 12,809 reals.[1]

Thus, within the short space of eighteen months, the Netherlands
East India Company had been challenged successively by Perak,
Acheh and Kedah, and on each occasion had been obliged to back
down. The Company's prestige suffered, since the rulers of Malaya
drew the lesson—on inadequate evidence, perhaps—that Dutch power
was not so much to be feared as they had thought. The Company's
confidence also suffered. After 1652 Governors of Malacca no longer
wrote sanguine reports about the commercial prospects of their
settlement, and in Batavia's thinking the Malay Peninsula began to
be pushed into the background. In his annual commercial reviews,
prepared for the Directors at home, the Governor-General no longer
quoted from 'the Malacca letters' at length; from mid-century
onwards a laconic reference to 'the accompanying papers' sufficed.

The Dutch, indeed, never did obtain satisfaction for the massacre at
Perak. In 1659 a treaty negotiated with Acheh stated that the sum of
50,000 reals would be paid by Perak as compensation for the destruction of Company property, but the Sultan could not produce the
required cash. It was then agreed that the debt should be gradually
amortized by a reduction in the price of tin: the Dutch would pay 30
reals per *bahar* instead of the contract price of $31\frac{1}{4}$ reals. The arrange-

[1] Generale Missive, 31 January 1653. Coolhaas, II, pp. 641–5.

ment obviously encouraged Perak to get a better price whenever possible by selling to other purchasers.[1] In the end the Company had to admit defeat. The 'still outstanding debt of f. 130,885 . . . due from the king and nobles of Perak' was written off by the Council at Batavia in September 1694.[2]

The failure of the Dutch to impose their will on the Malayan tin quarters was due only in part to their unwillingness to commit the resources needed to carry out the task. The weapon they chose, naval blockade, would in any case have been difficult to employ effectively. The large Dutch ships could not penetrate far up the western Malayan rivers,[3] and could not therefore be used to bombard an enemy into submission. There were numerous creeks and inlets into which 'smugglers' could escape,[4] and Malay prahu captains showed much ingenuity in devising methods of getting the tin out unobserved. At one time, when Perak was under blockade, tin was even being carried overland from the Perak uplands to be exported from Kedah.[5] When a vessel suspected of 'illegal' trading was captured, moreover, the Dutch could not always prove it had committed an offence. By treaty Acheh shared equally with the Company in Perak tin, and Indian traders sailing for the Malayan coast from Acheh were often given passes by the Achinese court. Such traders, although operating on their own account and not on that of Acheh, could not legally be molested.[6] Captains of vessels, too, who did admit Dutch monopoly claims could readily make false declarations of cargo. Since the Dutch did not, by treaty, have boarding rights, the word of such captains had to be accepted.[7] There was also a great deal of private trading on the part of the Company's factors,[8] which not only harmed it commercially but brought it into disrepute: a protest against a Malayan ruler's contract infringement came ill from a commercial concern which apparently could not even keep its own servants in check.

[1] Generale Missive, 26 December 1662. *BPO*, 1663, Boek 1.
[2] Generale Resolutiën, 6 September 1694. Rijksarchief, *Kol.* 609.
[3] Generale Missiven, 31 January 1653 and 1 April 1655. Coolhaas, II, pp. 643 and 822.
[4] Generale Missive, 19 January 1654. *BPO*, 1654, Boek 1.
[5] Generale Missive, 7 November 1654. *BPO*, 1655, Boek 4.
[6] Instructie voor den Gouverneur–Generaal, 26 April 1650. J. A. van der Chijs, ed., *Nederlandsch-Indisch plakaatboek, 1602–1811*, II, Batavia, 1886, p. 145.
[7] Generale Missive, 17 December 1657. *BPO*, 1658, Boek 1.
[8] *D-R, 1666–1667*, p. 179. William Dampier, *A Supplement to the Voyage Round the World*, London, 1729, pp. 111, 166. Dampier visited Malacca in 1689.

During one brief period of just over a decade (1664–75) the annual trade balances at Malacca showed a profit,[1] and the Governor of the day began to hope for better things. Batavia authorized an increase in the purchase price of tin, which stimulated voluntary, as opposed to compulsory, sales to the Company's factors.[2] In Perak a *bendahara* had come to power who proved to be unusually favourable to the Dutch interest—so favourable, indeed, that in 1667 there was a rebellion against his authority, his opponents maintaining that he had been selling too much tin to Malacca. He had to hurry down from the tin mountains, where he had been urging the miners on to greater production, to quell the disturbances.[3] The Dutch also profited from a weakening in the competition offered by their rivals. During the Anglo-Dutch wars English ships and Indian vessels sailing under English colours were reluctant to venture into Malayan waters because of the increased danger of Dutch attack. Nor was Acheh so much of a trade rival as it had been in the past. By the 1660s the decline of that once great state was well under way, and the Achinese were not only less capable than before of shielding Perak from Dutch demands but less able to finance their own share of the Malayan tin trade.

Malacca's interlude of prosperity, however, was short-lived. It had been caused by a chance combination of circumstances which did not occur again. The pro-Dutch *bendahara* died in 1674,[4] and the Governor of Malacca was soon voicing the familiar complaint that where once Perak had produced seven or eight hundred *bahar* of tin a year, the quantity now available for purchase by his factors was 'no more than two hundred to two hundred and fifty *bahar*'.[5] By 1680 competition from English, Portuguese and Indian traders had increased to the point where they were undercutting the Dutch at will.[6] At Kedah the Sultan felt so sure of English and Indian support against the Dutch that year after year, on one pretext or another, he avoided paying his debts

[1] The Malacca accounts showed deficits from 1641–2 to 1648–9, surpluses in 1649–50 and 1650–51, deficits again from 1651–2 to 1663–4, surpluses from 1664–5 to 1675–6, and deficits thereafter until the end of the century. In the 1664–75 period much of the profit came from the gold trade with Indragiri, which was under Malacca's control at that time.

[2] W. Ph. Coolhaas, 'Malacca under Jan van Riebeeck', *JMBRAS*, xxxviii, pt. 2, December 1965, p. 177.

[3] Generale Missive, 5 October 1667. *BPO*, 1668, Boek 1.

[4] Generale Missive, 17 November 1674. *BPO*, 1675, Boek 1.

[5] Generale Missive, 19 March 1683. *BPO*, 1683, Boek 1.

[6] Generale Missive, 13 March 1680. *BPO*, 1680, Boek 1, vervolg.

to the Company and refused to sell it any tin. At Ujong Salang and Bangeri little tin was to be had by anybody, since these areas were fast falling into chaos caused by civil war.

Finally, the Company's claims to 'possess' the Malayan export trade were challenged by a new rival, and in a region the Dutch had some reason to consider their own, the open sea. By the 1690s piracy had become a serious problem in Malayan waters, especially along the northwest coast. It was a pirate, *panglima* Kulup, who burnt the Dutch redoubt (by then abandoned) in Dinding Island in 1692,[1] and the free burgers of Malacca were so fearful of his power that they refused to sail for Perak to trade except in convoys protected by Dutch warships.[2] By this time all pretence of enforcing by naval blockade the agreements made in the 1640s between the Company and the rulers of the tin quarters had been abandoned. The twice-a-year commercial mission lapsed in 1687 'because of the lack of a suitable vessel',[3] and the blockade ship off the mouth of Perak River was withdrawn, because it served no useful purpose, in 1689.[4]

Thus, by the end of the seventeenth century the attempt of the Netherlands East India Company to engross the tin trade of western Malaya had failed. The Dutch were defeated partly by the superior resources, tactics and persistence of their rivals, but even more by the rigidity of their own economic policies. Having learned by mid-century that a mercantilist-style regulation of commerce was both unacceptable to the rulers of the tin quarters and unenforceable without great expenditure of men and money, they might well have been content with a share of the trade purchased under competitive conditions. But they adhered to a system of fixed prices, annual quotas and exclusive privileges long after it had become plain to all that they could not enforce their demands. The Company never formally abandoned its treaty rights in Malayan tin, but ultimately became reconciled to the fact that these rights had no practical significance. 'It has been known for a long time', wrote the Governor-General and Council in 1698, 'that Malacca has been more a place of necessary residence and garrison than of trade.'[5]

---

[1] Generale Missive, 14 March 1693. *BPO*, 1693, Boek 4.
[2] Generale Missive, 8 December 1693. *BPO*, 1694, Boek 1.
[3] Generale Missive, 23 December 1687. *BPO*, 1688, Boek 1.
[4] Generale Missive, 30 December 1689. *BPO*, 1690, Boek 1.
[5] Generale Missive, 6 December 1698. *BPO*, 1699, Boek 1.

EARLY CHINESE MIGRATION
INTO NORTH SUMATRA

BY ANTHONY REID

Victor Purcell's *The Chinese in South-east Asia* was the more impressive an achievement in view of the absence of detailed regional studies on which to base such a vast coverage. Even today, fifteen years after that work was first published, one looks in vain for a scholarly treatment of any of the 'secondary' Chinese centres in Indonesia, outside the main base in Java. The most sizable of these communities is that in the province now called Sumatera Utara. This province includes the sparsely populated former Dutch residency of Tapanuli, and the former Government of the East Coast of Sumatra, which had a Chinese population of 99,000 in the 1905 census and 193,000 in that of 1930.

The most interesting aspect of the history of this community is not how it came to be, but why it did not become greater; why, despite the apparent trend of the nineteenth century, Deli, Langkat, and Serdang did not follow the pattern of Perak and Selangor in Malaya, with Chinese immigrants coming to form the major racial group. The planters of Sumatra made no secret of their preference for Chinese labour over Javanese, and the massive annual influx of Chinese to Singapore and Penang between 1880 and 1930[1] would appear to have provided a ready source of supply. Yet difficulties in the way of recruiting this labour eventually persuaded the planters to substitute Javanese,

---

OFFICIAL PRINTED SOURCES frequently cited include:

Straits Settlements Legislative Council Proceedings (*SSLCP*), especially Appendix 22 of 1876: 'Report of the Committee appointed to consider and take evidence upon the Conditions of Chinese Labourers in the Colony', 3 November 1876.
Annual Reports of the Protector of Chinese, Straits Settlements, in *Straits Settlements Government Gazette* (*SSGG*).
Straits Settlements Labour Commission Report, Singapore, 1890 (*SSLCR*).
Koloniale Verslagen, The Hague.
Verzameling van Consulaire en andere Verslagen en Berigten (*Consulaire Verslagen*), The Hague.

[1] Between 1882 and 1932 the annual influx fell below 100,000 only in the years 1918–19.

who now form the largest single component of the population of the *cultuurgebied* (cultivation district).

What was the cause of these difficulties? Dutch writers have generally ascribed them to the obstructionism of British officials and the intrigues of 'coolie-brokers' in the Straits Settlements.[1] Writers from the British or Malayan side who have noted the problem incidentally have been inclined to blame the Sumatra planters for giving their district a deservedly bad name among Chinese immigrants.[2] In reality, of course, the problem cannot be answered by any such categorical solutions, yet a careful examination of it is of considerable importance for an understanding of migration patterns in the Nanyang.

Before the middle of the nineteenth century, Chinese played a very limited rôle in Sumatra, and especially its northern part.[3] The energetic people of the Acheh Sultanate, in the northwest, brought their own pepper to market in Penang or sold it on the spot to American, European, or Indian buyers. Further south, isolated Chinese traders were to be found, but they formed no substantial or permanent part of the economy of any district. In the early decades of the nineteenth century the produce of the Deli-Asahan area was still carried to market by the Minangkabau traders of Batu Bara.[4] At the river ports further south—Rokan, Siak, Kampar and Jambi—Bugis, Arab, Indian and local craft still dominated the trade in the 1820s.[5] Anderson, touring the east coast states in 1823, saw 'a very few Chinese' in Deli,[6] but did not think them worthy of notice elsewhere.

The growth of Chinese merchant communities in the fast-expanding

---

[1] W. H. M. Schadee, *Geschiedenis van Sumatra's Oostkust*, Amsterdam, 1918–19, II, pp. 34–35. H. J. Bool, *De Chineesche immigratie naar Deli*, Utrecht, 1904, pp. 1–2.

[2] R. N. Jackson, *Pickering, Protector of Chinese*, Kuala Lumpur, 1965, pp. 70–72. Ng Siew Yoong, 'The Chinese Protectorate in Singapore 1877–1900', *Journal South-east Asian History*, II, no. 1, 1961, pp.99.

[3] The important Chinese connection with Sri Vijaya, culminating in the apparent establishment of Chinese rulers in Jambi and Palembang at the end of the fourteenth century, is of course a remarkable exception. This connection did not survive the Ming abandonment of state trading after 1435.

[4] [John Anderson], *An Exposition of the Political and Commercial Relations of the Government of Prince of Wales' Island with the States on the East Coast of Sumatra from Diamond Point to Siak*, Penang, 1824, pp. 22 and 37.

[5] Anderson, p. 39. William Milburn, *Oriental Commerce*, revised ed., London, 1825, p. 375. J. H. Moor, *Notices of the Indian Archipelago, and Adjacent Countries*, Singapore, 1837, pp. 101–02. John Anderson, *Mission to the East Coast of Sumatra in 1823*, Edinburgh/London, 1826, pp. 172, 352–3, 394–6.

[6] Anderson, *Mission*, p. 296.

entrepôts of Penang and Singapore brought about a major change which was fully evident by about 1860. Straits Chinese traders had established strong links with all the Malay states of the east coast between Siak and Temiang by the time the Dutch extended their influence to the district (1858–65). This was particularly the case in Asahan, where the import and export duties, as well as the opium and gambling monopolies, had been entrusted to the Penang merchant Boon Keng. The Dutch considered that Boon Keng's influence, and the support he could muster in Penang, were principally responsible for the Raja's resistance to Dutch overtures until 1865, when the Dutch army was sent in.[1] One of the major reasons advanced in favour of a permanent Dutch occupation of Asahan was that otherwise 'the Chinese traders would spread British influence and exploit the country even more than before'.[2]

Despite this early antagonism, the gradual establishment of Dutch power in the East Coast of Sumatra provided a further opportunity for Chinese enterprise. Straits-based Chinese firms continued to operate the opium, spirit, and gaming monopolies of most states, and even the import and export duties of some, including Siak and Asahan. By 1876 the Resident could report that 'the trade of this Residency is exclusively in the hands of the Chinese', most of whom were connected with firms in Singapore or Penang.[3] As for Western enterprise, there was no European-owned shipping link to the East Coast of Sumatra until the Dutch mails began in 1873, and no serious commercial competition for the Chinese steamers and tongkangs until the Ocean Steamship Company began its Singapore–Deli service in 1880.[4] From the point of view of commercial connections, therefore, the East Coast of Sumatra had become as much an economic hinterland for the Straits Chinese as the Malay Peninsula.

Permanent Chinese settlement in large numbers began soon after the

[1] C. A. Kroesen, 'Geschiedenis van Asahan', *Tijdschrift voor Taal-, Land-, en Volkenkunde*, XXXI, 1886, pp. 105 and 111.

[2] M. Hamerster, *Bijdrage tot de Kennis van de Afdeeling Asahan*, Amsterdam, 1926, p. 50, Schadee, I, pp. 141–2.

[3] *Koloniaal Verslag*, 1876, p. 18.

[4] *Verzameling van Consulaire en Andere Verslagen en Berigten* 1876–86: Consular reports, Penang and Singapore. Holland destroyed Achinese vessels after declaring war on Acheh in 1873, leaving this field almost equally in the hands of Chinese traders. The war, however, prevented the establishment of resident Chinese traders in any numbers, while it also gave a larger rôle to the European firm which acted as provisioner for the Dutch forces.

establishment of Dutch authority. By 1875 there were already sizable communities at Bengkalis, where the important fishing and lumbering resources soon became a Chinese preserve; at Tandjung Balai (Asahan) and Labuan Bilik (Panai), centres of trade with the Batak districts inland; and especially in the agricultural enterprises of Deli.[1]

When the colonial government at Batavia sent its first nervous representative to Deli in 1864, there were about twenty Chinese in the place—mostly goldsmiths and small shopkeepers.[2] This official lodged at first with the Dutch pioneer of Deli, J. Nienhuys, who had arrived the previous year in search of tobacco. He had just decided to grow his own crop with hired labour, having received poor returns from buying up the inferior tobacco which the Bataks of Hamperan Perak had grown for years. Neither Bataks nor Malays would work as wage labourers, and Nienhuys resorted to bringing some Javanese *hajis* from Penang, who were probably still in debt for their passage to Mecca. As a former tobacco-planter in Java Nienhuys turned first to this familiar source of labour. However, one disappointing season was enough to make him experiment again. In 1865 he brought 88 Chinese and 23 Malays from Penang as wage labourers. This brought the pay-off. Nienhuys's 1865 crop received recognition in Amsterdam as the finest quality, and sold for the remarkable price of 1·49 guilders per half-kilo.[3]

This success began a twenty-five-year period of uninterrupted expansion in the Deli tobacco industry. Capital flowed rapidly into the area, which soon included Serdang and Langkat as well as Deli. Much of the capital came from nearby Penang. Chinese entrepreneurs were prominent at first, and in 1867 three of them were busy planting their leasehold with tobacco as well as copra and nutmeg.[4] But within a few years the need for large-scale investment and sophisticated technical and sales management made the tobacco industry a European preserve. Leading the field from 1869 was the Deli Maatschappij, a marriage of Nienhuys's local experience and the capital of the N.H.M.

Following Nienhuys's lead, all the new firms used Chinese exclusively for cultivating the tobacco plant, though Indians, Javanese,

[1] *Koloniaal Verslag*, 1875, p. 18.
[2] J. A. M. Cats baron de Raet, 'Vergelijking van de vroegeren toestand van Deli, Serdang en Langkat met den tegenwoordige', *Tijdschrift voor Taal-, Land-, en Volkenkunde*, XXIII, 1876, p. 30.
[3] Schadee, I, pp. 171–7.   [4] De Raet, p. 31.

Bataks, and Malays were often employed for more routine labour. The Deli Maatschappij alone brought 900 Chinese from Penang when it began operations in 1869.[1] The Chinese population of Deli climbed from the twenty of 1864 to nearly 1000 in 1867[2] and over 4000 in 1872.[3] Every year throughout the 1870s and 1880s thousands of Chinese labourers were brought from the Straits Settlements to support the most spectacularly expanding economy of Southeast Asia.

Nienhuys and the other pioneers of the 1860s had acquired their Chinese labour through the *kongsi* system so well established in the Straits Settlements. The *kongsi*-head was allocated part of a virgin land concession and some seedlings, and the finished tobacco leaf was bought from him at the end of the year. This system was discontinued by about 1870, however, in favour of a direct contract between a European manager, assisted by his Chinese *tindals* (headmen), and the individual labourer. Advances were made to the field-worker throughout the year at half-monthly intervals, until in December he brought his crop to the European assistant who paid him according to his estimate of the quality of the crop. The planters maintained: 'The first essential for a successful cultivation of tobacco is to ensure soundness of leaf . . . and unless the remuneration of the labourers is based upon the condition in which he delivers his produce, the cultivation of good tobacco becomes impossible.'[4] Deli thus brought the Chinese labourer into much closer relation with a European employer than any of the other major avenues of employment in the Nanyang.

Before plunging into a description of the complex pattern of Chinese labour recruitment, one must sound a note of caution. Like previous studies of the subject, this paper is based entirely on colonial sources, which give a very inadequate picture of a phenomenon whose complexity they hardly understood. This is particularly evident in the case of the reports of the Straits Settlements Protectors of Chinese, who were so burdened by the immense but routine task of registering the influx of migrants that they could give little attention to more fundamental matters.[5] The two main sources of information, the reports of

[1] Schadee, I, p. 181.   [2] De Raet, p. 33.
[3] Schadee, I, p. 186. A much more accurate figure was the number of Chinese employed on Western plantations—4476 by the end of 1874. *Koloniaal Verslag*, 1875, p. 196.
[4] Planters' Committee to Read, 31 May 1882, *The Deli Coolie Question*, Singapore, 1882, pp. 10–11.
[5] Moreover, the early Protectors of Chinese were not men of outstanding ability or imagination. Significantly, they took no part in the various attempts during the late

the 1876 and 1890 Labour Commissions in the Straits Settlements, do supply a range of statements from Chinese involved in labour recruitment. These conceal more than they reveal, however, unless read with a full understanding of the economic and clan structure of the time, and the way each witness fitted into it. The writer is acutely aware that this paper is largely based on the same uncertain foundation of rumour and speculation as that on which colonial officials made their judgments in matters Chinese.

Following the Anglo-Franco-Chinese Convention of 1866 governing Chinese emigration, the recruitment of labourers in China and their passage to the Straits Settlements were conducted in a tolerably civilized manner. With the exception of a small and decreasing number who sailed to Singapore on Hainan junks, the migrants travelled on chartered steamers which reached Singapore in six to eight days. A firm in one of the treaty ports would publicise the coming departure of one of its chartered ships, and prospective migrants would be brought in by *khehtaus*—usually men of the same area who had themselves returned from the Nanyang. By the 1866 Convention no advances could be given or contracts signed in China, and Singapore's reputation as an eldorado attracted hungry Chinese without any need for press-gang methods.

On the other hand few emigrants could personally afford the six to eight dollars for their fare to Singapore, and therefore most were probably obligated to somebody on arrival in the Straits Settlements.[1] In many cases, no doubt, this obligation was no more than an informal one towards a relation or other associate already established in the Straits Settlements, for whom the *sinkheh* (new arrival) would work. Of the real nature and extent of such ties there can be no certain knowledge, for British officials did not concern themselves further with those who gave an affirmative answer to the question, 'Have you paid your own passage?' The majority always answered affirmatively, which meant they did not have to be detained in a depôt or to sign a contract at the Chinese Protectorate. Hokkiens in particular were seldom put

nineteenth century to reform the system of immigration. See, for example, Powell's strained defence of the *status quo*, in *Straits Settlements Labour Commission Report*, 1890, pp. 69–72.

[1] This is the impression given by the *SSLCR*, 1890, pp. 8–11, though earlier sources were more ready to accept the category of 'paid passengers' at face value. See especially Report of Protector of Chinese 1883, *SSGG* 1884, pp. 453–4.

in the official category of 'unpaid passengers', because the Chinese authorities in Amoy forbade the emigration of *sinkhehs* who had not at least nominally prepaid their passages.[1]

Before the establishment of the Protectorate of Chinese in 1877 probably more than one quarter of the total immigrants were indebted to the supercargo of the ship on arrival. The *khehtau* of such migrants travelled with the *sinkhehs* he had recruited and was responsible to the supercargo for payment of their fares. On arrival in Singapore or Penang such *sinkhehs* were detained on board until the *khehtau* had arranged for a prospective employer to pay the fares. The fare on this credit basis was usually about $12, and the *khehtau* would expect a further profit for himself of $5–8. Though no written contract was signed, the *sinkheh* was then bound to his employer for at least a year by a mixture of loyalty, fear and force.[2]

The 1877 Chinese Immigrants Ordinance (superseded by Ordinance IV of 1880) provided for a category of 'unpaid passengers' who were to be registered and admitted to licensed 'coolie depôts' which had legal power to detain them subject to government inspection. Initially this category was understood to mean those immigrants indebted to the supercargo of the ship for their passage. Most such passengers had begun their journey in Swatow. Before long, however, steamers on the Swatow run abandoned the speculative practice of carrying credit passengers, as the Hong Kong steamers had done some time earlier. The whole migrant traffic became more highly organized to cope both with this change and with the vastly increased volume of migrants in the 1880s. By 1890 recruiting firms in the treaty ports generally paid the passages of migrants in advance and recovered the sum later from a firm of 'coolie-brokers' in the Straits Settlements, to whom the *sinkhehs* were consigned. An occasional variant of this practice was for the *khehtau* in charge of a group of *sinkhehs* to pay the fares and receive the due reimbursement plus profit from the consignee broker.[3]

[1] Reports of Protector of Chinese for 1878 and 1883, *SSGG* 1879, p. 113 and 1884, pp. 453–4.
[2] Report of the Committee appointed to consider and take evidence upon the Condition of Chinese Labourers in the Colony, 3 November 1876 [1876 Report on Chinese Labourers], Appendix 22 of *SSLCP*, pp. ccxlii–iv.
[3] The Protectorate of Chinese continued to base its classification on the *sinkheh's* answer to the question, 'Have you paid your own passage?' so that the change in the organization of the traffic was not officially noted until June 1890. The Court of Appeal then reverted to the original definition in a judgment on a case of forcible detention

Although the status of those who gave a negative answer to the question, 'Have you paid your own passage?' changed fundamentally between 1877 and 1890, this group continued (until 1888, when official pressure in Swatow became too strong) to consist mainly of migrants from the port of Swatow, destined for the plantations of Sumatra, Sabah, Province Wellesley and Johore. This only strengthens the suspicion that the category 'unpaid passengers' was determined less by the poverty of the emigrant than by the practice of the recruiting firms involved in that particular branch of the traffic. The European planters of Sumatra, Sabah and Province Wellesley were dependent on the Chinese Protectorate for their labour, because they lacked the necessary direct contacts. Many, perhaps most, Chinese employers in Malaya, on the other hand, must have preferred to bypass the Protectorate. This was no difficult matter if the *sinkhehs* were instructed to state that they had paid their own passages. Official records have little to say about such systematic evasion of the regulations. It is, however, indicative of the mood on both sides that one Chinese employer did divulge his systematic frustration of the Act to the 1890 Labour Commission as if this were nothing extraordinary, and that his methods earned special commendation by that Commission. This was Gan Eng Seng, whose *sinkhehs*, destined for the Tanjong Pagar Dock Company, signed a contract in China which of course had no validity in the eyes of any government. Their passages were all paid in advance in China, but only those *sinkhehs* who could not otherwise be trusted were brought before the Protector of Chinese to sign a legally valid contract.[1]

In the view of the 1876 Labour Commission, abuses occurred less in the immigration to the Straits Settlements than in the emigration therefrom, particularly to Sumatra. Indeed abuses in recruitment for Sumatra, both real and alleged, were the main spur behind agitation leading to the establishment of the Chinese Protectorate. This agitation was begun by Chinese employers of Singapore and Johore motivated, as

Since no *sinkheh* was any longer indebted to the ship on arrival, the effect of this judgment was to remove the legal power of depôt-keepers to detain any immigrants. The *status quo ante* was restored by Ordinance I of 1891. *SSLCR* 1890, pp. 8–12. Report of Protector of Chinese for 1890, *SSGG* 1891, pp. 1084–5.

[1] *SSLCR* 1890, p. 62 of evidence. On this question, as on others, the Chinese Protectors in Singapore and Penang were curiously obscure. On the other hand W. Cowan, Acting Secretary for Chinese Affairs in Perak, told the 1890 Commission: 'The men who come down nominally as free passengers are really in debt to the brokers.' *Ibid.* p. 128.

Eunice Thio has said, 'by self-interest and perhaps philanthropy'.[1] Their principal organ in this was the Gambier & Pepper Society, dominated by Teochiu planters. Its members suffered from the general labour shortage of the early 1870s, and particularly from the competition for Teochiu labourers offered by the new plantations of Deli. They petitioned government in 1871 against the forcible detention and disposition of *sinkhehs*, and followed this in 1873 with a request for 'arrangements to prevent bad characters from kidnapping the newly-arrived immigrants'.[2] Further pressure led at last to the appointment of the 1876 Commission into 'the Condition of Chinese Labourers in the Colony', which heard much evidence concerning 'kidnapping' for Sumatra.[3]

One of the witnesses before this Commission, Penang Police Commissioner Plunket, gave the impression that there was an organized system of kidnapping *sinkhehs* in Penang for service in Deli during the early 1870s. There were, he said, over a hundred 'bad characters' in Penang whose sole occupation was to obtain labour for Sumatra, and who were constantly convicted for 'kidnapping'.[4] In suggesting the image of a press-gang plucking unwitting Chinese from the streets, shop-houses, and brothels, Plunket is here rather misleading. All the victims of 'kidnapping' brought to light by the 1876 Commission or otherwise were in fact indebted immigrants who had perforce lost some of their freedom of movement. Their wretchedness was no less because of that, but to call them victims of 'kidnapping' was to confuse the issue—intentionally in the case of some interested parties.

Though always a few migrants had through tickets from China to Penang, most left their homeland with the intention of going to Singapore. If their *khehtau* succeeded in finding them work in the city or nearby in the plantations of Johore or Riau, they appear to have accepted this without much protest. If, however, there was insufficient

---

[1] E. Thio, 'The Singapore Chinese Protectorate: Events and Conditions leading to its establishment, 1823–1877', *Journal of the South Seas Society*, XVI, 1960, p. 64.

[2] *SSLCP* 1873, Appendix 33.

[3] *SSLCP* 1873, pp. 139–49. Thio, pp. 64–65. Jackson, pp. 49–64. Another, and more obviously self-interested, lobby against 'kidnapping' for Sumatra was the sugar planters of Province Wellesley. Petition of 25 October 1876, *SSLCP* 1876, Appendix 23.

[4] *SSLCP* 1876, Appendix 22, pp. cclxxx–xxxi. See also the evidence of Captain Ellis, *ibid.*, p. cclxvii, and the divergent views expressed in the Legislative Council Meeting of 9 September 1873, *SSLCP*, 1873, pp. 140–1 and 149.

demand from such employers, the *sinkhehs* were either forcibly detained on shore or sent on to Penang where the process was repeated. In either port they were kept under guard until somebody could be found to pay their fares. With the bill for their maintenance rising every day, abuses were frequent. *Khehtaus* used force or deception to compel the immigrants to go to a distant place of which they had heard nothing good, and to work in occupations they had never contemplated.[1]

Though most evidence before the 1876 Commission related to Singapore, there is an interesting glimpse of the system in Penang, the main base for recruitment to Deli. E. Karl, Chinese interpreter in Penang, related how 'Tan Tek' (Khoo Thean Tek, sentenced to deportation in 1867 for leading the Toh Peh Kong Society during the Penang riots but later pardoned as a British subject) had a virtual monopoly over the disposition of indebted immigrants. 'Tan Tek is a kind of protector of Chinese Coolies, and is paid a thousand dollars a year or more by parties in Swatow. He has a house on purpose to receive them. He is the chief of the Toh Pek Kong Society, and the most powerful man in the place.'[2] According to Karl all indebted migrants were detained in the depôt of 'Tan Tek' until redeemed by the agents of employers. The various Penang 'coolie-brokers' who supplied *sinkheh* labour for the Deli planters must therefore have been in close contact with Khoo Thean Tek. These brokers would supply labourers to the Penang agents of Sumatra tobacco firms for a cost of $40–50, of which $25–30 was an advance to the *sinkheh*. After paying the expenses of the passage, the profit of the *khehtau* and the cost of accommodation in Khoo Thean Tek's depôt, the *sinkheh* would be left with only a few dollars, and the broker often tried to cheat him out of that. Whatever was received by the *sinkheh*, he had ultimately to repay the full sum fixed as the advance. The remaining $15–20 in the cost provided the profit of the broker—much higher in the case of Sumatra labourers than those for the Malay Peninsula.[3]

Almost from the beginning of the Deli tobacco plantations, they acquired an extremely bad reputation among immigrants. As a British

---

[1] 1876 Report on Chinese Labourers, *SSLCP*, 1876, Appendix 22, pp. ccxliii–iv.

[2] *Ibid.* p. cclxxx. Though smaller numerically than the Ghee Hin in Penang, the Toh Peh Kong included most of the wealthy merchants, mainly Hokkien. C. D. Cowan, *Nineteenth-Century Malaya*, London, 1961, p. 48.

[3] Lavino to Wiggers van Kerchem, 5 October 1876. Consulaat Penang 102, Algemeene Rijksarchief, The Hague. 1876 Report on Chinese Labourers, *SSLCP*, 1876, Appendix 22, ccxlvi–vii, cclxvii–iii, and cclxxx.

planter with interests in both Province Wellesley and Sumatra complained in 1875:

> There exists, in the Chinese labour market, a perfect hatred of the name of 'Deli', which operates not only inimically to that particular place, but also as regards the whole Island—so much that Chinese who will ship willingly to Langkat or Serdang, in ignorance of the precise 'locale' of those places, will become perfectly mad if the word 'Deli' be heard on board.[1]

As early as 1871 this bad name was being fostered in China as well as the Straits Settlements. In that year the British Consul in Swatow sent to Singapore translations of placards erected in the streets 'by certain Chinese in the habit of sending Chinese labourers here', protesting at the way *sinkhehs* were forcibly sent from the Straits Settlements to Deli and other places.[2]

Whatever the original cause of this reputation, it was greatly exaggerated by the force and deception used to make immigrants go to Deli against their will. The unpleasant nature of the migrant business attracted some of the most unscrupulous men as recruiting agents, and violence bred further violence. In 1874–5 in particular, when demand for labour greatly exceeded supply, there was a spate of complaints in the Straits press against 'kidnapping' for Deli. Late in 1875 there were two cases in which labourers bound for Sumatra plantations overpowered the crews of the small steamers taking them across the Strait, and escaped with their advances. Subsequent investigation suggested that the mutineers were thugs making a business of collecting advances rather than unwary *sinkhehs* deluded about their destination.[3] Tan Seng Poh, the Singapore Teochiu leader and a leading advocate of protection for *sinkhehs*, admitted: 'Most of the men who take advances to go away from here are bad characters, and many ship intending to rob and run away. Singapore is relieved of many of its bad characters in this way.'[4] Nevertheless publicity obtained by these outrages only strengthened the adverse impression about Deli among Chinese.

[1] Walter Knaggs to Lavino, 23 August 1875, copy in Bylandt to Willebois, 28 September 1875, Buitenlandse Zaken Dossier Atjeh, Algemeene Rijksarchief.
[2] Statement of Colonial Secretary in Legislative Council meeting of 9 September 1873, *SSLCP*, 1873, p. 141. I am indebted to Dr Eunice Thio for this reference, and much incidental help.
[3] Singapore report in *Verẓameling van Consulaire en andere Verslagen en Berigten* 1876 p. 113. Schadee, II, pp. 14–15. Schadee asserts that the offenders in one of the mutinies were part of a group who had already escaped from contract labour in Deli in order to collect a second advance in Penang, and so repeat the offence.
[4] *SSLCP*, 1876, Appendix 22, cclix.

How far did labour conditions in Sumatra justify its unsavoury reputation in the 1870s? In attempting to answer this question we are faced with some confusion as to the exact grievance against Deli. Singapore Chinese witnesses before the 1876 Commission made most play with its unhealthy climate, but also mentioned the difficulty of returning.[1] The English and Dutch commentators were in general more concerned about allegations of ill-treatment by planters.[2]

There was certainly truth in all these complaints. But it would be difficult to argue that Deli was in any important respect worse than other 'frontier' communities of the time such as Perak and Selangor. The allegation of unhealthiness seems a particularly strange one. Deli was exemplary if compared with Perak, where about 3,000 tin-miners died of beri-beri every year in the period 1879–82.[3] The larger tobacco plantations were in a position to provide hospital facilities for their workers, and had an interest in doing so.

There is more cause for complaint against ill-treatment by employers, though again it is difficult to find clear evidence in relative terms. Like other frontier societies, early Deli lacked an established judicial and police system, or even a code of civilized conduct. Holding complete economic power over their employees, the planters tended to assume equal judicial power. The Sultan of Deli had initially given the planters wide powers over their employees, though reserving for himself the trial of the most serious offenders. In practice almost all offences were, however, dealt with on the spot. The Sultan was certainly not lacking in goodwill towards the planters, but his police force was woefully inadequate and planters were reluctant to lose the services of both the offending worker and someone sent to guard him throughout the lengthy procedure in the capital. Abuses were to be expected, but as in the similar case of mining *towkays* in Malaya there is little recorded evidence on which to make a judgment.

Rapid expansion made government intervention long overdue by 1874, when a judicial apparatus was at last set up to regulate the

---

[1] *Ibid.* p. cclxvi (Tan Hong Moh): 'They don't like going to Deli because it is very hot, and they don't get back from there, and if they fall sick they don't get enough treatment.' *Ibid.* p. cclxvii (Lim Kah Kway): 'They don't like going to Deli because the water is bad and makes their bodies swell up.'

[2] Walter Knaggs to Lavino, 23 August 1875, *loc. cit.* Lavino to Wiggers van Kerchem, 5 October 1876, *loc. cit. Koloniaal Verslag* 1875, p. 196. *Ibid.* 1876, p. 198.

[3] Annual Report on Revenue and Expenditure of Perak for 1882, *SSGG* 1883, pp. 1105–06. See also Wong Lin Ken, *The Malayan Tin Industry to 1914*, Tucson, 1965, p. 74.

immigrant population of the East Coast of Sumatra. In theory the planters were shorn of their judicial powers, which had included punishments for labourers attempting to leave the plantation. But the government machinery set up in replacement was altogether inadequate. Only twelve armed policemen were stationed in Deli, and none at all in Langkat and Serdang, where plantations were fast developing.

During the period 1874–7 Deli acquired a name for violence even in European circles. Attacks on planters and traders became a matter of frequent occurrence, culminating in the death of several planters in 1876–7. Ill-treatment of workers by planters was probably not the main cause. Gayos and Bataks initiated most of the attacks, though local Malays and runaway Chinese workers increasingly joined in as the absence of settled authority became apparent. The need for reform in labour relations was in any case glaringly apparent, and a legal commission was sent from Batavia at the end of 1876 to investigate labour conditions. It brought charges against four planters accused of ill-treatment, of whom one committed suicide soon after. At the same time considerable police reinforcements were sent to the *cultuurgebied*.[1]

On the judicial side, the 1870s witnessed a battle by the Deli planters, led by the redoubtable J. T. Cremer, against a motion introduced into the States-General by Mirandolle seeking the abolition of the penal sanction attached to labour contracts. As a result of this controversy, special labour regulations were framed for the East Coast of Sumatra in 1875, amplified in the famous 'coolie ordinance' of 1880. The latter became the model for all plantations outside Java. It preserved the penal sanction (abolished in Java) but stipulated definite conditions which were if anything advanced for their time. All labour contracts were to be registered with government, and could not bind the labourer after three years. On expiry of the contract (or after three years if the labourer had not repaid his debt to the planter before then) the labourer was to be returned to the place where he was recruited. The employer was obliged to give regular bi-monthly advances to the worker, to provide adequate housing, water, and medical attention, and to allow him to bring his complaints before the nearest government official.[2]

---

[1] Schadee, II, pp. 10–18 and 32–4. *Koloniaal Verslag* 1878, p. 22. Lavino to Van Lansberge, 4 February 1877, Consulaat Penang 102, Algemeene Rijksarchief.

[2] Schadee, II, pp. 33–39. A. Vandenbosch, *The Dutch East Indies: Its Government, Problems, and Politics*, Los Angeles, 1944, pp. 285–7. J. H. Boeke, *The Structure of the*

On paper therefore, and probably also in practice, contract labourers were less open to ill-treatment than those in Malaya after the mid-1870s.[1] The 1876 Labour Commission felt

bound in fairness to say that, whatever may have been the case in former times, we believe that the welfare of the labourer is as well assured there as here, and indeed that there is far more interference on the part of the Dutch Government than there is on the part of our own to secure that welfare.[2]

This judgment ignores one vital factor. With the partial exception of those on Penang sugar plantations, Chinese contract labourers in Malaya almost never had anything to do with anyone not of their own race. Tobacco workers, on the other hand, were directly responsible to European assistant managers, from whom they received their advances and their final payment. The European planter class of Deli, moreover, was portrayed by most outside observers as unusually arrogant, 'demanding a great deal in the way of servile respect for their personal dignity'.[3] During the first decades of the twentieth century there is enough evidence, for example in the constant attacks by workers on planters and headmen, to suggest that plantation workers in Deli were subjected to an unusual degree of personal humiliation, if not physical cruelty.[4] Probably these disadvantages were already evident

---

Netherlands Indian Economy, New York, 1942, p. 142. The highly controversial penal sanction gave rise to an extensive literature, some of which is reviewed in A. D. A. de Kat Angelino, *Colonial Policy*, The Hague, 1931, II, pp. 497–531.

[1] Only after 1889 did the governments of the British-protected Malay states issue a series of ordinances to protect labour, which were 'honoured more in the breach than in the observance'. Government had much less contact with employers in Malaya than in Sumatra, and was reluctant to interfere in a field where it had so little experience. Wong Lin Ken, pp. 73–74. For agricultural labour the Straits Settlements were brought up to the standard of Sumatra by an ordinance of November, 1891, *SSGG*, 1891, p. 2582.

[2] *SSLCP*, 1876, Appendix 22, p. ccxlvi.

[3] P. Endt, *Wanderarbeiterverhaeltnisse*, 1919, quoted in Bruno Lasker, *Human Bondage in South-east Asia*, Chapel Hill, 1950, p. 221.

[4] The attacks on plantation personnel, numbering as many as eighty in 1929, are listed in the annual *Kroniek* of the Oostkust van Sumatra–Instituut. For impressions of conditions in Deli during the early decades of this century see Lasker; W. F. Wertheim, *Indonesian Society in Transition: A study of social change*, The Hague, 1964, pp. 250–3; Ladislao Szekley, trans. Marion Saunders, *Tropic Fever. The Adventures of a Planter in Sumatra*, London, 1936. A similarly critical opinion of 1888 is quoted in A. G. de Bruin, *De Chineezen ter Oostkust van Sumatra*, Leiden, 1918, p. 81. In complete contrast, however, is the enthusiasm of an official British report of 1900. *Parliamentary Papers, House of Commons*, 1900, LXXXVII, p. 103. It seems possible that the predominance of Javanese labour in twentieth-century Deli may have encouraged more servility in labour relations, as opposed to an earlier pattern borrowed from the Straits Settlements.

in the 1870s, when evidence is scarcer. Even were this not the case, it is easy to imagine that a *sinkheh* with absolutely no experience of the 'red-haired devils' felt less secure placing himself in their power than in that of an employer with shared standards of behaviour.

The final grievance commonly mentioned against Deli was the difficulty of returning. In part this complaint was simply a function of the distance from one of the centres of Chinese life—particularly Singapore.[1] In part it referred to the fact that some contract workers in Deli escaped from debt only after a very long period, if at all.

In the plantations and many of the tinfields of Malaya, the general pattern was for the *sinkheh* to work virtually without pay for a year, to pay off his passage money. After this, if he survived on the meagre diet provided, he was theoretically a free agent.[2] In the tobacco plantations, however, everything depended on the worker's performance. The most successful might leave his estate after a year with a discharge notice and as much as $100 in his pocket. The least successful might never escape from debt, until the legal three-year maximum was introduced in 1880. The average return for the harvest of one cultivator in Deli was estimated at $45 (on one estate) in 1869,[3] $68 in 1874,[4] and $78 in 1882.[5] Since the crop cycle only occupied 8 or 9 months of the year, labourers were given other work for the remaining months at a wage averaging $6 per month. In 1882, the usual amount debited against a labourer at the end of his first year was $93 (or $78 for *laukhehs* re-engaged in Sumatra), made up as follows:[6]

	$
Advance to *sinkhehs* in Penang	30
(or in case of *laukhehs* $15)	
Regular bi-monthly advances of $2	48
Special advances at Chinese New Year, etc.	7
Cost of clearing jungle before planting	5
Cost of tools, etc.	3
	93

[1] The tobacco industry in Sabah suffered from all the difficulties of early Deli when trying to establish itself in 1888–90, including remoteness; Tongkah (Siam) suffered from similar factors in 1876. *SSLCP*, 1876, Appendix 22, p. cclxiv.

[2] *Ibid.* pp. cclix–x. *SSGG*, 1883, p. 1105. *The Deli Coolie Question*, pp. 19–20. Wong Lin Ken, pp. 71–76. *SSLCR*, 1890, p. 24 of evidence.

[3] *Straits Times and Singapore Journal of Commerce*, 24 April 1869.

[4] *Koloniaal Verslag*, 1874, p. 211.

[5] *The Deli Coolie Question*, pp. 5–6.   [6] *Ibid.*

In 1882, therefore, the *average* labourer in Deli could do no more than meet his debts, assuming he had incurred no additional ones, and expect five or ten dollars profit. At the lower levels prevailing in the 1870s, it is probable that the majority in fact failed to meet their commitments after one year. On the other hand, as the tobacco industry consolidated, higher productivity was achieved, until by 1890 it was acknowledged by many witnesses before the Labour Commission that Deli tobacco offered the best remuneration available to the *sinkheh*. Their evidence suggested that about 75% of *sinkhehs* then made a profit in their first year, and that in the case of Teochiu labour the figure was as high as 90%.[1]

The number of Chinese who left Sumatra with discharge tickets from their plantations was not great—2,101 in 1881, compared with about 8,000 who had immigrated the previous year. But the planters argued that many re-engaged on the estates, 'because they are unable in any neighbouring country to obtain equal remuneration', or remained in the area as traders. In 1881 there were already 4,597 'free Chinese' in the *cultuurgebied* who paid the trade tax.[2]

In sum, it would appear that Chinese labourers in Sumatra were comparatively well provided for in terms of welfare services, and that the most fortunate of them were also well remunerated. The most unsuccessful or improvident, on the other hand, were liable to a much longer term of virtual servitude in an environment affording little pleasure. It was common for workers who failed to clear themselves in their first year to lose heart and take increasingly to opium. They were then likely to fall into debt to the farmers of the opium, spirit, and gaming monopolies. In such a case the three-year maximum clause of the 'coolie ordinance' could not help them, since their creditors would insist on their signing a new contract and beginning the process again.[3]

These factors taken together may partly explain the bad reputation of Deli among labourers in the early 1870s. When Deli is objectively compared with other employment opportunities, however, it appears that the persistence of this reputation into the 1880s must be explained

---

[1] *SSLCR* 1890, pp. 8, 13–14, 16–17, 24, 108, of evidence. Also Wong Lin Ken, p. 67.
[2] *The Deli Coolie Question*, pp. 9–10.
[3] *SSLCR*, 1890, p. 16. Most observers stressed the rapacity of the Chinese *tindals* in endeavouring to keep unlucky workers in debt; e.g. the Imperial Chinese Commission of 1886, *SSGG*, 1887, pp. 243–4; and John Parker (1888), quoted in De Bruin, p. 82. And for a later impression see Szekely, pp. 176–7.

in part by the influence of Malayan Chinese employers with vested interests.

In 1875–6 the reputation of Deli was at its worst, and was accentuated by the violence so often used by *khehtaus* and brokers to compel unwilling *sinkhehs* to board the ships for Deli. The brokers in Penang required $40 to 50 for the supply of each *sinkheh* to the agents of Deli companies, compared with only $22–26 for labour in Penang or $32–36 for Perak.[1] The difference was not an extra inducement to the *sinkheh*. It went to the brokers as profit or possibly to some other source involved in the business. To some extent it certainly induced the least reputable brokers and *khehtaus* to use the more dangerous methods of intimidation or deceit to send the *sinkhehs* on their way. It seems likely also that this extra profit margin was an inducement to more powerful figures such as 'Tan Tek'—employers of labour and society headmen —to part with labour which might have been useful to themselves.

Even with these higher costs it was impossible for the Sumatra planters to fill their labour requirements under the conditions of 1875–6. In those years, therefore, they began attempting to bring Chinese direct from China, and employing Javanese more widely in the fields.[2] They were, it seems clear, saved temporarily from these difficult courses by the establishment of the Protectorate of Chinese in the Straits Settlements.

As a result of the report of the 1876 'Chinese Labourers' Commission two ordinances were passed the following year. The Chinese Immigrants' Ordinance provided for a Protector of Chinese Immigrants, and the Crimping Ordinance for a Protector of Emigrants. The two offices were for all practical purposes amalgamated with the appointment of Pickering as Protector of Chinese in Singapore in May 1877, and Karl to a similar post in Penang soon after. The ordinances provided for Government Immigration Depôts, where

[1] Lavino to Wiggers van Kerchem, 5 October 1876, Consulaat Penang, 102, Algemeene Rijksarchief. The brokers also charged $50 for *sinkhehs* recruited to work for the Dutch army of occupation in Acheh before 1877. As was the case for Deli, $25 of this was listed as an advance to the *sinkheh* which the latter was obliged to repay, but almost all of this advance was used to meet the expenses of the *khehtau*. *Consulaire Verslagen* 1878, p. 758. This differential was maintained throughout the 1880s. In 1890 brokers were charging $35–8 for Teochiu *sinkhehs* if for Province Wellesley, and $80–90 if for Sumatra or Sabah. The 1890 Labour Commission considered the profit of the brokers was roughly double in the case of Sumatra and Sabah, but that most of the differential went to meet extra expenses in China. *SSLCR* 1890, p. 17.
[2] See below, pp. 314 and 318.

immigrants indebted for their fares would be detained under supervision until employers were found for them. Such depôts were never
built, however. Instead the existing depôts of the 'coolie-brokers'
were licensed by government subject to certain standards of maintenance. Detention in unlicensed premises was made illegal. When
employers were found, legally binding labour contracts were signed in
the presence of the Protector, and the contracting *sinkhehs* were given
some idea of their rights and duties under the law.[1]

TABLE 1 *Labour contracts for Langkat, Deli, Serdang and Asahan
made before the Protectors of Chinese, Penang and Singapore*[2]

	Penang	Singapore	Total
1879	3,529	500*	4,000*
1880	6,600*	1,381	8,000*
1881	7,426	2,378	9,804
1882	5,990	1,498	7,488
1883	6,740	1,977	8,717
1884	8,540	2,464	11,004
1885	11,434	3,617	15,051
1886	12,391	4,317†	16,708†
1887	11,953	4,811	16,764
1888	10,913	7,439†	18,352†

* Estimates only, based on figures for *all* Sumatra.
† These figures include a substantial proportion of Javanese and Bandjarese. The number
of Indonesians signing contracts in Singapore for work in the *cultuurgebied* was 1726 in
1887, and increased in the following two years.

The Protectorate broke the vicious circle of violence associated with
labour recruitment for Sumatra. On the one hand, more satisfactory
machinery was instituted for prosecuting against forcible and illegal
abduction. On the other, a section of the labour market—that of the
'unpaid passengers'—was to some extent removed from the control of
the Chinese societies. In this sector a certain amount of price competition became possible, both among the *sinkhehs*, who were made
aware of the relatively favourable terms in the Sumatra contracts, and
among the brokers, who could still expect a higher commission from
the agents of the tobacco companies. Thus the supply of Chinese labour
from the Straits Settlements to the plantation district of Sumatra, which

[1] Wong Lin Ken, pp. 69–71. Jackson, pp. 66–70.
[2] Compiled from Annual Reports of the Chinese Protectorate in *SSGG*, and Annual
Reports of the Netherlands Consulate in Penang in *Consulaire Verslagen*.

had been no more than three or four thousand per year in the 1870s could expand rapidly in the 1880s (see Table 1).

Opposition to Deli among interested parties continued, however. In 1880 Pickering was complaining that the *khehtaus* kept the prejudice against Sumatra alive, in order to dissuade their *sinkhehs* from accepting in Singapore 'the liberal terms offered by the Deli planters'. The *sinkhehs* then moved on to Penang, where 'exorbitant squeezes' were possible because of the weakness of the Protectorate staff. Having refused in Singapore an advance of $24 of which the *khehtau* would have taken $16 as expenses, the *sinkheh* was compelled to accept the same contract in Penang with an advance of $30, of which the *khehtau* pocketed $26.[1] Pickering probably exaggerated here the rôle of the *khehtaus* as against the secret society headmen and brokers in Penang,[2] but his experience emphasized the difficulty of substituting an open labour market for the established Chinese channels of recruitment.

As the largest and best-organized group of European employers of Chinese labour, the Deli planters initially enjoyed the great advantage of cordial cooperation from Pickering.

> Believing that the prospects of a Chinese going to labour in Deli were really favourable [wrote Pickering], I devoted some time to visiting the Depots with the planters and their agents and issued placards to inform the Immigrants and other Chinese of the advantages they would gain by engaging for Sumatra.[3]

But the Protector of Chinese was after all a British employee. His benevolent attitude soon altered under pressure from Penang employers, led by the Province Wellesley sugar magnate Khaw Boo Aun and supported by Karl.[4] In September 1881 they urged Pickering to

---

[1] *SSGG*, 1881, pp. 354–5.

[2] The Deli Planters Committee were nearer the mark, when regretting their inability to recruit large numbers in Singapore, 'for it appears that the connexions, between Penang and the Hong Kong coolie Hongs, are so strongly established as to direct the stream of emigration via the northern port'. *The Deli Coolie Question*, pp. 6–7.

[3] Minute by Pickering, 13 June 1882, *ibid.*, pp. 13–14.

[4] The planters of Province Wellesley were always in the vanguard of opposition to what they called 'crimping', which meant anything from enticing labourers away from their plantations to Deli before the expiry of their contracts to merely recruiting at the expense of the Province Wellesley recruiters. See e.g. the petition from eleven Province Wellesley sugar planters to the Legislative Council, 25 October 1876, *SSLCP*, 1876, Appendix 23. The presence of Khaw Boo Aun in this delegation may suggest that he, as a Teochiu and a Ghee Hin leader, could not rely on labour through the sources controlled by the Toh Peh Kong. For Khaw see C. S. Wong, *A Gallery of Chinese Kapitans*, Singapore, 1963, pp. 81–3.

give local employers first choice of the *sinkhehs* and prevent Deli recruiters from entering the depôts until their demands were met. The *sinkhehs*, they argued, 'had no real wish to go out of British territory, but were induced by delusive promises and large advances to go to Sumatra'. As a result of this pressure Pickering ceased encouraging immigrants to go to Sumatra.[1]

The request of the Penang employers for first choice in the depôts was refused by Pickering in 1881. The official attitude on this point appears to have weakened by 1890, however, to judge from the evidence of W. Cowan before the Labour Commission. Asked why all *sinkhehs* were not attracted to Deli by the higher wages there, he replied, 'Because Province Wellesley planters were allowed to redeem coolies first.'[2]

The Deli planters were particularly annoyed by Pickering's attitude on the question of through passengers from China to Sumatra. The Ocean Steamship Company, which already ran steamers from China to Singapore, opened a Singapore–Belawan (Deli) service in 1880, and offered through tickets from China to Sumatra for Chinese migrants. Pickering ruled that such migrants transshipping in Singapore nevertheless had to come before him to sign regular contracts. But this defeated the purpose of the Sumatra planters, which had been to keep the *sinkhehs* they had recruited in China away from the brokers, employers, and secret societies of the Straits Settlements. Although they continued sending old hands to China to recruit for Sumatra, it could no longer be considered a direct emigration if all *sinkhehs* had to pass through the licensed depôts of Singapore or Penang.[3]

These and other minor differences caused annoyance on both sides,

[1] *The Deli Coolie Question*, pp. 14–15.
[2] *SSLCR*, 1890, p. 130 of evidence.
[3] Bool, p. 6. *The Deli Coolie Question*, pp. 6–7, 14, 17–18. Another cause of friction was the tendency of Sumatra planters to send back to the Straits Settlements labourers whom they considered unfit. In justification of thus breaking their side of the contract, the planters claimed that substitutions were often made after the contracts had been signed. After an ultimatum from Pickering in 1881, a system of medical inspections for all labourers signing contracts was evolved. The Kapitan China of Labuan (Deli) was charged with checking against substitutions on arrival there. Old or sick relations of the workers could come without medical certificates only if they comprised no more than 15% of the total contract workers. Finally in 1886 the Protectorate agreed to provide photographs of all those signing contracts. Bool, pp. 2–3. P. W. Modderman, *Gedenkboek uitgegeven ter gelegenheid van het Vijftig Jarig Bestaan van de Deli Planters Vereeniging*, Batavia, 1929, pp. 33–4. *SSGG*, 1887, p. 244.

but they had little to do with the crisis in the labour supply which finally decided the Deli planters to bypass the Straits Settlements altogether as a source of labour. This crisis of the late 1880s was caused in part by economic conditions, in part by the hardening attitude of officials in China.

TABLE 2

	Straits tin price, per pikul[1] ($)	Tobacco price Amsterdam per ½ kg[2] (guilder cents)	Immigrants landed in Penang and Singapore[3]	Of whom admitted to depôts as 'unpaid passengers'
1881	27.74	115	89,803	32,316
1882	30.85	137·5	101,009	28,415
1883	30.29	134	109,136	26,446
1884	25.14	144	106,748	24,871
1885	23.53	141·5	111,456	26,391
1886	33.82	154	144,517	39,192
1887	36.89	121	166,442	42,400
1888	42.10	128·5	166,353	34,607
1889	35.52	146	146,820	21,213
1890	31.97	72·5	132,274	14,335

Tobacco prices were at peak levels during 1884–6, and more and more Sumatran jungle was burned to make way for plantations. Production increased steadily from 93,500 packs in 1883 to 236,300 in 1890, with a consequent demand for labour.[4] The same years witnessed the beginning of a period of sustained high prices and rapid expansion in the Malayan tin industry, which lasted from 1886 to 1895.[5] The supply of immigrant labour expanded rapidly in response to these boom conditions in 1886–7, though not rapidly enough to meet demand at the existing wage levels. The result was not, unfortunately, a rise in wages to an economic equilibrium, but spectacular profits for the brokers and others involved in the migrant business. They pushed up their premiums and commissions to unprecedented levels, especially for European employers like those in Sumatra. After 1887 immigration ceased to increase and even fell off, despite the continued high demand for labour during the following two years. The figures in Table 2 show the disparity between supply and demand in the major sectors.

[1] *Ibid.*   [2] Schadee, II, pp. 20 and 181.
[3] Annual Reports of Protectorate of Chinese, in *SSGG*.
[4] Schadee, II, pp. 20 and 181.
[5] Wong Lin Ken, Appendix A, tables 'c' and 'e'.

The failure of the labour supply to keep pace with demand was most marked in the category judged to be 'unpaid passengers', on which European employers were dependent. Most of the decline between 1887 and 1890 was in fact in this category. The main cause was to be found in the attitude of Chinese officials.

The emigration of Chinese under conditions bound to lead to indentured labour was naturally looked down upon by progressive-minded Chinese officials. The traffic in indebted *sinkhehs* was generally regarded as dishonourable, and was even sometimes referred to disparagingly as 'buying and selling little pigs'. It was for this reason that the Amoy authorities had made it compulsory for emigrants nominally to have paid their fares in advance. For the Sumatra plantations the most important port was Swatow. Teochius were regarded as the best agriculturalists, followed by the Hai-lok-hongs, who are often also categorized under the broad heading of Teochius. Both groups usually emigrated from Swatow. The only other dialect group employed widely in tobacco cultivation, though less highly regarded, were Khehs, who might embark either at Swatow or Hong Kong.[1] The Sumatra planters depended for their labour first on the cooperation of the Straits Settle-

---

[1] The occupational structure of the different dialect groups in northern Sumatra differed widely. While Teochius, followed by Hakkas, predominated on the estates, there were always a substantial number of Hokkiens in trade. As a result of the gradual integration of Deli into the economy of Netherlands India, where Hokkiens were the largest and longest-established group, they numbered 24·3% of Chinese in the *cultuurgebied* by 1930. Cantonese came to the area mainly as craftsmen, and by 1930 formed 21·1% of the total, as against 21·8% Teochius. Hakkas were active in small trade as well as estate labour. Though only 8·7% of the Chinese in the *cultuurgebied* in 1930, they had long held a virtual monopoly of official positions throughout northern Sumatra—as *kapitans china*. This tradition probably began with the predominance of Chang Chen-hsun (alias Thio Tiau Siat), a Batavia Hakka who went to Acheh as contractor to the Dutch army, and by 1877 was farming most of the government monopolies of the east coast.

The Chinese communities of the Bengkalis district (Kampar, Siak, and Rokan), occupied in fishing, lumbering, and trade, were overwhelmingly Hokkien (82% in 1930). The smaller group of Chinese in Acheh (21,795), on the other hand, was predominantly Hakka (40·8%) and Cantonese (27·7%) in 1930.

Though Chinese secret societies were forbidden in Netherlands India, branches of Penang societies certainly existed among plantation workers of the *cultuurgebied*. In the period 1881–4 there was a series of violent incidents between the Ghee Hin, which in Sumatra represented primarily Teochius, Hakkas, and Hailams, and the Ho-seng, representing Hokkiens and Hakkas from Fiu-chew. Sterner measures were taken in 1884 to suppress these societies. De Bruin, pp. 38–52. Bool, pp. 27–82. Schadee, II, pp. 45–6. Lavino to Governor-General 17 February 1877 and 22 April 1884. Consulaat Penang 102, 13, Algemeene Rijksarchief. Wen Chung-chi, *The Nineteenth-Century Imperial Chinese Consulate in the Straits Settlements: Origins and Development*, unpublished thesis, University of Singapore, 1964, pp. 235–8.

ments Protectorate of Chinese, but ultimately on the co-operation, indifference or venality of imperial officials in Swatow, who allowed *sinkhehs* to emigrate openly in the 'unpaid passengers' category.

Sporadic movements for reform on the part of senior officials in Swatow were never completely effective, largely because the whole system of emigration relied heavily on corruption and subterfuge. They could, however, seriously reduce the number of migrants arriving in the category of 'unpaid passengers'. Early in 1879, for example, the authorities of Chaochou (Swatow region) forbade indebted emigration from the port, on the ground that indentured *sinkhehs* were 'sold in a manner not differing much from cattle' on arrival in Singapore. Straits pressure through the British Consul in Swatow had this order revoked after a few months. But the incident substantially reduced the number of 'unpaid passengers' and of contracts for Sumatra in that year.[1]

A more sustained attempt at reform in the late 1880s was largely attributable to Tso Ping-lung, the second Chinese Consul in Singapore (1881–91).[2] After unsuccessfully suggesting to the British that they ban indebted immigration to the Straits Settlements, Tso began in June, 1885, to put pressure on the Chinese authorities of Chaochou. He described to them in exaggerated terms the maltreatment of indebted migrants on arrival in the Straits. As a result a proclamation was again issued in Swatow forbidding indebted emigration, but again withdrawn after pressure from the British Consul, who had been urged into action at the behest of Pickering.[3]

Tso then turned to less direct forms of pressure against indentured labour, particularly in Deli. The Singapore daily *Lat Pau*, which he had been instrumental in founding and supporting, published two leading articles during 1886 attacking labour conditions in Deli.[4] Tso

---

[1] *SSGG*, 1879, pp. 113–14. *Ibid.* 1880, pp. 225 and 751.

[2] The first consul, and one of the first Chinese representatives abroad, was Hoo Ah Kay ('Whampoa'), the greatly respected Singapore merchant, who had been made a C.M.G. and a member of the Legislative and Executive Councils by the British. During his tenure from 1877 to his death in 1880 he did nothing to disturb the British authorities. Tso by contrast was a bright young Chinese official and scholar, though unusually well versed in Western affairs. Wen Chung-chi, pp. 86–89.

[3] *Ibid.*, pp. 121–3. *SSGG*, 1886, p. 133.

[4] Bool, p. 4. Modderman, p. 45. The increased hostility towards Deli about this time may have owed something also to the tour of two Chinese Government Commissioners, who visited Deli among other places in 1886. There is a wide discrepancy between the favourable impression which they told Pickering they had of Deli (*SSGG*, 1887, pp. 243–4) and the extremely critical one quoted by Wen Chung-chi (p. 132) from a Chinese printed source of 1928.

also cooperated with the authorities of Chaochou in a series of actions against dealers alleged to have kidnapped workers from China against their will. The main target was the Swatow firm of E Kee, the largest recruiters of Teochiu labour for the Straits Settlements. In 1886 this firm was accused of having kidnapped seven men for Singapore, who subsequently signed contracts for Deli. The men concerned denied the charge, but the pressure from their relatives in Swatow, and from officials, was such that E Kee had to spend $500 bringing them back to China, including the expense of bribing some of them.[1] The same firm was forced to bring a *sinkheh* home from Serapong (Bengkalis) in June 1888 to testify that he had emigrated freely. Soon after this the firm was dissolved. A European agency house in Swatow was also forced to bring home two emigrants in 1888. The most devastating example to other agents, however, was the beheading of Siau Khai in Swatow in September 1888. He had been accused by two emigrants just returned from the Nanyang of having kidnapped them years before.[2]

In all these cases the Chinese Protectors, and of course the Dutch, claimed that the charges were false, and made only for purposes of extortion. It was undeniable that widespread corruption dissipated any reforming impetus on the part of individual officials. Indeed many commentators considered that much of the huge commissions being charged by 'coolie-brokers' in Penang and Singapore during this period went as bribes and inducements to interested parties in Swatow and Hong Kong.[3] For this, however, the Straits Settlements Government was above all responsible through its refusal to cooperate openly and emphatically with reforming Chinese officials for the termination of a recognized evil.[4]

[1] *SSGG*, 1887, p. 244.   [2] *Ibid.*, 1889, p. 221.

[3] Pickering, in *SSGG*, 1889, pp. 222–3. *SSLCR*, 1890, pp. 17 and 19, and pp. 14–15 of evidence.

[4] Pickering's 1883 report (*SSGG*, 1884, pp. 453–4) looked forward to the banning of indebted immigrants, who were subject to so many abuses. Subsequently, however, neither he nor his successors reverted to the subject, even when the 'unpaid passengers' became an unimportant fraction of the total arrivals in the 1890s. On the contrary, the British Government refused to take up the recommendations of the 1890 Labour Commission for a cooperative Anglo-Chinese regulation of the migrant traffic, on the ground that the credit-ticket system would never obtain official Chinese recognition. Wong Lin Ken, p. 69. The reports of the Protectorate suggest that a genuine concern to assist Chinese immigrants in its earliest years gradually gave way to a defence of its own vested interests, which included the fees (25 cents on contracts for British Malaya, $1 on those for elsewhere) accruing as a result of the indentured labour system.

All the main employers of *sinkheh* labour were affected by the short supply which resulted from this renewed Chinese pressure after 1885, but those who were obliged to rely on the 'unpaid passengers' who came before the Chinese Protector were much the worst hit. The commissions of the 'coolie-brokers' mounted steadily. In March 1885, the Deli Planters Union (D.P.V.) resolved that all members should pay no more than $50 premium for each *sinkheh* recruited. The brokers were in too strong a position, however, and the attempt was abandoned in January 1887. Immediately the fee jumped to $60–70. By the end of that year it had risen further to $110–115 in Singapore and $125 in Penang.[1] Of this no more than $30 was ever used to cover the advance to the *sinkheh* and the expenses of the passage.

Since Sumatra tobacco-growers had no alternative source to Chinese labour, and could afford to pay the premiums, their share of the indentured labour supply remained high, as the following figures show:

TABLE 3 *Labour contracts signed before the Protector of Chinese,*
Straits Settlements[2]

	All destinations[3]	Penang and Province Wellesley	Malay States	East Coast of Sumatra	(Plus direct recruitment in China)[4]
1886	45,717	6,221	16,721	16,757	—
1887	51,859	5,464	21,397	17,489	—
1888	44,451	2,476	16,367	19,561	(+ 1152)
1889	32,666	3,170	7,071	11,793	(+ 5176)
1890	26,211	1,880	5,104	8,972	(+ 6666)

The share going to Malayan tin mines was reduced by the gradual fall in the tin price after 1888, but probably even more by the substitution of nominally 'free' immigrants for those who had been obtained from the licensed depôts. The European sugar planters of Province Wellesley suffered the most severely.

[1] Bool, p. 4. *Consulaire Verslagen*, 1887, p. 435; 1888, pp. 790 and 1073.
[2] From annual reports of Chinese Protectorate in *SSGG*.
[3] These figures are larger than those in the final column of table 2 because they include (*a*) 3000–5000 Indonesians each year, (*b*) some *laukhehs* who had already worked for some time in the Nanyang. The only region taking an increasing number of contract labourers during this period was Sabah, where tobacco was being established. Taking fewer than 500 before 1888, Sabah recruited 3,028 in that year, 6,321 in 1889 and 7,223 in 1890. *SSGG*, 1891, p. 1087. Wong Lin Ken, p. 67.
[4] See below, pp. 314–17.

The Deli tobacco industry was at the height of its prosperity in 1887–9. Previously the desire of the planters to break free from dependence on the Straits Settlements brokers had been damped only by the extreme difficulty attending other methods. During this crisis in the labour supply they succeeded in breaking away.

The solution dearest to the hearts of the planters was to bring labour directly from China to Sumatra. This, however, necessitated the sanction of the Chinese Government. To this end Holland had in 1873 signed the Anglo-Franco-Chinese protocol of 1866 which, among other provisions, entirely ruled out any advances to the labourer, or charge against him of the cost of recruitment. J. T. Cremer, the energetic manager of the Deli Maatschappij, tried to implement these terms by travelling to China himself in 1875. He then found a general reluctance to permit emigration to Deli on any terms whatever. Cremer's conclusion was that the Deli firms should send trusted *laukhehs* (experienced migrants) back to China to persuade their friends to migrate to Sumatra without any contracts. In this way the most successful companies, particularly the Deli Mij., succeeded in influencing a growing number of emigrants to opt consciously for Deli when the scramble for labour began in the Straits Settlements.[1]

Five Sumatra tobacco concerns,[2] led again by the Deli Mij., joined forces in 1886 in a more earnest attempt to bring about direct migration. Dr J. J. M. de Groot, official Chinese interpreter in Batavia, was then making a study tour of South China. At the request of the five firms, he was instructed to try to arrange direct emigration to Sumatra at the same time.

After consultation with the planters, De Groot decided to avoid contact with the British, whom he considered to have a vested interest in opposing direct migration. Instead of working through Swatow, therefore, where the Netherlands Consul was an Englishman, De Groot decided to try to recruit Teochiu labourers through the German firm of Pasedag & Co. at Amoy, whose principal, Piehl, was the Netherlands Consul there. This firm in turn called in the assistance of Lauts & Haysloop, a German firm in Swatow, and of the German Consul in Swatow. The eventual success of the scheme

[1] Bool, pp. 5–6. Schadee, ii, pp. 35 and 44.
[2] The Deli Mij., the Deli Batavia Mij., the Tabaksmaatschappij Arendsburg, the Amsterdam Deli Compagnie, and Messrs Naeher & Grob.

owed more to German pressure on the Chinese Government than to Dutch.[1]

De Groot and his supporters quickly realized the impossibility of obtaining permission for emigration under contract—particularly from Amoy. Early in 1887 they directed their efforts to obtaining permission for emigration to Sumatra on a basis similar to that for 'unpaid passengers' to the Straits Settlements. The authorities were still reluctant. Peking was anxious to force the Dutch to allow Chinese Consuls in Netherlands India, and pointed out that the strictest precautions had to be taken in the case of emigration to countries where no Chinese Consuls were stationed.

The German Consul in Canton obtained a breakthrough in late 1887, by making much of the appointment of a government adviser for Chinese Affairs at Medan, whom he portrayed as a sort of Protector of Chinese. The Viceroy of Kwangtung softened to the extent of asking for a report from Swatow on the subject. Meanwhile De Groot and the German Consuls used all their influence on the higher officials of Chaochou, and bribed some of the junior ones. As a result, official permission was obtained for free emigration to Sumatra in April 1888.[2]

The five participating Deli concerns had already signed a contract the previous February with Lauts & Haysloop for recruiting and carrying free immigrants to Deli. In May 1888 the first two ships arrived at Belawan, the *China* bringing 70 migrants from Swatow and the *Glucksburg* 68 from Amoy. The following month the *Duburg* brought 60 more from Swatow, although some had fled in Singapore where the ship had called as a result of a cholera outbreak.

The cost of chartering these three steamers—over $11,000—fell on the five firms supporting the venture, though the migrants were under no obligation to sign contracts with these or any firms on arrival. Twenty-seven of the immigrants on the *China* signed no contracts at all, because brokers had shipped with them, and were able to prevent their signing contracts unless the brokers were given large commissions.[3] Brokers were prevented from joining subsequent ships, and few *sinkhehs* thereafter refused to sign a contract on arrival in Sumatra.

[1] Commercially Germany was the country most interested in breaking British predominance in Asian trade. Germans also had a large share in Deli tobacco. Among the 688 European residents of Sumatra's East Coast in 1884 were 390 Netherlanders, 123 Germans, and 88 British. Schadee. II, p. 41.

[2] Bool, pp. 6–10. Schadee, II, pp. 219–20.   [3] Bool, p. 11.

Technically they were still 'free' immigrants, at least as far as dealings with the Chinese Government were concerned. From the *sinkheh's* point of view, however, the main advantage over the old system was that he could send his $30 advance back to relatives in China instead of seeing it go into the pockets of the brokers and *khehtaus*.

In the early years of direct migration the cost to the planters for each *sinkheh* brought in directly was about $100, whereas the brokers in the Straits Settlements immediately dropped their charges to $85. Nevertheless the planters were unwilling to return to their old dependence on the Straits Settlements, and hopeful that costs would drop as trade developed to fill the empty steamers on the Sumatra–China run. At their annual conference in July 1888, the Planters Union established an Immigrants' Bureau to relieve the five pioneer firms of their financial responsibility. Members of the D.P.V. undertook to recruit labour only through this bureau, which would in turn recruit in the Straits Settlements whenever the supply direct from China was insufficient. The sum to be paid for each *sinkheh* so recruited was first fixed at $60 (or $40 for those recruited in the Straits), raised to $85 (or $50) in 1889, and finally settled at $75 (or $40) in 1891.[1] Of this amount, $20 was an advance given to the *sinkheh* on arrival at the plantation, and repayable by him. These sums failed to cover costs, but the losses were distributed amongst members.

In 1890 the planters ceased chartering special migrant vessels and contracted with the Hong Kong agents of the Aziatische Kustenfahrte Gesellschaft of Hamburg, which put two vessels permanently on the China–Sumatra route.[2] Lauts and Haysloop continued as recruiting agents, and in turn made an arrangement with the Swatow 'cooliehong' Heng Thye. The latter undertook to have nothing to do with the Straits brokers, and to recruit exclusively for Deli. Trusted *laukhehs* were sent home from Sumatra to assist in recruitment at a village level.[3]

Despite all these efforts, the planters never succeeded in filling their needs. The established brokers had an interest in upsetting the new

---

[1] Bool, pp. 28 and 40. Modderman, pp. 50–4. *Consulaire Verslagen*, 1889, II, pp. 35–36; 1890, II, pp. 37–38. The planters differentiated between so-called 'first class coolies' recruited in Swatow, who were mainly Teochiu, and 'second class coolies', recruited locally, who were usually Hakkas or Hokkiens, and were often *laukhehs* rather than *sinkhehs*.

[2] Bool, p. 26. Jebson & Co. (Hong Kong) took over this contract in 1904, and the K.P.M. in 1914.   [3] Bool, pp. 11–12.

system, by playing on old prejudices against Deli. Dutch commentators always claimed that agents of the Straits brokers had shipped along with 270 *sinkhehs* on the Sumatra-bound S.S. *China* in Hong Kong in March 1889.[1] When near Singapore these *sinkhehs* began to attack their *khehtaus*, claiming that they had been duped into going to Sumatra. The *China* was obliged to call at Singapore to avoid a general mutiny. There the *sinkhehs* came before the Protector of Chinese, and were lost to the Deli planters. Similar disturbances took place on two other steamers in 1889–90, but each managed to take on troops from Riau or Singapore to restore order without having to call at the British port.[2]

In China, too, there was continued pressure against emigration to Deli. The Heng Thye recruiting house, for example, was plagued by people threatening to complain to officials about the kidnapping of a relative unless they were paid to keep quiet. Early in 1890 placards were privately posted in Swatow warning that Heng Thye was about to lose his head for trafficking in men. These moves were officially denounced the following May after pressure from Hoetink, the Chinese adviser in Medan who had been sent to lobby for Deli interests in South China.[3] Despite the cordial tone of this declaration, however, Peking itself was involved in the opposition to emigration, partly because of its growing desire to place Consuls in Netherlands India. In a formal pronouncement of 4 October 1891, the Chinese Government imposed three conditions for the continuance of emigration: the appointment of Consuls; the abolition of opium and gambling dens in Deli; and the assurance that financial remittances would flow into China from the emigrants abroad. The last point was to be achieved by the compulsory remittance home of all the earnings of labourers above their minimum needs. This proclamation caused great alarm but little action, and was gradually forgotten after 1892.[4]

By about 1897 the direct immigration to Sumatra could be said to be on a permanent basis, no longer threatened with immediate termination by official opposition or natural disaster. But the continuing current of opposition prevented the planters from ever obtaining as full or as sure a supply of labour as they required. Attempts to begin

[1] In a proclamation of May 1890, the Provincial authorities of Kwangtung endorsed this by stating the disturbance on the *China* was solely the work of the Straits brokers. Bool, p. 17.
[2] *Consulaire Verslagen*, 1890, II, p. 37. *SSGG*, 1890, p. 847. Bool, p. 13.
[3] Bool, p. 17.   [4] Bool, pp. 19–21.

direct migration from Hong Kong, Macao, and Hainan were unsuccessful, while the migrant ships from Amoy did not operate after 1889. Swatow had more than ever a monopoly of the labour supply for the *cultuurgebied*.[1]

Despite the establishment of direct migration, the planters were obliged increasingly to look to other sources to fill their labour requirements. Indian workers, so important for Malayan plantations, had never been numerous. The few Indians who signed contracts in the Straits Settlements for work in Sumatra were breaking the laws of the Indian Government. Fitful negotiations between Batavia and Calcutta in the 1870s had not succeeded in reaching agreement over the migration of workers. In 1887, as a result of the labour crisis in Deli, the Netherlands Indian Government made a more serious overture by sending a commission to India. It failed, however, to alter Calcutta's demand for a British protector of Indian labour to be resident in Sumatra.[2] This the Dutch would not allow.

Javanese labour, on the other hand, was readily available. There were established recruitment offices in Java, a huge reservoir of underemployed labour, and ample co-operation from Dutch officials. But the planters resisted switching over to Javanese, particularly for the cultivation itself, where the Chinese were regarded as being more responsive to the money incentive. In periods such as the first years of the Chinese Protectorate, when Chinese labour was readily available from the Straits Settlements, Javanese were not recruited and their numbers declined.[3] In the late 1880s, on the other hand, Javanese began to be employed on all tasks except cultivation. In 1887 2,210 Javanese passed through Singapore with contracts already signed for work on Sumatra plantations, and a further 1940 'natives of Netherlands India' (Banjerese and Boyanese, as well as Javanese) signed contracts at the Singapore Chinese Protectorate for work there.[4] These numbers continued to increase until 1890, when the drastic halving of the tobacco price stopped expansion temporarily. Javanese immigration recommenced in the mid-1890s, and quickly surpassed that of Chinese. Coffee, and later tea and rubber, broadened the economic base of the plantation district after 1890, and in these new crops Javanese predominated from the beginning.

[1] Bool, p. 22. [2] Schadee, II, pp. 223–4. *Consulaire Verslagen*, 1888, p. 790.
[3] *Koloniaal Verslag*, 1880, p. 192. Schadee, II, p. 44.
[4] *Consulaire Verslagen*, 1888, p. 1076. Also Schadee, II, p. 223; *SSGG*, 1891, p. 1087.

The following table[1] shows the changing composition of the plantation labour force in the East Coast of Sumatra Residency:

TABLE 4

	1874	1884	1890	1900	1916	1926
Chinese	4,476	21,136	53,806	58,516	43,689	27,133
Javanese	316	1,771	14,847	25,224	150,392	194,189
Indian	459	1,528	2,460	3,270	—	—

Chinese immigration had been at its peak during the period 1886–9, when more than 16,000 entered each year. For the 1880s as a whole, when labour was being recruited in the Straits Settlements, there was an average of about 12,000 indentured Chinese immigrants per year. This compares with rather less than 7,000 per year brought in by the Immigrants Bureau over the period during which it operated, 1888–1930.[2]

Though the indentured Chinese labourers gradually dwindled in number, the total Chinese population of the East Coast of Sumatra continued to grow. A more balanced community emerged, of traders, shopkeepers, small farmers, fishermen and lumbermen. It remained, however, a small minority.

In retrospect, it appears that the greatest impediment to the Sumatran tobacco industry in recruiting Chinese labour was that the Malayan Chinese who controlled most of the labour supply had no particular interest in it. In the early stages of the industry, when this disadvantage was coupled with prejudice against Deli as a strange and distant field of employment, the tobacco planters had great difficulty attracting enough labour even after paying exceptionally high commissions to the brokers in control. It seems probable that the Deli employers would have had to switch away from Chinese labour before 1880 but for the establishment of the Protectorate of Chinese in the Straits Settlements. The great advantage of European employers was their greater influence with colonial governments, as opposed to the influence Chinese

---

[1] From *Koloniale Verslagen*, relevant years.
[2] The majority of these were brought directly from Swatow. After 1899 the Immigrants Bureau ceased to recruit from the Straits Settlements, though planters who were not members of the D.P.V. continued to do so in small numbers.

employers exercised over the workers themselves. By means of the Chinese Protectorate a section of the migrant traffic was partially removed from the control of the Chinese societies, and became available to price competition among the European employers. This section was, however, limited to labour supplied by those groups in Swatow which had already established some relationships with European employers, and which it suited to work through the Chinese Protectorate. The vast majority of immigrants continued to escape the scrutiny of the Protectorate as nominally 'free' migrants, and were employed for the most part on the older pattern.

The Protectorate also proved unable to provide adequate numbers to meet increasing demand in the late 1880s. The main obstacle was opposition by the Chinese Government, for whom the Deli branch of the emigration system became the main object of attack because it was the most obvious beneficiary of the open credit-ticket system.

The purpose of this paper is not to whiten the reputations of the Deli planters. As a class they probably deserved most of the criticism levelled against them for their arrogance and harshness. Moreover, they showed very little interest in attempting to substitute a genuinely free and stable labour force for the rapid turnover of indentured *sinkhehs*. They were quick to point out that increases in wage levels had very little effect on labour supply, which could be increased much more cheaply by giving larger premiums to the brokers.[1] The preference constantly expressed for *sinkheh* labour over that of experienced hands suggests that planters encouraged a pattern of social and economic relationships which was actually inimical to the development of a stable labour force.

---

[1] Bool, p. 24; Boeke, pp. 74–5.

REVOLUTION IN EDUCATION

BY KENNETH ROBINSON

Of all the revolutions which are changing the face of the world, perhaps the revolution in education will be the most far-reaching in its effects. This revolution is proceeding in all countries, Communist and non-Communist alike, on fairly similar lines, a most heartening fact: for if a similar ferment is at work the world over, the end-product is likely to be similar; and if the end-product is similar, the opportunities for co-operation between countries and continents are likely to be increased.

What are the significant features of this revolution? First, there is the desire of parents at every level of society that their children should receive an education. This in itself is something quite new in the history of the world. It is very rare now to meet a parent who says, 'What was good enough for me is good enough for my son', although it was a common attitude among uneducated people of many nations fifty years ago.

No matter how slender the resources of a developing country may be, few governments dare allocate less than a fifth of the budget to education, and in many cases they spend much more. In Malaysia, for example, in 1966 the proportion was between one-fifth and one quarter, or to be precise 7/32. In countries that do not need to spend money on armaments, it may even approach a third of the total budget.

The first demand is for universal primary education: justice combines with national interest to satisfy it. Modern society requires everyone to be able to read and write. Moreover, very clever children who have been given only these rudiments nevertheless stand a good chance of forcing their way to the top, even if they receive no further help. The developing countries of the world can show many examples today of ministers of state who have arrived with only a sketchy education, but very few who cannot read or write at all.

While the greater part of a nation's effort is being put into achieving universal primary education, it is usually necessary for secondary education to be limited for lack of funds, and at this stage only children who are very able or whose parents are reasonably well off are likely to get into secondary schools.

As primary education begins to take effect the nation slowly becomes more productive. The increase in productivity helps to pay for more secondary education, and in due course all children begin to benefit from it. At intervals, as the nation's wealth increases, secondary schooling is extended, usually by a year at a time. Compulsory schooling slowly creeps up from the thirteenth to the fourteenth and then from the fourteenth to the fifteenth year, as now in Britain, or even higher in a few fortunate states.

In developing countries the number of children who receive secondary education is usually between 10 and 50% of those who complete their primary schooling. Unfortunately, long before national production has reached a point at which it can afford to finance universal secondary education, without starving some other sector, there is a very lively demand from the majority of the population that all children should be given a secondary education too. Then those who are directing affairs have to make an agonizing decision. Either they must concentrate their resources so as to be able to guarantee a first-class higher education to the small number of able children needed to supply the state with administrators, scientists, doctors, technicians, teachers, and so on; or they must spread the butter universally but so thinly that they risk entrusting the state in the next generation to ill-trained or untrained and unqualified people.

The facts of this situation have been well put by Dr Hla Myint when writing about his own country, Burma:[1]

When we started the post-war period, with very few trained people . . . there was a great demand for education. Parents wanted their sons and daughters to get better jobs, therefore they wanted to put them into schools. The reasonable thing to my mind would have been to choose the cleverest children, whether they came from rich or poor families, and to teach them so that they could become the teachers of the future, and to progress in this way. But no, the general political opinion was that it was unequal and undemocratic to discriminate: everyone had the basic right to education, not only at school level but also at university level. This meant that there was wholesale crowding of schools and universities, with only limited teaching resources, so that the cleverest children could not be taught properly and existing intelligence potential and skills never had the chance to develop. The aim was to extend education to all, and while certain experts in education say this is a very good thing and that where in the old days education was very restricted and narrow now it is extended to all, the trouble now is that there

[1] *Overseas Quarterly*, March 1964, p. 12.

is less chance to produce the sort of skilled people these countries need because of lack of selection. And the drive to get education is simply that parents want their children to attain middle-class standards of living by means of getting good jobs, because middle-class people have about five or six times the average income of the country. Of course it is not possible for everyone in the country to have five or six times the prevailing average income. Only a limited number of such people can be supported, and it must be ensured that those who do get the high incomes are very good. With the departure, after the war, of colonial administrators, there were a certain number of well-paid jobs available, but they were soon filled and the countries have not advanced enough for the creation of many more of such high-level jobs for graduates. Theoretically, these graduates should have helped to quicken the rate of progress, but in practice they are not of sufficient quality to be of much help. In fact, many of them, because of insufficient training and ability, may hinder the process. So there is this unsatisfactory situation—of a great deal of talent being wasted, countries being unable to offer enough jobs to graduates, and a storm-centre for future political tensions being created thereby.

It is not politically easy to say to an elector: 'Your child cannot go to a secondary school because we need the money for improving agriculture, but So-and-So's can, because he is very clever.' But the alternative is likely to be ineffective secondary education due to dilution and excessively large classes, leading to university degrees which are not recognized by the established academic world, and graduates unable to perform what is expected of them; scientists, for example, who are unable to use expensive equipment, or doctors whose training is based on mass instruction and book learning only.

The second factor in the educational revolution is the new emphasis on science. Not so long ago children entering a secondary school had to choose whether to become 'classical' or 'modern', and if they chose 'modern', they had to decide whether to study modern languages or science. This sharp division into compartments has now largely gone. Even in primary schools children now learn to observe, measure and record, as a first step in scientific training. Science is more and more becoming the backbone of all education, with the language of speech and the language of numbers as its left and right hands. Even in such subjects as history the effect of science can be felt, for there is now greater emphasis on the history of transport, of medicine, of technology and of science itself at the expense of political, constitutional and military history.

For developing countries this emphasis on science is particularly important not only because it is the young scientists and technicians who will make the country rich, but because training in science completely alters the attitude of the new generation to their world. Superstition and belief in magic lose their grip and make it possible for farmers and others to try out innovations without fear of heaven's reprisals or the hostility of neighbours who resent the upsetting of the old ways. Schools are mobilized for this purpose as in Communist China's 'Anti-Superstition Weeks'.

In time the new attitude of science will even affect governments. They will realize that it is no less grotesque to attempt to teach children to hate other countries and governments than to attempt to train doctors to hate diseases. The idea of a Hate Cancer Week is already laughable. Nor would a surgeon whose hands were quivering with anger as he operated do a particularly good job. One day the idea of 'Anti-Communism' or of a 'Hate America Week' will also be unthinkable.

One quite remarkable development in the educational revolution is to be seen in the education of armies. The proverb from Imperial China was that one does not use good iron to make nails, nor good men to make soldiers. Wellington's armies were seen as the brutal and licentious soldiery. Today soldiers not only start with what schooling the state has given them before they enter, but schooling is continued during their service. Thus a modern army, in countries where the whole population is not yet highly educated, can be used as an instrument for development or enlightenment in addition to its usual rôle. So we find soldiers in mainland China teaching peasants and helping in rural work, and similarly the troops deployed in Malaysia against the Indonesian threat helped to make improvements in rural life and performed errands of mercy. The result is that when a people is not racked by hot war, it is no longer opposed to the presence of the military, whose coming in former ages had always meant trouble, looting and death. Soldiers are beginning to be thought of as instruments of social advance. This has been carried to its logical conclusion in Iran,[1] where doctors and other suitable persons are conscripted for national service not into the army but into the Health Corps and do their service in those parts of the country which most need help.

[1] *Facts About Iran*, Special Issue, Ministry of Information, Teheran, July 1965.

Service to the community from men under arms is only one aspect of that type of service which has been steadily developing over the last hundred years as a result of the spreading of education.

Voluntary groups and single volunteers in democratic countries, and political groups in authoritarian societies, work for the improvement of the nation. Their motives are often different but the productive result is likely to be similar. Aspects of this phenomenon include such things as youth work in poor districts: the Hitler Youth who dug ditches for the fatherland; singing and dancing groups in Communist organizations; Voluntary Service Overseas from Britain and the Peace Corps from the United States of America, Japan and elsewhere. If nothing else, it indicates something of the ferment in people's minds which wider education has started, and the desire of young people to give themselves to a good cause. It may be a little startling to see grouped together in one category the youngsters of the Hitler Youth, the Communist organizations, the Peace Corps, V.S.O. and so on. Yet it would be presumptuous of an adult to deny that the motives of a young man or woman of eighteen in any one of these were or are less generous than those of the young people in another, whatever the political framework in which they have grown up.

Certainly the movement on a large scale of young people from one country or continent to another is bound to have a great long-term effect not so much on the country for which they have worked as on their own country when they return. The next generation in the donor countries can scarcely fail to be better informed about the world than the generation which preceded it.

A fourth factor in the educational revolution which gives great encouragement is the emergence of a more balanced view of world history and the gradual coming into focus of the idea of a world civilization.

There was a time when the West was exclusively concerned in its schools with the West and with the various extensions of Western power. All else was outer darkness. This attitude goes far back into history and has its roots perhaps in the concept of Rome dispensing the Eternal Light. It was understandable. The brilliance of Persia was a hostile glare, too close for comfort. The Han court in China, almost as distant as Neptune or Uranus, flickered fitfully across the void, and was little more than fable. All else, the hinterlands of Africa and Russia, the German forest, frozen Scandinavia, Scotland and Ireland blanketed in rain and fog, all these were areas of darkness to which one did not go. It is not surprising that with the passing of centuries the inheritors of the Roman Empire thought of themselves as the heirs of the only true light.

Nor was it so very different in China, where isolation and a cohesive civilization had given its people a similarly self-centred attitude. This attitude was given a rude knock when it was found that the West was armed with artillery and scientific method. But a rude knock induces a desire to give a counter-knock. Artillery is not the best way of helping a nation to make an adjustment in its view of the world, even when the adoption of scientific method must form part of that adjustment.

Although world politics present a somewhat dismal scene, one need not be without hope, for the revolution in our thinking is continuing rather more hopefully in the world's classrooms. The pendulum is swinging back, and in time equilibrium will be found. Already there are many parts of the world where children no longer begin their study of history with the statement that Gaul consisted of three parts, or that Julius Caesar landed in Britain in 55 B.C. Little by little each nation is learning to look more critically at its past, to understand how it fits into an agglomeration of states, and to wish to make some contribution from its own stock to the culture of others.

Part of this process of adjustment involves exaggerations. For example some nations develop a morbid desire to prove that all the most famous inventions originated with their own people. When such nations have produced an ample number of genuine inventions, they will no longer need to have recourse to fantasy. A new generation trained by research to accept nothing but the truth will throw out the lumber.

What is vital is that children should have access to truth, and be free to ask questions. Without these liberties they can never become good scientists, and that is something no nation dare go without. Throughout the world the movement in teaching is away from authoritarian lecturing and towards individual discovering.

When education first begins to develop in a country, the teaching has to be authoritarian. One need only think back to such giants of the early nineteenth century in Britain as Andrew Bell and Joseph Lancaster who pioneered new ways of teaching in their developing country, to realize how far we have travelled from the old authoritarian systems under which one teacher controlled eight hundred children like an officer commanding his regiment.

The teachers in a developing country have not the experience and skill to teach except on rather rigid lines. But little by little, as teachers are trained and standards rise, liberty comes creeping in, a sure foundation for the greater liberty of a democratic state.

For young people one of the most important freedoms is freedom of movement. Some idea of the health of nations can be gauged from the extent to which young people are allowed to travel without hindrance, both inside their own country and outside as well, in order to see how other nations live. Even more important is the free flow of ideas.

Once again, science is a great force for breaking down barriers. All nations wish to enjoy the technical advantages of their neighbours, but technical developments are rooted in the societies which produce them. It is difficult to import a technical innovation without altering society as well. At the very least it must add to and possibly alter the language which that society uses.

The humble aspirin, for example, first adds its name to the language. But its cheapness affects the attitude of customers to their own in-digenous pills, each of which is made by hand. Its effectiveness modifies the patient's attitude to pain. Is it really necessary to endure pain when all one has to do is to swallow a little white pill with some water? Inevitably society is altered once a technical innovation has gained a foothold.

A further factor in the revolution in education is linguistic. Until the early eighteenth century education was intended to meet the needs of churchmen, bureaucrats or gentlemen. In Europe and China the attitude was similar. A boy went to school in order to learn to express himself in dignified prose, to be at home with quotations in classical language deriving from the civilization of the preceding two thousand years, and to behave according to the established code.

Modern education began in the Charity schools which were founded not in the pattern of the old grammar schools, but in sympathy with the age of joint stock companies, for the production of useful people. By 1701 there were more than 25,000 children in England attending such schools. They were not only trained in cleanliness and godliness, but also made literate and taught useful work leading on to apprenticeship;

and a place was found in their scheme of education for science and modern languages.[1]

The idea spread, until eventually, more than a century later, Dr Thomas Arnold introduced mathematics, modern history and modern languages into the curriculum at Rugby. Since that time the science of teaching languages has been greatly developed, and with good reason. A monoglot nation is doomed to backwardness. A nation whose scientists, doctors and businessmen can only manage their own mother tongue will be outclassed. In science, and in medicine in particular, it is essential for the leading men to keep themselves informed of what is being done in other countries. The man who relies on translations has to wait until the translations are published. When they are published they may be inaccurate or abbreviated. But in any case only a fraction of all the original work published is translated even into the major languages.

It is therefore essential for the leaders of a nation's thought to be familiar with at least one of the world's major scientific languages, that is to say, the languages in which the most important scientific contributions are written. Among the languages at the top of the list are English, Russian, German, French, Japanese and Chinese. At least one of these languages must be studied in the schools of every state in the world that does not wish to be outstripped in the race towards the new form of society which is evolving.

In countries which are only just coming to nationhood the question of languages is critical. In South-east Asia the pattern is to develop a national language to serve as the language of the region. In Indonesia Malay was chosen because it was the language of a minority and unlikely to provoke the resentments in the other islands which might have been stirred up if the language of Java had been chosen. In Malaysia, on the other hand, it was adopted for precisely the opposite reason, because it was the language familiar to the largest number of people not only in Malaya but in the 'Maphilindo' region.

There is a slight contradiction in the early days of building up a national language. It is in the nation's interest not to damage the teaching of English or whatever the world language may be, but it is also in the nation's interest to build up the national language as an

---

[1] G. M. Trevelyan, *Illustrated English Social History*, Harmondsworth 1964, III, pp. 66, 124-5. M. G. Jones, *The Charity School Movement*, London, 1938, p. 4.

instrument of national solidarity. It is scarcely possible to build up a national language without damaging the teaching of the world language, if the developing nation is also straining its resources to expand its education system at the same time. It can only be done by increasing the amount of time spent on the national language at the expense of the world language or of some of the other subjects.

But as teaching methods improve this state of affairs is corrected. A language can still be well learnt in a reduced number of hours when the teaching is efficient. The developing countries which have built up a national language will then be no worse off than, say, Holland or the countries of Scandinavia, which all have strong national languages, yet are forced to use English and German as their world languages.

The chief source of friction is with the people of the region who do not speak the new national language as their mother tongue and would prefer to by-pass it and go straight to English as the common or official language, as has been done in nine African states since they achieved independence.[1] A Dayak child in Sarawak, for example, will need to learn his mother tongue, Malay and English if national language is made compulsory, whereas a Malay child need only learn his mother tongue and English. A Chinese child must also carry the learning load of three languages, though he has the reward of knowing two of the world's great scientific languages at the end of it, and will have this advantage over a Malay child, in addition to the toughening process of a harder school discipline on the way up.

The world today presents a strange linguistic spectacle. At the top there are the two giants, English and Russian, fighting it out for supremacy. Russian is handicapped by having an alphabet whose geographical distribution is far more limited than that of the Roman alphabet. On the other hand English is handicapped by a system of spelling, if one can call it a system, which represents the sounds of words as they were spoken in an amalgam of dialects four or five centuries ago.

At the other end of the scale we find an exuberant proliferation of little literatures. The literature of the Sea Dayaks, for example, is only now beginning to be written down, drawing on a vast oral literature from the past which is recorded in people's memories. There seems to

[1] Nigeria, Uganda, Kenya, Ghana, Zambia and Sierra Leone, where it is the sole official language, and Cameroon, Malawi and Tanzania, where it is one of two official languages.

be little point in building up very small literatures. The Kelabits of Sarawak, for example, only number some 2000 people: even the three Land Dayak languages have a combined strength of only approximately 60,000 speakers. Publication for such small numbers is not economic. Yet the production of these little literatures serves a purpose. Perhaps the small races who find themselves hammered by the advance of the twentieth century discover in the production of their literatures some guarantee or reinforcement for their racial identity which is in such mortal danger of assimilation.

English plays an important part in the school systems and the commerce of South-east Asia, but it is most beneficial as a purveyor of new ideas.

In terms of sheer numbers the English-speaking world, by which is meant the world of people that use English as one, though not necessarily the first, of their languages, is rather smaller than the Chinese-speaking world.[1] But whereas Chinese speakers are concentrated in East and South-east Asia, English speakers are found in large numbers in all the continents, and particularly along the most important seaways. There are large blocs of English speakers not only in Britain and Scandinavia, Canada and the United States, but in the West Indies, in many states of Africa, in several states from Pakistan to Malaysia and so down to Australia and New Zealand. It is in fact the only globe-encircling language.

Its great strength is in the number of universities to be found in the English-speaking world.[2] The fact that the universities of the English-speaking world are closely interconnected, pouring out their ideas, as it were, into a single grid system even though they have their being in different nations, is an additional source of strength.

Members of the English-speaking world are also fortunate in having a large literature in the colloquial language. Many of the new national languages are in process of building up their literatures almost from the beginning. Although China, for example, has a vast and ancient classical literature, the literature of the modern colloquial language can be said to have begun only in 1911.

[1] Perhaps 5–600,000,000 people speak English as compared with some 7–800,000,000 including overseas Chinese, who speak the National Language of China or one of the Chinese dialects.
[2] There are, for example, 373 universities in those five countries to which the majority of Malaysian students go for higher education outside Malaysia, namely: United States 291; Canada 33; United Kingdom 32; Australia 12; New Zealand 6.

In some instances, on the other hand, the classical language has been made colloquial, as in Israel where Hebrew is again spoken as a living language. Where this is done people without a classical education are not wholly cut off from the literature of their past, but neither the new literatures nor the ancient literatures provide in themselves a bridge to the industrial revolution or the ferment of ideas that followed the French revolution. The beginnings of modern economics, political theory and scientific discovery were not made in these languages, and therefore the bridge has to be made by translation.

All the new nations put much effort into translating the great established works of the modern world. Large nations such as China have done this very thoroughly. But small nations with only a small reading public cannot afford to carry out translation projects on a vast scale. For them English is a bridge to world civilization, since the main works of all nations are translated into English.

Another remarkable feature of the present century is the building up of a two-tier literature. In the past, it was the practice for a child to work away at grammar and composition in school till he reached a level where he could read Daniel Defoe or Jane Austen in the original. This took many years. Children who left school before they had reached the level went empty away. There were no books of quality sufficiently simple for them to read.

This is no longer the case. The great works of English literature have not only been translated horizontally across into other languages, but vertically downwards into simpler forms of English. The greater the simplification of the vocabulary and grammar the greater the loss in the way of style. But though there may be a loss in style there is no corresponding loss in ideas. Darwin, for example, had an excellent literary style. In a simplified version *The Origin of Species* might lose some of the balance and neatness of Darwin's phrasing, but it would lose none of its ideas.

A man who has had only eight or nine years of schooling might well be daunted by the vocabulary of Darwin and similar great thinkers of the past. But he is well able to assimilate these ideas in a simplified version, and it is for ideas rather than for style that he reads such books. English, more than any other language, has been translated vertically downwards to accommodate readers at different levels, and now possesses an extensive literature at many different levels of simplification.

The pattern in schools is no longer to study a few books, which are generally too difficult, until they are known by heart but scarcely appreciated. Rather it is to begin reading good literature in simplified versions at an early age, and year by year to raise the standard till eventually the reader can tackle a work in the original quite painlessly. The large number of books already read in simplified form then provides a solid basis for appreciating the niceties and refinements of style thereafter.

Today there are probably more people in the English-speaking world who are acquainted with English literature through simplified versions than there are who have read great works in the original. This is a quite revolutionary development which in time is likely to react on the whole of the English-speaking world and modify the common spoken language.

One may imagine a new language developing out of it, greatly simplified in grammar and structure, with a smaller but better-organized vocabulary. Such a language will have been hammered into shape by international airways and telecommunications, by commercial and industrial practices, by the functioning of law and the movement of tourists in staggering numbers. It is not unreasonable to believe that there will be some among its speakers who will be born poets and writers, who will use it to fashion a new literature with possibilities as yet undreamed of.

There remains, however, a major difficulty in the transmission of ideas. The ideas themselves are available whether translated from one ancient culture to another, or new-born as a result of international co-operation. World languages exist for the transference of ideas, and are being learnt by ever larger numbers of people. The great nations and power blocs are well aware that new ideas must be speedily assimilated. Yet, although the quickest way for a nation to assimilate new ideas is to feed them into schools, so that children aged 12 to 15 may absorb them into their thinking processes and a few years later emerge into adult life no longer regarding them as revolutionary, there is an appalling time-lag between the acceptance of an idea by a nation's thinkers and its digestion by the mass of the people. The reason for the delay is the difficulty in providing textbooks suitable for children of this age.

To take one example. It is now perfectly clear that the technical achievements of the West are not the product of Greek genius and the brains of Western nations alone.[1] There has been an interdependence and cross-fertilization of ideas between East and West for some two thousand years. Each has been a giver and each a receiver. Appreciation of this fact is essential for a healthy world society.

The story of *Heavenly Clockwork*[2] shows how Greek ideas of time measurement were reactivated by the Chinese invention of the escapement to produce modern clocks. Retold in the language of children in their early teens, this story would fascinate young scientists, and also alter their attitude to the great civilizations of East and West. The idea has been available already for ten years. It may well be a full quarter of a century or more before it begins to have any impact on young minds.

Unfortunately books containing new ideas are written at a high academic level. Before their ideas become assimilable for schools they must be predigested. To select their essentials, to divide them into topics suitable for lessons, and to rewrite them interestingly in simple language without distortion or inaccuracy is a difficult, expert, and ill-paid undertaking. Until this obstacle is removed the pace of the world's progress towards a new and rational society is likely to be unnecessarily slow.

[1] This may be regarded as the central theme running through all the volumes of Joseph Needham's *Science and Civilization in China*, a series with which school-textbook writers would do well to make themselves familiar.

[2] J. Needham, Wang Ling, and D. J. de S. Price, *Heavenly Clockwork, the Great Astronomical Clocks of Medieval China*, Cambridge, 1960. First published as a monograph by the Antiquarian Horological Society in 1956.

SIKH IMMIGRATION INTO MALAYA DURING THE PERIOD OF BRITISH RULE

KERNIAL SINGH SANDHU

PROLOGUE

No separate worthwhile records relating to Sikh migration were kept either in India[1] or in Malaya.[2] The following account of Sikh immigration into Malaya from its inception in the mid-nineteenth century to its virtual cessation in the 1950s is almost wholly based on fragmentary evidence in Malayan and Indian records pertaining to Indian migration as a whole, on sample surveys, and on the oral testimonies of a number

ABBREVIATIONS used in the footnotes throughout this paper:

C.O. 273 The Colonial Office's (London) Straits Settlements (and Malay States) original correspondence, followed by number of volume.

FMSAR Federated Malay States annual report (Kuala Lumpur), followed by year and page.

F.O. Foreign Office (London) correspondence, followed by number of correspondence.

IO:FP India Office (London): Foreign proceedings of the Government of India, followed by number of volume and year.

JAR Johore annual report (Singapore, Johore Bahru), followed by year and page.

MSGAR Malay States Guides annual report (Kuala Lumpur), followed by year and page.

NAI:EP National Archives of India: Emigration proceedings of the Government of India, followed by month and year.

NAI:FPP National Archives of India: Foreign political proceedings of the Government of India.

NAI:HDPP National Archives of India: Home Department political proceedings of the Government of India.

PLCSS Proceedings of the Legislative Council of the Straits Settlements (Singapore), followed by year and page.

SSAR Straits Settlements annual report (Singapore), followed by year and page.

SSGG Straits Settlements government gazette (Singapore), followed by year and page.

[1] For present purposes 'India' includes both the present-day Union of India (Bharat) and Pakistan.

[2] Unless otherwise stated, the term 'Malaya', or 'British Malaya' as it was called before independence, is used throughout the text to include both West Malaysia and the Republic of Singapore. Although separated politically from each other, these two territories have nevertheless traditionally functioned together.

of Sikhs interviewed by the writer in Malaya and India in 1962, 1965 and early 1966.

The Indian immigrants into Malaya during the period of British rule (1786–1957) were predominantly South Indian, principally Tamil, labourers and, to a lesser extent, clerks and administrative, technical and business assistants, who were mainly brought in to work on some plantation or government or commercial project. Although North Indian immigrants were fewer, they exercised a degree of economic and social influence in the Indian community and in the country as a whole out of all proportion to their small numbers. Prominent among the North Indian immigrants were the Sikhs from the Punjab.

CAUSES OF SIKH IMMIGRATION

Just as South Indians proved to be invaluable in the labouring and subordinate administrative and technical services,[1] similarly North Indians, particularly the tall, turbaned, sturdy Sikhs, were much sought after as soldiers, policemen, watchmen and caretakers.

The problem of providing adequate internal security in early British Malaya, a *sine qua non* for the cherished economic development of the country, appears to have been more difficult than usual with such pioneer areas. The population was largely transitory, widely dispersed and extremely mixed, consisting of such elements as Muslim Malays and Indians, ancestor-worshipping Chinese, Hindu Tamils, Christian Europeans and Eurasians and Buddhist Siamese and Sinhalese. The numerous Chinese with their secret societies were a special problem and a major source of disorders and crime. Quite apart from the difficulties of ordinary policing, they were also regarded as a political threat, to the extent that if not controlled they might 'take possession' of the country. These fears and the problem of controlling the Chinese increased with their growing numbers and with the reduction in the Indian military garrison following the transfer in 1867 of the Straits Settlements from Indian to Colonial Office control. The situation was further aggravated by the British assumption of paramountcy in the Malay states, for this not only vastly extended the area to be policed but also introduced a new problem of security in the form of dispossessed

[1] K. S. Sandhu, 'Indians in Malaya', unpublished Ph.D. thesis, University of London, 1965, pp. 216–91, 483–553.

Malay chiefs who had to be watched, at least in the early stages of British hegemony. But the early British administrators had no intention of handing over the country to the Chinese immigrants or letting it fall back under the control of the Malay rulers; they wanted instead to see it developed under their direction as a British asset, and they set about taking the necessary measures to ensure this. One such measure was the organization and maintenance of a modern efficient military and police force for internal law and order, external security being left to Britain.[1]

Several avenues were explored to meet the security needs. Malays, Javanese, Filipinos, Boyanese and Bugis were experimented with. There was, however, a general reluctance on their part to serve in these branches of government service. This was partly, it appears, because of the general turbulence that marked the early phase of British rule, and partly because of the nature of police work, involving as it did considerable discipline and odd hours of work—rather irksome and alien concepts to their traditional mode of life. Anyway, they could earn a reasonable, if not comparable, living in other and more amiable and safer occupations. Consequently, it was difficult to get sufficient numbers of recruits from the local Malays, at least in the early days of the British administration. Then, too, even if they had been available, it was the considered opinion of British police officers that they would not be at all effective in dealing with the Chinese, who had little or no respect for the military or police capabilities of the Malays. Finally, recruits from amongst the people of the Malay world, especially indigenous Malays, were regarded as altogether 'too close' to the local populace. Thus, although Malays could be usefully employed to some extent in ordinary police duties, the British Government and Residents considered it generally 'objectionable' and 'undesirable' to leave any substantial security arrangements, particularly those of a 'decidedly military character', in their hands.[2]

Opinion on the employment of *Jawi Pekans* and South Indians as

---

[1] *SSAR 1856–66*, pp. 20–22. Collyer to Government of India, 4 February 1858, *C.O. 273/2*. Governor-General in Council to Secretary of State for India, 29 July 1863. *C.O. 273/6*. Ord to Colonial Office, 20 April 1867. *C.O. 273/10*. Straits Settlements to Colonial Office, 4 November 1875. *C.O. 273/81*. Straits Settlements to Colonial Office, 18 October 1876. *C.O. 273/85*.

[2] Straits Settlements to Colonial Office, 26 February 1868. *C.O. 273/17*. Straits Settlements to Colonial Office, 18 October 1876. *C.O. 273/85*. *PLCSS 1872*, p. 18; *PLCSS 1876*, Appendix 3, pp. ccii–iv.

policemen was also unfavourable, although for somewhat different reasons. They were tried in the Straits Settlements in the nineteenth century. They proved quite 'active and intelligent', but they did not have even 'the slightest confidence' of their officers or the general public, many of them being members of secret criminal societies. Moreover, the British officers and the Straits Settlements Police Commission of 1879, set up to observe and recommend improvements in the police force, considered them 'very corrupt, thoroughly untrustworthy' and totally unsuited for dealing with the troublesome Chinese, who appeared to pay only the scantiest attention to the South Indian and *Jawi Pekan* policemen.[1] There was constant agitation by officials and members of the public that the 'ranks of the force ought to be carefully weeded' of South Indian and *Jawi Pekan* policemen, and this was finally achieved towards the end of the nineteenth century.[2]

Since most of the disorders and crimes were associated with the Chinese community, it was also suggested that Chinese should be employed for police work. But the weight of opinion was almost wholly against their employment in police duties other than as detectives. No 'respectable' Chinese would consider becoming a constable, the social stigma attached to such work being a powerful deterrent. Anyway, more money could be made in other and more honourable undertakings. Only *samsengs* (gangsters) would be attracted and they were expected, by the Chinese community leaders themselves, to be 'ten times more corrupt than the Tamils or Malays'. Finally, most important of all, since much of the rationale for the organization of the police was the supervision and control of the Chinese community, especially its secret societies, it was feared that there might be collusion between it and the local Chinese constables.[3]

It was thought for a while that the above objections would perhaps be overcome if, instead of being drawn from the local Chinese, recruits who had no local connections were obtained from Hong Kong. This was attempted in 1891 when fifty men were thus engaged. But the experiment ended in total failure, the men proving thoroughly

[1] *PLCSS 1872*, pp. 18–19; *PLCSS 1873*, Paper no. 27, p. 5; *PLCSS 1879*, Paper no. 32, pp. cclxxi–viii. *Jawi Pekan* was a local term for the offspring of intermarriage between Indian and Malay.

[2] *PLCSS 1879*, Paper no. 28, p. ccxliii; *SSAR 1894*, p. 19; *SSAR 1899*, p. 417.

[3] *PLCSS 1872*, pp. 18–33; *PLCSS 1873*, Paper no. 27, pp. 1–3.

'untrustworthy'. They were dismissed in 1894[1] and thenceforth, until after World War II, no Chinese are known to have been employed in police work other than in such rôles as detectives, officers and clerks.

Europeans, too, were thought of as constables and in fact a force of twenty-one trained British policemen was recruited in England. They arrived in Singapore in 1881. But they were soon dissatisfied with the conditions of service and pay. It became increasingly difficult to control them and they had finally to be shipped back a few years later.[2] Anyway, the whole idea of Britons working as common constables was considered 'impolitic', embarrassing and highly damaging to the prestige of the white man by the *Tuan Besars*, whose sentiments could not be lightly ignored.[3] The experiment was never attempted again.

In these circumstances where Malays, other South-east Asians, Chinese, *Jawi Pekans*, South Indians and Europeans were unavailable, impracticable or unsuitable, except for certain specific duties, the government had of necessity to turn to alternative possible sources of police and military recruits. It turned to the Northern Indian provinces, particularly the Punjab and North-west Frontier. Amongst the inhabitants of these areas, the Sikhs were particularly sought after.

They were sufficiently mobile and poor at home and were quite prepared to migrate and work for three to five years for such low wages as M$9–15 per month, in the hope of living frugally and saving enough to return home to buy new land or redeem the mortgaged family plot. If promised steady increments of about a dollar a year, with the prospects of a pension thrown in and suitable leave arrangements enabling them to visit their homes periodically, they could be persuaded to serve for much longer periods. Being wholly reliable, 'fairly uncorruptible', conscientious and generally quick to learn, they were considered quite good workers for all branches of the security services, but especially so for armed police work or for military and para-military duties, where their stature, bearing and martial traditions and reliability were invaluable.[4]

---

[1] *SSAR 1890*, pp. 570–1; *SSAR 1891*, p. 142; *SSAR 1894*, p. 19.

[2] *SSGG 1882*, p. 365; *SSAR 1890*, pp. 570–1; R. Onraet, *Singapore—A police background*, London, 1947, pp. 82–3.

[3] Labour Research Department, *British imperialism in Malaya*, London, 1926, p. 14; *British Malaya* (Singapore), May 1926, p. 6; J. Cameron, *Our tropical possessions in Malayan India*, London, 1865, pp. 281–2.

[4] *SSGG 1880*, p. 496; *SSGG 1881*, p. 422; *SSGG 1882*, p. 365; *SSGG 1883*, pp. 1097–8; *SSAR 1888*, p. 69; *PLCSS 1879*, Paper no. 28, p. ccxliii; Paper no. 32, p. cclxxviii.

They had been tried in police work by the British in Hong Kong as early as 1867, and had worked exceedingly well amongst the Chinese population.[1] The Chinese appeared to have a healthy respect and fear for the strong-arm police and military capabilities of the *Bengali Kwai* ('Bengali [Sikh] Devils'). In these circumstances they thus appeared to be just the right 'means of fully over-awing' the Chinese population in Malaya too. Moreover, they had little connection with the rest of the people, and were, therefore, equally suitable for dealing with them. Finally, they appeared to have the confidence of the European and other community leaders who had by this time apparently heard of the exploits of the Sikhs in Hong Kong and elsewhere.[2]

The Straits Settlements received their first batch of Sikh policemen in 1881. The fame of the effectiveness of these men as security guards, and that of their colleagues in Perak and other parts of the country, spread in Malaya. As a result they were also eagerly sought after by private employers for such jobs as caretakers, watchmen, guards and dunners.[3]

[1] *PLCSS 1879*, p. cclxxviii; G. B. Endacott, *A History of Hongkong*, London, 1958, p. 153.

[2] In fact, while the government was still debating the value of the different ethnic groups as police and military material, a Malay chief, Ngah Ibrahim, the Orang Kaya Mantri of Larut, Perak, commissioned one Captain Speedy, a former Superintendent of Police, Penang, to go to Northern India and enlist a force of fighting men to help him to save his tin mines from the depredations of Chinese insurgents. Speedy returned with 95 men, mainly Sikhs, Pathans and Punjabi Muslims, and on 29 September 1873 proceeded to Larut to put down the disorders caused by feuding Chinese clans. At about the same time, the British intervened and took control of the affairs of Perak and also Selangor and Sungei Ujong (Negri Sembilan). Speedy was appointed Assistant Resident of Perak and instructed to re-enlist as many of the Mantri's force as would be possible as 'Residency Guard', the nucleus of the proposed Perak police. This was done and the Residency Guard and a number of other Northern Indians who followed in the wake of their relatives and friends in this force were subsequently absorbed into the Perak Armed Police. Others found employment in the police forces of the other Malay States and in the Malay States Guides, a military regiment created in 1896. Straits Settlements to Colonial Office, 18 October 1876; Straits Settlements to Colonial Office, Confidential, 18 October 1876; Colonial Office Minute no. 13901. *C.O. 273/85*. Straits Settlements to Colonial Office, Confidential, 24 July 1894. *C.O. 273/196*. Straits Settlements to Colonial Office, Confidential, 5 March 1896. *C.O. 273/213*. Colonial Secretary, Singapore, to Government of India, 16 September 1873; District Superintendent of Police, Lahore, to Deputy Inspector-General of Police, Lahore Circle, 3 October 1873. *IO:FP 770/1873*. Speedy to Commissioner of Police, Calcutta, 16 September 1873; Commissioner of Police, Calcutta, to Government of Bengal, 25 September 1873. *IO:FP 771/1873. Kelantan administrative report, 1909*, Kuala Lumpur, 1910, pp. 8–10; *JAR 1913*, pp. 14 ff.; *Yearly report on the administration of the State of Kedah, 1905–1906*, Penang, 1906, p. 13; *The Times*, London, 19 September 1902.

[3] *SSGG 1882*, p. 365; *FMSAR 1915*, p. 8; C. W. Harrison, *Some notes on the government services in British Malaya*, London, 1929, p. 57; *Malayan Police magazine*, Kuala

In addition to the foregoing migration stream there was a fairly continuous influx of Sikh petty entrepreneurs, merchants, traders and suchlike, who followed in the wake of their potential security-force brethren. They found increasing scope in Malaya, catering for the special needs of their countrymen and in many other fields.[1]

They in turn imported, assisted or encouraged a number of assistants and underlings to come to Malaya to help them in their undertakings.

With a growing horde of graduates being turned out by the numerous schools, colleges and universities in India, the English-educated Sikhs, like the other Indians, began to find it extremely difficult to get into the cherished, but comparatively limited and highly competitive, government services or obtain other similarly desirable jobs. Prospects in Malaya for such classes of Sikhs were by no means rosy, being limited to subordinate rôles in a European-dominated government and professional world until after World War II. But even such opportunities were apparently, in some cases at least, sufficiently attractive compared with those in India,[2] because English-educated Sikhs, such as teachers and clerks, began to trickle into Malaya from about the end of the nineteenth century.

Finally, following the designation in the 1820s of the Straits Settlements as penal stations for the Government of India and the latter's annexation of the Punjab in 1849, a number of Sikh convicts also began to arrive in Malaya.[3]

TYPES OF MIGRANTS AND RECRUITMENT

Potential militiamen, policemen and similar immigrants

Sikhs entering Malaya to join the security forces were almost all from the Mahja, Malwa and Doaba areas of the Punjab. The proportion of immigrants from each of these areas in the total Sikh movement of this type is uncertain, but it is estimated that the Mahja and Malwa areas

Lumpur, I, 1928, pp. 17–525; III, 1930, p. 160; Straits Settlements to Colonial Office, 9 July 1894. *C.O. 273/193.* High Commissioner to Colonial Office, Secret, 12 September 1902. *C.O. 273/291.* High Commissioner to Colonial Office, Confidential, 30 December 1904. *C.O. 273/303.* Secret memorandum by Swettenham, 12 August 1903. *NAI:EP,* December, 1904. Secret file no. 154, serial no. 1. *NAI:EP,* October, 1915.

[1] Gurdit Singh, *Voyage of Komagata Maru,* Calcutta, n.d., pp. 2–16. Secret file no. 154, serial no. 1. *NAI:EP,* October, 1915.

[2] *Statement exhibiting the moral and material progress and condition of India, 1911–12,* London, 1913, pp. 164, 368–77.   [3] See p. 347 below.

were approximately equally represented with about 35% of the total immigrants each; about 20% came from the Doaba region.

Although a number did subsequently send for them, few such Sikh migrants arrived in Malaya with their womenfolk before World War II. The migrants of this type found their way to Malaya mainly through three channels. The first to enter Malaya were those recruited by Captain Speedy in 1873 to combat Chinese insurgency among the tin mines of Perak. Some of these pioneer recruits were subsequently drafted into the government service to form the nucleus of the police and para-military forces of that state, following its passing under British control. Furthermore, the government, to meet its growing need for Sikh recruits for the security forces, now began to recruit Sikhs in India on its own. This the government did for some time through the Indian Government but later on through its own officers, usually Sikh non-commissioned officers on furlough in India.[1] The common practice in recruiting Sikhs, however, was to enlist them in Malaya, because, as the word spread of the opportunity in Malaya, more and more Sikhs were coming into the country on their own or, more correctly, were being brought along by relatives and friends returning from a visit to India, or were in other ways assisted by such people to reach Malaya.[2] Not all such immigrants were absorbed by government and quasi-government departments. At times for every candidate accepted another was rejected, partly because only a limited number was needed in any one year and partly because of strict physical requirements.[3] Those who failed in their bid for the cherished government jobs either drifted, occasionally, out of the country to such places as Sumatra and Thailand or, more usually, into the private sector of the Malayan economy, to assume such rôles as caretakers, watchmen, bullock-cart drivers, dairy-keepers and mining labourers.[4]

The total number of these Sikh immigrants into Malaya is unknown

[1] Secret memorandum by Swettenham, 12 August 1903. *NAI:EP*, December, 1904. *MSGAR 1913*, p. 1.
[2] *MSGAR 1899*, p. 1; *MSGAR 1900*, p. 5; *SSGG 1882*, p. 365; *JAR 1926*, p. 27. High Commissioner to Colonial Office, Secret, 12 August 1902. *C.O. 273/291*.
[3] *MSGAR 1908*, p. 2; *MSGAR 1909*, p. 1; *Federated Malay States Police Force annual report, 1909*, Kuala Lumpur, 1910, p. 1; *JAR 1927*, p. 27; *JAR 1931*, p. 31.
[4] Secret memorandum by Swettenham, 12 August 1903. *NAI:EP*, December 1904. Secret file no. 154, serial no. 1, *NAI:EP*. October, 1915. W. L. Blythe, *Methods and conditions of employment of Chinese labour in the Federated Malaya States*, Confidential print, Kuala Lumpur, 1938, pp. 19 *et seq.*

but, judging from the number of candidates offering themselves for recruitment into the country's military and police forces in certain years, it would appear that the movement was not large, at the most only a couple of thousand arrivals in any one year, and generally much less than this.[1] But these Sikhs nevertheless represented the major stream, in terms of numbers, of all Sikh immigration until the 1930s. Thereafter, with increasing numbers of other Sikh immigrants and changes in employment opportunities in the country, the proportion of these Sikhs in the total Sikh immigration into Malaya appears to have gradually declined.

There was no such movement between India and Malaya during the Japanese occupation (1942–5) because of the disruption of communications. After the war this immigration was resumed but it did not last for long. Firstly, the policy of the British Malayan Government *vis-à-vis* the employment of Sikh immigrants in the government forces had undergone a drastic change since the war, in so far as it now no longer appeared keen to have such recruits. The reasons for this virtual *volte-face* are not wholly clear, but the consensus of opinion of those interviewed on this topic and the little written evidence that is available suggest that it was principally the result of the following developments.

Up to the war, Sikhs arriving in Malaya from India were moving from one British area to another. The emergence of an independent India ended this and it meant that henceforth Malaya, still a British colony, would have to deal with a foreign Indian Government, which in any case did not appear at all sympathetic to the emigration of its citizens for the purpose of taking up such low-income jobs as labourers, policemen, watchmen and so on.[2] Then there was the fact that many Sikhs, including members of the British Malayan police force, had espoused the cause of the wartime anti-British Indian National Army, and as such were considered 'politically tainted and a security risk'.

Moreover, some of them were either known or suspected of 'collaborating' with the Japanese and 'ill-treating' British prisoners of war. More important, there was an intensification after the war of

[1] *JAR 1927*, p. 27; *JAR 1930*, p. 33; *FMSAR 1900*, p. 5; *FMSAR 1902*, p. 15; *MSGAR 1909*, p. 1.
[2] Sandhu, pp. 322–5, 650–739; *Straits Times* (Singapore), 26 and 27 April 1949.

the policy, apparently begun in the 1920s,[1] of limiting government employment to locally domiciled people, especially Malays, as far as possible. With the rapid growth and increasing stabilization of the country's population, larger numbers of locally domiciled people were available for government jobs. In any case, if some special para-military recruits were required and could not be acquired locally, they could be more conveniently drawn from the ranks of the Gurkhas, whose loyalty was above reproach and with whose government Britain still had a treaty allowing it to recruit its citizens for British military needs. Some Gurkhas were in fact recruited for service in Singapore as a 'Special Force' or 'Reserve Unit', that is, as an anti-riot unit.

Secondly, employment in the private sector also became more difficult for new Sikh immigrants after the war. Perhaps partly because of the government's lead and partly because of the increasing availability of local Malay-speaking candidates, commercial organizations also began to limit their recruitment largely to locally domiciled elements. This tendency strengthened after 1948 when, with the outbreak of an armed Communist-led revolt, a number of Sikh policemen with sufficient years of service to exercise their pension options began leaving the government service for the comparatively safer commercial sector.

Finally, there was the general immigration restriction brought in by the Malayan Government in 1953. This was the *coup de grâce*, for it completely stopped the entry of potential policemen and similar immigrants.

Commercial immigrants. It is not known when the first Sikh commercial immigrants followed their potential security force brethren into Malaya, but until the early years of the present century the Northern Indian commercial immigrants consisted almost wholly of Bengalis, Parsis and Gujeratis. With increasing Sindhi and Sikh immigration in the ensuing years, however, the Gujeratis, Parsis and Bengalis were superseded by these newcomers, together with Marwaris, as the largest group in terms of numbers, and gradually in terms of scale of business too.

The Sikh commercial immigrants were mainly from the Rawalpindi, Lahore, Ludhiana, Jullundur and Amritsar urban centres of the Punjab

[1] *FMSAR 1924*, p. 35.

and their environs. While the majority of them arrived in Malaya directly from India, substantial numbers also came from such places as Rangoon and Bangkok, where they had first settled prior to moving to Malaya.

The vast majority of the Sikh commercial immigrants were salesmen, pedlars, petty entrepreneurs, traders, shopkeepers and suchlike. Merchants, financiers and contractors of substantial means were few, estimated to be less than a fifth of the total Sikh commercial movement into Malaya. But despite the great disparity in capital assets amongst the different categories of commercial immigrants, they nevertheless had at least two notable features in common. In the first place, like their potential security force countrymen, they were predominantly adult males, there being little family movement until the 1940s. Secondly, they usually came on their own or family resources, invariably with some capital, however small, and experience in the kind of trade they sought to practise. Accustomed to travel, and resourceful, aggressive and ambitious, the more successful amongst them, in conjunction with others like them from such classes as the professional groups, gradually assumed the rôle of a *petite bourgeoisie* among the Sikh community of Malaya.

It is impossible to know exactly how many Sikh commercial immigrants arrived in Malaya during the period of British rule, because no separate account was ever taken of such immigrants in India or Malaya. However, on the basis of interviews and the statistical data available for the other types of Indian immigrants, it is estimated that their numbers seldom exceeded a few hundred in any one year. With the exception of occasional fluctuations and the total cessation of the movement during the Japanese occupation, the annual movement of commercial immigrants into Malaya increased substantially from the early years of the present century. This was particularly so in the late 1930s and the early post-war years. Far more economically minded than their militia and caretaker countrymen, the commercial immigrants were influenced to a considerable extent not only by conditions in Malaya but also by those in India. For instance, there were big influxes of these immigrants, many of them refugees, in 1947–8, 1951 and 1953, following, respectively, the political unrest in the Indian subcontinent just before and after its partition into India and Pakistan, the trade boom generated by the war in Korea, and the Malayan Government's notification to restrict immigration in general with effect from 1 August

1953. The *Straits Times*, a Singapore daily, in discussing the increased movement of commercial immigrants in 1948, described the arrival of Northern Indians as 'an invasion': 'Hundreds of Sindhis have arrived in Singapore in the last few months . . . Besides Sindhis, Sikhs have also been arriving in large numbers, some of these Sikhs . . . [are from] Bangkok . . . Other Sikhs are from West Punjab . . .'[1] However, this movement was drastically reduced with the 1953 immigration restrictions and even more so with the 1959 amendment of them;[2] and thenceforth fresh immigration of commercial classes was limited almost entirely to a few highly paid executives and wealthy capitalists, and wives and children below twelve years of age of such people and of those already in Malaya.

Professional, clerical and other similar immigrants. Unlike their commercial countrymen, some of the Sikhs who came to Malaya to join a government department or private undertaking as technicians, priests, clerks, teachers or doctors were recruited in India and assisted to migrate by their employers. This was usually so in the case of the clerks for the Sikh firms and the temple priests. The government for its part too, from time to time obtained some of its Sikh staff either through secondment or recruitment in India. The former practice, however, virtually ceased with the emergence of an independent India. The latter practice continued. Only a few years ago the government, faced with an acute shortage of such people following the rapid expansion of services and the departure of many of its expatriate officers under the policy of Malayanizing the services, secured about one hundred Indian doctors and highly qualified secondary school teachers, including some Sikhs, on three- to five-year contracts. But generally most of these immigrants either came on their own or, as was more usual, were 'sent for', with the necessary provision of money, by relatives or friends already in Malaya. However, this practice also virtually ceased

[1] *Straits Times* (Singapore), 6 December 1948.
[2] This amendment required every new immigrant entering Malaya for the purpose of employment to furnish proof that he was 'entitled to a salary of not less than one thousand and two hundred dollars (Malayan) a month'. Furthermore, the government had to be satisfied that such an entry would not be prejudicial to any local interest. Even if an applicant fulfilled all the above conditions the government still reserved the right to refuse admission. Federation of Malaya, *Immigration Ordinance, 1959,* Kuala Lumpur, 1959, paras. 5 ff.; Singapore, *The Immigration (Amendment) Ordinance, 1959,* Singapore, 1959, paras. 3 ff.

with the implementation of the 1953 and 1959 immigration restrictions of the Malayan Government.

The few such Sikh immigrants were from approximately the same areas of the Punjab as their commercial brethren or those entering the country to fit themselves into the ranks of the military, the police, the prison-guards, and other such pursuits.

Sikh convicts. The first Sikh convicts to arrive in Malaya were two political prisoners, Nihal Singh (popularly known as Bhai Maharaj Singh) and Kharak Singh, who were sentenced to exile for life for their part in the Sikh wars against the British in the 1840s. They landed in the Straits Settlements in 1850.[1] Subsequently other classes of Sikh convicts also began to arrive in Malaya. This movement continued until 1860 when, following mounting agitation by the local European residents against the use of the Straits Settlements as dumping grounds for the 'concentrated scourings of the Indian jails', the Government of India agreed not to send any more Indian convicts to the Straits. Finally, following the British Government's decision in 1866 to transfer the Straits Settlements from India to Colonial Office control, the Indian authorities also agreed to remove all Indian convicts still under sentence to the Andamans: this was done on 8 May 1873.

Exactly how many Sikh convicts entered the Straits Settlements during their tenure as penal stations is unknown, no continuous record being maintained of the number of Sikh prisoners arriving in the Straits annually. However, on the basis of the available figures for some years, it would appear that there were seldom more than a few arrivals in any one year.

Some three-quarters of the Sikh convicts are estimated to have been those sentenced to transportation for life, the remainder being those serving terms ranging from seven to twenty-five years. The fate of the Sikhs set free at the end of their terms is unclear, but it is not impossible that the hundreds of discharged Indian convicts who, instead of returning to India, were settling down in the Straits Settlements included a few Sikhs too.[2]

[1] Secret consultations, nos. 46–57, 25 January 1850; nos. 27–8, 26 January 1850; nos. 89–94, 22 March 1850; nos. 27–8, 26 July 1850; Political consultations, nos. 225–7, 29 August 1856; nos. 17–20, 2 October 1857; nos. 296–8, 17 February 1860. *NAI: FPP.* Kirpal Singh and M. L. Ahluwalia, *Punjab's Pioneer Freedom Fighters*, Calcutta, 1963, pp. 42–54.   [2] Sandhu, pp. 632–49.

FLOW AND CHARACTERISTICS OF MIGRATION

One significant feature of the Sikh movement into Malaya during the period of British rule was the remarkably small volume of immigration in relation to the Sikh total numbers. Secondly, the movement was of an ephemeral character. Finally, it was essentially a movement of male adults.

The exact total of Sikhs arriving in Malaya between the 1850s and 1950s is unknown, but it was not very large. An estimate would place the number of Sikh immigrants at about one hundred thousand, or less than 5% of the total Sikh population of India in 1900. In this sense Malaya's case, however, was not unique because the number of Sikh immigrants into other countries was also small in terms of the total Sikh population. Indeed the same could be said of all types of Indian emigrants, both to Malaya and elsewhere. For instance, Davis has estimated that the number of Indians leaving India between 1834 and 1937 did not exceed thirty-one million, or less than 11% of the total population of the country in 1900.[1] This compares most unfavourably with the similar figures for, say, the British Isles and Italy, where the overseas departures during roughly the same period are estimated to represent more than 43% and 31% respectively of their total population in 1900.[2]

The most common explanation given in official publications for this comparative inertia amongst the Sikhs and other Indians was that it was the result of their 'innate love of home', which precluded their leaving on the same scale as the Europeans.[3] At the best this is only a half-truth and at the worst it is a gross fallacy.

In the first place, there was the traditional conservatism of an essentially agrarian society. The general mode of life, tied as it was to a farm and to centuries of isolated living in the customary and familiar environment of virtually one and the same village, appears to have endowed the Indian peasant with more than the usual reluctance to move associated with his kind. Moreover, inheritance laws in India called for an equal division of property, and so no group of sons was forced to leave by an inferior right to inherit. Social customs and

---

[1] K. Davis, *The Population of India and Pakistan*, Princeton, 1951, pp. 27–99.

[2] A. M. Carr-Saunders, *World Population*, Oxford, 1936, p. 49; Davis, p. 98.

[3] *Census of India, 1911*, Delhi, 1911–15, I, pt. I, p. 91; *Census of India, 1921*, Delhi, 1921–4, I, pt. I, pp. 62–83; *Census of India, 1931*, Delhi, 1932–7, XXI, pp. 33–4.

institutions militating strongly against emigration further reinforced this stay-at-home attitude: for instance, the joint-family system which, while granting security to its members, also imposed certain obligations that required their presence at home. Consequently, the peasant needed far stronger forces of propulsion and attraction than normal in many other societies. More important, a potential Sikh migrant making his own way, say, to South-east Asia or eastern Africa, in the pre-World War II period, needed to have about Rs. 40–60 in cash—the approximate cost of travel expenses between the Punjab and these areas. Few Sikh potential emigrants had ready cash even of this 'magnitude'. In most cases their only hope of getting it was to wait for some more fortunate (and sympathetic) relative or friend to make the trip, earn sufficient and send them the necessary money for the passage. Needless to say this was a slow process. Another possible avenue of raising the fare was to mortgage, that is if they still had it, the family plot of land to the local money-lender. This most Sikhs were reluctant to do: the reason for emigrating and enduring all the imaginary and real hazards of foreign travel was to make sufficient money either to buy a few acres of land or to redeem the already mortgaged family plot. In any case, those still in possession of their plots of land were not the ones most likely to migrate.[1]

Then, with the expansion of the armed forces in India, and the increasing emphasis by its government on recruiting these from the 'martial races' of the country, Sikhs found considerable employment opportunities in India itself.[2]

There was also a change for the worse in the British Indian Government's attitude towards Sikh emigration in general. Up to about the turn of the century it had not discouraged Sikh emigration. Indeed, it had itself recruited Sikhs for security duties on behalf of the Malayan and other governments. But about this time its attitude began to change. In the first place, it ceased to recruit for other governments. It also began to frown upon recruitment by other means too.[3] The reasons for this change in policy are unclear, but four possibilities may be suggested.

[1] *Report of the Punjab provincial banking committee, 1929*, Calcutta, 1930, I, pp. 129–45, 163–5, 377; *Report of the Royal Commission on agriculture in India*, London, 1927–8, VIII, pp. 622–78.
[2] *SSAR 1897*, p. 61; *SSAR 1915*, p. 1; *FMSAR 1918*, pp. 8–11. Curzon to Hamilton, 3 and 24 September 1902. *Hamilton Collection.*
[3] *SSAR 1897*, p. 61. Curzon to Hamilton, 24 September 1902. *Hamilton Collection.* B proceedings nos. 12–4, file no. 40/22. *NAI: EP*, May, 1922.

First, the Government needed Sikhs for its own armed forces and the comparatively better terms offered by the colonial and other governments were leading to a Sikh 'brawn drain'. Secondly, there was the danger that Sikh emigrants, once abroad, would enlist in foreign armies, which could one day conceivably be opposing their British counterparts.[1] Thirdly, many Sikh emigrants were a constant source of administrative trouble and political embarrassment to their home government. For example, a number of Sikh emigrants were entering or trying to enter 'white' countries, such as South Africa, Canada, the U.S.A. and Australia, which were far from anxious to have them. As British subjects they expected and demanded that the British Government should support their case on the same basis as it would have done, say, that of their United Kingdom fellow citizens.[2]

This position also applied to the extraterritorial agreements that Britain had with some countries, for instance Thailand and China. One of the reasons for these agreements was the protection of the interests of the British people there. The entry of substantial numbers of Indians, predominantly Sikhs and other Punjabis and Pathans, into such countries as Thailand, and their insistence on equal treatment, threatened to queer the pitch of extraterritorial privileges, for, although these were meant for the British people, this term was, at least in practice, apparently intended to mean whites only.[3]

These developments created a serious problem for the British Indian Government: political expediency, in the context of the Indian nationalist movement and the security of British interests in India, demanded that the myth of equal rights with the people of the United Kingdom, conferred by the status of British subjects, be maintained; but at the same time, especially in view of the ambivalent position of the Indian Government within the British Empire, the wishes and sentiments of white settlers and the foreign governments could not be lightly nor safely ignored. Maintenance of this double policy was becoming increasingly difficult.

[1] High Commissioner to Colonial Office, Secret, 12 August 1902; Colonial Office Minute no. 33335. *C.O. 273/291.*

[2] Confidential file no. 3, serial nos. 17–18. *NAI:EP*, May, 1913. *Report of Royal Commission on agriculture in India*, VIII, pp. 630–1. One of them, *The Sikh at home and abroad*, Vancouver, 1917, pp. 3 ff. 'Emigrant', *Indian emigration*, London, 1924, pp. 76–77.

[3] Lyall to Sanderson, 21 January 1891; Bayley to Sanderson, 4 March 1891. *F.O. 69/145.* Maurice de Bunsen to Salisbury, 17 August 1895. *F.O. 69/168.*

Finally, Sikh emigrants, particularly those in the United States, Canada and South-east Asia, were becoming an increasingly dangerous source of supply of arms, recruits and money to the Indian revolutionary movement, dedicated to the overthrowing of the Raj by force of arms.[1]

This dampening of enthusiasm for Sikh emigration as a whole on the part of the British Indian Government to some extent inhibited the movement of Sikhs out of India.[2] These factors in the general immobility of the Sikhs and other Indians do not exhaust the topic. They nevertheless serve to set up some of the main features and to show that the lack of large-scale emigration amongst the Sikhs and other Indians was not due, in any appreciable degree, to something mystic in their character or their 'innate love of home', as some officials would have us believe.

In the case of Malaya, there were other obstacles besides the factors operating against Sikh emigration from India in general. These included changes in the Malayan Government's employment policy and the competition from the other immigrant-receiving countries.

We have noted above that the policy of the Malayan Government *vis-à-vis* the employment of Sikh migrants in the government forces began to change from the 1920s, after which the emphasis was on limiting government employment to locally domiciled people, particularly Malays, as far as possible. Moreover, the Malay States Guides and the Straits Settlements Sikh Contingent—two of the principal government bodies employing Sikhs—were disbanded in 1919 and 1946 respectively. About the same time employment in the private sector also became increasingly difficult for new Sikh arrivals, partly as a result of the growing availability of local Malay-speaking candidates.

Then, too, Malaya had to compete with other equally, if not more, desirable areas of Sikh immigration. For example, if they were able to raise the necessary passage money, it was not Malaya but 'Miriken' (America) or 'Kaneida' (Canada)—lands of fabulous wealth in their

---

[1] Confidential A proceedings nos. 97–177, November 1914. *NAI: HDPP.* Director of Intelligence of the Admiralty War Staff to Colonial Office, 10 August 1915; Colonial Office Minute no. 38661. *C.O. 273/429.*

[2] Confidential A proceedings nos. 1–2. *NAI: EP*, November 1915. A proceedings nos. 8–22. *NAI: EP*, June 1917. Confidential B proceedings no. 27. *NAI: EP*, August, 1919. Confidential B proceedings no. 27. *NAI: EP*, November, 1919. B proceedings nos. 12–4, file no. 4 of 1922. *NAI: EP*, May 1922.

estimation—that was the first choice of many Sikh emigrants. The fascination of America and Canada persisted even after the discriminatory restrictions imposed on their entry and employment there by the American and Canadian Governments from about the beginning of the second decade of the present century, as witnessed by the 'Komagata Maru' incident when some 380 Sikh immigrants, denied entry into the country by Canadian law, tried to land—albeit unsuccessfully—at Vancouver in 1914.[1]

Needless to say, each one of the above developments in its own way would have tended to reduce the number of Sikhs arriving in Malaya. So much for these probabilities; now for the actual Sikh movement between India and Malaya. The great bulk of this movement was of an ephemeral character, with some one hundred thousand entering and about seventy-five thousand leaving the country between 1850 and 1959. Moreover, much of the net immigration appears to have been wiped out, mainly by disease, for the present-day Sikh population of Malaya is mostly local-born.

With the exception of occasional fluctuations and the total cessation of the movement during the Japanese occupation, the annual movement of Sikh immigrants into Malaya increased substantially from the last few years of the nineteenth century. This was particularly so in the years immediately preceding and following World War I and World War II respectively. It will be recalled, however, that the post-World War II revival of Sikh immigration was soon cut short by the inauguration in the 1950s of a stringently selective immigration policy by the Government of Malaya. Thenceforth fresh Sikh immigration virtually came to an end. The movement of Sikhs into Malaya after this was confined almost wholly to those going to India to visit relatives and homes and returning to their place of domicile or work in Malaya.

These changes in the current of Sikh immigration appear mainly to have been the result of fluctuations in employment opportunities and general economic conditions in Malaya, and of immigration restrictions, initially in India and subsequently in Malaya.

With the increased movement into Malaya from about the turn of the century the already exceptionally high percentages of the return movement also increased: in some years those returning home appear

---

[1] Confidential A proceedings nos. 97–177, November 1914 and nos. 1–13, March 1915. *NAI:HDPP.*

to have exceeded 80% of the total immigration. The large percentage of returnees among the Sikhs was chiefly due to the fact that most of the Sikhs migrating to Malaya came primarily as short-term entrants, 'to make a quick buck' and return home to their family hearth.

The total current of Sikh migration to Malaya was a summation of the several lesser currents generated by and distinguishing the different categories of migrants in and out of Malaya. The trends and characteristics of these lesser currents were by no means uniform, because dissimilar economic, social and other conditions affected the different sections in both India and Malaya. But one of the features common to all categories of Sikh migrants was the preponderance of males amongst them. The cumulative total of the main stream quite naturally reflects this pattern. Females seldom appear to have exceeded 20% of the total Sikh immigration till after the Japanese occupation. The predominantly male character of the Sikh immigration was mainly due to the fact that almost all the migrants appear to have been leaving the Punjab not initially in any permanent sense, but rather with the idea of returning to it as soon as possible. In the meantime the family could best remain in India where maintenance was simpler, safer and less costly.

EPILOGUE

We have seen that much of the Sikh movement to Malaya during the period of British rule was a short-term migration with an extremely high proportion of returns. The flow of migration was primarily affected by migration restrictions in India and Malaya and the state of employment opportunities prevailing in Malaya from time to time. Within this framework probably the peak of Sikh immigration was reached in the first decade or so of the present century, for since then migration restrictions in India and Malaya, coupled with the growth of a local supply of security personnel and strident nationalism, have led to a decline and finally a virtual cessation of fresh Sikh immigration into Malaya.

The present movement of Sikhs to and from Malaya is limited almost wholly to Sikhs of Malayan domicile. The factors which contributed to the decline of Sikh immigration show no real sign of slackening in the future. Thus there appears to be little likelihood of fresh Sikh immigration even in small numbers, let alone on the scale of the period prior to World War I. In the meantime, however, a number of the Sikh immigrants did bring their womenfolk and settle in Malaya. The ranks of such Sikhs steadily increased, especially after the Japanese occupation. About two-thirds of the Sikhs in the country today are estimated to be Malayan-born.

The exact number of Sikhs at present in Malaya is unknown, but it would amost certainly exceed 30,000, compared with the estimated 15,000 in 1947 and 10,000 in 1931. Initially concentrated in such services as the police and military forces, Sikh immigrants and their descendants are today found in almost every major sphere of the country's economy, being particularly prominent in the professional, mercantile and money-lending groups.

THE ENTREPÔT AT LABUAN
AND THE CHINESE

BY NICHOLAS TARLING

The British Government began to consider abandoning the Crown Colony of Labuan within a decade of its foundation in 1846. 'The settlement', wrote Herman Merivale at the Colonial Office, 'is nothing unless coal is found and worked.'[1] Without it, the revenue was deficient, since it derived from royalties on the coal, and from excise farms whose income a mining population would expand. A further trial was resolved upon, and in 1857 the colony was again put into the budget estimates, despite a display of impatience from another official, Frederick Elliott, who referred to 'unhealthy jungles like Labuan'.[2] 'If the coal could have been properly worked and conveniently shipped', he wrote in 1858, 'this Island would have been a valuable Station. As it has been demonstrated that neither one nor the other can be accomplished, it is a failure ...'[3] In 1860, however, a new company was formed to work the coal, with a capital of £100,000 and a 21-year lease.[4]

Certainly the attempts to secure Labuan coal had so far failed. The Eastern Archipelago Company which held the initial lease suffered from the quarrel between Henry Wise, its first managing director, and Sir James Brooke, Governor till 1852. By 1857 only advances from the colonial treasury by his successor, G. W. Edwardes, were keeping the mines in operation.[5] It was not merely a matter of capital, nor even of mismanagement: the mines had been damaged by surface working, which increased the already high risk of flooding. Indeed the later coal companies were also unsuccessful. In 1875 there were only some six hundred Chinese on the island,[6] and in 1879 the mines were closed, to remain so for some years. Another problem was the dubious quality of the coal, coupled with the expense of transporting it to a major

[1] Minute on Low to C.O., 26 June 1856. *C.O. 144/13*, Public Record Office.
[2] Minute on Edwardes to C.O., 8 December 1856. *C.O. 144/13.*
[3] Minute on St John to F.O., 11 January 1858. *C.O. 144/15.*
[4] Board of Trade to C.O., 25 June 1860. *C.O. 144/14.*
[5] Edwardes to C.O., 5 August, 14 September, 23 November 1857. *C.O. 144/14.*
[6] Low to C.O., 25 November 1875. *C.O. 144/45.*

commercial centre like Singapore or Hong Kong. Labuan itself had not become such a centre. But originally the colony was intended as an entrepôt and not merely as a mine.

In the 1840s, in a period of commercial difficulty, and in face of Dutch restrictions on British trade in Java, the Foreign Office had determined on a limited intervention in the Borneo region designed, in particular through the suppression of piracy, to create conditions under which commerce might expand. The major instruments of this policy were James Brooke, who had become Raja of Sarawak in 1841, and the Royal Navy. Brooke secured from the government of Brunei—where he sought to increase the influence of his friend the *bendahara*, Raja Muda Hassim—the offer of the island of Labuan as a naval base and a possible commercial entrepôt. Following the overthrow of Hassim in 1846, ships of the Royal Navy seized Brunei and, though the Sultan was subsequently restored, the operations of that year, as Hugh Low was to put it in 1875, 'laid the foundation of the quiet which now prevails along the coast'.[1] Subsequently Labuan was made a Crown Colony, Grey, the Colonial Secretary, seeing it 'as a station where Chinese merchants and various other persons of that sort might settle with advantage, with perhaps a small number of persons from commercial houses at Singapore'. He saw it too, as an entrepôt for Borneo.[2] The treaty made by Brooke in May 1847 with nearby Brunei declared that trade should be free (article 4), provided for a general import duty of one dollar per ton (article 5), and prohibited export duties (article 6). Another article, the ninth, gave British officers power to enter Brunei ports and rivers to seize vessels engaged in piracy and slave-dealing, and an Additional Article gave the Consul-General jurisdiction over all cases involving British subjects.

For Brooke and the Foreign Office, this treaty was a model for treating with neighbouring states, and in 1849 Brooke concluded a similar one with the Sultanate of Sulu. Spanish protests, and a naval expedition to Sulu, prevented its ratification, while the British Government, concerned to avoid extensive intervention in these regions and apprehensive over Radical attacks on some of Brooke's proceedings in Borneo, began to qualify its policy on the suppression of piracy. Brooke argued that there were

---

[1] Low to F.O., 6 July 1875, confidential. *F.O. 12/41*, Public Record Office; *C.O. 144/44*.
[2] Grey's replies, 14 June 1850. *Parliamentary Papers, House of Commons*, 1850, x (662), nos. 8266, 8270.

two courses open to the government—the independence of Sulu—the ratification of the treaty—the maintenance of Labuan—the increase of trade from that place and the determined and systematic suppression of Piracy on the one hand: or, on the other, the sacrifice of Sulu—the abandonment of Labuan and the discontinuance of our efforts to eradicate Piracy. There can be no object in retaining Labuan after the field for the extension of Commerce has been lost; and the possession of a coal mine would hardly warrant the expenses of the settlement . . .[1]

During the 1850s, however, Spanish claims were not challenged, and traders in that region could not therefore rely on British protection. But the Spaniards, though concerned at European intervention, did not succeed either in establishing an effective political control over the Sulu archipelago or in concentrating its commerce upon their port at Zamboanga in Mindanao. Indeed their attempts to do so perhaps encouraged traders to go to Labuan, as a later Governor, Henry Bulwer, suggested:

The settlement planted in remote waters and amidst a wild, neglected, and oftentimes oppressed people, in no long time acquired their confidence and commanded their respect by the power with which it was known to be associated and by the shelter and protection it afforded against oppression.
. . . a trade sprang up which has gradually extended itself along the north west and north coast as far as the northeast coast of Borneo, and the group of the Sulu islands, the people of the latter preferring the risks and delays of a long voyage in order to barter their pearls and tortoiseshell in the English settlement to the enforced market of the Philippine islands . . .[2]

In the 1870s, fearing a new phase of European intervention and the penetration of Islamic reformism, the Spaniards began to adopt more vigorous measures in the Sulu archipelago. These included a semi-blockade, enforced with considerable violence, which affected the resort of traders to Labuan. At the Colonial Office, this was a subject of concern: but its call for action rested also upon humanitarian grounds, and perhaps, too, upon the recognition that Britain had millions of Muslim subjects. Robert Meade referred to the 'events in this unhappy group of Islands and the spectacle afforded to orientals of a Christian Power murdering pillaging and burning with no adequate excuse—and that Power so weak that the slightest intimation from us that these proceedings must cease, would no doubt be attended to . . .'[3] Joining with

---

[1] Brooke to Addington, 26 January 1852. *F.O. 71/1*, Public Record Office.
[2] Bulwer to C.O., 12 November 1872. *C.O. 144/38*.
[3] Minute, 12 August, on F.O. to C.O., 4 August 1874. *C.O. 144/43*.

the German government, the British induced the Spaniards to assent to a *modus vivendi*, the tripartite protocol of 1877.[1]

Labuan's trade to north-east Borneo and to the Sulu archipelago was also affected at this time by Governor John Pope-Hennessy's attempts to increase the colony's revenue. 'Some of the Chinese merchants', he reported in 1868, 'have recently built schooner prahus in Labuan with which they carry on a good trade with Bengkoka in Marudu Bay', with the northeast coast, and with Palawan.[2] Traders also came to Labuan, bringing coastal produce, taking away opium and Chinese tobacco. 'It was upon the value in the Singapore market of the coast produce that the Labuan traders hoped to make their large profits and therefore in order to obtain it they were generally contented with small profits on the opium or Chinese tobacco, which they gave in exchange ...' But in 1868 Pope-Hennessy established a tobacco excise, and the farmer secured a virtual trade monopoly; and from 1870 the opium farmer also secured a virtual trade monopoly.[3] The prices rose, and the profits on the trade to the north fell.

These difficulties were compounded by the establishment of a rival trading station. In 1872 a German barque from Singapore went to Sulu and the northeast coast and disposed of opium and tobacco more cheaply than the Labuan traders. Willi Schück, the German agent, established a depôt at Sandakan the following year. Its position was also strengthened by its connection with Sulu, since from it 'a small steamer ... runs the Spanish blockade of that island ...'[3] That blockade, Pope-Hennessy's successor complained, stopped

all regular communication and in a great measure hinders the collection of the produce of which the trade thence is composed. What escapes the Spanish ships is all or mostly secured by the Sandakan traders and as they run the risks no one can grudge them the profits. Were it not for the small steamer with which they successfully run the blockade very little trade would either enter or leave Sulu. What did escape would probably find its way to Labuan, and to that extent our traders are losers both by the blockade and by the rival trading station ...[4]

1 For the negotiation of this protocol, see S. C. Hunter, *English, German, Spanish Relations in the Sulu Question, 1871–1877*, unpublished M.Sc. (Econ.) thesis, University of London, 1963.
2 Pope-Hennessy to C.O., 17 August 1868. *C.O. 144/27*.
3 Bulwer to Kimberley, 6 January 1874. *C.O. 144/42*.
4 Bulwer to Kimberley, 14 January 1874. *C.O. 144/42*.

Henry Bulwer had been well aware that Labuan's position in the trade of the region could be damaged by enterprising rivals, by the establishment of another entrepôt, by the introduction of steam.[1] The Colonial Office, though prepared to resist the Spanish blockade, did not think Britain 'would be justified, for the sake of fostering the trade of Labuan, in throwing any obstacles in the way of the developing of the trade and prosperity of other neighbouring places . . .'[2] In other words, once Spain had been restrained, it was the business of the Labuan traders to retain their share in regional commerce in the new circumstances if they could.

No great capital or enterprise had so far, however, been attracted to Labuan. The financial crisis of 1848 damped its early development, while the Europeans at Singapore were initially jealous of an entrepôt that might compete with a city 'dependent wholly upon its external resources, and drawing the ingredients of its prosperity from many and widely scattered sources . . .'[3] Labuan's early experiences gave it an insanitary reputation. Brooke himself referred to 'the decided unhealthiness' of the situation first chosen for the township of Victoria. 'Report, too, magnifies the evil a hundred-fold, and settlers and citizens will not adventure here . . .'[4] The Eastern Archipelago Company, while perhaps deterring others, did not engage in general traffic, as one acting Governor regretted.[5] No doubt the prospects were not particularly attractive. The fact remains that Labuan merchants disposed of too little capital even to make the most of the opportunities there were. In 1856 prahus from Sulu and north-east Borneo, laden with pearl and birds' nests, found their cargoes too valuable for the Labuan market.[6]

In subsequent years the position rather improved. The prospects in the Sulu and east coast trade 'induced one or two respectable and enterprising though small Chinese traders from Brunei and Singapore to come to Labuan . . .' One was Choa Mah Soo who, born in Malacca, 'had some years before come to Brunei in a very humble position'. In

[1] Bulwer to C.O., 12 November 1872. *C.O. 144/38.*
[2] C.O. to F.O., 2 October 1872. *C.O. 144/39.*
[3] Napier to C.O. 30 March 1849. *C.O. 144/3.*
[4] Brooke to Templer, 26 November 1848. J. C. Templer, ed., *The Private Letters of Sir James Brooke,* London, 1853, II, pp. 230–1.
[5] Scott to C.O., 25 March 1851. *C.O. 144/7.*
[6] Edwardes to C.O., 8 December 1856. *C.O. 144/13.*

1858 Edwardes induced him to open an establishment in Labuan and subsequently he moved to the island. Pope-Hennessy described him ten years later as the principal Chinese merchant, worth £4,000 a year, and his carriage and pair as 'far superior to those of the Governor'. He made him a J.P. Frederick Rogers at the Colonial Office thought it 'most important . . . to get the Chinese under an authority of this kind, i.e. Chinese in nationality but part of the regular Governmental system': it might anticipate 'the growth of those secret societies (at least called secret) which give us so much trouble and are really so formidable at Penang . . .'[1] In fact Choa Mah Soo was described by Bulwer as the head of one of the secret societies in Labuan. The other was headed by Lee Cheng Ho, a native of Malacca who had apparently come to Labuan in 1848, had later become the opium farmer, and was connected with a large Singapore Chinese firm. This firm in 1869 placed a sailing ship, the *Cadovius*, on the line to Labuan, which had come to serve as a collecting post for Singapore. The ship was the sole rival to the *Samson*, run by John Dill Ross, who, established in the Singapore-Labuan trade around 1860, was by 1871 worth about £25,000. To him many of the local merchants were indebted, and he was strongly entrenched.

These were the rival interests that Bulwer believed must unite if Labuan was to benefit from the introduction of steam. But the owners of the *Cadovius* would not co-operate, Ross did not wish to risk the change, and the Labuan merchants had no adequate resources of their own. All were dependent on Singapore houses or under obligations to Ross. Even Choa Mah Soo could raise only $5,000, and he died in March 1872. Finally Ross decided himself to make the experiment by chartering the steamer *Cleator*.[2] The result was the completion of his monopoly of the trade to Singapore.[3] The next Governor, H. T. Ussher, indeed believed that Ross did not wish for the success of the Labuan mines, for his 'prospects would be injured by the local competition which a large supply of coal would surely attract . . .'[4]

[1] Bulwer to C.O., 9 May 1874. *C.O. 144/42*. Pope-Hennessy to C.O., 18 September 1868, and minute thereon. *C.O. 144/28*.
[2] Bulwer to C.O., 27 November 1871. *C.O. 144/35*; 9 November 1872. *C.O. 144/38*; 9 May 1874. *C.O. 144/42*. On Lee Cheng Ho, see Pope-Hennessy to Stanley, 23 September 1868. *F.O. 12/34 A*.
[3] Bulwer to C.O., 4 July 1874. *C.O. 144/42*.
[4] Ussher to C.O., 6 May 1876. *C.O. 144/46*.

Ross had been alarmed over the Sandakan traders, and at Labuan had undertaken himself to set up in opposition. In fact he came to an agreement with them whereby the Sandakan trade should be trans-shipped at Labuan to Ross's steamer: 'no Labuan trader was to be allowed a passage or to send or receive goods by the Sandakan station ships ...'[1] In face of this combination one major attempt was made to retain the northern trade for Labuan. This was the formation in 1874 of the Victoria Trading Company, consisting of three Labuan Chinese merchants, including Lee Cheng Ho, two Chinese merchants residing at Brunei, Kim Swee and Lee Cheng Lan, and John Raw Howard, an Englishman who had been Surveyor-General of Labuan. The Company chartered the Sultan of Brunei's steamer, the *Sultana*. But the venture was brought to an early end when the Spaniards seized the *Sultana* at Sulu as a blockade-runner.[2]

The activities of the Sandakan station undoubtedly attracted the attention of the American adventurers who held the Sabah leases of 1865. In a sense, therefore, those activities initiated the series of steps by which the British North Borneo Company was set up. Again, the Colonial Office realized that they could not oppose a new settlement on the ground that it might destroy Labuan's commerce. 'Labuan no doubt would be extinguished by a great and prosperous Company established in its own neighbourhood—but Labuan hardly exists as it is, & cannot pretend to stop the way if any good scheme for developing Borneo is set on foot ...'[3] The establishment of the Company was also to affect Labuan's relations with the west coast. Upon that region its Governors had indeed increasingly concentrated their attention.

Labuan, of course, had a rôle in Brooke's initial plans for Brunei. He intended, he told his friend John Templer in 1844, 'to extirpate piracy ... I wish to correct the native character, to gain and hold an influence in Borneo Proper. To introduce gradually, a better system of government. To open the interior. To encourage the poorer natives. To remove the clogs on trade. To develop new sources of commerce ...'[4] The instruments of the policy were Hassim and his half-brother, Budrud'in. Labuan would exert an influence, and it would benefit by a

[1] Bulwer to C.O., 4 July 1874. *C.O. 144/42.*
[2] Treacher to F.O., 22 January 1877. *F.O. 71/10.* Low to F.O., 15 July 1875, and enclosures. *F.O. 71/6.*
[3] Minute by Herbert, 6 April, on Ussher to C.O., 15 March 1878. *C.O. 144/51.*
[4] Brooke to Templer, 31 December 1844. Templer, II, p. 42.

reform of the Brunei administration and a regularization of its taxation system. Many of the rivers were in the hands of nobles or *pengirans* either as hereditary estates or as appanages of office, and their population was subject to such demands as could be enforced. It was necessary

that the native governments be settled so as to afford protection to the poorer and producing classes ...

A post like Labuan, or Balambangan, would beyond doubt give an impetus to trade merely from the freedom from all restrictions, and the absence of all exactions which the natives would enjoy, and (Piracy being checked) countries which now lie fallow, would from its proximity be induced to bring their produce into market.

This limited expansion is however of little moment when compared with the beneficial results which must attend our exerting a beneficial influence over the Native Governments ...

Let our influence be of the mildest kind; let us, by support of the legitimate government, ameliorate the condition of the people by this influence. . . I have impressed upon the Raja Muda Hassim and Pengiran Budrud'in, that the readiest and most direct way of obtaining revenues from their various possessions will be by commuting all their demands for a stated yearly sum of money from each; and by this direct taxation, . . . the system of fraud and exaction would be abolished, the native mind tranquillised, and the legitimate government would become the protector rather than the oppressor of its dependencies . . .[1]

With the crisis of 1846, the scheme of indirect rule was defeated; and following the Radical attacks on Brooke not only the reform of Brunei, but even the suppression of piracy, became difficult to pursue. The development of Labuan was affected; indeed by 1853 Brooke felt that it 'ought to be abandoned, because the Government of England have not made, and will not make, the necessary exertions to develop its capabilities and to ensure its success . . .'[2] In the meantime his activities in Brunei had hinted at least at the exertions that were necessary. They were based above all on a wide interpretation of the treaty of 1847.

In 1848, the year the colony was set up, he had reported that the Brunei rajas were intriguing against it, disliking the idea of 'free trade' and fearing the escape of their slaves. He visited the capital, where the

<hr>

[1] Memorandum, 31 March 1845. H. Keppel, *The Expedition to Borneo of H.M.S. Dido*, second edition, London, 1846, II, pp. 189–208; *C.O. 144/1; F.O. 12/3; Board's Collections 102772*, p. 5, India Office Library; *Parliamentary Papers, House of Commons*, 1851, LVI, pt. I [1351], p. 12.
[2] Brooke to Templer, 22 July 1853. Templer, III, p. 263.

rajas promised to fulfil the treaty of 1847, and the Sultan proposed 'to address a circular letter to the inhabitants of the various rivers in his dominions, granting his permission for them to trade freely with the new settlement of Labuan . . .' Pengiran Mahkota, whom Brooke had displaced as governor of Sarawak, was now influential in Brunei.[1] The following year, the Lt-Governor of Labuan, William Napier, sent Hugh Low over to Brunei with a protest. Labourers from the Klias river had apparently been influenced to leave Labuan, and the murderers of a Labuan subject had fled to Klias. Mahkota went to Klias with Low, who invited the chiefs there to renew intercourse with Labuan.[2] In 1850 Brooke again referred to Brunei opposition inspired, he believed, mainly by concern over runaway slaves. The government there instigated crimes intended to prevent the advance of Labuan and 'hinder the poorer inhabitants of the coast from resorting to it'.[3] Early in 1851, Brooke urged the Sultan and *pengirans* to allow a free intercourse with Labuan. He also protested at the heavy taxation which had led the Muruts of the Limbang to revolt: 'the British Government must always regard with grave displeasure a system of misgovernment and oppression of the poorer classes, which not only obstructs but destroys the Commerce which the Government is bound by Treaty to encourage . . .'[4] Later that year the Brunei government denied attempting to prevent traders from coming to Labuan; but Spenser St John, Brooke's deputy, reported that it was ordering them 'to touch first at Brunei, which in practice amounts to a complete prohibition'.[5] Brooke was in England, and had told St John 'to interfere as little as possible with the direct acts of the Brunei Rajahs towards their own people; to maintain the spirit of the Treaty; and to remonstrate against gross instances of oppression, which are repugnant to humanity and an interference with trade . . .'[6]

Brooke ceased to be Governor of Labuan late in 1852, and after the Commission of Enquiry of 1853–4 his resignation was accepted as Commissioner and Consul-General to the Sultan and Independent

[1] Brooke, to C.O. 2 October 1848. *C.O. 144/2*. Brooke to F.O., 31 October 1848. *F.O. 12/6*.
[2] Napier to C.O., 17 November 1849, and enclosures. *F.O. 12/8*.
[3] Brooke to C.O., 9 January, 1 February 1850. *C.O. 144/4*. Brooke to F.O., 23 January 1850. *F.O. 12/8*.
[4] Brooke to F.O., 9 January 1851. *F.O. 12/9*.
[5] St John to F.O., 1 June 1851. *F.O. 12/9*.
[6] Brooke to F.O., 9 January 1851. *F.O. 12/9*.

Chiefs of Borneo. His deputy succeeded him merely as Consul-General. St John urged the Government, however, again to take up a decisive policy. As a result of some years of indecision, he argued, piracy had revived. Another result was the anarchy in the dependencies of Brunei: 'the Sultan's officers are murdered or plundered and traders are in an equal state of insecurity'. Thirdly, the Sultan had introduced 'into those districts that still practically acknowledge his sway' measures like 'the monopoly of pepper, the closing of certain valuable districts for the benefit of particular traders, the monopoly of salt, and the duty on iron . . .' The British Government, however, while concerned to suppress piracy, declined to intervene in Brunei. St John was simply instructed to call the attention of the Sultan's ministers to the infringement of the treaty of 1847.[1] But this gave him some scope.

In the latter part of 1856, St John took up residence at Brunei. Already he had begun to follow a policy of enforcing the treaty, particularly for the benefit of Chinese who might be British subjects in Labuan or elsewhere. Thus he remonstrated with the Brunei government over the obstruction of the Klias pepper trade carried on by Ting Wan and Company of Labuan, and against other commercial 'clogs' and monopolies. He also sought naval aid, offering the Sultan, for instance, the support of the steamer *Auckland*'s boats in capturing some Bajaus at Mengkabong who had murdered a Chinese trader from Labuan. In fact two of the boats were lost at the entrance to the river and the mission of the two *pengirans* the Sultan had sent failed.[2] St John believed that the Sultan was also trying to protect the 'aboriginal' tribes. 'Many of the evils of Brunei rule result from the poverty of the governing classes, and much amelioration may be expected should the revenues increase of which there is every prospect . . .'[3] In 1857 he felt less confident. The *pengirans* were anxious for quick riches and, despite St John's representations, fell back on oppression of the tribesmen. In their rivers, too, the Pengirans monopolized trade, encouraged by Mahkota, 'plausible, pleasant and clever'. The only remedy was 'constantly visiting the rivers of the coast, and inquiring on the spot into these evasions of treaty, and then remonstrating

---

[1] St John to F.O., 16 July 1855; reply, 30 November. *F.O. 12/22*.
[2] St John to F.O., 5 August, 11 October 1856. *F.O. 12/23*. Edwardes to C.O., 9 October 1856. *C.O. 144/13*.
[3] St John to F.O., 21 November 1856. *F.O. 12/23*.

strongly with each individual . . .¹' In 1858 he pointed out the way Brunei might be developed:

it is only necessary for Chinese or other capitalists to make advances to the natives, and as these capitalists will be British subjects assistance can be afforded them in securing their interests. Every noble will soon be aware of the great personal interest he has in encreasing the produce of his district, and directly he is convinced that he will not be allowed to interfere beyond his just rights, no further trouble will be given by these petty chiefs . . .²

Mahkota, presumably as the *shahbandar* of Brunei, rather curiously sat with St John in determining the Chinese cases.³

In mid-1856 Low had attributed some of the falling-off in Labuan's trade to the 'successful attempts' of Brunei *pengirans* 'at monopolizing the produce of the various rivers and exchanging it for British manufactures in the capital of Borneo, the trade of which town is now very considerable and owes its existence entirely to the protection afforded to British interests by the neighbourhood of this Colony'.⁴ Later in the year St John had sought to protect the interests of Labuan Chinese. But by 1857, Edwardes, who had succeeded Brooke in his capacity as Governor, was complaining of the effect of St John's policy on Labuan. In October, he visited Brunei himself, and told the Sultan of 'several cases of interference with the trade of Labuan from a restricted intercourse with the Coast of Borneo . . .' The Sultan had little power outside the capital:

the rivers are, with one or two exceptions, under the control of the Pengirans who, supported by the Consul-General's views of collecting the whole trade at Brunei, do not scruple to use every coercive measure to prevent all export to Labuan, where the natives would otherwise come, being secure from injustice and free from all exactions . . .⁵

Brooke had thought it advisable, when appointing St John to act as Consul-General in 1851, but appointing another to act as Governor of Labuan, that 'the Officer administering the Government of Labuan should always be invested with Consular Powers . . . for the encouragement of commerce in all cases which may arise affecting the

---

¹ St John to F.O., 10 April 1857. *F.O. 12/24.*
² St John to F.O., 8 January 1858. *F.O. 12/25.*
³ Treacher to C.O., 15 May 1879. *C.O. 144/52.*
⁴ Low to C.O., 26 June 1856. *C.O. 144/13.*
⁵ Edwardes to C.O., 23 October 1857. *C.O. 144/14.*

interests and well-being of this Island . . .'[1] Edwardes now felt that the *pengirans* were, as earlier reported, impeding intercourse with Labuan; but with St John as Consul-General, 'what influence the Governor of Labuan had with the Sultan to counteract these measures is subverted . . .'[2] And at the same time Labuan's coal mines were failing.

In 1859 St John went on leave, and Edwardes welcomed his idea that the Governor should act as Consul-General. For he was convinced

> that more frequent and closer connection with H.H. the Sultan of Brunei, and the Rajas of the Court, will materially ameliorate the relationship with the Governor of this Colony, and I hope secure a less restricted intercourse and commerce with the Natives of Borneo than has existed of late. A feeling of jealous distrust has, I regret to say, been too frequently exhibited . . .

The arrangement over the consulship should be made permanent, 'as the Colony has never ceased to feel the adverse influence of the present system . . .'[3] Earlier in the year he had brought before the Senior Naval Officer the murder on the Papar river of some twelve Chinese, employed as 'agents to collect trade for the merchants at Labuan who made advances to them . . .'[4] St John believed the Papar Dusuns had been provoked, and warned against considering all Chinese, British subjects or not, 'who leave our colony to settle on the coast as entitled to protection . . .'[5] Edwardes, as a later Governor put it, 'fought the battle of the Colony during the darkest days of its existence in a public-spirited and energetic manner',[6] and another of his measures was to encourage Choa Mah Soo to set up in Labuan. The latter's great success was as a sago trader with the Brunei coast.[7]

Following St John's departure, Edwardes's successors were Consul-General as well as Governor. Hugh Low, administering the government before Pope-Hennessy's arrival, intervened in a case which showed how the sago trade developed during the 1860s. The village of Mempakul had been founded at the mouth of the Klias, immediately opposite Labuan, and by 1867 about eighty Chinese lived there, having

1 Brooke to F.O., 9 January 1851. *F.O. 12/9.*
2 Edwardes to C.O., 29 April 1858. *C.O. 144/15.*
3 St John to F.O., 22 October 1859. *F.O. 12/26.* Edwardes to C.O., 24 December 1859 *C.O. 144/16.*
4 Edwardes to C.O., 19 August 1859; Admiralty to C.O., 30 December 1859. *C.O. 144/16.*
5 S. St John, *Life in the Forests of the Far East*, London, 1862, II, pp. 317–18.
6 Bulwer to Kimberley, 23 September 1873. *C.O. 144/41.*
7 Bulwer to Kimberley, 26 March 1872. *C.O. 144/36.*

come from Labuan. 'Several of the Labuan storekeepers have establishments there for the purposes of trade, and there are two or three sago manufactories also belonging to native merchants of this Colony ...'
A quarrel developed between the Chinese and the Bisayan inhabitants of the Padas Damit, and the Sultan's officer, despatched at Low's request, failed to prevent a Bisayan attack on Mempakul in which eighteen Chinese were killed.[1] Later in the year Low reported that two more Chinese had been murdered at Mempakul. The chief of the murderers was Pengiran Mumein, son of Mahkota, and he claimed to be carrying out a sentence passed on one of the Chinese by his secret society for fomenting differences with the Bisayas. Low found that the Sultan merely intended to fine the *pengiran* and the Padas chief.[2] On his arrival Pope-Hennessy received a deputation from Lee Cheng Ho and other merchants about the outrage at Klias.[3] Apparently on another occasion, the Chinese complained of the closure of the Klias by 'certain second-class Pengirans. . .' Pope-Hennessy went to Brunei, 'had an interview with the Sultan, and in a few days the trade was again free on the river...'[4]

In 1869 he was still more vigorous. Two Labuan merchants with establishments at Mempakul, Choa Mah Soo and Lim Tye Seng, complained that Pengiran Mumein had threatened to burn them down unless he was given certain 'presents'. Calling for naval aid, Pope-Hennessy proposed, under the Additional Article of the treaty of 1847, to capture the *pengiran* and try him in the consular court. The boats of H.M.S. *Elk* took Pope-Hennessy to Mempakul, and the *pengiran* was arrested. His trial was left at the Sultan's request to the Sultan's court, which banished him for life from Mempakul. Choa Mah Soo was made Capitan-China in Klias and Mempakul, Pope-Hennessy later claiming that he had 'induced the Sultan to restore the old system of "Capitans China" and to treat the Chinese well...'[5]

In 1871 Pope-Hennessy brought to book the Bisayan chief responsible for the murder of the eighteen Chinese in 1867, some of whom he pointed out, had been British subjects. Another murder had been

[1] Low to C.O., 22 August 1867. *C.O. 144/26.*
[2] Low to C.O., 25 October 1867. *C.O. 144/26.*
[3] Pope-Hennessy to C.O., 14 February 1868. *C.O. 144/27.*
[4] Pope-Hennessy to F.O., 23 April 1868. *C.O. 144/28.*
[5] Pope-Hennessy to C.O., 13 October 1869. *C.O. 144/30.* To F.O., 1 September 1869. F.O. *12/34B.* To Lord Knutsford, 25 May 1888. *C.O. 144/66.*

reported by Choa Mah Soo in 1870, that of Keng Wan, a native of the Straits Settlements, trading in sago at Menumbok at the mouth of the Klias. Pope-Hennessy went over in a gunboat, H.M.S. *Algerine*, and the *orang kaya* responsible gave himself up. The Sultan's court voted for the death penalty, an unprecedented punishment for murdering Chinese. 'I believe the development of Borneo depends solely on the Chinese,' Pope-Hennessy wrote. At the Colonial Office, Robert Herbert suggested that he should have 'abstained from mixing himself up with the affair', and that his interpretation of the Additional Article of the treaty of 1847 was strained. But the Foreign Office approved his proceedings.[1]

Pope-Hennessy, as Herbert observed, 'brought forward and utilized the intelligence and business ability of the Chinese who, being often far superior to many of the local Europeans, are generally in the East despised and thrust into the background . . .'[2] In fact, of course, this was not a novel policy. And his successor, Bulwer, also urged that the Navy should enable him occasionally 'to proceed to some of the principal trading stations on the coast for the purpose of establishing friendly relations with the people'.[3]

Again acting as Governor and Consul-General in 1875, Low reported the expansion of the sago trade in the Membakut: 'some of the Labuan merchants have, in order to secure larger and more regular supplies, sent Chinese to purchase the trees and work up the starch-bearing pith in the river, forwarding it to this place to be refined into the sago flour of commerce . . .' It was, he noted, 'the only branch of trade of any considerable importance which is left to Labuan now that the commerce with the Sulu islands and the coasts to the eastward has ceased'. But it was impeded by the levying of a poll-tax on the coolies, a payment per tree and an internal duty, with an export duty in addition, in place of the duty of one dollar per ton alone stipulated in the treaty of 1847. He urged the Sultan and the *pengirans*—'the sago producing rivers being the territorial possessions of different nobles'—to regulate and moderate their charges and so build up a revenue through which they might introduce a more orderly and reliable administration.[4]

---

[1] Pope-Hennessy to C.O., 10 August 1871, and minutes thereon. *C.O. 144/34.* To F.O., s.d.; reply, 4 December. *F.O. 12/37.*
[2] Minute, 30 October, on Pope-Hennessy to C.O., 3 August 1871. *C.O. 144/34.*
[3] Bulwer to Kimberley, 29 April 1872. *C.O. 144/36.*
Low to C.O., 9 March 1875. *C.O. 144/44.* To F.O., s.d. *F.O. 12/41.*

As the revenues of the Rajas will in all probability be chiefly derived from excise duties on the consumption of articles within their countries I think it would be good policy on their part to encourage by liberal terms the settlement and intercourse of Chinese with their Rivers. It is by means of the Chinese, under British direction, that the wealth of Johore and the Malay peninsula has been developed, and these are the people as useful settlers, in whom the hopes of the Rajas of Borneo ought chiefly to be placed.

He thus encouraged the rajas to levy a low and comprehensive duty. With the revenue gained, he hoped they might maintain an officer of rank, representing the government of Brunei, in each river. This was hard to arrange in most rivers, in view of their multiple 'ownership', but had been tried at Mempakul. 'The poverty of the Country presents the greatest obstacle to the introduction of settled Government, as the Revenue which could be raised from the greater number of rivers would scarcely meet the expenses necessary to be incurred . . .' There was no tin, as in Malaya. But much might be done from Labuan 'by judicious advice and kind encouragement . . .'[1] Here indeed were recommendations that recalled Brooke's policy before 1846, and an understanding attitude that suggests reasons for Low's later success as Resident in Perak.

The next Governor, Ussher, abandoned what he called the 'supine policy of late years followed by the Labuan Government . . .' During 1876, he pressed the Sultan to deal with 'Midin', 'alleged to be guilty of murder and robbery of British Chinese subjects' at Mengkabong. Under article 9 of the treaty of 1847, Ussher sent armed police to arrest him at Mempakul, but he was finally taken by the Sultan's officers in Brunei Town. The arrival of H.M.S. *Sheldrake*, acting Consul-General W. H. Treacher later reported, probably helped to induce the Sultan and *pengirans* to execute Midin, though he was, as Ussher put it, a member of 'a class which is the curse of Borneo, the river Pengirans and their relatives . . .' Treacher believed that trade would expand 'were a more vigorous and powerful form of government introduced in this part of Borneo, and in my opinion such a government could without much difficulty be established were Labuan in a position to bring to bear her influence through the Sultan upon the petty Pengirans . . .'[2] The

---

[1] Low to F.O., 26 April 1875, and enclosure. *C.O. 144/44, F.O. 12/41.* Low to F.O., 6 December 1875. *F.O. 12/41.*

[2] Ussher to F.O., 3 November 1876. *F.O. 12/43.* Treacher to F.O., 20 December 1876. *F.O. 12/43, C.O. 144/46.*

Colonial Office thought Ussher's policy 'if unsupported by a ship of war at frequent intervals may prove somewhat hazardous'.[1] The 'Perak war' in Malaya was no doubt much in mind. But Ussher denied there was 'the slightest probability of a repetition of such complications as resulted in the more powerful states of the Malay Peninsula'. Brunei was too divided, and the presence of Charles Brooke in Sarawak, 'and [that] of the semi-independent wild tribes about the capital, are very effectual checks to united action on the part of the decrepit and degenerate Malays in Brunei . . .' Indeed pressure by the Governor/Consul-General might 'strengthen the Sultan's hands . . .'[2] Lee Cheng Ho and others acknowledged Ussher's encouragement of their trade on the coast of Borneo.[3] This Treacher continued during 1878. He was anxious also to settle the government of the Padas region by inducing the Sultan to take it over from the chiefs and stop their 'undefined and increasing exactions . . .'[4]

This was again something constructive like Low's policy, and Treacher indeed praised the Sultan's governor of Mempakul, Pengiran Sabtu, as 'more enlightened than any other Brunei Chief . . .' Sabtu was the officer usually sent by the Sultan to inquire into complaints of ill treatment experienced by Labuan traders, and was another of Mahkota's sons.[5] The government of Mempakul was 'leased' to him—in other words he paid a fixed sum to the Sultan on account of its revenue—and on his death in 1880 Mempakul and Menumbok were leased to Lee Cheng Lan, a British subject of Chinese origin, 'long settled at Brunei as a trader and sago manufacturer . . .'[6] Ussher had indeed mentioned that, as a result of his policy, some of the Chinese proposed to 'rent or farm' various Brunei rivers.[7] The Mempakul lease was subsequently cancelled, and the then Governor/Consul-General, Peter Leys, told Lee Cheng Lan that 'he being a British subject could not be recognized as exercising such independent governing authority without the express sanction of Her Majesty'; and this was declined.[8] By this time, indeed, the North Borneo Company was

[1] C.O. to F.O., 7 February 1877. *F.O. 12/44.*
[2] Ussher to F.O., 11 April 1877. *F.O. 12/42.*
[3] Petition, 20 September, in Ussher to C.O., 21 September 1877. *C.O. 144/48.*
[4] Treacher to F.O., 3 December 1878. *F.O. 12/45.*
[5] Treacher to C.O., 15 May 1879. *C.O. 144/52.*
[6] Lees to F.O., 7 September 1850. *F.O. 12/50.*
[7] Ussher to C.O., 17 March 1877. *C.O. 144/48; F.O. 12/44.*
[8] Leys to F.O., 27 May 1883; reply, 14 November. *F.O. 12/59.*

established, and Charles Brooke had been allowed to extend up to the Baram river. What seemed in the case of Pengiran Sabtu to be a means of strengthening the Brunei Sultanate could be in other hands the means to its further break-up. The sort of lease offered was not apparently very different from those acquired by Brooke and the Company, and it might simply have led to the setting up of yet another more or less independent authority on the coast of Borneo.

Nevertheless this episode was a testimony to the strong position which a few Chinese had secured in the trade of Brunei, and perhaps affords evidence also of some of the ways in which it was threatened by the appearance of novel enterprises. Partly with British help, the Chinese had been put in a position to monopolize the trade of various rivers. This was the case, Treacher reported in 1884, with the sago trade of the Limbang and the Tutong as well as of Mempakul; while in Brunei dealing in many articles was 'farmed', or made a monopoly, as with opium, Java tobacco, Chinese tobacco, salt, curry stuff, tea, coconut oil, and gambier.[1] The Brunei government thus out-Hennessyed Hennessy, while in the rivers Chinese commercial monopoly was associated with the political power of Brunei *pengirans*.

There was little to distinguish Labuan and Brunei Chinese participation in these activities. Choa Mah Soo, though becoming established in Labuan, retained sago establishments at Brunei, as well as at Tutong and Mempakul.[2] Tan Kim Swee, the chief sago manufacturer at Brunei, made Capitan Temenggong by the Sultan, owned shops in Victoria, too.[3] The opium farmer of Labuan offered more because he held the farm under Sabtu on the opposite coast also.[4] Edwardes had perhaps hoped to create a separate Labuan interest, but his successors, Consul-General as well as Governor, had supported Chinese enterprise in general. But what St John had seen as a means of limiting the demands of the *pengirans* had to some extent become a means of profiting in association with them, of entrenching the Chinese in the system of farms and monopolies that Brooke counted among the 'clogs' on trade. The case of Pengiran Sabtu seems to have been an isolated one, and no general reorganization of Brunei government interposed.

[1] Treacher to Derby, 10 June 1884. *C.O. 144/58*.
[2] Bulwer to Kimberley, 26 March 1872. *C.O. 144/36*.
[3] Pope-Hennessy to C.O., 25 January 1870. *C.O. 144/31*.
[4] Treacher to C.O., 31 December 1876. *C.O. 144/46*. Treacher to C.O., 6 December 1878. *C.O. 144/50*.

The establishment and expansion of the North Borneo Company on the west coast meant for Labuan a loss of excise revenue. For the traders it meant problems of adaptation. Furthermore, the establishment of the Company also released the limits on the Brookes. As a result of the events of 1846–55, Sir James had concentrated on the expansion of Sarawak administration over neighbouring rivers. Edwardes, indeed, had hoped to win the sympathy of the Brunei *pengirans* by upholding their cause against Sarawak encroachments, for instance at the time of the blockade of Mukah in 1859.[1] This episode had, however, produced on the one hand, Edwardes's replacement and, on the other, Sarawak's extension to Bintulu. Further extension to the Baram was opposed by Pope-Hennessy and Bulwer partly in the interests of Labuan and Brunei traders.[2] But Charles Brooke maintained that Baram was bled to death by a Chinese farmer,[3] while, at the Colonial Office, it was felt that 'Labuan like everybody else will benefit by a settled instead of an unsettled state in her neighbourhood...'[4] The chances of the Labuan or Brunei traders' adapting to the circumstances were, however, reduced by Brooke's acquisition of Baram: 'it is probable that in future almost the whole of the Baram trade will find its way direct to Sarawak, to facilitate which result Raja Brooke has recently had built a light draught paddle-wheel steamer...'[5]

By 1886 Leys was speaking of Labuan in valedictory fashion: towards the Borneo coast 'she has albeit with a struggle, played well her part as a Pioneer, and introduced, directly and indirectly, civilization and British commerce along so many hundreds of miles of Bornean coast...'[6] Its administration was shortly after virtually made over to the British North Borneo Company, and a visitor was less sure that it had achieved its purpose:

Although it seems falling out of repair, still it looks like an old English place. When you get under the shadow of the wide-spreading trees, and see the lovely green turf around, the native houses standing back from the now

[1] N. Tarling, 'British Policy in the Malay Peninsula and Archipelago, 1824–71', *Journal of the Royal Asiatic Society Malayan Branch*, XXX, pt. 3, October 1957, pp. 207–8.
[2] Pope-Hennessy to Stanley, private, 30 September 1868. *F.O. 12/34 A*. Bulwer to C.O., 16 December 1874. *C.O. 144/43*. To F.O., s.d. *F.O. 12/42*.
[3] Brooke to Ussher, 20 February 1879. *F.O. 12/54*.
[4] Minute by Meade, 27 July, on F.O. to C.O., 18 July 1881. *C.O. 144/55*.
[5] Treacher to C.O., 14 August 1884. *C.O. 144/58*.
[6] Leys to C.O., 12 October 1886. *C.O. 144/61*.

grass-grown roadway, the brick-made gate-posts without any gates to support them, you begin to understand that this island was intended to show the Eastern Pacific England's greatness, but has never realized its dream . . .[1]

But while its greater hopes had always eluded Labuan, still its inhabitants were not altogether defeated by their permanent destruction. In the early years of the present century, the Company made strenuous efforts to open up Sabah's west coast. But 'the Labuan traders had a good year in 1901,' the Administrator reported. 'The existence of a progressive neighbour generally reacts on oneself unless indeed one is too lethargic to take advantage of his activity . . .'[2]

[1] W. J. Clutterbuck, *About Ceylon and Borneo*, London, 1891, pp. 200–1.
[2] Report by E. W. Birch, 1901, received 22 July 1902. *C.O. 144/76*.

CHINA AND SOUTH-EAST
ASIA 1402–1424

BY WANG GUNGWU

For the past few decades, a great deal of attention has been paid to the relations between China and other Asian countries and probably the most frequently discussed problem of China's traditional relations has been the maritime expeditions of Cheng Ho to the Indian Ocean during the years 1405–33. Because of the prominence of these expeditions, they have often been seen as the only significant feature of China's relations with South-east Asia during this period. This paper attempts to show that there are other important questions about China–South-east Asia relations which have been neglected in the past. It also attempts to compare China's policies towards South-east Asian countries with its activities elsewhere and to arrive at some assessment of the relative importance of South-east Asia to China. For this purpose, I have chosen the reign of Emperor Yung-lo (1402–24), the emperor who sent Cheng Ho to the Indian Ocean six times and who received missions from more foreign peoples and countries than any other emperor in China's history. And by South-east Asia, I refer to the area presently so called, covering both the mainland and island countries.

It should, however, be borne in mind that many levels of relationships between the Chinese and various groups of South-east Asians had been developing for several centuries before the Ming dynasty (1368–1644). By the T'ang dynasty (618–906), the Chinese were already aware of the great trading centres on the coasts of the Gulf of Siam and the Java Sea. Missions from these areas reached China throughout the seventh and eighth centuries and there were many more during the Northern Sung dynasty (960–1126), especially during the later half of the tenth and the first half of the eleventh centuries. After the fall of the Northern Sung, however, few missions were received until after the conquest of South China by the Mongols in 1276. The successors of the Mongols, the Chinese rulers of the Ming dynasty, therefore, inherited a long tradition of increasingly close relations with South-east

Asia. But, before the Ming dynasty, such relations were mainly un-official or semi-official and confined to the economic centres of South China. Imperial participation in either trade or even tribute was spasmodic and opportunistic. Rarely may initiatives be traced back to any of the Chinese rulers. The emperors received foreign missions and then responded or not more or less as they were advised to do by their ministers.

Thus for the long centuries from the early T'ang dynasty, it is not meaningful to discuss Chinese relations with South-east Asia during any single reign. Only the spectacular invasion of Java during Kubilai Khan's reign in 1292 and the missions sent out to the region by the first Ming emperor, Hung-wu (1368–98), can be identified with a particular emperor and neither of these can compare with the sustained efforts by Yung-lo to keep relations with South-east Asia open and meaningful. In fact, Yung-lo was the first Chinese emperor to allow so much attention to be paid to South-east Asia and to take initiatives which determined the pattern and nature of China's relations with the countries of the region. This is significant because imperial initiatives had long been crucial in China's foreign relations; therefore the absence of positive steps to encourage official relations with South-east Asia before Yung-lo marks out the importance of Yung-lo himself as the key figure in the extraordinary developments of the early fifteenth century. For this reason, there is special justification for the study of one reign in this essay. As will be shown later, China's involvement in South-east Asian history during the period 1402–24 was very much the product of the emperor's personal interest.

Confucian historians always emphasized the rôle and the archetype of the Emperor at the expense of the individuality and unorthodoxy of each emperor. Clear pictures of each emperor as a person, as an autocrat or a despot, or even as a weakling or a fun-loving playboy, are very rare. This was particularly true when the emperor was the founder of the dynasty and the historians had to write during the reigns of his descendants. Although Yung-lo was not the founder of the Ming dynasty, his usurpation of the throne in 1402 from his nephew (his elder brother's son) led to the founding of his own line of emperors. His temple-title of Ch'eng-tsu emphasized a degree of equality with his father as founder of the imperial house. Thus the official history of

Yung-lo is mainly one of an emperor of great personal courage, a skilled warrior and strategist, shrewd and stern and yet a lover of the common people. There are examples of his benevolence, of his wisdom and of his successful appointments of ministers and generals. But only between the dry and discreet lines can we also see his arbitrariness, his restlessness, his extravagance, his suspicious nature and his political manipulations.

His was a most eventful reign, yet the records succeed in making it less remarkable than it was. His was a strong and direct personal rule, yet it would be difficult to point to the events in which his feelings and calculations can be fully known. We are presented with long memorials and edicts but not shown how the decisions were made. We know that the senior ranks of the bureaucracy were weak after the wholesale executions, banishments and retirements following Yung-lo's usurpation, but we are not told how he made use of the scholar and eunuch cadres whom he personally selected to help him govern the empire. Most exasperating of all, we have several lists of the innumerable foreign missions to his court and notes on many decisions about what to do with them, but we are never given details about their significance to China, to the dynasty or to Yung-lo himself.

It is with this background in mind that we can understand why the events of his reign, especially the Cheng Ho expeditions, have been so puzzling for historians. All the speculation about what they mean has been handicapped by the lack of explicit statements of purpose. Hence the many attempts to explain China's policy towards South-east Asia and the Indian Ocean countries in terms of Yung-lo's whims and fancies, of Chinese expansionism and imperialism, and of the natural extension of the Chinese world order. None of these explanations is satisfactory in the light of the timing of the outward-looking policies and of the withdrawal into isolationism after 1435. It is significant that Yung-lo's policies towards the various Mongol confederations, towards Tibet, towards various kinds of Jurchen tribes, towards Korea and Japan, towards the numerous different peoples of South-western China, Burma and Laos and towards various countries in South-east Asia have never been seriously studied by those modern historians who have written on the spectacular voyages of Cheng Ho's fleets to the coast of East Africa. Instead, the scholars who have dramatized the expeditions have often likened them to the salt-water imperialism of the West in later centuries. Hence there is the tendency to interpret the Cheng Ho expeditions ominously in terms of past and future Chinese designs on South-east Asia.

But the facts do not support such an interpretation and it is necessary for us to be reminded that a more authentic picture of China's relations with South-east Asia in the fifteenth century is possible. This can be achieved by examining the reign of Yung-lo more closely. In this way, we can try to see what Yung-lo really intended, under what conditions he decided to send Cheng Ho and other missions to South-east Asia, what else he had to worry about, what he actually ordered to be done to South-east Asian countries, and, not least, how typical Yung-lo's decisions were in the context of Chinese history.

Let me now begin with the highlights of Yung-lo's reign.[1] He started inauspiciously. Having been passed over by his father in 1398, he had refused to accept his nephew's rule. Within months of his nephew's accession, he had resisted the new emperor's authority and started a civil war. For three years, from the middle of 1399 to the middle of 1402, the civil war dominated all events. Then on 17 July 1402, after defeating his nephew's army and capturing the capital of Nanking, he ascended the throne. Even this was inauspicious as his nephew's body could not be found and there was much speculation throughout the empire that his nephew, the legitimate emperor, had escaped and was in hiding. The repercussions of his accession were great. The court lost some of the ablest senior officials and no one could really be trusted apart from his loyal army officers and his eunuchs. The government had to be re-established afresh.

His first acts were to reaffirm his father's policies and argue that his nephew's advisers had perverted those policies. He promoted the remaining officials and appointed unknown new men to supervise them as well as the provinces and the border military regions. He hand-picked seven young scholars to be his private secretaries and, with their help, was able to rule directly and personally. He then rewarded all his loyal supporters with noble titles, promotions, grants and cash gifts.[2]

On 22 August, five weeks after his accession, he received his first mission, a mission from a minor chieftain in Yunnan in South-west

---

1 *Ming T'ai-tsung Shih-lu* (or *Yung-lo Shih-lu*), photolithographic edition, Taipei, 1962, hereafter abbreviated as *YLSL*, vols. 9 to 14; *Ming Shih* (hereafter *MS*), chuan 5–7; *Ming T'ung-chien* (Peking, 1959), chuan 14–18.
2 *YLSL*, chuan 9B–12A; *Ming T'ung-chien*, pp. 590–611.

China. A week later, as the last resistance to his rule was broken in Shantung province, he sent his first mission abroad. This was to Korea announcing his accession to the throne. Six days later, on 4 September, he sent a monk with his edict of accession to Tibet with rich gifts. About three weeks later, he sent missions to the various Mongol leaders.[1] Then on 3 October, he ordered envoys to go to the following countries:

An-nan (Annam)	Hsi-yang (South India)
Hsien-lo (Siam)	Liu-Chi'u (Ryukyu)
Chao-wa (Java)	Su-men-ta-la (Samudra)
Jih-pen (Japan)	Chan-ch'eng (Champa)

Significantly, he left policy instructions to the Ministry of Rites for these *overseas* countries, which read as follows:

During the reign of T'ai-tsu, when the various foreign countries sent missions, they were all treated with sincerity. Those who came with native produce to trade were all allowed to do so; and those who in ignorance broke the regulations were all generously pardoned—all this in order to care for those who came from afar. Now that the Four Seas are one family, it is the time to show no outer-separation (*shih wu-wai*). Let those missions which sincerely come with tribute do so freely. You should explain this to them so that they know my desire.[2]

The next day, Yung-lo had occasion again to lay down policy on places *overseas*. This was in connection with the return of Chinese envoys, presumably sent during his nephew's reign, from the 'south-east' islands who reported that Chinese adventurers were collaborating with the natives there in acts of piracy. Yung-lo immediately ordered a mission to go there again bearing the following edict:

To like good and dislike evil is common to men. To do evil because one is forced to does not mean one's nature [is bad]. In the past you have run away because you feared punishment or because of poverty and starvation to live among the various foreign peoples and have joined them in plunder in order to save your lives. The coastal defence forces not only were not helpful and sympathetic but also treated you harshly. Although you may regret [what you have done], you are unable to show this. We are very concerned about this.

We specially sent someone with our edict to inform you thus. Those foreigners should all return to their respective lands, those who wish to come to court should be generously treated and sent home. Those Chinese who

[1] *YLSL*, 10B, 5a–11, 8b.   [2] *YLSL*, 12A, 7a.

escaped to and hid in [foreign] lands are all pardoned for their past wrongs to enable them to return to their original occupations and become loyal subjects again. If they are still stubborn and refuse to reform because they rely on distance and remoteness, then we will order our forces to exterminate them. It will be too late to regret then.[1]

After this, Yung-lo sent envoys to the Urianghai in Western Manchuria, to various other Mongol tribes inviting trade, and to a place as far away as the Muslim state of Samarkand. In early 1403, there were further missions to Korea and Siam as well as Tibet and also, on 4 March, the first of the important missions to open 'diplomatic' relations with the most powerful of the Mongol confederations under the Tartar Great Khan.[2]

Thus within nine months of his accession, Yung-lo had sent successive missions to all the countries which mattered to his empire. But there was an important difference between those he sent to overland countries and those to countries overseas. The reasons for overland relations were obvious and no explanations were thought necessary. Only with the overseas missions were instructions given, instructions which emphasized the value of friendly trading relations and also touched upon the question of stopping Chinese participation in piratical activities. It is not surprising that, during the next few months, a comprehensive plan for grain transportation by sea to Peking and Manchuria was drawn up and there appeared many references to ship-building, to piracy between the Yangste mouth and Fukien, to the conditions of the Yangtse ports, to the establishment of a Bureau of Maritime Trade and even to a typhoon near Canton.[3]

I have discussed elsewhere the events leading to the major missions to Malacca and the Indian Ocean of 25 August, 1 October and 28 October 1403.[4] That they were follow-ups of the decisions of late 1402 and early 1403 pertaining to overseas relations there can be no doubt. What needs to be added here is that these events must be seen in the context of a series of decisions about foreign relations in all directions, both overland and overseas. The areas which preoccupied Yung-lo

---

1 *YLSL*, 12A, 9a–b. Cf. Hung-wu's policy of prohibiting private overseas travel, which Yung-lo re-affirmed on 30 July, 1402.

2 *MS*, 5, 8a–b; 6, 1a–b.

3 *YLSL*, chuan 18–27.

4 Wang Gungwu, 'The Opening of relations between China and Malacca, 1403–5', in *Malayan and Indonesian Studies*, ed. by J. Bastin and R. Roolvink, Oxford, 1964, pp. 87–104.

were the various Mongol centres, the western and southwestern frontier regions of Tibet, Yunnan, Burma, Laos and Annam, and the whole length of the southern and eastern coasts where trade and piracy had been hardly distinguishable since the Fang Kuo-chen rebellion in 1348.

This brings us now to the most important development which involved China with what we call South-east Asia during the early years of Yung-lo's reign. I refer to the Chinese embroilment in the affairs of Annam (now North Vietnam).[1] This had begun with Yung-lo's sending an envoy to Annam on 3 October 1402 and Annam's responding with its mission of 21 April 1403. Suspecting that a usurpation had taken place during the past four years when the Tran dynasty came to an end, the Ministry of Rites called for an investigation and on 5 May 1403 a special envoy was sent to report on the Annam succession.

On what basis was such an investigation called? What right did Yung-lo have to question the letter sent to him by the new ruler of Annam? We observe that the new ruler is recorded as calling himself Temporary Chief Administrator (*ch'uan-li kuo-shih*) and 'memorializing' (*chou*) that he be recognized with a grant of title (*feng-chueh*). Does this mean that Annam genuinely considered itself a vassal state (or submitted to China, *kuei-shun*) and accepted Yung-lo's right to investigate the legitimacy of its new ruler?

The investigation turned out to be a long-drawn affair in which Yung-lo first recognized the new king and then withdrew recognition when a surviving heir of the Tran royal house explained that a usurpation had taken place. He pardoned the usurper and sent back the rightful heir and, when the heir was murdered, was drawn into open conflict with Annam. For three years, from April 1403 to April 1406, elaborate negotiations about the succession took place. Then came the final break and preparations for war began in May. By November, the first campaign was fought in Annam. Twenty main crimes (*tsui*) against the usurper were listed as reasons for the campaign. It is interesting to list them here:

(1) For the murder of the Tran King who was properly recognized by China.

---

[1] *Ming Shih Chi-shih pen-mo*, chuan 22, also Li Cheng-fu, *Chün-hsien Shih-tai chih An-nan*, Shanghai, 1945, pp. 142–6, provide short accounts. Details are found in *YLSL*, chuan 20A–53.

(2) For the massacre of the Tran royal family.

(3) For not using the Chinese calendar and for using his own reign-period.

(4) For ill-treating the Annamese people (with details).

(5) For changing his own surname from Li to Hu.

(6) For deceiving the Ming emperor about his usurpation.

(7) For bluffing the Ming emperor and resisting Ming missions.

(8) For murdering the legitimate Tran heir.

(9) For taking Chinese tribal territory at Ning-yuan chou.

(10) For killing the tribal chief's son-in-law and related crimes.

(11) For disturbing the peace among other border tribes.

(12) For taking Ssu-ming fu territory and only returning parts of it.

(13) For inciting the tribes of Hsi-ping chou against the emperor.

(14) For invading Champa territory during the king's mourning period.

(15) For taking four *chou* from Champa and sacking them.

(16) For taking over one hundred elephants from Champa and some territory.

(17) For forcing Champa, a vassal (*fan-ch'en*) of China, to use Annam seals and ceremonial dress instead of Chinese ones.

(18) For invading Champa because it acknowledged China and not Annam.

(19) For capturing Chinese and Cham envoys at one of the Cham ports.

(20) For insulting China by sending a criminal as envoy.[1]

One of the key words in the declaration of war appears to be that Annam was *mi-mi*, or 'very closely related'. For it is in this context that the crimes can be seen as heinous. I have listed them fully to show what vassalage to China meant at the time. The first eight may be described as moral and ideological issues, the next five as security matters, the five after that as Annamese aggression against another vassal, and the final two as personal insults to the emperor.

There are thus four groups of issues which purported to have aroused Yung-lo to take strong action. From his point of view, it may well be argued that there was extreme provocation. From the point of view of the country attacked, the list reveals the extent to which Chinese claims to suzerainty denied freedom and independence of action to the

[1] *YLSL*, 60, 1b–4a.

vassal state. One may well ask whether any of the above 'crimes' could be applied to other countries in South-east Asia as well.

Before I try to answer that, let me return to what Yung-lo's policies were towards foreign countries in other parts of Asia. Annam was certainly one of the main problems of his reign. Even after the usurper was eliminated, national leaders emerged one after the other to challenge Chinese rule. This troubled Yung-lo throughout his reign and the country was finally abandoned in 1428 to the great Annamese national hero, Lê Loi, who had fought ten years for his country's independence. The other three major external matters were the Wako pirates raiding the Chinese coasts from the Liaotung and Shantung peninsulas down to the southern provinces of Fukien and Kwangtung; the naval expeditions of Cheng Ho to the Indian Ocean; and the revival of Mongol power to the north. Of these latter three, it is interesting to note that two had to do with the ocean and problems of coastal defence while only one was an overland problem. Yet it was soon clear to Yung-lo that, while Wako attacks were frequent and Cheng Ho's expeditions were expensive, his real problems were in the north. It was there that the empire was vulnerable and it was to the north that he went, in 1409–10 and 1413–16 and the third time in 1417, never to return to Nanking. With the new year in 1421, the capital was permanently shifted to Peking.[1]

Many historians have remarked on this move of capital and its consequences to Chinese interests in South-east Asia, including Annam. On the one hand, there were good historical and geographical reasons for the move northwards. On the other, in less deterministic terms, Yung-lo himself was much more at home at Peking where he had been a young man for over twenty years before his accession. At Nanking, he felt strange and helpless. At Peking, he was the soldier-emperor, leading his armies to the steppes, hunting Mongols, returning home victorious and satisfied each time. Also, it was manifest that, unlike most other people on China's borders, the Mongols would never accept the Chinese world order, however nicely that order was dressed. They recognized only force as the decider of events. It was necessary for Yung-lo to keep the Mongols fragmented, to divide them whenever a new leader appeared and, therefore, to stay close to the Great Wall alert and ready to fight, bribe and cajole them to weakness. From the time he

[1] *MS*, 6, 7b–10a; 6, 12a–7, 3b; 7, 4b and 7a.

became emperor, Yung-lo was personally on campaign in Mongolia for five months in 1410, for six months in 1414, for five months in 1422, four more months in 1423 and was on his fifth campaign in 1424 when he died at Yu-mu at the age of 64. On three of these campaigns, he won notable battles, but none of them was decisive.[1] The Mongols remained the chief enemy for another 180 years.

It is with this in mind that we can better picture the place of the sea in Yung-lo's calculations. The Wako pirates were not a serious threat to the empire, but their attacks disrupted the transportation of grain by sea from the Yangtse to the military centres in Peking and Manchuria. Curbing the Wako was therefore part of the defence of the northern land frontiers. Similarly, strengthening the fleet also became a function of imperial defence in the north. Although the fleets were so strong that most of the ships could be away on expedition without endangering the defence of the coasts, Cheng Ho's expeditions could be seen as an extension of the sea power needed for imperial security. But in so extending itself, that power became a major factor in China's relations with overseas countries.

In Yung-lo's lifetime, the major expeditions were sent six times, in 1405–7, 1407–9, 1409–11, 1413–15, 1417–19 and 1421–24 (Cheng Ho himself returned in 1422).[2] Their importance for relations with Southeast Asia cannot be doubted. This was indeed a considerable show of power at a time when there was no other power to stand up to it. Yet it is clear that the expeditions were not directed at South-east Asia. They were sent with diplomatic and trading functions to the countries further west and sailed through the Straits of Malacca to get there. Only three parts of the region were directly affected, the north coast ports of Java, the newly established entrepôt of Malacca and the kingdom of Samudra at the northern end of the island of Sumatra. Less directly, the Chinese-dominated port of Palembang survived awhile as an outpost of Chinese trading interests, but this was not vital to the Cheng Ho fleets, which found a safer haven at Malacca to await the change of monsoons.

I have shown elsewhere that the expeditions were important for

---

[1] *MS*, chuan 6 and 7.

[2] The 1407–9, 1409–11 expeditions have been carefully reconstructed by J. J. L. Duyvendak in *T'oung Pao*; see also Cheng Ho-sheng, *Cheng Ho I-shih Hui-pien*, Shanghai, 1948. Both authors have also examined the confused dates of the 1421–24 expedition in *YLSL*.

Chinese relations with Malacca and Samudra and that most of the missions from these two kingdoms to China were sent in response to Chinese initiatives. Twelve missions went from Malacca to China as compared with ten from China which passed through Malacca and one specifically to Malacca, and eleven went from Samudra as compared with eleven which stopped at Samudra; and, with only one exception, each of the Chinese missions was on its way to the Indian Ocean. On the other hand, there is almost no correlation between the great fleets and the twenty-one missions from Siam and the seventeen from Java during the same period. Both Cambodia and Champa had relations with China for different reasons and on a different basis. Further, there were distinct relationships between China and the kingdoms of the eastern archipelago, Brunei and Sulu, which had nothing to do with the Cheng Ho fleets or with Chinese interests on the Indo-Chinese mainland.[1]

The Cheng Ho fleets and their itineraries, therefore, provide us with the means to differentiate between the various segments of South-east Asia. Albeit important in their impact on the small South-east Asian countries, they were not directly involved in China's relations with South-east Asia and may serve to remind us that, to the Chinese at the time and to many others until recent times, there was no conception of South-east Asia as a whole. In short, it is necessary to see the various segments and their relations with China before we can arrive at a general picture of China's relations with the region.

I have already shown that the main foreign concerns of Yung-lo were those of Annam, the Wako, the Indian Ocean fleets and the Mongols. Of these, the Mongols were contemptuous of diplomacy and Annam was annexed as a Chinese province; neither could be used as models of international relations. Of the other two, however, they were directly and indirectly connected with China's relations with South-east Asia and we may usefully begin with them.

The Wako terrorized the whole China coast and must have caused anxiety to all ships bound for China which were not protected by armed fleets. They also involved Japan in Yung-lo's calculations and their activities resulted in one of the four Yung-lo inscriptions and poems to

---

[1] Wang Gungwu, 'Early Ming Relations with South-east Asia: a background essay', in *The Chinese World Order*, ed. by J. K. Fairbank, Cambridge, Mass., 1968, pp. 34–62.

foreign rulers. This is interesting because two other inscriptions and poems were sent to rulers in South-east Asia while the fourth was for the ruler of Cochin in South-west India. Although they were written at different times, two were closely linked with the Cheng Ho fleets, the one to Malacca and the later one to Cochin, and one was to Brunei at the south-eastern end of the known world. A comparison of the four show interesting similarities and differences.

The dates of the inscriptions and poems are as follows: (1) Malacca, 11 November 1405; (2) Japan, 6 February 1406; (3) Brunei, 20 December 1408; (4) Cochin, 28 December 1416. In the first, Yung-lo was doing something unprecedented in writing personally. It may be that he believed that Malacca was really seeking a special relationship and, as this was the first time it was happening with a country from outside the Chinese cultural orbit, he thought it appropriate to write the inscription himself. I have elsewhere suggested that this fitted in with Cheng Ho's plans to sail to the Indian Ocean and Yung-lo may have chosen to write to emphasize Malacca's strategic importance. But, most of all, he wrote because Malacca's ruler was the *first* to ask for Chinese support and protection. As he knew little about Malacca, he wrote mainly about his father's glorious reign and the harmony in the universe which had accompanied that reign. As this harmony had benefited everyone and everything that lived, he said he could understand Malacca's desire to want to be closely associated with the realm. He appeared to have been flattered and stressed the inclusiveness of Heaven's bounty through the principle of 'showing no outer-separation'. In the poem, he had little to add except to comment on the natural beauties of the tropics and the wisdom and discretion of the king of Malacca and he ended with a pious couplet about the hope of greater future prosperity for the Malacca ruler and his family and people for generations to come.[1]

For the second inscription and poem, it has been pointed out how flattering Yung-lo was to Minamoto Dogi, the 'king of Japan', because he had attacked the Wako pirates at Tsushima and Iki and destroyed them. After the preliminaries about Yung-lo's heritage from his great father whose virtues were unsurpassed and whose vision of impartiality was unmatched, he went on to flatter the Shogun Dogi personally:

[1] This is also briefly discussed in Wang, 'Opening of Relations', p. 101. See *YLSL, 38*, 46–56.

You, Minamoto Dogi, King of Japan . . . are gifted with sagacity and wisdom, and for generations [your family] has been in possession of this land, the most distinguished in the Eastern Sea, and one of which it may properly be said that it is possessed of rites and propriety. For this reason, you do not fail to send [representatives] to Our Court to present tribute, neither do you neglect the proper forms of offering congratulations and thanks. In this [the lands] of the four directions are alike, but you are most circumspect in your respect, most faithful in your sincerity, and most shining in your reliability. Throughout you have been unchanging in your attitude of fear of Heaven and service to your superior, your spirit of respect for yourself and protection of your country, and your determination to foster good and suppress evil. The more perfect you become, the less you pretend to perfection; the more thorough you are, the less you pretend to thoroughness . . .

Of late, there have been pirates hiding in Tsushima, Iki, and other small islands, who, from time to time, come out to commit robbery and pillage. You, Minamoto Dogi, have been able to follow Our order and annihilate them. You have stood firm as Our defence and are pledged to Our Court. Among the countries of the Eastern Sea, none is so wise as Japan.[1]

There was no flattery in the remaining two pieces. For Brunei, it was clearly the fact that its king was the *first* ruler actually to visit China to pay respect to the emperor which prompted Yung-lo to write. He made it clear that it was the late king's desire for a special relationship and the new king's persuasion which had caused him to write the imperial inscription. He was obviously himself flattered and made much of the 'no separating into inner and outer, all being seen as one whole' (*wu-chien nei-wai, chün-shih i-t'i*) principles of impartiality and no outer-separation which obliged him to respond.[2] The inscription reproduces a dialogue between the king and Yung-lo about whether Yung-lo should give Brunei the privilege of a personal inscription. He then persuades himself that the king's coming to the Chinese court with his wife and son, brothers and other relatives, as well as his ministers, was unique in history and therefore deserved an imperial response. Then he proceeded to write the poem praising the king for his sincerity and loyalty. The whole tone is condescending and perhaps reflects the suzerain-vassal relationship as Yung-lo saw it very accurately.[3]

As for the fourth, to the ruler of Cochin, written so many years

---

[1] Wang Yi-t'ung, *Official Relations between China and Japan*, Cambridge, Mass., 1953, p. 42. See *YLSL*, 40, 4b–6a.

[2] For a full discussion of the principles of impartiality and no outer-separation or inclusiveness, see Wang, 'Early Ming Relations', pp. 50–60.

[3] *YLSL*, 60, 4b–6b; *MS*, 325, 3a–5a.

later, it was more modest and also more formal. There was nothing in it that was directly meaningful to China's activities in the Indian Ocean. Apart from the flattering references to Yung-lo's great virtues purportedly made by the ruler of Cochin, there were no obvious reasons why Yung-lo should choose to write the inscription and poem for Cochin at that time. He had just returned to Nanking from Peking after a successful campaign in the north against the Mongols and was preparing to leave Nanking for the last time never to return. It reflected a loss of enthusiasm for all the numerous missions that continually waited for audiences and might have been a farewell gesture to the overseas connections as his mind turned north once and for all. The conventionality is unmistakable and there seems to have been no pretence that the piece was in any way significant.[1]

Yet there they were, four pieces nicely distributed from Japan to India with the eastern and western Malay archipelago in between. Was Cochin an afterthought to complete the image of his impartiality (the strong statements by him and his father about *i-shih t'ung-jen*) towards all foreign countries which accepted a place in his world order? How real was this impartiality, especially where the different segments of South-east Asia were concerned? Although both had sought China's protection, Yung-lo had a use for Malacca but was condescending to Brunei. Brunei's was the first royal visit to China (1408), but Malacca's king also paid homage three years later. And the only other identifiable South-east Asian country to make royal obeisance was Sulu; this was 'the visit of the three kings' in 1417.[2] All three, Brunei, Malacca and Sulu, were small and weak; they needed protection and a profitable trade and Yung-lo seemed willing to offer them what they wanted.

To what extent was this principle of impartiality a system of fragmentation, a means of preventing the consolidation of larger political units? Was Yung-lo deliberately ensuring that there would not be another Sri Vijaya or Majapahit empire, or, for that matter, a Siamese empire? Or was he really passively supporting those who needed help?

From the above, we can already see what South-east Asia looked like to the Chinese. There were the various tribal and political units of Burma and Laos which were overland vassals handled from Yunnan in South-western China. Their relationship resembled that of Annam, although Annam had, in addition, special historical and cultural

---

[1] *YLSL*, 103, 6b–7b; *MS*, 326, 3b–4b.   [2] *YLSL*, 192, 1a–4b.

connections with the Son of Heaven. There were the Brunei, Sulu and other kingdoms of the eastern archipelago. There were Malacca and Acheh astride the Straits of Malacca on the way to India. There were Champa, Cambodia and Siam each beyond Annam and yet landward and proximate. And there were Java and South-Central Sumatra, the seat of past empires, now weak and divided.

TABLE I *Chinese Missions, 1402–24*[1]

Champa	Cambodia	Siam	Malacca	Samudra	Java	Brunei
1403	1403	1402	*1403	*1402	*1402	1405
*1405 A	1405	1403 A	*1405	*1403	*1403	1408
1405 B	1414	1403 B	*1407	*1405	†(1404)	1411
1407 A		1403 C	*1409	*1407	*1405	
*1407 B		*1407	1412	*1409	*1407	
*1409		1408	*1413	*1413	1408	
1410		*1409	[1415]	[1415]	*1409	
1413 A		1413	*1417	*1417]	1410	
*1413 B		1416	[1420]	[1420]	1412	
1415		1419	*1421	*1421	*1413	
*1417		1420	1423	(1423)	*1417	
1418					*1421	
1421					(1423)	
(1423)						

* Cheng Ho missions and others which went on to the Indian Ocean.
† Mission to the 'East King' of Java.
(1423) A special mission to return the envoys to their countries.
[1415]/[1420] Hou Hsien missions to Bengala would have stopped at Malacca (possibly also Samudra).

But, looking at the international relations of the reign, this was a false view. For, apart from the units of Burma, Laos and Annam, there was a separate and distinct set of relationships which can be described as regional. From within South-east Asia, there was already a long history of political connections linking the eastern and western archipelago and also Java with the territories of Siam, Cambodia and Champa. Was Yung-lo not aware of this? Was he trying to manipulate these traditional connections and fashion a new order in which China must always be the arbiter in the region's affairs?

A closer examination of the relations between China and each of the

[1] Compiled mainly from *YLSL* and *MS*, but checked against several Ming sources and also the work of Duyvendak and Cheng Ho-sheng. See also Wang, 'Early Ming Relations', footnotes 63–70.

units in the region should give us some answers. This could be divided into two parts, the first studying the main Chinese missions to each unit and the other examining the missions to China from each of the units. First, the Chinese missions.

There is no need to elaborate further on the 'Western Ocean' missions, all of which stopped at Champa, Java, Malacca and Samudra. They probably also stopped at Palembang each time, though we read of at least two separate missions to Palembang, one in 1405 and one by Cheng Ho himself in 1424. There was no special significance in the stops at Champa (although Champa was warned in 1414 and 1415 not to help the Annamese and not to harass Cambodia) nor was it extraordinary for the expeditions to stop at Malacca and Samudra. The great fleets presumably stabilized the power structure to some extent, especially on both shores of the Malacca straits. The 1413–15 expedition was also a factor in the civil war in Samudra and may have been instrumental in ensuring that the friendly ruler remained on the throne.[1]

What was significant, however, were the trips to Siam in 1407 and 1409 and the stops at Java of each expedition. Where the Siamese were concerned, the 1407 expedition was a show of force to curb Siamese ambitions. There had been complaints from Champa about harassment of its envoys at Pahang and, even more serious, complaints from Samudra and Malacca that Siam had sent troops to confiscate Yung-lo's imperial seals. Evoking the principle of impartiality, Yung-lo sent a strong letter to the Siamese king which has been summarised as follows:

Champa, Samudra, Malacca and you all receive our recognition and stand equally [before us]. How can you use your superior strength to seize their envoys and take away their imperial seals? Heaven's way is clear in rewarding good and punishing evil. The warning example of Annam's Li father and son is before you. [It is best that] you immediately return Champa's envoys and Samudra's and Malacca's seals. From now on, mind your own affairs, be friendly to your neighbours and preserve your own lands, so that [you] may always enjoy the great peace.[2]

The warning was effective and the king apologized. All the same, Cheng Ho visited Siam again in 1409, and in 1413 also called on the riverine states of Kelantan and Pahang. Further, the later fleets passing

---

[1] Palembang, *YLSL*, 38, 4b and 267, 3a. Missions to Champa in 1414 and 1415, *YLSL*, 149, 2b; 170, 3b–4a. Cheng Ho and Samudra in 1413–15, *MS*, 325, 10b–11a; *YLSL*, 168, 1a–b. [2] *YLSL*, 72, 4b–5a.

2 Missions to China, 1402–24[1]

Siam	Malacca	Samudra	Java (West)	Brunei
1403	*1405	*1405	1403	1405
1404A	*1407	*1407	1404	1407
1404B	1409	1409	*1405	1408
1405A	*1411	1410	1406A	1410
1405B	1412	*1411	(1406B)	1412
1406A	1413	1412	(1406C)	1514
1406B	1414	*1415	*1407	1417
1407	*1415	(1416)	1408	1421
1408	(1416)	1418	1410	
1409A	1418	1419	1411	
1409B	*1419	1420	1413	
1411A	1420	*1421	1415	
1411B	*1421	*1422	*1416	
1413	*1423	*1423	1418	
1416	1424		1420	
1418A			1422A	
1418B			1422B	
1420				
1421A				
1421B				
1422				
1424				

...ns returning with 'Western Ocean' fleets, mainly Cheng Ho's.
... Missions recorded twice probably because of two audiences with emperor

...ates in italics were the years of royal missions (Malacca and Brunei only).

...mbodia, all the countries sent missions more or less regularly and ...untry, except possibly Brunei, seemed to have been put off in any ... by the fact that missions had always to go to Peking after 1416. ...e second point is that, apart from the Malacca and Samudra missions ...ich frequently came together, especially when they came with ...hinese fleets returning home, all other missions seem to have gone to China on their own and for their own reasons. The following account may be given of the relations of each of the states in the table above.

Champa. The same king ruled throughout Yung-lo's reign. On four occasions (1406, 1408, 1415, 1418), he sent different grandsons as envoys and each time there were banquets and special gifts. Two

[1] Like Table 1 (see note 1, p. 389), compiled mainly from YLSL and MS. Also see footnotes on p. 396, footnote 3 on p. 397, and footnotes on pp. 398, 399.

through Samudra and Malacca were reminders that Chinese protection was still to be reckoned with.

Similarly, the visits to Java had political consequences. Up to 1406, a civil war was being fought and Yung-lo's first missions distinguished clearly between the East King and the West King. In 1404, there was a separate mission to the East King. Some 170 members of this (or of the first Cheng Ho mission of 1405–06) had been killed by the West King. An apology was sent back with Cheng Ho in 1407 and Yung-lo ordered the following letter to be sent, presumably with Cheng Ho's 1407 fleet:

Situated in the Southern sea, you have normal tributary relations [with us]; envoys come and go and are met and sent off with due respect. We have appreciated this. Now, in your war with the East King, you have involved us and all our 170 odd envoys have been killed, indeed a serious crime. Furthermore, both you and the East King have received our noble titles; yet you through greed and anger have destroyed him and taken his lands without authority. Is there anything more contrary to Heaven's wishes than this? [We were] about to raise armies to punish [you], when your envoy A-lieh chia-en arrived to admit your guilt. We note that you regret your actions and have for the time being stopped our forces. But thinking upon the 170 men who were killed for no reason, how can we stop there? [You should] immediately send 60,000 ounces of gold to compensate for their lives and to redeem your crime, so that you may preserve your lands and people. Otherwise we cannot stop our armies from going to punish you. The warning example of Annam is there.[1]

Here again, as with Siam, the arrival of Cheng Ho's fleet was a clear evidence of the readiness to use force. In both cases, the example of Annam was quoted in the letters. Also, in both cases, the 'crimes' listed could be compared with some of those of Annam. Although there were no moral or ideological issues or security matters involved, both Siam's and Java's crimes were akin to the Annamese aggression against other vassals and the personal insults to the emperor.

Cheng Ho's expeditions were sent for many reasons: state trading, show of majesty and force, geographical knowledge, intelligence about the western nations, Yung-lo's anxiety about his nephew and so on. What is clear here is that they could also act as an expeditionary force 'to protect the weak and deter the greedy', even as an extension of the force used to conquer Annam. Did this mean that Yung-lo was

[1] YLSL, 71, 6a–b.

deliberately equating Siam and Java (and also other South-east Asian countries) with Annam and that he intended to extend vassalage over all countries with the same implications as those for Annam? There seems to be little doubt that, in the first flush of the Annam victory, this was what Yung-lo wanted to do.[1]

The years following, however, were to change that. As the Chinese armies struggled to maintain control in Annam, as the northern frontiers remained unsettled and as Cheng Ho's expedition kept the *status quo* in South-east Asia unchanged, Yung-lo turned away from further ambitions overseas to concentrate on the real threats to his empire. From the table of Chinese missions, I would date the change of emphasis from Cheng Ho's fourth expedition in 1413–5. Although two more expeditions were to be sent after this, there were no further missions to any other South-east Asian country except to Siam. The mission to Champa in 1418 was merely to accompany the Cham envoys home, there were no more missions to Cambodia or Brunei and, even in the case of Siam, the mission of 1416 was a ceremonial one on the occasion of the death of the king and that of 1420 was to accompany Siamese envoys home.[2] Only the 1419 mission to Siam was significant.

This was a reminder of the principle of impartiality enunciated in the warning of 1407, but to the new king who had succeeded his father in 1416. It warned the king not to interfere with Malacca's affairs as follows:

We respectfully received the Mandate of Heaven to become lord over Chinese and barbarian. We appreciate Heaven and Earth's love of life to be the basis of good government and look upon all with impartiality and do not discriminate between one and another. Your Majesty is able to respect Heaven and serve the great (*shih-ta*), perform your duty and send tribute. We have appreciated this for some time.

Recently, the King of Malacca, Iskandar Shah, succeeded to the throne and followed his father's wishes. He personally came with his wife and son to the court with tribute. His sincerity to serve the great (*shih-ta*) was no different from yours. But [we have] heard that your Majesty intends to use force on him without any cause. Now arms are evil instruments. When two armies are opposed, the clash must harm both sides. That is why the good do not like to resort to arms.

[1] It is interesting to note that the two letters were written within four weeks of each other (23 October to Java and 20 November to Siam) and the first 3½ months after the Annam victory report reached the court on 4 July 1407.

[2] Mission to Champa, *YLSL*, 204, 1b; Mission to Siam, *YLSL*, 176, 1a and 224, 2a.

Furthermore, the King officer of our court. If he ha reports to us. Not to do this court. It must be that this w officers have, in your name, u Your Majesty should consider this befriend your neighbour and never benefits—this never fails! Your Maj

This is much softer than the lette far cry from the fierce words in the appears that Yung-lo realized the Malacca was planned, only the exerci ruler. Cheng Ho had just returned from h earlier and the Malacca royal family had c may have been mainly to elicit from Yung Siamese king that Malacca was still a protec does not show that he was willing to comm defence and reflects his preoccupations with nor certainly be dated from his 1413–16 visit to Pe campaign against the Mongols in 1414.

To sum up, Chinese missions were particularly half of Yung-lo's reign, especially between 1403 and ten years, Yung-lo vigorously extended the boundari world order into South-east Asia and appreciated the p Siam and Java. There was the need to show majesty (*we status quo*. After 1413 until his death in 1424, Chines South-east Asia were less purposeful and Yung-lo himsel and aloof. It was as if he thought that, having shown hi majesty, it was enough to maintain his moral power (*te*). He be arbiter and protector, but there was no further need for involvement. The later expeditions of 1417–19 and 1421–4, th could more appropriately be called the voyages of the 'treasure The politics of South-east Asia were already less of their conc

What about the missions to China from the various South-east A countries during the same period? The following table briefly su marizes the material about them.

Two general points may be immediately made. With the exceptio

[1] *YLSL*, 217, 1a–b.

envoys were sent more than once, the same man in 1409, 1410 and 1412 and another in 1419 and 1420. In 1403–6, the missions complained of Annamese aggression and their complaints were incorporated as Annamese 'crimes' in Yung-lo's declaration of war in 1406. The 1406 mission was also told of the Annam campaign and asked to help the Chinese. After 1414, however, relations were strained. The Chinese had not returned the lands taken by the Annamese. Instead, they had incorporated them as imperial prefectures and counties. This led to Cham attacks and resistance for the next few years. Although tribute was regularly sent, the Chams secretly supported the Annamese guerillas fighting to throw off Chinese rule. Also in 1414, Champa was warned not to harass Cambodia's envoys.

There can be no doubt that Champa's missions were sent for political and diplomatic reasons. For the first time since the tenth century, it had a common land frontier with China. Of course, China was useful as the big neighbour who restrained the aggressive Annamese. But as a neighbour, China was too strong for comfort and the local officials too avaricious to be endured. In this context, the Chinese gifts of the gold-bordered silver seal of 1406 and gold seal of 1408 with 100 ounces of gold, 500 of silver and fine silks and brocades which only kings who personally went to court were given (for example, Malacca and Brunei rulers) were flattering but not too reassuring. Fortunately the Annamese tied the Chinese invaders down successfully and the tributary system was flexible enough for Champa to survive within it without losing too much of its freedom of action. Yung-lo was asked to attack Champa but he wisely refused to do so.[1]

Cambodia. Yung-lo sought out Cambodia almost from the start of his reign, in 1403, but soon found that it was not really relevant to his plans. Cambodia itself had withdrawn from the main scene of action about this time. The old king soon died, in 1405, and a Chinese mission formally installed the new king. Thereafter, there were no incidents apart from a complaint to Yung-lo about Champa interference with its envoys to China in 1414. Cambodia may well have been content with the *status quo* and the safety of a Pax Yung-lo. It suggests that a minimal connection with China was helpful if not necessary, but the protection

---

[1] Champa's missions to China, *YLSL*, 21, 12b; 33, 4b; 44, 4a; 58, 2b–3a; 70, 1b; 84, 1a; 95, 1a; 108, 1b; a31, 2a–b; 143, 1b; 163, 2b; 181, 1b; 194, 4a; 198, 2b; 210, 2a; 225, 1b; 250, 4a; 259, 2b; 273, 1a.

did not depend on how much Cambodia had done for China in return.[1]

Siam. Here was the continuation of a long association with the Chinese. The Siamese knew the Chinese well from centuries of close contact even before they arrived at the Menam valley. They understood the tributary system perfectly. They were far enough from China not to fear it and yet near enough to profit from a flourishing trade. They sought to expand their territory but were always heedful of Chinese warnings not to go too far. Although they were twice warned by Yung-lo, in 1407 and in 1419, they behaved as if they knew there was no danger from China as long as they accepted the emperor's admonition or advice. Their missions did not falter and no other Southeast Asian country sent as many, twenty-two in just over twenty-two years. They were not favoured by China in any way—the gifts to the king and the envoys were most ordinary and the number of banquets recorded was moderate (of the twelve banquets given, only two were specifically for the Siamese envoys).

Siam lost its old king in 1416 and the new king was installed by a special mission. None of the envoys were members of the royal family, although one person who was sent twice (once in 1405 and once in 1411) was of Chinese origin (a certain Tseng Shou-hsien). There were three others who were also each sent twice as chief envoy, but there seem to have been no special reasons why they were. On the whole, the period of Siamese-Chinese relations was incident-free and there would have been no trouble with China at all if Siam had really left Malacca alone. Siam had no threatening enemies at the time and did not need Chinese protection. The tributary system was useful because, although slightly restrictive, it provided Siam with close trading contacts with the Southern Chinese coasts. It is therefore not surprising that it sent two missions a year for seven of the years of Yung-lo's reign. It could count on Yung-lo not to refuse audience even if no vital interests to China were involved.[2]

Malacca and Samudra. It has been established that it was China which

---

[1] Cambodia's missions to China, *YLSL*, 34, 1a; 44, 4a; 56, 5a; 86, 3b; 148, 1b; 190, 2b; 210, 1a.

[2] Siam's missions to China, *YLSL*, 23, 5a; 34, 3a; 36, 6a; 44, 3a; 48, 1a; 52, 3b; 59, 3a; 72, 4b–5a; 86, 3b; 87, 3b; 97, 1b; 112, 2a; 121, 4b; 135, 1b; 176, 1a; 195, 1a; 200, 1b; 224, 2a; 236, 4a; 242, 1a; 250, 4a; 268, 1b.

opened relations with Malacca and that the relationship became profitable and necessary for both during Yung-lo's reign. Samudra had earlier connections with Yung-lo's father and sought nothing special with Yung-lo. As a stop on the way to India, it was, like Malacca, happy to take advantage of Chinese ships whenever they were available to take its missions back with them to China. In addition, the two sometimes travelled with Bengala ships to China and at least once Samudra and Malacca missions went to China on their own.

The significant difference between the two was that China gave Malacca a special status, while Samudra did not seem to need it. That special status was reinforced by four royal visits from Malacca to the Yung-lo emperor, by three Malaccan kings, Parameswara in 1411, Megat Iskandar Shah in 1414 and 1419 and Sri Maharaja in 1424.[1] How important these royal visits were may be seen when it is noted that the only other South-east Asian country to make such visits was Brunei. Yung-lo was flattered by the Brunei king, even more so by the three rulers of Malacca. In Malacca's case, he had good reason to show special favour as it was invaluable to the success of the Cheng Ho expedition, but this was not enough to overcome the principle of impartiality. For when Malacca asked him to remove Palembang from Javanese control, Yung-lo assured the Javanese in 1413 that he did not agree to this.[2]

Malacca not only had four royal missions. Three others were each headed by a member of the ruling family, a nephew in 1412 and another in 1413 (both of Parameswara) and an elder brother of Megat Iskandar Shah (a son of Parameswara) in 1418. Samudra, too, was ready to send members of the royal house. The ruler, Zainal Abidin, sent his son in 1415 with Cheng Ho to deliver a Samudra rebel and pretender for execution, and in both 1419 and 1420 he sent his younger brother, Mahmud Shah.[3] It should be noted that no royal envoys were ever sent by Siam, Java or Cambodia.

[1] Wang Gungwu, 'The first three rulers of Malacca', Annual Lecture, Malaysian Branch Royal Asiatic Society, 11 February 1968, shows that Chinese sources are reliable on this point and that R. O. Winstedt was wrong to think that the first ruler, Parameswara, ruled to about 1424. There was a second ruler who reigned from about 1414 to 1423. The lecture is published in the *Journal* of the Society, XLI, pt. I, 1968, pp. 11–22.

[2] *YLSL*, 143, 1 b.

[3] Malacca's missions to China, *YLSL*, 46, 2a–b; 71, 1a; 88, 2a; 117, 2a; 129, 3a; 142, 2b–3a; 155, 2b–3a; 169, 1b; 203, 1b; 216, 1a; 229, 1a; 233, 5a; 263, 2a; 269, 3b.

Samudra's missions to China, *YLSL*, 46, 2a–b; 71, 1a; 97, 4a (with Bengala); 111, 3b (with Bengala); 117, 2a; 132, 2a; 200, 1b; 218, 1b–2a; 229, 1a (with Malacca); 233, 5a; 250, 8b; 263, 2a.

Java. During the first four years of Yung-lo's reign, Java was divided and the West King was about to destroy the East King. Yung-lo sent three missions to the West and one to the East and by 1406 received four from the West and three from the East. Soon after, the West King was victorious. Immediately there arose, as mentioned earlier, the question of compensation for the killing of 170 members of Yung-lo's mission to the East King. The West King could only send 10,000 ounces of gold and Yung-lo decided to accept this partial payment and remit the remaining five-sixths of the sum demanded. By this time, Cheng Ho's fleets had been to the Java coasts and five more were to go before the end of Yung-lo's reign. Java, under the shadow of the great fleets, sent missions regularly to China thereafter. There were at least fifteen missions altogether in twenty-two years. Of these, one chief envoy was a Chinese by the name of Ch'en Wei-ta and three envoys headed two missions to China each. For each mission, Yung-lo's gifts for the king and for the envoys were unremarkable, possibly even less than normal, and after the first years, 1403–6, there were only two banquets given for eleven separate missions. Java was, of course, very weak at this time, and Yung-lo had no reason to show it any favour.[1]

Brunei. The first foreign ruler to visit Ming China from South-east Asia was Manara Kananai of Brunei. He went with his whole family in 1408 and was received by Yung-lo at Nanking. It was a splendid occasion during which Yung-lo gave rich gifts and grand feasts. Unfortunately the king died forty days after the audience. Yung-lo then recognized the son Shawang as king and gave his father a most elaborate official burial. The rituals connected with the funeral and interment and the watch on the grave were so unusual that they have been recorded in detail. Four years later, Shawang came again with his mother and family. Again there were fine banquets and splendid gifts. Since Brunei was not important to Yung-lo's maritime or political interests as Malacca was, it is interesting that so much was expended on the two royal visits. Indeed it confirms that Yung-lo believed in his universal authority and delighted in the bounty he had to offer. It is interesting

---

[1] Java's missions to China, *YLSL*, 23, 1b–2a; 34, 2b; 46, 3b; 49, 2a; 50, 3a–b; 57, 4b; 71, 6a–b; 86, 3a–b; 111, 1b; 115, 2a; 143, 1b; 162, 3b; 182, 1a; 200, 2b; 225, 1b; 249, 1a–b; 253, 1a.

to note that, as with other smaller countries, three of the five known Brunei envoys were relatives of king Shawang, one was an uncle and two were grand-uncles.[1]

It remains to draw a few conclusions about these missions in the light of Yung-lo's imperial policies as a whole as well as his personal interest in missions to and from South-east Asian countries.

I have suggested earlier that by examining the reign of Yung-lo closely, we can see what he intended and what he had to do and perhaps even how much was peculiar to Yung-lo and how much was the result of traditional Chinese policy. It has been shown that Yung-lo was an unusual Chinese emperor, a usurper through open conflict with his own nephew, an active border general for twenty-two years before his accession and an emperor who began by southern involvements but ended his reign fully committed to northern frontier affairs. A number of major decisions early in his reign affecting relations with South-east Asia were personally made by him. It was Yung-lo who ordered communications with the region and beyond to India in 1402–3; he ordered the investigations in 1403 about usurpation in Annam (indeed he was sensitive to the question of legitimacy!) which led to deep involvement and the twenty-two years' war; he ordered the strengthening of the fleet to fight off the Wako pirates, to defend the transportation of military supplies and ultimately to form the expeditions he sent across the Indian Ocean; he personally committed himself to the protection of Malacca, the recognition of the South-east Asian *status quo* and the splendid treatment afforded the Brunei and Malacca kings. In addition, he reaffirmed his father's policy of state trading through the tributary system and prohibition of private Chinese travel overseas; he asserted the newly defined ideology of impartiality and no-separation towards all countries big or small, old or new; he found satisfaction in meeting all foreign missions—the more numerous the more reassuring—and delighted in the exotic new countries contacted and the products they sent to him. He was proud of his cosmic power and majesty, but was also shrewd enough to know how much armed might was needed to sustain it.

For each of these decisions, Yung-lo could have done otherwise and

[1] Brunei's missions to China, *YLSL*, 48, 3a; 62, 5a; 82, 7b–8a; 108, 2b; 131, 2a; 161, 5a; 193, 2b; 237, 1b–2a.

ordered alternative courses of action. Only in the case of Annam could it be said that he was trapped into war and even here it was open to him to pull out in his lifetime. But his earlier decisions had set the framework for the rest of his reign. His relative success in South-east Asia and the 'Western Ocean' ensured that he stayed with the policies to the end. When the perspectives changed and events drew him to the north, especially after 1413, the shift in policies could only be seen through his move of the capital from Nanking to Peking. This was far from a merely symbolic move; it was a change in the centre of gravity that was the result of changes in Yung-lo's preoccupations and attitudes. Nor was it really a later decision, a change of mind on the part of Yung-lo himself. The roots of this move lay deep in his recent history, and in the five centuries of Khitan, Jurchen, Tangut and Mongol invasions along the long land frontiers in the north. In his own reign, it was immediately noticed in the news he received of Timur in Central Asia when he first came to the throne, in his own first attempts to seek out friendly relations with northern and north-western countries and, most of all, in his unsuccessful efforts to practise 'diplomacy' with the new Mongol confederations. His three attempts in 1402, his unsuccessful effort on 4 March 1403 and another on 2 August 1403 to deal with the Mongol Great Khan, and again another attempt in 1404 came to nothing. In 1409, Yung-lo went personally to Peking to conduct northern affairs. When the new Great Khan also rejected Yung-lo's overtures and the Chinese envoy was killed, Yung-lo abandoned diplomacy and sent General Ch'iu Fu to punish the Mongols. When Ch'iu Fu was defeated, Yung-lo decided to lead a new campaign himself. The fateful moment was 14 October 1409, the decision to go himself. From that time, it must have been obvious to Yung-lo what a big contrast the north was compared to all other regions. Elsewhere, and especially in South-east Asia, the tributary system was working perfectly. China was safe and his authority seemingly supreme. Only in the north was the issue open, the situation fluid and the frontiers really threatened. It is not surprising that by 1413 when he once again went north to campaign personally, he was convinced that the future lay in the north. South-east Asia, therefore, as with all other regions, could be handled 'loose rein' (*chi-mi*) and occasionally visited by the great fleets. The scene of the real action was the Sino-Mongol boundary over which no diplomacy, no world-order ideology, no bribes or persuasion would work. Nothing less than full attention could make China safe for his dynastic line. The relations with South-east Asia, therefore, were pleasant, even profitable, but not vital. He was the first emperor to pay so much attention to South-east Asia. For the best of reasons, as the events of his reign proved without doubt, he was also justified in being the last.

WRITINGS BY THE LATE
DR VICTOR PURCELL

This bibliography is designed to show Dr Purcell's more important works and the range of his literary activities rather than give full information on his writings.

I NOVELS, TRAVEL BOOKS, POETRY, AND ESSAYS

The Further Side of No Man's Land. London: Dent, 1929.

The Dog and the Don. Singapore: privately printed, 1938.

Chinese Evergreen, the story of a journey across south China. London: Michael Joseph, 1938.

Cadmus: The Poet and the World. Melbourne: Melbourne University Press, 1944.

The Sweeniad, signed Myra Buttle. Privately printed, 1957; London: Secker & Warburg, 1958.

Toynbee in Elysium, a fantasy in one act, signed Myra Buttle. London: Thomas Yoseloff, 1959.

The Bitches' Brew or the Plot against Bertrand Russell, signed Myra Buttle. London: C. A. Watts, 1960.

II SCHOLARLY WORKS ON THE FAR EAST AND SOUTH-EAST ASIA

A   *Books of which Dr Purcell was sole author*

Early Penang. Penang: Penang Gazette Press, 1928.

An Index to the Chinese Written Language on a New Non-radical System with Reference to the Dictionaries of Kanghsi and Giles. Singapore: Singapore Government Printing Office, 1929.

The Spirit of Chinese Poetry, an original essay. Singapore: Kelly and Walsh, 1929.

Problems of Chinese Education. London: Kegan Paul, Trench, Trübner and Co., 1936.

Malaya: Outline of a Colony. London: T. Nelson, 1946.

The Chinese in Malaya. London: Oxford University Press, 1948; Chinese translation, Singapore, 1950.

The Position of the Chinese in South-east Asia. 11th Conference, Institute of Pacific Relations, Lucknow, India, October 1950. New York: IPR, 1950.

The Chinese in South-east Asia. London: Oxford University Press, 1951; 2nd impression 1952; new edition 1964.

The Colonial Period in South-east Asia, a historical sketch (mimeograph). International Secretariat, Institute of Pacific Relations. New York: IPR, 1953.

Malaya: Communist or Free. London: Victor Gollancz, 1954.

The Chinese in Modern Malaya. Institute of Pacific Relations, 1954; Singapore: Donald Moore, 1956.

China. London: Ernest Benn (in the Nations of the Modern World series), 1962.

The Revolution in South-east Asia. London: Thames & Hudson (in the Great Revolutions series), 1962.

The Boxer Uprising, a background study. Cambridge: Cambridge University Press, 1963.

Malaysia. London: Thames and Hudson (in the New Nations and Peoples series), 1965.

Memoirs of a Malayan Official. London: Cassell, 1965.

South and East Asia since 1800. Cambridge: Cambridge University Press, 1965.

B   *Contributions to volumes published under other editorship*

'The Chinese in South-east Asia', in Lennox A. Mills, *The New World of South-east Asia*, 1949, pp. 273–87.

Sections on Siam, Indo-China, Malaya, Indonesia, and Philippines, in Arnold Toynbee, *Survey of World Affairs, 1939–1946*, 1952, pp. 76–104.

'Crowther or Helvetius', in *Yearbook of Education: Concepts of Excellence in Education*, 1961, pp. 12–17.

'Malayan Politics', in Saul Rose, *Politics in Southern Asia*, 1963, pp. 218–34.

Section on Asia in 'Economic Relations with Asia and Africa', in *The New Cambridge Modern History*, vol. VII, 1963, chapter XXIV, pp. 579–92.

C   *Pamphlets*

War Settlement in the Far East? London: National Peace Council, 1952.

The Rise of Modern China. London: Routledge & Kegan Paul, 1962.
The Possibilities of Peace in South East Asia. London: Bertrand
Russell Peace Foundation, 1964.

III UNPUBLISHED WORKS COMPLETED

Gibbon and the Far East, typescript 419 pp., quarto, 1952. 'Notes for
Gibbon readers who may be curious to know with regard to his
references to China, Central Asia (as it impinges on China), India,
and Ceylon, the general state of present knowledge. The notes make
no claim to meet the needs of specialist students of the area. The
introduction, however, has a weightier purpose. In it I aim to show
that the nexus of relationships between Rome, Gibbon and his age,
and the Far East in our age, has a vital contemporary significance.'
Asia Redux: The Far East Revisited, typescript 420 pp., quarto, date
of completion uncertain. 'Based on four month journey in 1956
through China and South-east Asia, set against a background of 35
years association with the region.' 14 chapters and epilogue. [China,
pp. 161–298.]
Willie, the Dragon and the Witch, a fairy-story for Willie by his
grandfather, 5–7 November 1964. 'Adventures of a small boy whose
ship returning from a holiday in Persia, strikes a mine in the
Mediterranean.'
What Russell Has Meant to Me, typescript 40 pp., quarto, 1964 (?).
China and Japan in the Twentieth Century, typescript 84 pp., quarto, 1964.
Aere Perennius, a fantasy by Myra Buttle, 1964.

IV WORKS IN PREPARATION OR CONTEMPLATED

History of the Chinese Revolution—planned to be in three volumes:
  Vol. I. From Boxer Protocol 1901 to death of Yuan Shih-k'ai (13
      chapters).
  Vol. II. From Yuan's death in 1916 to the Northern Expedition and
      purge of KMT in 1927.
  Vol. III. 1927 to Communist triumph 1949.
Modern China for use in secondary modern schools, Hamish Hamilton,
contract signed on 1 January 1965.

INDEX

Acapulco, 228, 237, 239
accountancy, 129–30, 132
Acheh and the Achinese, 268, 276, 278 ff.,
    290, 389
    trade agreement with, 280
    treaty (1659), 284
administration, problems of, 127–8, 129,
    131
Adrianszoon, Jacobus (1608), 203, 205
Afghanistan, 136, 140, 148
Africa, 329, 349, 350
    East, 377
Agricultural Department's Broadcasting
    Bureau, 181
agricultural equipment, 123–4, 130, 132,
    162
Agricultural Producers Co-operatives,
    88 ff., 103–4, 107 ff.
    collectivization of, 91–2, 98, 107, 109–
    11, 129, 133–4
    degree of 'spontaneity' in, 94–5
    in north China, 126; in south China,
    111–12, 114–15, 126
    increasing scale of, 116 ff.
    objections to, 91–2, 102, 104
    pace of development, 126
    potential support for, 96 ff., 132
    standards of communal responsibility
    in, 120–1
agriculture, 85 ff., 115
    emulation campaigns, 172, 180–1
    slogans, 181–2, 185
Ai Lao-mei (militia instructor), 70
Ai Sheng, 78
Aigun, treaty of (1858), 152
Aksai Chin plateau, 149–50, 152
Alatau range, 137
Albuquerque, 271
Alexandrian force-pumps, 209
Alma Ata, 151
America, see United States
Americans, 361
    in China, 34–5, 37
Amoy, 295, 310, 314, 315, 318
Amritsar, 344
Amu Darya, see Oxus
Amur river, 137, 138, 141, 142, 143, 148,
    151, 152
Andamans, 347

Anderson, John, 270, 290
Andes, 136
Anglo-Bhutanese war, 146
Anglo-Chinese Convention (1890), 149
Anglo-Dutch wars, 286
Anglo-Franco-Chinese Convention (1866)
    294, 314
Anglo-Nepalese war, 146
Anglo-Sikkimese war, 146
Anhwei, 63
Annam, 379, 381–3, 385, 388–9, 391–2,
    395, 399, 400
Anthoniszoon, Adrian (mathematician,
    1527–1607), 203–4
anti-imperialism, 23–56
    reinterpretation of, 53
Anti-Japanese League, 50
anti-Japanese movement, 55, 56
'Anti-Superstition Weeks', 324
Arab traders, 290
Aral Sea, 137, 141
Arandia, Governor, 239, 243
Argun river, 137, 142, 143
armillary sphere, 198
army
    and political work, 194–5
    education, 173, 184, 324
army slogans, see slogans
Arnold, Thomas, 328
Asahan, 290, 291, 292, 306
aspirin, 327
Assam Himalayas, 149
astigmatism, 210
astronomical instruments, 211–12
astronomy, 198, 206, 207–8, 211, 220
Australia, 253, 350
authoritarianism, 50, 56
Aziatische Kustenfahrte Gesellschaft, 316

bahar (measure of weight), 269
Bajaus (tribal people), 364
Balambangan, 262
Balkhash, Lake, 137, 141
Baltis (frontier people), 140
Baltistan, 140
bandits, 60, 63–4, 68–9, 81
    religious, 68–9, 70
Bandjarese, 306, 318
Bangeri, 269, 279, 287

INDEX

Bangka, 247, 270
Bangkok, 345, 346
bankruptcy, 261–2
banks, 162, 258
Baram river, 371, 372
barter, 256
Bataks (tribal people), 292, 293, 301
Batavia, see Jakarta
Batu Bara, 290
Bauer, Colonel, 53
Beeckman, Isaac (1618), 203, 215
Belawan, 315
Belgian treaty (1928), 50–1
Bell, Andrew, 326
Bengal, 243, 244, 267, 269, 275, 280
  Bay of, 267, 271
Bengalis, 344
Bengkalis, 292
Bengkoka, 358
beri-beri, 300
Bhai Maharaj Singh, see Nihal Singh
Bhutan, 139, 145, 146, 149
Big Swords (secret society), 75
bilenticular combination, 201, 202, 205
bilharzia, 172
Billiton, 247, 270
Bintulu, 372
Bisayas, 367
Bisson, T. A., 153
Black Banners (militia group), 70, 71–2
Black Tiger (militia group), 70–1
Board of Rites, see Ministry of Rites
Boon Keng (Penang merchant), 291
borders, see frontiers
Borel, Pierre (1591–1689), 204
Borel, William (1619), 215
Borneo, 247, 255, 267, 356 ff., 361, 370–1, 372
Borodin, Michael, 10, 26, 39
botany, 220
boundary definition, 146–7, 148
bourgeoisie, 29
Bourne, William (sixteenth century), 202
Bowrey, Thomas (1677), 274
Boxer Movement, 8, 19, 57 ff.
  'bogus', 73
  deities of, 82
  leaders of, 80
  magical powers, 58, 60, 72, 74, 81
  membership of, 80–1, 84
  origins of, 72 ff.
  Plum Flower, 82
  religious character of, 81

social composition, 81
  White, 73
boxing, 71–2, 73, 77, 78
Boyanese, 318, 337
boycotts, 23, 32, 35, 36, 41, 46
van Braam Houckgeest, A. E., 270
Brahmaputra, 138
Brewster, David (1817), 212
bribery, 243, 245, 312
bridges, 197
brigades, 116 ff., 121, 128, 185–6
Britain, see Great Britain
British, 314
  and frontier formation in Asia, 138–9, 147 ff.
  Nationalist offensive against, 34–5, 40
British Empire, 52, 350
British North Borneo Company, 361, 370–3
brokers, see coolie-brokers
bronze-founding, 208
Brooke, Charles, 370–1, 372
Brooke, Sir James, 355–6, 359, 361 ff., 369, 372
Brunei, 356, 359, 361 ff., 370–1, 385, 392
  missions to and from China, 389, 394, 397, 398–9
  treaty with, 356, 362–3, 364, 367–8, 369
  Yung-lo's inscription to, 386–7
Buddhism, 82, 139, 336
  Zen, 82
Buddhist monks, 214
Budrud'in, 361, 362
Bugis (tribal people), 270, 290, 337
Bulwer, Henry, 357, 359–60, 368, 372
Bureau of Astronomy, 206, 208
Bureau of Maritime Trade, 380
Burma, 135, 377, 381, 388–9
  education, 322–3
  trade, 228
Burma–Assam border, 139
burning-glass, 211
Buttle, Myra (pseudonym of Victor Purcell), 9

Cadovius (sailing ship), 360
cadres, 127, 131, 167, 181 ff., 188–9
  complaints against, 194
  lack of experience, 129–30
  lower-level, 191–3
Cambodia, 385, 389, 390, 392, 394–6, 397
Cambridge, 7–8
campaigns, see emulation campaigns

camphor, 267
Canada, 351–2
cannon, 198, 208
Canton, 31, 34, 35, 36, 180, 182, 315
  Communist rising in, 42
  Portuguese expelled from, 229
  trade, 228 ff., 232, 236, 244, 245, 276
Canton Strike Committee, 32
capital and capitalism, 162, 256–7, 292,
  346, 365
  concentration of, 116
  foreign, in China, 28, 36
central government, and Nationalist poli-
  tics, 51
Ceylon, 19, 271, 275
Chambers of Commerce, 32
Champa, 379, 382, 385
  missions to and from China, 389–90,
  392, 394–5
Ch'ang-ch'iang-hui, *see* Long Spears
Chang Chih-tung, 67
Chang Ju-mei's memorial to the throne
  (1898), 59, 60
Chao San-tuo (Boxer leader), 76
Chaochou, 311–12, 315
Charity schools, 327
Chekiang, 90, 93, 104, 112
chemistry, 220
Ch'en, Eugene, 37–8, 39–40
Ch'en Kung-po (Kuomintang politician),
  48
Ch'en Pu-lei (Chiang Kai-shek's aide), 45
Chenab river, 136
Cheng Ho, 375, 377–8, 383–5, 386, 389 ff.
  397–8
Ch'i Shu-fen, 29
Chia-ch'ing rising, 73
Chiang K'ai, 75–6
Chiang Kai-shek, 37–8, 42, 50–1, 52, 155,
  159, 160–1
Ch'aoliangts'e, 100, 127, 128
Ch'ien Chien (leader of the Ch'ing-men,
  1725), 66, 83
Chihli, 63–4, 75
children, gifted, *see* gifted children
China, 11–12, 324
  foreign pressures in, 23, 26, 28–9, 33
  foreign relations, 236, 375 ff.
  trade, 247 ff., 267, 270, 276, 380, 384
China (steamer), 315, 317
Chinese:
  in Labuan, 364–5
  in Malaya, 5, 11–12, 289, 336 ff.

  in Manila, 242–5
  murders of, 366–9
  and police work, 338–9
  in north Sumatra, 289 ff.
Chinese characters, 10
Chinese Evergreen (Purcell), 10
Chinese Government, and emigration,
  314–16, 317, 320
Chinese immigrants:
  in Malaya, 289
  in Manila, 242–4
  in north Sumatra, 289 ff.
Chinese Immigrants Ordinance (1877),
  295, 305
Chinese import-export firms, 257–8
The Chinese in South-East Asia (Purcell),
  289
Chinese labourers, 289, 292–3, 299, 301–2,
  304, 313, 318–19
  European employers of, 293, 307, 319–
  20
  recruitment of, 293 ff., 299, 306–7, 314,
  316
Chinese language, 330
Chinese literature, 330
Chinese merchants, 255–7, 260, 290–1
Chinese Protectorate, 296, 312–13
Ch'ing dynasty, 25, 53, 82
Ch'ing government, 65–6, 73, 76
Ch'ing-ch'a-men-chiao, *see* Clear Tea
  Sect
Ch'ing-men (secret society), 65 ff., 72,
  82–4
Ching Shih (History of Optick Glasses),
  199, 200
Chinhsiang, 66, 67
Ch'iu Fu (general), 400
Chiu-shih chen-pien (methods to save
  society), 67
Choa Mah Soo, 359–60, 366, 367–8, 371
Chou En-lai, 158
Christian missions, 58, 79
Christians and Christianity, 15–16, 59, 76,
  79, 82, 157, 244, 336
Chu'anchow, 229
Chu Hung-teng (Boxer leader), 73, 74–5,
  76, 77
Chu Te (Communist leader), 158–9, 161
circumpolar constellation template, 211
'city and commerce', 239 ff.
class structure and co-operativization,
  98 ff.
class struggle, 134, 155, 170, 176–7

Clear Tea Sect, 66
Cleator (steamer), 360
clocks, 209, 333
clockwork, 209
closed-door policy, 227–8
cloth, as exchange commodity, 273, 274, 277, 280
Co-Hong, 231, 234, 236
coal mines, 355–6, 360, 366
Cochin, 386, 387–8
coconut oil, 371
Codex Atlanticus, 218
coercion, 89, 92–4, 100, 124, 132
coffee planting, 255, 318
collective consciousness, 119–21, 134
collective farms, 133
collectivization, see Agricultural Producers Co-operatives, collectivization of
colonial movements, 34
colonialism, 14–15, 19
Comintern, 39, 44
commerce, see trade
commercial campaigns, 178
commercialism and agriculture, 115
Commission into 'the Condition of Chinese Labourers in the Colony' (1876), 297–8, 300, 305
Commission on Extraterritoriality, 35
Common Programme (1949), 188
common property, 121–2
communes, 91, 179, 180–1, 183, 184, 190
Communist Party of China, 23, 25, 30, 151, 165 ff.
    and agricultural reform, 85 ff., 93 ff., 97, 110 ff., 115, 120–1, 123, 125 ff., 131
    duties of members, 130–1
    increase in membership, 31, 128
    rural members of, 128
Communist Youth Corps, 31
Communists and Communism, 29, 32, 42, 43, 55, 86, 91, 97, 135, 153 ff.
    in Malaya, 11–12
compradores, 29
compromise, and Communist Party policy, 114, 115, 122, 125
Consoo Fund, 234
Constitution of the People's Republic of China, 188
contracts
    short-term agricultural, 116–17, 119
    with immigrants, 293, 296, 301, 306–7, 308, 312, 315, 318
convicts, 341, 347

'coolie-brokers', 290, 295, 298, 305–6, 308, 312–13, 315–17, 319–20
'coolie ordinance' (1880), 301, 304
co-operative agriculture, see Agricultural Producers Co-operatives
co-operatives, 162
copra, 292
Coromandel, 243, 267, 269, 271, 274, 280
cost accounting, 130
costs, agricultural, 103, 106
cotton, 104, 105, 133, 184
Cowan, W., 308
credit, 260–1, 265
credit co-operatives, 122, 124, 125
Cremer, J. T., 301, 214
Crimping Ordinance (1877), 305
crops, 120, 190
    double, 105
    rotation of, 103, 123
cross-talk performers, 182
Cuba, 184
cultivation, intensification of, 103, 106
Cultural Revolution, 91, 188
Curre, Michiel (1651), 281–2
customs dispute (1923), 27

Da jai, see Tachai
Dalai Lama, 149
dams, repair of, 105
Danes, trade, 232
Danish East India Company, 273
Dardic (language), 140
dark glasses, 213, 219
dark lantern, 218, 219
Dayaks, 329–30
De Vero Telescopii Inventore, cum Brevi Omnium Conspiciliorum Historia (Borel), 203
debt, imprisonment for, 261–2; see also immigrants, indebted
Dee, John (sixteenth century), 202
deities of the Boxer Movement, 82
Deli, 289, 290, 292, 293, 297, 306 ff., 314
    bad reputation of, 298 ff., 317, 319
    Chinese population in, 293
    firms, 314–15, 316
    labour conditions in, 311
    planters, 320
Deli, Sultan of, 300
Deli Maatschappij (Deli-Mij.), 292–3, 314
Deli Planters Union, 313, 316
Descartes, R., 204

developing countries
  and education, 321–2, 324, 327
  language problem in, 328–30
deviations, from Party policy, 129
Diaz, Emmanuel (Jesuit missionary, 1615), 205
dictatorship of the proletariat, 194–5
Digges, Leonard (maker of optical instruments, b. c. 1510), 201–2, 205
Digges, Thomas (c. 1571), 201
Dinding Island, 287
diplopia, 210
dividends, 123, 133
Doaba area, 341–2
Dogras, 140, 146
Doi Toshitsuru (1789–1848), 217
Drebbel, Cornelius (1619), 203, 217–18
drought, 110, 115
Dunstheimer, G. G. H., 57, 64
Dusuns, 366
Dutch, 203–4, 312
  blockade, 279, 280, 283, 285, 287
  in Malaya, 268 ff., 291
  in Sumatra, 291–2, 302
  'naval supremacy', 277
  trade, 232, 247, 276, 356
Dutch Company, see Netherlands East India Company
Dutch mails, 291
duties, see import and export duties
Dzungarian peoples, 141, 144

East India Companies, 236, 248, 269
Eastern Archipelago Company, 355, 359
economic difficulties, 167, 194
economic exploitation, 28–9
economic work and ideology, 191 ff.
education, 5–6, 184
  army, 173, 184, 328
  in co-operative agriculture, 114, 131
  primary, 321–2, 323
  secondary, 321–2, 323
  socialist, 176–7, 192
  university, 322–3
Edwardes, G. W., 355, 360, 365–6, 371, 372
Eight Diagrams sect, 58–9, 69 ff., 75, 81–4
E Kee (Swatow firm), 312
elections, 160
elephant trade, 275
Elliott, Frederick, 355
emigration, 310–11, 317
  China to Sumatra, 314–16, 317
  Indian, 348–9, 351

emulation campaigns, 121, 170 ff., 175, 178, 180, 183, 185, 189–92, 194
Engels, F., 186, 191
England, see Great Britain
English East India Company, 234, 235, 236, 269
English language, 329–31
English literary works, simplified versions of, 331–2
Eredia (1618), 268
erosion, 102
escapement, 209, 333
d'Este, Cardinal (c. 1586), 203
ethnic minorities, 151
Euclid, 209
eunuchs, 229, 377, 378
Europe
  optics, 210, 215, 219
  trade with Asia, 227, 229 ff., 232 ff., 242, 244–5, 247 ff., 291–2
European import-export firms, 251–5, 257 ff.
exclusionist policy, see closed-door policy
expeditions, see maritime expeditions
experimentalism, 115
experiments with multiplied images, 212
extortion, 233–5, 245, 312
extraterritoriality, 24, 47, 50, 53–4, 55, 350
eye-glasses, 213
eye inflammation, 213

Faber, John (1625), 215
factories, 184, 185–6, 190
family ties, and co-operative agriculture, 97–8
famine, 162
Fan Ching-t'ang (leader of militia group), 71
Fan Wen-lan, 73
Fang Kuo-chen rebellion, 381
The Far Eastern Crisis (Stimson), 159
farmers, 86–7, 89, 98, 102, 120, 126
  commercial, 112–13
  individual, 132
Federated Malay States, see Malaya
Fei-chien (flying swords), 74
'feria' system, 243
fertilizers, 102, 103, 105, 106, 113, 114, 123, 125
'feudal' princes, 143
filial piety, 83
Filipinos, 337

'fire-engines', 198, 209
firms, see import-export firms
first world war, 3–4, 352
fishing resources, 292
fishponds, 105, 122
five-year plan, 189, 191
flax, 105
flies, 182
floods, 115
  control of, 103
fodder crops, 105
foreign capital, in China, 28, 36
foreign policy, 179–80, 193
  Kuomintang, 42–3
  Nationalist, 23 ff., 33–5, 37, 41, 44,
    45 ff., 55 ff.
  and the principle of impartiality, 388,
    390, 392, 397, 399
foreign relations, 236, 375 ff.
foreign trade, see trade
foreigners, hostility to, 32, 37–8, 51, 82, 84
forestry, 122, 182
Formosa, see Taiwan
fortifications, against nomadic tribes, 142
Franklin, Benjamin, 213
free market, 102
free trade, 227, 246
French trade, 232
frontier peoples, 138–42, 147
frontier policy, 142, 147
frontiers, 135 ff.
  Burma–Assam, 139
  Russo-Manchurian, 150
  Russo-Mongol, 150
  Russo-Sinkiang, 150
  Sikkim–Tibet, 146, 149
  Sino-Indian, 135 ff.
  Sino-Pakistani, 136, 140
  Sino-Russian, 135 ff.
  treaties, 149–52
Fu-fei (turbaned bandits), 68–9, 72
Fukien, 183, 185, 242, 380, 383

Galileo, 203, 204–5
galleon trade, 238 ff., 245–6
gambier, 257, 371
Gambier and Pepper Society, see Pepper
  and Gambier Society
gambling dens, 317
gambling monopoly, 291, 304
Gan Eng Seng (Chinese employer), 296
Ganges, 136, 138
Gayos (tribal people), 301

'gazetteers', 197
Geneva, Musée d'Histoire des Sciences,
  207, 216
geometry, 198, 209–10
German import-export firms, 261, 314–15
German military mission (1928), 53
gifted children and education, 321–3
Giles, Lionel, 10
Gilgit region, 140
Glaisher, James (1855), 217
Goa, 278
gold, 267
Gorchakov Memorandum (1864), 147
government services, see Malayan govern-
  ment services
graduates, 341
Grain Tribute, 63, 65, 68, 83
  transportation by sea, 380, 384
Grand Canal, 64
gradualism, 107 ff., 126
  and the problems of increasing scale,
    116 ff.
graft, see bribery
gratuities, 230, 233, 245
Great Britain, 35–6, 37, 157, 325, 344
  education, 322, 326, 327
  trade in Asia, 247 ff., 287, 356
Great Khan, 380, 400
Great Leap Forward, 91, 166–7, 189
Green Banners, 231
Groot, J. J. M. de, 314–15
Gujerat, 267
Gujeratis, 271, 344
Gulab Singh, 146
gunpowder weapons, 198, 208
guns, 208
  spring-trap, 198
Gurkhas, 139–40, 145, 344

Hai-lok-hongs (dialect group), 310
Hainan, 318
Han Kung-Lien (clock-maker, 1086), 209
Hankow, 36, 42
Hankow Incident (1927), 39–40
harvests, 109, 114–15, 132
Hassim, Raja Muda, 356, 361, 362
Heavenly Clockwork (Needham), 333
Hebrew language, 331
Heilungkiang, 90, 129
Heng Thye ('coolie-hong'), 316–17
Herbert, Robert, 368
heretical sects, 57–8, 60, 74
Hermansen, Jan, 273

The High Tide of Socialism in the Chinese Countryside, 90–1
Himalayas, 135 ff., 145, 148 ff.
Hindu Kush, 148
Hinduism, 139, 140, 336
Historia Generalis ofte Algemeene Verhandeling der Bloedeloose Dierkens, 217
history, study of, 325–6, 328
Hitler Youth, 325
Hla Myint, 322
Ho Ying-ch'in (general), 46
Hoetnik (Chinese adviser in Medan), 317
Hokkiens (dialect group), 294
Holland, 203, 314; *see also* Dutch
Holt, R. D., 266
Honan, 63–4, 90, 99, 101, 110
Hong Kong, 35, 310, 312, 317, 318, 338, 340
    strike and boycott, 32
Hong system, 228, 231, 232 ff., 244–5
Hopei, 90, 94, 98–9, 105, 111, 175, 185
Hoppos (revenue commissioners), 230–2, 234
Howard, John Raw, 361
Howqua (Hong merchant), 234
Hsin i hsiang fa yao (Design for a New Armillary Clock), 209
Hsisohsiang, 112, 127
Hsü Kuang-ch'i (minister, 1629), 206, 209
Hu-ch'iu Shan, 199, 207
Hu Han-min, 53–4
Huai River, 104
Huang Fu (foreign minister, 1927), 44
Huang Lü-chuang (scholar, 1656 to *c.* 1684), 206, 207, 218
Huang San-t'ai, 82, 83
Huang T'ien-pa, 82
Huang-yai-chiao, *see* Yellow Rock
Hung-ch'üan-hui, *see* Red Fists
Hung-men (Hung League), 65–6, 81–2, 83, 84
Hung-wu (emperor, 1368–98), 376
Hunza (state), 145
Hupeh branch of the Kuomintang, 30
Hupeh General Trades' Union, 33, 40
hygiene, 182
hypermetriopa, 210

I Ho Ch'üan, 58, 59, 60, 66, 67
I-ho-t'uan, 58, 59, 81
I-ho-t'uan yen-chiu (Tai), 58
ideological campaign, 191–3, 194

Iki, 386–7
Ili river, 141, 142, 144, 145, 151
images, infinite regress of, 214
immigrants
    and extraterritorial privileges, 350
    Chinese, 242–4, 289 ff.
    indebted, 297–8, 303–4, 311
    Indian, 335–6
    Javanese, 318
    Sikh, 335 ff.
Immigrants' Bureau, 316, 319
immigration restrictions, 344, 345–6, 347, 352, 353
impartiality, principle of, 388, 390, 392, 397, 399
imperialism, 15, 19, 23, 161
    and the Kuomintang, 26 ff., 44
import and export duties, 291, 356
import-export firms, 251
    Chinese, 255, 257 ff., 266
    European, 251–5, 257 ff., 266; agencies of, 254–5; Chinese employees in, 255
    Indian, 259–60, 266
    Japanese, 251
    Russian, 251
incentives, 106, 116–17, 121, 123
income, 107 ff., 118
    distribution of, 107, 122, 129
    inequalities of, 117–18
    level of, 106
India, 139, 379, 386, 399
    British in, 138–9
    education, 341
    frontiers, 135–6
    independence of, 343, 346
    inheritance laws, 348
    trade, 228, 237, 242, 247–8, 277, 278, 280, 285, 286, 290; tin, 267, 268, 270–1, 273, 280
Indian Government
    and emigration, 342, 343; British, 349–50, 351, 353; Netherlands, 318
Indian import-export firms, 259–60
Indian National Army, 343
Indian nationalist movement, 350–1
Indian Ocean, 375, 377, 380, 383, 385, 386, 388, 389, 399
Indians
    immigrants, 335–6, 348, 350
    labourers, 318–19
    merchants, 271, 273 ff., 278–9
    rights as British subjects, 350

Indochina, 247, 256, 385
Indonesia, 247, 267, 272, 328
  Chinese centres in, 289
Indonesian labourers, 306
Indragiri, 280
Indus, 136, 140, 146
Indus–Tarim waterparting, 136, 137
industrial and agricultural development,
  interdependence of, 120–1
industrial campaigns, 171, 178, 182, 185–6
insecticides, 132
instruction, methods of, see teaching
  methods
insurance companies, 254, 258
intellectuals, 154
  and foreign policy, 24
interest, 124
international understanding, 324
inventions, 326
investments, 121–5, 130
Iran, 324
iritis, 213
iron, duty on, 364
irrigation, 103, 104, 106, 114, 122
Irtysh river, 137
Islam, 16, 140, 357
Israel, 331
Issyk-Kul, Lake, 137, 141
Italian treaty (1928), 50
Italy, 200, 202, 203

Jaffe, Philip, 153
Jakarta, 247, 269, 275, 276, 285, 286, 301
Jambi, 290
Jammu, 140, 146, 149
Jansen, Zacharias (1588 to c. 1631), 203,
  204–5
Japan and the Japanese, 24–5, 32, 35, 36,
  38, 39, 44, 52, 55, 56, 325, 377, 379,
  385 ff.
  in China, 25, 34, 37, 41, 50, 157
  trade, 228–9
  war against China, 45 ff., 86, 154–5,
  159 ff., 184
Japanese import-export firms, 251
Japanese occupation (1942–5), 11, 343,
  345, 352, 353, 354
Java, 247, 267, 276, 289, 301, 328, 356, 379,
  384, 392, 393, 397–8
  invasion of, 376
  missions to and from China, 385, 389–
  91, 397
Java Sea, 375

Javanese, 337
  immigrants, 318
  labourers, 289, 305, 306, 318–19
Jawi Pekans, 337–8
Jaxartes river, 137, 140
Jesuits, 206, 209, 212
Jhelum river, 136
Johore, 247, 254, 257, 296, 369
  joint-family system, 349
Judaism, 16
judges, 211, 213
Jullundur, 344
Jumna river, 136
juntas regulating trade, 238 ff., 242, 243,
  245
Jurchen tribes, 377, 400

K'aifeng, clock-tower at, 209
kaleidoscope, 212, 214
  technical term, 219
Kampar, 290
Kansu, 159
Karakoram range, 136, 138, 140, 141,
  144–5, 148, 149
Karl, E., 298, 305, 307
Kashgar, 140–1, 144
Kashgaria, 141, 145
Kashmir, 136, 140, 146, 149
Kazakh people, 141, 151
Kazakhstan, 137, 141
Kedah, 269, 271–2, 275, 278, 280, 283–4,
  285
  Sultan of, 279, 284, 286–7
Kelabits (tribal people), 330
Kelantan, 390
Kellogg Pact, 53
Keng Wan (trader, 1870), 368
Kepler, J., 202, 205, 217
Khabarovsk, 151
Kharak Singh, 347
Khaw Boo Aun (sugar magnate), 307
Khehs (dialect group), 310
khehtaus, 294–5, 297, 298, 305, 307, 316,
  317
Khitan invasions, 400
Khoo Thean Tek, see 'Tan Tek'
Khotan, 140
Kiangsi, 157, 160, 185
Kiangsi Soviet, 188
Kiangsu, 90, 100, 105, 110–11, 185
'kidnapping' of immigrants, 297, 299, 312,
  317
King, H. C., 203

Kircher, Athanasius (1646), 212, 217
Kirgiz (tribe), 141, 144
Kirgizya, 137
Kirin, 90, 107
Klias, 363, 364, 366–7
Kiukiang, 36
Kokand, 141
'Komagara Maru' incident, 352
Komo Zatsuwa (Miscellaneous Information about the Red-Haired People, i.e. Europeans, especially Dutch), 216
Kongkek, see Pepper and Gambier Society
kongsi system, 293
Korea, 377
  missions to, 379, 380
Korean war, 345
Koxinga (1661–83), 230
Ku Jui-hsiang (militia leader), 78
Ku Yen-wu, 91
Kuanhsien incident, 82
Kubilai Khan, 376
Kuldja, 144
Kulup (pirate), 287
K'unlun mountains, 140
K'unshan, 112–14, 127
Kuo Mo-jo, 29
Kuo T'ai-ch'i, 42
Kuomintang, 10, 23 ff., 160, 162
  anti-Communists in, 37–9
  breach with Soviet Union, 42
  conflict within, 48 ff., 54
  Fifth Plenum, 49, 51
  foreign policy, 43
  ideology, 52
  increase in membership, 30–1
Kuomintang Political Council, 40
Kuomintang's First National Congress, 26
Kuomintang's Second National Congress, 34
Kwangtung, 31, 90, 104, 111–12, 114, 130, 242, 383
  rebellion, 61
  Viceroy of, 315
Kweichow Province, 184

labour
  and agriculture, 103–5, 116
  contracts, see contracts
  indentured, 310–11, 313, 319
  recruitment, see recruitment of labourers
  regulations, 301–2
  remuneration, 116–18, 120, 293
  shortage of, 101, 104, 133, 305, 313
  specialization of, 116
  supply and demand, 309–10, 318
  surplus, 104
Labour Commission (1876), 294, 296, 302
Labour Commission (1890), 294, 296, 304, 308
Labuan, 254, 355 ff.
Labuan Bilik, 292
Ladakh, 135, 140, 146, 149, 152
Lahore, 344
Lama incarnations, 143, 145
Lancaster, Joseph, 326
land
  investment of, 123
  reclamation of, 105, 122
  redistribution of, 118
  reform, 85, 86, 87, 113, 118, 161–2
  'retained', 123–4, 134
  tax, 110
land use, specialization of, 116
landlords, 114, 118, 133, 154, 161–2
landowners, 110
Langkat, 289, 292, 299, 301, 306
languages
  and education, 327–8
  national, 328–9
  world, 328–9, 332
Lao Nai-hsüan, 58, 59, 72, 74, 77
Laos, 377, 381, 388–9
Lat Pau, 311
laukhehs (experienced migrants), 314, 316
Lauts and Haysloop, 314 ff.
law codes, 50, 53–4
Lê Loi (Annamese national hero, 1428), 383
leadership methods, 185, 194
Leagues of All Sectors of the People, 32
'Learn from Lei Feng' campaign, 170
'Learn from the Liberation Army' campaign, 173–5, 177, 191–2, 194
Lee Cheng Ho (trader, 1848), 360, 361, 367, 370
Lee Cheng Lan, 370
van Leeuwenhoek, 211
Lei Feng, 173, 176
Lena river, 137
Lenin, V. I., 186, 191
lenses, 200, 202, 205, 210–11, 215, 218
Leonardo da Vinci, 218
Leur, J. C. van, 272
Leys, Peter, 370, 372
Lhasa, 140, 145, 146
Li-men, 69, 70

Li Tzu-ch'eng (rebel leader), 208
Li Wen-ch'eng (rebel leader, 1813), 66, 67
Liang Chao-hsiang (leader of militia group), 71
Liaoning, 185
Liberation Army Daily, 186
Ligor, 270
Lim Tye Seng (Labuan merchant), 367
Limbang, 371
Lin Ch'ing (rebel leader, 1813), 66, 67
Lippershey, J., 200, 203–4, 205
Liu Hou-i (rebel, *c.* 1860), 72
Liu K'un-i, 67
Liu Kuo-t'ang (magistrate of Tientsin), 78
Liu Shao-ch'i, 166
Liu T'ang, 75
Lo-chaio, 66
Lo Ying, 197
Lock, Edward, 275
loess plains, 122
Long March, 157, 160
Long Spears (secret society), 69
Low, Hugh, 356, 363, 365, 366–7, 368–9, 370
Lü Chen-yü, 73
Ludhiana, 344
lumbering resources, 292
Luzon, 247

Ma Ching-san (leader of militia group), 71
Ma Chün (third-century engineer), 219
Ma Kuang-jen (leader of militia group), 71
Macao, 229, 278, 318
McMahon Line, 149–50, 152
Madras, 244
Magia Naturalis (della Porta), 202
Magia Universalis (Schott), 203
magic lantern, 215, 217–18
    technical term, 219
magical powers, 58, 60, 72, 73–4, 81
magnification, 204
magnifying glass, 210–11
Mahja area, 341
Mahmud Shah, 397
Mahkota (*pengiran*), 363, 364–5
Malabar, 243, 267
Malacca, 247, 249, 267 ff., 271, 274 ff., 277 ff., 384–5, 386, 389, 391, 392–3, 396, 399
    Captains, 268
    import-export firms in, 258
    missions to and from China, 380, 385, 390, 394, 396–7

Malacca, Straits of 384, 389, 390
Malacca Sultans, 267, 271
Malay language, 328, 329
Malay States Guides, 351
Malaya, 4 ff., 11–14, 19, 255 ff., 300–1, 313, 324, 328, 369, 370, 388
    British administration in, 336 ff.
    Chinese in, 5, 11–12, 289, 296, 302, 336 ff.
    education, 32
    employment opportunities in, 352, 353
    Indian residents in, 273–4
    plantations, 303, 318
    population, 336
    Sikh immigrants in, 335 ff.
    trade, 255, 291; tin, 267 ff., 303, 309, 313
Malayan Chinese Association, 13
Malayan Civil Service, 4–5
Malayan government
    employment policy, 343–4, 351
    immigration policy, 352
Malayan government services, 341–2, 344
Malays, 336, 337, 344, 351
Malwa area, 341
Manara Kananai (king of Brunei), 398
Manchu Court edicts, 76–7
Manchu Empire, 135
Manchu government, 67
Manchuria, 44, 104, 137, 142, 143, 154, 380, 384
Manchurian armies, 155
Manchus, 142, 144, 148, 149–50, 200, 230, 231
mandarinate, 233
Mandate of Heaven, 91
Manila
    Chinese settlers in, 242 ff.
    trade, 228, 237 ff.
Manileño Spaniards, *see* Spain and Spaniards
manures, *see* fertilizers
Mao Tse-tung, 86, 88, 90, 91–2, 104, 111, 115, 126, 152, 158–9, 160, 165–6, 179, 193
Maoist thought, 105–6, 134, 171, 173, 175–6, 179, 182, 188, 191 ff.
'Maphilindo' region, 328
Marco Polo Bridge incident, 154
maritime expeditions, 375, 377–8, 383–5, 390, 392, 393, 397, 399
    reasons for, 391–3
Martini, Martin (Jesuit, 1654), 218

Marudu Bay, 358
Marwaris, 344
Marx, Karl, 186, 191
Marxism, 28, 135
mass consciousness, 166–7
mass mobilization, 179, 191
mass movements
   Chang Kai-shek's attitude to, 51, 54
   Communist Party's attitude to, 165
   revival of, 48, 49
   suspension of, 42
mathematics, 220, 328
May Fourth Movement (c. 1919–23), 23–4, 56
May Thirtieth Movement (1925), 30–1, 34
Meade, Robert, 357
Medan, 315, 317
medicine, 220
meetings, 172, 182
Megat Iskandar Shah (king of Malacca), 397
Membakut, 368
Mempakul, 366–7, 369, 370, 371
Mengkabong, 364, 369
Menumbok, 370
merchants, 32, 230 ff.
   at Canton, 229, 244
   Chinese, 255–7, 260, 290–1
   European, 260, 271
   Hong, 232, 234–6
   Indian, 271, 273 ff., 278–9
   in Manila, 240, 243
   Portuguese, 209, 271
Merivale, Herman, 355
Mexico and Mexicans, 237–8, 241–2, 246
Miao P'ei-lin, 63
microscope, 203, 206, 210–11, 212, 216–17
   compound, 215
   technical terms, 219
Midin (Brunei chief), 369
migrant ships, 315, 316, 318
migration, see immigration, emigration
militarism, 27, 30, 33
military force, in Malaya, 337
military training, see army, education
militia, 60 ff., 68–9
   'bogus', 62
   government-sponsored, 62, 78–80
   and the origin of the Boxers, 57, 72, 77 ff., 84
   and rebels, 70 ff.
   village, 59–60, 61, 69, 78
Minamoto Dogi, 386–7

Mindanao, 357
mines (explosive), 198
Ming dynasty, 229, 375–6
Ministry of Rites, 229, 379, 381
minorities
   ethnic, 151, 162–3
   Moslem, 159, 162–3
Mirandolle, 301
mirrors, 200, 214
   concave, 218
   distorting, 212, 214
   'light penetration', 215
   'magic', 214–15
   silvering of, 212
   technical terms, 219
missionaries, 79, 82, 157
missions, 388, 389, 392–3
   from China, 379 ff., 385, 390 ff.
   to China, 375 ff., 378, 385, 393 ff.
mnemonics, 173
'models', 187–8, 192, 193
Mombers, Nicolaes (1651), 281
Mongolia, 137, 138, 142–3, 144, 150, 384
Mongols, 162–3, 375, 377, 379, 380, 381, 383–4, 385, 388, 393, 400
Monkey (Chinese novel), 82
monocles, 213
monopolies, 228, 232, 233, 243, 244, 257, 270, 272, 277, 285, 287, 364, 371
   gambling, 291, 304
   opium, 291, 304, 358, 371
   pepper, 364
   salt, 364
   Singapore trade, 360
   spirit, 291, 304
   tin, 268
monsoons, 103, 139, 384
Moreland, W. H., 271
Morishima Churyo (physician, 1754–1808), 216–17
Moscow, 34, 38
Moslems, 159, 162, 336
mosquitoes, 182
Mu Ching-hua (leader of militia group), 70
Mukah, 372
Mukden Incident, 54, 55, 56
mulberries, 105, 122
Mumein (Pengiran), 367
murders of Chinese in Borneo, 366–9
Muruts, 363
mutiny, 317

Mutual Aid Teams, 87, 89, 93–4, 95, 98, 99–100, 101–2, 116–17, 126, 131, 132, 133
mutual benefit, 120, 122–5, 129
myopia, 199, 210

Na-yen-ch'eng, his memorial to the throne (1915), 58
'nakama', 232
Nanchang, 36
Nanking, 38, 155, 159 ff., 378, 383, 388, 398, 400
Nanking Government, 38, 39–41
and the student movement, 43
and the Western Powers, 44, 54
Nanking Incident (1927), 37–8, 39, 44
Nanp'ing Special Area, 183
Nanyang ('South Ocean'), 247, 290, 293, 294, 312
Napier, William, 363
National Government, 35, 145
National Revolution, 23, 40, 55–6
nationalism, 5, 52, 86, 155
Malayan, 13
Sun Yat-sen's lectures on, 28, 52
Nationalist movement, 25, 29 ff., 41, 86, 135
tension between Left and Right in, 37–9
Nationalist Party, 86
natural disasters, 114–15, 124, 132, 167, 188
naval blockade, see blockade
Needham, Joseph, 333
Negapatam, 268
Nepal, 139–40, 145, 146, 149
Nerchinsk treaty (1689), 143, 151
Netherlands East India Company, 275, 277, 279, 280, 282, 284–5, 287
Netherlands India, 315, 317, 318
newspapers, 168
Niceron, J. F. (1638), 218
Nien rebellion, 60, 62, 63, 65, 68, 69, 72
Nienhuys, J., 292–3
Nihal Singh, 347
Ninghsia, 159
Ningpo, 229
Nishihara loans, 50
nomads, 141, 142, 144–5, 147
North China Campaign, 44
North China Plain, 103
North East Frontier Agency, 139
North-west Frontier, 339
Northern Expedition, 36, 44, 45, 55, 86

Northern Indian provinces, 339
Northern Sung dynasty, 375
novels, 82–3
on supernatural performances, 74
nutmeg, 292

Obando, Governor, 239, 240
Ocean Steamship Company, 291, 308
Okhotsk, Sea of, 143
Old Liberated Areas, 101, 126, 127
opium, 358, 360
monopoly, 291, 304, 358, 371
opium dens, 317
Opium Wars, 7
optical apparatus, 197, 199, 207, 212
technical terms, 199, 210 ff.
Ordos deserts, 162
organism, philosophies of, 16
Ostenders, 232
Oxford, Old Ashmolean Museum, 207, 214, 215
Oxus river, 137, 140

Padas Damit, 367, 370
Pahang, 390
Painan treaties (c. 1660), 276
Pakistan, 145, 345
frontiers, 135
Palawan, 358
Palembang, 247, 280, 384, 390, 397
Pamirs, 137, 138, 140, 141, 144, 148, 150
P'an Ch'ing (leader of the Ch'ing-men, 1725), 66, 83
Panai, see Labuan Bilik
Panama, 179–80
Pantometria (Digges), 201
Papar river, 366
para rubber, 255
Parameswara (king of Malacca), 397
parents and education, 321–3
Parsis, 344
partnerships, registration of, 262–5
Pathans, 350
Peace Conference (1919), 24
Peace Corps, 325
Pear Garden Village, 59
Pearl River, 122
peasant-farmers, 117
peasants, 120, 122, 161–2, 184, 190, 192
and the modern revolution of China, 85 ff.
Pegu, 269, 280
Peiyang period, 54, 55

Peking, 10, 75, 76, 133, 154, 208, 380, 384, 388, 393, 394, 400
  capital moved to, 383, 400
  treaty of (1860), 152
Peking Educational Association, 47
Peking Government, 35, 47
Peking Teachers' Training College, 179
Pen-ming (monk and Boxer leader), 73, 74, 76, 77
Penang, 247, 249, 255, 256, 289–90, 292, 293, 294, 297–8, 305, 307, 312, 313, 360
  Chinese merchants in, 290–1
  employers, 307–8
  riots, 298
  sugar plantations, 302
P'eng-kung An (Prefect P'eng's cases), 61, 82–3
pengirans, 364, 366, 369, 371–2
People's Convention, 27, 33
The People's Daily, 167–8, 174, 176, 186–7, 192, 194
pepper, 257, 267, 276, 280, 290, 364
Pepper and Gambier Society, 257, 297
Perak, 267 ff., 276, 278, 280, 284, 285, 287, 289, 300, 305, 340, 369, 370
  Chinese insurgents in, 342
  massacre of, 281–4
  rebellion in, 286
  Sultan of, 279, 280, 282–3
Persia, 148, 273, 280
Philippines, 240, 244, 246, 247, 357
photophobia, 213
Phuankhequa (family of Hong merchants), 234–5
Phuket, *see* Ujong Salang
physical work, 184, 188
physics, 220
Pickering (Protector of Chinese), 305, 307–8, 311
piecework, 117, 118, 119, 121, 132, 134
Piehl (Netherlands Consul at Amoy), 314
P'ingyüan incident (1899), 74, 76–7
piracy, 272, 287, 356–7, 362, 364, 379, 380, 381, 383–4, 385, 386–7, 399
Pires, Tomé, 267
planetarium, 198, 209
planters, 296, 289–9, 307 ff.
  attacks on, 301, 302
  ill treatment of labourers by, 300–1, 302
Planters Union, 316
planting industry, 255
Plum Flower Boxers, *see* Boxer Movement
Plunket (Police Commissioner), 297

Po Yü (maker of optical instruments, b. *c.* 1610), 197–8, 200, 205, 206, 208, 219
police, 337 ff., 342, 344
political campaigners, 179–80, 193
political work, primacy of, 175–6, 182, 193
Pope-Hennessy, John, 358, 360, 366, 367–8, 372
popular organizations, repression of, 42
della Porta, G. B. (1535–1615), 202
Portuguese, 229, 247
  in Malaya, 267 ff., 275–6, 278–9
  merchants, 209, 271
  trade, 241, 242, 286
poverty, 114–15
presbyopia, 210
Price, D., 203
prices, control of, 228, 234, 246
prism, 214
production
  and co-operative agriculture, 89, 102
  and ideology, 193–4
  auxiliary, 104, 107
  campaigns, 170–1, 175
  increase of, 102 ff., 107 ff., 123
  means of, 117–18, 134
  organization of, 114
  planned, 116, 119, 125, 130, 131, 189
production teams, 118
profits
  division of, 110, 116, 130, 132
  in tobacco industry, 309
propaganda, 120, 129, 158, 167
property, *see* common property
Protectorate of Chinese, 295, 305–6, 307, 312–13, 317
'protectorate' systems, 142 ff.
Province Wellesley, 296, 299, 307–8, 313
provinces, social development in, 166
public opinion, 55
public works, 103
Puijt, Jan Dirksz., 278
pumps, 198, 209
Punjab, 336, 339, 344, 346, 347, 349, 353
Purcell, Victor, 3–20, 57, 77, 289

Rangoon, 345
Ranzan, Ono (naturalist, 1799), 217
Raskam, 145
rats, 182
Rawalpindi, 344
rearmament, 52–3, 54

rebellions and riots, 61 ff.
  Chia-ch'ing, 73
  Fang Kuo-chou, 381
  Hung-men, 65
  Penang, 298
  Perak, 286
  T'aip'ing, 61, 72
  Wang Lun's, 63
reconstruction, 43
recruitment
  of labourers, 293 ff., 299, 306–7, 314,
    316
  of Sikhs, 342, 346, 349
rectification campaign, 167
Red Academy, 157, 159
Red Armies, 155, 157, 159, 160, 162
Red Fists (secret society), 69, 70, 75
red thorn, 105
reflection phenomena, 200
refraction, 200, 204
religious orders and trade, 240–1
religious sects, 57, 64
religious tolerance, 16
remuneration of labour, 116–18, 120, 293
de Resende, Barretto, 268
revenues, maritime, 230 ff.
revolution
  'forward-going law of', 166–7, 188, 194
  'uninterrupted', 166–7
revolutionary democracy, 56
'revolutionary diplomacy', concept of, 48
'revolutionary discipline', policy of, 40
de Rheita, Schyrlaeus (1645), 204
Ricci, Matteo (Jesuit), 209
rice, 103, 105, 112, 114
rock crystal, 199, 214
Rogers, Frederick, 360
Rokan, 290
Rosen, E., 203
Ross, John Dill, 360–1
Royal Navy, 356
Royal Philippine Company, 241–2, 245
rubber companies, 255
rubber plantations, 318
Rugby school, 328
rural conditions, 85 ff.
rural revolt, 85
Russell, Bertrand, 9, 16, 20
Russian import-export firms, 251
Russian language, 329
Russian Revolution, 28
Russians, and frontier formation in Asia,
  138, 143, 147–8

Russo-Manchurian border, 150
Russo-Mongol border, 150
Russo-Sinkiang border, 150
Ryukyu, 379

Sabah, 296, 361, 373
Sabtu (Pengiran), 370–1
sago trade, 366–7, 368, 371
St John, Spenser, 363 ff., 371
sakoku rei, 228, 229
salt monopoly, 364, 371
salvage rights, 272
Samarkand, 380
Samson (sailing ship), 360
Samudra, 379, 384–5, 389–90, 391, 394,
  396–7
Sandakan, 358, 361
sandalwood, 267
São Tomé, 268
Sarawak, 254, 329–30, 370, 372
de Saussure, Léopold, 207, 216
Sayan range, 137, 143
Schall von Bell, Adam (Jesuit, 1626),
  205
scholar-gentry, 61–2
school-leaving age, 322
schools, 5, 163
  Charity, 327
Schott, Caspar (c. 1657), 203
Schück, Willi, 358
Schwenter, Daniel (1636), 217
science
  in modern education, 223–4, 327–8
  modern universal, 220
scientific experiment, 170, 181, 184
Scientific Technical Alliance, 181
Scoresby, William, 217
sea power, 384, 399
sea transport, 380, 384
searchlight, 218, 219
second world war, 6, 86, 103, 339, 341 ff.,
  352
secret societies, 5, 57 ff., 64, 78, 367
  and the Boxer Movement, 65 ff., 72,
    81 ff.
  decline in moral standards of, 67
  in Labuan, 360
  in Malaya, 336, 338
  in Penang, 307
  in the Straits Settlements, 308, 338
'security merchant' system, 233
Sekka Zusetsu (Illustrated Discussion of
  Snow Blossoms), 217

Selangor, 289, 300
'self-strengthening' policy, 46, 51–2, 56
'semi-colonialism', 161, 163
Serapong, 312
Serdang, 289, 292, 299, 301, 306
Shakee Incident, 31, 34, 35
Shanghai, 36, 39, 41, 45, 172, 175, 200
   Chinese banks, 162
   import-export firms in, 258
   International Settlement in, 35
Shanghai Defense Force, 37
Shansi, 184, 186
Shantung, 41, 45, 172, 379, 383
   Boxers in, 57
   forts (*yü*) in, 60–1
   militia of, 60 ff., 68, 70
Shantung t'ung-chih, 61
Shawang (king of Brunei), 398–9
Sheldrake, H.M.S., 369
Sheng Hsüan-huai, 67
Shensi, 106, 155–6, 159–60, 162
Shih Ch'un, 73
Shih-kung An, 82–3
Shih Shih-lun (director-general of Grain Tribute transport), 83
ship-building, 380
Shu ching (Book of History), 211
Shun Tien, chapter of the *Shu ching*, *q.v.*
Siak, 290, 291
Siam and the Siamese, 270, 336, 342, 350, 379, 380, 389, 391–3
   missions to and from China, 385, 390, 392, 394, 396, 397
   trade, 228, 396
Siam, Gulf of, 375
Sian, 155, 160, 247
Siau Khai, 312
Siberia, 143, 147
Sikh immigrants, 335 ff.
   and police work, 339–40
   as short-term entrants, 353
   commercial, 344 ff.
   convicts, 341, 347
   decline in numbers, 353
   English-educated, 341
   preponderance of males among, 348, 353
   recruitment of, 342, 346, 349
Sikh wars, 347
Sikkim, 139, 145, 146, 149
Sikkim–Tibet border, 146, 149
silk, 228
silt, 105

silver, 228, 237
   mines, 246
Sindhis, 344, 346
Singapore, 289, 294 ff., 303, 307, 311 ff., 315, 317, 339, 344, 346, 358 ff.
   Chinese merchants in, 290–1
   trade, 247 ff.
Singapore Chamber of Commerce, 261, 264
Singer, Charles, 201, 203
singers, 182
Sinhalese, 336
sinkhehs, 294 ff., 304 ff.
   in Malaya, 303
Sinkiang, 137, 138, 140, 141, 144–5, 150
Sino-American Tariff Treaty (1928), 47
Sino-Indian border, 135 ff.
   Chinese objections to, 150–2
Sino-Japanese relations, 47, 54
Sino-Japanese Treaty (1896), 47
Sino-Pakistani border, 136, 140
Sino-Russian border, 135 ff.
   Chinese objections to, 150–2
Sino-Russian border agreements, 142, 143, 144
Sino-Russian relations, 151
Sino-Soviet alliance, 11
Sirturi, Girolamo (1618), 203, 205
slaves, 356, 362, 363
slogan-fatigue, 190–1
slogans, 155, 165–95
   agricultural, 181
   army, 173–5, 180, 186
   'background', 168 ff., 172, 189
   industrial, 178, 182, 185–6
snails, 182
Snow, Edgar, 153
snow-flake patterns, 216, 217
social development, 165–6
socialism, 16, 166, 168, 170, 172, 191
socialist education, 176–7, 192
soil, deterioration of, 102
soldiers, education of, *see* army, education
South Indians, 337–8
sovereignty, Chinese concept of, 143
Soviet collectives, 87
Soviet Union, 25, 27–8, 34, 35, 41, 42, 49, 155, 160
   frontiers, 135, 151
Spain and Spaniards, 239, 245
   Manileño, 238, 241, 242, 243
   in the Sulu archipelago, 356–9, 361
   trade, 241–2, 245

Spanish America, 228
Spanish American independence revolts, 246
spectacles, 197, 199, 200, 210
  origin in Europe, 200
  semi-discoidal, 213, 219
  spectral colours, 214
Speedy, Captain, 342
Spencer-Jones, Sir Harold, 203
spices, 267
spirit monopoly, 291, 304
'split bifocals', 213
Sri Maharaja (king of Malacca), 397
'ssu-fen huo-p'ing' system, 117, 119
Stalin, J., 186, 191
state, problems of the, 52
steam, introduction of, 360
Steiger, G. N., 57, 58
Stelluti, F., 202
Stimson, 159
stimulus diffusion, 205, 219–20
story-tellers, 182
Straits Settlements, 5, 261, 265, 290, 293 ff., 305–6, 311–12, 314 ff., 336, 338, 340
  as penal stations, 341, 347
  emigration from, 296
Straits Settlements Legislative Council, 252, 257
Straits Settlements Police Commission (1879), 338
Straits Settlements Protectors of Chinese, 293, 310–11, 319–20
Straits Settlements Sikh Contingent, 351
strikes, 36, 189
'Student Army', 46–7
student unions, 32
students, 154, 179
  and the Nationalist movement, 24, 31–2, 43
study, methods of, 176, 186–7, 191
Su Sung, 209
Suchow, 197, 200, 206
sugar plantations, 302, 313
Sultana (steamer), 361
Sulu archipelago, 356 ff., 361, 368, 385, 389
  treaty (1849), 356–7
Suma Oriental (Pires), 267
Sumatra, 255, 267, 276, 342, 384, 389
  Chinese migration into, 289 ff.
  labour conditions in, 300, 304
  planters of, 289–90, 293
'sun-glasses', 213

Sun Ju-ching (rebel, c. 1860), 72
Sun Kai-ti, 74
Sun Yat-sen, 10, 25–8, 33, 34, 39, 52, 53, 86
Sun Yün-ch'iu (maker of optical instruments, c. 1630 to c. 1663), 197, 199–200, 206, 207, 210, 215, 218, 219
Sung Ching-shih (bandit leader), 69, 70–2
Sungei Ujong, 267
Superintendency of Foreign Trading Junks, 228
superstition, 324
supply and demand, 227, 246
Surat, 269, 280
Sutlej river, 136, 139–40, 149
Swammerdam, J. (1669), 217
Swatow, 295–6, 298, 299, 310 ff., 314–15, 317 ff.
Swedish trade, 232
Syr Darya, see Jaxartes
Szechuan, 184

Ta-tao-hui, see Big Swords
Tachai, 172, 187–8, 193
Tachai Production Brigade, 107
Tach'ing, oilfield of, 187–8, 193
Tadzhikstan, 137
Taghdumbash Pamir, 145
Tai Chi-t'ao, 28, 52
Tai Hsüan-chih, 58–9, 72 ff., 77–8, 82
T'aip'ing rebellion, 61, 72
Taiwan, 230, 280
Tamils, 336
Tan, Chester, 57–8
Tan Kim Swee, 371
Tan Seng Poh (Singapore Teochiu leader), 299
'Tan Tek', 298, 305
T'an T'ing-hsiang (governor of Tsouhsien, 1861), 68, 73
Tandjung Balai, see Asahan
T'ang dynasty, 375–6
T'ang Shao-yi, 29
Tangut invasions, 400
Tanjong Pagar Dock Company, 296
Tannu Ola range, 137
Taoists, 59, 82
Tapanuli, 289
Tarbagatay range, 137
Tariff Conference (1926), 35, 47
tariffs, 26, 47, 54
Tarim, 136, 138, 140
Tashkent, 140

taxation, 41, 47, 62, 63, 68, 71, 72, 78, 86,
113, 120, 228–9, 236, 246
in Brunei, 362–3
in Canton, 244–5
in Labuan, 368
in Malaya, 272
in Manila, 237, 243–4
on land, 110
tea, 228, 318, 371
teaching methods, 184, 326, 329
technical innovations, 327
technical terms, 211
magnifying glass, 211
optical equipment, 199, 210 ff., 219
telescope, 207, 219
telescopes, 198, 199, 206, 207
application to gunnery, 198, 208
first mention of, in China, 205
invention of, 201 ff.
technical terms, 207, 219
*Telescopium, sive ars perficiendi novum illud
Galilaei Visorium Instrumentum ad
Sidera* (Sirturi), 205
Temiang, 291
Templer, General Sir Gerald, 12–13
tenant farming, 85–6, 112–13, 161
Teng, S. Y., 60
Teochiu labourers, 297, 304, 310, 312, 314
territorial expansion, 33
textbooks, 5, 332–3
textiles, 228, 237
Thailand, *see* Siam
Thio, Eunice, 297
Thorstenson, Simon, 273
Tibet, 138, 140, 143–3, 145, 146, 149, 150,
152, 157, 377, 379, 380, 381
Tibetan–Dogra peace treaty (1842), 146
Tibetan plateau, 135–6, 138–9, 140
T'ien-li-chiao, 66
T'ien Shan, 137, 138, 140, 141, 144, 148,
150
T'ien-ti-hui, *see* Hung-men
T'ien Wen Lüeh (Explanation of the
Celestial Sphere), 205
Tientsin, 36, 133, 154
Timor, 267
Timur, 400
tin-miners, 300, 342
tin trade, 255, 256, 267 ff., 276, 309, 313
Ting Pao-chen (commissioner of law,
1863), 63
Ting Ping-t'ang (leader of militia group),
71

Ting Wang and Company, 364
tobacco, 292–3, 358, 371
industry, 304, 306, 309, 314, 318, 319
plantations, 298, 300, 302, 303, 310, 313
Toh Peh Kong Society, 298
Tongking, 276
Tore del Campo, Governor, 238
tractors, 104, 105
trade, 40, 228, 237 ff., 376, 380
concessions, 227, 229, 246
control systems, 32, 227 ff., 236, 246
foreign, 228–9, 232, 236
laws on, 236
Labuan, 355 ff.
Singapore, 247 ff.
trade agreements (1650), 279, 280, 281
trades' unions, 32, 39
Tran dynasty, 381
transmissions and communications, 205–6,
219, 332–3
translation projects, 331
transport workers, 65, 68, 83
travel
and education, 327
foreign, prohibition of, 399
Treacher, W. H., 369 ff.
'treasure-ships', 393
treaties
with Acheh (1659), 284
of Aigun (1858), 152
of Amity and Commerce, 47
Belgian (1928), 50–1
on border settlements, 149–52
with Brunei (1847), 356, 362 ff., 367 ff.
Italian (1928), 50
Painan (c. 1660), 276
Peking (1860), 152
Sino-American Tariff Treaty (1928), 47
Sino-Japanese (1896), 47
with Sulu (1849), 356–7
Tibetan–Dogra peace treaty (1842), 146
'unequal treaties', 26, 35, 42, 151
treaties question, 47, 49, 50–1
Treaty Powers, 24, 35, 48
tribal peoples, 138, 142, 144, 147, 370
Bajaus, 364
Baltis, 140
Bataks, 292, 293, 301
Bugis, 270, 290, 337
Dayaks, 329–30
Dogras, 140, 146
Dusuns, 366
Dzungarian peoples, 141, 144

tribal peoples (*cont.*)
Gayos, 301
Jurchen, 377, 400
Kazakhs, 141, 151
Kelabits, 330
Khitan, 400
Kirgiz, 141, 144
Tangut, 400
Tungusic groups, 142
Turcic peoples, 140, 144
tributary system, 228–9, 396, 399, 400
tribute, 230, 236, 267, 269, 376, 395
Truijtman, Joan (Commissioner), 282–4
Tsai-li-chiao (Observe Rites), 69
Tsangpo-Brahmaputra river, 136
Tsinan Incident (1928), 45–6, 47, 48
Tso Ping-lung (Chinese Consul in Singapore), 311
Tsouhsien, religious bandits of, 68–9
Tsushima, 386–7
Tu Ch'iao (commissioner of Shantung militia, 1860), 62
T'ung Chih Restoration, 52
Tungusic tribal groups, 142
turbaned bandits, *see* Fu-fei
Turcic peoples, 140, 144
Turkestan, 136, 140, 141, 142, 145, 150
Tutong, 371
Tuvinians, 144
Twist, Johan van (1641), 277

Uda river, 143
Ujong Salang (Phuket), 269, 273, 279, 280, 287
massacre at, 274
underemployment, 104, 106, 115, 117, 122, 133
unemployment, 40, 68
'unequal treaties', 26, 35, 42, 151
United Front, 24, 29, 31, 36, 43, 86, 155, 158, 159, 160–1, 163
United States, 35, 38, 44, 47, 178–80, 325, 350–2
universities, 322–3, 330
'unpaid passengers' (category of immigrants), 295–6, 306, 310–11, 313, 315
Urals, 148
urban markets, 87, 97, 104
Urianghai, 144, 380
Ussher, H. T., 360, 369–70
U.S.S.R., *see* Soviet Union
Ussuri river, 137, 142
usury, 85, 109

Valdés, Governor, 239
vassalage, 382–3, 387, 392
vegetable production, 105, 107
Venice, 204
Victoria, 359, 371
Victoria Trading Company, 361
village militia, *see* militia
vision, defects of, 199, 210
Vladivostok, 137, 151
de Vlamingh van Oudshoorn, Governor (1646), 280
voluntarism, principle of, 88–9, 92 ff., 167
Voluntary Service Overseas, 325

Wakhan, 136
Wakos, 229, 383–4, 385, 386, 399
Walgenstein, Thomas (1651), 218
Wang, C. T., 47–8, 49, 50
Wang Chan-ao (militia instructor), 71
Wang Chan-chi (militia instructor), 71
Wang Cheng-chi (rebel leader, 1813), 66, 68, 72
Wang Chin-kuang, 199, 206, 212
Wang Ch'ing (Boxer leader), 76
Wang Chiu-ling (leader of militia group), 71
Wang Fu-chih, 91
Wang Hsi-lu (militia instructor), 70
Wang Kuo-fan, 107
Wang Li-yen (Boxer leader), 76
Wang Lun (rebel leader), 73
Wang Pai-ling (leader of militia group), 71, 72
warlords, 26, 28, 29, 37, 54, 154
Washington Conference, 24–5, 28, 35–6
'Washington Formula', 54
water conservancy, 103, 116, 122
Water Margin, 77
water-raising machinery, 198, 209
waterpartings and international boundaries, 136–7, 140
wealth, redistribution of, 102
weather conditions and agriculture, 114–15
weeds, control of, 103
wells, 103
Wen-ch'ing (Grand Secretary) memorial to the throne (1855), 61
Wen-hsien sect, 68
Weng Yai (leader of the Ch'ing-men, 1725), 66, 83
Westernization of China's institutions, 53
Whampoa (Hoo Ah Kay), 257

wheat, 105
White Boxers, *see* Boxer Movement
White Lotus (secret society), 59, 70, 72–3, 75–6, 81–2, 84
Wise, Henry, 355
women, and co-operative farming, 97, 98, 104
Woolf, Leonard, 19
World Revolution, 33–4
World War I, *see* first world war
World War II, *see* second world war
Wright, Mary, 52
Wu chih-hui, 29
Wu hsien chih (History and Topography of Wuhsien, i.e. Suchow), 198–9
Wu K'ai (magistrate of Chinhsiang), 58
Wu San-kuei (general), 208
Wuhan, 33, 36, 37, 38, 179
Wuhan Government, 39–40, 41

Yang Ch'un-shan, 70
Yang Ming-ch'ien (leader of militia group), 71
Yangtse river, 380, 384
Yangtse Valley, 103, 122
Yarkand, 140
Yellow River, 63–4
Yellow Rock (secret society), 69, 70
Yen Ching-ming (acting governor of Shantung, 1862), 63, 70

Yen Lung-hsiu (leader of militia group), 71
Yenan, 153, 156–8, 167, 187
Yenchiaying, 72
Yenisey river, 137, 141
Yi Ho Boxers, 59
Yin and Yang, 198
Young Communist League, 178, 181
youth
    and co-operative agriculture, 97–8
    and service to the community, 325
Youth League, 127, 128, 182
Yü-hsien, 76
Yü-huang Miao (Taoist temple), 59
Yü-lu, 77
Yu-mu, 384
Yüan Chia-san, 68
Yuan ching shuo (Account of the Far-Seeing Optick Glass), 205
Yüan Shih-k'ai (governor of Shantung, 1899), 77, 79
Yung-lo (emperor, 1402–24), 375 ff.
    his inscriptions and poems, 385–8
    'impartiality' of his foreign policy, 388, 390, 392, 397, 399
Yunnan, 381, 388
    mission from, 378

Zainal Abidin (king of Samudra), 397
Zamboanga, 357
Zen Buddhism, *see* Buddhism